Encyclopedia of Northwest Native Plants
for Gardens and Landscapes

Encyclopedia of
Northwest Native Plants
for Gardens and Landscapes

KATHLEEN A. ROBSON, ALICE RICHTER & MARIANNE FILBERT

Timber Press

Published in 2008 by

Timber Press, Inc.
The Haseltine Building
133 S.W. Second Avenue, Suite 450
Portland, Oregon 97204-3527, U.S.A.

www.timberpress.com

For contact information regarding editorial, marketing, sales, and distribution in the United Kingdom,
see www.timberpress.co.uk.

Printed in China

Library of Congress Cataloging-in-Publication Data

Robson, Kathleen A.
  Encyclopedia of northwest native plants for gardens and landscapes /
Kathleen A. Robson, Alice Richter, Marianne Filbert.
    p. cm.
  Includes bibliographical references and index.
  ISBN-13: 978-0-88192-863-1
  1. Native plants for cultivation--Pacific, Northwest--Encyclopedias.
  2. Native plant gardening--Pacific, Northwest--Encyclopedias. 3.
Landscape plants--Pacific, Northwest--Encyclopedias. I. Richter, Alice.
II. Filbert, Marianne. III. Title.
  SB439.24.N673R63 2007
  635.9'51795--dc22   2007019030

A catalog record for this book is also available from the British Library.

CONTENTS

PREFACE AND ACKNOWLEDGMENTS

A few years ago, as a vendor at the Hardy Plant Society of Oregon's fall sale, I was chatting with author Susan Narizny. "We need another book on gardening with Northwest natives," Susan said. "You should write one. Call Timber Press." Surely, I thought, someone else is already doing this, but the possibility was worth checking into. I submitted a proposal, and, with infinite politeness, Timber Press informed me that while my writing was acceptable and my credentials as a botanist were excellent, my casual photography was not up to their high standards. By this time I had gotten to know Alice Richter; we first met when she visited my nursery, and by now I had seen a few gorgeous examples of her many wildflower portraits. Luckily for us all, Alice was thrilled at the prospect of collaborating on a book, and Timber Press had nothing but praise for her work.

I adore pen-and-ink drawings and, although we all love the botanical illustrations originally created for *Vascular Plants of the Pacific Northwest* (Hitchcock et al. 1969), it was time for some new ones. I had worked on a few articles with artist Marianne Filbert and had seen some of her technical drawings of grasses and other difficult subjects. Her work combines beauty with anatomical accuracy, and I am delighted she agreed to join in this project.

My thanks, too, to my friend and former student Sally Simmons, who let me talk her into photographing some of the additional shrub-steppe species that gardeners in the arid regions of the Pacific Northwest will want to grow; and to Bill Rickard, who knows the flora of the Columbia Basin better than anyone, and Dave Simmons, for assisting Sally in the field.

I am endlessly grateful to my husband, Tom Henn, and to Jack and Ellie Maze. This project would not have been possible without their support and patience. ~ *Kali Robson*

Alice Richter adds:
My interest in wildflowers started when my mother first showed me a lady's slipper orchid in the woods in northern Idaho. As a young parent, I was quick to include and protect native plants in my landscaping; a neighbor introduced me to the Native Plant Society, an association I have kept up over the years, and while living in Coos Bay, I treasured a circle of friends who were interested in photography. So, photographing native plants was natural and a joy for me, and close-ups became a specialty.

Thanks are due to so many people who were willing to put up with my stopping and setting up a tripod over the years that I cannot begin to name everyone. One friend that enjoyed both hiking and photography was Archi Davenport; my thanks to her for our many discussions of the fine art of photography. Another friend with whom I explored many areas of the Northwest was Carolyn Jenkins; from the Kalmiopsis Wilderness to southwestern Washington, we encountered many rare and intriguing wildflowers together. But a special thanks goes to my husband, Larry, and family for indulging me in my hobby, accompanying me on many excursions, and halting even casual trips long enough for me to photograph a native plant along the roadside. It has been a life-long pursuit, and I am pleased to be sharing some of my favorite photographs with a wider audience, in this book. Thanks to Kali Robson and the many friends who encouraged me and spurred the thought into action.

Marianne Filbert adds:
I want to thank Kali Robson for inviting me to work on this project and for being a pleasure to work with. Thanks also to my friends and family for their encouragement, especially my parents, Joe and Marion Cha; and to my husband, Randall, and Ivan and Lucy, for their patience.

Collectively, we would like to thank Dale Johnson, Eve Goodman, Franni Bertolino Farrell, and all the great people at Timber Press. Diana Reeck and Bill Janssen of Collector's Nursery, Julie Lockwood of Shadylane Nursery, and Judith Jones of Fancy Fronds Ferns generously supplied plants and growing tips. Pollock's Nursery, Wild Ginger Farm, and Watershed Garden Works were additional suppliers of specimens. Julie Whitacre of Fourth Corner Nurseries was a fine source of information on plants that can be grown in northwestern Washington. Scotty Fairchild of Leach Botanical Gardens in Portland, Oregon, steered us to some lovely subjects; we also found fine trees at the Hoyt Arboretum in Portland with the help of Lynn Wilson and Melba Dlugonski. Ed Guerrant of the Berry Botanic Garden in Portland offered advice on additional sources of information. In Longview, Washington, the lovely native garden of Shirley Lutz and the woodland where Ruth Deery lives were great sources of plants and portraits. The members of the Longview Lunch Bunch were most supportive of this project.

INTRODUCTION

This is a book for gardeners, landscape architects and designers, and watershed or habitat managers; it provides information on how and where to grow plants, and where they grow in the wild. It is not intended as an identification reference; readers with that aim will want to use an illustrated field guide or a flora with technical keys. Several such good books are listed in the references.

The backyard ecosystem

An ecosystem is a specified area, all the creatures living in the area, the physical characteristics of the area (precipitation, temperatures, soils), and the interactions among all these components. Most of us think of a wild, woodsy place filled with an assortment of native species, but an ecosystem can be more broadly defined. The entire planet Earth is an ecosystem (with the components interacting on a larger, global scale) as is a community of mosses, lichens, insects, and microbes living on a single, slowly decomposing rock. Even a lawn or ball field, or an agroecosystem such as a field of wheat, can be considered an ecosystem, albeit a very simplified one. But simple systems fed on synthethic fertilizers and pesticides tend to be weaker and more prone to disease and other disasters.

Gardeners love a diversity of plants, so most gardens are far more complex than lawns or cornfields. And more gardeners are interested in the life beyond the plants—they think about worms and birds and bacteria, pollinating and predatory insects, and all the other species in the garden ecosystem. Such gardeners use compost tea as a remedy for many plant diseases and as a great fertilizer. Compost tea doesn't work as a pesticide; it doesn't directly kill disease-causing microorganisms. The trick to compost tea is that it populates the microscopic universe with so many different bacteria and fungi that they crowd out the pathogens. The pathogenic creatures may not disappear, but increasing the biological diversity of the whole system reduces their numbers to the point where they cause little harm. This same approach works on a larger scale: diversity of garden species, whether microscopic or macroscopic, leads to strong, resilient ecosystems in the backyard or wild place. Birds and insects will live happily in these places, and—although there will still be chewed leaves and some black spot—major disease problems will be few.

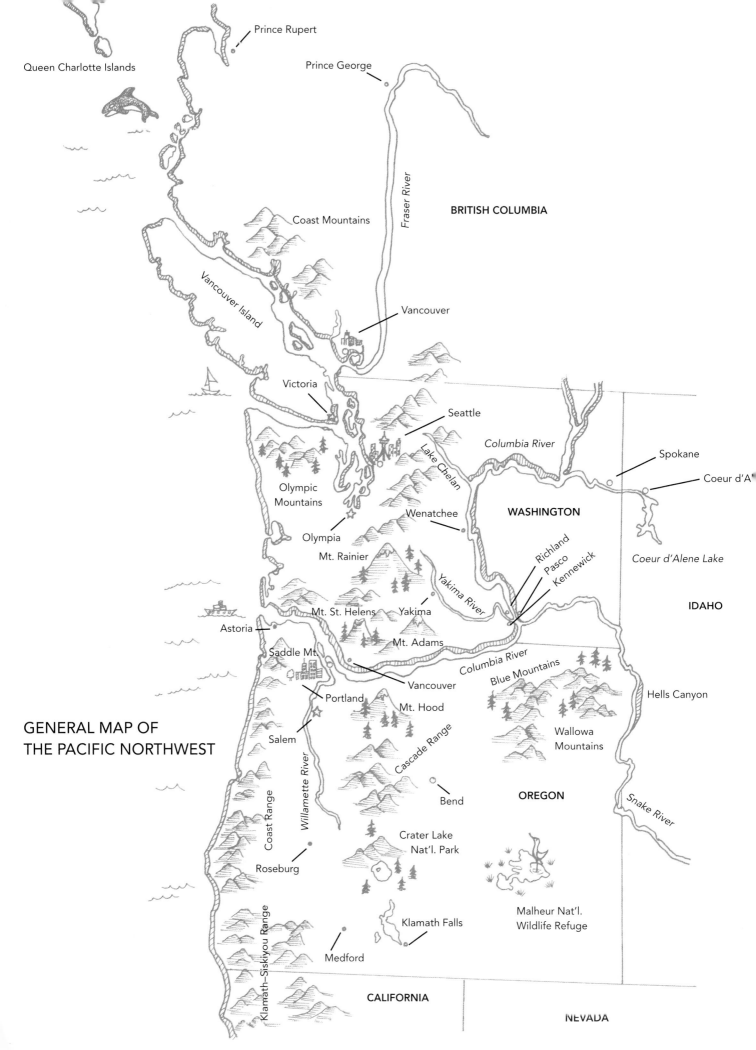

GENERAL MAP OF
THE PACIFIC NORTHWEST

Gardening in the Pacific Northwest

The Pacific Northwest has a wide variety of physical conditions and climates, ranging from the lush coastal rainforests, to the mountain meadows of the Cascades, to the arid shrub-steppe east of the mountains. Areas west of the Cascades are dominated by Sitka spruce (*Picea sitchensis*) and western hemlock (*Tsuga heterophylla*); the Columbia Basin is characterized by big sagebrush (*Artemisia tridentata*). Douglas fir (*Pseudotsuga menziesii*) grows through much of the Cascades and the mountainous areas to the east, transitioning to ponderosa pine (*Pinus ponderosa*) on drier sites. The composition of other species growing among these dominant species is quite variable. Although gardeners will have little impact on the general climate, soils, or precipitation, they can alter, to a large degree, important microclimate features such as the amount of direct sunlight or soil drainage. Many of the plants described in this book, although they may not be locally native, can nevertheless be grown in the garden.

The barrier of the Cascade Mountains creates the coldest, driest climates in the Pacific Northwest; southwestern Oregon has a dry but warmer climate, with a flora in many ways more similar to northern California. In general, the wettest conditions occur from southwestern Alaska, south along the coast and west slope of the Cascades to central Oregon; within this area there are many drier microclimates created by rain shadows on the leeward side of Vancouver Island and the Olympic Mountains. Many of the plants from cold, arid regions tolerate hot, dry conditions in southwestern Oregon, but may have trouble in the wet parts of northwestern Washington. Determined gardeners with unusually sandy soil or rock garden conditions often can compensate for the excessive amounts of rain. Gardeners on the east side of the Cascades will be concerned with the cold hardiness and heat tolerance of the plants they grow. Some specimen plants may need protection from winter weather, and sometimes also from summer heat.

Although many plants native to the wetter west side of the Cascades will not survive in the arid shrub-steppe east of the Cascades, and vice versa, quite a few species are found on both sides of the mountains. Some native plants have a long history of use as ornamentals; others are underused (though often excellent) garden subjects. Some plants were and still are used by indigenous tribes, and many are important components of wildlife habitat.

This book describes plants native to the Pacific Northwest that are both ornamental to the garden and useful for conservation, plants that can be grown to add beauty and improve habitat. We encourage diversity in the garden, not an absolute faithfulness to the surrounding native vegetation; though a reintroduction of at least some natives is always helpful, most backyards have been so highly altered it may be impossible to know exactly what grew there prior to disturbance. The Pacific Northwest is defined in the broad sense—mainly from southwestern Alaska and British Columbia, south to the California border, and from the Pacific coast to western Idaho.

Naturalized, not native

Only native plants are described or mentioned in this book—that is, species that were already here, in the Pacific Northwest, when the first non-indigenous human explorers collected and catalogued them. It is entirely possible that the first people in North America brought plants and seeds with them many thousands of years ago, or that people acquired different species from each other, and these plants became integrated into the flora as the millennia passed; however, we have no evidence of this and are left with the conclusion that the plants we include here evolved in place. Some exotics—plants that originated elsewhere but are now established in the Pacific Northwest—are well known. Almost everyone is aware that English ivy (*Hedera helix*), Scotch broom (*Cytisus scoparius*), Himalayan blackberry (*Rubus armeniacus*), and Russian thistle (*Salsola tragus*) either escaped from cultivation or their seed came into the region accidentally. Other garden escapes, such as foxglove (*Digitalis purpurea*) and Queen Anne's lace (*Daucus carota*), are often thought to be native—they have incorporated themselves into relatively undisturbed sites where they appear to belong. These plants are now naturalized, but we know they are not indigenous, and they are not included in this book.

Don't we wish . . .

Certain plants are the targets of great gardening lust. These are usually the plants that are the most difficult to grow, requiring special conditions or relationships with mycorrhizal fungi or other soil microorganisms. We don't yet have a good understanding of the needs of some plants, but we are discovering more about these mutualistic relationships, and helpful mycorrhizal spores are now commercially available. A few extremely uncooperative species can be grown "in captivity," but cheap they are not! Others persist in rejecting cultivation.

Native orchids are the best known of the difficult plants, and some real gems occur in our region. Fairy's slipper or calypso orchid (*Calypso bulbosa*) is a small, magenta beauty often seen along trails. We have several species of lady's slipper orchid, including California lady's slipper (*Cypripedium californicum*), clustered lady's slipper (*C. fasciculatum*), mountain lady's slipper (*C. montanum*), and yellow lady's slipper (*C. parviflorum*). Attempts are being made to propagate these and other lovely plants (gentians, for example) by tissue culture of the seed or vegetative cells. They may soon be available commercially; meanwhile, enjoy them in their wild homes. A few orchids, such as giant helleborine (*Epipactis gigantea*), western rattlesnake plantain (*Goodyera oblongifolia*), and hooded lady's tresses (*Spiranthes romanzoffiana*), are more easily propagated, and these are described in the perennials section of the encyclopedia.

As our knowledge of native orchids increases, so may our success in growing them. Many orchids are increasingly rare, due to a combination of habitat destruction and poaching. Many species are legally protected, but even when they are not, they should never, ever be dug from the wild.

Other notoriously difficult plants include *Lycopodium clavatum* and other club-mosses. Some orchids, ericads (heather and rhododendron relatives), and other species lack chlorophyll and are either parasitic on other plants or are saprophytes, living entirely off of decomposing material. These plants too are uncooperative in the garden: if you are lucky enough to have them growing, do not disturb them. As our understanding of the biology and growth requirements of these plants improves, they may become available to gardeners, but for now, enjoy the sight of them in their wild homes and leave them unmolested.

Several species described in this book are quite rare in nature but are easily cultivated. There is no rational reason why these plants shouldn't be grown. They must be maintained in the wild and should be protected in their small native ranges, but growing them in our gardens does no harm that we can see. There is no evidence that cultivating rare, easily grown species leads to introgression, causes genetic "contamination," or reduces "fitness." On the contrary, growing such plants helps ensure the continuation of the species, and we learn more about them as we grow them.

About the encyclopedia

The encyclopedia of plants is divided into five main categories: ferns (including horsetails and other spore-bearing vascular plants), conifers, annuals (those we couldn't resist), perennials (including grasses, rushes, and sedges), and shrubs and trees (including the occasional woody vine). The familiar flowering plants of these last three groups (often called the angiosperms, classified in the division Magnoliophyta) share certain unique characteristics, among them

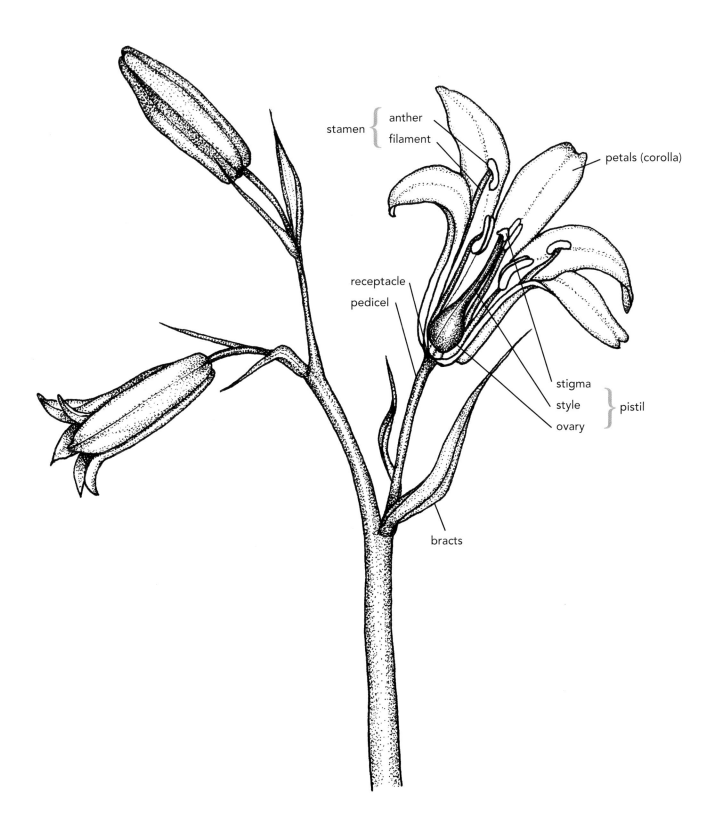

stamen { anther
          filament

petals (corolla)

receptacle
pedicel

stigma
style
ovary
} pistil

bracts

FLOWER PARTS

double fertilization: two sperms are involved in every fertilization event in flowering plants. One sperm fuses with an egg cell to form a zygote; the other fuses with two or more cells of the egg sac to form a polyploid tissue (where each cell now has more than two sets of chromosomes), the endosperm, which provides nutrients for the developing embryo. The formation of flowering parts, especially fruits, or ripened ovaries containing seed, is another characteristic unique to flowering plants.

In many angiosperms, the flower parts are obvious. In others—sedges, rushes, and wind-pollinated trees (birches, cottonwoods, oaks)—the sepals and showy petals are absent or reduced to small structures. In grasses, for example, the tiny florets are arranged into spikelets, each with two bracts, or glumes, at the base. Two additional bracts, the lemma and palea, surround each floret. The lemma often has a long awn, or bristle, at the tip. The typical fruit of the grasses is a grain, or caryopsis, one-seeded and dry, with the ovary wall fused to the seed coat.

The plants in each of the five main categories are presented alphabetically by scientific name. Recent and historical taxonomic name changes are occasionally addressed; and both newer and older names are listed in the index. Each description provides practical information on how to grow and where to site the featured native plant. Plant height and details of foliage, flowers, and fruits (or other reproductive structures) are also provided, as are flowering times, where appropriate. Measurements are given in metric units with approximate English equivalents in parentheses. General information on the genus and its world distribution; other Northwest native species in the genus, including cultivars, that the gardener may want to grow; and occasional brief discussions of natives in related genera are offered. Uses of plants, especially by indigenous people, are also noted.

Propagation advice is directed to gardeners rather than to professional propagators. For instance, the seeds of many plants require a cold, moist period of stratification before they will germinate; instead of stratifying seeds in a refrigerator, they can be planted into flats and left outside for the winter—an easier, less expensive method. Many plants can be propagated by layering, or from cuttings or divisions; specific information on the time of year and where on the plant to take cuttings, or when to divide perennials, is provided. Where more than one species in a genus is discussed, the generic information and methods of propagation are included in the introduction to the genus.

The information on native habitat and range describes where these plants are found in nature and what sort of conditions they live in. General elevations are also provided. In most cases, it is not necessary to exactly recreate a plant's wild habitat in the garden, but many plants will not thrive unless natural conditions are approximated. For example, most plants that live only in rocky, dry, serpentine soils do not require a serpentine substrate, but they probably do require a rocky, very well-drained place in the garden.

Finally, climate zones are based on the Plant Hardiness Zones developed by the United States Department of Agriculture. This climate information, keyed to average annual minimum temperatures, is helpful but sometimes a bit misleading—a plant native to the east side of the Cascades would not be killed by the west-side temperatures but possibly by the far greater amounts of rain, and this is not reflected in these climate ratings.

People have different reasons for gardening with native plants. Some desire a low-maintenance garden that will, once established, require no water in the summer and no protection in the winter. Others want to recreate habitat that will attract the native animals (especially birds and butterflies) to their gardens. Some gardeners focus on plants for a shady woodland or pond, drought-tolerant plants, plants for alpine and rock gardens, or other garden themes. A few try to fully recreate the effect of a rocky trail in the Cascades, a ferny clearing in the coastal forest, or a deer trail surrounded by sagebrush and bunchgrasses, depending on where they live. We hope this book will offer something to all these gardeners, and also serve as a reference to professional landscape designers, horticulturists, land managers, and students.

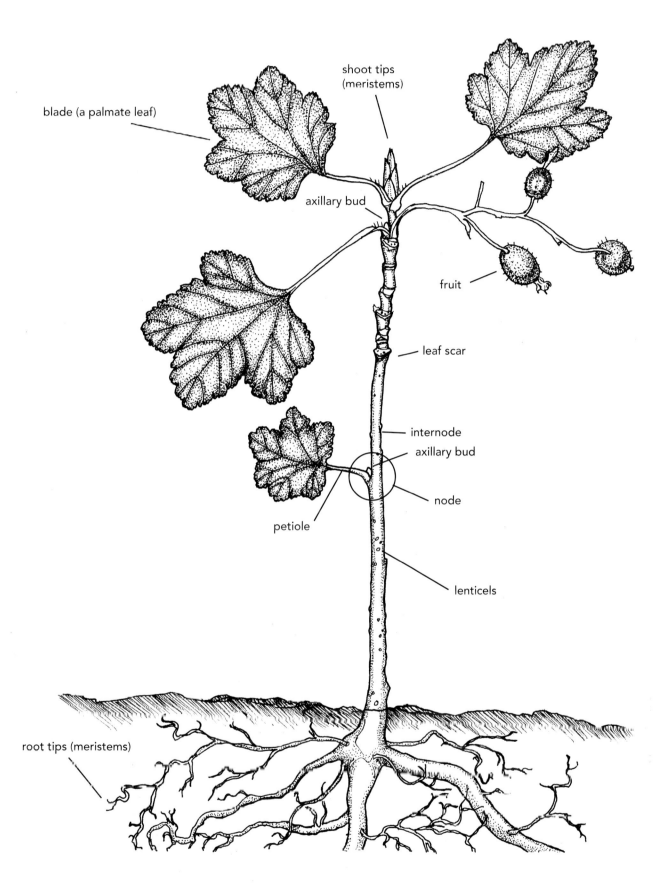

shoot tips
(meristems)

blade (a palmate leaf)

axillary bud

fruit

leaf scar

internode

axillary bud

node

petiole

lenticels

root tips (meristems)

GENERAL PLANT STRUCTURES

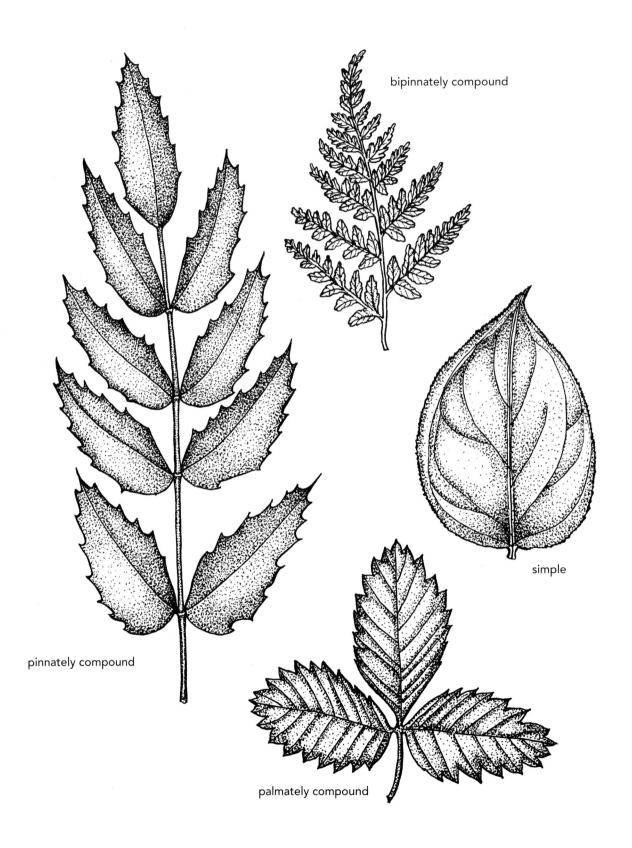

bipinnately compound

simple

pinnately compound

palmately compound

LEAF SHAPES

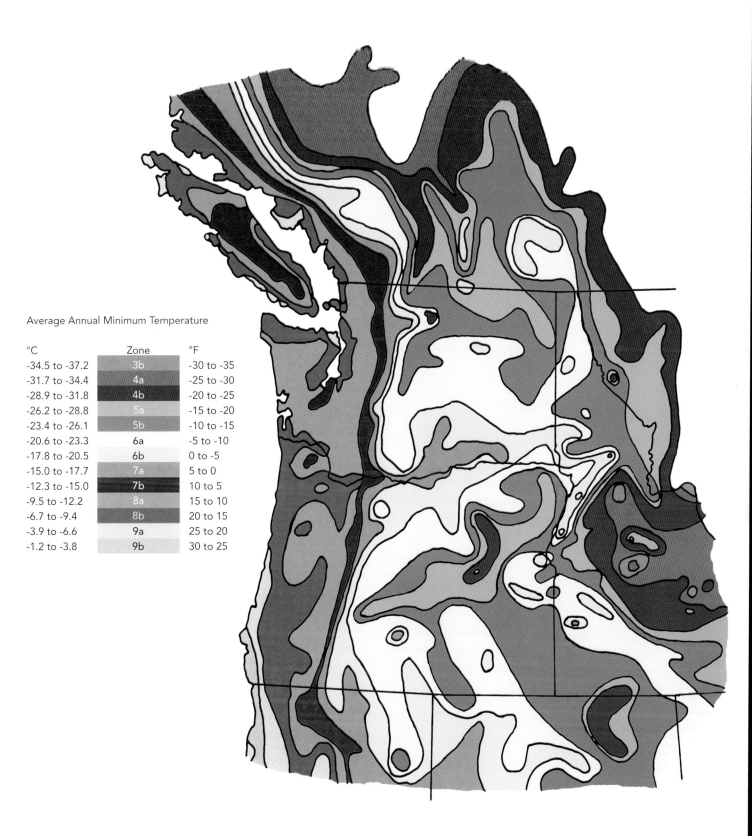

Average Annual Minimum Temperature

°C	Zone	°F
-34.5 to -37.2	3b	-30 to -35
-31.7 to -34.4	4a	-25 to -30
-28.9 to -31.8	4b	-20 to -25
-26.2 to -28.8	5a	-15 to -20
-23.4 to -26.1	5b	-10 to -15
-20.6 to -23.3	6a	-5 to -10
-17.8 to -20.5	6b	0 to -5
-15.0 to -17.7	7a	5 to 0
-12.3 to -15.0	7b	10 to 5
-9.5 to -12.2	8a	15 to 10
-6.7 to -9.4	8b	20 to 15
-3.9 to -6.6	9a	25 to 20
-1.2 to -3.8	9b	30 to 25

CLIMATE ZONE MAP

Encyclopedia of Plants

FERNS (including horsetails)

Ferns and horsetails are ancient vascular plants that reproduce by spores, not seeds. Ferns develop spore-bearing sporangia in groups (sori); a flap of tissue, the indusium, usually covers each sorus. In many ferns, the sori look like rounded or elongated dots on the underside of the leaves; in others, the sorus runs along the leaf margin, forming a row of sporangia protected by the rolled edges. Once dispersed, the spores germinate on moist soil to form a mass of young haploid gametophytes, tiny organisms with only one set of chromosomes, which produce gametes, eggs and sperm. The male gametes swim until they find an egg and fuse with it, forming a new diploid (two sets of chromosomes) sporophyte cell; the embryo absorbs nutrients from the gametophyte and finally develops into the familiar fern.

Some native ferns are difficult to propagate from divisions or cuttings, but most can be grown from spores. Gather some pieces of fronds with ripe sporangia and put them into an envelope kept at room temperature for a week to dry and release the spores. Fill a flat or other container with moist, sterile planting medium, but leave some space at the top. The planting mix can consist of two-thirds peat moss and one-third perlite; half ground leaf mold mixed with half sand and loam; or some other medium. Scatter spores evenly over the medium and cover the container with glass or plastic. Keep the medium warm, around 18 to 24C (65 to 75F), and moist at all times. After two or three months, tiny fronds will be visible, and small clumps of new ferns can be transplanted. Ferns often propagate themselves in a moist, relatively sheltered greenhouse and in appropriate conditions in the garden.

Adiantum aleuticum	Zones 3b to 9b	Pteridaceae

northern maidenhair fern, five-finger fern

This delicate, perennial fern develops annual fronds from clumps of short rhizomes. The wiry, black rachis (stem) is split into two distinctive, curved branches with the fronds palmately divided into filmy leaflets (pinnae). Sori form along the rolled margins of the leaflets. Fronds can reach 30 to 80cm (1 to 2.5ft) in height and 30cm (1ft) in width during the growing season.

Cultivation. Full to part shade or dappled light, and very moist to wet soil. Not fussy about soil quality but prefers a good amount of organic matter. Lovely among the rocks at the edge of stream, pond, or waterfall, or in moist stumps in the woodland garden. Does well in containers but must be kept watered.

Propagation. Grow from spores or divide larger clumps in late winter or early spring, before the new fronds expand.

Native Habitat and Range. In shady, moist woods, streambanks, seeps, and waterfall splash zones at low to mid elevations, from Alaska south through California, and from the coast, east to Montana and Colorado, the Great Lakes, and parts of eastern North America.

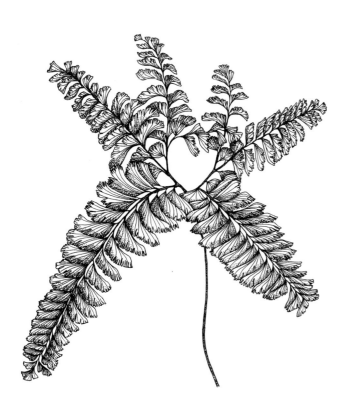

Adiantum aleuticum

Adiantum aleuticum with *Prosartes smithii*

Notes. Sometimes classified as a subspecies or variety of *A. pedatum*, a species that occurs in eastern North America. *Adiantum* is a genus of around 200 species, most of which are native to tropical parts of the Americas; fewer than ten species occur in North America, and only two others sparsely in our area. Both are distinguished by having an unbranched central rachis and feather-like fronds. California maidenhair (*A. jordanii*) occurs in moist rocky sites from southern California north to the canyons of the Rogue River in southern Oregon. Venus-hair or southern maidenhair fern (*A. capillus-veneris*), widespread throughout warmer parts of the Americas, is also known from hot springs in British Columbia.

Asplenium trichomanes	Zones 4a to 9b	Aspleniaceae

maidenhair spleenwort

This charming little evergreen fern grows from short rhizomes and produces dense tufts of leaves reaching 7 to 35cm (3 to 14in) tall. The petioles (extending to include the rachis where leaflets are attached) are wiry, shiny, and reddish. The leaves are once-pinnate, and the leaflets are oval with rounded teeth. The sori on the undersides of the leaflets are elongated, and the sporangia are covered with a flap-like indusium, which disappears as the sporangia mature.

Cultivation. Part to full shade or dappled light, and moist soil. Likes limestone or other alkaline substrates. Lovely in the shady rock garden or tucked into the cracks of a stone wall on either side of the Cascades.

Propagation. Grow from spores. The rhizomes of plants originally grown from spores can be divided in late winter or early spring.

Native Habitat and Range. In moist talus and cliff crevices (especially in limestone), at mid elevations, more or less circumboreal and scattered south to California, Arizona, Texas, and Florida.

Asplenium trichomanes

Notes. Two subspecies, *A. t.* ssp. *trichomanes* and *A. t.* ssp. *quadrivalens*, occur in the Pacific Northwest. *Asplenium* is a large, cosmopolitan genus of several hundred species, many of them tropical; fewer than 30 species occur in North America. Only two other spleenworts occur in our area. The circumboreal *A. trichomanes-ramosum* (*A. viride*; green spleenwort) is found in rocky crevices, often at timberline, ranging south to central Washington, northeast Nevada, Colorado, and New York; the petioles of this species are brownish, and the leaves, usually deciduous, are relatively short at 5 to 15cm (2 to 6in). *Asplenium septentrionale* (forked spleenwort), native mainly to the Southwest, ranges into Oregon.

Athyrium filix-femina ssp. cyclosorum	Zones 3b to 9b	Dryopteridaceae

lady fern

This deciduous fern can reach about 2m (6ft) in height, producing tall clusters of lacy fronds from the scaly rhizomes. The fronds are two to three times pinnately compound and broadest in the middle, tapering at the base and tip. The fronds die back in cold weather; they are fragile and easily broken but lush and intricate during the growing season. The sori on the undersides of the leaflets are oblong, elongate, and curved. Each sorus is covered with a flap-like indusium that disappears as the sporangia age.

Cultivation. Part to deep shade or dappled light, and wet or moist soil. This fern has a tendency to grow where it wasn't planted and is sometimes considered aggressive, but it is beautiful near the shady bog or stream, or in the wetland or woodland garden.

Propagation. Grow from spores, or divide rhizomes when plants are dormant. Once appropriately sited, this fern will probably spread by spores or rhizomes without assistance.

Native Habitat and Range. Common in bogs and wet woods at low to mid elevations, circumboreal, from Alaska south into California and east to Idaho, Colorado, and New Mexico.

Athyrium filix-femina ssp. *cyclosorum*

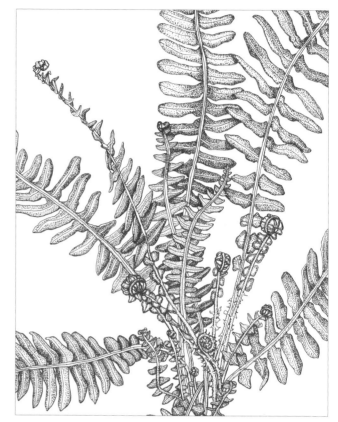

Blechnum spicant

Notes. This subspecies is our northwestern taxon. Most cultivars of *A. filix-femina*, including 'Frizelliae' (dwarf, with spherical pinnae) and 'Vernoniae Cristatum' (with crested fronds), were developed from European stock. *Athyrium americanum* (*A. distentifolium*, *A. alpestre*; alpine lady fern) is another, smaller circumboreal species native to the Pacific Northwest; it is found at mid to high elevations in the mountains. *Athyrium* is a primarily tropical genus of maybe a dozen species.

| ***Blechnum spicant*** | Zones 5b to 9b | Blechnaceae |

deer fern

This graceful fern can reach 1m (3ft) in height and width, though it is often a bit smaller. The fronds are widest in the middle and once-divided into simple, round-tipped pinnae (leaflets). Sterile fronds are evergreen; fertile fronds are deciduous and grow from near the middle of the plant, with narrower pinnae and a continuous, sporangia-filled sorus running along the narrow leaflet margins.

Cultivation. Full or part shade, or dappled light, and wet or moist soil. Retains its good looks year-round with enough shade and moisture. Cold weather may burn some of the fronds. An excellent addition to the shade or woodland garden and handsome enough to be a featured species. Plant it near a path, next to a log or stump, or near a bog.

Propagation. Grow from spores cultivated on wet soil.

Native Habitat and Range. On wet or moist shady sites, lowlands to mid-elevations from Alaska south to northern California, mostly west of the Cascades, but also east to northern Idaho; circumboreal, but disjunct.

Blechnum spicant

Cheilanthes gracillima

Notes. *Blechnum* includes around 200 species, mostly native to the Southern Hemisphere. In some areas deer fern is an important winter food plant for wildlife; it has also been used as livestock forage.

Cheilanthes gracillima	Zones 4b to 9b	Pteridaceae

lace lip fern

This charming fern produces evergreen fronds from a short, branching rhizome. The petioles of the fronds are dark brown, sometimes hairy or scaly, and up to 12cm (5in) long. The leaf blades are about 10cm (4in) long by 2cm (1in) wide. They are two or three times pinnate into tiny leaflets with inrolled margins, green above and with rusty, woolly hairs beneath. Sori form near the leaf margins, and the sporangia are often distinctly exserted.

Cultivation. Full sun to part shade, and rocky, well-drained, rather dry soil. Slow-growing but choice, and less difficult than some ferns. May need protection from excessive moisture in wetter areas. For the rock garden, trough, or stone retaining wall on either side of the Cascades.

Propagation. Grow from spores.

Native Habitat and Range. In cliff crevices, often on volcanic rock, at mid to high elevations from southern British Columbia, south through the mountains to central California, and from near the coast, east to Idaho, Nevada, and Utah.

Notes. Slender lip fern (*C. feei*) and coastal lip fern (*C. intertexta*) also occur in our area. *Cheilanthes* includes some 100 species, distributed throughout the world and most common in dry, rocky habitats; nearly 30 species are North American natives.

| *Cryptogramma acrostichoides* | Zones 3b to 9b | Pteridaceae |

American parsley fern or rock-brake

Both the sterile and fertile leaves of this small evergreen fern arise in tufts from short, branched rhizomes. Sterile fronds grow to 20cm (8in) and are three times pinnate with rounded leaflets; fertile leaves are taller, to 30cm (1ft), with divided blades. The margins of the fertile leaflets are rolled under, covering the continuous sori that run along their margins.

Cultivation. Part shade, and fast-draining soil. This is an excellent little fern, easier to grow than most other ferns of rocky habitats. Plant it in the rock garden or stone wall, or in the richer soil in front of logs, where its yellow-green foliage will add color.

Propagation. Grow from spores. Alternatively, divide rhizomes in late winter or early spring, but this should be done only with plants originally grown from spores.

Native Habitat and Range. On rocky, open, rather dry sites at various elevations, circumboreal but scattered, common in mountainous areas from Alaska and the Yukon south through California and New Mexico, east to southern Ontario and northern Michigan; eastern Asia.

Notes. Sometimes classified as *C. crispa*. There are only a few species in the genus, but they are widespread and complex. *Cryptogramma stelleri* (Steller's parsley fern or rock-brake) is another circumboreal species with fronds growing singly from a slender rhizome; it lives at high elevations south to northeastern Nevada, Colorado, Iowa, and the east coast. Cascade parsley fern (*C. cascadensis*) has thin, deciduous leaves and occurs at high elevations from British Columbia to California and east to Montana. *Aspidotis densa* (*Cryptogramma densa*; Indian's dream) is another small, evergreen fern of dry, rocky places; it has fronds with dark brown petioles, and most of the leaves bear sporangia.

| **Cystopteris fragilis** | Zones 3b to 9b | Dryopteridaceae |

fragile or bladder fern

This delicate species produces deciduous fronds to 30cm (1ft) from short, scaly rhizomes. The petioles are short, and the fronds are two or three times pinnate, widest in the middle and narrowed at both ends. The sori on the undersides of the leaflets are small and rounded. A hood-like indusium covers part of the sorus, drying up as the spores are released.

Cultivation. Part shade or dappled light, and moist to rather dry, rocky soil. This is a charming little fern for the rock garden, especially where calcium content is high. Plant it in the cracks of a stone wall, on an outcrop in the woodland garden, or among moist rocks near a pond.

Propagation. Grow from spores.

Native Habitat and Range. On talus, cliffs, and rocky, forested openings at low to high elevations throughout the Northern Hemisphere and occasionally beyond.

Notes. Ten of the approximately 12 species of *Cystopteris* occur in North America. Mountain bladder fern (*C. montana*) lives in moist places in southern Alaska and ranges south to Montana. *Woodsia* (cliff fern) is a similar genus of small or medium rock lovers; *W. oregana* (Oregon cliff fern) and *W. scopulina* (Rocky Mountain cliff fern), both native to areas east of the Cascades, are interesting additions to the rock garden.

| **Dryopteris expansa** | Zones 4a to 9b | Dryopteridaceae |

shield or spiny wood fern

This deciduous fern produces clusters of fronds to 1m (3ft) tall from thick rhizomes. The lacy leaves are triangular in outline and three times pinnate. The sori on the undersides of the fronds are rounded and have a persistent indusium.

Cystopteris fragilis

Cryptogramma acrostichoides

Dryopteris expansa

Cultivation. Full shade to almost full sun, and moist soil. A good fern for the moist woodland garden, tall enough to act as background for smaller plants. The fronds often remain more or less evergreen in mild winters.

Propagation. Grow from spores, or divide rhizomes in late winter or early spring.

Native Habitat and Range. In moist woods and along streambanks, at low to fairly high elevations; circumboreal, south on the west side of the Cascades to California, east to northern Idaho, Colorado, and the Great Lakes.

Notes. Sometimes classified as *D. spinulosa* or *D. dilatata*. This complex genus of more than 100 species of temperate and tropical regions has often been the subject of taxonomic dispute; around 20 species occur in North America, five of them in our area, including coastal wood fern (*D. arguta*), a species with evergreen fronds. It is most common west of the Cascades, in relatively dry, open woods from southern British Columbia to northern California and east to Arizona. Male fern (*D. filix-mas*) is circumboreal and occurs in moist woods throughout the west. Toothed wood fern (*D. carthusiana*) and crested wood fern (*D. cristata*) range into the Pacific Northwest, but are more common to the east.

Equisetum   Equisetaceae

horsetail, scouring-rush

Equisetum, a genus descended from ancient vascular plants, includes about 30 species of cosmopolitan distribution; most of the approximately fifteen that are native to North America occur in the Pacific Northwest. These rhizomatous, colony-forming perennials produce spores in sporangia organized into cone-shaped structures (strobili). The deciduous horsetail species are often dimorphic: the reproductive shoots, first to appear in the spring, are brownish, lack chlorophyll, and look like elongated cones; the vegetative shoots have whorls of green branches. Other species, often called scouring-rushes, are frequently evergreen and monomorphic, with spore-producing cones at the tips of slender, green shoots; these species are less aggressive and make interesting ornamentals. The epidermal cell walls of all species contain silicon dioxide, giving them a rough surface. Many groups of native people in the Northern Hemisphere used these plants for scouring dishes and polishing wooden tools.

Propagation. Easy by dividing the clumps of rhizomes in late winter or early spring. Plants can probably be grown from spores using the same methods suggested for ferns.

Equisetum hyemale   Zones 3b to 9b

common scouring-rush, Dutch rush

The hollow, evergreen stems of this perennial are unbranched, with 15 to 45 longitudinal ridges. The bluish green shoots grow to 1.5m (5ft) tall and up to 1cm (.5in) thick. The leaves are connate (fused together), condensed, and arranged in whorls, forming short, grayish sheaths topped with blackish teeth around the stems at each node. The spore bearing cones at the shoot tips are dark brown or blackish and persistent, with a sharp point at the tip (apiculate).

Cultivation. Full sun to part shade, and moist to wet soil. A beautiful plant for the pond margin or bank. Plant this species among pebbles or between stream-smoothed rocks for a striking effect. Not especially fast-growing or aggressive, but over time a single clump can form a large colony; if this is a concern, keep the plant in a buried container.

Equisetum hyemale

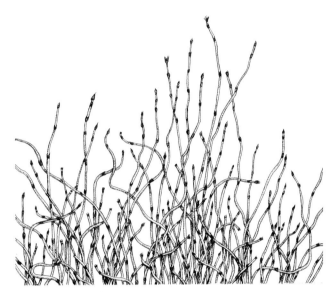

Equisetum scirpoides

Native Habitat and Range. Streambanks, roadsides, and other moist to wet sites at low to mid elevations, circumboreal, south to California and Florida.

Notes. The North American taxon is *E. h.* var. *affine*. *Equisetum laevigatum* (smooth horsetail) is similar, but its shoots are deciduous and the spore-bearing cones are generally blunt-tipped.

Equisetum scirpoides   Zones 3b to 9b

sedgelike or dwarf scouring-rush or horsetail

The shoots of this delicate, evergreen perennial are firm but often gracefully curved, and sometimes prostrate. The diminutive stems, which lack a central cavity, grow 7 to 25cm (3 to 10in) tall and only about a millimeter wide, with six longitudinal ridges. The tiny leaf sheaths that surround the stems have green bases with black bands above and bristled teeth. The spore-bearing cones are tiny and have pointed tips.

Cultivation. Sun or part shade, and wet or moist soil. This is a fine plant for unusual containers, such as small tabletop pools and trickling waterfalls, and well suited to the margin of a small pond, moss garden, or other miniature setting.

Native Habitat and Range. In moist to wet places, often in coniferous forests at low to mid elevations, circumboreal, south to Washington, Montana, the Great Lakes, and New York.

Notes. The evergreen *E. variegatum* (northern scouring-rush, variegated horsetail) is taller, to 50cm (20in).

Gymnocarpium dryopteris

Gymnocarpium dryopteris	Zones 3b to 9b	Dryopteridaceae

oak fern

This charming deciduous fern produces fronds to 15cm (6in) tall on light brown petioles. The blades are triangular in outline and two or three times compound into small pinnae. Fronds usually grow singly from the slender, spreading rhizomes, eventually forming extensive carpets. The sori are round dots on the undersides of the leaves, and they lack indusia.

Cultivation. Full shade to part sun, and moist soil. This delicate, creeping fern makes an excellent groundcover for damp places in the garden; it can eventually blanket the floor of the woodland shade garden, but it is not especially competitive. Though deciduous, it is lovely among the taller perennials and shrubs during the growing season.

Propagation. Easy from divisions of the slender rhizomes in early spring. Can also be grown from spores.

Native Habitat and Range. Along streambanks, seeps, and in moist woods, circumboreal from Alaska south to Oregon and east to Arizona, Iowa, and Virginia; Eurasia.

Notes. Sometimes classified as *Dryopteris* because of its similarity to that genus. This species is listed as rare in some of the eastern parts of its range. Pacific or western oak fern (*G. disjunctum*) has larger leaf blades. *Gymnocarpium* is a genus of the Northern Hemisphere, with less than six species in North America.

Pentagramma triangularis   Zones 6a to 9b   Pteridaceae

goldback fern

This small, evergreen fern puts up tufts of triangular leaves from short rhizomes. The fronds grow to 35cm (14in), and the wiry petioles are dark brown and glossy. The blades are two or three times divided and green on the upper surface. The undersides of the leaves are covered with a white to golden waxy powder, hence the common name. The sporangia are not grouped into distinctive sori, but run in lines along the veins, without indusia. The fronds curl up in dry weather, revealing their golden "backs."

Cultivation. Sun to part shade, and fast-draining soil. This species presents a challenge. Keep it on the dry side during the summer. A spot in the rock garden with an overhang will help protect it from excessive rain. It can also be grown in a trough or other container.

Propagation. Grow from spores. Rhizomes of plants originally grown from spores can be divided in late winter or early spring.

Native Habitat and Range. In rocky, open, dry sites and thin-soiled meadows at low to mid elevations, mainly west of the Cascades from southern British Columbia to Baja California and east through the Columbia River Gorge to Utah, Arizona, and New Mexico.

Notes. Sometimes classified as *Pityrogramma triangularis*. Only *P. t.* ssp. *triangularis* occurs in the Pacific Northwest. *Pentagramma* includes only a few species; another genus of rock-loving ferns, similarly challenging in cultivation, is *Pellaea* (cliff brake). These ferns have wiry, dark stems and should only be propagated from spores. *Pellaea andromedifolia* (coffee fern), *P. brachyptera* (Sierra cliff brake), *P. breweri* (Brewer's cliff brake), and *P. bridgesii* (Bridges' cliff brake) occur in rocky habitats in the Pacific Northwest.

Pentagramma triangularis

Polypodium   Polypodiaceae

licorice fern, polypody

Polypodium is a large cosmopolitan genus of mostly tropical, mostly epiphytic ferns. Half of the approximately ten North American species occur in the Pacific Northwest.

Propagation. Grow from spores. The stout rhizomes can be divided in spring or fall, but this should be done only with plants originally grown from spores or rescued from certain destruction.

Polypodium glycyrrhiza   Zones 7a to 9b

licorice fern

This perennial fern unfurls its fronds in the fall and remains green throughout the winter; in the spring the leaves usually turn brown. The creeping rhizomes are brownish, stout, and taste like licorice. The largest fronds can grow to 70cm (28in) long, but are often shorter. The leaf blades are once-pinnate, and the longest pinnae are about 5cm (2in) long with pointed tips. The sori on the undersides of the leaves are rounded and have no indusia.

Cultivation. Shade to part sun or dappled light, and moist soil. This fern grows on all sorts of substrates, including moist streambanks, rocks, logs, and the living boughs of deciduous trees. It is dormant during the dry summer months but a welcome splash of green in the winter landscape.

Native Habitat and Range. On a variety of substrates, including tree limbs, rocks, and moist banks at low elevations, from Alaska south to California, west of the Cascade crest and east in the Columbia River Gorge.

Polypodium glycyrrhiza

Notes. The licorice-flavored rhizomes were eaten by many of the coastal tribes as a treat and also used as a medicine. *Polypodium vulgare* (European polypody), from which many cultivars with finely dissected or crested foliage are derived, has sometimes included *P. glycyrrhiza*.

Polypodium hesperium	Zones 3b to 9b

western polypody

This deciduous fern produces fronds up to 20cm (8in) long in the spring from tough rhizomes. The leaflets are rounded at the tip and up to 2.5cm (1in) long. The sori on the undersides of the leaves are round or somewhat elongate.

Cultivation. Part sun or dappled light, and moist, well-drained soil. This fine little fern for the rock garden remains green all summer. Plant it near the rocky, drier margin of the pond or stream, in the cracks of a stone wall, or on a rock outcrop in the woodland garden.

Native Habitat and Range. In moist rock crevices and cliffs, occasionally on moist soil in woods, at low to high elevations, from Alaska south to California, on both sides of the Cascades, east to Montana, Colorado, and New Mexico.

Notes. *Polypodium amorphum* (*P. montense*; Pacific polypody) is another small fern of rocky places, with short leaves and rounded leaflets; it often grows at high elevations, occurring as far south as northwestern Oregon.

Polypodium hesperium

Polypodium scouleri   Zones 7b to 9b

leathery or Scouler's polypody

This rhizomatous, evergreen fern has thick, leathery leaves that can grow to 70cm (28in) long and to 18cm (7in) wide. The stout, pale rhizomes have little flavor. The fronds are once-pinnate; the pinnae have rounded tips and are up to 9cm (3.5in) long. The round sori generally develop only on the upper pinnae, near the tip of the frond.

    Cultivation. Part sun to shade, and moist (not wet) soil. The most difficult species of polypody to grow, it nevertheless tolerates a variety of substrates once established. It grows more slowly than the smaller *P. glycyrrhiza* but makes an interesting—and this time, evergreen—addition to many garden situations. Plant it on tree trunks, stumps, or logs in the shady woodland garden or among the moist rocks of a water feature.

    Native Habitat and Range. On moist banks, tree trunks, and cliffs near the coast from southern British Columbia to southern California.

    Notes. Common California or nested polypody (*Polypodium calirhiza*) is another coastal species with a range in western Oregon and California.

Polystichum   Dryopteridaceae

sword, Christmas, or holly fern

Polystichum encompasses some 100 species of tufted, evergreen ferns distributed throughout the world; around 15 species occur in North America, most in the Pacific Northwest.

Polypodium scouleri

Polystichum andersonii

Propagation. Grows quite easily from spores, and existing plants often produce little ferns where the soil is moist. Some species can be propagated from the small bud-like structures that develop on the frond tips; a piece of leaf with buds can be placed into loose potting soil and kept moist until small plants form. Dividing the short rhizomes in the early spring is another method, but the resulting ferns are uneven and may not survive.

Polystichum andersonii	Zones 5a to 9b

Anderson's sword or holly fern

The evergreen fronds of this laciest sword fern grow to 1m (3ft); they are soft and almost bipinnate, with the primary leaflets very deeply lobed. The rachis is scaly and produces small bud-like structures toward the tip of the leaf. Each round sorus has an umbrella-like indusium that quickly disappears.

Cultivation. Full to part shade or dappled light, and moist soil. This is a lovely evergreen fern for the shade or woodland garden. Plant it with other perennials near the shady bog or pond.

Native Habitat and Range. In shady forests and thickets at mid elevations from southern Alaska, south in the mountains to northern Oregon, east to northern Idaho and Montana.

Notes. Other native species of *Polystichum* with the primary leaflets deeply lobed or divided include Braun's holly fern (*P. braunii*), California sword fern (*P. californicum*), and Lemmon's holly fern (*P. lemmonii*); Kruckeberg's holly fern (*P. kruckebergii*) and rock or mountain sword fern (*P. scopulinum*) are smaller plants with deep lobes only on the lower leaflets.

Polystichum munitum

Polystichum munitum	Zones 5a to 9b

western sword fern

This big, evergreen fern can grow to almost 1.5m (5ft) from a compact, woody rhizome. Fronds arise from the crown in clusters, and the lance-shaped blades are once-pinnate. The leaflets have sharp teeth; each has a lobe at the base, like the toe of a boot. The sori on the undersides of the pinnae are round, and each has an umbrella-like indusium that soon withers.

Cultivation. Part sun to full shade, and moist to dryish soil with plenty of compost. Survives full sun but will not look its best. Tolerates the seasonally dry conditions under big conifers once established. An excellent and very tough fern for any shade or woodland garden, especially west of the Cascades, and useful as a background for other shade-loving plants. This fern has shallow roots and is easily transplanted, and it readily self-propagates from spores. Many gardeners remove the old fronds each spring as the new leaves unfurl, but this is not necessary.

Native Habitat and Range. In moist, coniferous woods from Alaska to California, east across northern Washington to northern Idaho and northwestern Montana, occasional in northeastern Oregon.

Notes. Very common on the west slope of the Cascades. Other sword ferns of the Pacific Northwest with once-pinnately compound leaves are narrow-leaf sword fern (*P. imbricans*) and northern holly fern (*P. lonchitis*).

Pteridium aquilinum

| ***Pteridium aquilinum*** | Zones 4a to 9b | Dennstaedtiaceae |

bracken fern

The huge, deciduous leaves of bracken arise singly from the branched rhizomes, which spread under the surface of the ground. Each frond is triangular in outline and may grow to more than 2m (6ft) tall and 1m (3ft) across. The blades are two or three times pinnate. The sori are continuous, running under the inrolled leaflet margin, which acts as an indusium.

Cultivation. Full sun to part shade, and wet to moist or rather dry soil. Many gardeners dislike bracken because it can be aggressive and difficult to eradicate, but it adds ferny laciness to the native meadow and looks beautiful with big perennials or grasses. A good plant for large meadows and forest edges.

Propagation. Rhizomes can be divided in the early spring but may be difficult to dig. Can also be propagated from spores.

Native Habitat and Range. In dry to moist woods, roadsides, fields, and burned sites, at low to fairly high elevations, widespread through much of North America and beyond.

Notes. This species has the largest range of any fern on the planet; *P. a.* var. *pubescens* is the western North America native. It can poison livestock, and eating young bracken fiddleheads—even after boiling—is not recommended: they are reputed to contain carcinogens.

Woodwardia fimbriata   Zones 6a to 9b   Blechnaceae

giant chain fern

This big, evergreen fern usually grows to 1.5m (5ft) in the garden but can grow to twice that size in the wild. The fronds are widest in the middle, erect and bipinnate, arising in clusters from a branched, woody rhizome. The sori are oblong and arranged along the midveins of the leaflets, end to end, like links in a chain. The indusia are flap-like and open toward the midrib.

Cultivation. Full to part shade, and moist or wet, organic soil. Will take sun if the soil is wet. This is a large, choice fern for the pond, stream margin, or moist to wet area of the shade or woodland garden. Potentially sensitive to winter cold and may need some protection.

Propagation. Grow from spores. The woody rhizomes can be divided in early spring, but plants may be slow to recover. Often self-sows under favorable conditions.

Native Habitat and Range. Along streambanks and other wet to moist places, from lowlands to mid elevations, mainly near the coast from southern British Columbia to southern California and occasionally inland to Arizona and Nevada.

Notes. *Woodwardia* includes about a dozen species of large ferns native to North America, Europe, and Asia. Three species occur in North America; this is our only native.

Woodwardia fimbriata

CONIFERS

Conifers generally have simple; tough; needle-, awl-, or scale-like leaves. Most have cones and are monoecious, with male and female cones in different structures, but on the same plant. The pollen-producing cones are usually small; seed-bearing cones are larger and generally somewhat woody, composed of seed scales and bracts set on a stalk. Although conifers are seed plants (a seed is an embryonic plant surrounded by parental tissues that form the seed coat), they are not flowering plants, and produce neither flowers nor fruits. Because their seeds are not enclosed within an ovary (a fruit is a ripened ovary containing seed—a structure unique to flowering plants), these plants are sometimes called gymnosperms, the "naked-seeded" plants.

Abies	Pinaceae

fir

Abies includes about 40 species, mostly native to the cooler regions of the Northern Hemisphere. Of the fewer than ten species that occur in North America, most are native to the Pacific Northwest. True firs can be difficult to identify because the female cones, which stand upright on the branches, shatter apart at maturity, releasing seed. Cones consist of an axis with seed-bearing scales and a bract beneath each. In some species the bracts are longer than the seed scales; in others, the bracts are short and not visible until cones shatter. The shape of the needles and their placement on the branches helps in identification of firs. Firs have silvery lines of stomata (pores that function in gas exchange) that run the length of the needles; whether the lines of stomata cover both upper and lower surfaces of the needle, or are restricted to the lower surface, helps distinguish one species from another. When fir needles fall, no woody peg remains on the twig. Both birds and aphids are attracted to firs.

Propagation. Usually grown from seed planted soon after it has been collected in autumn. Sow seeds into containers of well-drained potting soil and leave them outside to cold stratify over winter for spring germination. Seedlings are susceptible to damping-off and need some protection from the sun. Cuttings taken in winter and treated with hormones may strike roots, but this is a less successful method.

Abies concolor

Abies concolor	Zones 3b to 9b

white fir

In the wild, this tree reaches 70m (230ft) or more in height and around 7m (20ft) in width, but it is much smaller when cultivated. The needles are relatively flat and wider than they are thick. They tend to be arranged horizontally on either side of the twig. White lines of stomata are present on both upper and lower needle surfaces. The female cones vary from greenish purple to yellow or brown, and the bracts are not visible.

Cultivation. Full sun to part shade, and rather dry soil with good drainage. The silvery-blue foliage of this symmetrical, slow-growing conifer makes it a popular garden tree, and it can also be grown as a container plant.

Native Habitat and Range. On dry slopes and rocky places at fairly low to mid elevations in the Blue Mountains of southeastern Washington, northeastern Oregon, and adjacent Idaho, and on the east slope of the Cascades from Oregon to California, Nevada and Arizona, east to Wyoming and New Mexico.

Notes. A common conifer in the Sierra Nevada of California and often grown as a Christmas tree; 'Candicans' is a selection with striking bluish white foliage. *Abies amabilis* (Pacific silver fir) occurs from southern Alaska, south to northern California in the Coast Ranges and the west slope of the Cascades. Wild specimens can reach a height of 70m (230ft), but cultivated trees reach only a quarter of that height, with a spread of about 5m (15ft); this shade-tolerant conifer prefers a cool spot in the garden and moist, well drained soil.

Abies grandis

Abies grandis	Zones 3b to 9b

grand fir

Even in cultivation, grand firs can grow to more than 30m (100ft) tall and 7m (20ft) across. This fir is recognized by the flattened, blunt-tipped needles that spread horizontally on either side of the twigs. Needles are dark green on the upper surface with white lines of stomata beneath. The female cones are light green, and the bracts are hidden between the longer cone scales.

Cultivation. Full sun to part shade, and well-drained, moist soil. A good tree for the wildlife, woodland, or shade garden. Some gardeners prune the lower branches to create more room for understory plants.

Native Habitat and Range. In forested areas, among other conifers, at low to mid elevations in the mountains, from British Columbia south to California, and east to Idaho and Montana.

Notes. This species intergrades with *A. concolor* in northeastern Oregon. The cultivar 'Johnsonii' is smaller, reaching about 20m (60ft) in height and 3m (10ft) in width.

Abies lasiocarpa	Zones 3b to 9b

subalpine fir

Subalpine fir grows to 30m (100ft) in nature but is often dwarfed on alpine sites. Trees in cultivation are usually much shorter and often wider, to 5m (15ft) across. The bark is thin and gray, with resin-filled blisters. The blue-green needles are flattened but thickest in the middle, and tend to turn upward, brush-like, from the twigs. They have rows of white stomata on both

Abies lasiocarpa

surfaces. The erect seed cones are cylindrical, usually purple when young, and 6 to 11cm (2.5 to 4.5in) long. The short bracts are hidden among the seed scales.

Cultivation. Full sun to part shade, and moist, well-drained soil. This is usually a slow-growing fir, making it a good tree for the large rock garden. It makes a fine addition to the wildlife garden and can also be grown in containers or trained as a bonsai subject.

Native Habitat and Range. In somewhat dry habitats, at low elevations near major rivers and, more typically, at mid to alpine elevations, from Alaska and the Yukon south to southern Oregon, in the Olympic and Cascade Mountains, east to central Idaho and Montana, south to Arizona and New Mexico.

Notes. Cultivars include the dwarf 'Compacta' and the pale, waxy-needled 'Glauca'. Our native variety is the widespread *A. l.* var. *lasiocarpa*.

Abies procera	Zones 6b to 9b

noble fir

This beautiful, symmetrical tree can reach 70m (230ft) tall and 10m (30ft) across in the wild and may eventually approach this size in cultivation. The bark of young trees is smooth and gray with bumpy resin blisters. Older trees have gray-brown, flaking bark with reddish layers beneath. The branches tend to be stiff, giving the tree a tiered look. The needles are blue-green to silvery, thick, and somewhat four-sided. There are rows of white stomata on both sides of the needles. The needles are about 2cm (1in) long, and all tend to turn upward, like a brush. The seed cones grow to 15cm (6in) long. The bracts are straw-colored, with ruffled margins and a long, pointed tip. They are longer than the reddish seed scales and usually conceal them.

Abies procera

Cultivation. Full sun or part shade, and deep, moist soil. Plant it as a specimen tree and give it room to show off its natural stateliness and minimize pruning. A beautiful tree for the woodland or wildlife garden, or even as a container plant.

Native Habitat and Range. In moist forests and deep soils at mid elevations in the Cascades from central Washington south to the Siskiyous of northern California, west to southwestern Washington and northwestern Oregon.

Notes. Often grown as a Christmas tree. The cultivar 'Glauca' has especially bluish white foliage. The similar *A. magnifica* (red fir) is native at mid to high elevations from southwestern Oregon to the mountains of California; it usually grows poorly in the lowlands. *Abies* ×*shastensis* (Shasta red fir) is a hybrid between the two species.

Calocedrus decurrens	Zones 5a to 9b	Cupressaceae

incense cedar

This lovely tree has a dense, narrow conical shape and grows to 30m (100ft) in height and 4m (12ft) in width. It has purplish to reddish brown bark. The yellowish green leaves are tiny scales, usually with incurved tips, arranged so that there are four at about the same level at each node. The foliage tends to form flat sprays. The distinctive seed cones are cinnamon-colored, composed of six scales, the largest ones flattened and about 2.5cm (1in) long, looking something like a duck's bill.

Cultivation. Full sun or light shade, and well-drained, rather dry soil. This species resists most pests, tolerates poor soils, and takes fairly dry conditions. Give incense cedar a spot where its fragrance can be enjoyed in the summer heat. After the first year or two, it grows quickly and

Calocedrus decurrens

symmetrically, making a fine specimen tree, or use it in a windbreak, large hedgerow, or wildlife grove.

Propagation. Grow from seed collected and planted in autumn. Sow seeds into flats of potting soil and leave them outside to stratify in cool, moist winter conditions for spring germination.

Native Habitat and Range. In open, rather dry areas at fairly low to high elevations from northern Oregon, south and west through the Coast Ranges and Cascades, south through the Sierra Nevada of California, east to western Nevada.

Notes. Sometimes classified in *Libocedrus*. The wood of this species is resistant to fungal decomposers, making it valuable for fences and other structures. 'Compacta' is an especially dense, dwarf form.

Chamaecyparis	Cupressaceae

cedar, cypress

Although commonly called cedars, these conifers are more closely related to cypress (*Cupressus*), while the true cedars (*Cedrus*) are in the pine family. Juvenile leaves of *Chamaecyparis* are needle-like; the leaves of older plants consist of tiny scales. The female cones are small, woody, and rounded. Fewer than ten species are native to temperate North America and northeastern Asia, but these trees have a long history of horticultural use, with several hundred cultivars available.

Propagation. Grow from seed collected in the fall and kept under warm conditions for a few weeks after harvest. Sow the seeds into containers of potting soil in the late fall or winter and leave them outside to cold stratify for germination in the spring. Plants can also be grown from cuttings taken in fall or winter and treated with rooting hormones.

Chamaecyparis lawsoniana

Chamaecyparis lawsoniana	Zones 7a to 9b

Port Orford cedar, Lawson's cypress

This pyramidal tree can reach 50m (150ft) in native stands, but usually grows to 20m (60ft) in the garden. The fine foliage consists of small, scale-like leaves. Sprays of foliage have a pattern of Xs on the back, and the smaller branches droop gracefully with age. The female cones are woody and spherical, a bit less than 1cm (.5in) in diameter.

Cultivation. Sun or part shade, and well-drained, moist soil. Although the species itself may be difficult to find, nurseries stock cultivars for every garden situation, including dwarf forms for the rock garden or shrub bed. Plants can be sheared but shouldn't be pruned back into leafless wood.

Native Habitat and Range. On moist slopes at low elevations near the coast and in the Coast Ranges of southwestern Oregon and northwestern California.

Notes. Slow-growing and dwarf cultivars include 'Globosa', 'Nana', and 'Minima Glauca'; color forms include silvery 'Argentea', blue-green 'Glauca', and golden-yellow 'Aurea'. In 'Ellwoodii' and others, the needle-like juvenile leaves are retained; mutants offer odd shapes, twisted branches, and dense cockscombs of foliage. This species is susceptible to a species of *Phytophthora*, a fungus-like pathogen that is common in some areas and is usually lethal to the tree.

Chamaecyparis nootkatensis

Chamaecyparis nootkatensis	Zones 3b to 9b

Alaska yellow, Nootka, or Sitka cedar or cypress

This conifer typically grows to 35m (115ft) in the wild. The tiny, scale-like leaves have pointed, spreading tips. Leaves are opposite, arranged in four rows, and are prickly to the touch when brushed back from the tip. The branches are typically flattened and drooping. The seed cones are small and round, about 1cm (.5in) across, and covered with a waxy bloom when young, becoming woody when ripe. Seeds are released from the umbrella-like cone scales.

Cultivation. Sun or part shade, and well-drained, moist or even wet soil. Tolerates poor soils and low temperatures but should be protected from winter winds in the coldest areas. The graceful, weeping shape of this tree makes it a good backdrop or specimen tree. It can be lightly shaped or sheared.

Native Habitat and Range. In moist to wet, often rocky areas near the coast in southeastern Alaska, and at mid to high elevations in the mountains of Washington and Oregon, south to northern California.

Notes. Sometimes classified as *Cupressus nootkatensis*. The wood of Alaska yellow cedar is very tough; it was used in tools, decorations, and trade by Native American tribes living within its range, and continues to have commercial value. Cultivars include 'Compacta' (rounded, dwarf), 'Viridis' (bright green, narrowly columnar), and 'Pendula' (strongly weeping). ×*Cupressocyparis leylandii* (Leyland cypress) is an intergeneric hybrid between this species and *Cupressus macrocarpa*.

Cupressus bakeri

Cupressus bakeri   Zones 6a to 9a   Cupressaceae

Modoc cypress

This conifer usually attains 10 to 20m (30 to 60ft) with a narrow shape and shiny, reddish bark. Small, slender branchlets grow on all sides of the larger branches. The foliage is gray-green, composed of tiny, scale-like leaves. The rounded cones are about 1cm (.5in) long.

Cultivation. Full sun, and well-drained or rocky soil. It is a drought-tolerant tree, good for a large, sunny rock garden or hot, dry wildlife areas.

Propagation. Easiest from seed. Keep seeds warm for a few weeks after collecting them in the fall, and then plant them into containers of potting soil and leave them outside to cold stratify over winter. May be grown, with difficulty, from cuttings taken in fall or winter and treated with rooting hormones.

Native Habitat and Range. On dry, often volcanic or serpentine soils at mid elevations in southwestern Oregon and northern California.

Notes. *Cupressus* includes around 25 species native to western North America, Asia, and Europe; most of the other North American natives occur to the south of us, especially in California.

Juniperus   Cupressaceae

juniper

Junipers are probably the most familiar conifers used in landscaping; hundreds of cultivars have been developed over the years. More than 50 species of *Juniperus* are native to the Northern

Juniperus communis var. *saxatilis*

Hemisphere; about a dozen occur in North America, half in our area. Young plants have needle- or awl-shaped juvenile leaves; many species subsequently develop scale-like leaves, but in some the juvenile needles persist. Many species are dioecious, with male and female cones on separate plants. The small, round female cones are fleshy and berry-like. Juniper foliage gives off a fragrance that some gardeners find offensive, and they can also be a fire hazard. Still, the hardy junipers are fine additions to the garden as evergreen groundcovers, shrubs, or relatively small trees.

Propagation. Difficult from seed, which require a few months of warm conditions or pre-treatment with sulfuric acid. Pour boiling water over the seeds to encourage germination before planting them into flats of potting soil in the fall or spring. Semi-hard cuttings taken during the summer and treated with hormones usually root well; keep the cuttings humid and the rooting medium moist but not wet. Hardwood cuttings can be taken in the spring.

Juniperus communis	Zones 3b to 9b

common juniper

Common juniper is a woody, usually prostrate shrub to 1m (3ft) tall with branches spreading to 2m (6ft). The leaves are sharp needles, usually arranged on the stems in whorls of three. They are green on the upper surface and white on the underside. The round, berry-like cones are pale and covered with a waxy bloom when young, blue-black when ripe, and produced only on female plants.

Cultivation. Full sun, and dry soil. This drought-tolerant juniper can take part shade and poor soils, but won't survive in poorly drained or wet soils. All junipers become gnarled with age, but the same effect can be created with artistic pruning, making this low-growing species a popular choice for rock gardens and bonsai containers. This is a good plant for dry banks and parking areas, or around logs at the edge of the dry wildflower meadow.

Native Habitat and Range. On rocky sites, dry hills, and open woods at mid to high elevations from Alaska south to the mountains of California, east across much of North America.

Notes. *Juniperus c.* var. *saxatilis* (*J. c.* var. *montana*; mountain juniper) is found in the higher Cascade and Olympic mountains; *J. c.* var. *depressa* is more widespread. Populations with especially long, spreading branches that live near the coast in southwestern Oregon and northwestern California are sometimes recognized as *J. c.* var. *jackii*. Other naturally occurring varieties of *J. communis* occur throughout the large range of the species. Cultivars include 'Ashfordii' (columnar), 'Compressa' (dwarf), and 'Aurea' and 'Aureospica' (yellowish).

Juniperus scopulorum	Zones 3b to 9b	

Rocky Mountain juniper

This small, rounded tree grows to 10m (30ft) in height. The juvenile leaves are needle-like and may persist on older trees, especially in coastal populations. Mature leaves are tiny, scale-like, and arranged in pairs. The small, spherical female cones are bluish purple with a waxy surface.

Cultivation. Full sun, and fast-draining or dry soil, especially in gardens west of the Cascades. This juniper is able to tolerate cold winters and hot, dry summers, making it especially useful east of the Cascades. Use it as a specimen tree in the garden, or as a screen or part of the wildlife hedgerow.

Native Habitat and Range. On rocky, dry sites near the coast and inland through the lower mountains from Vancouver Island and parts of Puget Sound, east in British Columbia and Washington to northeastern Oregon, east to the Great Plains, New Mexico, and Texas.

Notes. 'Pathfinder' (gray-blue) and 'Wichita Blue' (silvery) are conical forms; 'Skyrocket' (blue-gray), 'Gray Gleam', and 'Cologreen' (bright green) are columnar selections. 'Tolleson's Green Weeping' has bluish foliage and gracefully drooping branches. Western juniper (*J. occidentalis*), a drought-tolerant tree growing to 15m (50ft) tall, lives in the dry foothills east of the Cascades from central Washington south through California and east through the Blue Mountains to southwestern Idaho and Nevada; many gardeners find the foliage of this species more fragrant than foul-smelling, and it can become massive and picturesque with age.

Larix occidentalis	Zones 3b to 9b	Pinaceae

western larch or tamarack

In the wild, this deciduous conifer can reach 80m (260ft) in height; in cultivation it is typically 20m (60ft) tall and 5m (15ft) wide. The needles are about 2cm (1in) long and spirally arranged on growing shoots as well as crowded into tufts at the tips of short spur branches. New spring growth is lime-green, and the needles turn golden in the fall. The small cones are about 2.5cm (1in) long and are red when young, brown when mature. The thin, long-tailed bracts extend from beneath each seed scale. Cones persist on the branches, creating interesting winter patterns.

Cultivation. Full sun to part shade. Although it is not fussy about soil, this species prefers moist to wet conditions and is more tolerant of cold winters than hot, dry summers. Makes a good specimen tree near the pond or bog and a fine addition to the wildlife garden, as it is attractive to birds. Especially beautiful when planted among evergreen conifers for the seasonal contrast.

Propagation. Easiest from seed collected in the fall, planted into flats of potting soil soon after harvest, and left outside to let the cool, moist winter conditions break dormancy for germination in the spring. Semi-softwood cuttings can be taken from young trees in the late summer, treated with hormones, and rooted under mist, but this is a less successful method.

Juniperus scopulorum

Larix occidentalis

Native Habitat and Range. On moist to swampy sites in the foothills to mid elevations in the mountains from southern British Columbia, south to central Oregon and east through northwestern Idaho to western Montana.

Notes. Larches are the only deciduous conifers native to the Pacific Northwest. The genus includes about eight other species native to the chillier parts of the Northern Hemisphere.

Picea   Pinaceae

spruce

Picea encompasses around 40 species of evergreen conifers native to the cool regions of the Northern Hemisphere; fewer than ten species of spruces occur in North America, half in our area. Spruce needles are generally four-sided, each sitting on a woody peg that remains on the twig after the old needle falls; they are arranged in all directions around the twigs and are usually sharply pointed. The female cones of *Picea* are generally cylindrical and hang downward from the branches. The seed scales are woody but thin, and the bracts are shorter than the seed scales. Spruces are excellent additions to the wildlife garden, providing food and shelter for birds.

Propagation. Grow from seed collected in autumn. Plant the seeds soon after harvest into flats of potting soil and leave them outside to stratify over the winter for spring germination. Keep seedlings moist and shaded. Cuttings taken in late winter or early spring and treated with hormones may produce some rooted plants.

Picea breweriana   Zones 6a to 9b

Brewer's or weeping spruce

In the wild, this spruce grows to 35m (115ft) but reaches only about a third of that size in a garden setting. The bark is red-brown with long scales. In older trees the larger boughs tend to grow horizontally with the smaller branches weeping. The needles are 2cm (1in) long, whitish above and dark green beneath. The female cones are up to 10cm (4in) long, with thin, rounded seed scales.

Cultivation. Full sun or part shade, and moist soil. Older specimens of Brewer's spruce are graceful and make a beautiful focal point in the garden, but they are intolerant of extreme heat or drought.

Native Habitat and Range. On cool, north-facing slopes at mid to fairly high elevations in the Siskiyou Mountains from southwestern Oregon to northwestern California.

Notes. *Picea glauca* (white, Canada, or Black Hills spruce) is a northern species, ranging as far south as Idaho, Wyoming, and South Dakota and east to the Atlantic. Engelmann spruce (*P. engelmannii*), a slender, densely branched tree with four-angled, blue-green needles, grows to 50m (150ft) tall; it inhabits boggy sites in the mountains at mid to high elevations east of the Cascades from British Columbia, south to California and east to Alberta, Montana, and New Mexico.

Picea sitchensis   Zones 6a to 9b

Sitka spruce

This gray-barked spruce can reach 70m (230ft) in height and 10m (30ft) or more in width. The needles are four-angled but somewhat flattened on the upper surface. They are about 2cm (1in) long, sharply pointed, silvery with broad lines of stomata above, and green beneath. The seed

Picea breweriana

Picea sitchensis

cones are cylindrical, reddish when young, turning brown as they ripen, and to about 8cm (3in) in length.

Cultivation. Full sun or part shade, and moist soil. This big tree is happiest near the coast and in other cool, moist climates. Sitka spruce can help create a shade garden and makes excellent bird habitat. It is a surprisingly good conifer for a container.

Native Habitat and Range. In moist areas and near bogs at low to mid elevations, from Alaska south to northern California, and from the coast east to the west slope of the Cascades.

Notes. Some of the biggest forest trees on the Olympic Peninsula are Sitka spruce. It is a valuable timber tree, but its use as an ornamental is limited by its susceptibility to spider mites and to adelgids, a kind of aphid, which cause the formation of cone-like galls on young shoots. Cultivars include the slow-growing 'Speciosa' and dwarf 'Papoose.'

Pinus   Pinaceae

pine

Approximately 90 species of *Pinus* are distributed throughout the Northern Hemisphere; roughly 40 occur in North America, ten or so in the Pacific Northwest. The needles of pines are relatively long and usually grouped into clusters, or fascicles. The species encountered in our area have two, three, or five needles in each fascicle. The female cones of pines, though sometimes small, are woody, and the small bracts are fused to the thick seed scales. Some of the five-needled pines are susceptible to white pine blister rust and may contract this fungal disease when currants or gooseberries (*Ribes* spp.), the alternate host in the fungal life cycle, are present. Aphids, air pollution, and the larvae of the European pine shoot moth can also damage pines.

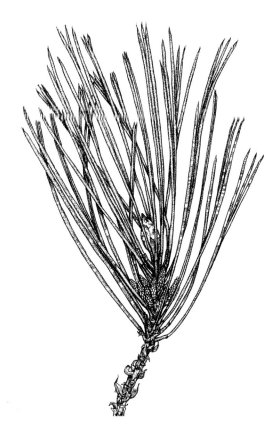

Pinus attenuata

Propagation. Collect seeds from ripe cones in the fall, plant them into containers of potting soil soon after harvest, and leave them outside over winter for germination in the spring. The fascicles of needles taken from young trees are sometimes treated with hormones and rooted in pumice, but this method meets with less success.

Pinus attenuata	Zones 6a to 9b

knobcone pine

This quick-growing species eventually reaches 5 to 20m (15 to 60ft) in height and width. The bark is gray, grooved, and scaly. Young trees are rounded, but open in age. The yellow-green needles are in fascicles of three and grow to 15cm (6in) long. The female cones are as long, and lopsided, often growing in whorls and remaining on the tree for many years.

Cultivation. Full sun, and well-drained soil. This pine tolerates poor, rather dry soils, making it a good tree for difficult places in the garden. Plant it in a rocky area or as part of the wildlife garden, where it will provide habitat for birds.

Native Habitat and Range. In rocky, rather dry places, at low to mid elevations from southwestern Oregon, south through parts of California.

Notes. The cones of this species usually remain closed until the heat of a fire causes the scales to open and release the seeds, which germinate the following spring, regenerating the burned-over forest. It may take heat or boiling water poured over the cones to release the seeds.

Pinus contorta var. contorta

Pinus contorta var. latifolia 'Chief Joseph'

Pinus contorta var. contorta   Zones 7a to 9b

shore or beach pine

Another fast-growing pine, but this species reaches only about 15m (45ft) in height and width; it is compact and rounded when young to more open in age. The dark green needles are usually in clusters of two per fascicle and short at around 5cm (2in). The bark is dark brown, and the seed cones are small, about 5cm (2in) long. They are prickly and yellow brown, usually lopsided, and may remain on the tree for years.

Cultivation. Full sun. It will tolerate almost any dry to wet soil, but prefers good moisture or even somewhat boggy conditions. This conifer does well in the rock garden or in containers, as it can be pruned or trained in various ways. Be sure to keep it in mind when planning a wildlife garden, especially in a small yard. It's an excellent conifer for a large hedgerow.

Native Habitat and Range. In dunes, bogs, and rocky hillsides at low elevations near the coast from Alaska south to northern California.

Notes. This is the only coastal variety of the species that occurs in our area.

Pinus contorta var. latifolia   Zones 3b to 9b

lodgepole pine

Lodgepole pine is very similar to shore pine, but it grows more slowly, has a narrower, more open habit, and eventually becomes taller, reaching 30m (100ft). There are usually two yellow-green needles per fascicle, and the bark is thin and reddish. The prickly, curved seed cones are about 5cm (2in) long and shiny brown, tending to persist on the tree.

Pinus jeffreyi

Pinus lambertiana

Cultivation. Full sun. It is not particular about soils but prefers moist conditions and will tolerate boggy sites. This is a good, open tree for bird habitat in the wildlife garden or wildflower meadow, especially east of the Cascades. It can also be planted in a large rock garden.

Native Habitat and Range. Near bogs and on dry mountain slopes, at mid to high elevations (but not near the coast), from Alaska and the Yukon south through north central and northeastern Oregon, and east through the mountains to Alberta, Saskatchewan, South Dakota, and Colorado.

Notes. This naturally occurring interior variety of the species varies mainly in size and needle color; its selection 'Chief Joseph' turns golden in the winter. A tall variety, *P. c.* var. *murrayana* (Sierra lodgepole pine), occurs away from the coast, from southwestern Washington, south through the Cascades of Oregon and through California; it has yellow-green needles, thin bark, and only slightly lopsided cones.

Pinus jeffreyi   Zones 6a to 9b

Jeffrey pine

Jeffrey pine is a symmetrical tree growing 20 to 50m (60 to 150ft) tall and around 5m (15ft) wide at a moderate rate. The bark of older trees is dark and furrowed, breaking off in scales to reveal pinkish surfaces and giving off a delicious fragrance. The blue-green needles, three to a fascicle, are up to 25cm (10in) long, as are the oval seed cones. The seed scales are thick at the tip, with curved points.

Cultivation. Full sun, well-drained soil, and, if possible, a high elevation, in the mountains. It is a lovely specimen tree with bluish foliage and a sweet fragrance in age, but it may not do well at low elevations.

Native Habitat and Range. On open, dry slopes at high elevations from the mountains of southwestern Oregon, south through the Sierra Nevada of California and east to western Nevada.

Notes. Jeffrey pine is very similar to ponderosa pine (*P. ponderosa*), but the cones of *P. jeffreyi* tend to be longer and smooth to the touch, without prickles.

Pinus lambertiana	Zones 6a to 9b

sugar pine

Sugar pine grows quickly when young, reaching an eventual height of around 80m (260ft) and a width of 15m (45ft), at least in the wild. It is narrow in youth, more open and flat-topped in age. The dark gray bark becomes thick and furrowed, peeling in reddish flakes. Each fascicle holds five slender, blue-green needles to 10cm (4in) long. Large, cylindrical seed cones to 40cm (16in) long are produced at the tips of the upper branches.

Cultivation. Full sun or light shade, moist soil, and a bit of room: this is a big pine for warmer areas. It makes a beautiful specimen tree and will attract birds.

Native Habitat and Range. In moist forests with other conifers at mid elevations from southwestern Oregon, south through the mountains of California and east to western Nevada.

Notes. Sugar pine is the tallest of all pines and produces high quality wood.

Pinus monticola	Zones 3b to 9b

western white pine

This pyramidal conifer grows quickly when young, eventually reaching about 35m (115ft). The bark of young trees is gray, breaking into reddish scales with age. There are five soft, slender needles per fascicle, blue-green with pale stripes of stomata beneath and about 7cm (3in) long. The slender cones have thin seed scales and lack prickles; they are light brown and around 20cm (8in) long.

Cultivation. Full sun or light shade. It is not fussy about soil and can tolerate moist to fairly dry sites. This lovely, symmetrical pine has a soft, silvery-blue appearance, and the pale bark adds to the effect. This is a fine pine for background plantings or wildlife gardens and makes excellent bird habitat.

Native Habitat and Range. From dry slopes to moist valleys, at low to high elevations, from southern British Columbia, south through the Olympics and Cascades to California and east to Idaho, western Montana, and western Nevada.

Notes. Western white pine is an important timber tree in some areas; it is susceptible to white pine blister rust, but some trees are naturally resistant. Whitebark pine (*P. albicaulis*), another five-needled pine, is slow-growing to 15m (40ft) or less; it occurs at high elevations in the mountains from southern British Columbia, south through the Cascades to California and east to northeastern Oregon, Idaho, western Montana, and northern Nevada. This is a great pine for bonsai, alpine, and rock gardens and does well in a container; give it full sun and fast drainage. The very similar alpine species *P. flexilis* (limber pine) lives at high elevations throughout the western mountains.

Pinus ponderosa	Zones 3b to 9b

ponderosa or western yellow pine

Ponderosa pines grow quickly when young, reaching about 70m (230ft) in nature but typically only half that size in cultivation. The bark of young trees is blackish, but old trees develop

Pinus monticola

Pinus ponderosa

beautiful, cinnamon-orange bark. The needles are usually arranged three to a fascicle; they are around 20cm (8in) long, glossy, and yellow-green to dark green. The seed cones grow to 12cm (5in); they are symmetrical and woody, and the seed scales have a thick, prickly tip.

Cultivation. Full sun and good drainage. This species is not particular about soil but prefers it on the dry side. It can be planted as a single tree or as part of a grove in the wildlife garden. Can also be grown in containers and used as bonsai material.

Native Habitat and Range. On open, dry sites at low to high elevations from British Columbia, south through California, east to Montana and the Dakotas, and south to Texas and Mexico.

Notes. *Pinus p.* var. *ponderosa*, the northwestern taxon, usually occurs east of the Cascades, with scattered populations in the Willamette Valley and other sites west of the Cascade crest in southern Oregon. It is an important timber tree in many parts of the interior west.

Pseudotsuga menziesii	Zones 3b to 9b	Pinaceae

Douglas fir

In wild coastal and Cascade populations, Douglas firs can reach 90m (300ft); in cultivation, heights of 40m (120ft) and widths of 10m (30ft) are more typical. The bark is rough and dark brown. The needles are flat, green above and with white stripes of stomata beneath; they are about 2cm (1in) long, soft to the touch and arranged in all directions around the twigs. New needles are bright green. The female cones average about 6cm (2.5in), and are woody, but thin-scaled. The bracts have three teeth and are longer than the seed scales, exserted from the cones. Seed cones hang downward from the branches and fall from the tree soon after maturity. Young trees are fast-growing, pyramidal, and densely branched.

Cultivation. Full sun, and well-drained, rather dry to moist (but not wet) soil. Many gardeners west of the Cascade crest have Doug fir in the yard, and it makes the perfect setting for shade plants. This is an excellent tree for the wildlife garden and birds find it most attractive.

Propagation. Usually grown from seed planted in containers in the fall and left outside to stratify over winter in moist, cool conditions for germination in the spring. Alternatively, take winter cuttings from different young trees and treat with hormones; rooting success will vary from tree to tree.

Native Habitat and Range. On moist to dry, open sites at low to fairly high elevations from southwestern British Columbia, south to California, and from the coast, east to southwestern Alberta and Montana, south to Texas and Mexico.

Notes. This species (not a true fir) is the state tree of Oregon. It is a very important timber tree and is often grown as a fragrant Christmas tree. *Pseudotsuga m.* var. *menziesii* is the taller, more western variety; *P. m.* var. *glauca* ranges east through the Rocky Mountains and rarely exceeds 40m (120ft). Cultivars include 'Argentea' (silvery); 'Caesia' (blue-green); 'Densa' and 'Globosa' (dwarf); and 'Pendula' (with drooping branches). There are only a couple of other species of *Pseudotsuga*, native to California and eastern Asia.

Sequoia sempervirens	Zones 7a to 9b	Taxodiaceae

coast redwood

In the wild, this species grows to 110m (360ft) but reaches only about a third of that size in cultivation. Young trees are fast-growing, dense, symmetrical, and conical, with fibrous red bark. The flat needles, about 2cm (1in) long with pointed tips, are medium green on the upper surface and waxy and whitish beneath; they are arranged horizontally, flattened on either side of the twig. The small seed cones are elliptic and about 2cm (1in) long, with umbrella-like scales.

Pseudotsuga menziesii

Sequoia sempervirens

Pseudotsuga menziesii

Sequoia sempervirens

Cultivation. Sun to part shade, and good, moist soil mulched with compost that will supply nutrients, including iron. Site coast redwoods where they will get plenty of moisture. If you live in the wetter, mistier regions of the Northwest, they will do fine on their own, once established; if you live in a drier climate, they may need additional water. Popular in landscaping, they do well as specimen trees or planted in a grove.

Propagation. Usually grown from seed, which will germinate without special treatment and can be planted in fall or early spring. Cones can be collected and dried to release the seed. The cuttings most likely to form roots come from the shoots that grow from the burls at the bases of older trees.

Native Habitat and Range. In moist coastal mountains at low to mid elevations from southwestern Oregon to central California.

Notes. This species, the world's tallest tree, is related to California's giant sequoia (*Sequoiadendron giganteum*), the world's most massive tree. Cultivars of coast redwood include several bluish or silvery-leaved forms ('Aptos Blue', 'Majestic Beauty', 'Filoli', 'Woodside', 'Simpson's Silver') and such dwarf forms as 'Adpressa' and 'Albo-Spica', both of which grow a mere 1m (3ft) tall and 2m (6ft) wide with white-tipped new growth. Coast redwood is the only species in the genus and is highly valued for its beautiful, decay-resistant wood. This tree, along with its relatives, is sometimes placed in the cypress family, the Cupressaceae.

Taxus brevifolia	Zones 3b to 9b	Taxaceae

Pacific or western yew

This shrub or small tree grows to a maximum height of about 15m (50ft). The trunk may be straight or contorted, and the bark is thin, peeling on older trees to reveal the deep red inner bark. The needles are flat and usually arranged in two flat rows on either side of the twigs; they are about 2.5cm (1in) long, green above and pale beneath with rows of stomata. The needle tips are abruptly pointed. Plants are either male or female (dioecious) and, although yews are conifers, they lack the typical woody cones. Female trees produce single seeds, each surrounded by an aril, a fleshy, red, cup-like structure.

Cultivation. Full to part shade or dappled light. Although not fussy about soils, this tree of the forest understory prefers a moist location. The wildlife gardener with a forested yard will want to create a complex habitat with multiple layers, and Pacific yew is a good evergreen species to plant under the larger trees.

Propagation. Easiest from cuttings taken in fall. Make cuttings from new growth with a bit of older wood at the base, treat them with rooting hormones, and set them to root in pumice or some other medium. Protect cuttings from excessive cold; they should root by the following spring or summer. Seeds are difficult to germinate, but can be harvested and planted outside in the fall to cold stratify over the winter; they may germinate after the weather warms in the spring.

Native Habitat and Range. In moist forests and along streambanks near the coast in Alaska and British Columbia, and through the Cascades at low to fairly high elevations, south to the Sierra Nevada of California, east to eastern British Columbia, Idaho, and Montana.

Notes. All eight species of *Taxus* are native to the Northern Hemisphere. As with other yews, the wood of Pacific yew is beautiful and very tough. It was used for all sorts of tools by Native American tribes and was also a valuable item of trade. The berry-like arils surrounding the seeds are poisonous to humans, but the cancer-fighting drug, taxol, was originally derived from yew bark. Yew is also poisonous to horses and cattle, but the seeds are attractive to birds. Only a few cultivars of Pacific yew have been developed, including 'Erecta' (columnar), 'Nana' (dwarf), and 'Nuttallii' (weeping).

Taxus brevifolia

Thuja plicata   Zones 3b to 9b   Cupressaceae

western red cedar

In nature this forest tree can reach 70m (230ft), but it usually grows to half that height in cultivation and to 20m (60ft) wide. The bark is gray or reddish and fibrous. Trunks of older trees are ridged and grooved. The tiny, scale-like leaves are arranged in flattened sprays, some of which will turn brown before dropping in autumn. The leaves are opposite and arranged in pairs, making up four rows. The tips of each pair of scale leaves are free at the same level and they appear to be arranged in twos. The seed cones are small at about 1cm (.5in) and are composed of eight to 12 flat scales; they are brown and woody when ripe, tending to turn upward on the branches.

Cultivation. Full sun or part shade, and moist soil. This species makes an excellent wildlife tree for the large yard, and its several cultivars serve other purposes, such as screening. Gardeners east of the Cascades will want to be sure their plants came from an interior source, so the trees will be adapted to the colder winters.

Propagation. Fairly easy from seed collected in fall and either planted immediately or stored in cool, dry conditions and planted in the spring. Cuttings taken in fall or winter and treated with hormones should slowly form roots.

Thuja plicata

Native Habitat and Range. Along streambanks and moist or boggy sites at low to mid-elevations from Alaska to northwestern California, and from the coast east to southeastern British Columbia and western Montana.

Notes. *Thuja* is a genus of five species native to North America and eastern Asia. Some cultivars of western red cedar are used for tall hedges: the columnar 'Fastigiata', the fast-growing 'Spring Grove', and the densely branched 'Hogan'. 'Hilleri' is oddly shaped; 'Pendula' has a weeping habit. Cultivars with yellow or variegated foliage include 'Aurea', 'Rogersii', 'Stoneham Gold', and 'Zebrina'. The species was extremely important to the coastal tribes of the Pacific Northwest; its rot-resistant wood had many uses as building material, and the long-fibered bark was used for clothing, rope, mats, and baskets.

CONIFERS   63

Tsuga   Pinaceae

hemlock

Tsuga includes around ten species native to the cooler parts of temperate North America and eastern Asia, some to Japan, where the generic name originates. As with *Picea* (spruce), the needles sit on tiny, woody pegs that remain on the twigs after the needles fall. The seed cones have woody but thin scales and are among the smallest cones in the Pinaceae. Hemlocks are valuable as ornamentals and are also a source of timber.

Propagation. Easiest from seed. Collect cones in fall before they open, and dry them in paper bags until they release their seed. Sow the seeds into containers of potting soil and leave them outside over winter for spring germination. Protect seedlings from full sun and keep them moist. Hemlocks can also be propagated from cuttings or by layering. Cuttings can be taken at any time of year, treated with hormones, and set into pumice or some other medium.

Tsuga heterophylla   Zones 4a to 9b

western hemlock

This graceful tree grows to 50m (150ft) tall and about 10m (30ft) in width with a distinctive drooping tip. The bark is reddish brown, becoming furrowed with age. The needles are flat and blunt-tipped, green on top, with two white lines of stomata beneath. The needles on each twig vary in length from 5 to 20mm (.25 to 1in), and are arranged on the sides and upper parts of the twig. The seed cones are small, only about 2cm (1in) in length, with thin, woody scales; they are purplish green when young, turning brown when ripe, and are often produced in large numbers.

Cultivation. Full sun to full shade, and moist, deep soil with lots of humus. Tolerates drier sites and mineral soils. Make sure young plants in full sun have sufficient water until they are established. Western hemlocks make beautiful background trees and are graceful against the sky; they are fine trees for wildlife but, given their shallow roots, can blow down in high winds. Susceptible to damage from hemlock woolly aphids.

Native Habitat and Range. A common tree on moist, organic soils at low to mid elevations in the mountains from Alaska south to northern California and from the coast, east to southeastern British Columbia, northern Idaho, and northwestern Montana.

Notes. In some spots near the coast this species, one of the most shade-tolerant in the Northwest, is the dominant forest tree. It is often seen growing on nurse logs and stumps, an interesting arrangement that can be duplicated in the garden. Coastal tribes used this tree for many purposes, including tools, medicines, and dyes.

Tsuga mertensiana   Zones 3b to 9b

mountain hemlock

This conifer can reach 40m (120ft), but it is often stunted on alpine sites. In the garden it usually grows to 10m (30ft) tall and half as wide. The tip of the tree droops only slightly, and the furrowed bark is dark brown. The needles, blunt-tipped and somewhat four-sided, are bluish green and have whitish lines of stomata on both surfaces; they are about 2cm (1in) long and surround the twigs, giving the foliage a tufted appearance. The seed cones are greenish or purplish when young, brown when ripe; they are 4 to 8cm (1.5 to 3in) long and relatively slender.

Tsuga heterophylla

Cultivation. Sun or part shade, and moist to wet soil with lots of organic matter and a cool location. Give this species shade where summers are hot. An excellent, slow-growing conifer for the large rock or alpine garden. It can also be grown in containers and makes a good bonsai subject, easily pruned and shaped to give it a windswept, alpine look.

Native Habitat and Range. On moist to boggy sites with organic soils at mid to high elevations in the mountains, often to timberline, from southern Alaska and British Columbia, south to California, in the Olympic and Cascade Mountains, east to northern Idaho, western Montana, and northeast Oregon.

Notes. 'Argentea' is a selection with bluish white foliage. *Tsuga ×jeffreyi* is a hybrid between this species and *T. heterophylla*.

Tsuga mertensiana

ANNUALS

Although perennials are the primary focus of this book, many native annuals are worthy of a place in the garden. These colorful flowering plants are useful in wildflower meadows, dry banks, roadsides, and parking areas, often reseeding and establishing themselves without assistance; in some situations, however, you may have to sow new seed each year. Genuine native seed may be difficult to find—"wildflower" mixes often contain all sorts of plants, even weeds. Better to try the numerous seed exchanges organized by botanical gardens, native plant societies, and alpine and rock garden enthusiasts; such groups are often good sources for native seed, as well as resources for plant lovers.

| *Amsinckia menziesii* | Zones 3b to 9b | Boraginaceae |

Menzies' fiddleneck

This annual reaches about 80cm (2.5ft) in height and may be branched or single-stemmed. The whole plant is covered with long, rough hairs. The leaves are usually lance-shaped, growing to 12cm (5in) long. The small, tubular flowers are orange or yellow and arranged in an inflorescence coiled like a fiddlehead or a scorpion's tail. They bloom through the spring, and the fruits are single-seeded nutlets.

Cultivation. Full sun, and dry to moist soil. Tolerates poor soils and neglect. This is a good plant to include with other species in the sunny wildflower meadow.

Propagation. Sow seed in place in the garden during fall or spring.

Native Habitat and Range. In fields, roadsides, and other open places at low to mid elevations from Alaska south to California and Texas, on both sides of the Cascades, east through much of North America to the Atlantic coast.

Notes. Both *A. m.* var. *menziesii* and *A. m.* var. *intermedia* occur in our area, as do the wide-ranging *A. lycopsoides* (tarweed fiddleneck) and *A. tessellata* (bristly fiddleneck). *Amsinckia spectabilis* (seaside fiddleneck) is another western species that occurs along our coast from British Columbia to California. The genus encompasses about dozen species, all native to North America.

| *Calandrinia ciliata* | Zones 4a to 9b | Portulacaceae |

red maids

This branched annual is low-growing, to 30cm (1ft). The linear to lance-shaped leaves are succulent and up to 7cm (3in) long. The leaves are alternately arranged and entire except for the coarse hairs along the margins. The flowers usually have two sepals and five deep magenta

Amsinckia menziesii

Calandrinia ciliata

(occasionally white) petals to 1cm (.5in) long, blooming from mid to late spring. The shiny, black seeds ripen in small capsules.

Cultivation. Full sun to part shade, and heavy or stony soil that is moist in the early spring. This is an attractive, spring-blooming annual for difficult spots in the garden with poor soil. Lovely along the sunny pond margin or vernal pool, or at the edge of a camas meadow.

Propagation. Collect ripe seeds in summer and plant them in the fall.

Native Habitat and Range. In open, poorly drained or gravelly soils, often on disturbed sites that are moist in spring, at low elevations from southwest British Columbia south to southern California, and from the coast, east to Idaho and Arizona.

Notes. The only other North American species in the genus is restricted to California.

Castilleja ambigua ssp. ambigua	Zones 7b to 9b	Scrophulariaceae

johnny-nip, paintbrush owl-clover

This annual produces simple or branched, hairy stems to 30cm (1ft). The leaves are lance-shaped to ovate and up to 5cm (2in) long. The lower leaves are often entire, and the upper leaves have one or two pairs of lobes. The showy, leafy bract beneath each flower has rounded lobes tipped with white, purple, or yellow. The tubular calyx has four lobes and is similar in color to the bract. The three-lobed, tubular corollas are yellow, blooming from early summer to late fall. The fruits are capsules containing many tiny seeds.

Cultivation. Full sun, and moist soil. Tolerates salty soil. Site this long-blooming partial parasite near grasses, sunflower relatives, or other species to act as hosts. An interesting addition to the coastal meadow or wildflower garden.

Castilleja ambigua ssp. *ambigua*

Propagation. Harvest seeds in the fall and scatter them into the garden or onto the surface of potting soil with grasses or other plants present. Press the seeds into the soil near the roots of host plants and leave them for the winter.

Native Habitat and Range. Along the upper edges of salt marshes and other places with saline soils at low elevations from southern British Columbia to the central coast of California.

Notes. Sometimes classified as *Orthocarpus castillejoides*. *Castilleja a.* ssp. *ambigua* occurs throughout the range; it is a partial parasite on the roots of other plants. See *Castilleja*, in the perennials section, for more details on the genus.

Centaurium muehlenbergii	Zones 5b to 9b	Gentianaceae

Monterey centaury

This slender annual usually produces a single stem to 30cm (1ft) tall. There are a few oblong leaves to 1.5cm (.5in) long at the base of the stem and several pairs of narrow, opposite leaves on the stem. Small clusters of flowers, usually with very short pedicels, bloom at the stem tips. Each flower has a calyx with five narrow lobes. The funnel-shaped corollas are about 1.5cm (.5in) long, with a tubular base and five flared petal lobes. The flowers, which vary from deep pink to white, bloom from early to late summer. The tiny seeds ripen in slender capsules.

Cultivation. Full sun to part shade, and moist soil, at least in the spring. Include this charming annual in the wildflower meadow on either side of the Cascades.

Propagation. Collect the small capsules in the fall and scatter the tiny seeds on the soil surface, into containers of potting soil or directly into the garden, in the fall or spring.

Centaurium muehlenbergii

Native Habitat and Range. In moist places, often in open woods at low elevations, scattered in eastern Washington and Oregon, west through the Columbia River Gorge and south through western Oregon, where it becomes more common, to west central California.

Notes. Of the approximately 25 species of *Centaurium* that occur worldwide, about half are native to North America. The only other Pacific Northwest native is *C. exaltatum* (desert centaury), with white or light salmon flowers; it lives near hot springs and alkaline lakes east of the Cascades and east through the Rocky Mountains.

Clarkia   Onagraceae

Clarkia includes some of our most beautiful native annuals, a great tribute to explorer William Clark. As with most plants in the evening-primrose family, the flower parts of *Clarkia* are in fours or multiples of four, with four petals, four sepals, eight stamens, and a four-parted capsule. In many older references, the genus included only those species with clawed petals (those that become very narrow at the base); species with broader petal bases were placed in *Godetia*. All these lovely annuals are now placed in *Clarkia*, a genus of some 40 species, almost all native to western North America, especially California.

Propagation. Collect seeds from the ripened capsules and sow some of them in the garden in the fall, and the rest in early spring, to help extend the bloom period. They can also be sown in flats of potting soil, and the seedlings planted out when large enough.

Clarkia amoena ssp. huntiana

Clarkia amoena ssp. lindleyi

Clarkia amoena   Zones 3b to 9b

farewell-to-spring

This annual grows simple or branched stems up to 1m (3ft). The alternate leaves are narrow and can reach 7cm (3in) in length. The flower buds are erect, and the sepals remain fused to each other on one side of the flower. Petals vary from pale to deep pink, often with a darker red spot in the center; they are up to 4cm (1.5in) in length. Plants begin to bloom in early summer (hence the common name), continuing through late summer. The fruits, dry capsules, are straight or curved.

Cultivation. Full sun or light shade, and well-drained to rather dry soil. Choose this lovely annual for the wildflower meadow, dry bank, or rock garden. If plants are in a location to their liking, they will self-sow.

Native Habitat and Range. On open slopes, dry meadows, and bluffs, often near the coast, from southern British Columbia at low elevations west of the Cascades, south to the coast of central California and east in the Columbia River Gorge.

Notes. Hunt's clarkia (*C. a.* ssp. *huntiana*) includes slender plants with shorter, pinkish petals with a red central spot; it ranges north as far as southwestern Oregon. Lindley's clarkia (*C. a.* ssp. *lindleyi*) has larger petals to 4cm (1.5in) long, pink and usually with a red central blotch; the plants of this subspecies tend to be larger and well branched, and they range north as far as British Columbia. *Clarkia a.* ssp. *caurina* also occurs in the Pacific Northwest. All the subspecies are lovely.

Clarkia gracilis ssp. *sonomensis*

Clarkia gracilis ssp. sonomensis   Zones 3b to 9b

slender clarkia

This graceful annual grows to about 60cm (2ft) with simple or branching stems. The alternate leaves are linear, and the flower buds arch downward. The pink petals are up to 2cm (1in) long and usually have a darker red spot in the middle. Flowers bloom from early to mid summer, and the capsules are straight.

Cultivation. Full sun or light shade, and well-drained to rather dry soil. Include this beauty in the wildflower meadow, rock garden, or oak woodland. With luck, plants will propagate themselves from seed.

Native Habitat and Range. In meadows and open woods at low to mid elevations from the Willamette Valley of Oregon, south to central California, occasionally west of the Cascades in Washington.

Notes. The petals of *C. g.* ssp. *gracilis*, also native in the Pacific Northwest, are usually without the reddish central spot.

Clarkia pulchella   Zones 3b to 9b

pink fairies, beautiful clarkia

This striking annual, one of the most beautiful clarkias, produces simple or branched stems up to 50cm (20in) tall. The leaves are linear or narrowly lance-shaped, up to 7cm (3in) long, and entire or with some small teeth. The racemes are few-flowered, and the buds are nodding. Each of the

Clarkia pulchella

Clarkia purpurea ssp. viminea

four petals is deeply three-lobed, narrow at the base and dark rose to lavender. Flowers bloom from late spring to early summer, and the capsules may be straight or curved.

Cultivation. Full sun or light shade, and well-drained to rather dry soil. Plant it in the wild-flower meadow, dry bank, or rock garden. Will self-sow if in a location to its liking.

Native Habitat and Range. In dry meadows and open ground at low to mid elevations, near the Columbia River in southern British Columbia, south on the east side of the Cascades to southeastern Oregon and east to Idaho and Montana.

Notes. This species is often used as a parent in developing clarkia hybrids. Mt. Lassen clarkia (*C. lassenensis*) and diamond clarkia (*C. rhomboidea*) are also native to the Pacific Northwest.

Clarkia purpurea ssp. *viminea*   Zones 3b to 9b

winecup, purple, or large clarkia

This annual produces stems up to 80cm (2.5ft) that are usually branched above the middle. The narrow leaves grow to 5cm (2in) in length. The petals are up to 2.5cm (1in) long and vary from light pink to rose or purple, often with a darker reddish spot in the center or toward the tip. Flowers bloom from late spring to mid summer, and the capsules are four-angled and sometimes ribbed.

Cultivation. Full sun or light shade, and well-drained to rather dry soil. Site in the wildflower meadow or rock garden, dry bank, or parking area. May self-sow.

Native Habitat and Range. In meadows and dry, open areas at low to mid elevations from southern British Columbia, south on both sides of the Cascades to southern California and Arizona.

Claytonia exigua

Notes. *Clarkia p*. ssp. *purpurea* and *C. p*. ssp. *quadrivulnera* also occur in our area. All three subspecies are sometimes granted specific status in older references.

Claytonia   Portulacaceae

spring beauty, miner's lettuce, candy flower

Claytonia and *Montia* have an intertwined taxonomic history. Formerly, all species that lacked corms or fleshy taproots were placed in the genus *Montia*. In this book, *Claytonia* includes plants that, like *Montia*, have two sepals and five petals. Species of *Claytonia* have one pair of opposite stem leaves, sometimes fused into a single blade perforated by the stem. *Claytonia* has fewer than 50 species, mostly native to the temperate or chillier parts of the Northern Hemisphere; nearly 30 occur in North America, more than half of these in the Pacific Northwest.

Propagation. Collect seeds in the summer and plant them outside soon after harvest. Seeds can be sown into containers or directly into the garden and left outside for the winter. They will germinate in spring. Once established in the garden, plants may seed themselves.

Claytonia exigua   Zones 6a to 9b

pale spring beauty or miner's lettuce

This little annual produces simple stems and basal leaves both to about 6cm (2.5in) tall from a thin taproot. The plant is grayish or bluish with a waxy coating. The basal leaves are linear or narrowly spoon-shaped (spatulate), and each flowering stem has a single pair of narrow leaves,

Claytonia perfoliata

sometimes fused along one side for almost half their length. Tiny white or pinkish flowers bloom in racemes to 2cm (1in) long from early spring to early summer. The fruits are little capsules containing a few black seeds.

Cultivation. Full sun, and moist to rather dry soil. This is a tiny but interesting addition to corners of the rock garden. Plant it with other small annuals near the trail through the wildflower meadow or on a slope or bank.

Native Habitat and Range. On dry or moist slopes and open places at low to mid elevations from southern British Columbia, south through western Washington and through the Columbia River Gorge, western and central Oregon to southern California and western Nevada.

Notes. Sometimes classified as *Montia spathulata*.

Claytonia perfoliata	Zones 4a to 9b

miner's lettuce

This fleshy annual produces basal leaves and flowering stems from a thin taproot. It is variable in size, but the lance or spoon-shaped (spatulate) basal leaves can grow to 10cm (4in) long, and the stems can reach 30cm (1ft) tall under favorable conditions. The flowering stems have a single pair of opposite leaves fused together to form a rounded blade with the raceme of flowers growing from the center of the disk. Small white to pinkish flowers, a bit less than 1cm (.5in) long, bloom from early spring to mid summer. Capsules produce a few shiny, black seeds.

Cultivation. Part shade or dappled light, and moist soil. Tolerates sunnier, drier conditions, but plants will be dwarfed. Site in moist places at the edge of the woodland garden or any partly shaded spot. Often self-sows.

Native Habitat and Range. In woods, meadows, and thickets where moist in the spring, often in sandy soil, at low to mid elevations, from British Columbia south, on both sides of the Cascades through California, east to Montana, South Dakota, Colorado, and Arizona.

Notes. Sometimes classified as *Montia perfoliata*. This succulent, oddly shaped annual is edible and can be used in salads. Both *C. p.* ssp. *perfoliata* and *C. p.* ssp. *intermontana* occur in the Pacific Northwest.

Claytonia sibirica   Zones 4a to 9b

spring beauty, Siberian candy flower

This succulent plant is usually an annual with a slender taproot, but sometimes develops rhizomes to become a short-lived perennial. The flowering stems can grow to 40cm (16in) in height, and each stem has an opposite pair of ovate or lance-shaped leaves up to 7cm (3in) long. The basal leaves, often spoon-shaped (spatulate), have long petioles and are up to 30cm (1ft) long; they sometimes have small bulbs at their bases. Each stem produces one or more racemes with many white or pink flowers with pink veins, and each blossom is about 1cm (.5in) long. Plants often bloom over a long period, from early spring to early fall. A few shiny, black seeds ripen in small capsules.

Cultivation. Part to full shade or dappled light, and moist soil. Some consider this a weedy species, but it blooms generously and makes a fine addition to the woodland garden.

Native Habitat and Range. In moist woods, meadows, and streambanks at low to mid elevations from Alaska, south on both sides of the Cascades to southern California, east to Montana.

Notes. Sometimes classified as *Montia sibirica*. Spring beauty is edible; excess plants can be used in salads. Both *C. s.* var. *sibirica* and *C. s.* var. *bulbifera* (with small bulblets at the leaf bases) occur in the Pacific Northwest. Other native species of *Claytonia* include Washington claytonia (*C. washingtoniana*) and red-stem miner's lettuce (*C. rubra*).

Collinsia grandiflora   Zones 3b to 9b   Scrophulariaceae

giant or large-flowered blue-eyed mary

This annual develops erect, simple or branched stems up to 40cm (16in) tall. The opposite leaves are oblong to linear, sometimes toothed, and up to 1.5cm (.5in) long. The flowers tend to grow in whorls. The base of the corolla is tubular and bent at a right angle. The petals are two-lipped (bilabiate) with a two-lobed upper lip and a three-lobed lower lip. The flowers, up to 1.5cm (.5in) in length, are blue with a whitish upper lip. Plants bloom from mid spring to early summer, and seeds ripen in small, rounded capsules.

Cultivation. Full sun to part shade, and moist to somewhat dry soil. This charming plant makes an excellent addition to the wildflower meadow, rock garden, or annual border. Clip spent flowers back to initiate new growth.

Propagation. Collect seeds from the ripened capsules and sow them directly into the garden in the fall, and again in the spring, to extend the blooming season. Seeds can also be sown in flats, and the seedlings planted out once developed. Often self-sows in the garden.

Native Habitat and Range. In open meadows, rocky flats, or slopes that are moist in spring, at low to mid elevations from southern British Columbia, south to northern California, mostly west of the Cascades, but occurring in the Columbia River Gorge, parts of eastern Washington, Idaho, and southeastern Oregon.

Notes. *Collinsia* includes around 20 species, most of them annuals native to western North America. Narrow-leaf blue-eyed mary (*C. linearis*), small-flowered blue-eyed mary (*C. parviflora*),

Claytonia sibirica

Collinsia grandiflora

Collomia grandiflora

Coreopsis tinctoria var. atkinsoniana

sticky blue-eyed mary (*C. rattanii*), few-flowered blue-eyed mary (*C. sparsiflora*), and Torrey's blue-eyed mary (*C. torreyi*) also occur in the Pacific Northwest.

| **Collomia grandiflora** | Zones 3b to 9b | Polemoniaceae |

large-flowered collomia

This annual produces a taproot and simple, sometimes branched stems up to 1m (3ft) tall. The alternate leaves are lance-shaped, reaching about 7cm (3in) in length. Tubular, five-lobed flowers are produced in clusters at the tips of the branches. The corollas grow to 2.5cm (1in) long and are salmon-colored or pale orange, blooming from late spring to late summer. The fruits are small capsules.

Cultivation. Full sun to part shade or dappled light, and moist to rather dry soil. This is an excellent, tall annual for the wildflower meadow, dry bank, parking area, woodland margin, or annual bed.

Propagation. Collect seeds in late summer or fall and plant them directly into the garden. This taprooted species would rather be seeded in place than transplanted from flats but you can try sowing seeds into tubes or other deep, narrow containers. Often self-sows once established.

Native Habitat and Range. In open woods and clearings, often where rather dry, at low to mid elevations on both sides of the Cascades, from southern British Columbia south to California and Arizona and east to Montana and Wyoming.

Notes. *Collomia* includes more than a dozen species of annual or perennial herbs, native to temperate parts of North and South America, especially western North America; nine other species occur in our area. The perennial *C. debilis* (alpine collomia) is found growing in talus; the other species are annuals, including *C. heterophylla* (varied-leaf collomia), *C. tinctoria* (yellow-staining collomia), *C. tenella* (diffuse collomia), and the widespread *C. linearis* (tiny trumpet, narrow-leaf collomia).

| **Coreopsis tinctoria var. atkinsoniana** | Zones 3b to 9b | Asteraceae |

Columbia coreopsis, Atkinson's tickseed

This slender annual or biennial grows to 1m (3ft) tall. The opposite leaves are pinnately divided into linear leaflets. Tiny flowers bloom in sunflower-like heads. The petal-like ray florets have corollas up to 2cm (1in) long, orange-yellow with darker patches of reddish brown at the base. Flowers bloom from early summer to early fall. The fruits are small, black, one-seeded achenes.

Cultivation. Full sun, and moist to wet soil. This is a cheerful orange-yellow daisy for the edge of the pond, wetland, or ditch. It offers late-season color, and the achenes are attractive to many seed-eating birds, making it a good choice for wet places in the wildlife garden.

Propagation. Collect seeds in late summer and plant them in the fall, winter, or early spring directly into the garden or into containers of wet soil. Once established in the garden, they may self-sow.

Native Habitat and Range. In wetland margins and moist banks along the Columbia River and major tributaries, from near Portland, Oregon, north and east to British Columbia, Saskatchewan, and North Dakota.

Notes. Sometimes classified as *C. atkinsoniana*. Around 30 species of *Coreopsis* are native to North America, most to the east of us.

Crocidium multicaule

Crocidium multicaule	Zones 5a to 9b	Asteraceae

spring gold, gold star

This delicate annual generally produces several stems and grows to 15cm (6in) tall. The basal leaves are rounded and about 2.5cm (1in) long. The few stem leaves are linear, and plants are glabrous (hairless) except for woolly tufts in the leaf axils. Single, golden daisy heads up to 2.5cm (1in) across, composed of many tiny florets, bloom singly at the stem tips from early to late spring. The fruits are tiny, dark achenes.

Cultivation. Full sun, and well-drained or sandy soil. These little sunflowers put on a bright show early in the season. Plant them at the edge of the rock garden or other sandy or stony site, or in the dry wildflower meadow or parking strip.

Propagation. Collect seeds in the late spring or early summer and scatter them thickly in the garden from fall to mid winter. Often self-sows and establishes dense populations under favorable conditions.

Native Habitat and Range. On outcrops, cliff ledges, sandy flats, and other open, dry places at low elevations from southern British Columbia, south through much of California, east through the Columbia River Gorge, south central Washington and north central Oregon.

Notes. This distinctive little plant is the only species in the genus.

Gilia capitata

Helianthus annuus

| *Gilia capitata* | Zones 3b to 9b | Polemoniaceae |

bluefield or bluehead gilia

This annual produces stems up to 1m (3ft) tall, simple or with a few branches. The leaves are alternate and pinnately or bipinnately divided into linear leaflets; they are largest at the base of the stem, becoming smaller toward the top. Dense, rounded heads of 50 to 100 flowers bloom at the stem tips from late spring to mid summer. Each flower is light blue, five-lobed and tubular at the base, and up to 1cm (.5in) long. The fruits are small, few-seeded capsules.

Cultivation. Full sun to light shade, and moist to rather dry soil. This delicate, blue flowered annual is lovely at the edge of the woodland garden and an excellent addition to the wildflower meadow, rock garden, roadside, or dry bank.

Propagation. Collect seeds in late summer and plant them in the fall, winter, or early spring, directly into the garden or into flats of potting soil for later transplanting. Plants will generally reseed themselves once established in the garden.

Native Habitat and Range. In moist to dry meadows, forest clearings, rocky slopes, and outcrops at low to mid elevations, from southern British Columbia south, especially west of the Cascades, to central California, east to northern Idaho.

Notes. Both *G. c.* ssp. *capitata* and *G. c.* ssp. *pacifica* occur in the Pacific Northwest. This species is sometimes added to commercial wildflower mixes. Most of the approximately 30 species of *Gilia* are native to western North America, with close to ten in our area; many of those previously classified as *Gilia* have been moved to different genera, including *Ipomopsis* and *Linanthus*.

| **Helianthus annuus** | Zones 3b to 9b | Asteraceae |

common sunflower

This roughly hairy, branched annual can grow to 2m (6ft) or more. Most of the leaves are alternate, with long petioles. The blades are heart-shaped to oval and have toothed margins. The tiny flowers are condensed into a typical sunflower head with small, tubular disk florets surrounded by the ray florets, each ray with a yellow, petal-like corolla, and the whole head subtended by green involucral bracts. Wild plants develop branched stems and several flowering heads, blooming from early summer until early fall. The fruits are single-seeded achenes, "sunflower seeds."

Cultivation. Full sun, and dry to moist soil. This is a good, tough annual for the dry wildlife garden, where seed-eating birds will enjoy the achenes. Site it on a dry bank, roadside, or parking area.

Propagation. Collect seeds in the late summer and fall, if you can beat the birds to them. Plant them in place in the garden in the spring. They can also be sown into containers of potting soil and planted out when large enough. Will usually self-sow in the garden.

Native Habitat and Range. On open, dry to somewhat moist sites, often along roadsides and other disturbed areas, usually at low elevations east of the Cascades; throughout much of North America.

Notes. This species is an important oil and seed crop, and many cultivars—including giant forms and ornamentals in such shades as cream and mahogany—have been developed from it. See *H. cusickii*, in the perennials section, for more on the genus and other sunflowers native to the Pacific Northwest.

| **Impatiens capensis** | Zones 3b to 9b | Balsaminaceae |

Cape jewelweed, touch-me-not, orange balsam

This succulent, glabrous (hairless) annual produces branched stems to 1m (3ft) tall or more. The alternate leaves have petioles to 4cm (1.5in) long. The blades are elliptic to ovate, up to 12cm (5in) long, and have shallow teeth along the margins. Flowers tend to bloom in pairs on well-developed peduncles from the leaf axils; they are broadly tubular and about 2cm (1in) long. One of the three yellowish sepals forms a curved spur at the base of the flower. The corolla has five fused petals, orange and heavily mottled with maroon. Flowers bloom from mid summer to early fall. The fruit, an elongated capsule, opens explosively to release several seeds, whether touched (note one of the common names) or not.

Cultivation. Full shade to part sun or dappled light, and wet to very moist soil. This orange-flowered annual is attractive along the margin of the pond, stream, ditch, or wet place in the wildflower meadow. Established plants will typically reseed themselves in the garden; they are somewhat aggressive but are easy to pull.

Propagation. Collect seeds in the fall and plant them soon after harvest, either directly into the garden or into flats of wet potting soil. Leave the planted seeds outside over winter; germination occurs when the weather warms in spring.

Native Habitat and Range. In moist to wet streambanks, wetlands, and thickets at low to mid elevations from southern British Columbia, south in western Washington to northwestern Oregon, absent from parts of the Southwest and most of the Rocky Mountains, but widespread throughout eastern North America.

Notes. Most of the several hundred species of *Impatiens* are native to the warmer parts of Asia and Africa. Of the five species native to North America, three others occur in our area: pale yellow touch-me-not (*I. aurella*), spurless touch-me-not (*I. ecalcarata*), and western touch-me-not (*I. noli-tangere*), a plant very similar to *I. capensis*.

Impatiens capensis

Lasthenia californica

Lasthenia californica	Zones 6b to 9b	Asteraceae

California goldfields

This charming plant produces simple or branched, sometimes succulent stems to 30cm (1ft) tall. The leaves are opposite, about 3cm (1.5in) long, and linear to oblong in shape with smooth margins. The flowering heads are bright yellow daisies with ray corollas up to 1cm (.5in), blooming from early to late spring. The fruits are small achenes.

Cultivation. Full sun, and wet or very moist soil. Site near the margin of a pond, wetland, sunny bog, or vernal pool. This is a beautiful little annual for the poorly drained spot in the wildflower meadow, where it will produce a carpet of tiny yellow daisies in the spring. Will probably do best in areas with warmer winters and earlier springs.

Propagation. Collect seeds in summer and sow them in the garden in fall; they typically germinate and begin to grow over the winter. They can also be planted into containers, left outside for the winter, and the seedlings transplanted early the following spring. Plants may self-sow.

Native Habitat and Range. In grasslands, oak woodlands, and other places where the heavy soils are wet in spring, at low to mid elevations, from southern Oregon, south through California to Arizona and New Mexico.

Notes. *Lasthenia c.* ssp. *californica* and *L. c.* ssp. *macrantha* range north into Oregon. This genus includes fewer than 20 species, most of them native to western North America, especially California. In addition to *L. californica*, four other species occur in the Pacific Northwest. Coastal or woolly goldfields (*L. minor*) lives mainly on the California coast, except for a disjunct population on Whidbey Island, Washington. Seaside goldfields (*L. maritima*) and smooth goldfields (*L. glaberrima*) have very short ray corollas. Orndull's goldfields (*L. orndujjuli*) is endemic to southwestern Oregon.

Limnanthes douglasii

Lupinus bicolor

Limnanthes douglasii   Zones 7b to 9b   Limnanthaceae

Douglas' meadowfoam

This charming hairless (glabrous) annual produces branched stems up to 40cm (16in) tall. The leaves are pinnately compound and up to 10cm (4in) long. Flowers bloom on slender peduncles up to 10cm (4in) long. The charming, bowl-shaped flowers are about 1.5cm (.5in) long, and the five yellow petals have notched, white tips. Flowers bloom from early to late spring, and the fruits are small nutlets.

Cultivation. Full sun, and soil that is wet or very moist, at least during the spring. Often cultivated and fairly easy to grow. Plant it near the margin of a sunny wetland, pond, or bog garden.

Propagation. Collect seeds in summer and plant them outside in fall or early winter. Sow in place, or plant into flats and transplant seedlings in the spring. May self-sow.

Native Habitat and Range. Moist or wet meadows, vernal pools, and seeps at low elevations from southwestern Oregon, south to west central California.

Notes. Of the four subspecies, only *L. d.* ssp. *douglasii* ranges into southwestern Oregon. There are around ten species of *Limnanthes*, all annuals native to western North America and several listed as rare. Hairy-leaved meadowfoam (*L. floccosa*) and slender meadowfoam (*L. gracilis*) also range into southern Oregon; Macoun's meadowfoam (*L. macounii*) is known only from the vicinity of southern Vancouver Island, British Columbia, though it may have been introduced elsewhere.

Lupinus bicolor   Zones 4b to 9b   Fabaceae

two color or miniature lupine

This single-stemmed or branched, usually hairy annual can grow to 40cm (16in) tall. The palmately compound leaves produce up to eight leaflets, each about 2.5cm (1in) long. The flowering racemes produce blue pea flowers with a white patch on the upright banner petal that turns violet with age. The flowers are a bit less than 1cm (.5in) long and are scattered or whorled on the peduncles, blooming from mid spring to early summer. The hairy pods contain up to eight seeds.

Cultivation. Full sun, and soil that is moist early in the year. Tolerates thin, poor, gravelly soils and makes a beautiful show in the wildflower meadow or parking area. Excellent for the butterfly garden, where it may provide food for the larvae of some butterflies.

Propagation. Collect seeds in the summer, before the dry legumes dehisce, and store them in a cool, dry place. They can be sown in the fall or spring, directly into the garden or into flats of potting soil. If planting in the spring, germination may be improved by placing seeds in a dish and pouring boiling water over them; let them cool before planting. With luck, established plants will reseed themselves in the garden.

Native Habitat and Range. In meadows and disturbed areas at low to mid elevations from southern British Columbia, south to California and Arizona, mainly west of the Cascades, but east through the Columbia River Gorge.

Notes. Two subspecies, *L. b.* ssp. *bicolor* and *L. b.* ssp. *microphyllus*, range north from California into our area. Small-flowered lupine (*L. polycarpus*) is another annual species native to the Pacific Northwest.

Madia elegans   Zones 7a to 9b   Asteraceae

autumn showy tarweed, common madia

This hairy, glandular annual produces stems to 1m (3ft) tall or more. The stems bear alternate, linear or lance-shaped leaves to 20cm (8in) long by up to 2cm (1in) wide. Flowering heads are produced in an open, branched inflorescence at the top of the stem. Each head has about 13 ray florets with yellow, three-lobed corollas to 1.5cm (.5in) long. The rays sometimes have a maroon blotch at the base. Flowers bloom from mid summer to early fall, often closing during the middle of the day. The disk florets are generally sterile, but the ray florets produce flattened, one-seeded achenes.

Cultivation. Full sun or light shade, and rather dry soil. This is a good fall-blooming species for the dry wildflower meadow, parking area, butterfly garden, or dry bank. Established plants often self-sow and may become somewhat aggressive.

Propagation. Collect achenes from the heads in the fall and plant them into flats of potting soil or directly into the garden in the fall or spring.

Native Habitat and Range. In rather dry meadows and disturbed areas at low to fairly high elevations near the Columbia River Gorge in southwest Washington, south through western Oregon and California, east to western Nevada.

Notes. *Madia e.* ssp. *elegans* ranges north to Washington; *M. e.* ssp. *densifolia* and *M. e.* ssp. *vernalis* occur as far north as Oregon. *Madia* is a genus of fewer than 20 species, most of them annuals native to western North America, with seven of these occurring in our area. Some species are fragrant (*M. elegans* tends to be) or lemon-scented, but others have a tar-like smell that many people dislike. Both the widespread *M. sativa* (coast or Chilean tarweed) and *M. gracilis* (slender tarweed) have showy heads with lobed, yellow ray corollas.

Madia elegans

Mimulus alsinoides

Mimulus alsinoides   Zones 5b to 9b   Scrophulariaceae

chickweed monkey-flower

This annual produces simple or branched stems to 30cm (1ft) tall. The opposite leaves are elliptic and up to 2cm (1in) long. They have toothed margins and distinct veins. The bright yellow, tubular corollas are about 1cm (.5in) long, each with a reddish blotch at the base of the lower lip. They bloom from mid spring to early summer. The fruits are small capsules containing tiny seeds.

   Cultivation. Full to part shade, and moist soil. This is a lovely little annual for the mossy rocks around the pond, stream, or bog. It can also be planted along a woodland path or tucked in a shady part of the rock garden.

   Propagation. Collect seed capsules in paper bags and plant them in the garden or into flats of potting soil in autumn. Scatter seeds onto the soil surface without burying them; let them stratify outside in the cool, moist winter for spring germination. If conditions are to their liking, plants may reseed themselves.

   Native Habitat and Range. In mossy, moist, shady places among rocks and on cliffs, mostly at low elevations, from southern British Columbia south to northern California, mainly west of the Cascades but also east in northern Idaho.

   Notes. Other yellow-flowered annual species include Washington monkey-flower (*M. washingtonensis*) and Suksdorf's monkey-flower (*M. suksdorfii*), both of which occur in wet or seasonally moist places east of the Cascades. Purple-flowered annuals include Brewer's monkey-flower (*M. breweri*) and Cusick's monkey-flower (*M. cusickii*), native to drier habitats east of the Cascades. Tricolor monkey-flower (*M. tricolor*) has purple flowers with white and yellow markings; it grows in vernal pools and seasonally wet clay soils of Oregon's Willamette Valley, south to California

Nemophila menziesii

Nemophila menziesii	Zones 6b to 9b	Hydrophyllaceae

large-flowered nemophila, baby blue-eyes

This delicate, taprooted annual produces branched, lax to erect stems to 30cm (1ft) long. The plants are succulent, and the opposite leaves grow to 5cm (2in) long. The blades are deeply pinnately lobed. Flowers bloom singly on peduncles to 6cm (2.5in) long, developing from the leaf axils; they have a saucer-shaped corolla to 2.5cm (1in) across, consisting of five petals fused at the base. The petals are commonly white, sometimes with lavender veins or tints, and lined with small, blackish purple dots. The flowers bloom from early to late spring, and several seeds ripen in rounded capsules.

Cultivation. Full sun to part shade or dappled light, and moist soil. A common element of "wildflower" seed mixes, this is a charming addition to the wildflower meadow, annual border, parking area, or woodland margin.

Propagation. Collect seeds from the ripened capsules in the summer and plant them in the fall or early spring. Plants prefer to grow in place, from seed sown directly into the garden, but it may be possible to grow them in tubes of potting soil for later transplanting. Populations often reseed themselves in the garden.

Native Habitat and Range. In moist meadows or shady places at low to mid elevations west of the Cascades and to the coast in Oregon, south through California.

Notes. The white-petaled, speckled *N. m.* var. *atomaria* is most widespread in our area; *N. m.* var. *integrifolia* and *N. m.* var. *menziesii* (with blue and white petals and often with darker veins or dots) generally occur to the south. *Nemophila* is a genus of 11 annual species, all native to North America, mainly in the west. About half of these occur in our area; they are charming but tend to have tiny flowers. Kirtley's nemophila (*N. kirtleyi*) has flowers up to 1.5cm (.5in) across; the petals are blue toward the tips and white at the center. This plant grows in part shade on rocky slopes at low elevations in eastern Oregon, western Idaho, and southeastern Washington.

Phacelia linearis	Zones 4a to 9b	Hydrophyllaceae

slender-leaved phacelia

This erect annual produces simple or branched stems to 50cm (20in) tall. The stem leaves are alternate, growing to 10cm (4in) long. The blades are narrow and often have a pair of lobes at the base. The flowers, which bloom from mid spring to early summer, are crowded into clusters at the stem tips. The corollas are bowl-shaped, and the five blue-lavender petals are fused at the base. Several seeds with a pitted surface ripen in small capsules.

Cultivation. Full sun or light shade, and rather dry, well-drained or sandy soil. This is a beautiful annual for the dry, sunny wildflower meadow, parking area, or large rock garden on either side of the Cascades.

Propagation. Collect capsules in the summer, and plant the seeds in the fall, either directly into the garden or into flats of well-drained potting soil. Leave the planted seeds outside over winter for germination in the spring. Established populations often self-sow.

Native Habitat and Range. Open, dry places, usually with sandy soils at low to mid elevations from southern British Columbia, south to northern California, on both sides of the Cascades (more common to the east), east to Wyoming and Utah.

Notes. *Phacelia humilis* (low phacelia) is somewhat similar but has smaller blue-violet flowers. Most of the other annual species of *Phacelia* that are native to our area have tiny, inconspicuous flowers. See the perennials section for more information on the genus.

Platystemon californicus	Zones 6b to 9b	Papaveraceae

creamcups

This charming annual produces a cluster of stems to 30cm (1ft) tall. The leaves are narrow, opposite, and up to 5cm (2in) long. The plants usually have long, soft hairs. Single flowers develop on peduncles up to 20cm (8in) long. The buds are nodding, and the flowers usually have six petals and many stamens. The flowers, around 2.5cm (1in) across, vary from cream-colored to white or yellowish and bloom from early to late spring. The seeds develop in capsules that break apart into pieces when ripe.

Cultivation. Full sun to light shade, and dry to somewhat moist soil. This is a beautiful, early-blooming annual for the dry meadow, oak grove, bank, or parking area.

Propagation. Collect the single-seeded fruit segments in summer and plant them in the fall, leaving them to stratify in cool, wet winter conditions. They are best sown directly into the garden. With luck, plants will reseed themselves and form drifts.

Native Habitat and Range. In open, oak woodlands, grasslands, and burns at low to mid elevations from southwest Oregon, south through California and east to Arizona and southwestern Utah.

Notes. This is the only species in the genus. *Meconella* is another genus of small annuals related to poppies. *Meconella oregana* (white meconella, fairy-poppy) occurs in parts of western Washington (where it is listed as threatened), and south to Oregon and California; *M. californica* ranges as far north as southwestern Oregon.

Phacelia linearis (photo by Sally A. Simmons)

Platystemon californicus

| *Plectritis congesta* | Zones 6a to 9b | Valerianaceae |

sea blush

This variable annual can grow to 60cm (2ft) tall. The plants are generally hairless, and the opposite leaves are spoon-shaped (spatulate) to elliptic, the largest up to 6cm (2.5in) long. The tiny pink or whitish flowers bloom in head-like clusters at the stem tips. The corollas are less than 1cm (.5in) long, with a tubular, spurred base and five bilabiate (two-lipped) petal lobes. Flowers bloom from mid spring to early summer, and the fruits are one-seeded, generally winged and achene- or nutlet-like.

Cultivation. Full sun, and soil that is moist during the spring. This annual forms gorgeous drifts and is lovely in the wildflower meadow, parking area, stony bank, or large rock garden. Established populations often maintain themselves from seed.

Propagation. Collect the small achenes and plant them in the fall or spring. It is probably easiest to sow the seed in place, directly into the garden.

Native Habitat and Range. In meadows, bluffs, and rocky slopes that are moist in the spring at low elevations from southwestern British Columbia, south to northern California, mainly west of the Cascades, but east in the Columbia River Gorge and parts of Oregon.

Notes. There are only two other species in the genus, both also annuals, and native to moist places in the west. The pink-flowered *P. ciliosa* (long-spurred sea blush) is more common in southern Oregon and California but ranges north to the Columbia River Gorge. White or longhorn plectritis (*P. macrocera*) has white flowers and the largest range, from southern British Columbia south to California, and on both sides of the Cascades, east to Montana and Utah.

| *Triphysaria eriantha* | Zones 7a to 9b | Scrophulariaceae |

yellow johnny-tuck, butter-and-eggs

This annual produces branching stems up to 30cm (1ft) tall. Plants are hairy, glandular, and purplish. The alternate leaves are up to 5cm (2in) long and pinnately divided into several linear lobes. The flowers are up to 2.5cm (1in) long and bloom in spikes at the stem tips. The corollas are bilabiate (two-lipped), with a narrow, purple, beak-like upper lip and a lower lip composed of three sac-like, inflated lobes with the lateral lobes usually white and the middle lobe yellow. Flowers bloom from early to late spring, and many tiny seeds ripen in oblong capsules.

Cultivation. Full sun, and moist to rather dry soil. Site this probable partial root parasite near grasses, sunflower relatives, or other species to act as hosts. With its tendency to form drifts, it is a charming addition to the wildflower meadow or grassy bank.

Propagation. Collect seeds in the summer and plant them in the fall, scattering them into the garden or onto the surface of potting soil, with grasses or other plants present to provide host roots for the seedlings. Press the seeds into the soil near the roots of host plants and leave them for the winter. Populations may reseed themselves, especially in southwestern Oregon.

Native Habitat and Range. In open grasslands and slopes at low to mid elevations from southwestern Oregon, south through California.

Notes. Sometimes classified as *Orthocarpus erianthus*. *Triphysaria e.* ssp. *eriantha* is yellow-flowered; *T. e.* ssp. *rosea* is pink-flowered. There are four other species of *Triphysaria* in western North America; two others, *T. pusilla* (*O. pusillus*; dwarf owl-clover) and *T. versicolor* (yellow-beak owl-clover), reach our area.

Plectritis congesta

Triphysaria eriantha

PERENNIALS (including grasses, rushes, and sedges)

Abronia   Nyctaginaceae

sand verbena

Abronia encompasses approximately 25 species, both annuals and perennials, and all native to western North America. Plants have fleshy, opposite leaves and a prostrate or spreading habit. The showy, tubular flowers are grouped into heads. The fruits are achenes surrounded by an inflated, winged calyx.

Propagation. Grow from seed collected and planted in fall. Survival may be better when seeds are planted directly into the garden, but they can also be planted into tubes or other deep containers of sandy potting soil and left outside for the winter, with seedlings transplanted after germination in the spring.

Abronia latifolia   Zones 8a to 9b

yellow or coastal sand verbena

This taprooted perennial produces trailing stems to 1m (3ft) long. The plants are glandular and hairy. The opposite leaves are thick and fleshy, varying in shape from rounded to triangular, and up to 5cm (2in) long. The flowering heads develop on stout peduncles to 8cm (3in) long. The bright yellow or orange-yellow flowers are tubular at the base, with five flaring lobes; each flower is about 1cm (.5in) long, and the heads bloom from late spring to early fall. The fruits are achenes surrounded by a winged calyx.

Cultivation. Full sun, and very well-drained soil. Tolerates moderate watering if drainage is very sharp. This is a beautiful plant for beaches, dunes, or other sandy sites, blooming throughout the summer.

Native Habitat and Range. In dunes and sandy beaches along the immediate coast from British Columbia, south to southern California.

Notes. *Abronia fragrans* (fragrant white or snowball sand verbena) is a taprooted perennial with sweetly-scented, white flowers; it occurs on sandy soils and is scattered from central Washington, east to North Dakota and south to Arizona and Texas. *Abronia turbinata* is an annual species of southeastern Oregon, Nevada, and California.

Abronia latifolia

Abronia umbellata

Abronia umbellata	Zones 8a to 9b

pink sand verbena

This herbaceous perennial produces prostrate stems to 1m (3ft) long. Plants are glandular and hairy, and the opposite leaves are fleshy but thin. The blades are oblong to elliptic and up to 6cm (2.5in) long with equally long petioles. The flowering heads develop on peduncles about as long as the leaves. The reddish purple flowers are tubular at the base, with five flaring lobes; each flower is about 1cm (.5in) long, and the heads bloom from late spring to early fall. The fruits are achenes surrounded by a calyx with three or four wings.

Cultivation. Full sun, and very well-drained, sandy soil. Tolerates watering when planted in sand, but won't survive in poorly drained soils. This is a beautiful plant for beaches or dunes, or sandy sites.

Native Habitat and Range. Rarely found on sandy, coastal beaches from British Columbia, south to southern California.

Notes. An uncommon species, considered endangered in Oregon and on the brink of extirpation in Washington, unable to hold its own against plantings of nonnative dune grasses. *Abronia u.* ssp. *breviflora* occurs along the coast in the Pacific Northwest. *Abronia mellifera* (white sand verbena) is native to dunes, sandy soils, and washes in arid habitats of the Columbia River Gorge and east through central and southeastern Washington, northern and eastern Oregon, through Idaho; it grows from a woody taproot, and its white flowers bloom in heads from late spring to mid summer. This is an unusual perennial for gardeners with sandy soils east of the Cascades.

Achillea millefolium	Zones 3b to 11	Asteraceae

yarrow

The stems of this rhizomatous, aromatic perennial grow from 10 to 100cm (4 to 36in). The leaves are alternately arranged and pinnately compound, divided multiple times to form a finely dissected, ferny leaf. The tiny flowers are grouped into many small sunflower heads, and these are arranged in flat-topped clusters. The petal-like ray florets are usually white in wild populations (sometimes pinkish), and flowers bloom from mid spring to mid fall. The fruits are small, one-seeded achenes.

Cultivation. Full sun to part shade, and moist to rather dry soil. Yarrow is one of our best-known and most common wildflowers, thriving in almost any situation. It is often used as a lawn substitute and can be mowed to form a soft, fragrant carpet. An excellent plant for the butterfly garden or wildflower meadow.

Propagation. Easy from seed sown in fall or spring, or by dividing clumps in early spring.

Native Habitat and Range. In moist to dry, open habitats, including roadsides, meadows, open forests, and rocky slopes at low to high elevations, on both sides of the Cascades and through North America; circumboreal.

Notes. Reputedly a fire retardant and used medicinally by many groups of people in the Northern Hemisphere. Around 75 species of *Achillea* are native to the temperate regions of the Northern Hemisphere. Six of the 11 varieties of *A. millefolium* occur in the Pacific Northwest; selections include 'Cerise Queen', 'Lavender Beauty', and 'Salmon Beauty' (pink to lilac flowers); 'Hoffnung' (yellow); and 'Fire King' and 'Paprika' (red).

Achlys triphylla	Zones 6a to 9b	Berberidaceae

vanilla-leaf, sweet-after-death

This striking perennial produces basal leaves to 30cm (1ft) tall from spreading rhizomes. The leaves are large, up to 20cm (8in) across, and divided into three fan-shaped leaflets with lobed margins. Small, white flowers bloom on narrow, leafless spikes up to 40cm (16in) tall from mid spring to mid summer. The fruits are single-seeded, dry, reddish berries.

Cultivation. Full to part shade or dappled light, and moist soil high in organic matter. Plants spread slowly but once established form a luxuriant groundcover. This species is a graceful addition to the shady woodland garden, pond, or stream margin but does poorly in containers.

Propagation. Grows most easily from rhizome divisions made in early spring. Ripe (or almost ripe) seeds can be planted into flats of potting soil soon after harvesting and left outside over winter for germination the following spring.

Native Habitat and Range. In moist woods, forest edges, and near streams at low to mid elevations from southern British Columbia south to northwestern California, and from the coast to the west slope of the Cascades in Oregon, through the Columbia River Gorge and along the east base of the Cascades in Washington and northern Oregon.

Notes. Dried leaves give off a sweet fragrance, hence the common names. *Achlys californica* (deer's foot), which also occurs near the coast, is distinguished from this species by having a longer central leaflet, with more numerous lobes, and brown fruits. The only other species in the genus is native to Japan.

Achillea millefolium

Achlys triphylla

Achnatherum hymenoides (photo by Sally A. Simmons)

Aconitum columbianum

Achnatherum hymenoides   Zones 3b to 9b   Poaceae

Indian ricegrass

This perennial bunchgrass grows to about 60cm (2ft) tall. Plants are smooth to finely hairy, and the narrow leaves are curled inward (involute). Each spikelet is about 1cm (.5in) long and contains a single floret; the lemma is densely hairy and has a long awn at the tip. The spikelets are arranged in an open, airy panicle to 15cm (6in) long, with fine, hair-like branches. The flowers bloom from late spring to early summer, but remain attractive through most of the season. The fruit is a grain, or caryopsis.

Cultivation. Full sun or light shade, and well-drained, sandy or rocky soil. This is an important rangeland grass, essential to many species of wildlife and perfect for native gardens east of the Cascades. Include this drought-tolerant species in the dry wildflower meadow or with sagebrush.

Propagation. Seeds germinate with difficulty. Collect seeds in the summer and scarify them by rubbing them between pieces of sandpaper or shaking them in a jar of coarse sand. Plant them outside in the fall, either into flats or directly into the garden, and leave them outside over winter to help break dormancy. Seeds can be stored for several years, which may improve germination.

Native Habitat and Range. On dry grasslands, arid plains, and foothills, especially in sandy or rocky soils at low to fairly high elevations east of the Cascades from British Columbia, south through California, east to Alberta and Minnesota, south through the Dakotas to New Mexico and Texas.

Notes. *Achnatherum* ×*bloomeri* is a natural hybrid between this species and western needlegrass, *A. occidentale*. Members of the genus *Achnatherum* (needlegrass) are widespread in western North America, where there are around 25 species; about a dozen occur in the Pacific Northwest, mostly in arid climates. Wide-ranging species include Thurber's needlegrass (*A. thurberianum*), Richardson's needlegrass (*A. richardsonii*), Columbia needlegrass (*A. nelsonii*), and Lemmon's needlegrass (*A. lemmonii*). These bunchgrasses generally occur in open ponderosa pine woods and sagebrush-dominated habitats; all can be grown from seed.

Aconitum columbianum   Zones 3b to 8b   Ranunculaceae

Columbian monkshood

Stems of this monkshood reach .5 to 2m (1.5 to 6ft) with alternately arranged, palmate leaves up to 20cm (8in) wide. The showy, uniquely shaped flowers can grow to 3.5cm (1.5in) long and bloom in racemes along the tall stems from early to late summer. The small petals are hidden within the hooded, petaloid sepals, which are pale blue to deep blue-purple, occasionally yellowish or white. The fruits are dry follicles.

Cultivation. Full sun to part shade, and wet or moist soil. This is a beautiful plant for perennial beds, moist edges of the shade garden, or wildflower meadows on either side of the Cascades. Protect them from slugs.

Propagation. Plant seeds into flats of potting soil as soon as they are collected in fall and leave them outside to stratify in the cool, moist winter weather. They should germinate the following spring, but plants may take a few years to reach flowering size.

Native Habitat and Range. In moist woods and mountain meadows at mid to high elevations, from Alaska, south through the Cascades to California, and east to southwest Alberta, Montana, South Dakota, Iowa, Colorado, and New Mexico.

Notes. *Aconitum c.* ssp. *columbianum* occurs throughout the range; *A. c.* ssp. *viviparum* is native in Oregon and California. *Aconitum delphiniifolium* (mountain or larkspurleaf monkshood) is native to Alaska and British Columbia. The approximately 100 species of *Aconitum* are native

Actaea rubra

Actaea rubra, fruits

to the temperate areas of Asia and Europe, with only six species in North America; all contain highly poisonous alkaloids and are especially toxic to livestock.

| **Actaea rubra** | Zones 3b to 9a | Ranunculaceae |

baneberry

This perennial reaches 40 to 100cm (1.5 to 3ft) during the growing season. The flowering stems bear compound leaves, pinnately divided two or three times into toothed segments. Numerous delicate flowers, with short, white petals and longer white or purplish sepals, are clustered at the stem tips; they bloom from late spring to mid summer and are followed by bright red (occasionally white) berries.

Cultivation. Part to full shade or dappled light, and moist soil high in organic matter. A lovely addition to the woodland or shade garden, attractive in flower and in fruit. The ripe berries, which hang on through the fall, are attractive to birds but poisonous to humans: do not site baneberry where small children might be tempted to eat its berries.

Propagation. Easy from seeds collected in fall, removed from the pulp, and planted into flats or directly into the garden. Leave them outside to stratify over winter. Will self-sow once established, but it is not aggressive.

Native Habitat and Range. In moist wooded areas and along streams at low to fairly high elevations from Alaska south to California, and east through Canada and the northern United States to the Atlantic coast; south in the Rocky Mountains to New Mexico, and to Kansas and Illinois.

Notes. Only *A. r.* ssp. *arguta* occurs in the Pacific Northwest. As its common name suggests, this species is highly poisonous, although it was used topically as a medicine. There are probably fewer than ten species of *Actaea*, native to temperate areas of the Northern Hemisphere with only a couple of others in North America. *Cimicifuga* (bugbane) is sometimes included in the genus *Actaea*. Both *C. elata* (tall bugbane), with shoots to 2m (6ft) tall, and *C. laciniata* (Mt. Hood or cutleaf bugbane) are rare plants of moist or boggy, shady places at low to mid elevations west of the Cascades; their inflorescence is a simple to branched raceme. The tiny flowers lack petals, but have attractive, white or pinkish sepals and numerous, showy stamens; they bloom from early to late summer, and the fruits are beaked follicles. Bugbanes can be grown from seed collected and planted outside in autumn. The white flowers of *Trautvetteria caroliniensis* var. *occidentalis* (western bugbane) are similar, but they are arranged in flat-topped clusters, and each flower produces several one-seeded achenes.

Agastache   Lamiaceae

giant hyssop or horsemint

In all, *Agastache* encompasses 20 or more species, mostly native to North America (with 16 species) and eastern Asia. Three or four are native to our area. The flowers of these aromatic herbs are crowded into spike-like verticils (whorls) at the stem tips; they have tubular, bilabiate (two-lipped) corollas with five short petal lobes.

Propagation. Collect seeds in the fall, store them dry, and plant the following spring. They can also be planted outside after harvest for germination the following spring. Do not plant seeds too deeply, as germination appears to be stimulated by light.

Agastache occidentalis   Zones 5b to 9b

western giant hyssop or horsemint

This perennial grows from a woody crown. The stems are often simple or with a few branches, growing to 1m (3ft) tall. The opposite leaves have deltoid (triangular) to ovate leaf blades to about 6cm (2.5in) long and 4cm (1.5in) wide on 5cm (2in) petioles. The undersides of the leaves are covered with short, fine hairs. The small, tubular flowers bloom in crowded whorls in a spike-like inflorescence up to 15cm (6in) long. The corollas are pale pink or whitish, and the tubular, five-toothed calyces are pinkish purple. Flowers bloom from early to late summer, and the fruits consist of four small nutlets.

Cultivation. Full sun or light shade, and well-drained, rather dry soil. This is an aromatic, summer-blooming perennial for the rock garden, dry slope, or parking area. Plant it with other tough, drought-tolerant species in the hummingbird and butterfly garden or rocky place in the wildflower meadow.

Native Habitat and Range. On open slopes and rock ledges at low to fairly high elevations on the east slope of the Cascades in Washington.

Notes. Cusick's giant hyssop (*A. cusickii*) has flowers with lavender calyces and whitish corollas; it lives in dry, rocky habitats at mid elevations in the mountains of central Idaho, southeastern Oregon and northern Nevada.

Agastache urticifolia   Zones 4a to 9b

nettleleaf giant hyssop or horsemint

This fibrous-rooted perennial grows stems, often branching, to 1.5m (5ft) or more from a woody crown. The opposite leaves are petiolate and ovate to heart-shaped (cordate). The leaf margins are serrate with somewhat rounded teeth. The largest leaves grow to 10cm (4in) long by 8cm (3in) wide. Small flowers bloom in crowded, spike-like whorls in an inflorescence up to 15cm (6in) long. The corollas are whitish or purplish, and the calyces are pinkish purple, blooming

Agastache occidentalis (photo by Sally A. Simmons)

Agastache urticifolia

from early to late summer. The fruits are small nutlets that ripen within the tubular calyx after the corolla fades and falls away.

Cultivation. Full sun or part shade, and moist, well-drained soil. This is a tall, aromatic plant for the perennial border, hummingbird and butterfly garden, or wildflower meadow.

Native Habitat and Range. On moist open slopes, woods, and washes from southeastern British Columbia, south through eastern Washington and Oregon to southern California and east to Montana, Wyoming, and Colorado.

Notes. Both *A. u.* var. *urticifolia* and *A. u.* var. *glaucifolia* occur in the Pacific Northwest.

Agoseris aurantiaca	Zones 3b to 9a	Asteraceae

orange agoseris, mountain dandelion

This taprooted perennial grows a basal rosette of lance-shaped leaves, often with a few lobes along the margins. Leaves can grow to 20cm (8in) or more, and the whole plant has milky sap. The leafless flowering stalks (scapes) can grow to 60cm (2ft). Each stem bears a single, dandelion like head of tiny ray florets, each with a burnt-orange corolla, blooming from early to late summer. The fruits are single-seeded achenes with fluffy, white pappus hairs (from a modified calyx) at the top of the fruit.

Cultivation. Full sun to part shade, and well-drained, moist to fairly dry soil. An unusual addition to the rock garden or wildflower meadow.

Propagation. Grow from seed collected in the late summer or fall. Seeds can be planted in the fall or spring. They can be planted into the garden or into flats for later transplanting.

Native Habitat and Range. In moist to rather dry meadows and woods at mid to high elevations in the mountains, British Columbia, and Alberta south to California and Arizona, east to South Dakota and New Mexico.

Notes. *Agoseris a.* var. *aurantiaca* occurs throughout the range. The roughly ten species of *Agoseris* are mostly native to western North America; a handful of these live in the Pacific Northwest. Tall agoseris (*A. elata*) and pale agoseris (*A. glauca*) are two natives listed as rare in parts of their ranges.

Allium	Liliaceae

onion

Allium includes at least 400 species, distributed throughout the Northern Hemisphere; more than 80 are native to North America, about half of these to the Pacific Northwest. Some species occur in moist meadows; others inhabit dry, rocky sites. Several are listed as rare. Alliums are bulb-bearing perennials with narrow leaves and an onion fragrance. The flowers bloom in umbels and are composed of six colored (petaloid) tepals or perianth parts (petal and sepals). Each flower has six stamens, and the fruit consists of a three-celled capsule.

Propagation. Collect seeds after the capsules ripen in late summer and sow them in the fall, soon after harvest, either into flats of potting soil or directly into the garden, leaving them outside over winter for germination the following spring. Seedlings will take a few years to reach flowering size. Offset bulbs can be removed or clusters of bulbs divided and transplanted in the spring, but this should be done only with cultivated plants originally grown from seed.

Allium acuminatum	Zones 4a to 9b

Hooker's or taper-tip onion

This little onion grows from a rounded bulb. A few narrow, grass-like leaves appear first, then wither as flowering begins. The leafless flowering stalk (scape) can grow to 30cm (1ft) in height and is topped by an umbel of eight to 30 bright magenta (sometimes lighter pink or white) flowers. The flowers bloom from late spring to mid summer and are around 1.5cm (.5in) long with strongly flared tepals. The fruits are small capsules.

Cultivation. Full sun, and well-drained, rocky, rather dry soil. An excellent species for the rock garden or dry meadow on either side of the Cascades. The little plants form rosy pink drifts over time and provide nectar for butterflies.

Native Habitat and Range. On rocky hills and dry plains at low to mid elevations on both sides of the Cascades from southern British Columbia, south to California and Arizona, east to Montana, Colorado, and New Mexico.

Notes. Narrowleaf onion (*A. amplectens*), Olympic onion (*A. crenulatum*), rock onion (*A. macrum*), and Robinson's onion (*A. robinsonii*) are a few of our other native species that occur in rocky, dry habitats.

Allium cernuum	Zones 3b to 9b

nodding onion

This perennial grows from elongated bulbs that often form clusters. The narrow leaves are basal and remain green during flowering. The flowering stems can grow from 15 to 50cm (6 to 20in) tall. Ten or more nodding, pink (sometimes white) flowers bloom in umbels at the shoot tips from early to mid summer. The old flowers turn upright and the tepals become papery as the capsules ripen.

Cultivation. Full sun or part shade, and well-drained, moist to fairly dry soil. This species is a graceful addition to the perennial bed, rock garden, or pond margin, and a good choice for the wildflower meadow or butterfly garden, as a nectar plant. Can spread aggressively by seed.

Agoseris aurantiaca

Allium cernuum

Allium acuminatum

Allium falcifolium

Anaphalis margaritacea

Native Habitat and Range. In moist meadows to rather dry, open woods and rocky or sandy sites at low elevations on both sides of the Cascades from British Columbia, Washington, and Oregon, east and south through much of North America to the Atlantic.

Notes. The bulbs can be cooked and eaten if they become too numerous. The widespread *A. c.* var. *cernuum* is the only one of the three varieties that occurs in our area. Other species of moist or seasonally wet habitats include white- to pink-flowered *A. madidum* (swamp onion), purple-flowered *A. validum* (Pacific onion), and *A. geyeri* (Geyer's onion), with light rose flowers.

Allium falcifolium	Zones 6b to 9b

sickle-leaved onion

This perennial produces two thick, sickle-shaped leaves to 15cm (6in) or longer from an oval bulb. The leafless scape grows to 12cm (5in) and is flattened below the umbel of flowers. Each umbel produces ten to 30 flowers on pedicels to 1.5cm (.5in) long; the six tepals are as long, usually deep rose, but occasionally greenish white with rosy tints. The flowers bloom from early spring to mid summer, depending on elevation. The fruit is a rounded capsule.

Cultivation. Full sun or light shade, and rocky soil that is moist in the spring but rather dry by summer. Butterflies visit this species for nectar. It is effective in the rock garden or dry patch of the wildflower meadow, or tucked into the crevices of a stone retaining wall. With luck, plants will reseed themselves and form small drifts.

Native Habitat and Range. In rocky or heavy soil, often on serpentine, on dry slopes and forest openings at low to fairly high elevations, from southwestern Oregon, south to west central California.

Notes. Sierra onion (*A. campanulatum*), another species with rosy flowers, lives in dry woods from southern Oregon to California. The pink flowered *A. brandegei* (Brandegee's onion) inhabits dry slopes in the mountains east of the Cascades. Bolander's onion (*A. bolanderi*), with pink or white flowers, lives on gravelly flats from southern Oregon to California. The flowers of Tolmie's onion (*A. tolmiei*) vary from light rose to almost white; it grows on stony flats and slopes east of the Cascades.

Anaphalis margaritacea	Zones 3b to 9b	Asteraceae

pearly everlasting

The stems of this rhizomatous perennial grow to 1m (3ft) tall. The narrow leaves, up to 12cm (5in) long, are usually green above but white (or rusty) with woolly hairs below. The tiny flowers are clustered into numerous small heads at the tips of the stems. Each flower head is surrounded by many papery, white bracts that persist beyond blooming time, from mid summer through early fall. The fruits are small achenes.

Cultivation. Sun or part shade, and moist to fairly dry soil. This species is happy in most any spot: some gardeners consider it weedy, but it's an excellent plant for the butterfly garden, wildflower meadow, dry bank, or parking area. Pearly everlasting also makes a great cut flower and is useful in dried bouquets, as its common name suggests.

Propagation. Divide rhizomes in spring or summer. Alternatively, collect seeds from female plants (this species is dioecious) and plant them in fall or early spring.

Native Habitat and Range. On roadsides, open forests, fields, and rocky slopes at low to fairly high elevations; circumboreal, ranging across North America, south to New Mexico, Kansas, Tennessee, and North Carolina; eastern Asia.

Notes. This is the only North American species of *Anaphalis*, a genus of 30 or so species native to temperate parts of North America, Europe, and especially eastern Asia.

Anemone		Ranunculaceae

windflower

The approximately 100 species of *Anemone* are mostly native to the chillier parts of the Northern Hemisphere; of the 20 or so that occur in North America, around a dozen are native to our area. Some species of the Pacific Northwest live in open mountain meadows; others are woodland species. The leaves are compound and sometimes finely dissected. The flowers lack petals, but the sepals are petaloid and showy. The stamens are numerous, as are the small pistils, which ripen into one-seeded achenes. The styles are short (plants with long, plumose styles are now placed in the genus *Pulsatilla*).

Propagation. Collect ripened seeds in the late summer or fall, sow them soon after harvest, either into containers of potting soil or directly into the garden, and leave them outside to stratify in cool, moist conditions for spring germination. Rhizomatous species can be propagated from divisions made in the fall or early spring, but this should be done only with plants originally grown from seed.

Anemone deltoidea	Zones 6b to 9b

Columbian windflower, western white anemone

This perennial grows to 30cm (1ft) from slender, spreading rhizomes. A few basal leaves grow singly from the rhizomes, each with three oval, coarsely toothed leaflets around 5cm (2in) long.

Anemone deltoidea

Anemone multifida

Each flowering stem has a whorl of three toothed leaflets to 8cm (3in), topped by a solitary, showy flower, usually with five white sepals, blooming from mid to late spring. The many small achenes at the center of the flower are hairy at the base.

    Cultivation. Full shade to part sun, and moist soil. This delicate perennial is a good addition to woodland gardens west of the Cascades. It is rhizomatous but not aggressive, and is charming among other shade-loving plants.

    Native Habitat and Range. Often among shrubs in dry to moist woods at low to mid elevations, west of the Cascades from Puget Sound south to northern California and in the Columbia River Gorge.

    Notes. Piper's anemone (*A. piperi*) is another woodland species with white or pinkish flowers and a range east of the Cascades. Drummond's anemone (*A. drummondii*) and Teton anemone (*A. tetonensis*) are also native to parts of the Pacific Northwest, especially high mountain meadows.

Anemone multifida	Zones 3b to 9b

Pacific or cliff anemone

This perennial produces hairy shoots and basal leaves from a branched crown. The basal leaves are rounded in outline and up to 10cm (4in) across; they are deeply divided into narrow lobes and set on long petioles. The flowering shoots grow to 50cm (20in) tall, and the blades of the stem leaves are similar to the basal ones. One or a few flowers bloom on long peduncles; each has as many as nine sepals, up to 1.5cm (.5in) long, ranging in color from creamy or yellowish to red, purplish, or bluish. Flowers bloom from late spring to late summer. The fruits, small achenes, have short styles but are densely hairy and arranged in a cottonball-like cluster.

Anemone occidentalis

Anemone occidentalis, fruits

Cultivation. Full sun to part shade or dappled light, and well-drained, rocky, moist to rather dry soil. This species tends to bloom periodically during the season, and the clusters of woolly achenes are as attractive as the flowers. A charming plant for the rock garden, wildflower meadow, or opening in the woodland garden on either side of the Cascades.

Native Habitat and Range. In open forests and rocky slopes at low to high elevations from Alaska south to northern California, east across the continent to the Atlantic and south through the mountains of the west to Arizona and New Mexico.

Notes. At least two varieties, *A. m.* var. *hudsoniana* and *A. m.* var. *saxicola*, occur in our area. *Anemone parviflora* (northern or small-flowered anemone), another species with woolly-haired achenes, grows to 20cm (8in) tall from slender rhizomes and has white or bluish flowers; it lives in meadows and near streams in Alaska and British Columbia, ranging south in the mountains of Washington and Oregon and in the Rocky Mountains.

Anemone occidentalis	Zones 4a to 9b

western anemone, white pasqueflower

This silky-haired perennial produces shoots to 50cm (20in) from a stout, sometimes branched crown. The basal leaves and the leaves of the flowering stems are two or three times compound into small, linear segments. Each flowering shoot has a single, relatively large flower to about 7cm (3in) across. The sepals are rounded and white or tinged with purple, blooming from late spring to late summer. The fruits, dense clusters of silky, long-styled achenes, are as showy as the flowers.

Cultivation. Full sun to part shade, and well-drained soil. This perennial is lovely in the wild-flower meadow, or in the rock or alpine garden. It sometimes blooms sporadically throughout the season, and the attractive clusters of achenes add to its beauty.

Native Habitat and Range. In mountain meadows and rocky slopes at mid to fairly high elevations from British Columbia south, in the Olympic and Cascade Mountains to the Sierra Nevada of California, east to Alberta, the Wallowa Mountains of Oregon, northern Idaho, and Montana.

Notes. Sometimes classified as *Pulsatilla occidentalis*. Similar is *P. patens* ssp. *multifida* (cut-leaf anemone), which ranges from southern Alaska to north central Washington, east through Alberta and the Great Lakes, and south to New Mexico and Texas.

Anemone oregana	Zones 5a to 9b	

blue windflower, Oregon anemone

This perennial produces flowering shoots and a few palmate basal leaves from a stout rhizome. The single-flowered shoots can grow to 30cm (1ft), and each shoot bears a whorl of three leaves near the top, below the flower. Each leaf of the whorl is divided into three lobed and toothed leaflets. The showy flowers have numerous stamens and five sepals to 2cm (1in) long, varying from bluish to reddish purple to pale pink or occasionally white. The flowers bloom from early spring to early summer. The fruits are finely hairy achenes with short styles.

Cultivation. Part to full shade or dappled light, and moist soil high in organic matter. This is a lovely anemone for the woodland or shade garden on both sides of the Cascades, but it is difficult to coax plants into vigorous flowering.

Native Habitat and Range. On brushy hillsides, moist thickets, and woods at low to mid elevations in the Olympic Mountains and Cascades of Washington, south through the Cascades and Coast Ranges of Oregon to northern California, east to the Blue Mountains of northeastern Oregon.

Notes. *Anemone o.* var. *oregana* is widespread; *A. o.* var. *felix*, with pinkish flowers, lives in marshes along the Washington and Oregon coasts. Lyall's anemone (*A. lyallii*) is very similar but has fewer stamens and narrower sepals that are usually white (sometimes pinkish or bluish); this species lives in shady forests, open prairies, and high mountain ridges from southwestern British Columbia south to northern California, and from near the coast up the west slope of the Cascades.

Angelica lucida	Zones 3b to 9b	Apiaceae

sea-watch, seacoast angelica

This glabrous (hairless) perennial produces a single, stout stem up to 1.5m (5ft) from a thick taproot. The large, alternate leaves are two or three times pinnately compound and have well-developed, often clasping petioles. The leaflets are broadly ovate, up to 7cm (3in) long by 6cm (2.5in) wide, and the margins have coarse teeth. The inflorescence is a compound umbel composed of up to 45 rays to 10cm (4in) long; each ray is tipped with a smaller umbel of tiny, white flowers. Flowers bloom from mid to late summer, finally ripening into a ridged, oblong schizocarp, to 1cm (.5in) long, a dry fruit that splits into single-seeded halves at maturity.

Cultivation. Full sun or part shade, and moist soil. This is a bold plant for the pond margin, streambank, perennial bed, or moist wildflower meadow. Sea-watch and other angelicas make good nectar plants in the butterfly garden.

Propagation. Grow from seed collected in the fall and planted soon after harvest. Soak the seeds in water the day before planting, and sow them into containers of potting soil or directly

Anemone oregana

Angelica lucida

into the garden, leaving them outside to cold stratify over the winter for germination in spring. Plants may take a couple of years to reach flowering size.

Native Habitat and Range. In moist meadows, beaches, and streambanks, mainly near the coast at low elevations from Alaska, south to northern California, but sometimes ranging inland and to higher elevations, especially in British Columbia and the northern parts of the range, and also along parts of the east coast, from Labrador to Virginia.

Notes. The stems and petioles of sea-watch were eaten by indigenous people, but they were careful—many other, similar plants in the celery and carrot family are extremely poisonous. *Angelica* includes around 50 species, mostly native to the Northern Hemisphere; around 20 species are native to North America, with about half of these occurring in the Pacific Northwest. Sharptooth angelica (*A. arguta*) grows in meadows, wetlands, and along streams at low to mid elevations from southern British Columbia, south on both sides of the Cascades to California and east to Montana and Wyoming; this robust species, which can grow to 2m (6ft) tall, bears large umbels of white flowers from early to late summer and is a good addition to sunny, wet places on either side of the Cascades. Kneeling angelica (*A. genuflexa*) is shorter, to 1.5m (5ft) tall, and its compound leaves tend to curve downward; widely distributed in southern British Columbia and mainly west of the Cascades in Washington and Oregon, it lives in moist places at low elevations from Alaska to northern California. Henderson's angelica (*A. hendersonii*) is found on coastal bluffs and dunes from southwestern Washington to California. Canby's angelica (*A. canbyi*) lives near streams on the east slope of the Cascades and Columbia Basin, in central Washington and Oregon.

Antennaria rosea

Apocynum cannabinum

| **Antennaria rosea** | Zones 4a to 9b | Asteraceae |

rosy pussytoes or everlasting

This perennial produces mats of leafy stolons with white-haired, spoon-shaped (spatulate) leaves about 2.5cm (1in) long. Flowering shoots grow to 40cm (16in) tall and produce a flat-topped cluster of small flowering heads at the tips. The heads consist of small disk flowers, either male or female, each with a pappus (modified sepals) of white hairs. Each head is surrounded by papery bracts less than 1cm (.5in) in length that vary from white to dark pink. The papery flowers are long-lasting, blooming from late spring to late summer; the fruits are tiny achenes.

Cultivation. Full sun to part shade, and well-drained, rather dry to moist soil. This charming mat-former is excellent in the rock garden or as a groundcover between paving stones.

Propagation. Divide the clumps of creeping stolons in early spring; or grow from seed, planted into flats in the fall and left to spend the winter outside for germination in the spring.

Native Habitat and Range. In open woods and dry meadows at low to fairly high elevations, from Alaska south through the Olympics and Cascades to California, east to New Mexico, Colorado, and the Great Lakes.

Notes. Sometimes confused with *A. microphylla*, which also occurs in our area, as do alpine pussytoes (*A. alpina*), pearly pussytoes (*A. anaphaloides*), silver pussytoes (*A. argentea*), low pussytoes (*A. dimorpha*), and small-leaf pussytoes (*A. parvifolia*). All would be good plants for the woodland path or rock garden. Raceme pussytoes (*A. racemosa*) is an attractive woodland species. Shrubby or evergreen pussytoes (*A. suffrutescens*) is woodier than most species and is endemic to southwestern Oregon and northwestern California. *Antennaria* debatably includes around 50 species, with a distribution centering in the mountains of western North America and extending through much of the continent.

Apocynum cannabinum   Zones 3b to 9b   Apocynaceae

Indian hemp, hemp dogbane

This rhizomatous perennial produces leafy, simple or branched stems with milky sap up to 1m (3ft) tall. The opposite leaves are upright, yellow-green, and oblong to lanceolate. They have short petioles and blades up to 11cm (4.5in) long with entire (smooth) margins. The tiny flowers, with tubular, five-lobed white or greenish white corollas, bloom in small clusters from the stem tips and from leafy lateral shoots from early summer to early fall. Seeds with a coma (a tuft of long, white hairs) ripen in long, slender follicles to 15cm (6in) or longer.

Cultivation. Full sun to part shade, and moist soil. Plant at the edge of the wetland or wildflower meadow. Though its flowers are not showy, this species is attractive, especially in the fall, with yellow leaves and reddish stems. It can become weedy and is toxic to livestock, and probably also poisonous to humans.

Propagation. Collect seeds in the fall and plant them soon after harvest, either into containers of potting soil or directly into the garden for germination in the spring. Well-developed plants can be propagated by dividing the rhizomes in winter or early spring.

Native Habitat and Range. Near streams and along moist roadsides and cultivated areas at low to mid elevations throughout most of North America.

Notes. The long, strong fibers in the stems of this species were used by various tribes to make nets, thread, and other products. The only other species in this North American genus, *A. androsaemifolium* (spreading dogbane), is shorter, and its leaves tend to droop on the branching stems. The bell-shaped flowers are pink or whitish. Plants occur in dry woods, slopes, meadows, and roadsides at low to fairly high elevations throughout much of North America. The fibers of spreading dogbane are strong, but shorter than those of Indian hemp. *Apocynum ×floribundum*, the naturally occurring hybrid between the two species, is also wide-ranging.

Aquilegia   Ranunculaceae

columbine

Aquilegia is a genus of more than 50 species, mostly native to the temperate parts of the Northern Hemisphere; about 20 occur in North America, with only a few species reaching the Pacific Northwest, in its broadest sense. In *Aquilegia* the five petals and five sepals are both petaloid (colored other than green), and the petals form long, nectar-producing spurs. The flowers have numerous stamens, and the fruits consist of five dry follicles. Columbines are short-lived, lasting only a few years, but generally reseed themselves in the garden. They are promiscuous, hybridizing at every opportunity.

Propagation. Grow from seeds planted in the spring or summer after they have been harvested. They usually respond to warm conditions and germinate in a month or so.

Aquilegia caerulea   Zones 3b to 9b

Rocky Mountain columbine

The leafy, flowering stems of this perennial can reach 60cm (2ft) or more. The leaves are twice ternately (divided into threes) compound. The sepals vary from white to blue, and the petals are white with long, blue or white spurs. The flowers can reach 5cm (2in) in length and width, blooming from early to late summer. Fruits are dry follicles that split open when ripe to release black seeds.

Aquilegia caerulea var. ochroleuca

Aquilegia formosa

Cultivation. Full sun to part shade, and moist, well-drained soil. Beautiful in the rock garden or meadow. Hummingbirds will visit this charming wildflower for the nectar in its long spurs, and other birds will eat the seeds.

Native Habitat and Range. In rocky slopes and meadows at mid to high elevations from Idaho to South Dakota and south through the mountains from Montana to Nevada and New Mexico.

Notes. Only one variety of this species, the state flower of Colorado, reaches our area, occurring west through Idaho; the other varieties range to the south and east of us.

Aquilegia formosa	Zones 3b to 9b

red or western columbine

The flowering stems of this taprooted perennial can reach 1m (3ft). The leaves are twice ternately (divided into threes) compound and clustered at the base of the stem. The nodding flowers, blooming from late spring to late summer, can reach 5cm (2in) in width and are often numerous on robust plants. The sepals are pale to deep red-orange; the yellow petals have nearly straight, short, red to orange spurs. Fruits are dry follicles that split to release black seeds.

Cultivation. Full sun to part shade, and moist, well-drained soil. Hummingbirds and butterflies visit red columbine, one of our most charming native wildflowers, for its nectar-producing flowers, while many other birds enjoy the seeds. An excellent addition to the wildlife garden, wildflower meadow, sunny streambank, or thicket.

Native Habitat and Range. Moist meadows, open forests, and rocky slopes, at low to high elevations, southern Alaska south through California and east to western Alberta, Montana, and Utah.

Notes. The yellow-flowered *A. flavescens* (yellow columbine) is an alpine species that occurs in the Cascades from southern British Columbia to Washington and Oregon, east to Montana and south to Utah and Colorado.

Arabis aculeolata	Zones 6b to 9b	Brassicaceae

Waldo rockcress

This perennial produces shoots to 30cm (1ft) tall from a simple or branched crown. The hairy leaves of the basal rosettes are spoon-shaped (spatulate), up to 2.5cm (1in) long, sometimes with a few teeth. The flowering stems have narrow leaves, and the inflorescence is a few-flowered raceme. The four sepals are purple, as are the four petals, which grow to 1.5cm (.5in) long. The flowers bloom from early to late spring, and the fruits, typical of the mustard family, are erect, slender siliques (a long, dry fruit that splits open along two margins at maturity), up to 6cm (2.5in) long.

Cultivation. Full sun or light shade, and well-drained, rather dry, rocky or gravelly soil. With its tufted rosette of basal leaves and delicate flowers, this is a charming addition to the rock, alpine, or trough garden. It can also be planted in the crevices of a stone retaining wall, or in the dry, rocky corner of the wildflower meadow. This and all rockcresses are easier to grow in drier climates.

Propagation. Grow from seed collected in the summer and planted soon after harvest. Sow seeds into flats of potting soil or directly into the garden in late summer, and leave them outside over winter for germination in spring. Specimens with branching crowns can be propagated from basal cuttings made in the summer, but this should be done only with plants originally grown from seed.

Native Habitat and Range. In rocky or gravelly places, usually derived from serpentine, at mid elevations, endemic to the Siskiyou Mountains in southwestern Oregon and northwestern California.

Notes. Most of the 100 or more species of *Arabis* are native to mountainous or dry places in the Northern Hemisphere; of the 80 species that occur in North America, approximately 40 are native to the Pacific Northwest. These include the white- or pink-flowered Drummond's rockcress (*A. drummondii*), a widespread but short-lived plant of gravelly places. Holboell's rockcress (*A. holboellii*) is another interesting, sometimes biennial, species with pinkish purple or white flowers and long siliques curved downward. Lemmon's rockcress (*A. lemmonii*), littleleaf rockcress (*A. microphylla*), and Lyall's rockcress (*A. lyallii*) are low, tufted perennials; they have pink or purple flowers and inhabit rocky sites and well-drained meadows in the west. Woody rockcress (*A. suffrutescens*) is a shrubby perennial with pink or purple flowers; it lives in rocks and talus near sagebrush or in dry woods in the southern parts of our area.

Aralia californica	Zones 7a to 9b	Araliaceae

western aralia, California spikenard

This big perennial reaches 1 to 3m (3 to 10ft). The large leaves are pinnately compound with toothed leaflets. Many small, greenish flowers make up each rounded umbel, and many umbels are borne in each branched inflorescence. Plants bloom from early to late summer. Purplish black, berry-like fruits follow the flowers.

Cultivation. Part to full shade, and moist soil. This is a bold, almost tropical-looking background or specimen plant for the woodland or shade garden.

Arabis aculeolata

Aralia californica

Argentina egedii

Armeria maritima

Propagation. Collect ripened fruits in late summer, remove the seeds from the pulp, plant them outside into containers of potting soil, and leave them to stratify in cool, moist conditions. They will germinate when the weather warms in the spring.

Native Habitat and Range. In moist, shady woods at low to mid elevations in the Cascades and Coast Ranges from central Oregon south to southern California.

Notes. *Aralia* is a genus of around 30 species, mostly native to Asia, with six species in North America. *Aralia nudicaulis* (wild sarsaparilla) is a rhizomatous perennial that occurs in moist, shady places from eastern British Columbia and northeastern Washington, east through North America to the Atlantic coast, and south to Colorado, Missouri, and Georgia.

Argentina egedii	Zones 6a to 9b	Rosaceae

Pacific silverweed

This taprooted perennial herb spreads by long, reddish stolons that root where they touch the ground. The basal leaves are pinnately compound and can grow to 40cm (16in). Each leaf has 15 to 25 leaflets with sharply toothed margins. The leaves are usually green on the upper surface and white with long, silky hairs beneath. Single flowers bloom on leafless peduncles to 10cm (4in) long. The flowers have five bright yellow petals and are about 2.5cm (1in) across, blooming from late spring to late summer. The fruits are small achenes.

Cultivation. Full sun to part shade, and moist to wet soil. Tolerates but does not require very sandy soil. Although deciduous, this is a fine little groundcover for the edge of a path or among the stones of a water feature, stream, or rock wall. It competes with weeds and can become aggressive in moist habitats.

Propagation. Simply detach and plant the small plantlets that form along the stolons, just like strawberries. Alternatively, make cuttings in spring or fall, or collect and sow the tiny achenes into flats of potting soil in the fall.

Native Habitat and Range. Sandy beaches and dunes and the wet edges of marshes and streams, from Alaska south along the coast to southern California, inland along rivers to eastern North America; Asia.

Notes. Sometimes classified as *Potentilla anserina* ssp. *pacifica* or *P. pacifica*. Of the two subspecies, only *A. e.* ssp. *egedii* occurs near our coast, with a small distribution in the east. *Argentina anserina* (*P. anserina*; silverweed cinquefoil) is similar but occurs away from the coast, usually east of the Cascades, and east to the southwestern states, Rocky Mountains, northern Great Plains, and the east coast. *Comarum palustre* (*Potentilla palustris*; marsh cinquefoil) has a similar growth habit and red flowers; it grows in our wetlands, sometimes floating on the surface of shallow water, and has a circumboreal distribution.

Armeria maritima	Zones 4a to 9b	Plumbaginaceae

thrift, sea pink

This evergreen perennial forms a dense mound, spreading to 30cm (1ft). The tufted leaves are needle-like and linear, reaching 10cm (4in) in length. The tiny flowers are usually pink (sometimes white) and crowded into head-like clusters on leafless stalks (scapes), 10 to 30cm (4 to 12in) tall. Thrift blooms most profusely in spring, but may continue to produce flowers throughout the year, especially where the climate is mild. The fruits are one-seeded and achene-like.

Cultivation. Full sun, and well-drained, moist to rather dry soil. Tuck this tidy, slow-growing species in the rock garden or at the edge of the perennial border. Thrift also makes an excellent container plant or groundcover for a small area.

Propagation. Easiest by dividing clumps in the spring or fall. Seed planted in spring germinates in three or four weeks.

Native Habitat and Range. On coastal bluffs and beaches, and along inland streams and prairies, not far from salt water, at low elevations, circumboreal, Alaska to southern California; Europe.

Notes. Two subspecies occur in our area. *Armeria m*. ssp. *sibirica* (Siberian sea thrift) has the more northern range, from Oregon to Alaska; *A. m*. ssp. *californica* (California sea pink) has longer leaves, fewer flowering heads, and a range from British Columbia to southern California. Selections of the species include 'Cotton Tail' (white flowers), 'Bloodstone' (rosy flowers), and 'Rubrifolia' (reddish foliage and pink flowers). This is the only North American species in the genus; some 30 others are native to Europe, northern Africa, and parts of Asia and Chile.

Arnica   Asteraceae

Arnica is a genus of around 30 species of perennials with opposite leaves and yellow-flowered daisy-like heads. They are distributed throughout the cooler parts of the Northern Hemisphere and are especially diverse in western North America; about 20 species are native to the Pacific Northwest, common near streams and in woods. Species are known to hybridize, and some are apomictic, producing viable seed without sex. Arnicas have medicinal properties but they are also poisonous and are mainly used externally.

Propagation. Grow from seed collected in the late summer or fall and planted outside after harvest. Sow seeds into flats or directly into the garden, cover them very lightly with soil, and leave them outside to cold stratify over the winter for germination the following spring. Alternatively, divide rhizomes in the spring.

Arnica amplexicaulis   Zones 4a to 9b

streambank or clasping arnica

This species spreads from rhizomes and produces leafy shoots to about 80cm (2.5ft). The plants have a few, small basal leaves and several pairs of opposite, lance-shaped stem leaves that usually lack petioles. The leaves are up to 12cm (5in) long and have toothed margins. Plants produce several flowering heads with light yellow ray and disk florets. The heads have up to 14 ray florets with corollas to 2cm (1in) long, toothed at their tips. The flowers bloom from early to late summer. The fruits, single-seeded achenes, are topped with a light brown, feathery pappus, the modified calyx.

Cultivation. Full sun to part shade, and moist to wet soil. This large, spreading perennial is a good summer-blooming species for the sunny pond margin or streambank. Plant it in the bog garden or in the wetter parts of the wildflower meadow or butterfly garden.

Native Habitat and Range. Along streams and in moist forests and glades at low to mid elevations, from Alaska south to central California, and from the coast, east to Montana and Utah.

Notes. Meadow or Chamisso's arnica (*A. chamissonis*) is a similar but taller species of moist habitats; it too has several pairs of lance-shaped stem leaves. Both *A. c*. ssp. *chamissonis* and *A. c*. ssp. *foliosa* occur in the Pacific Northwest. *Arnica longifolia* (seep-spring or spearleaf arnica) also has several pairs of stem leaves; it lives in well-drained, often rocky sites near seeps and springs in the mountains of the west.

Arnica amplexicaulis

Arnica cordifolia

Arnica cordifolia	Zones 3b to 9b

heartleaf arnica

This arnica produces shoots up to 60cm (2ft) tall, singly or in small clusters. Short, leafy, sterile shoots also grow from the rhizomes. The leaves are heart-shaped (cordate), and the blades can reach 12cm (5in) long by 9cm (3.5in) wide. The leaves have long petioles, and the blade margins are usually coarsely toothed. The flowering stems have up to four pairs of opposite leaves. Each flowering shoot produces one to three heads, each head surrounded by involucral bracts with spreading, white hairs. Each head has up to 15 ray florets with yellow corollas about 2.5cm (1in) long. Flowers bloom from mid spring to early summer, sometimes longer. The pappus (modified sepals) at the top of each achene consists of long, whitish hairs.

Cultivation. Part shade or dappled light, and moist to rather dry soil high in organic matter. This charming yellow daisy forms an open groundcover, often growing among other plants. Site it in an opening or glade in the woodland garden or at the margin of the meadow.

Native Habitat and Range. In open, moist to rather dry woods and meadows, at low to fairly high elevations, from Alaska south through California, mainly east of the Cascades, east to New Mexico, Colorado, and Michigan.

Notes. Broadleaf arnica (*A. latifolia*), Nevada arnica (*A. nevadensis*), and hairy arnica (*A. mollis*) are similar native species with broad, mostly basal leaves.

Artemisia	Asteraceae

wormwood, mugwort

Artemisia encompasses more than 100 species of shrubs and herbs that occur throughout the Northern Hemisphere as well as in South America and Africa. Nearly half of these are native to North America, almost 30 to the Pacific Northwest. The plants have tiny flowers clustered into small heads, and these are often arranged into larger inflorescences. Many, but not all, species have aromatic foliage. Most of the shrubby species occur in the mountains or east of the Cascade crest (see the last A-to-Z section, of shrubs and trees, for information on these), but several of the herbaceous species are native near the coast and along streams west of the Cascades. Members of this genus have been used medicinally by many groups of people; one common name refers to its usefulness in killing worms and other intestinal parasites.

Propagation. Herbaceous species can be grown from seed collected in the fall and planted outside for germination the following spring. Many species can be propagated by dividing the rhizomes in spring or summer, or by removing shoots formed at the base of the plant during the summer.

Artemisia dracunculus	Zones 3b to 9b

tarragon

This perennial herb can reach 1.5m (5ft), producing several stems from a thick rhizome. The alternate leaves are linear and mostly entire, but sometimes with a few lobes. The largest leaves develop near the middle of the stem and grow to 8cm (3in) long by 1cm (.5in) wide. The inflorescence is a large panicle of small, nodding flowering heads. The tiny florets within each head are yellowish and bloom from mid summer to mid fall. The fruits, tiny achenes, are produced only by the outer florets in each head.

Cultivation. Full sun, and moist to rather dry, well-drained soil. A leafy plant for the dry meadow, sandy or rocky streambank, or butterfly garden.

Native Habitat and Range. In rather dry, open areas, often near streams at low to mid elevations, east of the Cascades from British Columbia, south to Mexico and east across much of North America to the Great Lakes; Eurasia.

Notes. Although tarragon is commonly used in cooking, particularly in poultry and fish dishes and for flavoring vinegar, the aromatic properties of the individual plants can be highly variable, ranging from strongly fragrant to almost odorless. *Artemisia campestris* (field sagewort) is shorter, growing to 1m (3ft) or less, generally from a taproot, and is not strongly fragrant; plants have pinnately compound leaves with the basal ones well developed. A highly variable, circumboreal species, it is often encountered in sandy, open places in our area.

Artemisia lindleyana	Zones 4a to 8b

Columbia River wormwood

This species grows to about 60cm (2ft) tall and tends to have a shrubby base, sometimes with a cluster of roots but usually without well-developed rhizomes. The alternate leaves are narrow, up to 5cm (2in) long, with entire or toothed margins. The leaves have dense, woolly hairs on the undersides but tend to be greenish above. Small clusters of flowering heads form spike-like inflorescences at the branch tips. Flowers bloom from mid summer to mid fall, and the fruits are tiny achenes.

Cultivation. Full sun to light shade, and well-drained, moist soil. This silvery plant is a good addition to the rocky streambank or lake margin. Plant it a sandy, moist spot in the wildflower meadow or butterfly garden.

Artemisia dracunculus

Artemisia lindleyana

Artemisia suksdorfii

Aruncus dioicus

Native Habitat and Range. In sandy or rocky shores of lakes and streams, especially along the Columbia River and its tributaries, from southern British Columbia, mainly east of the Cascades, south through Oregon and perhaps east to Idaho.

Notes. *Artemisia ludoviciana* (western mugwort, white sage) is similar, but its stem bases are not woody. The leaves have entire to toothed margins and are grayish, with woolly hairs; it grows to 1m (3ft) tall and lives in open, rather dry places through most of North America. *Artemisia frigida* (prairie sagewort) is a mat-forming perennial with a woody crown, growing to 40cm (16in) tall; its aromatic leaves are finely divided and covered with white hairs. These two silvery natives are often cultivated.

Artemisia suksdorfii	Zones 7b to 9b

coastal or Suksdorf's wormwood or mugwort

This large, aromatic perennial produces a cluster of stems to 1.5m (5ft) from short, thick rhizomes. The leaves are lance-shaped to elliptic, the largest ones up to 15cm (6in) long and 5cm (2in) wide; they usually have some coarse teeth along the margins and are dark green on the upper surface, white with woolly hairs beneath. Tiny, greenish flower heads are produced in long, branching, plume-shaped clusters at the stem tips and bloom from early to late summer. The fruits are tiny achenes.

Cultivation. Full sun or light shade, and well-drained, moist to rather dry soil. The flowers are not showy, but the attractive foliage and big fountain shape make this a good background plant for the perennial bed or butterfly garden, especially in sandy soils or near the coast.

Native Habitat and Range. On sandy or rocky beaches and bluffs, mainly near the coast and in valleys at low elevations west of the Cascades from southwestern British Columbia, south to California.

Notes. The similarly sized *A. douglasiana* (Douglas' sagewort) has lance-shaped leaves that are entire or have a few lobes; this species occurs near streams and in other moist places, generally on both sides of the Cascades, and south to California and Nevada. Michaux's wormwood (*A. michauxiana*) is a herbaceous species with pinnately compound leaves, growing only to 40cm (16in) tall; it lives in rocky places, usually at high elevations in the mountains of the west.

Aruncus dioicus	Zones 4a to 9b	Rosaceae

goatsbeard

This robust perennial can reach 2m (6ft) in height and 1.5m (5ft) in width from short, stout rhizomes. The large leaves are usually three times pinnate, and the leaflets are ovate with sharply toothed margins. The plants are dioecious (either female or male) and produce many tiny, white flowers in plume-like panicles to 50cm (20in) from late spring to mid summer. The fruits, small follicles, are produced in large numbers on female plants. Flowers of male plants are considered by some to be showier, but the differences are minor.

Cultivation. Part to full shade or dappled light, and moist soil. Tolerates almost full sun where summers are not too hot. Not fussy about soil, but benefits from additional compost. This large, graceful species is a welcome addition to the woodland garden or tall perennial border and a fine background or specimen plant.

Propagation. Easy from seed. Collect seeds from the follicles and plant them outside in fall or spring. Young plants will reach blooming size in a couple of years. Garden plants will probably produce seedlings on their own, if both sexes are present.

Native Habitat and Range. In moist woods, shady roadsides, and along streambanks, at low to mid elevations from Alaska south to California, and from the coast, east to the west slope of the Cascades.

Notes. Sometimes classified as *A. sylvester*. Only *A. d.* var. *acuminatus* occurs in our area; the other two varieties are eastern. The genus has only two or three species, all native to the Northern Hemisphere.

Asarum caudatum	Zones 4b to 9b	Aristolochiaceae

wild ginger

This lush, slow-growing groundcover forms a low carpet from shallow, creeping rhizomes and remains evergreen where winters aren't too fierce. The heart-shaped leaves are shiny and dark green, 4 to 10cm (1.5 to 4in) long and up to 15cm (6in) wide. The odd flowers bloom singly from mid spring to mid summer and are often hidden under the leaves. They are usually maroon (sometimes whitish) with three long, tapered calyx lobes up to 8cm (3in). The entire plant has a delicious ginger aroma, and the fruits are capsules.

Cultivation. Part sun to full shade, and moist soil. It looks its glossy best in soil with high organic content. Wild ginger is a wonderful plant for carpeting the woodland garden or edging the shady perennial bed. Site it near the garden path or bench, where the occasional bruised leaf will add fragrance to the air. Slugs and snails will crawl across hot coals to get to this plant.

Propagation. Easy. Plant rooted sections of the rhizomes in spring or summer, or grow from seed collected from ripened capsules. Seeds germinate without treatment. Young seedlings often appear in spring and summer next to existing plants, and these can be transplanted.

Native Habitat and Range. In moist, shady woods at low to mid elevations in the mountains, British Columbia to California, on both sides of the Cascades and east to northern Idaho and western Montana.

Notes. Not related to the common culinary ginger root, *Zingiber*. *Asarum marmoratum* (marbled wild ginger), with mottled leaves, occurs in Oregon and California; *A. wagneri* (*A. caudatum* var. *viridiflorum*; longtailed wild ginger), with light green flowers, is native to southern Oregon. *Asarum* includes about 20 species native to the Northern Hemisphere, especially Japan; the closely related *Hexastylis* (heartleaf) has sometimes been included in it.

Asclepias   Asclepiadaceae

milkweed

Asclepias includes about 200 species worldwide, including Africa, with the majority (more than 70) native to North America. They are mostly perennial and have simple, opposite (sometimes whorled) leaves and milky sap, the source of their common name. The flowers of *Asclepias* are uniquely formed. The sepals and five fused petals are reflexed, and in the center of the flower the corolla tube and stamens have additional appendages that form a structure called a corona. Each anther has two chambers, where the pollen is fused into a waxy mass called a pollinium. Each pollinium has an arm at the top, and a gland attaches the two pollinia where the arms meet. When an insect visits the flower, the gland catches on the leg of the pollinator, and it carries off the pair of pollinia to deposit on another flower. The fruits are follicles that split along one margin when ripe to release seed. Milkweed seeds are flattened and have a coma (a tuft of long silky hairs) at one end, which functions in seed dispersal. Milkweeds are good plants for the butterfly garden, supplying nectar for adults and edible foliage for some larvae, such as monarch butterflies. Though some species were used medicinally, most are poisonous to humans.

Propagation. Collect seeds when the follicles begin to split open in the fall, store them in paper bags, and plant them in the spring when the soil begins to warm. Plants may take a few years to reach flowering size. Larger plants can be propagated from divisions of the rhizomes made in the spring.

Asclepias fascicularis   Zones 5a to 9b

narrowleaf milkweed

This deciduous, rhizomatous perennial grows to 80cm (2.5ft). The narrow, linear leaves are scattered or whorled on the stems, reaching up to 15cm (6in) in length. The flowers are arranged in umbels and are purplish pink, blooming from early summer to early fall. The fruits are narrow, smooth follicles to 10cm (4in) long.

Cultivation. Full sun, and fast-draining, moist to dryish soil. A fine addition to the butterfly garden or wildflower meadow.

Native Habitat and Range. In dry to moist soil, often near streams, but in various open habitats, at low to mid elevations, northeastern Washington, south to Utah, Arizona, and Mexico, west to the coast in Oregon.

Notes. Heartleaf milkweed (*A. cordifolia*) occurs in southern Oregon; swamp milkweed (*A. incarnata*) ranges west as far as western Idaho.

Asarum caudatum

Asclepias speciosa

Asclepias fascicularis

Asclepias speciosa   Zones 4a to 9b

showy milkweed

This deciduous perennial develops shoots up to 1m (3ft) from rhizomes. The opposite, ovate leaves are up to 15cm (6in) long, and the plant is generally covered with woolly hair. The pink or purplish flowers are arranged in umbels of 15 to 25 blossoms each, blooming from late spring to mid summer. The oblong follicles are woolly and covered with spiny warts; each produces numerous flattened seeds, each with a coma.

Cultivation. Full sun or very light shade, and fast-draining, moist or rather dry soil. A beautiful plant for the sunny butterfly garden or wildflower meadow on either side of the Cascades.

Native Habitat and Range. On open, often rocky or sandy, dry to somewhat moist sites at low to mid elevations, mainly east of the Cascades from British Columbia to California and east to Illinois and Texas.

Notes. Pallid milkweed (*A. cryptoceras*) is another native species with broad, opposite leaves and yellowish pink flowers; it grows from enlarged, tuber-like roots in clay or gravel from southeastern Washington and eastern Oregon, east and south to Idaho, Wyoming, Colorado, California, and Arizona.

Aster   Asteraceae

Aster has been taken apart and dispersed into several different genera by recent systematists. At one time the genus contained more than 250 species, mostly native to North America but also to South America, Europe, Asia, and Africa. Each "daisy" consists of many tiny flowers (florets) condensed into a head and subtended by a set of herbaceous to somewhat papery bracts. The center of the flowering head is made up of many disk florets with tubular, yellow corollas. The ray florets are on the outer margin of the head; they are usually purple, blue, pink, or violet. Asters are often difficult to identify, but they are generally easy to grow and add beauty to the landscape in late summer and autumn. They are an essential part of any butterfly garden, providing both a late-season source of nectar for adults and leafy food for larvae.

Propagation. Grow from seed collected in fall and either planted outside soon after harvest or stored for spring planting. Plants can also be grown from divisions of the rhizome made in the early spring.

Aster modestus   Zones 3b to 9b

great northern aster

The leafy flowering stems of this aster develop from spreading rhizomes and reach up to 1m (3ft) in height. The lanceolate leaves have a few teeth along the margins and grow to 13cm (5in) long and up to 4cm (1.5in) wide. The disk florets are yellow, and the ray florets, as many as 40 per head, are violet to purple and about 1.5cm (.5in) long. Some of the herbaceous bracts are also purplish. Plants generally bloom from mid to late summer. The achenes are sparsely hairy with a pappus of thin bristles.

Cultivation. Full sun to part shade, and moist soil. This is an excellent, late-blooming plant for the butterfly garden, streambank, pond margin, perennial bed, or wildflower meadow.

Native Habitat and Range. In moist wooded areas at low to mid elevations, often along streams, from Alaska, south through the mountains to Oregon, east to Alberta, Idaho, and Montana, and to Ontario and Michigan.

Notes. Also classified as *Canadanthus modestus*.

Aster modestus

Aster subspicatus

Aster subspicatus   Zones 6a to 9b

Douglas' aster

This deciduous perennial grows from creeping rhizomes and leafy flowering shoots can reach 1m (3ft) or more. The leaves are oblong or lanceolate and generally have a few teeth along the margins; the larger ones are about 10cm (4in) long. The ray florets are blue or violet. The flowering heads are about 2cm (1in) wide and bloom from mid summer to mid fall; the bracts are yellowish at the base. The fruits are small achenes, and the pappus (modified calyx) is sometimes reddish.

Cultivation. Full sun to part shade, and moist soil rich in organic matter. This is an excellent aster for the butterfly garden or perennial bed, where it will attract many insects. It is also beautiful near a stream, pond, or any other moist to fairly wet location.

Native Habitat and Range. Near streambanks, seashores, woods, and other moist to wet places at low to mid elevations from the coast of Alaska, south to coastal California and east to Alberta, northern Idaho, and northeastern Oregon, but most common west of the Cascades.

Notes. Also classified as *Symphyotrichum subspicatum*. Several other Pacific Northwest asters would add beauty to gardens. *Aster chilensis* (*S. chilense*; Pacific aster) and *A. campestris* (*S. campestre*; western meadow aster) are both native to open, sometimes rather dry habitats. *Aster eatonii* (*S. eatonii*; Eaton's aster) and *A. frondosus* (*S. frondosum*; alkali aster) are often pink-flowered and prefer moist places. *Aster foliaceus* (*S. foliaceum*; leafy bract aster) is a species of moist, wooded places in much of the west.

Astragalus   Fabaceae

milkvetch, locoweed

Astragalus is a genus of more than 1,000 species, native to the chillier, drier parts of the Northern Hemisphere. Milkvetches reach their greatest diversity in Asia, but there are around 350 species in North America and nearly 100 native to the Pacific Northwest, many of them rare endemics. Most occur in dry climates east of the Cascades, and some are quite showy, making good additions to the desert planting or rock garden. These annual or perennial herbs usually have pinnately compound leaves. Plants produce racemes of typical pea flowers in shades of white, yellow, red, or purple. The fruits, dry legumes, are sometimes as attractive as the flowers, inflated, mottled, or coiled in some species. A few species are considered good forage, but many contain toxic compounds (hence, locoweed); in other cases, the plants may be poisonous because they take up selenium from soils with high concentrations of this element. Some of the Asian species have long been used as medicinal herbs, especially in traditional Chinese medicine.

Propagation. Harvesting milkvetch seeds is difficult: insect larvae quickly eat almost all of them. Collect seeds just as soon as the legumes ripen, and don't expect a high percentage of viable seed. The seed coats are hard and may require nicking or scratching with a file. To further increase chances of germination, place seeds in a bowl and pour hot water (just below boiling) over them to break dormancy. Plant seeds in tubular containers or directly into the garden in the fall, and leave them outside for the winter. Seeds may germinate sporadically the following spring.

Astragalus purshii   Zones 3b to 9b

woollypod milkvetch

This cushion-forming perennial grows from a taproot and produces a branched crown. The prostrate stems grow to 10cm (4in) long, and the crowded, pinnately compound leaves are up to 15cm (6in). The entire plant is covered with woolly, white hair. The short racemes have up to ten flowers. The corollas grow to 3cm (1.5in) long and vary from reddish purple to pink or cream, blooming from mid spring to early summer. The attractive fruits are fuzzy pods up to 2.5cm (1in) in length.

Cultivation. Full sun or part shade, and well-drained, rather dry or gravelly soil. This is a charming, silvery perennial for the rock garden, dry prairie, or sagebrush planting. Tolerates cold but does not do well in wet climates and is therefore easier to grow east of the Cascades.

Native Habitat and Range. In arid sagebrush-steppe and prairies at low to mid elevations east of the Cascades from southern British Columbia to southern California, east to Alberta, the Dakotas, and Colorado.

Notes. Six of the eight varieties of this variable species occur in some part of our area. *Astragalus kentrophyta* (spiny milkvetch) is another interesting cushion-forming species with rigid, needle-like leaflets and creamy flowers with purple tints; *A. newberryi* (Newberry's milkvetch) is low-growing and silvery with purplish flowers and a wide distribution in the Southwest, ranging north to Oregon and Idaho.

Astragalus spaldingii   Zones 5a to 7b

Spalding's milkvetch

This taprooted perennial produces several generally erect stems to 40cm (16in) from a branching crown. Plants are grayish with woolly hairs, and the pinnately compound leaves grow to 12cm (5in) long with about 15 narrow leaflets. The racemes are densely flowered with up to 60 small

Astragalus purshii (photo by Sally A. Simmons)

Astragalus spaldingii (photo by Sally A. Simmons)

blooms. The corollas are about 1.5cm (.5in) long, white, with bluish lines and purplish tips. The flowers bloom from late spring to early summer, and the fruits, small, rounded pods, are densely woolly.

Cultivation. Full sun or light shade, and well-drained, sandy or dry soil. This is a taller perennial for the large rock garden or dry meadow. Plant it with sagebrush and other drought-tolerant shrubs in the wildlife garden east of the Cascades.

Native Habitat and Range. In grasslands and with sagebrush at low to mid elevations east of the Cascades from central Washington, south to northeastern Oregon and east to western Idaho.

Notes. *Astragalus canadensis* (Canadian milkvetch) is an even taller upright species, to about 80cm (2.5ft). The racemes are densely flowered and spike-like, sometimes with more than 100 white to creamy flowers. This widespread species includes three varieties, all of which occur in the Pacific Northwest, usually near streams, from the east slope of the Cascades, east through much of North America. Blue Mountain milkvetch (*A. reventus*) is another robust perennial with garden potential. This species produces multiple stems to 40cm (16in) and creamy or purplish flowers; it lives near sagebrush or ponderosa pine, ranging from southeastern Washington to northeastern Oregon and adjacent Idaho.

Astragalus succumbens   Zones 5b to 7b

crouching or Columbia milkvetch

This perennial usually produces a reclining, branching main stem to 50cm (20in) long from a deep taproot. The plants are grayish with fine hairs and the pinnately compound leaves are somewhat fleshy and up to 10cm (4in) long. The racemes are densely flowered with up to 60 blossoms, each up to 2.5cm (1in) long. The corollas are light pink or white with purplish tips, blooming from mid spring to early summer. The interesting pods grow to 4cm (1.5in) long and are heart-shaped in cross-section.

Cultivation. Full sun or light shade, and well-drained, dry, sandy or rocky soil. This is a relatively tall milkvetch, and the large clusters of pink flowers make it one of the loveliest. Plant it among the taller perennials in the rock garden or dry meadow, or near a path among sagebrush in the wildlife garden. As with other milkvetches, this species is difficult to grow west of the Cascades.

Native Habitat and Range. In sandy, dry soils, often with sagebrush, at low to mid elevations, east of the Cascades from central Washington, south to northern Oregon.

Notes. Balloonpod milkvetch (*A. whitneyi*) grows to 30cm (1ft) and has creamy flowers washed with purple. It too has interesting fruits, strongly inflated pods up to 6cm (2.5in) long and half as wide; they have a shiny, membranous texture and are mottled with reddish purple. This is a species of rocky slopes east of the Cascade crest from Washington to northeastern California, and east to Idaho and Nevada.

Balsamorhiza   Asteraceae

balsamroot

Balsamorhiza is a small, distinctive genus of taprooted perennials with leaves in basal rosettes and sunflower-like, mainly yellow, flowering heads. The flowering shoots have only a few bract-like leaves, and the achenes lack a pappus (modified calyx). There are about a dozen species, all native to western North America, and most of them occur in the Pacific Northwest. Some species produce clusters of large, arrow-shaped leaves and flowering shoots from a branched root crown; others are smaller and have toothed or divided leaves. Balsamroots are long-lived but

Astragalus succumbens (photo by Sally A. Simmons)   *Balsamorhiza careyana* (photo by Sally A. Simmons)

slow-growing, and the leaves of seedlings and young plants are elliptic in shape, taking on adult characteristics as they age.

Propagation. Grow from seed collected after the flowering heads ripen in summer. Plant the achenes soon after harvest in deep containers or directly into the garden for germination in fall or spring. In their first year of life, balsamroots begin to form an extensive taproot but only a single leaf. Be prepared to wait three years for plants to reach flowering size.

Balsamorhiza careyana   Zones 5b to 7b

Carey's balsamroot

This taprooted perennial produces basal rosettes of leaves and numerous flowering shoots to 1m (3ft) tall. The large triangular basal leaves grow to 30cm (1ft) long by 15cm (6in) wide. The leaves have a veiny, firm texture and well-developed petioles, and are mostly entire but sometimes with a few rounded teeth. The flowering shoots have a few small, narrow leaves, and each produces one to several heads. The ray and disk florets are both bright yellow, and the involucral bracts surrounding the heads are green, but not usually leafy. Each head produces around 13 ray florets with corollas up to 4cm (1.5in) long, tending to turn white and papery, remaining on the heads as they age. Flowers usually bloom from early to late spring, but sometimes into summer. The achenes are mostly, but not always, hairy.

Cultivation. Full sun to part shade and dry, well-drained soil. This is a big, bold, drought-tolerant perennial, especially suited to the arid climates east of the Cascades. Plant this species with sagebrush, bunchgrasses, and other desert taxa. It is also a good plant for the rock or butterfly garden.

Balsamorhiza deltoidea

Balsamorhiza rosea (photo by Sally A. Simmons)

Native Habitat and Range. In open, dry places with fairly deep soil at low to mid elevations east of the Cascades in eastern Washington and north central Oregon.

Notes. This species has two varieties, *B. c.* var. *careyana* and *B. c.* var. *intermedia*, a taxon endemic to Oregon with some characteristics similar to *B. deltoidea*. Carey's balsamroot is strongly associated with the path of the Missoula floods, the drenching of parts of eastern Washington and Oregon that took place at the close of the last ice age. Very young shoots and petioles have a delicate flavor and are harvested, peeled, and eaten as "Indian celery" by some of the Columbia Basin tribes.

Balsamorhiza deltoidea   Zones 6b to 9b

deltoid or Puget balsamroot

This taprooted perennial produces clusters of basal leaves and many flowering shoots to 1m (3ft) tall. The large triangular basal leaves are finely hairy and grow to 30cm (1ft) long by 20cm (8in) wide. The leaf margins usually have shallow, rounded (crenate) teeth and long petioles. The flowering shoots have several narrow, bract-like leaves, and each produces multiple heads with the central head the largest. The flowers are yellow, and the central head produces up to 20 ray florets with corollas to 5cm (2in) long, falling from the heads as the hairless (glabrous) achenes ripen. The involucral bracts surrounding the heads are well developed and leafy. Flowers usually bloom from early to late spring, but sometimes to mid summer.

Cultivation. Full sun or light shade, and well-drained, fairly dry soil. Plant with camas and other prairie species for a beautiful spring display. This is a big, beautiful perennial for the dry wildflower meadow on the west side. Slugs and snails are not a problem east of the Cascades, but on the west side, where they are all too numerous, they will go to great lengths to feast on young foliage.

Native Habitat and Range. Open, rather dry, grassy places with deep soils at low elevations from southwestern British Columbia, south through the Puget trough and west of the Cascades (east through much of the Columbia River Gorge) to southern California.

Notes. The most widespread balsamroot, *B. sagittata* (arrowleaf balsamroot), is another large plant with deep taproots and arrow-shaped leaves; its flowering shoots usually produce single heads, and plants are often silvery with white, felt-like hairs. It grows at low to fairly high elevations from southern British Columbia, south through California, east of the Cascade and Sierra Nevada crests, and east through the mountains to Montana, South Dakota, Colorado, and Arizona.

Balsamorhiza rosea	Zones 5a to 7b	

rosy balsamroot

This balsamroot usually has a simple, unbranched crown and a carrot-like taproot. The lance-shaped leaves have well developed petioles and grow in a basal rosette. The blades are up to 20cm (8in) long by 10cm (4in) wide, and their margins vary from being deeply lobed to crenate (having rounded teeth). The flowering stems grow to 30cm (1ft) tall and usually have a pair of small bracts near the base. Each shoot bears a single flowering head with up to 15 reddish yellow ray corollas. The ray corollas are relatively short, about 2.5cm (1in) long, and broad, about 1cm (.5in). Flowers bloom from mid to late spring, and the achenes have long hairs.

Cultivation. Full sun, and very well-drained, rocky or gravelly soil. A beautiful, unusual perennial for rock gardens and patient gardeners east of the Cascades.

Native Habitat and Range. In thin, rocky soils at low to mid elevations east of the Cascades; known from only a few locations in south central and eastern Washington to north central Oregon.

Notes. An endemic species with a small range. Though not listed as rare, plants should never be removed from the wild; they will not survive transplanting. Several other smaller balsamroots have pinnately toothed, lobed, or divided leaves; these include Hooker's balsamroot (*B. hookeri*), hoary balsamroot (*B. incana*), silky balsamroot (*B. sericea*), and serrate balsamroot (*B. serrata*), all native to rocky habitats or dry meadows, mostly east of the Cascades. The tall, large-leafed species of balsamroot often hybridize with such smaller, cutleaf species where populations meet.

Bensoniella oregana	Zones 8a to 9b	Saxifragaceae

Oregon bensoniella

This delicate perennial produces shoots to 40cm (16in). The leaves are mostly basal, palmate, and ovate, with heart-shaped (cordate) bases; the blades of the largest are 7cm (3in) long on petioles up to 12cm (5in). Many tiny, cup-like flowers with filament-like (filiform) petals bloom in racemes in the spring. The fruits are capsules with two elongated styles.

Cultivation. Full to part shade or dappled light, and moist, well-drained soil. An unusual species for the woodland or shade garden.

Propagation. Grow from seed planted in fall or early spring, either into the garden or into containers for later transplanting.

Native Habitat and Range. In moist woods at mid elevations from southwestern Oregon to northwestern California.

Notes. Sometimes classified as *Bensonia oregona*. It is the only species in the genus and is listed as rare in California.

Bensoniella oregana

Bolandra oregana

Boykinia major

| *Bolandra oregana* | Zones 4a to 8b | Saxifragaceae |

Oregon bolandra, northern false coolwort

This leafy-stemmed perennial grows to 40cm (16in) from short, bulblet-bearing rhizomes. The lower leaves are kidney-shaped (reniform), to 7cm (3in) wide; they are carried on petioles to 15cm (6in) long, with leafy stipules at the base. The upper leaves are palmate, with toothed margins; they lack petioles and clasp the stems. Purple flowers to 2cm (1in) long with slender petals bloom in few-flowered panicles from mid spring to early summer. The fruits are small capsules.

Cultivation. Full to part shade or dappled light, and moist soil with high organic content. This is an unusual and charming little plant for the shaded rocks around a stream, pond, waterfall, or other water feature. It can also be planted among mossy rocks in the shade or woodland garden.

Propagation. Grow from seed planted in fall or early spring.

Native Habitat and Range. Among damp, mossy rocks, usually near waterfalls and streams at low to mid elevations, in the western end of the Columbia River Gorge, and along the Snake River and its tributaries in southeastern Washington, northeastern Oregon, and central Idaho.

Notes. The only other species in the genus is native to California.

| *Boykinia major* | Zones 4b to 9b | Saxifragaceae |

large boykinia

This perennial grows to about 80cm (2.5ft) from short rhizomes. The palmate leaves are toothed, with the largest, petiolate leaves at the base of the plant, up to 20cm (8in) across. The small flowers have five white petals and are about 1cm (.5in) long, blooming in flat-topped clusters from early summer until early fall. The fruits are small, two-lobed capsules with many seeds.

Cultivation. Part to full shade or dappled light, and moist soil. This is a charming perennial for the woodland or shade garden, and it has a longer blooming season than many natives. Plant it near a path or bench.

Propagation. Grow from seed planted in fall or early spring. Plants can also be divided in fall or spring.

Native Habitat and Range. Near streams, moist forests, and meadows at low to mid elevations from western Montana, through Idaho and west to northeastern and western Oregon to California.

Notes. *Boykinia occidentalis* (*B. elata*; coastal brookfoam) and *B. intermedia* (*B. major* var. *intermedia*; Sierra brookfoam) occur in Washington and Oregon; *B. richardsonii* (Richardson's brookfoam) is a more northern species. There are fewer than ten species of *Boykinia* native to North America and eastern Asia.

| *Brodiaea* | | Liliaceae |

cluster lily

Brodiaea includes about 14 species, all native to western North America and especially California. These are showy, corm-forming perennials with six tepals (petals and sepals similar to each other and usually petaloid) that are fused to each other at the base. The long, linear leaves appear first and die back by flowering time in some species. Each flower has three functional stamens and three staminodes. Plants are occasionally placed in *Dichelostemma* or *Triteleia*; all are genera of graceful, corm-bearing perennials with grass-like leaves and umbels of tubular or trumpet-shaped flowers, but the seeds, styles, and stigmas vary among the three.

Propagation. Collect seeds in late summer or fall, when the capsules ripen and become papery. Plant the seeds within a couple of weeks of harvesting into containers or directly into the garden

Brodiaea coronaria

Brodiaea elegans

and leave them outside over winter for germination in the spring. Two or three years are needed before the corms become big enough to produce flowers. Mature corms can be transplanted to a depth of 7 to 10cm (3 to 4in) in autumn. Small corms, which sometimes form around the base of an older corm, can be detached and transplanted; but even these will take a year or two to reach flowering size, and they should be taken only from plants originally grown from seed.

Brodiaea coronaria   Zones 6a to 9b

harvest brodiaea

This corm-bearing perennial produces one to three linear leaves that die back before the flowers bloom. The leafless flowering stem (scape) grows 10 to 25cm (4 to 10in) tall, and produces three to nine flowers on unequal pedicels, varying in length from 2 to 9cm (1 to 3.5in). The violet-purple flowers are narrowly bell-shaped and about 2cm (1in) long. The tube (where the tepals are fused) is shorter than the free lobes and somewhat rounded at the base; the three flat staminodes curve toward the pollen-producing anthers. Flowers bloom from late spring to mid summer, and the fruits are oval capsules.

Cultivation. Full sun or part shade, and well-drained soil. Will grow in rocky or clay soil but prefers to dry out in the summer. If this species is planted in a moister spot, make sure it has good drainage. A lovely plant for the rock garden, dry meadow, or sharply drained slope.

Native Habitat and Range. In gravelly soil or dry clay on grassy slopes, rocky bluffs, or open woods at low to mid elevations from southern British Columbia, south, mainly west of the Cascades, to central California, east through the Columbia River Gorge.

Notes. Only *B. c.* ssp. *coronaria* occurs in the Pacific Northwest. Its scaly corms were eaten by some of the tribes living within its range.

Brodiaea elegans   Zones 5b to 9b

elegant or harvest brodiaea

The perennial corms produce one or two linear leaves up to 40cm (16in) long, which usually dry by the time the flowers appear. The leafless flowering stems vary from 10 to 40cm (4 to 16in). The flowers are usually violet or blue-purple and arranged in an open umbel with pedicels to 5cm (2in) long. The flowers are up to 4cm (1.5in) long and shaped like a funnel, with the tepals fused into a narrow tube at the base, opening to long lobes. The three flat staminodes are upright. This species blooms from mid spring to mid summer, sometimes later. The fruits are papery capsules.

Cultivation. Full sun or part shade, and dry soil. Plants go dormant after blooming and prefer to dry out. This is a lovely plant for the rock garden or dry, clayey slope, preferably away from irrigation. Plant it in drifts in the wildflower meadow along with other drought-tolerant perennials.

Native Habitat and Range. On dry, grassy plains and hillsides, sometimes moist meadows, usually in heavy soils, at low to mild elevations, mainly west of the Cascades from northwestern Oregon, south through Oregon to southern California.

Notes. Both *B. e.* ssp. *elegans* and *B. e.* ssp. *hooveri* occur in Oregon. Two other species range as far north as southwestern Oregon; these are *B. californica* (California brodiaea) and *B. terrestris* (*B. coronaria* var. *macropoda*; dwarf brodiaea).

Calochortus   Liliaceae

mariposa or sego lily, cat's ear, star tulip

Calochortus includes some of our most beautiful native lilies. Around 60 species are native to western North America, from southern Canada south to Guatemala, and especially California; nearly 20 are native to the Pacific Northwest, some of them listed as rare. These bulb-bearing perennials have linear, sometimes grass-like leaves. One to a few showy flowers bloom at the stem tips. Each flower has three narrow, green sepals and three broad, colored petals. The petals are often hairy on the inner surface, and each has a glandular depression at its base. Each flower has six stamens, and the fruits are capsules with three angles or wings, containing many seeds. Various Native American tribes ate the bulbs of some species, and the plants are, unfortunately, attractive to livestock. Mariposa lilies are beautiful but difficult to grow, requiring patience and perfect conditions.

Propagation. Grow from seed collected in late summer. Plant seeds in the fall, directly into the garden or into deep containers or flats filled with very porous soil high in pumice or sand. Leave the planted seeds outside to cold stratify over the winter for germination the following spring. Keep seedlings moist while they are growing but allow them to dry out as they become dormant in the late summer. Bulbs that survive their first few years can be transplanted in autumn. These lilies take three to five years to reach flowering size from seed.

Calochortus macrocarpus   Zones 4a to 7b

sagebrush mariposa lily

This bulbous perennial produces a stout, usually unbranched stem to 50cm (20in) tall. The narrow, linear leaves are curled at the tip and arranged alternately on the stems. The inflorescence bears one to three flowers and has two or more leaf-like bracts at its base. The flowers are erect, with narrow, green sepals and petals to 6cm (2.5in) long. The lavender petals are yellow at the base, and the gland at the base of each petal is surrounded by a fringed membrane and has a

Calochortus macrocarpus (photo by Sally A. Simmons)

Calochortus subalpinus

darker purple stripe above it. The glands are covered with branched, hair-like structures. Flowers bloom from late spring to mid summer, and the fruits are three-angled capsules containing straw-colored seeds.

Cultivation. Full sun to part shade, and well-drained, dry soil. In less well-drained soils, try planting it on a slope. This taller species of arid lands is for gardeners east of the Cascades, and it is particular about habitat. Plant among sagebrush, bunchgrasses, and other drought-tolerant plants in the wildlife or rock garden, away from irrigation, or try it in deep troughs or clay pots. It is a challenge compared to mariposa lilies of moister habitats.

Native Habitat and Range. In dry, loose, sometimes volcanic soil, often with sagebrush, at low to mid elevations, east of the Cascades from southern British Columbia, south to northeastern California, east to northern Nevada, Idaho, and western Montana.

Notes. This is one of the most common species of mariposa lily. The widespread *C. m.* var. *macrocarpus* generally has lavender petals with darker purple banding and thick fruits; the other variety, *C. m.* var. *maculosus*, with a small range in central Idaho and the adjacent corners of southeastern Washington and northeastern Oregon, is characterized by white petals, reddish purple banding, and narrow capsules. Lyall's mariposa lily (*C. lyallii*) has white or lavender flowers with long hairs on the inner surface of the petals; it lives in open, coniferous forest, sometimes with sagebrush, at mid to high elevations, mainly on the east slope of the Cascades, from southern British Columbia to south central Washington. Longbeard mariposa lily (*C. longebarbatus*) has lavender-pink flowers and also lives east of the Cascades, in low meadows from central Washington south to northern California.

Calochortus subalpinus   Zones 5a to 8a

subalpine mariposa lily, mountain cat's ear

This bulbous perennial produces flowering shoots up to 30cm (1ft) tall, usually with a single basal leaf up to 30cm (1ft) tall and 1.5cm (.5in) wide. The inflorescence has two or more bracts at its base and bears one to several flowers. The sepals usually have a purple spot at the base, and the petals often have a purple band above the gland at the base of the petal. The petals are typically pale yellow to creamy, sometimes with a lavender tint, and about 3cm (1.5in) long. Long hairs are scattered over the inner surface of the petals. Flowers bloom from early to late summer. The fruits are three-winged, nodding capsules containing pale yellow seeds.

Cultivation. Full sun to part shade, and very well-drained soil. This is a choice plant for the rock garden or trough, but protect it from excess moisture. Once past the seedling stage, it prefers to dry out in the summer.

Native Habitat and Range. In open forests and dry meadows with porous, well-drained volcanic soil at mild to fairly high elevations in the Olympic and Cascade Mountains from southern Washington, south to central Oregon.

Notes. Pointed-tip mariposa lily (*C. apiculatus*) is very similar, with pale yellow flowers; it lives on rocky slopes in dry, coniferous woods east of the Cascades. White mariposa lily (*C. eurycarpus*) has creamy or lavender flowers and upright capsules; it too lives east of the Cascades. Yellow mariposa lily (*C. monophyllus*) has bright yellow petals and sepals; it grows in the Sierra Nevada, ranging as far north as the mountains of southern Oregon. Bruneau mariposa lily (*C. bruneaunis*) and elegant mariposa lily (*C. elegans*) are also native to the Pacific Northwest; both have white petals with dark purple blotches at the base.

Calochortus tolmiei   Zones 6b to 9b

Tolmie's mariposa lily or cat's ear

This bulbous perennial produces a stem that is sometimes simple, but usually branched, up to 30cm (1ft) tall. Plants usually have a single basal leaf up to 40cm (16in) long and 3cm (1.5in) wide. The branched inflorescences are subtended by leafy bracts and bear one to several flowers. Flowers vary in color from white or creamy to purplish or pinkish. The petals are up to 4cm (1.5in) long, their inner surfaces covered with long hairs. The gland at the base of each petal is crescent-shaped and surrounded by a fringed membrane. Flowers bloom from late spring to early summer. The fruit, a three-winged nodding capsule, contains purple seed.

Cultivation. Full sun or part shade, and well-drained, rocky or sandy soil that is not irrigated. A good mariposa lily for gardeners west of the Cascades and a good plant for the rock garden or trough. Site it in a dry, stony meadow or among shrubs in the dry parts of the wildlife garden.

Native Habitat and Range. On dry, rocky slopes, often among shrubs, at low to mid elevations, west of the Cascades to the coast, from northern Oregon, south to central California.

Notes. Pink mariposa lily (*C. uniflorus*) has lilac or pink petals with a few hairs above the gland; it too lives west of the Cascades, in moist meadows and bog margins at low elevations from central Oregon, south to west central California. Broadfruit mariposa lily (*C. nitidus*) has showy, purplish petals with long, scattered hairs and upright capsules; it grows in meadows and swales in eastern Washington, northeastern Oregon, and adjacent Idaho. Howell's mariposa lily (*C. howellii*), Cox's mariposa lily (*C. coxii*), and Umpqua mariposa lily (*C. umpquaensis*) are rare endemics from southwestern Oregon.

Calochortus tolmiei

Caltha leptosepala

Caltha leptosepala	Zones 3b to 9a	Ranunculaceae

white, two-flowered, or broad-leaved marsh-marigold

This charming buttercup relative is a fleshy perennial growing to 40cm (16in) tall from short rhizomes. The leaves are mostly basal with long petioles and rounded leaf blades to 10cm (4in) long and at least as wide. The leaf margins usually have rounded teeth, and the lobes at the base of the blade sometimes overlap. There are usually two showy, white flowers to 4cm (1.5in) across on each stem, blooming from late spring through summer. The seeds develop in clusters of stalked follicles.

Cultivation. Sun to part shade, and wet soil with high organic content. This is a lovely, succulent plant for the pond margin or bog garden, especially in the cooler areas of the Northwest.

Propagation. Collect seeds from ripe follicles and plant them soon after harvest into a boggy site or wet, peaty medium, leaving them outside to stratify over winter. Germination should occur the following spring.

Native Habitat and Range. In bogs and seeps from lowlands (in the northern part of the range) to subalpine and alpine areas; Alaska south to California and east to Utah and Colorado.

Notes. Sometimes classified as *C. biflora*. Both *C. l.* ssp. *leptosepala* and *C. l.* ssp. *howellii* occur in our area. *Caltha palustris* (*C. asarifolia*; yellow marsh-marigold) is similar. There are probably less than 20 variable species of *Caltha* native to cold, marshy habitats in the Northern Hemisphere. The related *Trollius laxus* (globeflower), with palmately compound leaves and showy white or cream flowers, is another perennial with garden potential; it occurs in seeps and wet meadows at high elevations in the mountains of the west.

Calystegia soldanella

Calystegia soldanella	Zones 7b to 9b	Convolvulaceae

beach morning-glory

This succulent, glabrous (hairless) perennial produces prostrate stems that trail on the ground from deep rhizomes. The stems can grow to 50cm (20in) long, and the alternate leaves are kidney-shaped (reniform) to heart-shaped (cordate), up to 4cm (1.5in) across. The five petals are fused to form a funnel-shaped corolla up to 5cm (2in) long, purplish pink, with a white center and white streaking. Flowers are pleated and folded in bud, blooming singly from peduncles in the leaf axils from mid spring until early fall. The fruits are rounded capsules containing a few, large seeds.

Cultivation. Full sun, and sandy or rocky, well-drained soil. This plant prefers to sprawl on the ground, so plant it in the foreground of the rock garden or dune, where its lovely flowers and long bloom period can be enjoyed. Though native to beaches, it is worth trying in sandy, fast-draining soils away from the immediate coast and is tolerant of salty conditions.

Propagation. Usually grown from seed collected in the fall and planted soon after harvest; plant seeds where they are to grow or into well-drained potting soil in containers, and leave them outside to stratify in moist, cool winter conditions. Plants can also be propagated from cuttings made in the summer. Since they are prostrate, propagation by layering (nicking a stem and covering the cut segment with sand) should be successful. Another likely method would be to divide rhizomes in early spring from plants originally grown from seed.

Native Habitat and Range. On sandy or gravelly beaches and dunes, near the coast from southern British Columbia south to southern California and in many other parts of the world.

Notes. This species and its relatives are sometimes classified in the genus *Convolvulus*. The more than 20 species of *Calystegia* are all trailing or vining herbs native to temperate and tropical regions throughout the world. *Calystegia atriplicifolia* and *C. occidentalis* ssp. *occidentalis* are also Northwest natives.

Camassia   Liliaceae

camas

All six species in this genus of beautiful lilies are native to North America. The generic and common name are both derived from the word used by the tribes of the Pacific Northwest to refer to its edible bulb. Camas plants produce long, narrow leaves and flowering stems from bulbs. The flowers bloom in racemes and consist of six colored tepals (petals and sepals) and six stamens. A papery capsule containing many black seeds develops from the three-parted ovary. On their trek to the west coast, Lewis and Clark saw vast meadows filled with the blue flowers of camas, noting that they looked like lakes in the distance. The hospitable indigenous people rescued the expedition from starvation, offering them, among other foods, baked camas bulbs. Camas, a staple food plant for many tribes, was harvested in great quantities. Humans cannot easily digest raw camas bulbs, so they were always cooked first, and then eaten immediately or made into cakes and dried for later use. No matter how they were prepared, poor Meriwether Lewis found the bulbs indigestible, but they helped keep the Corps of Discovery alive during their long journey.

Propagation. Easy from seed, but be patient: it will take about three years for plants to be large enough to flower. Collect seeds from the ripe, brown capsules in the summer and plant them in the fall, into deep containers or directly into the garden. Seeds will germinate the following spring, looking much like onion seedlings or succulent bits of grass. If grown in containers, leave them for a few years until large enough to transplant, in autumn. If you buy bulbs or blooming plants, be sure they were grown from seed and not taken from the wild.

Camassia leichtlinii   Zones 7a to 9b

great camas

This perennial bulb produces several linear leaves to 60cm (2ft) long and up to 2.5cm (1in) wide. The inflorescence is a several-flowered raceme that can reach 1m (3ft). The flowers consist of six tepals, around 2.5cm (1in) long, and range in color from creamy white (in *C. l.* ssp. *leichtlinii*) to dark blue-violet (in *C. l.* ssp. *suksdorfii*). The tepals are evenly spaced and star-like, with regular symmetry; after flowering, from mid to late spring, the tepals twist together around the developing capsules.

Cultivation. Full sun, and soil that is moist or wet in the winter and fairly dry during summer. This is a beautiful bulb for many garden situations and far easier to grow than many native lily relatives. Plant in a sunny spot or near oaks and other deciduous trees, so that they will be able to leaf out and bloom before the trees shade them. These bulbs can be mixed with other flowering bulbs in the formal border or perennial bed, and they are a fine addition to the wildflower meadow or rock garden.

Native Habitat and Range. In meadows and hillsides that are moist in early spring, drier in summer, at low to mid elevations mainly west of the Cascade crest from southern British Columbia south through Oregon to California.

Notes. Sometimes flowers a bit later than *C. quamash*. *Camassia l.* ssp. *leichtlinii* is native to southwest Oregon; selections include 'Alba' (blue-tinted, white-flowered) and 'Semiplena' (semi-double, cream-colored flowers). *Camassia l.* ssp. *suksdorfii* occurs throughout the range; 'Blue Danube' is a dark blue selection. Howell's camas (*C. howellii*) is also native to the Pacific Northwest.

Camassia leichtlinii ssp. *leichtlinii*

Camassia leichtlinii ssp. *suksdorfii*

Camassia quamash   Zones 3b to 9b

common camas

The bulbs of this species produce several basal leaves up to 50cm (20in) long and 2cm (1in) wide. The inflorescence is a raceme that can grow to 80cm (2.5ft) tall, with five to many flowers blooming up the stem. The flowers consist of six tepals, around 2.5cm (1in) long, and vary in color from light to dark blue, and occasionally white. The tepals are somewhat bilaterally symmetrical, with five of the tepals curved upward and the sixth tending to turn outward. After flowering, from mid to late spring, the tepals usually curl and wither separately, but in some subspecies they twist together over the ripening, papery capsules.

Cultivation. Full sun, and soil that is moist or wet in the winter and fairly dry during summer. Tolerates the light shade of oaks and other deciduous trees that will not be in full leaf when it blooms. Mix with other flowering bulbs in the formal perennial bed, border planting, or rock garden. It is a delight in the wildflower meadow and can be mowed in the summer, when the bulbs are dormant. Given this species' wide geographic range, you'll have the best success with plants grown from a relatively local seed source.

Native Habitat and Range. In meadows and other moist, open areas that are usually dry by spring at low to mid elevations from southern British Columbia, south on both sides of the Cascades to the Sierra Nevada of California, east to southwestern Alberta, Montana, Wyoming, and Utah.

Notes. *Camassia q.* ssp. *breviflora* is a small plant with yellow anthers and blue tepals that twist together over the ovary; it is native east of the Cascades, ranging into California. Another subspecies from the eastern part of the range is the larger *C. q.* ssp. *utahensis*, with blue anthers and

Camassia quamash

Camissonia cheiranthifolia

tepals that twist together after flowering. *Camassia q.* ssp. *azurea* has pale blue-violet tepals that wither separately; it occurs in the northwestern part of the range, in the Olympic Peninsula and Puget Sound regions of Washington. *Camassia q.* ssp. *quamash* occurs in the northeastern part of the range, east of the Cascades from southern British Columbia and northeastern Washington to southwestern Alberta, northern Idaho, and Montana; the tepals are blue-violet and wither separately, and the pedicels curve sharply upward, pressing themselves to the main flowering stem as the capsules ripen. The pale blue tepals of *C. q.* ssp. *intermedia* wither separately, and the pedicels become erect or pressed to the stem as the fruits ripen; this plant is found west of the Cascades from central to southern Oregon. *Camassia q.* ssp. *walpolei* is also restricted to Oregon. *Camassia q.* ssp. *maxima* occurs close to the western slope of the Cascades from southwestern British Columbia, south through Washington and through the Willamette Valley of Oregon; its tepals are dark blue or violet and wither separately, and its pedicels often spread outward as the capsules ripen. *Camassia cusickii* (Cusick's camas), native to the Blue and Wallowa Mountains of northeastern Oregon, is similar to the variable *C. quamash*, but the plants are larger and more densely flowered; its bulbs are especially large and tend to grow in clusters connected by short rhizomes.

Camissonia cheiranthifolia   Zones 8a to 9b   Onagraceae

beach suncup

This perennial develops low-growing stems to 60cm (2ft) from a central rosette of leaves. The leaves of the rosettes grow to 7cm (3in), but the stem leaves are smaller, to 4cm (1.5in) and lance-shaped. The leaves and stems are pubescent with grayish hairs. The flowers have four bright yellow petals, sometimes with reddish spots near their bases, up to 1cm (.5in) in length; though small, they bloom over a long period, from mid spring to late summer. The fruits are coiled capsules.

Cultivation. Full sun, and sandy or well-drained soils, especially for gardens near the coast. Tolerates drought once established. With its silvery foliage and long bloom season, this attractive plant is worth trying in a sunny sand or rock garden away from the coast.

Propagation. Collect seeds in the late summer or fall, and plant them outside in the garden or in containers to spend the winter in chilly, moist conditions; expect the germination percentage in the spring to be low. Established plants may produce a few seedlings on their own.

Native Habitat and Range. On beaches and dunes along the coast from southwestern Oregon to southern California.

Notes. Sometimes classified as *Oenothera cheiranthifolia*. Only the more herbaceous type, *C. c.* ssp. *cheiranthifolia*, occurs in our area. There are more than 50 species of *Camissonia* in western North America, many of them annuals of arid habitats; more than a dozen species are native to the Pacific Northwest, and some of these are rare. Perennial species include *C. subacaulis* (*O. subacaulis*; northern suncup), a taprooted plant with yellow flowers arising directly from the basal rosette of elliptic, entire-margined or lobed leaves. This plant blooms from mid spring to mid summer and is widespread east of the Cascades, growing near streams or with sagebrush, in places that are moist in early spring. Another yellow-flowered perennial, *C. tanacetifolia* (*O. tanacetifolia*; tansy-leaved evening-primrose) produces basal rosettes of ferny, pinnately compound leaves and sometimes forms extensive mats; it lives in meadows, near streams and other places that are moist in spring, in the shrub-steppe and ponderosa pine habitats east of the Cascades. These are lovely plants for wildflower meadow in drier parts of the Pacific Northwest and can be grown from seed.

Campanula rotundifolia	Zones 3b to 9b	Campanulaceae

common harebell, bluebells of Scotland

This delicate perennial grows from a branched taproot or slender rhizomes. The leafy stems can reach 80cm (2.5ft) in height. The basal leaves have long petioles and rounded blades to 2cm (1in) with toothed margins, often withering by flowering time. The leaves of the flowering stems are linear and up to 8cm (3in) long. The nodding, bell-shaped flowers bloom on slender pedicels from early summer to early fall. The five fused petals are blue (occasionally white) and up to 3cm (1.5in) long. The fruits are small capsules containing many seeds.

Cultivation. Full sun or part shade, and moist soil. An excellent plant for the perennial border, rock garden, or wildflower meadow, or along a sunny garden path.

Propagation. Grow from seed, collected when the capsules ripen in fall. The seeds can be planted into flats in fall or early spring and will germinate when the weather warms. Plants should reach flowering size the following spring. Another method is to divide rhizomes in early spring or mid summer. Will self-sow once established.

Native Habitat and Range. On grassy hillsides, rocky clearings, and streambanks at low to mid elevations; circumboreal and extending south in the mountains to northern California, New Mexico, and Texas.

Notes. 'Olympica' is a selection with dark green, toothed leaves and medium blue flowers. *Campanula* encompasses around 300 species native to the arctic and temperate regions of the Northern Hemisphere, especially Europe. Several others are native to the Pacific Northwest. Among them, the blue-flowered (occasionally white) Piper's harebell or bellflower (*C. piperi*) may be most sought-after by alpine and rock gardeners; it is endemic to high elevations in the Olympic Mountains and grows in screes. Other blue-flowered species of high elevations include the

Campanula rotundifolia

Cardamine californica

dwarf mountain harebell (*C. lasiocarpa*), Parry's bellflower or harebell (*C. parryi*), and rough harebell (*C. scabrella*). *Campanula prenanthoides* (*Asyneuma prenanthoides*; California harebell) and *C. scouleri* (Scouler's bellflower or harebell) are species of lower elevations. The flowers of these two species are pale blue or almost white; the tips of the fused petals are flared back, and the long styles extend noticeably from the flowers.

Cardamine   Brassicaceae

bittercress, toothwort

Cardamine includes around 100 species of annual and perennial herbs, widely distributed in the temperate parts of the world. The flowers bloom in racemes and are typical of the mustard family, with four sepals, four pink or white petals, and six stamens. The fruits, again typical of the family, are long, slender siliques, a dry fruit that splits open along two margins at maturity. Some 30 species are native to North America, more than 15 to the Pacific Northwest.

Propagation. Grow from seed collected in the late summer and planted in the fall. Sow the seeds into flats of moist potting soil or directly into the garden, and leave them outside over winter for germination the following spring. Alternatively, divide rhizomes in the early spring or autumn.

Cardamine californica   Zones 7b to 9b

coast toothwort, milkmaids

This small, hairless (glabrous) perennial grows from fleshy, rounded tubers and slender rhizomes. The leaves are fleshy, sometimes purplish and variable in form. The basal leaves are rounded and toothed to deeply three-lobed, the blades up to 7cm (3in) long. The stem leaves are pinnately compound into three to five lanceolate or linear leaflets. The flowering shoot grows to 30cm (1ft), topped with a short raceme. The flowers are white to pinkish or lavender, and the petals are about 1cm (.5in) long. Blooming takes place from early to late spring, and the fruits grow to 5cm (2in) long.

Cultivation. Part to full shade or dappled light, and moist soil high in organic matter. This is a dainty plant for the woodland or shade garden west of the Cascades. It is one of the earliest wildflowers to bloom and makes a charming addition to the woodland trail or shady corner of the wildflower meadow.

Native Habitat and Range. In shady, moist woods, usually near the coast at low elevations, from northwestern Oregon, south through California.

Notes. Sometimes classified as *C. integrifolia* or *Dentaria californica*. *Cardamine c.* var. *integrifolia* and *C. c.* var. *sinuata* range to the north. Angled or seaside bittercress (*C. angulata*) produces shoots to about 60cm (2ft) from slender rhizomes; its white or pinkish flowers bloom from mid spring to early summer. This perennial lives in moist woods and near streams at low elevations from Alaska south to northern California and from near the coast, east to the west slope of the Cascades.

Cardamine nuttallii   Zones 6b to 9b

Nuttall's toothwort

This delicate species produces flowering stems and basal leaves from short, slender rhizomes. The basal leaves have long petioles, and the blades are generally rounded in outline. They vary from entire to shallowly lobed, or sometimes deeply lobed or compound into a few leaflets. The flowering stems grow to 20cm (8in) tall and bear a few leaves, divided into lanceolate leaflets to 4cm (1.5in) long. The inflorescence is a few-flowered raceme, and the flowers are pink or purplish, with petals about 1cm (.5in) long. Flowers open from early to late spring, and the fruits grow to 5cm (2in).

Cultivation. Part to full shade or dappled light, and moist soil rich in organic matter. This is a sweet, early-flowering perennial for the woodland, shade garden, or oak grove. Site it along the path among ferns and other shade-loving plants, where it will be noticed in the spring.

Native Habitat and Range. In moist to wet woods at low to mid elevations, mainly west of the Cascades from southwestern British Columbia, south to northern California.

Notes. *Cardamine n.* var. *nuttallii*, *C. n.* var. *covilleana*, *C. n.* var. *dissecta*, and *C. n.* var. *gemmata* all occur in the Pacific Northwest; all are characterized by variations of the basal leaves. *Cardamine cordifolia* var. *lyallii* (heartleaf bittercress), with rounded leaves and white flowers, lives near mountain streams and meadows at fairly high elevations in the mountains of the Pacific Northwest. Cuckoo flower (*C. pratensis*) is similar, but the pinnately compound leaves have more leaflets; it has white or pinkish flowers and a more northern range in southwestern Alaska and British Columbia, across Canada and south around the Great Lakes and Atlantic coast.

Cardamine nuttallii

Cardamine occidentalis

Cardamine occidentalis	Zones 6b to 9b

big western bittercress

This perennial grows from short, thin rhizomes that become tuberous at the bases of the leafy stems. The basal leaves are pinnately compound with rounded leaflets, the largest leaflet up to 2cm (1in) long, at the tip. The stem leaves are also pinnate, but smaller and with fewer, narrower leaflets. Flowering stems grow to 30cm (1ft) and are topped with a raceme of small, white flowers. Blooming occurs from mid spring to mid summer, and the fruits are about 2.5cm (1in) long.

Cultivation. Part shade or dappled light, and wet soil. This small perennial adds interest and diversity to the muddy margin of the pond, stream, or bog.

Native Habitat and Range. Along the margins of streams in flowing or standing water at low to mid elevations, mainly west of the Cascades from Alaska, south to California.

Notes. *Cardamine breweri* (Brewer's bittercress) is a similar, widespread species, occurring along shady streams and springs on both sides of the Cascades and through much of the west; small, white flowers top its leafy stems.

Carex	Cyperaceae

sedge

Carex is a huge, diverse genus; it is represented throughout the world, but the majority of its approximately 2,000 species are native to moist arctic and north temperate regions. Of the more than 500 species that occur in North America, around 200 are native to the Pacific Northwest, many of them listed as rare in parts of their ranges. Sedges are important wetland plants and are often used in restoration projects to help slow the movement of floodwater and control soil erosion; they provide excellent habitat for wildlife species that inhabit lakeshores, streams, and marshes. Other sedges live in drier, upland areas, so there is a suitable sedge for most any garden situation. All sedges are handsome plants; many species are graceful, similar to bunchgrasses in shape, and the tiny, rudimentary flowers are often combined into attractive inflorescences. The flowers are either female or male, subtended by bracts and arranged in spikes; female flowers produce a fruit, a single-seeded achene surrounded by a saclike bract, the perigynium.

Propagation. Grow from seed collected in the late summer and planted in the fall. Sow seeds directly into the garden or into flats of moist or wet potting soil, and leave them outside to cold stratify over the winter for germination the following spring. Most sedges can also be propagated from divisions of the rhizomes made during the spring.

Carex feta	Zones 6a to 9b

greensheath sedge

This sedge has a tufted habit and lacks creeping rhizomes. The leafy stems can reach about 1m (3ft) in height, and the narrow leaves grow from the lower half of the stems. Six or more rounded flowering spikes, each around 1cm (.5in), bloom at the shoot tips from late spring to mid summer. The fruits, small achenes, are lenticular (lentil-shaped).

Cultivation. Full sun to part shade, and wet soil. This is a fine sedge for the pond margin, bog, or ditch bank. Site in the wet spots of the wildflower meadow or wildlife garden, as a backdrop to other perennials.

Native Habitat and Range. In wet meadows, marsh edges, and ditches at low to mid elevations west of the Cascades from southern British Columbia, south to southern California and east through the Columbia River Gorge.

Notes. Bebb's sedge (*C. bebbii*) and meadow sedge (*C. praticola*) are similar to this species in form. Fragile sheath sedge (*C. fracta*), likewise similar, occurs in wet or dry soil east of the Cascades from central Washington, south through California; Henderson's sedge (*C. hendersonii*) prefers wet or moist woods to wetlands and is fairly common west of the Cascades. Long-stolon sedge (*C. inops* ssp. *inops*) lives in dry woods and meadows west of the Cascades.

Carex mertensii	Zones 4a to 9b

Mertens' sedge

This large, handsome sedge produces stems to 1m (3ft) or a bit taller from a short, stout rhizome. The leaves are broad, up to 1cm (.5in) wide, and well developed all the way up the stems. Plants produce several cylindrical flowering spikes up to 4cm (1.5in) long, usually nodding on thin peduncles. The uppermost spike and some of the other spikes have some male (staminate) flowers at their bases, but the majority of the flowers are female (pistillate). Each little flower is tucked into the axil of a brownish or blackish scale, much smaller than the light brown, saclike bracts (perigynia) that surround each female flower. The flowers bloom from late spring to late summer, and the fruits, tiny achenes, are three-sided.

Cultivation. Full sun or part shade, and moist to wet soil. Although this plant produces short rhizomes, the stems tend to be clustered, giving it a vase-like shape. This is an excellent sedge for the margin of the pond, stream, or ditch. It can also be planted in open, moist spots of the meadow, woodland, or wildlife garden.

Native Habitat and Range. In wet to moist streambanks, meadows, roadsides, and forest openings at low to fairly high elevations from southern Alaska, south in the Cascades and Coast Ranges to California, east to Idaho and western Montana.

Carex feta

Carex mertensii

Carex obnupta

Notes. Showy sedge (*C. spectabilis*) is a smaller, similar plant with leafy stems and nodding flower spikes; it lives in wet meadows at mid to high elevations in the mountains of the west. Lyngbye's sedge (*C. lyngbyei*) also has cylindrical flowering spikes that arch from slender peduncles. This species is rhizomatous, spreading by creeping rhizomes; it lives in estuaries, tidal marshes, and other wet places near the northern coasts, sometimes forming dense stands, ranging south along the coast to northern California. *Carex aquatilis* (*C. sitchensis*; Sitka or water sedge) is another tufted species, growing to 1.5m (5ft) or taller with long, cylindrical spikes; it grows on lakeshores and other wet places, mainly west of the Cascades, forming extensive populations—an important component of waterfowl habitat.

Carex obnupta	Zones 7b to 9b

slough sedge

This sedge produces tufts of shoots up to 1.5m (5ft) from thick, creeping rhizomes. The lowermost leaves are reddish and rudimentary, and the upper leaves are tough and grass-like. They are shorter than the flowering shoots and up to 1cm (.5in) wide, often remaining more or less evergreen during mild winters. The leafy bracts of the flowering shoots are often longer than the inflorescence. The inflorescence consists of several arching, cylindrical spikes, up to 12cm (5in) long, sessile (stalkless) or set on short peduncles. The uppermost spikes consist of male (staminate) flowers; the lower spikes are either female (pistillate) or have some male flowers at the tips. The scale-like bracts of the female flowers are dark brown with a pale midrib. They are longer than the female flowers and their straw-colored, saclike perigynia. The tiny flowers bloom from mid spring to mid summer, and the fruits, small achenes, are lenticular (lentil-shaped).

Cultivation. Full sun or part shade, and very wet soil or shallow, standing water. This is an excellent plant for the margins of ponds and wetlands, where it will provide food and cover for birds and other wildlife. Plant it along a ditch or wet slope, where its rhizomatous habit will help hold the soil in place and control erosion.

Native Habitat and Range. In shallow, standing water or very soggy ground along lakes, rivers, forest openings, and coastal swamps at low elevations from the west slope of the Cascades to the coast, and from southern British Columbia, south through much of coastal California.

Notes. This species was and still is used by some of the coastal tribes in the creation of baskets. Large-headed sedge (*C. macrocephala*) is another rhizomatous species that lives in coastal dunes; plants are shorter, up to 30cm (1ft), and the flowering spikes are crowded into dense heads up to 8cm (3in) long and 5cm (2in) thick. Many other sedges in our area have flowering spikes that are short and condensed instead of elongated; these include sawbeak sedge (*C. stipata*), thick-headed sedge (*C. pachystachya*), small-winged sedge (*C. microptera*), and many others. *Carex aurea* (golden sedge) has especially distinctive, relatively large, rounded, yellow perigynia; this species lives in moist or wet places at low to high elevations through much of western North America.

Castilleja	Scrophulariaceae

paintbrush

Most of the more than 150 species of *Castilleja* are native to western North America, more than 30 to the Pacific Northwest; the balance occur in eastern North America, South America, and northern Asia. Paintbrushes are perennial or annual herbs with alternate, often laterally lobed leaves. The petals are not especially showy and are fused into a greenish tube surrounding the style and stamens. The sepals are fused into a tubular, four-lobed calyx, and beneath each flower

Castilleja affinis ssp. litoralis

Castilleja hispida

there is a leafy, often lobed bract. The tips of the bracts and calyces are brightly colored with scarlet, pink, yellow, or white, giving the flowering spikes the look of a brush dipped in paint. The fruits are capsules containing many tiny seeds. Paintbrushes are some of our best-known wildflowers. They are partially parasitic on the roots of other plants, but they don't seem to be too particular about their hosts and are often found growing near grasses, penstemons, sunflower relatives, and other species.

Propagation. Harvest a few dried inflorescences in the late summer or fall, place them upside down in a paper bag, and collect the tiny seeds after they fall to the bottom of the bag. Seeds are best planted soon after harvest and left outside for the winter. Scatter them into the garden, near other plants, or sow them onto the surface of potting soil in containers with grasses or other host plants. Press the tiny seeds into the soil near the roots of host plants, but don't bury them. Paintbrushes can sometimes be grown from cuttings taken in late winter or very early spring and placed in the soil next to the roots of a host. Keep cuttings moist until roots form.

Castilleja affinis ssp. *litoralis*	Zones 7a to 9b

Pacific paintbrush

This perennial produces a few, usually branched stems that can grow to 80cm (2.5ft). The plants are covered with spreading hairs, and the leaves are ovate or lance-shaped, entire or with a few lobes. The inflorescences are tipped with scarlet, and the broad bracts beneath the flowers are rounded, with or without one or two pairs of lateral lobes. The colorful, tubular, four-lobed calyx can grow to 2.5cm (1in), surrounding the greenish flowers that bloom from mid spring to early fall. The fruits are two-celled capsules containing many tiny seeds.

Cultivation. Full sun to part shade, and well-drained soil. Be sure to position this lovely para-site close to grasses, sunflowers, or other species that will serve as hosts. This beauty is a fine addition to a sandy meadow or grassy dune, especially near the coast, and is attractive to hum-mingbirds.

Native Habitat and Range. On sandy bluffs, dunes, and open woods near the coast from northern Oregon to northern California.

Notes. Sometimes granted specific status, as *C. litoralis*.

Castilleja hispida	Zones 3b to 9b

rough paintbrush

This perennial produces multiple stems up to 60cm (2ft) tall from a woody base. The stems are usually not branched, and the plants are covered with stiff hairs. The leaves are broadly lance-shaped, and the upper ones have one or two pairs of lobes. The bracts beneath the flowers are deeply lobed and the four-lobed calyx grows to 2.5cm (1in) in length. The inflorescences are usually bright red, but sometimes yellow, blooming from mid spring to late summer. The flowering spikes produce many tiny seeds in capsules.

Cultivation. Full sun to part shade, and fairly well-drained soil. Position this showy root para-site near grasses, asters, penstemons, or other species that will serve as hosts. Include it in the butterfly garden or meadow, or along a path, where its relatively long and bright bloom period can be fully enjoyed.

Native Habitat and Range. In dry meadows, grassy slopes, and forest openings at low to mid elevations from southern British Columbia south to California and from the coast east to Alberta, Montana, and Nevada.

Notes. *Castilleja h.* ssp. *acuta* and *C. h.* ssp. *hispida* occur throughout the range; *C. h.* ssp. *brevilobata* has a relatively small range, in southwestern Oregon and California.

Castilleja miniata	Zones 3b to 9b

common red paintbrush

This perennial produces branched stems up to 80cm (2.5ft) from a woody base. Plants vary from pubescent with short or woolly hairs to hairless. The leaves are linear or lance-shaped and usually entire, but occasionally with a few lobes. The inflorescences are usually scarlet, occasionally yellow, blooming from late spring to early fall. The bracts and calyces have pointed or linear lobes, and the tiny seeds develop in capsules.

Cultivation. Full sun to part shade, and moist to fairly dry soil. Plant this showy wildflower near grasses, asters, penstemons, or other host species. It is lovely in the rock garden or meadow, or along a path, and a fine addition to the hummingbird garden.

Native Habitat and Range. In meadows, open woods, slopes, and roadsides at low to fairly high elevations from Alaska south to California and from the coast east to Montana and New Mexico.

Notes. The most widespread species of *Castilleja* in the Pacific Northwest. *Castilleja m.* ssp. *miniata* (*C. uliginosa*) occurs throughout the range; *C. m.* ssp. *dixonii* is native near the coast from Alaska to Oregon; *C. miniata* ssp. *elata* (*C. elata*) is found in wet habitats in southwestern Oregon and northern California. Golden paintbrush (*C. levisecta*) is a rare plant of low-elevation prairies on southern Vancouver Island, western Washington, and Oregon; it has become endangered due to habitat loss, but its numbers could be increased through cultivation. *Castilleja cryptantha* (ob-scure paintbrush) is another rare species, endemic to subalpine meadows on Mt. Rainier.

Castilleja miniata

Castilleja parviflora

Castilleja parviflora	Zones 3b to 8a

rosy or mountain paintbrush

This perennial produces a cluster of simple stems up to 30cm (1ft) tall from a woody base. The foliage may be hairless or softly hairy. The leaves are divided into three to five spreading lobes. The inflorescences are usually rosy pink but sometimes crimson or whitish, and the flowers bloom from early summer to early fall. Tiny seeds ripen in capsules.

Cultivation. Full sun to part shade, and moist to fairly dry soil. Position this colorful root parasite near other garden plants that will serve as hosts. Makes a fine addition to the perennial bed, hummingbird garden, or wildflower meadow.

Native Habitat and Range. Near streams and in meadows at mid to high elevations in the mountains from southern Alaska to California and east to the Rocky Mountains of British Columbia and Alberta.

Notes. *Castilleja p.* var. *oreopola*, with rose, crimson, or sometimes whitish bracts, grows in the Cascades of Washington and Oregon; *C. p.* var. *olympica* occurs in the Olympic Mountains and has dark pink or crimson inflorescences. The white *C. p.* var. *albida* is native in the Cascades of southern British Columbia and northern Washington. Rosy pink-flowered *C. p.* var. *parviflora* is apparently disjunct in the mountains of southwestern Alaska and California. Thompson's paintbrush (*C. thompsonii*), with cream-colored inflorescences, is a common species of arid regions east of the Cascades in British Columbia and Washington; plants are associated with big sagebrush (*Artemisia tridentata*), apparently its usual host.

| *Cerastium arvense* | Zones 3b to 9b | Caryophyllaceae |

field chickweed, mouse ear

This gray-green, tufted perennial develops trailing stems and sometimes forms clumps to 40cm (16in) across. The opposite, entire leaves are linear to oblong, up to 3cm (1.5in) long, and usually finely hairy. Small shoots and clusters of smaller leaves develop in the axils of the larger stem leaves. The flowering stems grow to 50cm (20in) tall and produce several flowers in an open, flat-topped cluster at the tip. Flowers bloom on pedicels about 2.5cm (1in) long. The five sepals are usually glandular, and the five petals are white, deeply two-lobed, and about 1cm (.5in) long. They bloom from mid spring to late summer, depending on elevation. The fruits are cylindric capsules containing many brownish seeds and opening by ten teeth at the tip.

Cultivation. Full sun or light shade, and well-drained, rocky or sandy soil. This is an attractive perennial for rock gardens throughout our area; plant it in the crevices of a rock outcrop or let it spill over a stone retaining wall. Good for sandy, rather dry soils in the wildflower meadow, low perennial border, rocky bank, or hillside.

Propagation. Grow from seed collected in the late summer or fall. Seeds can be sown into containers or directly into the garden in the fall or early spring, and should germinate when the weather warms. Plants often form roots where the trailing stems touch the ground, and these can be divided in the spring. Can also be propagated from basal cuttings made near the branched crown during the summer.

Native Habitat and Range. On cliffs, rocky hillsides, dry meadows, and clearings at low to fairly high elevations from Alaska south to California, and from the coast east across much of North America; Eurasia.

Notes. Both *C. a.* ssp. *strictum* and *C. a.* ssp. *maximum* occur in our area, as do many of the approximately ten species of *Cerastium* native to North America. Bering chickweed (*C. beeringianum*) is a mat-forming, white-flowered perennial; this alpine species occurs throughout the high mountains of western North America. Some of our native sandworts, family relations in the genera *Arenaria* and *Minuartia*, are also considered good rock garden plants for their evergreen mats of needle-like leaves and white flowers, and branching cushions of small, linear leaves, respectively.

| *Chamerion angustifolium* | Zones 3b to 9b | Onagraceae |

fireweed, blooming sally

The stems of this rhizomatous perennial can reach up to 2.5m (8ft) in height, under favorable conditions. The alternate, lance-shaped leaves can grow to 15cm (6in) or more in length. Many-flowered racemes develop at the stem tips. As is typical of the family, the flower parts are in fours, and the slender ovary, which will develop into a long capsule, is inferior. Magenta-pink (occasionally white) flowers up to 4cm (1.5in) across bloom from early summer to early fall. Ripe capsules split into four parts to release seeds. Each seed is equipped with a tuft of hairs (coma), allowing it to float on the wind.

Cultivation. Full sun or part shade, and moist to fairly dry soil. Fireweed is often too aggressive for the formal perennial bed; keep plants from becoming too large by keeping them on the dry side. This plant is sometimes grown as a honey source, and all sorts of flying creatures visit the flowers—great for the butterfly and hummingbird garden or wildflower meadow.

Propagation. Grow from seed collected and planted in fall, directly into the garden or into containers, and left outside over winter. Dividing rhizomes in the early spring is equally easy.

Native Habitat and Range. On roadsides, forest margins, and disturbed moist to rather dry sites, at low to fairly high elevations, Alaska to California and east to the Atlantic coast; Eurasia.

Cerastium arvense

Chamerion angustifolium

Cistanthe umbellata

Notes. Sometimes classified as *Epilobium angustifolium*, *Chamerion a.* ssp. *angustifolium* occurs from Alaska to Washington and the Rocky Mountains; *C. a.* ssp. *circumvagum* has a wider range in North America. *Chamerion latifolium* (dwarf fireweed) occurs near streams and on talus throughout the higher mountains; it grows to 30cm (1ft) from a woody crown and has blue-green, waxy (glaucous) foliage. The flowers are usually rosy pink and up to 6cm (2.5in) across. It is a choice plant for the rock garden and can be grown from seed. Around a dozen species are now placed in *Chamerion*, some of them recent transplants from *Epilobium*.

Cistanthe umbellata	Zones 3b to 9b	Portulacaceae

Mt. Hood pussypaws

This species grows from a branched crown, sometimes developing small mats up to 15cm (6in) across. The hairless, somewhat fleshy leaves are mainly basal and clustered into rosettes. They are up to 5cm (2in) long, entire and spatulate (spoon-shaped), tapered to broad petioles. The flowering stems grow to 10cm (4in) tall and are generally leafless. Numerous flowers bloom in dense, head-like clusters to 4cm (1.5in) across. Each flower has two rounded, white or pinkish, papery sepals to 1cm (.5in) across, larger than the four pinkish petals. Flowers bloom from early to late summer, and the fruits are flattened capsules containing several shiny, black seeds.

Cultivation. Full sun or light shade, and very well-drained soil. This is a charming perennial (occasionally annual) for the rock garden, rocky slope, or dry bank. Perfect for enlivening the sandy or gravelly, dry place near the trail in the wildflower meadow. This plant is usually happier in the drier parts of the Northwest.

Propagation. Grow from seed collected in the fall and planted soon after harvest. Sow seeds directly into the garden or into containers of well-drained potting soil and leave them outside to stratify over the winter for germination in the spring.

Native Habitat and Range. On sandy or gravelly flats and in ponderosa pine woodland at mid to high elevations from British Columbia, mainly east of the Cascade crest, south through California and east to Montana, Wyoming, and Colorado.

Notes. Sometimes classified as *Calyptridium umbellatum* or *Spraguea umbellata*. The shorter-lived plants that sometimes grow at lower elevations are *C. u.* var. *umbellata*, and the longer-lived specimens with smaller leaves and a branched crown are *C. u.* var. *caudicifera*. Similar is *C. rosea* (*Calyptridium roseum*; rosy pussypaws), a small annual to 8cm (3in) tall of sagebrush and dry forested habitats east of the Cascades, but it has two petals and a branched inflorescence of coiled (scorpioid) racemes. *Cistanthe* includes almost a dozen species in North America, with around four of these native to the Pacific Northwest.

Clintonia uniflora	Zones 4a to 9b	Liliaceae

bead lily, queen's cup

This deciduous perennial grows from spreading rhizomes. Oblong leaves around 15cm (6in) long and 5cm (2in) wide grow in clusters of two or three. Single flowers bloom on peduncles about 10cm (4in) long. The charming flowers are composed of six white tepals, about 2cm (1in) long, and bloom from early to mid summer. A shiny, deep blue berry follows the flower.

Cultivation. Full shade to part sun or dappled light, and moist soil high in organic matter. This is a lovely small lily, with fruits as pretty as the flowers, to tuck among the taller shade plants or along a path in the woodland garden.

Propagation. Remove the seeds from the ripe berry and plant them soon after harvest in the late summer. Sow the seeds into containers or directly into the garden, and leave them outside over winter for germination the following spring. As with many lilies, the seedlings will take

Clintonia uniflora

around three years to reach flowering size and should be protected from slugs. Can also be propagated from divisions of the rhizomes made in the early spring, but this should be done only with plants originally grown from seed.

Native Habitat and Range. In moist, shady coniferous forests at low to mid elevations from Alaska south into California, and from near the coast east to southwestern Alberta, Montana, Idaho and eastern Oregon.

Notes. Red clintonia (*C. andrewsiana*) is another bead lily native to the Pacific Northwest. Instead of single flowers, this rhizomatous perennial produces pink to red flowers in umbels. The fruit is a blue berry. This species is native to the damp forests dominated by coast redwood (*Sequoia sempervirens*) in southwestern Oregon and northwestern California. There are four additional species of *Clintonia*, two of them native to eastern North America and two from Asia.

| **Coptis laciniata** | Zones 7b to 9b | Ranunculaceae |

Oregon or cutleaf goldthread

This small perennial spreads by thin, yellow rhizomes, producing shiny, evergreen leaves that are divided into three main segments (ternate), each segment up to 4cm (1.5in) long. Each primary leaflet is further divided into three segments with lobed, toothed margins. The leafless flowering stems are up to 12cm (5in) long at flowering, increasing in length as the fruits ripen. The flowers consist of very thin sepals and petals, and bloom from mid spring to mid summer. The fruits, a ring of several-seeded follicles, each set on a slender stipe, are as interesting as the flowers.

Cultivation. Full shade to part sun or dappled light, and very moist soil high in organic matter. This charming, rhizomatous evergreen will carpet moist to fairly wet places in the woodland garden. Plant it by a shady pond or bog or under taller shade-loving perennials, or tuck it into a moist corner of the rock garden.

Coptis laciniata

Corydalis scouleri

Propagation. Grow from seed harvested from the follicles in the late summer or fall. Plant seeds into containers or directly into the garden soon after collecting. Leave them outside in cool, moist winter conditions for spring germination. Can also be propagated by dividing the yellow rhizomes, with shoots and roots attached, in the spring; this should be done only with plants already growing in cultivation.

Native Habitat and Range. In moist woods and seeps at low to mid elevations, west of the Cascades, from west central Washington, south to northern California.

Notes. The approximately ten species of *Coptis* are native to moist places in the northern parts of the Northern Hemisphere. Fern-leaf goldthread (*C. aspleniifolia*), three-leaf goldthread (*C. trifolia*), and Idaho goldthread (*C. occidentalis*) are also native to the Pacific Northwest. The yellow rhizomes of these plants have been used as a medicine and as a dye.

| *Corydalis scouleri* | Zones 7b to 9b | Fumariaceae |

Scouler's corydalis

This deciduous, succulent perennial produces hollow, erect stems to 1m (3ft) or more. Each stem usually bears three large leaves that are at least three times pinnate, giving them a ferny appearance. A many-flowered, sometimes branched raceme develops at the top of the stem. The showy, pink flowers bloom from mid spring to mid summer. They are spurred and about 2.5cm (1in) long. The fruits are capsules that open explosively to release shiny, black seeds.

Cultivation. Part to full shade or dappled light, and very moist soil with high organic content. The bog or moister parts of the woodland garden would suit this tall, lush perennial.

Propagation. Collect seeds from ripened capsules and plant them into containers or directly into the garden soon after harvest. Keep the planted seeds moist and leave them outside to cold stratify over the winter for germination the following spring. This species seems to dislike life in

Cynoglossum grande

Cyperus strigosus

a container, so transplant containerized seedlings as soon as they are large enough. It may take a couple of years for plants to reach flowering size.

Native Habitat and Range. In shady, moist or wet places, including streambanks and roadsides, from southwestern British Columbia south to west central Oregon, and from the coast to the west slope of the Cascades.

Notes. The more than 100 species of *Corydalis* are mostly native to the Northern Hemisphere, but also to southern Africa. A few others are native to the Pacific Northwest, including the yellow-flowered annual or biennial golden corydalis (*C. aurea*). Coldwater corydalis (*C. caseana* ssp. *aquae-gelidae*) is a rare taxon with pink or lavender flowers; it is endemic to northwestern Oregon and southwestern Washington. Cusick's corydalis (*C. caseana* ssp. *cusickii*) has white or pink flowers tipped with purple; it occurs near streams in northeastern Oregon and Idaho.

Cynoglossum grande	Zones 6b to 9b	Boraginaceae

great or Pacific hound's tongue

This taprooted perennial produces a few stems up to 80cm (2.5ft) tall. The leaf blades are ovate or triangular in shape, and up to 15cm (6in) in length. The largest leaves are at the base of the stem, set on long petioles. Flowers bloom in panicles and each flower has five fused blue or violet petals. At the center of the flower, where the tubular corolla base opens into five distinct petal lobes, there are five white projections, or fornices. The fruits are rounded nutlets with a few prickles. Blooming takes place from early to mid spring, and each flower produces up to four nutlets.

Cultivation. Full sun to part shade or dappled light, and fairly dry soil with good organic content. A medium-sized, early flowering perennial for the shade or woodland garden, forest edge, or herbaceous border. Plant this blue-flowered beauty under oaks and other deciduous trees.

Propagation. Grow from seed collected in summer when the nutlets are ripe. Plant seeds into the garden or into containers in the fall, and allow them to stratify outside in the cool, moist weather for spring germination. Seedlings will be small their first year and may not bloom until they are three, but plants are long-lived. Protect seedlings from slugs.

Native Habitat and Range. In rather dry woods at low to mid elevations west of the Cascades from western Washington, south through much of California and east through the Columbia River Gorge.

Notes. Western hound's tongue (*C. occidentale*) ranges from central Oregon south through the mountains of California; it has reddish or bluish flowers and lance-shaped leaves, tapered to the base. *Cynoglossum* encompasses around 80 species widely distributed in the temperate regions of the world.

Cyperus strigosus	Zones 3b to 9b	Cyperaceae

straw-colored flatsedge

This short-lived perennial lacks rhizomes, producing one or a few three-angled stems to about 60cm (2ft) tall from fibrous roots. The basal leaves and leafy bracts of the inflorescence are both narrow and grasslike. Tiny flowers bloom in narrow spikelets up to 2.5cm (1in) long. The spikelets are crowded into short, cylindrical spikes growing from slender peduncles of varying lengths. The inflorescences develop at the stem tips and are surrounded by the leafy bracts. Flowers bloom from mid summer to early fall, and the fruits are tiny, three-sided achenes.

Cultivation. Full sun or light shade, and wet soil. This is an interesting little papyrus-like plant for the margins of the pond, wetland, or sunny bog. It won't spread aggressively, and adds diversity to the wet places in the garden.

Propagation. Grow from seed collected in the fall. Sow seeds into containers of very wet soil or directly into the garden, and leave them outside to cold stratify over the winter for germination the following spring.

Native Habitat and Range. On the banks of rivers and other wet places, mainly at low elevations, in southeastern Washington, western Oregon, south through California and Arizona and east through much of North America.

Notes. *Cyperus* includes more than 500 species of annuals and perennials, most common in the tropics and warmer parts of the world but cosmopolitan in distribution. This species is quite attractive and the most garden-worthy of the approximately ten species native to our area.

Danthonia californica	Zones 4a to 9b	Poaceae

California oatgrass

This perennial bunchgrass grows to about 80cm (2.5ft) tall. The leaves generally have flat blades and are hairy at least at the collar, where the sheathing base of the leaf clasps the stem. The several florets are grouped into spikelets. Two bracts, or glumes, subtend each spikelet; they are about 1.5cm (.5in) long, as long as the spikelet. Each lemma has two long teeth at the tip, between which the awn is set. Each inflorescence consists of up to five spikelets arranged in an open, spreading panicle. Flowers bloom from early to mid summer, and the fruit is a grain, or caryopsis.

Cultivation. Full sun or part shade, and moist to rather dry, well-drained, sandy or rocky soil. Plant this charming bunchgrass on either side of the Cascades, in the wildflower meadow, wild life garden, or in the perennial bed, where birds and other small animals will eat the seed.

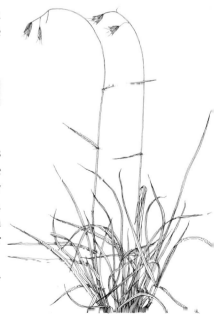

Danthonia californica

Darlingtonia californica

Darlingtonia californica, flowers

Propagation. Grow from seed collected in the summer and planted in the fall. Sow seeds into containers of moist potting soil or directly into the garden, and leave them outside over winter for germination in the spring. They can also be stored under cool, dry conditions and planted in early spring. Although this grass does not form extensive rhizomes, the clumps can usually be divided in the early spring.

Native Habitat and Range. In open meadows, rocky ridges, and ponderosa pine forest at low to mid elevations from southern British Columbia, on both sides of the Cascades, south to southern California, east to Wyoming, Colorado, and New Mexico.

Notes. Fewer than ten species of *Danthonia* are native to North America, only four to the Pacific Northwest. The other three, timber oatgrass (*D. intermedia*), poverty oatgrass (*D. spicata*), and one-spike oatgrass (*D. unispicata*) occur through large areas of North America in moist to rather dry, often rocky meadows, woods, and ridges.

| *Darlingtonia californica* | Zones 7b to 9b | Sarraceniaceae |

California pitcher plant, cobra plant

This rhizomatous perennial develops large, yellow-green, tubular, pitcher-like leaves modified to trap insects. The top of the leaf curves, like the head of a cobra, to form a purplish, translucent hood with an opening under the curve for the temptation of unwary insects. There is a two-lobed appendage at the forward tip of the hood. The leaf size varies depending on the age of the plant, but the tallest can approach 1m (3ft) in height. Single flowers, which bloom from mid to late summer, are produced on separate stems that can also grow to 1m (3ft); the nodding flowers have yellowish green sepals to 6cm (2.5in) long and shorter, dark purple petals. The fruit is a five-chambered capsule with many seeds.

Darmera peltata

Darmera peltata, flowers

Cultivation. Full sun to part shade, and a boggy spot. Acidic, mucky soil with sphagnum makes a good substrate. These plants appreciate a location with a slight trickle of water flowing across the ground surface.

Propagation. Grow from seed planted in spring and kept warm and humid under glass or plastic. Moist sphagnum is a good medium for starting seeds. Plants originally grown from seed can be divided in early spring.

Native Habitat and Range. In bogs and spongy, wet ground, often in serpentine substrates and usually growing in trickling streams, at low to high elevations, near the central Oregon coast, south into northern California and east to the northern Sierra Nevada.

Notes. *Darlingtonia* is a monotypic genus, and this odd, insect-trapping plant is the only representative of the pitcher plant family in the Pacific Northwest. Its native range is small, and plants should never be poached from the wild. Nurseries specializing in carnivorous plants sometimes offer this species. Make sure any plant you buy was originally grown from seed; plants raised "in captivity" will have a much better chance of survival.

Darmera peltata	Zones 6b to 9b	Saxifragaceae

Indian rhubarb, umbrella plant

This bold, deciduous perennial grows from large, tough rhizomes up to 5cm (2in) thick. The leafless flowering stems (scapes) appear before the leaves, growing to 1.5m (5ft). These hairy stalks produce a flat-topped, branched cluster of many flowers, each about 1.5cm (.5in) across, with live pink or white petals. The flowers bloom from mid spring to early summer, and the leaves appear as the fruits, a pair of purplish follicles for each flower, ripen. The leaves are basal, growing from the rhizomes on petioles up to 1m (3ft) tall. The leaf blades are nearly round and up to 40cm (16in) across, with lobed and toothed margins. The leaves are peltate, with the petiole attached at the center of the blade, like an umbrella.

Cultivation. Full sun or part shade, and wet or very moist soil. Despite its limited native range, this species is not fussy and will grow in just about any wet, sunny place in the garden, such as a pond margin or bog. Include it in the wild meadow or woodland clearing in a soggy spot. A spectacular specimen plant, impressive throughout the growing season.

Propagation. Easy from cuttings of the rhizomes made in late spring, just as the leaves begin to appear; cuttings with roots and buds can be planted into containers or directly into the garden, but this should be done only with plants grown in cultivation. Can also be grown from seed collected in the summer and planted in the fall. Leave planted seeds outside over winter for spring germination. Seedlings will take a few years to reach flowering size.

Native Habitat and Range. Among the rocks in and along cold streams at mid to high elevations in the Coast Ranges of west central Oregon, south to northwestern California and the central Sierra Nevada.

Notes. Sometimes classified as *Peltiphyllum peltatum*. This is the only species in the genus.

Delphinium　　　　　　　　　　　　　　　　　　　　　　Ranunculaceae

larkspur

Delphinium is a well-known genus, its members loved by gardeners and hikers alike. The showy, spurred sepals and two pairs of smaller petals both contribute to the colorful flowers, which bloom on racemes. Numerous seeds are produced in follicles, dry fruits that split along one margin when ripe. These annual or perennial herbs have distinctive, palmately compound leaves that are often further divided into narrow segments. There are somewhere upward of 200 species of *Delphinium* native to the temperate parts of the Northern Hemisphere; close to 60 species occur in North America, more than 20 in the Pacific Northwest, some of them rare. Species often hybridize in nature, and some have apparently evolved through these crosses. Larkspurs are toxic to humans, cattle, and horses.

Propagation. Grow from seed collected from the dry follicles in the summer or fall. Seeds do not store well but can be kept temporarily under cool, dry conditions. Plant them into containers or directly into the garden in autumn, and leave them outside over winter for spring germination. Seedlings will take at least a year to reach flowering size and may need protection from slugs. Plants can sometimes be propagated from basal cuttings of shoots made in the spring, but this should be done only with plants already under cultivation and originally grown from seed. Take care when handling, as the stems of some species are easily broken from the crowns during the growing season.

Delphinium glareosum　　　　　　　　　　　Zones 5a to 9b

Olympic or rockslide larkspur

This perennial produces one or more stout stems up to 30cm (1ft) tall from thick, woody roots. Leaves arise from the lower part of the stem, the lowermost with the longest petioles. The leaves are fleshy, and the blades are up to 6cm (2.5in) across, divided into five to seven main lobes that are further divided at the tips into long, narrow segments. The inflorescence is open and often branched, with up to 20 flowers about 2.5cm (1in) long. The sepals are usually bluish purple, but sometimes light blue or even white. The petals are blue or whitish and blooming takes place from late spring to late summer, depending on elevation. Numerous winged and angled seeds ripen in follicles.

Delphinium glareosum

Delphinium menziesii

Cultivation. Full sun to light shade, and rocky, well-drained, moist to fairly dry soil. This low-growing species tends to form a clump among rocks and is therefore excellent for the rock garden, gravelly hillside, or top of a stone retaining wall.

Native Habitat and Range. On talus slopes and rocky ridges, mostly at mid to high elevations in the Olympic Mountains and in the Cascades from southern British Columbia, south to the Columbia River Gorge and central Oregon.

Notes. Nuttall's larkspur (*D. nuttallii*) also lives in moist gravel and rocky cliffs, from southern Puget Sound, south and east through the Columbia River Gorge and on both sides of the Cascades in Oregon; it is about twice as tall, to 60cm (2ft), and its blue flowers have sepals and petals that tend to cup forward rather than spread outward.

| *Delphinium menziesii* | Zones 5a to 9b |

Menzies' or coastal larkspur

This perennial produces simple or branched stems to 50cm (20in) tall from one or more rounded tubers. The plants are hairless (glabrous) to hairy (pubescent), and most of the leaves are arranged alternately along the stems. The largest leaves have long petioles and blades up to 7cm (3in) across, two or three times palmately compound into narrow segments. The racemes are open and bear up to 20 flowers on pedicels the same length or much longer than the flowers. The flowers have deep blue sepals and are about 2.5cm (1in) long, including the spur. The lower petals are blue with shallow notches; the upper petals are white or light blue. Flowers bloom from mid spring to mid summer. The follicles are hairy and up to 1.5cm (.5in) long, containing seeds with narrowly winged margins

Delphinium nudicaule

Delphinium trolliifolium

Cultivation. Full sun or part shade, and well-drained, moist soil. This is a lovely plant for the sunny, moist places of the wildflower meadow, rocky hillside, or perennial bed.

Native Habitat and Range. On prairies and bluffs near the coast and moist meadows at low to mid elevations from southwestern British Columbia, south to northern California and from the coast to the west slope of the Cascades and east through the Columbia River Gorge to southeastern Washington and northeastern Oregon.

Notes. *Delphinium m.* ssp. *menziesii* occurs throughout the range; *D. m.* ssp. *pallidum* lives in the southern part of the range. *Delphinium nuttallianum* (upland or common larkspur) is similar, growing to 40cm (16in) tall. The sepals are open and spreading, sometimes hairy, and range in color from very pale to deep, purplish blue. The petals are almost white to yellowish or blue. This extremely variable species lives in well-drained soils of mountain slopes and valleys from southwestern British Columbia, south through the Olympic Mountains and west slope of the Cascades, through the mountains of southern Oregon to northern California and east through the ponderosa pine and sagebrush habitats to the Rocky Mountains. Meadow larkspur (*D.* ×*burkei*), thought to be a hybrid between it and slim larkspur (*D. depauperatum*), lives east of the Cascades, in swales and other places that are wet during the spring.

Delphinium nudicaule   Zones 7a to 9b

red larkspur

This delicate perennial produces stems up to 60cm (2ft) tall from clusters of fleshy roots. The leaves have long petioles and are produced at the base and lower part of the stem. The blades are up to 6cm (2.5in) across and palmately divided into three to five lobed leaflets. The open racemes bear spurred, scarlet (sometimes yellow) sepals up to 1cm (.5in) long. The petals are yellow with red tips and the flowers bloom from early spring to early summer. The fruits are glabrous follicles.

Cultivation. Part shade or dappled light, and moist to fairly dry soil. Red larkspur is a lovely and unusual addition to the hummingbird garden, hillside, or partly shaded edge of the wild-flower meadow.

Native Habitat and Range. In open woods and moist to fairly dry slopes at low to mid elevations from southwestern Oregon to central California.

Notes. 'Laurin' is a selection with particularly bright red flowers.

Delphinium trolliifolium   Zones 6b to 9b

Columbian, trollius-leaved, or poison larkspur

This perennial produces tall stems up to 1.5m (5ft) or more from woody roots and short rhizomes. The stems are leafy, and the leaves are alternate. The lowermost leaves are the largest, with blades up to 20cm (8in) across, set on long petioles. The leaf blades are palmate, lobed into five to seven main segments, with the segments more shallowly lobed and toothed. The long, open racemes produce flowers about 2.5cm (1in) long. The sepals are usually deep blue, occasionally pinkish or white. The two upper petals are whitish, and the two lower petals are generally blue. Flowering occurs from mid spring to early summer, and winged, brown seeds ripen in hairless follicles.

Cultivation. Full to part shade or dappled light, and moist soil. This tall, blue-flowered beauty is an excellent plant for the shady, woodland garden or forest glade, especially west of the Cascades. Plant it near the shaded margin of a pond, stream, or bog.

Native Habitat and Range. Along streams and in moist, shady woods at low to mid elevations from southwestern Washington, south through the Columbia River Gorge to northern California, and from the coast to the west slope of the Cascades.

Notes. *Delphinium glaucum* (Sierra larkspur) is another tall species of moist habitats, found in wet meadows and along streams at mid to high elevations in the mountains of the west.

Dicentra   Fumariaceae

bleeding heart

Dicentra includes around 20 species native to temperate North America and Asia; of the seven species that occur in North America, four are native to the Pacific Northwest. The plants are succulent and usually glaucous, covered with a whitish, waxy coating. The leaves are finely divided and ferny. The unusual flowers consist of four petals, the two outer petals with spurred or sac-like bases. The fruits are elongated capsules, and each seed has an eliasome, an oil-rich appendage that attracts ants, which aids in seed dispersal.

Propagation. Collect seeds when the capsules are ripe, and plant them outside in the fall to stratify them under cool, moist winter conditions; they should germinate by the following spring, but plants may take a year or so to reach flowering size. Bleeding hearts can also be grown from divisions of the rhizomes made in the spring.

Dicentra cucullaria

Dicentra formosa

Dicentra cucullaria   Zones 4a to 9b

Dutchman's breeches

This deciduous perennial grows from a short, bulb-like rhizome covered with small, rounded tubers. The leaves are basal, with long petioles and three or four times compound leaves. The leaves reach about 20cm (8in) in length, and the ultimate leaflets are linear. The leafless flowering stems grow to 30cm (1ft) tall and develop an open raceme with few to several flowers. The flowers are white or pinkish, and the petals have yellow tips. The flowers are about 2cm (1in) long with spreading spurs (they look somewhat like the legs of baggy pants) and bloom from early to late spring. The slender capsules produce shiny, black seeds.

Cultivation. Part shade or dappled light, and moist soil. This is an unusual, striking species for the edge of the woodland garden or perennial bed.

Native Habitat and Range. In wet gravel along riverbanks and moist woods near Saddle Mountain in northwestern Oregon; the Columbia River and its tributaries, from near Portland, Oregon, east through Washington and Oregon to Idaho; and from Kansas east to Nova Scotia and south to North Carolina.

Notes. Our populations are disjunct (geographically separated) from populations in eastern North America, where this species is more common. Because of this, our plants are sometimes considered a distinct variety, _D. c._ var. _occidentalis_ (western Dutchman's breeches).

Dicentra formosa   Zones 7a to 9b

Pacific bleeding heart

This herbaceous perennial grows from slender, spreading rhizomes. The plants are glaucous, and the leaves are all basal, finely divided and fernlike, growing to 30cm (1ft). Five to 15 flowers bloom at the tips of the leafless scapes, to 40cm (16in). The flowers are purplish pink and about 2cm (1in) long with rounded, heart-shaped spurs at the base, nodding gracefully from the pedicels. Bleeding hearts bloom from early spring to mid summer. The fruits are slender capsules containing several shiny, black seeds.

Cultivation. Full shade to part sun or dappled light, and moist to rather wet soil with good organic content. Plant along the path of the woodland garden or with other shade-loving bedding plants. Once established in good habitat, this species tends to spread aggressively; some gardeners find it a bit of a pest, but it does make a lovely carpet under trees, shrubs, and taller perennials.

Native Habitat and Range. Along streambanks and in moist forests from western British Columbia south to central California, and from the lowlands near the Pacific to mid elevations in the Coast Ranges and Cascades.

Notes. The white-flowered 'Alba' is sometimes available from nurseries. *Dicentra f.* ssp. *formosa* is the common pink-flowered form. The endemic *D. f.* ssp. *oregana* (*D. oregana*; Oregon bleeding heart), often found in serpentine soils in southwestern Oregon and northwestern California, has bluish foliage and creamy flowers with pink-tipped inner petals. Another native species, *D. uniflora* (steer's-head, long-horn steer's-head), may be tried in gardens east of the Cascades; it generally dies out when planted west of the Cascades. *Dicentra pauciflora* (few-flowered bleeding heart, short-horn steer's-head) grows in the high alpine areas in and around the Siskiyou Mountains of southwestern Oregon.

Dichelostemma   Liliaceae

blue dicks, ookow, wild hyacinth

Dichelostemma includes about five species, all native to western North America and four to the Pacific Northwest. The flowers have six tepals or perianth segments (petals and sepals that are similar to each other and petaloid) that are fused together at the base. The long, linear leaves are sometimes still green when the flowers open. In some species, each flower has three functional stamens and three staminodes. Plants are occasionally placed in *Brodiaea*; both are genera of graceful, corm-bearing perennials with grass-like leaves and umbels of tubular or trumpet-shaped flowers, but their seeds, styles, and stigmas vary.

Propagation. Collect seeds in the summer, after the capsules ripen. Plant them by fall, sowing them into flats or directly into the garden, and leave them outside over winter for germination in the spring. Two or three years of patience will be needed before the corms become big enough to produce flowers. Mature corms can be transplanted to a depth of 7 to 10cm (3 to 4in) in autumn. Small corms sometimes form around the bases of older corms; these can be detached during transplanting. Even small corms will take a couple of years to reach flowering size, and they should be taken only from plants originally grown from seed.

Dichelostemma capitatum

Dichelostemma ida-maia

Dichelostemma capitatum   Zones 6a to 9b

blue dicks, wild hyacinth

This corm-bearing perennial produces a few linear basal leaves, up to 40cm (16in) long, that sometimes wither by flowering time. The leafless flowering stems (scapes) grow to 60cm (2ft) tall. The flowers are arranged in a dense head-like umbel at the stem tip, subtended by (usually) purple bracts. The flowers are violet or blue, up to 2cm (1in) long, with the tepals fused at the base and with six fertile stamens, three of them longer than the other three. The flowers bloom from early to late spring, and the fruits are oval capsules.

Cultivation. Full sun or light shade, and fairly dry soil. This is a lovely spring-blooming species for the dry parts of the wildflower meadow, well-drained slope, or rock garden. It is tolerant of various garden conditions and can be planted with bulbs or other perennials in a border or bed.

Native Habitat and Range. In dry, open woods, grasslands, and deserts at low to mid elevations from northwestern Oregon, west of the Cascades, south and east to California, Nevada, Utah, Arizona, and New Mexico.

Notes. Sometimes classified as *D. pulchellum*, *Brodiaea pulchella*, and *B. capitata*. Only *D. c.* ssp. *capitatum* ranges into Oregon. *Dichelostemma congestum* (*B. congesta*; forktooth ookow) also has lavender to bluish purple flowers crowded into a dense, head-like umbel; it lives in prairies, grassy slopes, and meadows from northwestern Washington, south to central California and east through the Columbia River Gorge. *Dichelostemma multiflorum* (*B. multiflora*; roundtooth ookow, snakelily) has similar violet or purplish flowers arranged in umbels, where each flower sits on a short pedicel; this species lives on open or wooded slopes in clay soils, ranging as far north as southwestern Oregon from California.

Dichelostemma ida-maia   Zones 7b to 9b

firecracker flower

This unusual, corm-bearing perennial usually produces three leaves up to around 50cm (20in) long. The leafless flowering stalk can approach 1m (3ft) in length. Six to 20 flowers are arranged in an umbel at the tip of the scape, and each flower nods from a pedicel to 5cm (2in) long. The tepals are fused most of their length, forming a scarlet perianth tube to 3cm (1.5in) long. The perianth tube is rounded at the base and greenish at the tip, where the tepals become distinct and recurved (curved backward) during flowering. This species has three functional stamens and blooms from late spring to mid summer. The fruit is a small capsule set on a short stalk (stipe).

Cultivation. Full sun or light shade, and well-drained, rather dry soil. This is a stunning plant for the rock garden or dry wildflower meadow. It can also be planted at the edge of a dry shrub border or woodland, where the branches of open shrubs will help keep its tall stems erect during blooming.

Native Habitat and Range. On grassy slopes and open woods at fairly low to mid elevations, from southwestern Oregon to northwestern California.

Notes. Sometimes classified as *Brodiaea ida-maia* or *Brevoortia ida-maia*. This is an endemic species with a restricted range and should never be disturbed in the wild. *Dichelostemma* ×*venustum* (*B. venusta*), a naturally occurring hybrid between it and *D. congestum* has rose-colored flowers and a small range where the two parents meet, in southwestern Oregon and northwestern California.

Dodecatheon   Primulaceae

shooting star

This well-known genus of wildflowers includes about 15 species, primarily native to North America, with nine of these occurring in the Pacific Northwest. These perennial herbs produce a basal rosette of leaves from rhizomes or a short crown (caudex). The leafless flowering stems terminate in an umbel of one to several flowers. The showy purple to white flowers arch gracefully on curved pedicels. The style and stamens point forward, while the five (sometimes four) petals are flared back. The filaments of the (usually) five stamens are at least partly fused to each other, forming a tube. The style and stigma protrude from the ring of anthers, and the fruits are rounded capsules. The scientific name is derived from the Greek for "twelve gods," who apparently are the protectors of these lovely plants.

Propagation. Grow from seed collected in the late summer or fall and either planted in the fall or stored under cool, dry conditions for early spring planting. Seeds can be planted into containers or directly into the garden. The seedlings will take a couple of years to reach flowering size. Rhizomatous species can be propagated from divisions of larger plants made in the early spring. Any plants propagated by division should be individuals that were originally grown from seed; these plants should never be poached from wild places.

Dodecatheon dentatum   Zones 4a to 9b

white shooting star

This perennial produces basal leaves and flowering shoots from short, thick rhizomes. The leaves are ovate to oblong and up to 10cm (4in) long. The blades have toothed margins and are abruptly rounded at the base to a narrow petiole. The leafless flowering stems (scapes) can grow to 40cm (16in) in height, producing an umbel of up to 10 flowers, each from about 1.5cm (0.6in) long. The

Dodecatheon dentatum

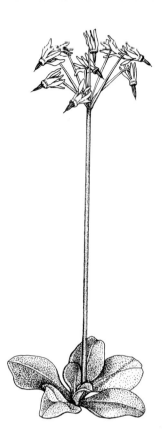

Dodecatheon hendersonii

petals are white with a purplish ring at the base where they are fused. Flowers bloom from late spring to mid summer, and seeds ripen in rounded capsules.

Cultivation. Part shade or dappled light, and well-drained, moist soil. Plants can be allowed to dry out during the late summer, when they normally go dormant. This is a lovely species for the shadier parts of the rock garden, or among the cobbles along a pond or stream on either side of the Cascades. Let it form clumps near the path or bench in the woodland garden.

Native Habitat and Range. Along streams, waterfalls, and moist, shady places at low to fairly high elevations, east of the Cascades from southern British Columbia, eastern Washington and central Idaho, south to northern Oregon and in the Columbia River Gorge, south and east in Utah, Arizona, and New Mexico.

Notes. This is the only species that typically has toothed leaves and white petals. *Dodecatheon d.* ssp. *dentatum* is the only subspecies encountered in the Pacific Northwest.

Dodecatheon hendersonii	Zones 7a to 9b

Henderson's or broad-leaved shooting star

This herbaceous perennial does not develop rhizomes, but produces bulblets around the crown at flowering time. The broadly spoon-shaped basal leaves are generally hairless (glabrous), up to 13cm (5in) long and almost as wide. The blades have smooth (entire) margins and are narrowed abruptly at the base to the petiole. The leafless flowering stalks (scapes) can grow to 30cm (1ft) in height, and each can produce up to 15 flowers in an umbel-like inflorescence. The corollas are up to 2.5cm (1in) long. The petal lobes vary from magenta to lavender, with yellow and reddish purple rings at their fused bases, where the petals meet. Flowers bloom from early spring to early summer, and seeds develop in rounded capsules.

Dodecatheon hendersonii

Dodecatheon jeffreyi

Cultivation. Full sun to part shade or dappled light, and well-drained soil that is moist early in the year. This is a beautiful perennial for the rock garden or dryish wildflower meadow in the warmer parts of our area; it is especially lovely under oaks and other deciduous trees, generally blooming before the trees leaf out.

Native Habitat and Range. In rather dry prairies and open woods at low to mid elevations, from southwestern British Columbia, south in the Coast Ranges and the west slope of the Cascades to California.

Notes. Of the four subspecies, only *D. h.* ssp. *hendersonii* is native to the Pacific Northwest.

Dodecatheon jeffreyi	Zones 5a to 9b

Jeffrey's shooting star

The leaves of this clump-forming rhizomatous perennial are lance-shaped but widest toward the tip (oblanceolate), tapering gradually to long petioles. The leaves can grow to 40cm (16in) long, but are much smaller on plants in drier habitats. The umbellate inflorescence can grow to 60cm (2ft) in robust plants and can produce up to 20 flowers. Flowers are up to 2.5cm (1in) long; the petal lobes may be magenta, purplish, or sometimes white, becoming yellow or whitish, and are marked with a purple or reddish band at the petal bases, where they fuse to form a tube. The style is tipped with a rounded stigma. Flowers bloom from early to late summer, and the seeds ripen in rounded capsules.

Cultivation. Full sun to part shade, and wet to moist soil. This is a beautiful perennial for the wetter parts of the wildflower meadow, streambank, or pond margin on either side of the Cascades. It blooms later than many shooting stars, adding summer color to wet areas. Given a good location and a bit of time, plants will spread by their thin rhizomes and also by seed, forming colonies.

Dodecatheon poeticum

Dodecatheon pulchellum

Native Habitat and Range. Near streams and in wet meadows at low to high elevations from Alaska south through the Cascade and Olympic Mountains to the southern Sierra Nevada, east to Idaho and Montana.

Notes. *Dodecatheon j.* ssp. *jeffreyi* occurs throughout the range. Alpine shooting star (*D. alpinum*) is another species of wet mountain meadows; it is native to Oregon and ranges south and east to California, Utah, and Arizona.

Dodecatheon poeticum	Zones 6a to 8b

poet's shooting star

This plant produces finely hairy, glandular leaves and shoots from a perennial crown without well-developed rhizomes. Basal leaves grow to 15cm (6in) long. The blades are spoon-shaped (spatulate) to oblong, tapered to the petioles, and often have toothed margins. Flowering umbels can grow to 40cm (16in) tall and bear up to ten flowers. The corollas are about 1.5cm (.5in) long, and the flared petal lobes are bright pink, yellow at their bases, with a purple ring where the petals are fused. Blooming takes place from early to late spring, and seeds ripen in rounded capsules.

Cultivation. Full sun to part shade or dappled light, and soil that is wet or very moist in the spring but dry later in the year. This is a good shooting star for gardeners east of the Cascades; the plants can be left to become dormant and dry after flowering. Site it in seasonally wet places in the rock garden, wildflower meadow, or pond margin.

Native Habitat and Range. Near streambanks, vernal pools, open woods, and other places that are wet in early spring, at low to mid elevations in the Columbia River Gorge, south central Washington, and north central Oregon.

Notes. Although it is not listed as rare, this species is endemic to a small area and should never be poached from the wild. Bonneville shooting star (*D. conjugens*) is found in seeps and other wet places in the arid sagebrush-steppe regions and mountain meadows along the east slope of the Cascades, from British Columbia, south to California and east to Alberta, Montana, and Wyoming.

Dodecatheon pulchellum	Zones 3b to 9b

pretty or few-flowered shooting star

This perennial produces glandular-hairy to hairless (glabrous) leaves and flowering shoots from short crowns without rhizomes. The basal leaves grow to 15cm (6in) long. The leaf blades are oblong or spoon-shaped (spatulate), gradually tapering to winged petioles. The margins are entire or with small teeth. Flowering umbels can grow to 40cm (16in) tall and produce up to 25 flowers. The corollas are about 1.5cm (.5in) long, and the petal lobes are magenta to purplish, sometimes white, changing to yellow at the bases of the petals, with a purplish ring where the petals are fused. The tube formed by the fused filaments of the stamens is often yellow in this species, but sometimes purple. Blooming takes place from mid spring to late summer, depending on habitat and elevation. Seeds ripen in rounded capsules.

Cultivation. Full sun or light shade, and wet to moist soil. This species often grows in moist, saline soils and is able to tolerate such conditions either near the coast or further inland, on both sides of the Cascades. An excellent perennial for the wet corner of the rock garden or wildflower meadow, or in plantings near the streambank or pond margin.

Native Habitat and Range. In wet, coastal or mountain meadows and near salt marshes and streams at low to high elevations, from Alaska south to Mexico and east to the Dakotas, Nebraska, and New Mexico.

Notes. *Dodecatheon p.* ssp. *pulchellum* has the largest distribution, but *D. p.* ssp. *cusickii*, *D. p.* ssp. *macrocarpum*, and *D. p.* ssp. *monanthum* are encountered here as well. All four subspecies are listed as rare in some part of their natural range.

Douglasia laevigata	Zones 4a to 9a	Primulaceae

smooth douglasia, dwarf-primrose

This mat forming perennial produces stems to 8cm (3in) tall with tufts of evergreen leaves at their tips. The small leaves are oblong and about 1.5cm (.5in) long. The flowers have five petal lobes and are fused into a tube at the base of the corolla. The corollas are about 1cm (.5in) across and are rosy pink on opening, fading to lavender as they age. They are produced in compact umbels of up to ten flowers each, blooming at the branch tips from early spring to late summer, depending on elevation. The fruits are few-seeded capsules.

Cultivation. Full sun to part shade, and well-drained but moist soil. A choice species for the alpine rock garden or trough planting on either side of the Cascades. This beautiful evergreen would also be welcome in the cracks of a retaining wall or other stone structure.

Propagation. Grow from seed collected in summer or fall and planted outside, in gritty soil, in the garden or in containers. Leave the planted seeds outside in the cool, moist winter weather for spring germination. Can also be propagated from cuttings taken near the base of the plant in mid to late summer, treated with hormones, and set to root under humid conditions in pumice or some other medium. Cuttings should be taken only from seed-grown garden plants, never from individuals in the wild.

Native Habitat and Range. On moist coastal bluffs, talus slopes, and rock ledges at low to (more commonly) high elevations, from Alaska south, west of the Cascade crest to the Columbia

Douglasia laevigata

River Gorge, east to Mount Hood, and also in the Olympic Mountains, on Saddle Mountain in northwestern Oregon, and other mountain peaks.

Notes. *Douglasia* encompasses fewer than a dozen species, most of them native to Alaska and the far northern parts of North America. Snow dwarf-primrose (*D. nivalis*) and Idaho dwarf-primrose (*D. idahoensis*) range south to Washington and western Idaho, respectively. *Primula* (primrose) is another genus in the Primulaceae favored by rock gardeners; violet-flowered *P. cusickiana* and magenta *P. parryi*, native to rocky streambanks and other moist places east of the Cascades, can be grown, with difficulty, from seed.

Drosera rotundifolia	Zones 3b to 9b	Droseraceae

round-leaved sundew

This interesting perennial herb produces a basal rosette of spreading leaves to 10cm (4in) long with slender petioles. The margins of the round leaf blades are covered with long-stalked, reddish, sticky, gland-tipped hairs that function as insect traps. The leafless flowering stems (scapes) grow to 18cm (7in) and bear three to ten small, white flowers 1cm (.5in) long, all secund (set along one side of the peduncle), blooming from early summer to early fall. The fruits are capsules with numerous seeds.

Cultivation. Full sun to part shade, and wet, acidic soil. Appreciates sphagnum added to its growing medium. This charming little plant for the bog garden, wet place in the wildflower meadow, or pond margin can be grown throughout our area if conditions are to its liking. Relatively easy to cultivate, it is often available from growers specializing in carnivorous plants.

Propagation. Grow from seed collected in the fall and sown on wet sphagnum in flats dur-

Drosera rotundifolia

Dulichium arundinaceum

ing fall or winter. Keep the growing medium saturated through spring germination and seedling growth.

Native Habitat and Range. In bogs and wet meadows at low to mid elevations, circumboreal, from Alaska south to California, east to Nevada, Idaho, Montana, the Great Lakes region, and Labrador, south to northern Florida; Eurasia.

Notes. *Drosera r.* var. *rotundifolia* occurs in our area, mainly west of the Cascades. *Drosera* includes around 100 species on every continent, with Australia, New Zealand, and southern Africa having the greatest diversity of species. *Drosera anglica* (*D. longifolia*; long-leaved, great, or English sundew), the only other species in the Pacific Northwest, is much like *D. rotundifolia*, but its leaves are upright and the blades longer and narrower. It has a similar habitat and occurs in some of the same areas as *D. rotundifolia*, but is not as common. The two species hybridize when given the opportunity, yielding *D. ×obovata*. Various peoples have used sundews medicinally and for other purposes.

| *Dulichium arundinaceum* | Zones 3b to 9b | Cyperaceae |

three-way sedge

This sedge produces leafy, sometimes three-angled shoots up to 1m (3ft) tall from rhizomes. The basal leaves lack blades, consisting only of sheathing leaf bases. The upper leaves are stiff and grass-like, up to 15cm (6in) long and evenly three-ranked along the stem. Each tiny flower is surrounded by a scale, and groups of these little florets are arranged into vertical rows, or spikelets, with each narrow spikelet up to 2.5cm (1in) long. The spikelets are arranged into spikes consisting of several spikelets each, these developing from the axils of the upper leaves. Flowers bloom from mid summer to early fall. The fruits are small one-seeded, lenticular (lentil-shaped) achenes.

Cultivation. Full sun or light shade, and very wet soil. This is an interesting, vaguely bamboo-like perennial for the margin of the pond, stream, ditch, or sunny bog. It will add diversity and improve wildlife habitat.

Propagation. Grow from seed collected in the fall and planted soon after harvest. Sow seeds into flats of wet potting soil or directly onto muddy ground, and leave them to cold stratify over winter for germination in the spring. Alternatively, divide rhizomes in the spring.

Native Habitat and Range. In wet meadows, streambanks, and marshy shores at low to mid elevations from southwestern British Columbia, south through northern California and east to western Montana; absent through the southwestern United States but widespread in eastern North America.

Notes. This is the only species in the genus. *Sparganium*, the lone member of the Sparganiaceae, is another genus of rhizomatous perennials of wet places; both *S. eurycarpum* (broadfruit bur-reed) and *S. angustifolium* (narrowleaf bur-reed) are widely distributed in our area and likewise add value to wildlife habitat.

Elymus elymoides	Zones 3b to 9b	Poaceae

squirreltail

This graceful, short-lived bunchgrass is usually somewhat hairy and grows to about 60cm (2ft) tall. The leaf blades are flat or sometimes folded. The small flowers (florets) are grouped into spikelets, the typical unit of the grass inflorescence. Two bracts, the glumes, subtend each spikelet. The inflorescence is a densely flowered spike with whorls of two or three spikelets at each node. Groups of four or six slender, sometimes two-forked (bifid) glumes to 10cm (4in) long subtend the spikelets. Each spikelet consists of up to six florets. Each floret is further enclosed in its own pair of bracts, the lemma and the palea. Each lemma has an awn, a long bristle, sometimes as long as the glume, at the tip. The inflorescence has the look of a fluffy squirrel's tail or a bottlebrush. The flowers bloom from late spring to mid summer, and the fruit is a grain, or caryopsis.

Cultivation. Full sun to part shade, and well-drained, moist to rather dry, rocky soil. Can be grown on either side of the Cascades, but seeds from relatively local populations will probably do best. The long glumes and awns attach themselves to the socks of visitors, so keep it away from garden paths. Best for the wildflower meadow or drought-tolerant wildlife garden.

Propagation. Grow from seed collected in the fall and sown into flats of potting soil or directly into the garden in the fall or early spring.

Native Habitat and Range. In moist to dry, often rocky habitats from coastal prairies to sagebrush plains and mountain ridges, at low to high elevations on both sides of the Cascades from British Columbia east to Alberta and the Dakotas, south to southern California, New Mexico, and Texas.

Notes. Sometimes classified as *Sitanion hystrix*. *Elymus e.* ssp. *californicus* and *E. e.* ssp. *elymoides* occur on both sides of the Cascades; *E. e.* ssp. *hordeoides* is more common on the east slope. *Elymus e.* ssp. *brevifolius* is more southern and eastern, ranging north into Oregon and east across much of North America. Along with other grass genera, *Elymus* has been the subject of much taxonomic revision, and some species have been moved to *Leymus* (which see). At present, more than 30 species of *Elymus* occur in North America, with about a dozen native to the Pacific Northwest, and some of these are widespread. Blue wildrye (*E. glaucus*) forms small clumps to 1m (3ft) tall, and the flowering heads are narrow spikes; this is an excellent grass for moist to rather dry meadows, open woods, and hillsides, ranging from southern Alaska south to California and east across much of North America. Canada wildrye (*E. canadensis*) and thickspike wheatgrass (*E. lanceolatus*) also occur in our area.

Elymus elymoides (photo by Sally A. Simmons)

Epilobium	Onagraceae

willowherb

Epilobium includes annual and perennial (sometimes a bit woody) herbs with four (sometimes petaloid) sepals and four petals, fused at their bases (along with the filaments of the stamens) into a floral tube, or hypanthium, that sits on top of the ovary and encircles the style. Of the approximately 40 species in North America, around 25 occur in our area. Willowherbs have eight stamens, a four-lobed stigma, and an inferior, four-celled ovary. The fruit, a four-celled capsule, splits lengthwise at maturity to release the hair-tipped seeds.

Propagation. Grow from seed collected in the fall. Plant seeds into flats of moist potting soil soon after harvest or in winter, and leave them outside to chill for germination in the spring. *Epilobium luteum* can also be propagated from divisions of the rhizomes or from cuttings made at the bases of the stems in spring. The slightly woody *E. canum* can be grown from semi-hard stem cuttings taken in the summer.

Epilobium canum ssp. *latifolium*	Zones 5b to 9b

hummingbird trumpet, California fuchsia

This slightly shrubby perennial produces clumps of branched, leafy, decumbent (relaxed and touching the ground, but usually not rooting) stems to about 60cm (2ft) long. The alternate (sometimes opposite) leaves are ovate to lanceolate and sessile (lacking petioles), up to 3.5cm (1.4in) long, sometimes with finely toothed margins. The foliage is woolly with long hairs, and flowers bloom in leafy spikes at the stem tips. The flowers are showy, with sepals, petals, and

Epilobium canum ssp. *latifolium*

Epipactis gigantea

Epilobium luteum

floral tube all bright scarlet. The flowers are up to 3.5cm (1.5in) long, and the narrow floral tube is swollen at the base, where it joins with the inferior ovary. The four petals are notched at the tips, and the stamens and style are well exserted. Blooming takes place from late summer to early fall. The fruits, oblong capsules, are about 2.5cm (1in) long, and each seed has a tuft of white hairs, the coma.

Cultivation. Full sun to light shade, and well-drained, moist to rather dry soil. This is a beautiful, easily grown plant for rock gardens on either side of the Cascades. As its common names suggest, this is a classic tubular, red-flowered plant, attractive to hummers. Plant it among rocks or in a large trough in the hummingbird garden.

Native Habitat and Range. On dry, rocky slopes and ridges at mid to high elevations in the mountains of southwestern Oregon, south to California, Nevada, and the Southwest.

Notes. Sometimes classified as *Zauschneria latifolia* or *Z. californica* ssp. *latifolia*. The many available cultivars differ in plant size and flower color.

Epilobium luteum	Zones 5a to 9a	

yellow willowherb

This perennial herb develops leafy shoots up to 60cm (2ft) from extensive rhizomes. The leaves are opposite and subsessile (lacking petioles, more or less). They are ovate to lanceolate, up to 8cm (3in) long and have finely toothed margins. Flowers bloom in small clusters from the axils of the upper leaves, on pedicels up to 2.5cm (1in) long. The hypanthium is cup-shaped and very short. The four lanceolate sepals are often yellowish or reddish, and the four petals are pale yellow, about 1.5cm (.5in) long, and notched at the tip. Flowers bloom from mid summer to early fall. The fruits are linear, four-celled capsules up to 8cm (3in) long, developing below the flowers. The seeds are tipped with a tuft of rust-colored hairs, the coma.

Cultivation. Part shade or dappled light, and moist to wet soil. Plant this lovely willowherb near a waterfall, among the rocks near a stream, pond, or bog, or among stones in the wet part of the wildflower meadow. A good species for late summer and fall color.

Native Habitat and Range. Along streams, lakes, forested springs, and seeps at mid to fairly high elevations from southern Alaska, south through the mountains of western British Columbia, Washington, and Oregon to northern California.

Notes. This is our only yellow-flowered willowherb. Siskiyou Mountains or stiff willowherb (*E. rigidum*) and rock or rose willowherb (*E. obcordatum*) are equally lovely, mat-forming species with deep pink flowers and glaucous foliage, bluish with a waxy surface. Both live in rocky, sometimes rather dry places, *E. rigidum* in southern Oregon and northern California, and *E. obcordatum* in alpine talus from eastern Oregon to Idaho, California, and Nevada. They are beautiful plants, very much worth cultivating, especially for the rock garden, and should be grown from seed.

Epipactis gigantea	Zones 3b to 9b	Orchidaceae

giant helleborine, stream orchid

This orchid produces one to several leafy stems up to 1m (3ft) from short rhizomes. The leaves are broadly lance-shaped, and the largest ones, up to 15cm (6in) long and 5cm (2in) wide, develop higher on the stem. Up to 15 flowers bloom in a leafy-bracted raceme. The three sepals are about 1.5cm (.5in) long and yellowish green with brownish veins. The two upper petals are flat, and the lower, pouch-shaped petal has a three-lobed lip. The petals are streaked with purple. Flowers bloom from mid spring to mid summer, depending on elevation. The inferior ovary develops into a curved capsule to 3.5cm (1.5in) long, containing many tiny seeds.

Cultivation. Part shade or dappled light, and moist soil high in organic matter. This is one of the easier orchids to grow, especially if you add the spores of mycorrhizal fungi to the soil when planting. Although the flowers are subtle, it makes a lush and attractive addition to the pond margin, bog garden, or streambank.

Propagation. Possible from seed collected from the capsules just before they are fully ripe and planted soon after harvest. Sow seeds (along with mycorrhizal spores) onto the surface of moist, sterile potting soil in flats. Protect the flats with glass or plastic, and keep them moist and out of direct sun. With luck, there will be seedlings large enough to transplant in a year. Alternatively, the short rhizomes can be divided in spring, but this should be done only with plants grown from seed. Even were they cooperative in cultivation, all wild orchids should be left alone unless they are being rescued from certain destruction.

Native Habitat and Range. Near seeps, streams, and lakeshores, often near hot springs, at low to fairly high elevations, on both sides of the Cascades from southern British Columbia, south to California and northern Mexico, east through the Rocky Mountains to South Dakota and Texas.

Notes. *Epipactis* includes fewer than 20 species native to the Northern Hemisphere, most of them Eurasian. This species is our only native.

Erigeron	Asteraceae

fleabane daisy

Erigeron is a genus of close to 200 species, most of them native to North America, with the greatest diversity in the mountains of the west: more than 60 species occur in our area. Flowers are similar to their sunflower relatives, but they tend to bloom earlier in the season. Each inflorescence consists of many tiny flowers (florets) crowded into a head and surrounded by a set of narrow bracts that are often green. The center of the flowering head is filled with tiny disk florets with tubular, yellow corollas. The ray florets are on the outer margin of the head; they look like the petals of a single flower, but are actually flowers themselves. The flat corollas of the ray florets are usually purple, pink, or white, sometimes yellow, and occasionally they are missing completely. Despite their unfortunate common name (they are not very effective as a flea repellant, though they were once used for that purpose in Europe), fleabane daisies are beautiful additions the garden and provide nectar for butterflies. Many species, including some rare ones, are native to dry habitats east of the Cascades; others occur in the mountains or near the coast. Wherever you garden in the Pacific Northwest, there are at least a few fleabane daisies that will be right at home.

Propagation. Grow from seed collected in late summer. Seeds can be planted into flats soon after harvest. Some will probably germinate and spend the winter as seedlings; these may need some protection from winter cold. The seeds can also be stored in cool, dry conditions and planted in the spring, after the soil warms. Rhizomatous species can also be propagated by dividing rooted pieces of the rhizomes in late summer. Plants with well-developed crowns can be propagated from basal cuttings made from young shoots as they begin to grow in the spring; treat the cuttings with hormones and set them into pumice or some other medium, keeping them humid until roots form.

Erigeron filifolius	Zones 4a to 9b

threadleaf fleabane daisy

This taprooted perennial produces slender, hairy shoots up to 50cm (20in) from a branched root crown. The basal and stem leaves are very thin and thread-like, up to 8cm (3in) long. The flowering stems produce one to several heads, and the ray corollas are often white (at least in

Erigeron filifolius (photo by Sally A. Simmons)

Erigeron glaucus

eastern Washington, where it is widespread), but sometimes blue or pink. The ray corollas are about 1cm (.5in) long, and flowers bloom from late spring to mid summer. The hairy achenes are topped with a pappus (modified calyx) of thin bristles.

Cultivation. Full sun or light shade, and well-drained, rather dry, sandy soil. This is an attractive daisy for wildflower gardens east of the Cascades. It can be planted with sagebrush or among the bunchgrasses and other perennials in the wildlife and butterfly garden.

Native Habitat and Range. In dry, sandy soils, often with sagebrush, at low to mid elevations, east of the Cascades from southern British Columbia east to Montana and south through eastern Oregon and Idaho to California, Nevada, and Utah.

Notes. The widespread *E. f.* var. *filifolius* occurs throughout the range; each of its flowering shoots bears multiple heads with 15 to 50 rays. *Erigeron f.* var. *robustior* consists of stouter plants that usually bear single heads with 50 to 125 rays; it is restricted to Washington and Oregon.

Erigeron glaucus   Zones 8a to 9b

seaside fleabane daisy

This perennial grows 30 to 60cm (1 to 2ft) in height and spreads by rhizomes to form clumps to 1m (3ft) across. The leaves are succulent, with the largest, up to 15cm (6in) long and 5cm (2in) wide, at the base of the plant, becoming smaller on the upper parts of the stem. The leaves are obovate (oval but widest toward the tip) and usually have some teeth along the margin above the middle of the leaf. One to 15 heads bloom on leafy stems from late spring to late summer. The heads, packed with yellow disk florets, are up to 3.5cm (1.5in) across. Each head has about 100 ray florets with slender, usually blue (sometimes white) corollas up to 1.5cm (.5in) long. The hairy achenes usually have four nerves and a pappus (calyx) of thin bristles.

Cultivation. Full sun to light shade, and moist to rather dry soil. Tolerates salt spray and sandy soil but is less tolerant of extreme heat and cold—a fleabane daisy for gardens west of the Cascades. An excellent addition to the butterfly garden, where it will provide nectar through much of the season. It is also lovely in the perennial border or on a dry bank or sandy site. Plants will be smaller in harsh conditions but will spread vigorously in the fertile perennial bed.

Native Habitat and Range. On bluffs and beaches at low elevations along the coast from northern Oregon to southern California.

Notes. 'Sea Breeze' is a selection with large, pink flowering heads. The compact 'Arthur Menzies' has pinkish lavender flowers and grows only to 20cm (8in) tall.

Erigeron linearis	Zones 4a to 9b

desert yellow fleabane daisy

This perennial produces many finely hairy shoots up to 30cm (1ft) tall from a branched crown. The leaves are narrow and linear with the longest, up to 9cm (3.5in), at the base of the plant. Each shoot usually produces a single flowering head with yellow disk and ray corollas. Each head has 15 to 45 ray florets with corollas about 1cm (.5in) long, blooming from late spring to mid summer. The hairy achenes have a pappus (calyx) of thin bristles and some shorter scales.

Cultivation. Full sun to light shade, and well-drained, rocky, rather dry soil. This is a species for gardens east of the Cascades. Plant it in the rock garden, with sagebrush, or among bunchgrasses and other perennials. The yellow flowers will brighten the dry wildflower meadow or butterfly garden.

Native Habitat and Range. In dry soils and rocky slopes at low to fairly high elevations, east of the Cascades from southern British Columbia, south through eastern Washington and Oregon to California and Nevada, east to Montana, Wyoming, and Utah.

Notes. Piper's fleabane daisy (*E. piperianus*), another yellow-rayed species, also lives in arid habitats east of the Cascades; it is an uncommon plant, endemic to eastern Washington. Alpine or golden fleabane daisy (*E. aureus*) is a low-growing species with spoon-shaped (spatulate) leaves and single heads with yellow rays; it lives on rocky ridges at high elevations in the Washington Cascades and the mountains of southern British Columbia and Alberta.

Erigeron peregrinus	Zones 3b to 9b

subalpine fleabane daisy

This variable perennial grows (usually) unbranched, leafy stems, 30 to 60cm (1 to 2ft) or a bit more, from a short rhizome or crown. The basal leaves are the largest, spoon-shaped (spatulate) or broadly lanceolate, and up to 20cm (8in) long in large plants. Stems produce one to few flowering heads, each with 30 to 80 ray florets. The disk florets are yellow, and the ray corollas are lavender, pink, or purplish, and up to 2.5cm (1in) long. Flowers bloom from mid to late summer, earlier at lower elevations. The achenes usually have five nerves running lengthwise and a pappus of long bristles.

Cultivation. Full sun to part shade, and moist to wet soil. This is an excellent species for gardens throughout our area, with larger heads than many fleabane daisies. Plant it near a pond, stream, or bog, in the perennial bed, or in the moist, sunny wildflower meadow or open glade in the woodland garden. A fine addition to the butterfly garden.

Native Habitat and Range. Along streams, near bogs, or in moist meadows and open woods at mid to high elevations, from coastal Alaska and British Columbia, south to northern California and east through the mountains to Montana, Colorado, and New Mexico.

Erigeron linearis (photo by Sally A. Simmons)

Erigeron peregrinus

Erigeron poliospermus (photo by Sally A. Simmons)

Erigeron speciosus

Notes. The wide-ranging *E. p.* ssp. *callianthemus* includes plants with darker ray corollas and glandular heads; this subspecies occurs more commonly in our interior mountains as *E. p.* ssp. *c.* var. *callianthemus*. Erigeron *p.* ssp. *peregrinus* includes more northern and western plants of the Cascades and the coast; it consists of three varieties, *E. p.* ssp. *p.* var. *peregrinus*, *E. p.* ssp. *p.* var. *dawsonii*, and the rare *E. p.* ssp. *p.* var. *thompsonii*, a taxon listed as sensitive in Washington. *Erigeron aliceae* (Alice Eastwood's fleabane daisy) is a similar but hairier species, native to rocky ridges and high mountain meadows.

Erigeron poliospermus   Zones 5a to 7b

purple cushion or desert fleabane daisy

This perennial grows from a taproot and produces a branched crown with many short, hairy stems to 15cm (6in) tall. The leaves are narrowly spatulate (spoon-shaped) to oblanceolate (lance-shaped but widest toward the tip). The basal leaves are usually the largest, up to 8cm (3in) long and about 1cm (.5in) wide. The flowering heads usually bloom singly at the stem tips. The disk florets are yellow, and the 15 to 45 ray florets have pinkish, purple, or violet corollas about 1cm (.5in) long. Flowers generally bloom from mid spring to early summer. The achenes are covered with silky hairs, and the pappus (calyx) includes long and short bristles.

Cultivation. Full sun or light shade, and well-drained, rather dry soil. This is another fine flea-bane for arid gardens east of the Cascades, where so many of these charming daisies are native. Plant it in the butterfly garden, wildflower meadow, or perennial bed among other herbaceous

America, it also does very well with sagebrush and other drought tolerant plants in the wildlife garden.

Native Habitat and Range. In dry foothills and plains, often with sagebrush, at low to mid elevations, from the east slope of the Cascades in southern British Columbia, south to central Oregon, and east to Idaho.

Notes. *Erigeron p.* var. *poliospermus* occurs throughout the range; plants are more hairy than glandular. *Erigeron p.* var. *cereus* is restricted to central Washington; plants are densely glandular but less hairy. Cutleaf fleabane daisy (*E. compositus*) is another low-growing plant, reaching up to 25cm (10in); its leaves are deeply divided into narrow lobes, and the ray corollas, when present, are pink, blue, or white. This species grows on rocky or sandy sites at mid to high elevations in the mountains of the west.

Erigeron speciosus	Zones 4a to 9b

showy or aspen fleabane daisy

This species produces a cluster of leafy, mostly hairless (glabrous) stems 30 to 80cm (1 to 2.5ft) tall from a woody crown. The lowermost leaves are spatulate (spoon-shaped), petiolate, and up to 15cm (6in) long. The stem leaves are shorter, sessile (lacking petioles), and lanceolate to ovate. Each shoot produces up to a dozen heads with yellow disk florets and blue or violet (occasionally white) ray corollas. The ray florets are numerous, each head producing 65 to 150 rays with corollas almost 2cm (1in) long. Flowers bloom from early to late summer. The achenes usually have two nerves, and the pappus (calyx) consists of longer bristles and some shorter scales.

Cultivation. Full sun to part shade, and moist to rather dry soil. This is a lovely daisy for the sunny perennial border, wildflower meadow, or butterfly garden on either side of the Cascades. It also does well in openings or near the edge of the woodland or shade garden.

Native Habitat and Range. In open woods, thickets, and forest clearings at fairly low to mid elevations from southern British Columbia, western Washington, and northwestern Oregon, east to Montana and South Dakota, south to Arizona and New Mexico.

Notes. *Erigeron s.* var. *speciosus* has narrower, hairier leaves; its range overlaps with the less hairy *E. s.* var. *macranthus*, with broader leaves. This species has been crossed with others to produce hybrids with large heads, including 'Darkest of All' (blue-violet flowers), 'Strahlenmeer' (lavender), 'Schneewittchen' (white), 'Pink Jewel', and 'Blue Beauty'.

Eriophorum	Cyperaceae

cotton-grass

Eriophorum encompasses fewer than 20 species, most of them native to chilly, wet parts of North America; around ten occur in the Pacific Northwest. The cotton-grasses are slender perennials, mostly with creeping rhizomes, angular stems, and narrow, grass-like leaves. The flowering stems terminate in one or more spikelets, collections of tiny florets, subtended by bracts. Instead of petals and sepals, the three stamens and three-sided ovary are surrounded by long, white to reddish bristles. These bristles expand as the fruit, a single-seeded achene, matures, forming a dense, cottony tuft.

Propagation. Grow from seed harvested in the fall and planted in the fall or spring. Sow seeds into containers of very wet soil or directly into a pond margin or other muddy place in the garden. Plants can also be propagated by dividing the rhizomes in fall or spring.

Eriophorum angustifolium

Eriophorum chamissonis

Eriophorum angustifolium	Zones 3b to 8b

tall or narrow-leaved cotton-grass

This perennial forms colonies from extensive rhizomes, producing shoots to about 80cm (2.5ft) tall. The leaves are well developed along the stems and have flat, grass-like blades that narrow and become channeled toward the tip. The tips of the flowering stems usually bear several spikelets, each one drooping from a peduncle. A few leaf-like involucral bracts, longer than the spikelets, subtend each umbel-like group of spikelets. The spikelets grow to 2.5cm (1in) long as the fruits ripen, and the bristles are generally white. Flowers bloom from mid to late summer, and the fruits, small achenes, are blackish.

Cultivation. Full sun to light shade, and very wet soil or shallow, standing water. This species spreads by rhizomes and may be too aggressive for the small bog or pond; keep it in control by planting it into sunken containers or into the soggy spot in the wildflower garden, where drier surroundings will keep it in check. An attractive plant for the larger pond margin, sunny bog, or streambank.

Native Habitat and Range. In wet meadows, cold bogs, and streambanks at mid to high elevations, circumboreal and widespread to the north, extending south through the mountains to northern Oregon, Idaho, and east through the Rocky Mountains to the Great Lakes and Atlantic coast.

Notes. Sometimes classified as *E. polystachion*. The wide-ranging *E. a.* ssp. *scabriusculum* is the tall cotton-grass that occurs in much of our area; *E. a.* ssp. *triste* and *E. a.* ssp. *subarcticum* are more northern taxa. *Eriophorum gracile* (slender cotton-grass) is another species with multiple spikelets; it occurs in wet places and has a range similar to tall cotton-grass. Fringed cotton-grass (*E. cringerum*) also produces rhizomes and tall stems, each with a head-like cluster of spikelets; it is more southern, occurring in swampy places from southwestern Oregon to northern California.

Eriophorum chamissonis	Zones 3b to 9b	

Chamisso's cotton-grass

This perennial can form large colonies from creeping rhizomes, producing flowering stems to 60cm (2ft) or more. The leaves are few in number and mostly basal. The leaf blades are about 10cm (4in) long, very narrow and channeled. The well-developed leaf bases sheathe the stems. The flowering stem bears a single spikelet subtended by dark, brownish scales. The cottony bristles of the spikelet vary from reddish to almost white, expanding to 5cm (2in) or more as the fruits ripen. Florets bloom from late spring to late summer, and the fruit, a dark, angular achene, has a sharp tip.

Cultivation. Full sun to light shade, and very wet soil or shallow, standing water. This is a distinctive, showy plant for the pond margin, sunny bog, or ditch. Can spread extensively; keep under control by planting it into sunken containers or in a wet depression surrounded by dry banks.

Native Habitat and Range. In bogs, wetland margins, and other wet places at low to mid elevations, circumboreal, extending south along the coast to southern Oregon, to northeastern Washington and east to the Rocky Mountains and Great Lakes.

Notes. Northland cotton-grass (*E. brachyantherum*) also has an inflorescence of only a single spikelet; it lives in cold, wet, mountain habitats, extending south in our area only to southwestern Alaska and British Columbia.

Eriophyllum lanatum	Zones 4a to 9b	Asteraceae

Oregon sunshine, common woolly sunflower

This variable perennial produces several stems 10 to 60cm (4 to 24in) tall, with leaves from 1 to 8cm (.5 to 3in) long, varying from alternate to opposite and from entire and linear to pinnately lobed. Plants are covered with white, woolly hairs. The stems produce bright yellow flower heads with ray corollas up to 2cm (1in) long. Flowers bloom from late spring to late summer. The fruits are achenes, sometimes with a pappus (calyx) of scales or teeth.

Cultivation. Full sun to light shade, and very well-drained, sandy or rocky, rather dry soil. Tolerates some summer water if the soil is well drained, and quite drought-tolerant once established. The small, compact forms are beautiful plants for the rock garden or trough; the taller varieties are excellent in larger rock gardens, stony banks, or sandy sites in the wildflower meadow or butterfly garden.

Propagation. Grow from seed collected in the late summer or fall when the heads are dry. Plant seeds into containers of potting soil or directly into the garden in the fall, and let them spend the winter outside to cold stratify for spring germination.

Native Habitat and Range. In dry, often rocky places at low to mid elevations from southern British Columbia, south to California, and from near the coast, east to western Montana, Wyoming, and Utah.

Notes. *Eriophyllum l.* var. *lanatum* and *E. l.* var. *achillaeoides* are taller plants with lobed leaves and rolled leaf margins, the leaves hairiest on the undersides. *Eriophyllum l.* var. *lanceolatum* has leaves that are densely hairy on both surfaces and not rolled under; it and *E. l.* var. *grandiflorum* with larger flowers, occur as far north as southern Oregon. *Eriophyllum l.* var. *integrifolium*, with

Eriophyllum lanatum

Erysimum capitatum

usually entire leaves, has a large range east of the Cascades. All the approximately 11 species in the genus are native to western North America, especially California. One other species, seaside woolly sunflower (*E. stoechadifolium*), ranges as far north as the coast of southern Oregon; this woody plant has densely clustered, rounded flower heads with short ray corollas.

Erysimum capitatum	Zones 3b to 9b	Brassicaceae

western or sand dune wallflower

This biennial or short-lived perennial produces a cluster or rosette of basal leaves and usually a single shoot up to 1m (3ft) tall. The basal leaves are linear or spatulate (spoon-shaped), up to 12cm (5in) long and 1cm (.5in) wide, with toothed to entire margins. The stem leaves are also narrow, and the foliage is sometimes grayish hairy. The inflorescence is a raceme and the flowers bloom on pedicels to 1cm (.5in) long. The showy flowers have four sepals, two of them saccate (sac-like) at the base. The four petals are yellow to orange or reddish and up to 2.5cm (1in) long, blooming from late spring to mid summer. The fruits are slender siliques (a dry fruit that splits open along two margins at maturity) up to 10cm (4in) long containing flattened seeds.

Cultivation. Full sun to light shade, and very well-drained, sandy or rocky soil. Tolerates drought but can take a bit of extra moisture if the soil is well drained. This is a beautiful plant for a sunny spot in gardens on either side of the Cascades, and excellent for a rocky bank or hillside. Plant it in the dry, sunny parts of the wildflower meadow, perennial border, or butterfly garden, where butterfly larvae can enjoy the foliage.

Propagation. Grow from seed collected in the fall. Seeds can be planted into flats of potting soil or directly into the garden, either in the fall or spring. The seeds will germinate when the weather warms in the spring. Established garden plants often self-sow.

Native Habitat and Range. On stony slopes and dry, sandy places at low to mid elevations from southern British Columbia, south in the Olympics and on both sides of the Cascades to California and Arizona, east through the Rocky Mountains and the Great Lakes region.

Notes. Sometimes included with *E. asperum* (rough or western wallflower or prairie rocket), a more eastern taxon, ranging west to Idaho. *Erysimum c.* var. *capitatum* is our most widespread variety; *E. c.* var. *perenne* occurs in Idaho and Oregon. *Erysimum* includes around 80 species of annual and perennial herbs native to the temperate regions of the Northern Hemisphere, mainly Europe and Asia. Around a dozen species are native to North America, around half of these to the Pacific Northwest. The perennial *E. arenicola* (Cascade wallflower), with lemon-yellow flowers, inhabits rock crevices, talus, and sandy sites at mid to fairly high elevations from southern British Columbia, south in the Olympic Mountains and through the Cascades of Oregon. Shy wallflower (*E. inconspicuum*), with small, pale yellow flowers, lives in dry soils east of the Cascades, ranging east through much of North America. Pale wallflower (*E. occidentale*) has pale to bright yellow flowers and lives in sagebrush habitats east of the Cascades in Washington, Oregon, and Idaho.

Erythronium   Liliaceae

fawn, trout, or avalanche lily, dog-tooth violet, adder's tongue

Erythronium is a genus of graceful, nodding lilies, much loved by hikers and gardeners. The pair of basal leaves is mottled with darker, purplish patches in many species (hence, fawn lily), and the corms develop a tooth-like projection (hence, dog-tooth violet). The showy flowers, which look nothing like violets, consist of six tepals or perianth segments (the sepals and petals are all similar in shape and color). Each flower has six stamens, and the stigmas have three deep or shallow lobes. The fruits are papery capsules. The genus encompasses around 25 species, nearly all native to temperate North America, especially California; about ten, some of them narrowly endemic, occur in the Pacific Northwest. Our native species bloom in early spring, usually becoming dormant by summer.

Propagation. Collect seeds as soon as the capsules have ripened and dried. Plant seeds in deep containers of potting soil soon after harvest, and allow them to spend the winter outside in cool, moist conditions for germination the following spring. The seedlings are tiny at first, and plants won't reach blooming size for at least the first few years. Small seedlings are easier to care for and protect from slugs if left in containers until the corms are large enough to plant out in autumn.

Erythronium grandiflorum   Zones 3b to 8b

yellow fawn, avalanche, or glacier lily

Yellow fawn lily produces annual leaves and shoots from an elongated corm. The basal leaves are oblong, up to 20cm (8in) long and solid green, with no mottling. The leafless flowering stem (scape) grows to 30cm (1ft) tall. The flowers are nodding, and the recurved (flared back) tepals vary from cream to light or deep yellow and are about 3cm (1.5in) long. The anthers vary from white or yellow to pink or purple. The slender style is tipped with three thick stigmas. Flowers bloom from early spring to late summer, depending on elevation. The cylindric to clavate (club-shaped) capsule can grow to 6cm (2.5in) long.

Cultivation. Full sun to part shade, and well-drained soil rich in organic matter that is moist early in the year. This species does not do well in low-elevation gardens; plants from a high-elevation seed source won't persist in lowland gardens, but gardeners east of the Cascades may have success with seed from foothills populations. Plant it in the wildflower meadow or near the edge of the woodland garden.

Erythronium grandiflorum

Erythronium hendersonii

Erythronium montanum

Erythronium oregonum

Native Habitat and Range. From moist meadows and avalanche tracks to mountain forests and sagebrush slopes at mid to high elevations from southern British Columbia, south through the mountains on both sides of the Cascades to northern California, east to Montana, Colorado, and New Mexico.

Notes. *Erythronium g.* ssp. *grandiflorum* occurs throughout the range; *E. g.* ssp *candidum*, with pale flowers, is restricted to eastern Washington and adjacent Idaho.

Erythronium hendersonii	Zones 7a to 9b

Henderson's fawn lily

This deciduous lily grows from a perennial corm. Plants usually produce a pair of basal leaves up to 20cm (8in) long and mottled with maroon. The leafless flowering stems (scapes) reach up to 40cm (16in) and bear one to six flowers from mid spring to mid summer. The tepals are lavender toward the tips and darker purple at the base. The anthers are purple, and the stigma has three shallow lobes. Erect, club-shaped (clavate) capsules follow the flowers.

Cultivation. Part shade or dappled light, and well-drained soil rich in organic matter. This is a lovely fawn lily for the woodland garden or shadier parts of the rock garden or wildflower meadow west of the Cascades.

Native Habitat and Range. In open woods and meadows at fairly low to mid elevations from southwestern Oregon to northwestern California.

Notes. Howell's fawn lily (*E. howellii*) is another endemic with a small native range, growing in forests at mid elevations in southwestern Oregon and northwestern California. Its leaves are mottled, and the tepals are white at the tips, streaked with yellow or orange at the base; the flowers become pinkish with age. Klamath fawn lily (*E. klamathense*) is native to open forest at high elevations in southern Oregon and northern California; its leaves are solid green, and the tepals are yellow at the base with white tips.

Erythronium montanum	Zones 4b to 7b

white avalanche lily

This perennial produces a pair of solid green, oblong leaves to 20cm (8in) long. The leafless flowering stems, to 25cm (10in) tall, are topped with one to three nodding flowers. The white tepals have a yellow band near the base and turn pinkish with age. The anthers are yellow, and the three stigma lobes curl back during flowering, from early summer to early fall, depending on elevation. The papery capsules are about 2.5cm (1in) long.

Cultivation. Full sun or part shade, and moist, well-drained soil. Another species for gardeners living at high elevations; it will not persist in lowland gardens.

Native Habitat and Range. In moist meadows and open woods at high elevations from southern British Columbia, south through the mountains of western Washington and Oregon.

Notes. *Erythronium citrinum* (lemon or cream fawn lily), in its var. *citrinum*, extends north into Oregon from northwestern California, living on brushy or wooded slopes at low to mid elevations; its leaves are mottled with maroon, and the tepals are creamy white with yellow or greenish banding at the base, becoming pinkish with age.

Erythronium oregonum	Zones 7a to 9b

white or giant fawn lily

This fawn lily produces a pair of leaves mottled with maroon from a perennial corm. The leaves are basal and can grow to 20cm (8in) long. The leafless flowering stems, to 30cm (1ft) tall, bear one to three nodding flowers. The flared tepals are white or slightly pinkish (especially as they dry) with a band of yellow on the inner base and often purplish on the outer surface of the tepal base. The anthers are white or light yellow, and the filaments widen at their bases, concealing the ovary. The long stigma lobes curl back with age. Flowers grow to 5cm (2in) long and bloom from early to late spring. The papery capsules are club-shaped (clavate) and up to 5cm (2in) long.

Cultivation. Full sun, part shade, or dappled light, and a moist, well-drained (even rocky) soil with a good amount of compost or mulch. This fawn lily is quite cooperative in woodland gardens west of the Cascades and often self-sows, forming showy colonies over time. Lovely with other spring-blooming bulbs, among ferns in the woodland garden, planted in an oak grove, or in the rock garden. May need protection from slugs.

Native Habitat and Range. In moist woods and rocky prairies at low elevations west of the Cascades from southwestern British Columbia south to northwestern California.

Notes. *Erythronium o.* ssp. *oregonum* occupies the northern parts of the range.

Erythronium revolutum	Zones 7b to 9b

pink or coast fawn lily

Two green leaves with maroon mottling grow from the perennial corms, reaching up to 18cm (7in) in length. One (sometimes more) nodding flowers bloom on scapes to 30cm (1ft) tall. The tepals are about 4cm (1.5in) long and flare back with age. The flowers are deep pink with yellow banding at the bases of the tepals; the yellow anthers and flattened filaments closely surround the ovary, style, and stigma branches. Flowers bloom from mid to late spring, and the fruits are papery, club-shaped (clavate) capsules.

Cultivation. Shade to full sun, and soil with a high organic content. Tolerates ground that is boggy, at least in early spring, but does best in soil with better drainage, eventually forming showy drifts. Allow plants to dry out later in the summer, when they become dormant. Lovely in the open parts of the woodland or rock garden west of the Cascades; grow with *E. oregonum* for a bicolor spring display.

Native Habitat and Range. Near streambanks, open woods, and meadows, often where boggy in spring, at low elevations west of the Cascades from southwestern British Columbia south to northwestern California; especially common near the Oregon coast.

Notes. Listed as sensitive in Washington. Cultivars include 'White Beauty' (with white flowers) and 'Pink Beauty' (solid pink tepals, with no yellow banding at the base). Various groups of indigenous people ate the scaly corms of this and other species of fawn lily.

Eschscholzia californica	Zones 3b to 9b	Papaveraceae

California poppy

This perennial develops one or more stems up to 50cm (20in) tall from a slender taproot. The ferny foliage is several times compound into narrow segments and is glaucous, bluish with a waxy coating. The flowers bloom on peduncles to 20cm (8in) from late spring to early fall. Each bloom has four petals up to 4cm (1.5in) long, usually bright orange, but varying to yellow or creamy white. Seeds ripen in linear, ribbed capsules to 6cm (2.5in) long.

Cultivation. Full sun or light shade, and moist to rather dry soil. A little extra water will prolong the blooming season but is not necessary. This is an excellent self-seeding perennial for a sunny wildflower meadow, dry bank, or parking area. It is sometimes grown as an annual where winters are cold.

Erythronium revolutum

Eschscholzia californica

Eupatoriadelphus maculatus

Propagation. Easy from seed. Collect seeds from the capsules in the summer or fall, and sow into containers or directly into the garden in the spring. Seeds germinate easily, and established plants will likely self-sow.

Native Habitat and Range. In fields, clearings, and roadsides at low elevations, from the Columbia River Gorge, south to southern California.

Notes. Yes, California poppy is easy. It has escaped cultivation, and its seeds seem to be included in every "wildflower" mix, but it's a beautiful plant and such lovely orange flowers are hard to resist. Many cultivars are available—some doubles, others with bronzy foliage, and in flower colors suggested by such names as 'Carmine King', 'Apricot Flambeau', 'Inferno', 'Cherry Ripe', 'Purple Cap', and 'Milky White'. All the approximately ten species in the genus are native to western North America; most are annuals native to California, with *E. caespitosa* (tufted poppy) ranging as far north as southern Oregon.

Eupatoriadelphus maculatus	Zones 3b to 9a	Asteraceae

spotted Joe Pye weed

This robust perennial produces shoots to 2m (6ft) from fibrous roots. The leaves are arranged in whorls of three or four at each node; they have short petioles, and the lance-shaped blades grow to 20cm (8in) long with sharply toothed margins. The small flowering heads are arranged into dense, flat-topped clusters. Each head has only disk florets, no rays. The involucral bracts surrounding each head are usually purplish, and the corollas of the florets are also purple. Flowers bloom from mid summer to early fall, and the fruits are small achenes topped with a pappus (modified calyx) of thin bristles.

Cultivation. Full sun or light shade, and moist to rather wet soil with lots of compost. This large, bold species is quite popular as an ornamental, in part for its late-season bloom, and an excellent nectar plant for the butterfly garden. Plant it with other tall perennials or near the edge of a sunny pond or bog.

Propagation. Divide rooted clumps in early to late spring. Plants can also be grown from seed harvested from the small heads in the fall and planted outside during fall or winter for germination the following spring.

Native Habitat and Range. In wetlands and other open, swampy places at low to mid elevations, from the east coast west through much of North America to Idaho and southwestern British Columbia, and dipping into adjacent northwestern Washington, south to Utah, and New Mexico.

Notes. Sometimes classified as *Eupatorium maculatum*. *Eupatoriadelphus maculatus* var. *bruneri* is the only variety that enters the Pacific Northwest. Another lovely but smaller rhizomatous perennial, *Ageratina occidentalis* (*Eupatorium occidentale*; western snakeroot), grows to about 60cm (2ft) in rocky places at low to fairly high elevations from the east slope of the Washington Cascades east to Idaho, and through southern Oregon to California, Nevada, and Utah; its leaves are broadly oval or deltoid (triangular), and the clusters of pink to reddish purple flower heads bloom from early to late summer. Species of *Brickellia* have a similar look: herbaceous or shrubby sunflowers with flowering heads composed of creamy to pinkish disk florets. Tasselflower brickellbush (*B. grandiflora*), littleleaf brickellbush (*B. microphylla*), Mojave brickellbush (*B. oblongifolia*), and California brickellbush (*B. californica*) all occur in our area, usually in rocky, dry habitats east of the Cascades.

Festuca idahoensis

| ***Festuca idahoensis*** | Zones 3b to 9b | Poaceae |

Idaho fescue

This densely tufted perennial grass produces a basal cluster of very slender leaves with blades to 10cm (4in) long and flowering shoots up to 1m (3ft) tall. The small flowers (florets) are grouped into spikelets, the typical unit of the grass inflorescence. Two short bracts, the glumes, subtend each spikelet, and each spikelet is made up of about six florets. The inflorescence is a narrow panicle with spikelets on slender branches. Each floret is further enclosed in its own pair of bracts, the lemma and the palea. Each lemma usually has an awn, a short bristle. The flowers bloom from late spring to mid summer, and the fruit is a grain, or caryopsis.

Cultivation. Full sun or part shade, and well-drained, moist to rather dry, rocky soil. This graceful bunchgrass would suit the wildflower meadow, perennial bed, or drought-tolerant wildlife garden on either side of the Cascades. Often self-sows.

Propagation. Most easy from seed. Collect seeds in the late summer, plant them in the fall, either directly into the garden or into flats of potting soil, and leave them outside over winter for germination in spring.

Native Habitat and Range. In rather dry grasslands, rocky slopes, and arid sagebrush plains at low to high elevations from southern British Columbia, south to northern California, and east through the Rocky Mountains.

Notes. *Festuca i.* ssp. *idahoensis* has a broad range, from eastern Washington to Idaho and the Rocky Mountains, south to Arizona and New Mexico. *Festuca i.* ssp. *roemeri* (*F. roemeri*; Roemer's fescue) has a more limited range, mainly west of the Cascades to northwestern California. The approximately 100 species of *Festuca* are widespread through the temperate parts of the world.

of the 30 some native to North America, half occur in the Pacific Northwest, where many are highly valued as pasture or range grasses. Rocky Mountain fescue (*F. saximontana*), bearded fescue (*F. subulata*), and alpine fescue (*F. brachyphylla*) have large ranges in the west. Western fescue (*F. occidentalis*) forms low tufts of hair-like basal leaves and long, drooping inflorescences; it lives on rocky slopes and meadows, often at low elevations, throughout our area. Red fescue (*F. rubra*) lives in various habitats from coastal marshes and dunes to mountain forests and meadows throughout much of North America. *Bromus* is a related genus; species native to our area include Columbia brome (*B. vulgaris*), Alaska brome (*B. sitchensis*), and Pacific brome (*B. pacificus*), all of which lack rhizomes and tend to form small clumps. The rhizomatous Pumpelly's brome (*B. inermis* ssp. *pumpellianus*) also occurs in our area.

Fragaria	Rosaceae

strawberry

The well-known genus *Fragaria* encompasses approximately a dozen species, most of them native to the temperate parts of the Northern Hemisphere but sometimes extending further south. All three of the wide-ranging North American species occur in our area. With five petals, five sepals, and many stamens, strawberry flowers are similar to many other members of the rose family. Strawberries are sometimes called accessory fruits because some structure other than the actual fruit contributes to its ripened state. The juicy, edible part we think of as the strawberry is not a berry but an enlarged receptacle. The true fruits are actually the tiny, brown achenes; each one has a dry fruit (ovary) wall topped by a style and stigma, where pollination took place. Inside each little achene is a single seed. In some species, the achenes are partly sunken into small pits in the fleshy receptacle. Plants have basal leaves divided into three leaflets (ternate). New plantlets are formed at the nodes of stolons, slender stems that grow across the ground surface. In addition to having sweet fruits, the leaves of strawberries possess medicinal properties.

Propagation. Easiest by removing the plantlets that form along the stolons in the early spring or late summer. Strawberries can also be grown from seed. Remove the tiny, brown achenes from the fleshy receptacle and plant them into flats of potting soil in the fall; leave the flats outside to stratify over the winter. Germination occurs after the weather warms in the spring.

Fragaria chiloensis	Zones 6a to 9b

beach strawberry

This trailing perennial develops reddish stolons that form new plants as they spread along the ground. The leaves are generally evergreen, often turning red in the winter; they grow in basal clusters on petioles to 10cm (4in) long. Each leaf consists of three dark green, leathery leaflets to 4cm (1.5in) long with serrated margins. The flowering stems are leafless and grow to 10cm (4in) long, producing five to 15 flowers. The flowers are about 3cm (1.5in) across with five showy, white petals, blooming from mid spring to early summer. The tasty strawberries are about 1.5cm (.5in) across.

Cultivation. Full sun to light shade, and well-drained soil. Excellent as a groundcover between paving stones or near a garden path, or tucked into the crevices of a stone wall, and makes an attractive sand-binder for gardens near the beach. Can be aggressive.

Native Habitat and Range. On seaside bluffs and sand dunes near the coast and island shores from Alaska south to California, Hawaii, and the coast of South America.

Fragaria chiloensis

Fragaria vesca (left) and F. virginiana

Notes. This species is the source of showy cultivars and a parent to some hybrid strawberries. *Fragaria c.* ssp. *pacifica* is the taxon native to northwestern beaches. *Fragaria* ×*ananassa* is a naturally occurring hybrid between *F. chiloensis* and *F. vesca*.

Fragaria vesca	Zones 3b to 9b

woodland strawberry

This deciduous perennial produces extensive stolons and flowering shoots from rosettes of basal leaves. The stems and petioles are greenish or faintly reddish and pubescent, with fine hairs. The petioles of the basal leaves are up to 10cm (4in) long, and the three leaflets are around 6cm (2.5in). The leaflets are broadly elliptic and coarsely toothed, with the tooth at the tip of the leaflet at least as long as the others. The leaflet blades tend to be yellow-green (not bluish) and veiny, the blade tissue sometimes bulging slightly between the larger veins. Three to 11 flowers bloom in an open cluster from mid spring to early summer. The five petals are white to pale pink and about 1cm (.5in) long. The small, sweet strawberries are about 1cm (.5in) across.

Cultivation. Full sun to part shade or dappled light, and moist, well drained soil. This strawberry is an attractive deciduous carpet for openings in the woodland garden, near the path in the wildflower meadow, or under taller species in the perennial bed.

Native Habitat and Range. In well-drained meadows, moist woods, and along streambanks at low to fairly high elevations throughout much of North America; Europe.

Notes. *Fragaria v.* ssp. *bracteata* occurs throughout the west. *F. v.* ssp. *californica* ranges into Oregon from California.

Fragaria virginiana

Fragaria virginiana	Zones 3b to 9b

wild or Virginia strawberry

This deciduous (to somewhat evergreen) perennial produces greenish or slightly reddish stolons and flowering stems from small crowns with clusters of basal leaves. The petioles of the leaves can grow to 15cm (6in) long. Leaves are divided into three leaflets (ternate), and each leaflet can grow to 7cm (3in) long. The leaflets are obovate (oval, but widest toward the tip) in shape, thick in texture, and coarsely toothed, with the terminal tooth of each leaflet generally shorter than the others. The leaflets are blue-green and glaucous, with a waxy, whitish coating on the upper surface, and usually silky-haired beneath, turning deep red in fall. Two to 15 flowers bloom in open inflorescences that are usually a bit shorter than the leaves. The petals are white, sometimes pinkish, and the flowers are about 2cm (1in) across, blooming from late spring to late summer. The sweet strawberries are about 1cm (.5in) across.

Cultivation. Full sun to part shade or dappled light, and moist, well-drained soil. This strawberry has attractive, bluish foliage, especially in sunnier sites. It makes a fine groundcover for the edge of the woodland garden, among paving stones, or in perennial borders. Plant it in the sandy or gravelly parts of the wildflower meadow.

Native Habitat and Range. In open woods, near streambanks and rocky or sandy meadows at low to fairly high elevations from Alaska south on both sides of the Cascades to California and east across most of North America.

Notes. *Fragaria v*. ssp. *platypetala* is widespread throughout our area and much of the west; *F. v*. ssp. *glauca* ranges west to Washington and Idaho from the Rocky Mountains and Great Plains.

Fritillaria   Liliaceae

fritillary, checker lily

Fritillaria includes more than 50 species native to temperate parts of western North America, Europe, Asia, and northern Africa; around 20 species occur in North America, around eight in the Pacific Northwest. These small lilies produce narrow leaves and nodding flowers from perennial bulbs. The flowers have three sepals and three petals (or, because they are all similar and petaloid, six tepals or perianth segments). Each flower has six stamens and produces a three-parted capsule containing many flat seeds. Many species produce edible bulbs and bulblets that were eaten by indigenous people.

Propagation. Not difficult, but a bit of patience is required. Fritillaries should be grown from seed and never be dug from the wild. Collect seeds in the summer after the capsules have dried, plant them soon after harvest into deep containers of well-drained soil, and leave them outside to stratify in the cold, moist winter weather for germination in the spring. As with most lilies, plants will take a few years to reach flowering size and will need protection from slugs in west-side gardens. Older bulbs will produce small bulblets around their bases; these can be separated and planted in late summer when plants are dormant, but this should be done only with plants originally grown from seed.

Fritillaria affinis   Zones 5a to 9b

checker or chocolate lily, rice root, mission bells

This bulbous perennial produces a leafy flowering stem to 1m (3ft) tall. The linear leaves are arranged in whorls on the lower part of the stem, becoming scattered toward the top. The longest leaves are 15cm (6in) long and 2.5cm (1in) wide. One to five nodding, bell-shaped flowers bloom at the top of the stem from mid spring to early summer. The six tepals (petals and sepals) are 3cm (1.5in) long and greenish purple with yellowish mottling. The fruits are angled, winged capsules.

Cultivation. Full sun, part shade, or dappled light, and well-drained, moist soil rich in organic matter. This graceful lily adds subtle beauty to the shade or woodland garden and can be planted with other spring bulbs. Does well under deciduous trees or in the rock garden.

Native Habitat and Range. In meadows and open woods from lowlands to mid elevations, southern British Columbia, south near the coast and west slope of the Cascades to southern California, less common east of the Cascades to northern Idaho.

Notes. Sometimes classified as *F. lanceolata*. *Fritillaria a.* var. *affinis* spans most of the range. *Fritillaria atropurpurea* (spotted fritillary) has greenish brown flowers with yellowish mottling; it occurs in open forests, grassy and rocky sites at mid to high elevations from central Oregon, east across Idaho to the Dakotas, Nebraska, Colorado, and Arizona. *Fritillaria camschatcensis* (Kamchatka fritillary, black lily, northern rice root) grows at low to fairly high elevations from coastal Alaska, south, sporadically to western Washington (where it is listed as sensitive) and northwestern Oregon, a plant of moist meadows, streambanks, and salt marshes, it grows to about 60cm (2ft) tall, with whorled leaves and bronzy, purple-brown flowers.

Fritillaria pudica   Zones 5a to 7a

yellow bells

This diminutive bulbous perennial develops a flowering stem up to 20cm (8in) tall. Each stem has two (sometimes more) linear leaves to 15cm (6in) long and 1cm (.5in) wide. The nodding flowers are usually solitary, to 2.5cm (1in) long; the tepals are yellow, sometimes purplish at the

Fritillaria affinis

Fritillaria pudica

base, turning reddish as they age. Angled, winged capsules follow the flowers, which bloom from early spring to early summer.

Cultivation. Full sun to light shade, and well-drained, rocky or gravelly soil. This delicate lily is for gardeners east of the Cascades; it usually fails on the wetter west side. Site it in the rock garden or dry meadow, or in clearings among sagebrush and other drought-tolerant natives.

Native Habitat and Range. In arid sagebrush-steppe and open forests east of the Cascades from British Columbia south to northern California, east to Alberta, Idaho, Montana, Utah, Wyoming, and Colorado.

Notes. What with habitat destruction and unethical bulb-digging, this wide-ranging little plant is far less common than it once was, and wild populations should be protected. Siskiyou fritillary (*F. glauca*) has yellowish flowers; it lives in rocky habitats, often at high elevations in the mountains of southwestern Oregon and northwestern California.

Fritillaria recurva	Zones 6a to 9b

scarlet fritillary

This beautiful lily produces a stem up to 60cm (2ft) tall from a perennial bulb. The linear leaves grow to 10cm (4in) and are arranged in whorls on the lower part of the stem, scattered toward the top. One to four nodding, narrowly bell-shaped flowers bloom from early spring to mid summer. The scarlet tepals are curved back at the tips and reach 3.5cm (1.5in) in length; they are spotted with yellow on the inside and purplish on the outside. The fruits are angled, winged capsules.

Cultivation. Full sun to part shade, and well-drained soil. A stunning lily for the rock garden, woodland edge, or the dappled light under an open tree canopy.

Native Habitat and Range. In dry, open woods and brushy areas at low to mid elevations,

Fritillaria recurva

Gaillardia aristata

from southwestern Oregon to northern California and a bit of adjacent Nevada.

Notes. Gentner's fritillary (*F. gentneri*) has similar purplish red flowers, but the tepals are not curved back at the tips; it is endemic to southwestern Oregon and is listed as endangered.

Gaillardia aristata	Zones 3b to 9b	Asteraceae

common blanketflower

This herbaceous perennial grows from a slender taproot and produces one to several stems, simple or with a few branches, to 60cm (2ft) or a bit taller. The leaves are narrowly oblanceolate (lance-shaped, but widest toward the tip) to oblong, with entire, toothed or lobed margins; they are hairy (pubescent) and usually grow to 10cm (4in) long. Each shoot produces one or a few flowering heads with both ray and disk florets. The small disk florets have purple or reddish corollas. Each head has around a dozen ray florets with broad corollas to 3.5cm (1.5in) long, each with three lobes at the tip. The ray corollas are mainly yellow, but usually purple or reddish at the base. Flowers bloom from late spring to early fall. The hairy achenes have a pappus (modified calyx) of long scales.

Cultivation. Full sun, and moist to rather dry soil. With its long bloom period, this species is frequently included in perennial borders throughout the Pacific Northwest. It is an excellent addition to the relatively dry parts of the wildflower meadow or butterfly garden. Established plants often self-sow.

Propagation. Easiest from seed collected in the fall and either planted outside soon after harvest, or stored in cool, dry conditions for spring planting. Alternatively, take cuttings of basal shoots in mid spring, treat with hormones, and set in pumice or some other medium to form roots.

Native Habitat and Range. In rather dry meadows, prairies, and other open places at low to mid elevations from British Columbia, south to central Oregon, mainly east of the Cascades, south to Utah and Colorado, east to Saskatchewan and South Dakota, possibly introduced further east.

Notes. Nearly all the approximately 12 species of *Gaillardia* are native to North America, from northern Mexico to southern Canada; this the only species that occurs in the Pacific Northwest. It is the parent, along with *G. pulchella* (firewheel), of *G. ×grandiflora* and its many popular cultivars.

Galium oreganum	Zones 5b to 9b	Rubiaceae

Oregon bedstraw

This deciduous perennial produces single, angled stems up to 40cm (16in) tall from slender, spreading rhizomes. The leaves are arranged in several whorls up the stem, four to each whorl; they are oval to elliptic and up to 5cm (2in) long. The leaves have firm, rough hairs along the margins and sometimes along the veins. Several small flowers bloom in branched clusters at the stem tips and also from the axils of the upper leaves. The tiny flowers are greenish white or yellowish, have four petal lobes, and bloom from early to late summer. The fruits are dry and two-lobed, splitting into two single-seeded halves at maturity; they are covered with hooked bristles, aiding in dispersal by fur or socks.

Cultivation. Full sun to part shade or dappled light, and moist soil. An airy addition to the sunny perennial bed or wildflower meadow. Plant it in clearings or at the edge of the woodland garden.

Propagation. Grow from seed collected in the fall and planted into containers or directly into the garden in the fall or spring. Seeds will begin to germinate when the weather warms. Plants can also be grown from divisions of the slender rhizomes made in the fall or spring.

Native Habitat and Range. In moist woods and meadows at low to fairly high elevations from the Cascades of northern Washington, west to the coast and south through western Oregon to the northwestern edge of California.

Notes. Boreal bedstraw (*G. kamtschaticum*) is similar in form, dipping south into Washington and some of the eastern states. *Galium boreale* (northern bedstraw) is taller, to 80cm (2.5ft), with four narrow leaves per node and many, tiny white or creamy flowers making a showy display all summer; it occurs in a variety of moist habitats at low to high elevations in our area and through much of the continent and other parts of the Northern Hemisphere. *Galium* includes some 300 species, widely distributed, mainly in temperate regions of the world; more than 60 are native to North America, almost 20 to the Pacific Northwest.

Gentiana	Gentianaceae

gentian

Gentians are herbaceous, mostly perennial plants, known for their intensely blue flowers. They have simple, opposite leaves, a five-lobed calyx, and corollas composed of five fused petals that are often folded or pleated between the lobes. The fruits are one-chambered capsules with many small seeds. The genus includes upward of 200 species native to the temperate and arctic regions of the planet; around 30 occur in North America, with fewer than a dozen of these native to the Pacific Northwest. Many gentians are notoriously difficult rock garden species, but the lovely flowers are hard to resist.

Propagation. Difficult but can be grown from seed. Collect seeds in mid to late fall and plant them outside immediately, either in containers or directly into the garden. The cold, moist winter weather will help break their dormancy, as will treating seeds with gibberellic acid. Keep seeds

Galium oreganum

Gentiana calycosa

moist or wet, for germination the following spring. Plants can also be propagated from basal cuttings made from shoots as they begin to grow in the spring, but this should be done only with plants originally grown from seed.

Gentiana calycosa	Zones 3b to 8a

mountain bog or explorer's gentian

This gentian produces shoots from fleshy roots. Clusters of stems with up to nine pairs of opposite, sessile (lacking a petiole), ovate leaves to 2.5cm (1in) long clasp the stems. The unbranched shoots grow to 30cm (1ft) tall, usually topped with a single flower. The sepals are fused to form a lobed calyx tube. The petals are also fused into a broadly tubular corolla up to 4cm (1.5in) long. The five free petal lobes usually have pointed tips, and the pleats between lobes are fringed. The deep blue corollas are spotted or streaked with green. Flowers bloom from mid summer to mid fall, and many small seeds ripen in capsules.

Cultivation. Full sun to part shade, and well-drained but moist to wet soil. If conditions resembling a cool mountain stream or moist, rocky meadow can be created in the garden, the plants may cooperate. A perennial for the determined, patient gardener.

Native Habitat and Range. Along streams, in wet meadows and bogs at mid to high elevations in the mountains from British Columbia, south in the Cascade and Olympic Mountains to California and east to the Rocky Mountains.

Notes. *Gentiana douglasiana* (swamp gentian) and *G. glauca* (pale gentian) are both rare species of alpine bogs and tundra that range south to Washington. Pleated gentian (*G. affinis*) is more widespread, a locally common beauty of moist meadows from fairly low to mid elevations, mainly east of the Cascades.

Gentiana sceptrum

Geranium viscosissimum

Gentiana sceptrum   Zones 6a to 9b

king's or king's scepter gentian

The thick fleshy roots of this gentian usually produce many stems up to 1m (3ft) tall, each bearing ten to 15 pairs of opposite, lance-shaped leaves up to 6cm (2.5in) long, with the largest leaves toward the top of the stem. A cluster of flowers is typically borne on each shoot. The sepals are fused to form a calyx tube with long lobes. The tubular corollas grow to 4cm (1.5in) long and are blue, often streaked with green. The five free petal lobes have pointed tips, and the pleats in the sinuses between the lobes are flattened at the top. Flowers bloom from mid summer to early fall, and many small seeds ripen in capsules.

Cultivation. Full sun to part shade, and wet soil. The flowers of this species are not as intensely blue as those of others, but this plant is better adapted to low elevations. It makes an uncommon and delightful addition to the wet corner of the wildflower meadow, sunny pond margin, or bog garden.

Native Habitat and Range. In wet meadows, bogs, and lake shores at low to mid elevations from British Columbia, south to northern California, from the west slope of the Cascades to the coast.

Notes. *Gentiana platypetala* (broadpetal gentian) is a northern species of lakeshores, meadows, and rocky slopes; it ranges from coastal Alaska, south to British Columbia. More widely distributed, in high mountain meadows and bogs, is pygmy gentian (*G. prostrata*); alpine gentian (*G. newberryi*) occurs in similar high-elevation habitats but has a smaller range in southern Oregon and northern California.

Geranium viscosissimum Zones 3b to 9a Geraniaceae

sticky purple geranium or cranesbill

This perennial produces one or a few stems that can approach 1m (3ft) in height from a simple crown. The plants are hairy and glandular, especially the inflorescence. The leaves are deeply palmate, with cuneate (wedge-shaped), sharply toothed lobes. The blades are up to 12cm (5in) wide and set on long, hairy petioles. The inflorescences branch into few-flowered clusters, and the flowers have five deep pink to purplish or lavender petals with darker veins, up to 2cm (1in) long, blooming from late spring to late summer. The fruits are capsule-like, with a ring of loosely connected carpels (the units of the ovary, like the sections of an orange), each with an elongated style, circling a narrow receptacle, this beaked stylar column, which looks like a crane's bill, grows to 5cm (2in) long. On maturity, the styles arch away from the receptacle, breaking apart explosively into individual carpels, each containing one or two seeds.

Cultivation. Full sun to part shade, and well-drained, moist to rather dry soil. This is an attractive, summer-blooming plant for the wildflower meadow, perennial bed, or sunny woodland clearing. Can be tried on the west side, in a sunny, sandy part of the garden, but is probably easier east of the Cascades.

Propagation. Collect seeds in late summer or early fall, capturing them before the fruits explode. Just before planting, in the winter, place seeds in a dish and pour hot (just below boiling) water over them; allow them to cool and then plant into flats of potting soil or directly into the garden. Leave the planted seeds outside to stratify in the cold weather for a month or so, for germination when the weather warms in the spring. Larger plants can be propagated from cuttings made at the bases of the stems during the spring or later in the growing season; treat the cuttings with rooting hormones, set them into pumice or some other medium, and keep them humid until roots form.

Native Habitat and Range. In open woods and meadows at low to fairly high elevations east of the Cascades from British Columbia, south to northern California and east to Saskatchewan, South Dakota, Colorado, and New Mexico.

Notes. *Geranium v.* var. *viscosissimum* is hairy and glandular; *G. v.* var. *incisum* is less hairy, often lacks glands, and ranges further south. A better choice for west-side gardens is Oregon geranium (*G. oreganum*). This species is slightly shorter, to about 80cm (2.5ft), with similarly sized showy red-purple flowers from late spring to mid summer; it lives in meadows and woodlands west of the Cascades from central Washington to northern California. Richardson's geranium (*G. richardsonii*) is another native perennial with stems to about 80cm (2.5ft) tall and white or pale pink flowers with purplish veins, blooming from early to late summer; this species lives in partly shaded, rather moist sites at mid to fairly high elevations, mainly east of the Cascades from southern British Columbia, south and east through the Rocky Mountains. The perennial *G. erianthum* (woolly or northern geranium), with pinkish purple or bluish flowers, lives in moist places in Alaska and British Columbia. There are more than 200 species of geraniums native to temperate regions throughout the world, with a few of the perennial species widely cultivated; only around a dozen species are native to North America, half of these occurring in the Pacific Northwest.

Geum Rosaceae

avens

Geum encompasses approximately 50 species, most of them native to temperate or arctic regions of the Northern Hemisphere; around a dozen species are native to North America, more than half to the Pacific Northwest. Plants have pinnately divided leaves with the basal largest the

Geum macrophyllum

Geum triflorum

largest. The flowers have five sepals, five petals, and many stamens. The fruits are single-seeded achenes, sometimes with an elongated, plumose style that makes the seed heads as decorative as the flowers.

Propagation. Grow from seed planted outside in the fall and left to chill over winter. Seeds should germinate when the weather warms in the spring. Plants can also be propagated from divisions of the clumps made in mid spring or late summer.

Geum macrophyllum	Zones 5a to 9b

Oregon or large-leaved avens

This herbaceous perennial grows from a short rhizome. The basal leaves are lyrate-pinnatifid, with a large, rounded leaflet at the tip of the leaf and smaller leaflets along the midrib (rachis). They grow to 30cm (1ft) long. The flowering stems can reach 1m (3ft). Several flowers with five bright yellow petals, about 2cm (1in) across, bloom at the stem tips from mid spring to late summer. The fruits consist of many small achenes, each with a persistent style that is bent at the tip; this hooked style serves as an effective dispersal mechanism, and seeds are likely to be carried away by the fur of animals and the clothing of gardeners.

Cultivation. Full sun to full shade, and moist soil. This is a good plant for the far corners of the woodland garden or for a moist wildflower meadow or streambank. Aggressive, especially west of the Cascades, but it does compete with weeds. Somewhat harsher conditions, such as the dry shade under big conifers, will keep it from becoming too rampant. Often self-sows.

Native Habitat and Range. Near streams, in meadows and moist woods at low to fairly high elevations, Alaska south to California and Mexico, east to New Mexico and Colorado, through Canada to the Great Lakes and Nova Scotia; Asia.

Notes. *Geum m.* var. *macrophyllum* has leaflets with shallow lobes and teeth; in our area, it is common west of the Cascades, ranging from Alaska to California and east to southeastern British Columbia and western Montana. *Geum m.* var. *perincisum*, with deeply lobed leaves with larger teeth, occurs from Alaska south, usually east of the Cascade crest, to California and east. Yellow avens (*G. aleppicum*) grows in damp woods and near streams east of the Cascades from British Columbia south to California, east through the Rocky Mountains and northeastern North America; caltha-leaved avens (*G. calthifolium*) also has yellow flowers and lives in moist or wet areas in Alaska and British Columbia. Yellow-flowered *G. rossii* (Ross' avens) lives in scree and stony meadows in arctic or high mountain habitats: *G. r.* var. *rossii* occurs in northern Asia, Alaska, and the Yukon, south into British Columbia; *G. r.* var. *depressum* is endemic to the Wenatchee Mountains of north central Washington, and *G. r.* var. *turbinatum* is an alpine plant of the Rocky Mountains, disjunct in the Wallowa Mountains of northeastern Oregon.

Geum triflorum	Zones 4a to 9b

prairie smoke, old man's whiskers

This perennial herb grows from thick rhizomes and forms clumps to 30cm (1ft) across. The leaves are mainly basal and usually grayish with long hairs. The blades are pinnately compound with deeply toothed leaflets, reaching 15cm (6in) in length. Flowering stems grow to 30cm (1ft) and bear clusters of one to nine blooms, usually in groups of three. Each nodding flower has a cup-shaped, reddish to yellow, purple-veined calyx of five fused sepals about 2cm (1in) long. The five small petals vary from creamy yellow to pinkish or purplish, and the flowers bloom from mid spring to late summer. As the achenes ripen, the graceful, plumose styles lengthen to 5cm (2in), and the old flowers turn upright, presenting a fluffy cluster of achenes, the source of the common names.

Cultivation. Full sun or light shade, and well-drained, moist to rather dry soil. This plant is as attractive in fruit as it is in flower, and with a little extra water, it will bloom for much of the season. A beautiful addition to the rock garden, sunny perennial border, or wildflower meadow on either side of the Cascades.

Native Habitat and Range. Rather dry meadows, talus, and moister spots in areas often dominated by sagebrush at fairly low to high elevations, from British Columbia south, mainly east of the Cascades to the Sierra Nevada, east through Canada to Newfoundland, south to Arizona, New Mexico, Illinois, and New York.

Notes. *Geum t.* var. *campanulatum* has especially long petals and a deciduous style tip; it is scattered in Washington and Oregon. Overlapping this taxon is the highly variable *G. t.* var. *ciliatum*, with short petals and a deciduous style tip; it occurs east of the Cascades, from British Columbia to California, and east through the Rocky Mountains. *Geum rivale* (purple avens) is a similar species that inhabits bogs, wet meadows, and lakeshores in British Columbia and north central Washington, east across Canada and the northern states, and through the Rocky Mountains.

Glehnia littoralis	Zones 6b to 9b	Apiaceae

beach silvertop, beach-carrot

This low, stout perennial grows from a woody taproot. The large, thick, prostrate leaves develop on petioles buried beneath the ground surface. The blades are once or twice divided into sets to three (ternate) lobed leaflets. The leaflets are broadly rounded, up to 7cm (3in) long with lobed or coarsely toothed margins. The stout peduncles grow no longer than 10cm (4in) and are tipped by the five to 13 rays of the umbel, each about 4cm (1.5in) long. At the tip of each ray a dense

Glehnia littoralis

Goodyera oblongifolia

cluster of small white flowers blooms from early to mid summer. The fruits are dry, rounded schizocarps, with longitudinal ribs expanded into wings.

Cultivation. Full sun or light shade, and well-drained, sandy soil. This is an unusual perennial for dunes near the beach, and perhaps for sandy soils away from the coast. It is bold but low-growing, and the winged fruits are at least as attractive as the flowers.

Propagation. Grow from seed collected in late summer and planted outside in the fall under cool, moist conditions. Seeds can probably be planted in the spring, but they may not store well and could lose some viability. Plant seeds of this taprooted species directly into the garden or into deep containers, where seedlings will have room to grow until transplanted.

Native Habitat and Range. Scattered on sandy beaches and dunes along the coast from Alaska south to northern California; Asia.

Notes. This is the only species in the genus, and our subspecies, *G. l.* ssp. *leiocarpa* (*G. leiocarpa*) grows in the same coastal habitats in eastern Asia.

Goodyera oblongifolia	Zones 3b to 9b	Orchidaceae

western rattlesnake plantain

Unlike most orchids, western rattlesnake plantain is rhizomatous but slow-growing, producing rosettes of leaves and flowering stems from short rhizomes. Flowers bloom from mid to late summer, but the evergreen leaves are the most interesting feature of this perennial. The leaves are thick and dark green, and usually striped and mottled with white, especially along the midrib; the blades are ovate to elliptic, about 7cm (3in) long, tapered to broad petioles. The leafless flowering stems (scapes) grow to 12cm (5in) tall, producing a spike crowded with small greenish white flowers. The upper sepal along with the two lateral petals are fused to form a hood over the lip. The inferior ovary ripens into a capsule, about 1cm (.5in) long, containing many tiny seeds.

Cultivation. Part to full shade or dappled light, and well-drained, moist but not wet soil high in humus. Often grows in rather dry conifer needles and forest duff. This is a charming orchid for the shade or woodland garden; plant it near the trail or bench with other small shade-lovers.

Propagation. Possible from seed collected from the capsules as soon as they begin to ripen. Gather a bit of native soil from the base of the plant as well. Soon after harvesting, mix the tiny seeds with the sample of soil and some mycorrhizal spores, and sprinkle the mix onto the surface of moist, fine, well-drained potting soil. Protect planted containers; keep them moist, and leave them outside. With luck, some seeds will germinate and the seedlings will survive. Alternatively, the short rhizomes can be divided in the spring, but this should be done only with plants grown from seed or rescued from destruction.

Native Habitat and Range. Among mosses and in the humus of rather dry to moist, open to dense forests at low to mid elevations from Alaska, east across much of Canada, and south through most of the west to California and New Mexico, also south to the Great Lakes and Maine.

Notes. *Goodyera* includes a couple of dozen species, most native to the chilly parts of the Northern Hemisphere. Four are widespread in North America, one other, *G. repens* (lesser rattle-snake plantain), occurs in the Pacific Northwest, in Alaska and British Columbia, east across Canada and the northern United States.

Grindelia stricta	Zones 6a to 9b	Asteraceae

coastal or Oregon gumweed or resinweed

This perennial produces stout branches up to 80cm (2.5ft) from a taproot. The plants vary in hairiness, and the leaves are sometimes toothed. Basal leaves are oblanceolate (lance-shaped, but widest toward the tip) and 30cm (1ft) or longer, by up to 4cm (1.5in) wide. The stem leaves are smaller, becoming sessile (lacking a petiole) and clasping the stem. Many slender, curved involucral bracts, usually with a resinous surface, surround the flowering heads. The ray and disk florets are both present, their corollas bright yellow. There are up to 35 ray florets with corollas up to 2cm (1in) long. Flowers bloom from early summer to mid fall. The fruits are achenes with a pappus (modified calyx) of deciduous awns.

Cultivation. Full sun or light shade, and moist to wet soil. Tolerates poor, sandy or salty soils. Plant near the edge of the pond, stream, or sunny bog, or add it to the taller, late-blooming species of the perennial bed, wildflower meadow, or butterfly garden. An excellent plant for gardens close to the coast. Established plants will self-sow.

Propagation. Easiest from seed. Harvest seeds in the fall and plant them into containers or directly into the garden, leaving them outside over winter to cold stratify for germination the following spring. Some seeds will germinate when planted in spring, but the percentage will be greater after a winter chilling period.

Native Habitat and Range. In salt marshes and rocky shores along the coast at low elevations from southern Alaska, south through coastal California.

Notes. Sometimes classified as *G. integrifolia* var. *macrophylla*. Only one of the three varieties, *G. s.* var. *stricta*, occurs in our area. *Grindelia* is a distinctive genus of around 50 species, native to the western regions (primarily) of North and South America, with five others native to the Pacific Northwest. *Grindelia integrifolia* (Puget Sound or Willamette Valley gumweed) also lives in wet meadows, but the plants are usually less maritime, ranging from southern British Columbia, south through the Puget Trough and Willamette Valley. Columbia River gumweed (*G. columbiana*) lacks ray florets and lives along streams from the Columbia River Gorge north and

Grindelia stricta

Helenium bolanderi

Helianthus cusickii (photo by Sally A. Simmons)

east to Idaho. Idaho gumweed (*G. nana*) has yellow ray florets and lives in dry, open places east of the Cascades and in southwestern Oregon. Curlycup gumweed (*G. squarrosa*) is a wide-ranging species of dry places across North America; hairy gumweed (*G. hirsutula*) lives in southwestern Oregon and California.

Helenium bolanderi	Zones 7b to 9b	Asteraceae

Bolander's sneezeweed

This perennial produces hairy stems up to 1m (3ft) tall from thick rhizomes. The basal leaves are obovate (oval, but widest toward the tip), up to 15cm (6in) long, and tapered to clasping petioles. The stem leaves are oblong and sessile (lacking petioles), with the base of the blade clasping the stem. Flowering heads are rounded and usually produced singly, on long peduncles. The disk florets have yellow or purplish corollas. The heads have 15 to 30 ray florets with showy, yellow corollas up to 2.5cm (1in) long and lobed at the tip. Plants bloom through most of the summer. The achenes are hairy along their longitudinal nerves and have a pappus (modified calyx) of pointed scales.

Cultivation. Full sun to light shade, and moist or wet soil. This is an excellent, yellow-flowered daisy for the butterfly garden, the perennial border, the wet spot in the meadow, or near a pond or bog.

Propagation. Grow from seed collected in the fall and stored under cool, dry conditions for planting in early spring. Plants can also be propagated from basal cuttings of new shoots made from mid to late spring. Rhizomes can be divided in mid spring or late summer.

Native Habitat and Range. In moist meadows, coastal bluffs, and bogs at low elevations from southwestern Oregon to northwestern California.

Notes. All the approximately 40 species of *Helenium* are native to North and South America. The well-known *H. autumnale* (common sneezeweed) occurs in moist, open places through much of North America; it has been used to develop many cultivars with flowers in rich shades of burgundy, gold, and copper. Bigelow's sneezeweed (*H. bigelovii*) is mainly Californian, but occurs in wet meadows as far north as southwestern Oregon. *Helenium puberulum* (rosilla) is another plant of California, ranging north to Klamath Lake and occasionally found in the Willamette Valley; it is distinguished by having very short ray corollas.

Helianthus cusickii	Zones 5a to 7b	Asteraceae

Cusick's sunflower

Clusters of prostrate to erect, branching stems grow to 1m (3ft) or a bit more from a thick taproot. Plants are hairy and rough to the touch (scabrous). The leaves have very short petioles and are narrowly lanceolate, up to 12cm (5in) long; they have entire margins and three distinct veins running up from the base. Narrow, hairy involucral bracts surround the flowering heads. The ray and disk florets are yellow, and each head has eight or more rays with corollas to 3.5cm (1.5in) long. Plants bloom from mid spring to late summer. The achenes are generally hairless (glabrous), and the pappus (modified calyx) consists of a pair of deciduous awns.

Cultivation. Full sun, and well-drained, sandy or rocky, rather dry soil. This is an excellent plant for the butterfly garden or dry wildflower meadow and a fine perennial in general for gardeners east of the Cascades; it may not flourish on the wet side. Plant it with sagebrush or other drought-tolerant plants in the native garden.

Propagation. Grow from seed collected in the fall and planted into containers or directly into the garden soon after harvest. Leave planted seeds outside to stratify in the cold, moist winter weather for germination the following spring.

Heracleum maximum

Native Habitat and Range. On rocky slopes and dry, often sandy plains at low to mid elevations east of the Cascades in central Washington, south through eastern Oregon and southwestern Idaho to northeastern California and adjacent Nevada.

Notes. *Helianthus* includes perhaps 100 species of annuals (see *H. annuus*) and perennials native to North and South America. Bolander's or serpentine sunflower (*H. bolanderi*) is a plant of dry meadows and flats in southern Oregon, ranging north from California. Nuttall's sunflower (*H. nuttallii*) lives in moist meadows in eastern Oregon and south central Washington, south and east to the Great Plains. *Helianthella* includes about a dozen species of similarly leafy perennials with yellow sunflowers, all native to western North America; one-flowered helianthella (*H. uniflora*) and five-nerved helianthella (*H. quinquenervis*) occur in the mountains throughout much of the west.

Heracleum maximum	Zones 3b to 9b	Apiaceae

cow parsnip

This big, hairy perennial produces single stems, 1 to 3m (3 to 10ft) tall, from a taproot or cluster of fibrous roots. The massive leaves are ternately compound into three leaflets; each leaflet is palmate and coarsely toothed, growing to 30cm (1ft) long and wide, though the lateral leaflets may be somewhat smaller. Small, white flowers bloom in large, flat-topped umbels. Each umbel consists of 15 to 30 rays to around 10cm (4in) long, with the largest, terminal umbel up to 20cm (8in) across. The flowers bloom from early to mid summer. The fruits are rounded, flattened schizocarps, splitting into single-seeded halves at maturity.

Cultivation. Full sun (where plants will stay shorter) to full shade or dappled light, and moist to wet soil. This is a beautiful, bold plant for the edge of the pond, bog, stream, or wetland, where it will have enough room. It's also great for the wet place in the butterfly garden or meadow, or as a striking background species in the woodland or shade garden.

Hesperochiron pumilus

Propagation. Collect seeds in late summer and plant them outside in the fall to spend the winter under cool, moist conditions. Sow directly into the garden or into deep containers, where seedlings will have room to grow until transplanted.

Native Habitat and Range. Along streams and wetlands, in moist thickets and roadsides, at low to fairly high elevations from coast to coast, Alaska south through California and New Mexico across much of North America to Newfoundland.

Notes. Sometimes classified as *H. lanatum*. *Heracleum* includes around 60 species of big perennials, all native to the Northern Hemisphere; this is the only North American native. This species can cause rashes, especially in people sensitive to light. Many tribes ate the peeled stems of young shoots as a vegetable, being careful not to confuse them with any of the several very poisonous members of the carrot and celery family.

Hesperochiron pumillus   Zones 3b to 9b   Hydrophyllaceae

dwarf hesperochiron

This small perennial produces basal leaves, flowers, and slender rhizomes from a shortened taproot. The basal leaves have elliptic blades to 5cm (2in) long on slender petioles to 2.5cm (1in). Flowers bloom singly on peduncles about as long as the leaves. The five petals are fused at the base to form a saucer-shaped corolla about 2.5cm (1in) across. The corollas are white or purple tinted with purplish penciling and yellow centers. Flowers bloom from mid spring to early summer, and the fruits are one-celled capsules containing many seeds.

Cultivation. Full sun or light shade, and soil that is moist in spring but dry in summer, when the plants are dormant. Under favorable conditions it may form white drifts in the spring, but will generally be happier east of the Cascades, in the rock garden or margin of a vernal pool in the wildflower meadow.

Propagation. Collect seeds from the capsules during the summer, before the plants become completely dormant. Sow them in the fall, into flats of potting soil or directly into the garden, and leave them outside over winter for germination the following spring.

Native Habitat and Range. On open slopes, swales, and rocky meadows that are moist in spring at fairly low to high elevations east of the Cascades in British Columbia and Washington, to both sides of the Cascades in southern Oregon, and south through California, east to Montana, Wyoming, and Arizona.

Notes. *Hesperochiron californicus* (California hesperochiron), the only other species in the genus, lives in flats and (often somewhat alkaline or saline) meadows at fairly low to high elevations, mainly east of the Cascades from eastern Washington south through eastern California and east to Montana, Wyoming, and Utah. It is slightly larger and forms its branched crown from a taproot. The basal leaves have elliptic blades to about 7cm (3in) long, a bit longer than the slender petioles. Several peduncles, shorter than the leaves, grow directly from the crown; each bears a single flower of five white to pale lavender petals, often with purplish veins, fused at the base to form a bell-shaped corolla about 2cm (1in) long. It too blooms from mid spring to early summer.

Hesperostipa comata	Zones 3b to 9b	Poaceae

needle-and-thread

This tufted grass produces a cluster of leaves and flowering shoots to about 60cm (2ft) tall. The leaf blades tend to be rolled inward (involute), and the inflorescence is a narrow panicle to 20cm (8in) long. The small flowers (florets) are grouped into spikelets, as is typical for grasses. Two narrow bracts, the glumes, subtend each spikelet. Each spikelet is made up of only a single floret, which is further enclosed in its own pair of bracts, the lemma and the palea. Each lemma is tipped with an awn, a long, slender bristle that can grow to 15cm (6in). The awn is twisted and sometimes bent, the source of the common name of this grass. The bloom season is late spring to mid summer, and the fruit is a grain, or caryopsis.

Cultivation. Full sun or light shade, and rocky, rather dry soil with good drainage. This is an excellent bunchgrass for gardens east of the Cascades; it does not thrive in wetter climates. Plant it in the dry wildflower meadow or with other drought-tolerant perennials and shrubs in the wildlife garden.

Propagation. Grow from seed collected in late summer. Before planting, try rubbing the seeds between pieces of sandpaper or shaking them in a jar full of coarse sand; scarifying will increase germination percentage. Plant seeds directly into the garden or into flats of potting soil in the fall or spring.

Native Habitat and Range. In dry, often rocky soil on sagebrush plains and forest openings at low to fairly high elevations east of the Cascades from British Columbia south to east central California and east to Texas, the Great Plains, and the Great Lakes.

Notes. Sometimes classified as *Stipa comata*. Both *H. c.* ssp. *comata* and *H. c.* ssp. *intermedia* occur in our area. *Hesperostipa* has only four species, all in North America; the other three have ranges to the east and south. In the related *Calamagrostis* (reedgrass), plants have spikelets with single florets, usually arranged into narrow panicles, and tend to form clumps, but many species are rhizomatous. One such is *C. rubescens* (pinegrass) which, like *H. comata*, is more common east of the Cascades; it is taller, to 1m (3ft), and is found on dry to moist forest slopes and sagebrush flats. Purple reedgrass (*C. purpurascens*) and bluejoint (*C. canadensis*) occur on both sides of the Cascades; Pacific reedgrass (*C. nutkaensis*) grows in seaside dunes and coastal foothills, sometimes forming large populations, from Alaska to California

Hesperostipa comata (photo by Sally A. Simmons)

| *Heterotheca villosa* | Zones 3b to 9b | Asteraceae |

hairy goldenaster

This variable species produces several stems with woody bases from a taproot. The leafy shoots grow to 50cm (20in), and the plants are hairy and often glandular. The leaves are generally oblong or narrower, grow to 5cm (2in) long and 1cm (.5in) wide, and sometimes have a short petiole. Several flowering heads bloom in clusters at the stem tips. The heads are about 1cm (.5in) tall and include ray and disk florets with yellow corollas. Each head has up to 25 ray florets with corollas up to 1cm (.5in) long. The flowers bloom from early summer to early fall. The fruits are flattened achenes with a pappus (modified calyx) of bristles and scales.

Cultivation. Full sun or light shade, and well-drained, moist to rather dry soil. This is a long-blooming, golden-flowered daisy for the rock garden, dry streambank, or stony slope. Plant it with other perennials in the dry, sandy parts of the butterfly garden or wildflower meadow.

Propagation. Grow from seed collected in the fall and planted into containers or directly into the garden in the fall or spring.

Native Habitat and Range. Along rocky streambanks, open slopes, and sandy, sometimes disturbed places at low to mid elevations, mostly east of the Cascades, from British Columbia south to California and Arizona, east to Texas, the Great Plains, and Great Lakes.

Notes. Sometimes classified as *Chrysopsis villosa*. *Heterotheca v.* var. *villosa* is probably the most common taxon in the Pacific Northwest; the widespread *H. v.* var. *foliosa* and *H. v.* var. *minor* also occur here. Oregon goldenaster (*H. oregona*) is another perennial, growing to 50cm (20in) from a shrubby base. The leafy stems are topped with clusters of flowering heads that lack ray florets, consisting only of yellow disk florets. This plant blooms from mid summer to

Heterotheca villosa

early fall and lives on sandy banks or gravel near rivers at low to mid elevations, mainly west of the Cascades from Washington, south to west central California. *Heterotheca* includes almost 20 species, all native to North America. *Hulsea* (alpinegold), another genus of golden-flowered daisies, encompasses some seven species, all native to western North America. Pacific hulsea (*H. algida*) grows in cliffs, crevices, and talus, especially in granite, at high elevations in northeastern Oregon, Montana, and California; it is 40cm (16in) tall, and its single flowering heads, up to 3cm (1.5in) across, bear up to 55 yellow ray florets with corollas to 1.5cm (.5in) long, from mid summer to early fall. Dwarf alpinegold (*H. nana*) is similar but smaller, only 10cm (4in) tall, with large, yellow heads but fewer ray florets; it prefers to live in pumice near volcanoes from Mt. Rainier to Mt. Lassen. These two species are sometimes grown in troughs or rock gardens and can be propagated from seed.

Heuchera   Saxifragaceae

alumroot

This well-known genus of perennial herbs includes around 35 species, all native to North America; around ten species occur in the Pacific Northwest and innumerable cultivars are available at nurseries, locally and worldwide, including selections of ×*Heucherella*, an intergeneric cross between *Heuchera* and *Tiarella*. Alumroots have branched crowns, thick rhizomes, and well-developed palmate basal leaves with long petioles. The upright inflorescence is either densely flowered and spike-like or open and panicle-like. The small flowers have a bell-shaped calyx with five lobes and (usually) five white or greenish yellow petals. The fruits are small two-beaked capsules containing many tiny seeds. Alumroots are sometimes susceptible to mealybugs. Yellow coralbells (*Elmera racemosa*) is a close family relation with rounded basal leaves and spike-like clusters of greenish white and creamy flowers to 25cm (10in) tall, blooming in summer; it grows on mountain cliffs and talus slopes from southern British Columbia to Oregon and is a good addition to the trough or rock garden.

Propagation. Grow from seed collected as soon as the capsules are ripe in the summer or fall, and planted soon after harvest. Sow seeds into flats of moist, well-drained potting soil, and leave them outside for the winter. Some seedlings may appear in the fall, soon after planting, but most will appear after the weather warms the following spring. It is also possible to sow in the spring. Keep seedlings moist until they are large enough to transplant; it will take a couple of years for them to reach flowering size. Heucheras can also be propagated from divisions of thick rhizomes, or from cuttings made of the branched crowns, rooted in pumice or sand; cuttings or divisions can be made in mid spring or late summer. Root weevil larvae sometimes chew the roots from the stems below the clusters of leaves, but chewed-off rosettes can be dipped in hormones and rerooted in pumice or sand.

Heuchera cylindrica	Zones 4a to 9a

lava or roundleaf alumroot

This species produces mostly evergreen leaves in basal clusters from short, thick rhizomes and a branching crown. The basal leaves have well-developed petioles and are glandular-hairy to nearly hairless (glabrous). The leaf blades are ovate to cordate (heart-shaped) or almost reniform (kidney-shaped), around 6cm (2.5in) wide, and about as long. They are palmate, with five or more main lobes, and the margins of these lobes have shallow lobes and teeth. The flowering stems can reach 1m (3ft) in vigorous plants, and the spike-like panicle grows to 12cm (5in) long. The pedicels and branches of the inflorescence are shorter than the small flowers. The petals are tiny and sometimes lacking, but the campanulate (bell-shaped), greenish yellow to creamy calyx grows to 1cm (.5in) long. The stamens are shorter than the calyx lobes and are not exserted from the tubular calyx. The flowers bloom from mid spring to late summer, depending on elevation, and the tiny seeds are oblong and dark brown with rows of conical spines.

Cultivation. Part shade or dappled light, and rocky, well-drained, moist to rather dry soil. Tolerates full sun, but prefers some shade where summers are hot. This is a beautiful plant for the rock garden or large trough. Plant it on a stony slope or gravelly place in the wildflower meadow, or tuck it under the edge of taller shrubs in the hummingbird and butterfly garden.

Native Habitat and Range. On talus, cliffs, and rather dry, rocky slopes at fairly low to high elevations, mainly east of the Cascade crest from British Columbia south to northern California, east to Alberta, Montana, and Wyoming.

Notes. Meadow or tall alumroot (*H. chlorantha*) and gooseberry-leaf alumroot (*H. grossulariifolia*) are similar species with narrow inflorescences and white to creamy or greenish flowers; they both occur in our area.

Heuchera glabra	Zones 5a to 9b

smooth or alpine alumroot

This perennial produces clusters of generally evergreen basal leaves and flowering stems up to 60cm (2ft) tall from a branched crown and short rhizomes. The blades of the basal leaves are oval to heart-shaped (cordate) in outline, up to 9cm (3.5in) across and a bit shorter in length. The leaf margins are palmate with around five deep lobes, these more shallowly lobed and toothed. The leaves are sometimes sparsely hairy and glandular underneath but otherwise mainly

Heuchera cylindrica

Heuchera glabra

glabrous (hairless). One or two smaller leaves develop on the lower part of the flowering stem. The inflorescence is open and panicle-like with slender branches and pedicels. The tiny flowers have five calyx lobes and five white petals less than 1cm (.5in) long. The petals are spoon-shaped (spatulate) and narrowed at the base (clawed). The five stamens are about as long as the petals. The flowers bloom from late spring to late summer, depending on elevation, and the beaked capsules contain many spiny, elongated brown seeds.

Cultivation. Part shade or dappled light, and well-drained, moist soil. Tolerates full sun but looks better with shade. With its low mound of evergreen leaves and delicate flowers, this is a lovely plant throughout the year. Plant it near the path at the edge of the woodland garden; among the wet rocks near a pond, stream, or waterfall; or in the rock garden, retaining wall, or stony wildflower meadow. It's also a good addition to the butterfly garden.

Native Habitat and Range. In stony meadows, and rocky streambanks, mossy talus, and moist rock crevices at low to high elevations from Alaska south through the Olympic Mountains, the Cascades of Washington and Oregon and scattered west to the coast.

Notes. This species was used medicinally by indigenous people and colonists; its dried roots were made into a poultice and used to stop bleeding and encourage healing of wounds.

Heuchera micrantha   Zones 5a to 9b

small-flowered alumroot

This (usually) evergreen perennial produces a branched crown and short rhizomes with clusters of basal leaves and taller flowering stems. The petioles of the basal leaves are well developed and usually have long, whitish hairs. The leaf blades are ovate-cordate (oval-heart-shaped) to

Heuchera micrantha

reniform (kidney-shaped) and up to 8cm (3in) wide, about the same in length, and sometimes hairy on both surfaces. The blades are palmate, with five or seven shallow or well-developed lobes, these with rounded or sharp teeth. The flowering stems grow to 60cm (2ft) tall, often with a few, small leaves toward the base. The inflorescence is open and panicle-like with thin branches and pedicels. The tiny flowers are similar to those of *H. glabra*, less than 1cm (.5in) long, but the five-lobed calyx is usually woolly. The five white petals are spoon-shaped (spatulate) and narrowed at the base (clawed). The five stamens are about as long as the petals. The flowers bloom from late spring to late summer, depending on elevation, and the tiny seeds are oblong, dark brownish purple, and covered with rows of tiny spines.

Cultivation. Part shade or dappled light (especially where summers are hot), and moist, well-drained soil. This is a versatile little evergreen for the perennial border, rock garden, or woodland. Plant it among the rocks near the pond or stream, or in the wildflower meadow or butterfly garden.

Native Habitat and Range. On mossy rocks and crevices and gravelly streambanks at low to fairly high elevations from southern British Columbia south through western Washington and Oregon to central California, east in the mountains of northeastern Oregon and adjacent Idaho.

Notes. A variable species, despite its relatively small overall range. *Heuchera m.* var. *diversifolia* has the most northern range, to British Columbia; *H. m.* var. *micrantha* occurs through the Columbia River Gorge and east; and the other three varieties range north into southern Oregon from California. Although it has a lovely, delicate inflorescence, this species is often grown as a foliage plant, and many selections may be traced to natural variations of its basal leaves, including the deeply lobed 'Ruffles'.

Horkelia fusca

Horkelia fusca	Zones 3b to 9b	Rosaceae

pinewoods horkelia

This delicate, taprooted perennial herb produces basal leaves up to 20cm (8in) long. The blades are pinnately compound, and the leaflets are ovate to wedge-shaped with toothed or narrowly lobed margins. The flowering stems can reach 60cm (2ft). The small, white or pinkish flowers are about 1cm (.5in) across and bloom in dense clusters from early to mid summer. The fruits are small achenes.

Cultivation. Full sun or light shade, and moist to fairly dry soil. This is a charming little species for the rock garden, wildflower meadow, or low perennial border. Plant it near rocks or in openings among pines and oaks.

Propagation. Quite easy from seed. Collect seeds in summer, plant them outside in the fall, and let the cold, moist conditions of winter help to break their dormancy, for germination the following spring.

Native Habitat and Range. Rocky slopes, moist meadows, and open forests in the foothills to mid elevations, from central Washington south along the east slope of the Cascades to the Sierra Nevada of California, east to Idaho, western Wyoming, and Nevada.

Notes. *Horkelia f.* ssp. *fusca* has deeply divided leaflets and green foliage; it occurs along the east slope of the Cascades from central Washington to north central Oregon. *Horkelia f.* ssp. *capitata* has relatively long petals and leaves with shallow lobes; it grows from southeastern Washington and Idaho, south through eastern Oregon to California and Nevada. *Horkelia f.* ssp. *parviflora*, with wedge-shaped leaflets and small petals, ranges from the Sierra Nevada of California, north through the Oregon Cascades to Montana. *Horkelia f.* ssp. *pseudocapitata* ranges from the east slope of the Oregon Cascades to California and Nevada; the undersides of the leaves have gray hairs, and the flowers are small. *Horkelia f.* ssp. *filicoides* has an open inflorescence and deeply toothed leaflets; it is endemic to southern Oregon. *Horkelia* includes more than a dozen species of western North America, most of them native to California. Sierra horkelia (*H. congesta*) occurs in Oregon and California, as does carrot-leaf horkelia (*H. daucifolia*). Henderson's horkelia (*H. hendersonii*) lives in the Siskiyou Mountains of southern Oregon and northern California; silky horkelia (*H. sericata*) and three-tooth horkelia (*H. tridentata* ssp. *tridentata*) live in open, dry places in southwestern Oregon and northern California.

Hydrophyllum   Hydrophyllaceae

waterleaf

Hydrophyllum is a genus of fewer than ten species, all native to North America. Most plants are rhizomatous perennial herbs with alternate, pinnately divided leaves. The sepals are joined at their bases to form a calyx with five hairy lobes. The bell-shaped corollas have five petals, also fused at the base. The five stamens have long filaments and protrude from the flowers. The fruits are few-seeded capsules.

Propagation. Grow from seed collected from ripened capsules in late summer or fall. Plant the seeds shortly after harvest, into containers or directly into the garden, and leave them outside in the cool, moist winter weather to improve germination in the spring. Seedlings may need protection from slugs. Alternatively, rhizomes can be divided in the early spring, but this should be done only with plants already in cultivation.

Hydrophyllum fendleri   Zones 4a to 9b

Fendler's waterleaf

This perennial grows single, hairy shoots up to 80cm (2.5ft) from short rhizomes. The alternate leaves are few but large, up to 25cm (10in) long, divided into lobed and toothed leaflets. Flowers are produced in dense clusters at the tips of the stems and on peduncles arising from the leaf axils. The bell-shaped flowers are white to purplish and up to 1cm (.5in) across. Plants flower from late spring to late summer, depending on elevation. A few seeds are produced in each small capsule.

Cultivation. Part shade or dappled light, and moist soil high in organic matter. This is a lovely, ferny plant for the woodland garden, but it tends to spread under ideal conditions. Plant it with other tall, aggressive shade lovers.

Native Habitat and Range. In thickets and moist openings at mid to high elevations, from southern British Columbia, south through the Olympic and Cascade Mountains to northern California, east in the mountains of southeastern Washington and northeastern Oregon, east and south to Idaho, Colorado and New Mexico.

Notes. *Hydrophyllum f.* var. *albifrons*, which is confined to the western part of the range, tends to be more densely, softly hairy; *H. f.* var. *fendleri*, with a thinner, harsher pubescence, occurs in the eastern and southern parts of the range. Ballhead waterleaf (*H. capitatum*), a smaller species with blue flowers, occurs in woods and moist, open places from the foothills to fairly high elevations mainly east of the Cascades, and east to the Rocky Mountains; it is a lovely plant for the rock garden, blooming in the early spring at low to mid elevations.

Hydrophyllum fendleri

Hydrophyllum tenuipes

Hydrophyllum tenuipes   Zones 7a to 9b

Pacific or slender-stemmed waterleaf

This species produces solitary, somewhat hairy shoots up to 80cm (2.5ft) from rhizomes. The few, large, alternate leaves grow to 15cm (6in) in length and width. They are divided into about five lobed leaflets with sharply toothed margins. Flowers are produced in clusters on peduncles about as long as the leaves, arising from the leaf axils. The bell-shaped corollas are usually greenish white, but are blue or purple in some populations. The flowers are about 1cm (.5in) across, with strongly protruding stamens. Plants flower from mid spring to early summer, and each small capsule produces a few seeds.

Cultivation. Full to part shade or dappled light, and moist soil high in organic matter. This is a lovely, lush perennial for the woodland or shade garden. It is beautiful in the spring but becomes less attractive after flowering; site it with other plants that will hide it later in the season. Under ideal conditions, it tends to spread, which is another reason to place it among other, preferably aggressive shade lovers.

Native Habitat and Range. In moist woods and shady places at low to mid elevations, from southern British Columbia, south to northern California, and from the coast to the west slope of the Cascades.

Notes. Western waterleaf (*H. occidentale*) lives in thickets and moist, open woods at mid to high elevations from the Coast Ranges and Cascades of Oregon, south to central California and east to Utah and Arizona; its flowers vary from white to blue-violet, blooming in compact clusters from mid spring to mid summer.

Hymenoxys hoopesii

Hymenoxys hoopesii	Zones 3b to 9b	Asteraceae

orange sneezeweed, tall mountain helenium

This perennial produces several stout stems to 1m (3ft) tall from a thick rhizome or crown. The lower leaves are the largest, narrowly oblong, up to 30cm (1ft) long, with the blades tapered to a clasping base. Clusters of yellow or orange, sunflower-like heads bloom at the stem tips. The many, small, tubular disk florets are surrounded by up to 20 ray florets with corollas to 2.5cm (1in) long. Flowers bloom from mid summer to early fall, and the fruits are small, hairy achenes.

Cultivation. Full sun, and moist soil. This is a fine plant for late-season bloom in the wildflower meadow or sunny perennial border and a good addition to the butterfly garden.

Propagation. Grow from seed collected in the fall and stored under cool, dry conditions. Sow into flats of potting soil in early spring. Alternatively, take basal cuttings of new shoots from mid to late spring, or divide rhizomes in mid spring or late summer.

Native Habitat and Range. Near streams, moist slopes and meadows at mid to high elevations in the mountains of southeastern Oregon, south through California and east to Wyoming and New Mexico.

Notes. Sometimes classified as *Helenium hoopesii*. This species is toxic to livestock, especially sheep. *Hymenoxys* (rubberweed) is a genus of approximately 20 species, 16 of them native to western North America, mainly to the Southwest; Cooper's rubberweed (*H. cooperi*) and Lemmon's rubberweed (*H. lemmonii*) range north to Oregon.

Hypericum anagalloides

Iliamna rivularis

Hypericum anagalloides	Zones 4b to 9b	Hypericaceae

bog St. John's wort, tinker's penny

This prostrate perennial forms dense mats from freely rooting stems and produces upright shoots to 15cm (6in) tall. The small, opposite leaves are ovate to elliptic and up to 1.5cm (.5in) long. The leaves are sessile (lacking petioles), and the plants are glabrous (hairless). The tiny flowers, less than 1cm (.5in) across, bloom in leafy, few-flowered clusters at the stem tips from early to late summer; they have five sepals, five yellow petals, and up to 25 stamens. The fruits are small capsules with three chambers and yellow seeds.

Cultivation. Full sun to part shade, and wet soil. This is a charming mat-forming species for the shallow margin of the pond, bog, or wetland; the low, wet place in the wildflower meadow; or along wet ditches. It can spread aggressively but is too low-growing to interfere with most plants.

Propagation. Grow from seed collected from the little capsules in the fall. Sow the seeds along a shoreline in autumn or winter or into flats of wet potting soil and leave them outside for germination in the spring. This little plant is also easy to propagate from rooted pieces of the stoloniferous stems divided in the spring.

Native Habitat and Range. In wet meadows, ditches, and wetlands at low to mid elevations from southern British Columbia, south to California, and from the coast, east to Idaho, Utah, and Arizona.

Notes. *Hypericum* includes some 200 species, most from the Northern Hemisphere; of the approximately 50 species that are native to North America, about six occur in the Pacific Northwest. Another is *H. scouleri* (*H. formosum*; western St. John's wort), a taller native species, forming stems to about 60cm (2ft) from underground rhizomes and aboveground stolons; the showy yellow flowers are about 2cm (1in) across and bloom from early summer to early fall. This species lives in moist meadows, along streams and in thickets at low to fairly high elevations, with populations scattered from southern British Columbia, south to Mexico, and from the coast east to the Rocky Mountains.

Iliamna rivularis	Zones 4a to 8b	Malvaceae

streambank wild hollyhock or globemallow

The stout stems of this perennial are often branched, growing .5 to 1.2m (1.5 to 3.5ft). The pubescent leaves are palmately five- to seven-lobed and up to 15cm (6in) across. The showy flowers bloom in open racemes from the leaf axils (nodes). The calyx consists of five short lobes with three small bracts (bracteoles) beneath them. The five petals are about 2cm (1in) long and pale pink to rosy purple. The filaments of the numerous stamens are fused into a tube around the style and round-tipped (capitate) stigmas. The flowers bloom from early summer to early fall. The fruit is a rounded capsule, a ring of stiff haired carpels (the units of the ovary, like the sections of an orange), each of which splits open to release a few seeds.

Cultivation. Full sun or light shade, and moist soil. Be sure to give it a sunny spot and good drainage on the west side; otherwise, a good perennial for gardeners on either side of the Cascades. Try it in the large perennial bed, the rock garden, or along a streambank or pond.

Propagation. Grow from seed collected from the capsules in the late summer or fall. Plant seeds into flats of moist potting soil or directly into the garden, and leave them outside to cold stratify over winter for germination in the spring. Dividing the crowns in early spring is another method.

Native Habitat and Range. Near streams and in moist canyons at mid elevations, mainly east of the Cascades, British Columbia to Oregon and east to Montana and Colorado

Notes. *Iliamna r.* var. *rivularis* occurs throughout the range. *Iliamna longisepala* (longsepal wild hollyhock or globemallow) is a similar but rare species, restricted to a few counties in central Washington. *Iliamna* is a genus of about six species, mostly native along streams in western North America. *Iliamna latibracteata* (California wild hollyhock, broad-bracted globemallow) and *I. bakeri* (Baker's wild hollyhock or globemallow) both range north into southern Oregon from California.

Ipomopsis aggregata	Zones 3b to 8b	Polemoniaceae

scarlet gilia, skyrocket

Scarlet gilia is a biennial or short-lived perennial that produces a basal rosette of leaves in its first year; the leaves are pinnately divided into narrow lobes and up to 10cm (4in) long. Flowering shoots can grow .5 to 1m (1.5 to 3ft) tall. The flowers have a five-lobed calyx and a five-lobed tubular corolla to 3.5cm (1.5in) long, brilliant orange-red with whitish dots; they bloom in a panicle-like inflorescence from late spring to late summer. The fruits are few-seeded capsules.

Cultivation. Full sun or very slight shade, and well-drained, moist to rather dry soil. Will probably do best in gardens east of the Cascades or in southwestern Oregon, but it can be grown in rainy climates when given sandy or gravelly soil and full sun. Plants typically die after flowering, but their intense beauty makes up for their short life span, and they often self-sow. With its tubular red flowers, this is a classic for the hummingbird garden and glorious in the rock garden or near the path through the sunny wildflower meadow.

Propagation. Grow from seed collected from the small capsules and planted in the fall or early the following spring, either into flats of potting soil or directly into the garden. Seedlings will grow a lacy rosette the first year and flower the following summer. After flowering, seeds can either be harvested or left to self-sow.

Ipomopsis aggregata

Native Habitat and Range. In dry, open, often rocky areas mainly east of the Cascades from southern British Columbia, south to California, west of the Cascades in Oregon, and east to the Rocky Mountains, New Mexico, and Texas.

Notes. Sometimes classified as *Gilia aggregata*. *Ipomopsis a.* ssp. *aggregata* and *I. a.* ssp. *formosissima* both have large ranges and occur in parts of our area, as do ballhead ipomopsis (*I. congesta*) and littleflower ipomopsis (*I. minutiflora*). *Ipomopsis* includes more than 20 species, most of them native to North America, with a few in South America.

Iris	Iridaceae

flag, fleur-de-lis

Around 200 species native to temperate parts of the Northern Hemisphere constitute *Iris*, with the greatest diversity in Eurasia. These are some of our best-known garden plants, and breeders introduce new cultivars every year. Irises are perennial monocots growing from rhizomes or bulbs. The leaves are long, sometimes narrow and grass-like, sometimes broader, folded and flattened from the midvein and sheathing the stems (equitant). The name *Iris* (Latin for "rainbow") reflects the variety of flower colors these plants can produce, often within the same species. The three (usually) upright petals, or standards, in the center of the flower are the true petals; the three outer structures, or falls, are colorful, petaloid sepals. The falls usually curve downward and are often marked with other colors and penciled with dark lines. The petaloid style branches are opposite the sepals and usually curve over them, with the stamens tucked in between the styles and sepals. The inferior ovary develops into a three-parted capsule and is connected to the other flower parts by a floral or perianth tube (hypanthium), which is very short or quite long, depending on the species. Around ten species are native in the Pacific Northwest; several of these have been used in developing the Pacific Coast iris hybrids. Species also hybridize with each other in nature; some are poisonous.

Propagation. Collect seeds in the summer or fall and plant them outside into flats of potting soil or directly into the garden soon after harvest. After spending the winter in cool, moist conditions, seeds will germinate in the spring, and seedlings may reach blooming size the following year. Plants can also be propagated by separating small side shoots from the rhizomes during the summer, after the flowers have bloomed, but this should be done only with plants originally grown from seed. Rhizomatous species such as *I. tenax* can also be propagated by divisions made in late winter or early spring, as new growth begins.

Iris chrysophylla	Zones 6b to 9b

slender-tubed or yellow-leaf iris

The leaves of this rhizomatous iris grow to 10 to 40cm (4 to 16in) and are narrow and grass-like, light green with pink to reddish bases. The flowering stems are generally shorter than the leaves, to 20cm (8in), with one or two flowers per stem. The flowers are usually yellowish white with purple penciling, but pale blue, lavender, and yellow forms also occur. The hypanthium is 4cm (1.5in) or longer. Flowers bloom from late spring to mid summer, and seeds ripen in three-celled capsules.

Cultivation. Full sun, part shade, or dappled light, and well-drained, moist to rather dry soil. This is a pretty iris for the rock garden, or with other species in the sunny perennial border. Plant it in a glade or near the edge of the woodland garden, or in the wildflower meadow.

Native Habitat and Range. In open, rather dry woods at low elevations west of the Cascades from western Oregon to northwestern California.

Notes. This species hybridizes with *I. tenax* when the opportunity presents itself, producing intermediate plants. *Iris tenuis* (Clackamas iris), another species with pale flowers, grows along streambanks and is endemic to a small area of northwestern Oregon.

Iris douglasiana	Zones 7a to 9b

Douglas' iris

This rhizomatous iris produces evergreen leaves up to 1m (3ft) long and 2cm (1in) wide, usually reddish at the base. Flowering stems are around 50cm (20in) tall, often branched, with one to several flowers. The hypanthium is 2.5cm (1in) long. The sepals are about 7cm (3in) long and vary in color, from cream to shades of lavender, bluish and reddish purple. This species blooms from early to late spring and produces a capsule up to 5cm (2in) long.

Cultivation. Full sun, and moist to rather dry, well-drained soil. Tolerates poor soils and salty, windy, sandy coastal conditions. Include this tough, aggressive iris in the dry wildflower meadow or hillside; it's also a good plant for the rock garden or perennial bed.

Native Habitat and Range. On open, grassy hillsides and cliffs near the coast, at low elevations from central Oregon, south to southern California.

Notes. This species has been used in breeding. Wild flag (*I. setosa*) also has blue or purplish flowers and relatively wide leaves, to at least 1cm (.5in); it is native to wet habitats at low to mid elevations in southwestern Alaska and British Columbia.

Iris chrysophylla

Iris douglasiana

Iris innominata

Iris missouriensis

Iris tenax

Iris innominata   Zones 7a to 9b

golden iris

This rhizomatous iris produces clusters of narrow, evergreen leaves with reddish bases to 30cm (1ft) long. Flowering stems grow to 20cm (8in) tall, each with one or two flowers. The flowers are usually pale to golden yellow, but sometimes lavender or purple. The sepals grow to 6cm (2.5in) long and usually have darker penciling. The hypanthium is usually less than 3cm (1.5in) long, and the flowers bloom from late spring to early summer. The oblong capsules are about 3cm (1.5in) long.

Cultivation. Full sun, part shade, or dappled light, and well-drained, moist to rather dry soil. Lovely for the rock garden, wildflower meadow, woodland garden, or perennial bed.

Native Habitat and Range. In thickets and open to partly shaded, rather dry slopes at low to mid elevations from southwestern Oregon, south to northwestern California.

Notes. *Iris bracteata* (Siskiyou iris) is another yellow-flowered species native to woodlands in southwestern Oregon and northwestern California.

Iris missouriensis   Zones 3b to 9b

western blue or Rocky Mountain iris

This iris grows from thick, spreading rhizomes, producing narrow leaves and flowering stems, both to .5m (1.5ft) tall. Each flowering stem has one to a few flowers, usually light blue to lilac, purple, or whitish, with sepals to 6cm (2.5in) long and a short hypanthium. Flowers bloom from late spring to early summer and are followed by three-angled capsules to 5cm (2in) long.

Cultivation. Full sun or light shade, and moist to wet soil. This is a great iris for wet places, such as the pond margin, streambank, or moister parts of the wildflower meadow. It's also a good addition to the sunny, moist perennial bed on either side of the Cascades.

Native Habitat and Range. In meadows, along streams and in seeps, at mid to high elevations, mainly east of the Cascades, from southern British Columbia, south to southern California and east through the Rocky Mountains to the Dakotas and New Mexico.

Notes. This species, ranked a noxious weed in California, has increased its range as a consequence of human activity. It competes with range grasses and is toxic to cattle.

Iris tenax	Zones 6b to 9b

Oregon or toughleaf iris

This small, deciduous iris grows 10 to 50cm (4 to 20in) from a dense cluster of rhizomes. The leaves are tough and narrow, to 40cm (16in) long, forming a grass-like clump. The flowers are lovely, generally purple or bluish but occasionally pink, yellow, or white, with sepals to about 6cm (2.5in) long and a very short hypanthium; they bloom from mid spring to early summer. Seeds ripen in capsules to 3cm (1.5in) long.

Cultivation. Full sun or part shade, and moist to rather dry soil. This low-growing, versatile iris is beautiful in the rock garden or wildflower meadow; among equally low plants in the sunny perennial border or bed; or in a glade or near the edge of the woodland garden or oak grove.

Native Habitat and Range. In meadows, roadsides, forest glades, and other open areas, at low to mid elevations, west of the Cascades, from west central Washington, south through Oregon to northern California.

Notes. *Iris t.* ssp. *tenax* is the most common native iris in western Oregon and adjacent Washington, and certainly one of the prettiest.

Juncus	Juncaceae

rush

Juncus is a genus of more than 200 species, widely distributed in the moist, temperate parts of the world; around half are native to North America, about 50 of these occurring in the Pacific Northwest. Rushes are annual or perennial herbs with rounded or flattened leaf blades and stem-sheathing bases. The tiny flowers are greenish or brownish, and the perianth segments or tepals (petals and sepals) are all similar, with an outer whorl and an inner whorl of three tepals each. There are usually either three or six stamens (sometimes fewer), and the fruits, small capsules, contain numerous tiny seeds. Flowers are usually arranged into clusters of two to many, and the inflorescences vary from closely flowered to open and panicle-like. *Luzula* (woodrush) is closely related to *Juncus*, with flat, grass-like leaves and similar flowers, reminiscent of tiny, brown lilies; our woodrushes, almost 20 native species, often occur in forested habitats and make small, graceful additions to the woodland garden.

Propagation. Grow from seed, collected and planted in the late summer or fall, and left outside over winter for germination in the spring. Scatter seeds over the surface of moist soil, either in flats or directly into the garden; they can be pressed into the surface of the soil but avoid burying them too deeply. Rushes can also be propagated from divisions of the rhizomes or clumps made in the spring, although the clump-forming species are sometimes tough and difficult to work with.

Juncus acuminatus

Juncus breweri

Juncus acuminatus   Zones 3b to 9b

tapertip rush

This tufted rush produces shoots up to 80cm (2.5ft) tall, sometimes from very short rhizomes. The leaves have rounded blades and sheathing bases. The flowering stem is topped with a short, leaf-like bract and a branched inflorescence to 12cm (5in) long. The tiny flowers are grouped into small heads, each with up to 20 flowers. The perianth (petals and sepals) is greenish brown or straw-colored, and the flowers bloom from late spring to late summer. The small, brown capsules are three-sided.

Cultivation. Full sun or light shade, and wet soil. Although not showy, this rush adds subtle grace and diversity to the pond margin, ditch, streambank, or wet place in the wildflower meadow.

Native Habitat and Range. On the shores of lakes and streams, wet meadows, ditches and other wet places at low to mid elevations, mainly west of the Cascades, from southern British Columbia, south through northern California, east to Idaho and throughout much of North America to the Atlantic coast.

Notes. Similar are jointed rush (*J. articulatus*), with a wide range through North America, and pointed rush (*J. oxymeris*), which is limited to the west coast; both plants have small clusters of flowers arranged into a larger, branched inflorescence and occur in wet places, often at low elevations.

Juncus breweri Zones 6b to 9b

Brewer's or salt rush

This rush produces stout, rounded stems to 60cm (2ft) from thick, elongated rhizomes. The leaves are all basal and reduced to bladeless sheaths. Small flowers bloom in a single, spherical cluster to 3cm (1.5in) long. The inflorescence appears to be lateral, developing from above a long involucral bract that appears to be a continuation of the stem. The tiny flowers bloom from early to mid summer. They have six stamens, and the perianth parts are green and brown. The fruits are small, rounded capsules.

Cultivation. Full sun or light shade, and wet soil. As one common name suggests, this rush will tolerate salty soils and is an unusual addition to the wet places in the coastal garden or wildflower meadow. Site along ditches or the pond margin.

Native Habitat and Range. In salty marshes, meadows, and dunes along the coast from southern British Columbia, south to California.

Notes. Sometimes classified as *J. lesueurii*. This species is closely related to the variable *J. arcticus* (*J. balticus*; arctic or Baltic rush), which has leaves reduced to sheaths and a condensed or open inflorescence that appears to grow from the side of the stem; it lives in wet places through much of North America and beyond, tolerating both saline and alkaline conditions. Mertens' rush (*J. mertensianus*), another interesting species, bears a single, densely flowered head from the tip of the stem; it lives along streams and ponds at mid to high elevations in the mountains from Alaska to California and east to the Rocky Mountains.

Juncus effusus Zones 3b to 9b

common or soft rush

This rush produces large tufts of rounded stems and leaves to 1m (3ft) tall from stout rhizomes. The inflorescence develops above a pointed bract that appears to be a continuation of the rounded stem; its tiny flowers are arranged in panicles that vary in shape from open and branched to congested and head-like. The perianth segments are narrowly lance-shaped and vary in color from greenish to deep brown. Flowers bloom from early to late summer, and the fruits are small, three-parted capsules.

Cultivation. Full sun or part shade, and wet to moist soil. A tough plant for the pond margin, ditch, streambank or wet place in the wildflower meadow. It can become invasive but won't spread where the ground is too dry: include its graceful, vase-shaped clusters in the perennial bed or the base of a hedgerow.

Native Habitat and Range. In moist to wet pond margins, pastures, roadsides, and coastal tideflats at low to mid elevations from southern Alaska, south along the coast to Mexico, east across much of North America.

Notes. Cultivars include the curly-leaved 'Spiralis' and plants with yellow ('Cuckoo') or whitish ('Zebrinus') variegation. Thread rush (*J. filiformis*) and spreading rush (*J. patens*) are similar wetland species with long involucral bracts and an inflorescence that appears to be growing from the side of the stem. Slender rush (*J. tenuis*) also has long involucral bracts and an open to condensed inflorescence; it too is often found in moist pastures and roadsides and other disturbed habitats.

Juncus effusus

Juncus ensifolius	Zones 3b to 9b

dagger-leaf rush

This perennial rush produces annual shoots to 60cm (2ft) from extensive rhizomes. Each shoot produces iris-like leaves, flattened from the midrib and clasping the stem (equitant). Flowers bloom in dense heads at the stem tips. Each inflorescence consists of up to ten heads and is subtended by a small, leaf-like bract. The attractive, spherical heads are up to 1.5cm (.5in) across and crowded with greenish brown to dark brownish purple flowers. Flowers bloom from early to late summer, and the fruits are small, oblong capsules.

Cultivation. Full sun or part shade, and moist to wet soil. This delicate looking rush adds interest and diversity to the pond margin, streambank, ditch, or wet place in the wildflower meadow, but it can reproduce aggressively, both by spreading rhizomes and from seed.

Native Habitat and Range. On moist to wet lake shores, streambanks, bog margins, and meadows at low to fairly high elevations, from Alaska south to California and Arizona and from the coast, east through the Rocky Mountains and rarely to the east coast.

Notes. Sickle-leaved rush (*J. falcatus*) has flattened, grass-like leaves and rounded heads of dark chocolate-brown flowers; it lives in tideflats and coastal marshes along the coast from Alaska to California. Bolander's rush (*J. bolanderi*) also has spherical heads of tawny to brown flowers, but its leaves are rounded, not flattened; it lives near tidal marshes and along rivers, mainly west of the Cascades from British Columbia, south to California.

Juncus ensifolius

Lathyrus vestitus ssp. *bolanderi*

Leptosiphon nuttallii

Lathyrus vestitus* ssp. *bolanderi	Zones 7b to 9b	Fabaceae

Pacific pea

This rhizomatous perennial produces climbing or somewhat erect stems to 1m (3ft) long. The pinnately compound leaves have leafy stipules at the base of the petiole and around ten oblong to ovate leaflets up to 6cm (2.5in) long. The tendrils at the tips of the leaves are well developed. Up to 20 flowers, each about 1.5cm (.5in) long, are produced in racemes. The flowers are white to cream, the banner petal sometimes washed and penciled with purple; they bloom from mid spring to early summer. The fruits, dry legumes, are up to 6cm (2.5in) long.

Cultivation. Full sun to part shade, and moist to somewhat dry, well-drained soil. Site this deciduous vining species near shrubs or small trees that will act as a trellis. Excellent for the margin of the hedgerow, wildlife planting, or woodland garden.

Propagation. Grow from seed collected in late summer and planted soon after harvest. As with many peas, the seeds have hard coats and will germinate more easily if they are scratched with a file, or placed in a dish and covered with hot (just below boiling) water, allowed to cool, and then planted. Sow seeds into containers of potting soil or directly into the garden, in fall or spring.

Native Habitat and Range. In woods, forest edges, and clearings at low to mid elevations from west central Washington, west of the Cascades and south to southern California.

Notes. Of the five subspecies, only *L. v.* ssp. *bolanderi* ranges north of California. *Lathyrus* includes approximately 100 species of annual and perennial herbs native to the temperate parts of the Northern Hemisphere and to some cooler, mountainous parts of South America and Africa; plants often grow as twining vines and usually have pinnately compound leaves tipped with tendrils. Close to 20 species are native to the Pacific Northwest, some of them very attractive plants, including silky beach pea (*L. littoralis*) with showy white and purple flowers, which lives in coastal dunes from southern British Columbia to central California. *Lathyrus japonicus* (beach pea) is another coastal species with pink and purplish flowers. Leafy pea (*L. polyphyllus*) and Torrey's pea (*L. torreyi*) mainly live west of the Cascades, while few-flowered pea (*L. pauciflorus*), stiff pea (*L. rigidus*), Sierra pea (*L. nevadensis*), and Nevada or mountain pea (*L. lanszwertii*) are often found in east-side forest or sagebrush habitats. *Vicia* is very similar to *Lathyrus*, but only a few of its more than 100 species are native. *Vicia americana* (American vetch), with purple flowers, is native to much of North America. *Vicia nigricans* ssp. *gigantea* (*V. gigantea*; giant or black vetch) has small, reddish flowers and can grow to 2m (6ft); it occurs along our coast and in forest clearings west of the Cascades.

Leptosiphon nuttallii	Zones 3b to 9b	Polemoniaceae

Nuttall's linanthus

This aromatic perennial produces multiple stems to 30cm (1ft) tall from a branching crown and a woody taproot. The leafy stems have opposite, sessile (lacking a petiole) leaves that are palmately compound into linear, spine-tipped leaflets up to 2cm (1in) long. Smaller leaves often grow from the axils of the larger stem leaves, and flowers bloom in leafy clusters, from very short peduncles, at the stem tips. The five-lobed calyx is about 1cm (.5in) long, and the woolly tube of the corolla is as long as the calyx. The five petal lobes are as long as the tube, spreading widely (salverform). The flowers are white or creamy with a yellow throat where the petal lobes meet the tube, blooming from early to late summer. The fruits are small, three-celled capsules, each chamber often containing a single seed.

Cultivation. Full sun or light shade, and well-drained, rather dry soil. This is a lovely addition to the sandy parts of the wildflower meadow, the drought-tolerant perennial border, or the stony rock garden slope on either side of the Cascades.

Propagation. Grow from seed collected in the late summer or fall and planted soon after harvest. Sow seeds into flats of potting soil or directly into the garden, and let them stratify over winter for germination in the spring.

Native Habitat and Range. On rocky, dry, sometimes brushy slopes at fairly low to high elevations in the Cascades of Washington and Oregon, south through California, east in the mountains of southeastern Washington, northeastern Oregon, and central Idaho to Wyoming, Colorado, and New Mexico.

Notes. Sometimes classified as *Linanthus nuttallii* or *Linanthastrum nuttallii*. *Leptosiphon n.* ssp. *nuttallii* is the most widespread subspecies in our area; the other three occur mainly to the south, but *L. n.* ssp. *pubescens*, a perennial of Nevada and adjacent eastern California, is apparently disjunct (geographically separated) in east central Washington. Close to 30 species of *Leptosiphon* occur in western North America, most in California and most of them annuals; about eight are native to the Pacific Northwest.

Lewisia		Portulacaceae

It's a great compliment to Meriwether Lewis, of the Lewis and Clark expedition, to have a genus of such unusual and stunning flowering plants named for him. *Lewisia* includes about 15 species, all native to western North America, with about ten occurring in the Pacific Northwest. These succulent, perennial herbs have fleshy roots or corms and basal clusters of thick, sometimes evergreen, entire leaves. Flowers come in brilliant shades of pink, magenta, and orange. Lewisias are much loved by alpine and rock gardeners, and many forms are readily available from nurseries. Some flowers, with showy pink or white flowers and dense cushions of narrow basal leaves, are in the same family as lewisias; *Phemeranthus sediformis* (*Talinum okanoganense*, Okanogan fameflower) and *P. spinescens* (*T. spinescens*; spiny fameflower) grow in arid, rocky habitats in British Columbia, Washington, and Oregon, and are attractive plants for rock gardens in dry climates.

Propagation. Generally not difficult from seed. Collect seeds from the capsules in late summer or fall. Plant them outside soon after harvest, directly into the garden or into containers with well-drained potting soil high in pumice, so that seedlings will be moist but not soggy. Winter weather will help break seed dormancy for spring germination. Seedlings are slow-growing and take a few years to reach flowering size. Most species are difficult to propagate vegetatively, but *L. cotyledon* can be grown from cuttings of the crowns made in spring. Rooted pieces of plants can be transplanted into pots; rootless sections can be treated with hormones and set into pumice or some other well-drained medium until roots form. This should be done only with plants grown from seed. Lewisias should never be dug from the wild.

Lewisia columbiana	Zones 5a to 9a

Columbia lewisia

This charming evergreen perennial grows from a fleshy, branched taproot. Shoots grow from simple, sometimes branched, crowns and produce many narrow, spoon-shaped (spatulate) leaves up to 10cm (4in) long. Flowering stems can grow to 30cm (1ft) tall, producing many flowers in branched panicles. Each flower is up to 2cm (1in) across and has up to nine petals, varying from magenta-pink to almost white with pink veins. Flowers bloom from late spring to late summer, and dark reddish black seeds ripen in rounded capsules.

Cultivation. Full sun or light shade, and very well-drained, gravelly soil. This is a beautiful, delicate plant for the rock garden or cracks in a stone wall. It's also a fine choice for a trough garden or clay pot. Although gardeners east of the Cascades will have an easier time growing this plant, it is reasonably tolerant of the wetter west-side climate. Adding a collar of small rock chips around its crown may help keep the plant from rotting. Do not water established garden plants.

Native Habitat and Range. On rocky slopes and open, gravelly banks at mid to high elevations from southern British Columbia, south through the Olympics, Cascades, and Coast Ranges to northern California, east to northeastern Oregon, adjacent Idaho, and western Montana.

Notes. *Lewisia c.* var. *columbiana* includes relatively large plants that occur in southwestern British Columbia and in the Cascades to California. *Lewisia c.* var. *wallowensis* includes smaller plants of northeastern Oregon and Idaho; *L. c.* var. *rupicola* grows in the Olympic Mountains of Washington and on Saddle Mountain in northwestern Oregon. *Lewisia pygmaea* (alpine lewisia) is a species of high mountaintops through much of the west; it produces several single flowers that can vary from white to lavender to dark pink. Nevada lewisia (*L. nevadensis*), another native of our western mountains, is considered a variety of *L. pygmaea* in some references. Threeleaf lewisia (*L. triphylla*) is native to vernally moist places in the arid parts of the west; unlike most lewisias, this species grows from a rounded corm, and instead of clusters of basal leaves, it produces three narrow leaves at the base of each flowering stem. The flowers are usually white with pink veins.

Lewisia cotyledon	Zones 4a to 9b

Siskiyou or imperial lewisia

This beautiful lewisia produces a thick, fleshy taproot and clusters of evergreen, spoon-shaped (spatulate) leaves up to 7cm (3in) long from a branching crown. Inflorescences are panicle or umbel-like and topped with numerous flowers, about 2.5cm (1in) across with up to ten petals. The petals are commonly whitish with a rosy central stripe, but cultivated plants come in various

Lewisia columbiana

Lewisia cotyledon

color forms. Blooming takes place from late spring to mid summer, and black, shiny seeds ripen in rounded capsules.

Cultivation. Full sun or light shade, and very well-drained, gravelly soil. Reasonably tolerant of the climate west of the Cascades; add a collar of small rock chips around the crown of the plant to help prevent crown rot in wetter gardens. Established garden plants are drought-tolerant. This popular rock garden plant also does well on a dry slope or between the stones in a wall, and it's an excellent choice for a trough garden or clay pot.

Native Habitat and Range. In open, rocky places at mid to high elevations in the mountains of southwestern Oregon and northwestern California.

Notes. *Lewisia c.* var. *howellii*, with wavy leaf margins, and *L. c.* var. *cotyledon*, with smooth to somewhat undulate leaves, occur in Oregon and California.

Lewisia rediviva	Zones 3b to 9a

bitterroot

Bitterroot is a small plant growing from a short crown and a branched, fleshy taproot. The leaves are basal, succulent, and almost linear, reaching 1.5 to 5cm (.5 to 2in) in length. They are the first parts to appear from the ground in the spring and begin to wither by flowering time. Each flowering stem grows to 3cm (1.5in) tall with a whorl of narrow bracts beneath the single flower. Each flower has up to nine sepals and around 15 petals that vary from almost white to light pink to deep rose, blooming from late spring to mid summer. Older plants may bear several flowers and produce dark, shiny seeds in papery capsules. Plants become dormant after blooming.

Cultivation. Full sun, and very well-drained, rocky soil. Bitterroot is a wonderful little plant for the rock garden or stone wall east of the Cascades. Gardeners west of the Cascades, except perhaps for southwestern Oregon, will have difficulty finding a sufficiently dry location in the garden. May be easier to grow in a trough or clay pot that can be sheltered from excessive rain. Adding a collar of small rock chips around the crown of the plant will also help keep it from rotting. Established garden plants should not be watered. Allow them to go dormant after flowering.

Native Habitat and Range. On stony, dry, and exposed sites in thin soils at mid elevations on the east side of the Cascades from British Columbia south into central California, and east to Montana, Colorado, and Arizona.

Notes. *Lewisia r.* var. *rediviva* shows variation in flower color and other features throughout its range in the west; populations to the east tend to have deeper pink flowers. Root diggers have harvested bitterroot from the same ancestral root grounds for many thousands of years, and it remains extremely important to many Native American tribes, both as a food and as a part of traditional cultures and religions. Bitterroot is the state flower of Montana.

Lewisia tweedyi	Zones 4a to 9b

Tweedy's lewisia

The thick, fleshy taproot of this perennial produces a branched crown and clusters of succulent, evergreen oblong to spoon-shaped (spatulate) leaves up to 20cm (8in) long. Flowering stems can grow to 20cm (8in) tall, each producing up to five flowers in a loose cluster. Each flower has around eight petals up to 4cm (1.5in) long, and flower color varies among individuals, from apricot or salmon to almost white. Flowers bloom from late spring to mid summer. Brownish seeds ripen in rounded capsules.

Cultivation. Full sun (in cooler climates) to afternoon shade or dappled light, and soil with excellent drainage. Some gardeners have success growing this lewisia by inserting plants horizontally, into the vertical face of a rock wall with overhanging rocks to provide protection from

Lewisia rediviva

Lewisia tweedyi

excess rain and sun. Plants in clay pots can also be protected from wet weather. Adding a collar of small rock chips around the crown of the plant may help keep it from rotting. Many gardeners consider this the loveliest of the lewisias, and nursery-grown plants are sometimes available.

Native Habitat and Range. In rock crevices, on talus, or on well-drained slopes, usually near open ponderosa pine woods at mid elevations, endemic to the Wenatchee Mountains of central Washington and adjacent British Columbia.

Notes. Often classified as *Cistanthe tweedyi*.

| **Leymus cinereus** | Zones 3b to 9b | Poaceae |

basin wildrye

This big bunchgrass produces clusters of flowering shoots to 2m (6ft) tall and 1m (3ft) across, the stems connected by short rhizomes. The leaf blades are tough and flat, up to 2cm (1in) across. The inflorescence is a dense spike to 20cm (8in) long. The small flowers (florets) are grouped into spikelets, the typical units of the grass inflorescence, and three or more spikelets are crowded around each node of the larger spike. Two narrow bracts, the glumes, subtend each spikelet. Each spikelet is made up of up to six florets. Each floret is further enclosed in its own pair of bracts, the lemma and the palea. The lemmas are sometimes tipped with an awn, a short bristle. The flowers bloom from early to mid summer, and the fruit is a grain, or caryopsis.

Cultivation. Full sun or light shade, and dry or somewhat moist soil with good drainage. This is a big, beautiful bunchgrass, mainly for gardens east of the Cascades. Makes a good screen or background for smaller perennials. Plant it at the edges of the dry wildflower meadow or with sagebrush and other drought-tolerant species in the wildlife garden.

Leymus cinereus (photo by Sally A. Simmons)

Lilium bolanderi

Propagation. Grow from seed collected in the late summer or early fall. Seeds can be planted into flats or directly into the garden in the fall and left outside for the winter, or they can be stored under cool, dry conditions and planted in the spring. Clumps connected by short rhizomes can be separated and transplanted in autumn.

Native Habitat and Range. Near streams and on gravelly slopes and sand dunes, often near sagebrush at low to fairly high elevations east of the Cascades from British Columbia, south to California and east through the Rocky Mountains.

Notes. Sometimes classified as *Elymus cinereus*. *Leymus* is a genus of approximately 50 species, a dozen native to North America, with half of these occurring in the Pacific Northwest. Both American dunegrass (*L. mollis*) and beardless wildrye (*L. triticoides*) likewise form clumps from thick rhizomes. *Leymus mollis* lives in sand dunes along the coast from Alaska through California and other parts of North America; *L. triticoides* lives in dunes and saline meadows in regions often dominated by sagebrush, mainly east of the Cascades, ranging east and south through much of the west.

Lilium   Liliaceae

lily

Close to 100 species of *Lilium* are native to the temperate regions of the Northern Hemisphere; around 20 of these are native to North America, with fewer than ten in the Pacific Northwest. These lovely, perennial herbs develop flowering stems with whorls of leaves from a bulb composed of fleshy scales. Lily flowers have three petals and three petaloid sepals (tepals or perianth parts). The flowers of some species are trumpet-shaped; in others, the tepals are curled backward (recurved). The fruits are three-parted capsules. Although our native lilies are stunningly beautiful, some of them require exacting conditions that are difficult to duplicate in the garden. They are often pollinated by hummingbirds and butterflies.

Propagation. Collect seeds in the late summer after capsules have ripened. Plant them within a few weeks of harvest, either directly into the garden or into deep containers, and leave them outside in the cool, moist winter weather for germination the following spring. Seedlings will take several years to reach flowering size. Those that were sown in containers can be left in them for part of that time; it may be easier to protect them from slugs. Most species can also be propagated in the late summer by removing some of the bulb scales and transplanting them, but this should be done only with plants originally grown from seed and never with plants poached from the wild.

Lilium bolanderi	Zones 7b to 9b

Bolander's lily

The stems of this lily grow to 1m (3ft) in height. The leaves are arranged in whorls of up to ten at each node. They are oblanceolate (lance-shaped, widest toward the tip), up to 5cm (2in) long, thick, and glaucous, whitish with a waxy coating. The flowers are slightly nodding or horizontal and about 3.5cm (1.5in) long, blooming from early to late summer. The tepals are crimson to purplish red with darker purple spots and funnel-shaped. The capsules contain many seeds and are about 3cm (1.5in) long.

Cultivation. Part shade or dappled light, and fast-draining, rather dry soil. May tolerate a somewhat wider range of conditions than its very restricted native habitat would suggest. Protect from extremes of moisture or cold. This is a beautiful lily for the hummingbird or rock garden. Plant it near shrubs on a dry slope or in the stony, open wildflower meadow.

Native Habitat and Range. In dry clay or rocky, serpentine soils of forest openings, often among shrubs at mid elevations in the mountains of southwestern Oregon and northwestern California.

Notes. Wild populations of this endemic lily require protection. Nurseries specializing in lilies may grow it from seed, and gardeners may be able to find it through a seed exchange. *Lilium parvum* (Sierra, alpine, or small tiger lily) has similar, bell-shaped, red-orange flowers with darker spots; it occurs as far north as southwestern Oregon.

Lilium columbianum	Zones 4b to 9b

Columbia or tiger lily

This charming lily produces hairless, flowering stems to 1.2m (3.5ft) or more from a bulb with thick scales. The main leaves are lance-shaped, to 10cm (4in) long, and arranged in whorls along the stem with six to nine leaves per whorl. Flowering shoots produce one to 20 flowers on long pedicels in late spring and summer; the recurved tepals are 4 to 6cm (1.5 to 2.5in) long and yellow-orange to red-orange with maroon spots. Numerous seeds ripen in capsules to 4cm (1.5in) long.

Cultivation. Full sun to part shade or dappled light, and moist soil with good organic content. This is a wonderful plant for recreating a mountain meadow or stream-side thicket; although the flowers are relatively small, they are graceful in shape and numerous on older plants. Plant it among the taller perennials in the hummingbird garden or near the pond margin (be careful when handling, as the stems are easily detached from the bulb). Openings and edges of the woodland garden are other good places for it.

Native Habitat and Range. In meadows, thickets, and open woods at low to fairly high elevations, on both sides of the Cascades from British Columbia south, through western Oregon to northern California, and east to Idaho and Montana.

Lilium columbianum

Lilium occidentale

Lilium pardalinum ssp. vollmeri

Lilium washingtonianum

Notes. The bulbs of this, our best-known native lily, were eaten by many indigenous tribes, primarily as a spice or condiment to accompany other foods.

Lilium occidentale   Zones 8b to 9b

western lily

This lovely perennial grows from a scaly, rhizomatous bulb, producing stems to 1.5m (5ft) or a bit more. The linear leaves, up to 15cm (6in) long, are often scattered on the stems rather than arranged in whorls. Each stem produces one to eight striking flowers on long pedicels. The tepals are green at their bases, changing to orange and then crimson at the recurved tips, and spotted with maroon. The stamens tend to hang downward, and the flowers bloom from early to mid summer. The capsules grow to 2.5cm (1in) long.

Cultivation. Part shade or dappled light, and wet, acidic soil. Plant this species in the bog garden or near the edge of the pond, near acid-loving shrubs or among ferns, to help prop up its weak stems.

Native Habitat and Range. In sphagnum bogs and wet, acidic places, often among ferns, at low elevations near the coast from southwestern Oregon to northwestern California.

Notes. This is an endangered species with a very small range, and the remaining wild habitat must be protected. The flowers should never be picked and the plants never dug; however, the species would benefit from cultivation, and motivated gardeners may be able to find seed from conservation groups or seed exchanges.

Lilium pardalinum ssp. vollmeri   Zones 8b to 9b

leopard lily, Vollmer's lily

This lily usually produces a cluster of stems to 1m (3ft) from scaly, rhizomatous bulbs. The leaves are narrowly lanceolate, up to 15cm (6in) long, and usually arranged in whorls at the middle of the stem. Up to several flowers, around 6cm (2.5in) long, nod from long pedicels. The tepals are strongly recurved, varying from yellow to orange, with reddish margins and maroon dots. The anthers tend to spread widely on long filaments. Flowers bloom from early to mid summer, and the fruits are angled capsules about 3cm (1.5in) long.

Cultivation. Full sun or part shade, and moist to wet soil. This is a beautiful lily for the bog garden or pond margin. Plant it in a wet to moist spot at the woodland edge, in the wildflower meadow, or among the other moisture loving perennials in the hummingbird garden.

Native Habitat and Range. Along streams and in boggy sites, often with *Darlingtonia*, near the coast at low elevations in southwestern Oregon and northwestern California.

Notes. This subspecies and *L. p.* ssp. *wigginsii* are sometimes given the rank of species. *Lilium p.* ssp. *pardalinum* is larger, with stems to 2m (6ft) and yellow flowers spotted with maroon; Wiggins' lily is similar but smaller. Both range as far north as southern Oregon. Leopard lily cultivars are often available in nurseries, especially from growers specializing in the genus.

Lilium washingtonianum   Zones 6a to 9b

Washington lily

The bulbs of this lily are somewhat rhizomatous, oblique in shape, and 10 to 20cm (4 to 8in) long with fleshy scales. Stems can reach 2m (6ft) tall, and the narrowly elliptic leaves, about 10cm (4in) long, are arranged in whorls of six to 12 at each node. Up to 20 flowers are arranged in a raceme along the stem. The flowers are trumpet shaped, fragrant and up to 10cm (4in) long. The tepals are white or pinkish with red dots, often fading to darker pink, and not strongly recurved. They bloom from mid to late summer and are followed by capsules to 3cm (1.5in) long.

Cultivation. Part shade or dappled light, and fairly dry, well-drained soil. Plant this lily in the woodland garden or border of the wildflower meadow, preferably near shrubs or low-branching trees that will help keep the stems erect.

Native Habitat and Range. In brush or open forests on dry slopes at mid to high elevations, near the Columbia River Gorge and north central Oregon, south on both slopes of the Cascades, through the mountains to central California.

Notes. *Lilium w.* ssp. *purpurascens* (Cascade lily) is the more northern subspecies. Kellogg's lily (*L. kelloggii*), with similarly whitish or purplish tepals with darker spots, ranges as far north as the southwestern corner of Oregon.

Linum lewisii	Zones 3b to 9b	Linaceae

Lewis' or wild blue flax

This slender perennial develops a cluster of stems reaching 20 to 60cm (8 to 24in) from a woody crown. Many linear leaves 2 to 5cm (1 to 2in) in length clothe the stems. Bright blue flowers with five petals about 2cm (1in) long bloom at the stem tips from late spring to mid summer. The fruits are small capsules.

Cultivation. Sun, and moist to rather dry, well-drained or rocky soil. This species makes an excellent addition to the perennial bed in gardens throughout our area, adds airiness to a wildflower meadow or sunny garden path, and does well in the rock garden, as a taller, graceful background plant.

Propagation. Easy from seed collected in late summer or fall and either planted soon after harvest or sown in spring. Seeds can be sown directly into the garden or into flats of potting soil. Plants are often short-lived, lasting only a few years, but they generally self-sow once established.

Native Habitat and Range. In open dry meadows and along roadsides, at mid to fairly high elevations from Alaska south, mainly east of the Cascade crest, to California and Arizona, east through the Great Plains to Texas.

Notes. Sometimes classified as *L. perenne* var. *lewisii*. The wide-ranging *L. l.* var. *lewisii* occurs in our area. *Linum* includes at least 100 species of herbs native to the temperate regions of the world, especially in the Northern Hemisphere; of the nearly 30 species of flax native to North America, only *L. lewisii* occurs in the Pacific Northwest.

Lithophragma	Saxifragaceae

woodland or prairie star

Lithophragma includes nine species, all native to western North America; five occur in the Pacific Northwest. Plants grow from slender rhizomes that bear small underground bulblets the size of rice grains. The showy flowers are carried in simple or sometimes partly compound racemes; they have ten stamens and a cup-shaped calyx with five lobes and five white or pink petals with lobed tips. The fruits are small capsules with three beak-like styles, containing many small seeds. Most of the leaves are basal, with long petioles and blades palmately divided into lobed leaflets. The stem leaves are smaller, often with slender petioles and membranous stipules.

Propagation. Grow from seed or (in *L. glabrum*) from the bulblets that replace some of the flowers. Collect seeds or bulblets in late spring or summer, and plant them after harvest in late summer, sprinkling them onto the surface of well-drained, moist potting soil in flats; leave them outside for the winter. It may take a couple of years to have plants of flowering size. Established garden populations may reseed themselves.

Linum lewisii

Lithophragma glabrum

Lithophragma glabrum   Zones 3b to 9b

smooth or bulbous woodland or prairie star

This delicate perennial produces flowering stems up to 25cm (10in) tall from thin rhizomes. The basal leaves have petioles about 2.5cm (1in) long and blades about 2.5cm (1in) across. The leaves are palmately divided, usually into five cuneate (wedge-shaped) leaflets, each leaflet with three lobes at the tip. The inflorescence is a few-flowered raceme, short and compact at first, but elongating with age. The flowers are set on slender pedicels, and the calyx is usually bell-shaped (campanulate) with five rounded lobes. The five petals are pinkish or purplish, and their tips are usually divided into five (sometimes three) deep lobes. The flowers are about 1.5cm (.5in) across, blooming in late spring, early spring at low elevations. Clusters of small, reddish purple bulblets replace the flowers in the axils of the stem leaves; bulblet-bearing plants are often purple-tinted. The seeds are brownish, with tiny spines.

Cultivation. Full sun to part shade or dappled light, and soil that is well-drained and moist early in the season. Plant this dainty perennial in the sunny or partly shaded wildflower meadow, rock garden, or at the woodland edge. It is tougher than it looks and able to survive summer drought. After setting seed it goes dormant and disappears, but it is lovely in the spring, especially in small drifts.

Native Habitat and Range. Among bunchgrasses and sagebrush in the arid shrub-steppe and in open, rather dry forest at low to mid elevations, mainly east of the Cascades from southern British Columbia, south to southern California, west to southern Vancouver Island and southwestern Oregon, east to Alberta, South Dakota, and Colorado.

Notes. Sometimes classified as *L. glabra* and presently includes *L. bulbiferum* (*L. bulbifera*). *Lithophragma tenellum* (slender woodland star), another species of arid shrub-steppe and forest habitats, has a wide range, mainly east of the Cascades to the Rocky Mountains, it grows to 25cm (10in) tall and has white or pale pinkish flowers.

Lithophragma parviflorum — Zones 4a to 9b

small-flowered woodland or prairie star

This tiny, purple-tinted ephemeral is perennial from the small bulblets. Plants are glandular-hairy and grow 10 to 40cm (4 to 16in) from slender rhizomes. Most leaves are basal, with petioles up to 6cm (2.5in) long and blades about 2.5cm (1in) across. The leaf blades are rounded in outline and palmately divided into five leaflets; the leaflets are further divided into narrow lobes. The flowering stem has smaller leaves, and the inflorescence is a raceme, condensed at first, but expanding up to 15cm (6in) as the flowers bloom. The flowers have short pedicels and are almost 2.5cm (1in) across. The calyx is conical and widest toward the tip, topped with five triangular lobes. The five petals vary from white to pink or purplish, and each petal has three (sometimes five) narrow lobes. Flowers bloom in early spring, after which the plant goes dormant, disappearing completely by summer. The seeds are brown and elliptical with a reticulate surface.

Cultivation. Full sun to part shade or dappled light, and well-drained soil that is moist early in the spring. Lovely in the sunny or partly shaded wildflower meadow or rock garden, along a dappled woodland path, or under deciduous trees.

Native Habitat and Range. In open meadows, rocky areas, dry oak woodlands, open forest and shrub-steppe at low to mid elevations on both sides of the Cascades from British Columbia south to northern California, east to Alberta, South Dakota, Nebraska and Colorado.

Notes. Sometimes classified as *L. parviflora*. *Lithophragma p.* var. *parviflorum* occurs throughout the range. Hillside woodland star (*L. heterophyllum*), San Francisco woodland star (*L. affine*), and Siskiyou Mountain woodland star (*L. campanulatum*) occur in southern Oregon.

Lithospermum ruderale — Zones 3b to 9b — Boraginaceae

western stoneseed, gromwell, puccoon

This perennial produces a cluster of leafy, hairy stems up to 60cm (2ft) tall from a woody taproot. The leaves are alternate and lance-shaped to linear, largest on the upper parts of the stem and up to 10cm (4in) long by 1cm (.5in) wide. Flowers bloom in small, leafy clusters from the axils of the upper leaves. The corollas are about 1.5cm (.5in) long, tubular at the base with five free lobes. The flowers are creamy or light greenish yellow and bloom from mid spring to early summer. Each flower produces up to four shiny, grayish nutlets.

Cultivation. Full sun or light shade, and well-drained, rather dry soil. Can be grown on either side of the Cascades, but may need especially sharp drainage on the west side. This is a pretty perennial for the rock garden or dry bank. Plant it in the gravelly place in the wildflower meadow or near the dry edge of the woodland garden.

Propagation. Grow from seed collected in the late summer and planted in the fall. Sow seeds into deep containers of potting soil or directly into the garden, and leave them outside to stratify over the winter for germination in the spring. Alternatively, take stem cuttings during the summer; treat with hormones, insert into pumice, and keep humid until roots form.

Native Habitat and Range. In open woods, dry hills, and plains at low to mid elevations from southern British Columbia, south to northern California and east to Montana, Wyoming, and Colorado, mostly east of the Cascades, but occasionally in dry places on the west side.

Notes. Various tribes used the roots of this plant as a source of dye. *Lithospermum* includes around 40 species widely distributed through much of the world. Fewer than 20 are native to

Lithophragma parviflorum

Lithospermum ruderale (photo by Sally A. Simmons)

North America, most of them south and east of our area. California stoneseed (*L. californicum*) has yellow flowers and ranges into southwestern Oregon from northern California.

Lomatium

Apiaceae

desert-parsley, biscuitroot

Lomatium is a taxonomically difficult genus with around 75 species, some of them highly variable. Lomatiums are native to western and central North America and probably reach their maximum diversity east of the Cascades, in the shrub-steppe regions of the Pacific Northwest, where there are around 50 species, several of them rare endemics. Those known as biscuitroots develop fleshy taproots that are dug in early spring and eaten by interior tribes of the Northwest; these plants continue to figure in religious ceremonies. The leaves of other species are harvested by Native Americans as "celery," and the dry, aromatic fruits are useful as medicine. Some are tastier than others, but all species are edible. This cannot be said for other genera of the Apiaceae, some of which are deadly poisonous. Don't try nibbling any carrot, celery, or parsley relative until you are quite certain of its identity. Legitimate tribal root diggers are the only people who should ever dig biscuitroots in the wild. Increasingly in demand for rock gardens and as a potential source of food for butterfly larvae, several seed grown lomatiums are now commercially available.

Propagation. Collect seeds in late spring or summer, and plant them outside in fall, either directly into the garden or into deep containers that will accommodate the young taproots. Leave planted seeds outside to cold stratify over winter for germination in the spring. Plants will take a few years to reach flowering size.

| *Lomatium columbianum* | Zones 5a to 9b |

Columbia desert-parsley

This perennial grows from a thick, woody taproot and generally reaches around 60cm (2ft) in height. The leaves are pinnately compound, very finely divided into linear segments. The ferny foliage is glabrous (hairless) and glaucous, covered with a waxy bloom, and purplish in hue. The numerous tiny flowers bloom from early to mid spring. They are usually purple and arranged into typical umbels. Each peduncle produces umbels with up to 14 rays, each to 20cm (8in) long, and each ray produces a cluster of flowers. The fruits are dry schizocarps, which split into single-seeded halves at maturity; they are elliptical in shape, have a thickened margin, and reach up to 2.5cm (1in) long.

Cultivation. Full sun or light shade, and very well-drained, rocky, rather dry soil. Needs no summer water (plants typically become dormant after fruits ripen). Though it will probably have a shorter life span, this species can be grown successfully west of the Cascades on a site with good drainage. A beautiful and unusual plant for the rock garden or butterfly garden when planted in a sunny, dry spot.

Native Habitat and Range. On rocky sites, usually at fairly low elevations, in the eastern part of the Columbia River Gorge, north near the eastern slope of the Cascades to south central Washington.

Notes. *Lomatium cous* (cous biscuitroot), *L. gormanii* (pepper and salt, Gorman's biscuitroot), and *L. canbyi* (Canby's biscuitroot) all have enlarged, tuber-like roots.

| *Lomatium dissectum* | Zones 3b to 9b |

fern-leaf desert-parsley

This large perennial grows from a woody taproot and produces flowering shoots to 1.5m (5ft) at maturity. The leaves are pinnately compound and fern-like, finely dissected into narrow lobes with a somewhat rough surface. The flowering umbels are composed of ten to 30 rays, the longest up to 10cm (4in) long. Tiny yellow or burgundy flowers bloom on short pedicels at the tips of the rays from mid spring to early summer. The flattened schizocarps are elliptic in shape and up to 1.5cm (.5in) long, with narrowly winged margins.

Cultivation. Full sun or part shade, and well-drained, rocky, rather dry soil. This beautiful species can be grown throughout our area. Try it in the dry, rocky place in the wildflower meadow, the large rock garden, the perennial border, or the butterfly garden, where its flowers will attract adults and its foliage may provide food for the larvae of some species.

Native Habitat and Range. In open, dry meadows, rocky slopes and talus, from fairly low to mid elevations, from southern British Columbia and Alberta, south on both sides of the Cascades to California and Arizona, and east through the Rocky Mountains to Montana, Colorado, and New Mexico.

Notes. *Lomatium d.* var. *multifidum* occurs over most of the range; *L. d.* var. *dissectum* is more western, ranging as far east as Idaho. Nine-leaf desert-parsley (*L. triternatum*), Martindale's or Cascade desert-parsley (*L. martindalei*), and bare-stem desert-parsley (*L. nudicaule*) all grow in suitably dry and rocky habitats on both sides of the Cascades; as with *L. dissectum*, their long, narrow taproots are too tough to be considered edible, but their foliage and fruits were used as food, flavoring, and medicine. The leaves of *L. nudicaule* are waxy and bluish (glaucous), with large oval or lance-shaped leaflets, up to 9cm (3.5in) long.

Lomatium columbianum

Lomatium grayi

Lomatium dissectum

Lomatium grayi   Zones 4a to 9a

Gray's desert-parsley

This perennial grows 15 to 50cm (6 to 20in) from a long taproot. The leaves are very finely dissected, and the ultimate segments bend at different angles to add to the fluffy effect. The tiny bright yellow flowers are arranged in umbels with rays up to 10cm (4in) at maturity. They bloom from mid to late spring. The fruits, dry schizocarps, are elliptical, flattened, and about 1cm (.5in) long with winged margins.

Cultivation. Full sun or light shade, and well-drained soil. Does best in the drier climates of the Pacific Northwest. Include this species in the rock garden for a lovely spring display. It is also a good choice for a stony, dry spot in the wildflower meadow or butterfly garden.

Native Habitat and Range. In dry, open, often rocky places at low to mid elevations, mainly east of the Cascade crest from central Washington, south to Oregon and Nevada, east to Idaho, Wyoming, Utah, and Colorado.

Notes. One of the most widespread species brightening the Columbia River Gorge and shrub-steppe areas east of the Cascades in the spring. *Lomatium g.* var. *grayi* in our area, often along roadsides. The similar *Pteryxia terebinthina* (*Cymopterus terebinthinus*; turpentine wavewing), another carrot relative, occurs throughout the east-side shrub-steppe; this aromatic plant has more coarsely divided leaves and fruits with several wings running along the ribs.

Lomatium utriculatum   Zones 6b to 9b

spring gold, fine-leaf desert-parsley

This perennial grows to about 60cm (2ft) tall from a slender taproot. The stems are leafy, and the leaves are soft-textured, pinnately dissected into narrow segments. The leaf blades are ovate in outline and up to 15cm (6in) long on petioles to 10cm (4in). The tiny yellow flowers are arranged in umbels on rays that vary in length, the longest ones up to 7cm (3in) at maturity. The bracts that subtend the flowers of each ray are rounded and leaf-like, tipped with shallow teeth or lobes. The flowers bloom from mid spring to early summer. The fruits, dry schizocarps, are about 1cm (.5in) long, and the margins have well-developed wings.

Cultivation. Full sun or light shade, and well-drained soil. An excellent ferny plant for rock gardens, stony banks, or dry, rocky places in the butterfly garden or wildflower meadow west of the Cascades.

Native Habitat and Range. On open, rocky slopes, bluffs, and meadows that are moist in spring at low elevations west of the Cascades from southwestern British Columbia, south through California.

Notes. Hall's desert-parsley (*L. hallii*) is another yellow-flowered species with a range west of the Cascade crest in Oregon. Bigseed desert-parsley (*L. macrocarpum*) is a white-flowered species of rocky places; it occurs on both sides of the Cascades and through much of the west.

Lotus formosissimus   Zones 7b to 9b   Fabaceae

seaside bird's-foot trefoil

This perennial produces lax stems to about 60cm (2ft) long from a taproot. The leaves are pinnately compound, with small stipules at the base of each petiole and around five leaflets, each about 1.5cm (.5in) long. Showy flowers, to 1.5cm (.5in) long, bloom in crowded umbels of up to a dozen flowers from late spring to mid summer. The banner petal is yellow; the other petals are pinkish or purplish. Fruits are slender legumes up to 6cm (2.5in) long.

Lomatium utriculatum

Lotus formosissimus

Cultivation. Full sun to part shade, and moist to rather wet soil. This is a charming perennial for the margin of the pond, stream, or wetland, or the wetter spots in the wildflower meadow or perennial bed.

Propagation. Difficult from seed: as with many peas, the seed coats are hard. Collect seeds in late summer or fall and plant soon after harvest. To help break dormancy, first place them in a dish and cover them with hot (just below boiling) water; after they have cooled, plant seeds into containers or directly into the garden, and leave them outside over winter for germination the following spring.

Native Habitat and Range. In moist soils near ponds and streams, often near the coast, at low to mid elevations, from the southern tip of Vancouver Island, southwestern Washington, west of the Cascades, south to central California.

Notes. *Lotus* encompasses around 100 species, widely distributed in the temperate regions; of the nearly 40 that occur in North America, about a dozen are Pacific Northwest natives. Other perennials with garden potential are *L. pinnatus* (meadow bird's-foot trefoil, bog deervetch), a species with showy yellow and white flowers, found in moist soils near lakes and streams on both sides of the Cascades, and *L. crassifolius* (big deervetch), which grows to 1m (3ft) or more along streams or in moist woods. Its flowers vary from whitish to greenish yellow, spotted or washed with purple. *Hedysarum* is another genus of perennial legumes with showy flowers, mostly in shades of pink and purple; our natives, which are usually found in rocky places and forest openings, include northern sweetvetch (*H. boreale*) and western sweetvetch (*H. occidentale*). *Dalea* (*Petalostemon*) is another genus of attractive legumes that inhabit arid regions, mainly in the Southwest. Pink-flowered *D. ornata* (Blue Mountain prairie-clover) lives east of the Cascades; its tiny flowers grow in dense spikes and are not typically pea shaped.

Lupinus   Fabaceae

lupine

Lupinus includes at least 165 species distributed throughout much of the world. The center of lupine diversity is western North America, with more than 50 species occurring in the Pacific Northwest alone. Lupines are some of our best-known wildflowers, recognized by hikers and gardeners everywhere; they are important food plants for the larvae of some butterflies, and many wildlife species eat their seeds. They and other legumes, both native and exotic, colonize sandy beaches, dredge spoils, and other areas that are too poor in nutrients for most plants. A bacterium (*Rhizobium* sp.) housed in nodules formed on their roots is able to fix atmospheric nitrogen into nitrate, a form that is chemically useful to the plants; in exchange for the nitrates, the legume supplies the bacterial colony with carbohydrates from photosynthesis. As garden plants, lupines are fast-growing but short-lived; happily, they often self-sow. The species are highly variable and tend to hybridize, making for some taxonomic difficulties; at least some contain toxic compounds, and all should be avoided as a food source for humans or livestock.

Propagation. Easiest from seed planted in fall or spring. Collect seeds in late summer, before the pods split open, and plant them in the fall, or store them in cool, dry conditions for spring planting. Before planting in the spring, put the seeds in a dish and pour hot (just below boiling) water over them. Let them cool and then plant them into flats of potting soil or directly into the garden, where they should germinate within a few weeks. Lupines can also be propagated from cuttings made at the base of the crown in the early spring. Treat the cuttings with rooting hormones, set them into pumice or some other medium, and keep them moist and humid until roots form.

Lupinus latifolius   Zones 5b to 9b

broadleaf or arctic lupine

This lupine can reach about 1m (3ft) in height, producing several stems from a woody crown. The plants are usually sparsely hairy, and the alternate leaves have long petioles. The palmately compound leaves generally have seven to nine elliptic leaflets up to 6cm (2.5in) long. Bluish lavender pea-like flowers, about 1.5cm (.5in) long, bloom in racemes up to 20cm (8in) in length, from early to late summer. The fruits are legumes, pea pods, up to 3cm (1.5in) long.

Cultivation. Full sun to part shade, and moist to rather dry, well-drained soil. This is an excellent addition to the tall perennials of the wildflower meadow or butterfly garden. Plant it along the sunny edge of the woodland garden or in the herbaceous border.

Native Habitat and Range. In open, wooded slopes and meadows, occasionally in the lowlands, but commonly at mid to fairly high elevations in the mountains from British Columbia to California, from the Cascade crest, west to the coast, and east to Utah and New Mexico.

Notes. Sometimes confused with *L. arcticus*, another native mountain species. *Lupinus l.* ssp. *latifolius* ranges through most of our area; *L. l.* ssp. *viridifolius* occurs in Oregon and California. Similar are two species that occur west of the Cascades, riverbank lupine (*L. rivularis*), a species of low elevations, and sickle-keeled lupine (*L. albicaulis*), with purple, yellow, or whitish flowers.

Lupinus latifolius

Lupinus lepidus (photo by Sally A. Simmons)

Lupinus lepidus   Zones 3b to 9a

Pacific or prairie lupine

This lupine grows to a maximum height of about 30cm (1ft) and tends to form mats. Plants are hairy with silky or rusty hairs. The palmately compound leaves grow on long petioles and have up to nine oblanceolate (lance-shaped, but broadest toward the tip) leaflets up to 4cm (1.5in) long. Densely flowered racemes are produced on peduncles up to 15cm (6in) long. The flowers, blue or purplish (occasionally white) and about 1cm (.5in) long, bloom from early to late summer. The fruits are small, hairy legumes, about 1.5cm (.5in) long.

Cultivation. Full sun, and well-drained, rocky or gravelly soil. Must be protected from excessive sogginess west of the Cascades. This is a lovely, low-growing lupine for the rock garden, trough, or dry, sandy place in the wildflower meadow.

Native Habitat and Range. In open and rocky, often arid habitats at mid to high elevations on both sides of the Cascades from British Columbia south through Washington and Oregon.

Notes. The dainty, silvery *L. sellulus* ssp. *sellulus* var. *lobbii* (*L. lepidus* var. *lobbii*, *L. lobbii*; dwarf prairie lupine) is a charming plant of talus slopes and rocky ridges, usually at high elevations in the Olympics and Cascades, south to California and Nevada. *Lupinus aridus* (*L. lepidus* var. *aridus*; desert lupine) grows in dry, often gravelly soils east of the Cascades from central Washington, south to California and east to Arizona, Utah, and Montana. Rock lupine (*L. saxosus*) is another low-growing perennial of dry, rocky habitats east of the Cascades; it is found at mid to fairly high elevations, often near sagebrush from central Washington, south through eastern Oregon to northern California and Nevada.

Lupinus leucophyllus

Lupinus leucophyllus   Zones 3b to 8b

velvet lupine

This lupine grows from a branched crown, producing shoots to 60cm (2ft) or more that are usually covered with grayish to rusty hairs. Each palmately compound leaf has up to ten oblong leaflets to 5cm (2in) long, hairy on both surfaces. Densely flowered racemes to 20cm (8in) long bloom on short peduncles. The pea-shaped flowers are about 1cm (.5in) long and vary from lavender to almost white, blooming from early to late summer. The hairy pods can grow to 2.5cm (1in).

Cultivation. Full sun to light shade, and well-drained, rather dry, rocky soil. This is an excellent lupine for the dry wildflower meadow or butterfly garden east of the Cascades. Plant it with sagebrush and other drought-tolerant plants in the wildlife garden.

Native Habitat and Range. On dry, rocky hillsides and among sagebrush at fairly low to mid elevations east of the Cascades from southern British Columbia, south to northern California and east to Montana, Wyoming, and Utah.

Notes. Two subspecies are recognized, *L. l.* ssp. *erectus* and *L. l.* ssp. *leucophyllus* (which itself is further divided into three varieties). Silky lupine (*L. sericeus*) is another species of dry habitats mainly east of the Cascades; it grows to about 60cm (2ft), and the flowers can vary in color, from blue or purple to white or yellowish.

Lupinus littoralis

Lupinus polyphyllus

Lupinus littoralis   Zones 7b to 9b

seashore lupine

This prostrate perennial often forms mats with branches up to 60cm (2ft) long. The plants are usually somewhat silvery with long hairs. The palmately compound leaves have long petioles and lance-shaped leaflets, broadest toward their tips (oblanceolate). The racemes are up to 15cm (6in) long and loosely flowered. The bluish or purplish flowers, about 1cm (.5in) long, bloom from late spring to late summer. The hairy pods are up to 3.5cm (1.5in) long.

Cultivation. Full sun, and sandy, moist to rather dry soil. This is an excellent perennial for sandy gardens and dunes, especially near the immediate coast. It is a fine addition to the well-drained parts of the wildflower meadow and will provide food for some butterfly larvae.

Native Habitat and Range. In dunes and beaches along the coast from southern British Columbia, south to northern California.

Notes. Various coastal tribes ate the roasted roots of this species.

Lupinus polyphyllus   Zones 3b to 9b

large leaved or bigleaf lupine

This perennial produces several stems up to 1.5m (5ft) from a branched crown. The plants are usually somewhat hairy, often with reddish hairs. The leaves are palmately compound, and the basal leaves are the largest, with petioles up to 30cm (1ft) long and ten to 15 leaflets up to 10cm (4in) in length. Numerous pea flowers are produced in dense racemes up to 40cm (16in) tall. The flowers, blue to violet and about 1.5cm (.5in) long, bloom from early to late summer. The fruits are hairy pods to 5cm (2in) long.

Cultivation. Full sun to part shade, and moist to rather wet soil. This is an excellent addition to the herbaceous border, the tall perennials of the butterfly garden, or the moist wildflower meadow on either side of the Cascades. Try it along the sunnier edge of the pond or wetland. Once established, this lupine often reseeds itself generously.

Native Habitat and Range. Along streams, in moist to wet meadows, fields and open forests, at low to mid elevations, from Alaska south to California, and from the coast, east to Alberta, Montana, the vicinity of the Great Lakes, and parts of the east coast.

Notes. Two varieties of *L. p.* ssp. *polyphyllus*, the most common and widespread taxon, occur in our area. This species is one of the original parents in the Russell hybrid series of cultivated lupines, and, although it does not produce their rainbow range of flower colors, it seems to be less susceptible than the hybrids to aphids and mildew.

Lupinus sulphureus	Zones 5a to 8b

sulphur lupine

This perennial produces simple stems up to 1m (3ft) from a branching crown. The plants are somewhat hairy, and the palmately compound leaves have up to 11 narrow leaflets to 4cm (1.5in) long. Flowering racemes grow to 15cm (6in) and produce numerous blossoms, each about 1cm (.5in). Flowers vary in color from yellowish to bluish and bloom from mid spring to early summer. Seeds ripen in pods about 2.5cm (1in) long.

Cultivation. Full sun or light shade, and well-drained, rocky, dry soil. This is an excellent lupine to plant with taller perennials in the dry parts of the wildflower meadow or butterfly garden in southwestern Oregon or east of the Cascades. Include it with sagebrush and other drought-tolerant plants in the wildlife garden.

Native Habitat and Range. On dry, gravelly slopes at mid elevations, mainly east of the Cascades in British Columbia, Washington, and Oregon.

Notes. *Lupinus arbustus* (*L. laxiflorus*; longspur lupine) has flowers that are variable in color, ranging from white or cream to pinkish, blue, or purple; it usually grows with ponderosa pine or sagebrush, east of the Cascades.

Lysichiton americanus	Zones 3b to 9b	Araceae

skunk cabbage, swamp lantern

This big, lush perennial, one of the very first to bloom, grows from fleshy, upright rhizomes. Flowering shoots push up out of the boggy ground in early or mid spring, often before the leaves appear. Small flowers are crowded into a large spike, the spadix. A showy yellow bract, the spathe, grows to 20cm (8in) long and surrounds the flower spike. The bold, glabrous (hairless) leaves can become huge, up to 1.5m (5ft) long by .5m (1.5ft) wide. The green or reddish, berry-like fruits develop along the spadix and are somewhat embedded in it.

Cultivation. Shade or part sun, and mucky, boggy soil. Every wet spot in the garden deserves a skunk cabbage. Some people find its smell unpleasant, but this species is bold enough to be enjoyed from a distance. Its yellow "lanterns" brighten the early spring garden, and all summer its leaves give the pond margin, bog garden, or wet place in the woodland or shade garden a tropical feel.

Propagation. Grow from seed collected in the summer and planted outside shortly after harvest, into containers of moist potting soil or directly into the garden. Leave the planted seeds out-

Lupinus sulphureus (photo by Sally A. Simmons)

Lysichiton americanus

side during fall and winter for germination the following spring. Alternatively, divide rhizomes in the spring.

Native Habitat and Range. In boggy areas, wet forests, and along streams at low to mid elevations from Alaska south to California, and from the coast east, in British Columbia and northeastern Washington to Idaho.

Notes. This beautiful plant is related to *Arisaema* (jack-in-the-pulpit), *Zantedeschia* (calla lily), and other aroids. There is only one other species in the genus.

Machaeranthera canescens	Zones 3b to 9b	Asteraceae

hoary aster, tansyaster

This biennial or short-lived perennial produces several branching stems, usually up to 60cm (2ft) tall, from a taproot. The plants are covered with fine, white hairs, and the leaves are narrowly oblanceolate (lance-shaped, but widest toward the tip). The leaf margins usually have teeth with small spines at their tips. The lower leaves are the longest, up to 10cm (4in). The branched stems produce many flowering heads, each bearing up to 25 ray florets with bright blue-purple corollas, about 1cm (.5in) long, and yellow disk florets. Flowers bloom from mid summer to mid fall. The fruits, small achenes, are topped with a pappus (modified calyx) of thin bristles.

Cultivation. Full sun to part shade, and well-drained, dry soil. This is a lovely, late-blooming, and very tough little blue and yellow daisy for gardens east of the Cascades or in dry parts of southern Oregon. Plant it with sagebrush or other drought-tolerant plants. Usually self-sows.

Propagation. Collect seeds in fall, and either plant them soon after harvest or keep them in cool, dry conditions until spring. They require warmth but not cold in order to germinate.

Maianthemum dilatatum

Machaeranthera canescens (photo by Sally A. Simmons)

Maianthemum dilatatum, fruits

Native Habitat and Range. Dry plains and gravelly slopes at low to fairly high elevations from southern British Columbia, east to Saskatchewan, south through eastern Washington, on both sides of the Cascades in southern Oregon, through California and east through much of western North America.

Notes. Sometimes classified as *Aster canescens*. Both *M. c.* ssp. *c.* var. *incana* and *M. c.* ssp. *c.* var. *canescens* occur through much of our area; a couple of other varieties of this wide-ranging subspecies occur in Oregon only. All the approximately 20 species of *Machaeranthera* are native to western North America, with the greatest diversity in the southwestern United States. *Chaenactis* (false-yarrow, pincushion, dusty-maiden) is another genus of short-lived composites often found in rather dry habitats. These plants lack ray florets and have white, pink, or yellow disk florets; most species have ferny, pinnately lobed leaves and are white with woolly or web-like (arachnoid) hairs. False-yarrows can be grown from seed and make attractive additions to the wildflower meadow in drier climates. Hoary false-yarrow or Douglas' dusty-maiden (*C. douglasii*) has the largest range, occurring in the mountains and east of the Cascades.

Maianthemum

Liliaceae

mayflower

Maianthemum is a genus of about 30 species of deciduous rhizomatous herbs distributed through North America, Asia, and Europe. The small white flowers consist of similar sepals and petals, or tepals, usually in multiples of three. The fruits are berries. Two of our best-known perennial native wildflowers, false Solomon's seal and star-flowered false Solomon's seal, have been moved to this genus from *Smilacina*; these species get their common names from their resemblance to another lily relative, *Polygonatum* (Solomon's seal).

Propagation. Easy by dividing rhizomes in early spring or late summer. Can also be grown from seed collected in the fall and removed from the berries; plant seeds into flats of potting soil soon after harvest and allow them to spend the winter outside in cool, moist soil for spring germination. Seedlings will take a couple of years to reach flowering size and may need protection from slugs.

Maianthemum dilatatum

Zones 5a to 9b

false lily-of-the-valley

This deciduous perennial grows from spreading rhizomes and produces upright stems to 35cm (14in). Each flowering stem usually has two heart-shaped leaves, with blades up to 10cm (4in) long and equally wide, on long petioles. The small, white flowers have only four tepals and bloom in racemes to 6cm (2.5in) long from late spring to early summer. Attractive red berries follow.

Cultivation. Full shade, part sun, or dappled light, and moist soil with a good amount of humus. Spreads too aggressively for some gardeners, tending to compete with other shade-loving perennials, but it will also compete with weeds. Makes a wonderful summer carpet under shrubs or along the path in the woodland or shade garden.

Native Habitat and Range. Along streams and in moist, shady woods at low to mid elevations, from Alaska south to central California, and from the coast to the west slope of the Cascades, occasionally east to south central British Columbia and northern Idaho.

Notes. Sometimes classified as *M. bifolium* var. *dilatatum* or *M. b.* var. *kamtschaticum*. Unlike true lily-of-the-valley (*Convallaria* spp.), this species is not poisonous. Some tribes ate the berries (without great enthusiasm), and the plants were used medicinally.

Maianthemum racemosum

Maianthemum racemosum   Zones 3b to 9b

false Solomon's seal

This tall, rhizomatous perennial develops stout, leafy stems up to 1m (3ft). The leaves are oval and can reach 20cm (8in) in length by 8cm (3in) in width; they are alternate, sessile (lacking petioles), and clothe the flowering stems. The tiny flowers have six white tepals and bloom in dense panicles to 12cm (5in) long. They are deliciously fragrant and bloom from mid spring to early summer. Fruits consist of few-seeded red berries.

Cultivation. Part shade or dappled light, and moist soil with good organic content. Tolerates full shade, but does best with a little sun. This is an excellent perennial for the edges of the woodland garden or perennial bed, showy in bloom and also beautiful in the fall, when the golden foliage is topped with red berries. Plant it near a path or bench where garden visitors can enjoy its fragrance.

Native Habitat and Range. Along streambanks, in moist forests and meadows at low to mid elevations, from Alaska, south to California and east to the Atlantic coast. Often seen at the forest margin.

Notes. Sometimes classified as *Smilacina racemosa*. The western subspecies, ranging from the coast to the Rocky Mountains, is *M. r.* ssp. *amplexicaule*.

Maianthemum stellatum   Zones 3b to 9b

star-flowered false Solomon's seal

This graceful rhizomatous perennial develops flowering stems to 60cm (2ft) with the upper part of the stem often showing a strong tendency to zigzag. The lanceolate leaf blades clasp the stem

Maianthemum stellatum

Mentha arvensis

and can grow to 15cm (6in) long by 5cm (2in) wide. Racemes of up to about ten small, white flowers top the stems from late spring to early summer. The star-like flowers have six tepals and are followed by berries that turn from greenish yellow to blackish red as they ripen.

Cultivation. Sun, shade, or dappled light, and moist soil with good amounts of organic matter. Forms a taller but less aggressive groundcover than *M. dilatatum*. Site it among other shade-loving plants, near a path or water feature, or in a moist wildflower meadow.

Native Habitat and Range. Streambanks, moist woods, and rocky hills at low to high elevations from Alaska to California, and from the coast, east to the Atlantic and south in the Rocky Mountains to Colorado, Arizona, and New Mexico.

Notes. Sometimes classified as *Smilacina stellata*. Not only does this species have a wide distribution, but it also lives in a variety of habitats and is highly variable in form; it has historically been split into different varieties based on flower size, extent that the stem grows in a zigzag shape, and other characters. Listed as endangered in some of the eastern parts of its range.

Mentha arvensis	Zones 3b to 9b	Lamiaceae

field mint

This aromatic perennial produces shoots up to 80cm (2.5ft) tall from spreading rhizomes. The plants have a strong, peppermint fragrance and are usually hairy (pubescent). The opposite leaves are ovate to lance-shaped, and up to 8cm (3in) long on short petioles. Flowers bloom in dense whorls (verticils) above the pairs of stem leaves. The calyx consists of a small tube, and the petals are fused at the base of the corolla, differentiated at the top into three narrower petal lobes and a larger, fourth lobe derived from the fusion of the fourth and fifth petals. The small corollas vary from white to light pink or purple and bloom from mid summer to early fall. The fruits are tiny nutlets, up to four per flower.

Mentzelia laevicaulis

Menyanthes trifoliata

Cultivation. Full sun or part shade, and moist to wet soil. As with most, this mint can be somewhat aggressive, but it tends not to spread into dry areas. Excellent for the margin of a wetland, stream, pond, or wet meadow, planted near a path or bench where its fragrance can be enjoyed.

Propagation. Easy by dividing clumps of rhizomes from late winter through spring. The tiny fruits are difficult to collect but can be planted in the fall or spring. Garden plants often self-sow.

Native Habitat and Range. In wet meadows, along streams, lakeshores, and seeps, at low to mid elevations, circumboreal, south in North America to California, Texas, and Georgia; eastern Asia, Europe.

Notes. Can be used to flavor drinks and desserts. Mints occur in temperate regions worldwide and have long been cultivated and used medicinally or as flavoring. All other species of *Mentha* growing wild in the Pacific Northwest are cultivated escapes, hybrids of cultivated escapes, or hybrids between *M. arvensis* and exotic species.

| ***Mentzelia laevicaulis*** | Zones 4a to 9b | Loasaceae |

great or smoothstem blazing star

This biennial or short-lived perennial develops a deep taproot and a branched stem up to 1m (3ft). The stems and leaves are harshly hairy, and some of the hairs are shaped like tiny grappling hooks. Bits of dry leaves will stick to clothing in a Velcro-like fashion. The leaves are alternate and the lowermost are largest, up to 15cm (6in) long, with deeply lobed margins. Flowers bloom from the upper leaf axils and stem tips. The five petals are lemon-yellow, narrowly oblong, and up to 8cm (3in) in length. The many long stamens add to the starburst effect of the flowers, which bloom from mid summer to early fall. The fruits are capsules containing many winged seeds.

Cultivation. Full sun or light shade, and dry, rocky soil. Can be grown under dry, sunny conditions in the wetter parts of the Pacific Northwest, but will be happiest in the arid regions east of the Cascades or in southwestern Oregon. Some consider this a rough-looking plant, but the flowers are gorgeous and the texture of the foliage is interesting. It is a fine choice for a dry meadow, bank, or parking area, or addition to the taller plants of the rock garden or near sagebrush.

Propagation. Collect seeds in fall and plant them directly into the garden (seedlings develop long taproots), leaving them to stratify during the cold, moist winter weather for germination the following spring.

Native Habitat and Range. In dry, open, often rocky or gravelly places at low to mid elevations from south central British Columbia, south through eastern Washington and on both sides of the Cascades in southern Oregon, south through California, and east to Montana, Wyoming, and Colorado.

Notes. *Mentzelia l.* var. *laevicaulis* occurs in most of the range; the only other variety, *M. l.* var. *parviflora*, with smaller flowers, is restricted to southern British Columbia and eastern Washington. *Mentzelia* includes around 50 herbaceous species native to deserts and drier parts of North and South America; about ten species, most of them annuals, are native to dry areas of the Pacific Northwest.

Menyanthes trifoliata	Zones 3b to 9b	Menyanthaceae

buckbean

This aquatic perennial grows from thick rhizomes, usually in shallow water, producing flowering stems and leaves above the water's surface. The alternate leaves are crowded at the base of the flowering stems; each leaf produces a petiole to 30cm (1ft) topped by three elliptic leaflets to 12cm (5in) long. Leafless flowering stems (scapes) grow to 30cm (1ft) or more, topped with a cluster of up to 30 blossoms. Each flower has five white petals with a purplish tint; the petals are about 1cm (.5in) long and covered with long, white hairs. Flowers bloom from late spring to late summer. Many shiny seeds are produced in capsules.

Cultivation. Full sun to part shade, and very muddy soil or shallow water. This is a large pond plant with bold leaves and unusual, showy flowers, suitable for a larger pond, lakeshore, or wetland. The flowers are beautiful, but flies pollinate them—and the smell that attracts flies is not attractive to humans. Enjoy them from a bit of a distance.

Propagation. Grow from seeds collected in fall and kept moist until they are planted into containers in late winter or early spring. Keep the surface of the potting soil in the container slightly submerged. Seedlings can be transplanted when large enough, but should be kept wet at all times. Plants can also be propagated from divisions of the rhizomes made in early spring; rhizome pieces should already have roots and shoots, and these can be planted directly into a pond, or into submerged containers. Another method is to take cuttings during the summer; these often root in wet mud without additional hormones.

Native Habitat and Range. In ponds, bogs, and lake shores at low to mid elevations, circumboreal, from Greenland to Alaska and south through North America to California, New Mexico, Missouri, and Virginia; Europe.

Notes. This is the only species in the genus. Buckbean has been used for its medicinal properties by various groups of people. *Nephrophyllidium crista-galli* (*Fauria crista-galli*; deer cabbage) is a related rhizomatous perennial native to bogs and wet meadows at low to high elevations, especially near the coast, from Alaska to northwestern Washington, occasionally Oregon; it has heart-shaped leaves and pretty, white flowers that attract flies with their foul smell—a lovely plant for the wet soils of the bog or pond margin, in sun to part shade.

| *Mertensia paniculata* | Zones 3b to 9b | Boraginaceae |

tall bluebells

This perennial produces few to several stems to 1m (3ft) or more from a short rhizome or branched base. The leaves have distinct lateral veins and are lance-shaped to ovate, sometimes with larger, heart-shaped (cordate) basal leaves. The largest leaves are up to 15cm (6in) long, becoming smaller, and with shorter petioles, toward the tip of the stem. Flowers bloom in branched inflorescences at the tops of the shoots. The bell-shaped corollas are more narrowly tubular at the base, flaring toward the five free petal lobes at the tip. The lovely flowers are blue or pinkish, up to 1.5cm (.5in) long, and bloom from late spring to late summer. Each flower produces four wrinkled (rugose) nutlets.

Cultivation. Sun or shade, and moist to wet soil. This is a lovely species for the woodland or shade garden, or among the taller plants in the perennial bed. It is also an excellent choice for the margin of the pond or bog, streambank, or wet to moist meadow. Slugs are fond of bluebells.

Propagation. Grow from seed collected in the fall and planted soon after harvest, directly into the garden or into containers of potting soil. Leave the planted seeds outside over winter for germination in the spring. Plants can also be grown from divisions made in the early spring.

Native Habitat and Range. In wet to moist meadows, streambanks, thickets, open woods, and wet cliffs at low to high elevations, Alaska south through Washington, Oregon, east to Montana and the Great Lakes.

Notes. *Mertensia p.* var. *alaskana* and *M. p.* var. *eastwoodiae* have ranges in the far north; *M. p.* var. *borealis* and *M. p.* var. *paniculata* occur as far south as Washington, Oregon, and Idaho. There are around 40 species of *Mertensia*, native to the temperate parts of North America, Asia, and Europe; about six are native to the Pacific Northwest. The taller species of streambanks and meadows include *M. bella* (beautiful bluebells), *M. ciliata* (tall fringed bluebells), and *M. platyphylla* (broadleaf bluebells); low-growers include *M. longiflora* (small bluebells) and *M. oblongifolia* (oblongleaf bluebells), both species of arid sagebrush regions. The prostrate *Mertensia maritima* (oysterleaf, sea bluebells) ranges along the coasts of the far north and south to Alaska and British Columbia.

| *Mimulus* | Scrophulariaceae |

monkey-flower

The more than 100 species of *Mimulus* are native to Asia, Africa, Australia, and South America, but the genus reaches its highest diversity in western North America, especially California; around 30 species are native to the Pacific Northwest. Monkey-flowers are herbaceous annuals, perennials, or shrubs, with opposite leaves. The five sepals are fused into a tubular calyx; the corolla is five-merous (consisting of five parts), tubular at the base and two-lipped (bilabiate), with the upper lip formed from two fused petals and the lower lip from the fusion of the remaining three. Numerous tiny seeds ripen in papery capsules. Many species are charming annuals (see *M. alsinoides* in that section).

Propagation. Easiest from seed. Harvest capsules and drop them into a paper bag to capture the tiny seeds. Scatter seeds on the soil in the fall or spring, either into flats or directly into the garden, and press them onto the soil surface without burying them. They will usually germinate a few weeks after sowing. Rhizomatous species can be propagated from divisions made in spring or summer. *Mimulus aurantiacus* can grown from semi-hard stem cuttings made during the summer.

Mertensia paniculata

Mimulus aurantiacus

Mimulus aurantiacus   Zones 8a to 9b

shrubby or bush monkey-flower

This branched, shrubby species grows to around 1m (3ft) tall. The thick leaves are lance-shaped, up to 5cm (2in) long, and sticky with glands. The corollas of the tubular flowers grow to 4cm (1.5in) long and vary in color from yellow to orange. Flowers bloom over a long season, from early spring to late summer.

Cultivation. Full sun to part shade, and well-drained, rather dry soil. This is a drought-tolerant plant, but it is not cold hardy and may be killed by winter temperatures, even west of the Cascades, except for the southwestern corner of Oregon. A mulch of leaves or needles will help keep it from freezing, or keep in a container and move inside for the winter. An excellent shrubby addition to the dry meadow or sunny hummingbird garden. Try it on coastal dunes and bluffs or in open woods.

Native Habitat and Range. In rocky places and slopes in open woods at low to mid elevations along the coast and in the Coast Ranges from southwestern Oregon, south to southern California.

Notes. Sometimes classified as *Diplacus aurantiacus*. This is the only woody monkey-flower that occurs in our area.

Mimulus dentatus   Zones 7a to 9b

tooth-leaved or coastal monkey-flower

This perennial grows to 40cm (16in) tall from shallow rhizomes. The opposite leaves are usually somewhat hairy, elliptic to ovate in shape, and up to 7cm (3in) long with pronounced lateral veins and toothed margins. Flowers bloom on well-developed peduncles from the leaf axils. The calyces are hairy on the five ribs and up to 1.5cm (.5in) long. The yellow flowers grow to 4cm (1.5in) long and are usually red-dotted, sometimes tinted reddish purple; they bloom from late spring to early fall.

Cultivation. Full sun to part shade or dappled light, and moist soil. This is a charming species for the pond margin, streambank, perennial border, or moist place in the wildflower meadow. Less aggressive than the larger *M. guttatus*.

Native Habitat and Range. Along streams and in moist woods at low to mid elevations west of the Cascades and mainly near the coast from southern Vancouver Island, south to northwestern California.

Notes. Similar to the yellow-flowered *M. moschatus* (musk-flower), a species with slimy (viscid) foliage, which lives in moist or wet places at low to mid elevations throughout the west.

Mimulus guttatus   Zones 4a to 9b

yellow monkey-flower

This extremely variable species grows either as a perennial from spreading rhizomes, or as an annual. The leafy, succulent stems are upright or trailing and can grow almost to 1m (3ft) in vigorous plants, but are often smaller. The opposite leaves are ovate, up to a maximum of 10cm (4in) long, with toothed margins and prominent veins. The corollas are bright yellow with some reddish spots; they can grow to 4cm (1.5in) in length and bloom from the leaf axils and shoot tips from early spring to early fall. The capsules develop within the tubular, papery calyx.

Cultivation. Full sun to light shade, and wet to moist soil. Could be considered vigorous and generous with its flowers, or weedy and aggressive, depending on the garden and the gardener's

Mimulus dentatus

Mimulus guttatus

Mimulus lewisii

Mitella ovalis

perspective. It is a cheerful plant for roadside ditches, wetlands, and pond margins, especially where it has room to spread and reproduce; it can also be planted in containers. This monkey-flower will happily seed itself in the garden, but plants will tend to be small if they grow in dry sites.

Native Habitat and Range. In seeps, near springs, streams, ditches, and other wet places at low to fairly high elevations, from Alaska south through California and east through western North America; introduced in Europe and other temperate areas.

Notes. Many of this species' subspecies and varieties are not distinct or are plastic, changing with environmental conditions. Other yellow-flowered species include Tiling's monkey-flower (*M. tilingii*) and primrose monkey-flower (*M. primuloides*), both smaller perennials of the mountains.

Mimulus lewisii	Zones 3b to 8b

pink monkey-flower

This rhizomatous perennial produces clusters of stems up to 1m (3ft) tall. The plants are covered with soft, sometimes sticky hairs. The opposite leaves are ovate, distinctly veined and usually have some teeth along the margins. The showy, tubular corollas are purple-pink with yellow markings; they can grow to 5cm (2in) long and bloom from early to late summer.

Cultivation. Full sun to light shade, and wet or very moist soil. Does best at higher elevations; it is often less vigorous in lowland gardens, and with lighter pink flowers. A beautiful native for the edge of the pond or stream, or wet spot in the hummingbird garden.

Native Habitat and Range. Along streambanks, in shallow streams, seeps, and other wet places at mid to high elevations in the mountains from Alaska south to California and east to Alberta, Montana, Wyoming, and Colorado.

Notes. This is the only pink-flowered perennial monkey-flower among our native species (other monkey flowers with pink flowers are discussed in the annuals section). Another perennial, *M. cardinalis* (scarlet monkey-flower) grows to 50cm (20in) tall and has a scarlet (sometimes yellowish), strongly two-lipped corolla to 4cm (1.5in) long; it blooms from mid spring to early fall, along streams and near seeps at low to fairly high elevations in southwestern Oregon and south and east, and makes a lovely addition to the wet places in the hummingbird garden or near the pond, in full sun or part shade.

Mitella ovalis	Zones 7b to 9b	Saxifragaceae

oval-leaved miterwort

This delicate perennial produces clusters of basal leaves and flowering stems from rhizomes. The basal leaves are rough with brown or whitish hairs, and the blades are cordate (heart-shaped) to reniform (kidney-shaped) with well-developed petioles. The leaf blades are about 2.5cm (1in) long with shallowly lobed and toothed margins. The flowering stems are usually leafless and grow to 30cm (1ft) tall. The inflorescence is a narrow raceme bearing 20 or more flowers on short pedicels. The tiny flowers are greenish yellow with a saucer-shaped calyx. The five stamens are opposite the calyx lobes. The five slender petals alternate with the stamens and are divided into uneven, threadlike lobes. The flowers bloom from early to late spring, and the fruits are small capsules containing many tiny, black seeds.

Cultivation. Full shade, part sun, or dappled light, and moist to rather wet soil high in organic matter. This charming perennial has a subtle beauty. Site it along the edge of the trail through the woodland or shade garden, or at the shady edge of the meadow, pond, or bog.

Propagation. Grow from seed collected when the capsules ripen in summer and planted in the fall. Sow seeds into flats of moist potting soil and leave them to stratify during the cold winter months for germination after the weather warms in the spring. Alternatively, the rhizomes of plants originally grown from seed can be divided in the spring or fall. Plants sometimes form stolons (aboveground rhizomes) in late summer, and these can also be used as propagation material.

Native Habitat and Range. On wet, shady streambanks and moist woods at low elevations from the coast to the west slope the Cascades, from southwestern British Columbia, south to west central California.

Notes. *Mitella* is a genus of around a dozen species, most of them native to western North America. Leafy miterwort (*M. caulescens*) is another species of shady woods and moist meadows from the coast to mid elevations west of the Cascades and scattered east in the mountains to Idaho; it is unusual in that its flowers bloom from the top down. Other species, including Brewer's miterwort (*M. breweri*) and five-stamened miterwort (*M. pentandra*), occur in moist places at mid to high elevations. The petals in these and other species are yellowish or green and pinnately divided into delicate, thread-like (filiform) segments. Three-toothed miterwort (*M. trifida*) occurs at low to mid elevations on both sides of the Cascades; the petals are white or purplish and three-lobed at the tip. Side-flowered miterwort (*M. stauropetala*) occurs in wet places from the Rocky Mountains, west to eastern Washington and Oregon and scattered in the Cascades; its flowers are arranged along one side of the stem (secund), and the tiny, white petals are tipped with three thread-like lobes. *Parnassia fimbriata* (fringed grass-of-Parnassus), another delicate member of the saxifrage family, has clusters of rounded leaves and showy white flowers with fringed petals from mid summer to early fall; it lives in bogs and wet meadows, usually at mid or higher elevations on both sides of the Cascades and east through the Rocky Mountains. It and the handful of other species of *Parnassia* that occur in our area can be grown from seed planted in the fall.

Monarda fistulosa

Monardella odoratissima

Monarda fistulosa	Zones 3b to 9b	Lamiaceae

wild monarda, bergamot, horsemint, or bee balm

This aromatic, rhizomatous perennial usually produces simple stems to 1m (3ft). The pairs of opposite leaves are lance-shaped to somewhat oval on short petioles to 1cm (.5in); the blades have toothed margins and grow to 8cm (3in) long by 2.5cm (1in) wide. Tubular, bilabiate (two-lipped) flowers bloom in dense heads surrounded by leafy bracts at the stem tips; the purple or lavender corollas are up to 3.5cm (1.5in) long, blooming from early to late summer. The fruits are small nutlets.

Cultivation. Full sun to part shade, and moist soil. This is an excellent plant for the sunny hummingbird or butterfly garden. Plant it with other late-blooming species in the moist parts of the wildflower meadow or near a pond margin.

Propagation. Grow from seed collected and planted in the fall, either sown in the garden or into flats of potting soil, and left outside to stratify over winter for germination the following spring. Alternatively, take basal cuttings in the spring or divide the rhizomes in spring or late summer.

Native Habitat and Range. In moist, open places, sometimes on slopes, at low to mid elevations, from British Columbia, extreme eastern Washington and northern Idaho, east across much of North America to the Atlantic.

Notes. *Monarda fistulosa* barely enters the Pacific Northwest, as *M. f.* ssp. *fistulosa*, but is widespread to the east. *Monarda* is a genus of mints with fewer than 20 species, native to North America.

| *Monardella odoratissima* | Zones 4b to 9b | Lamiaceae |

mountain monardella, coyote mint

These aromatic plants grow to 50cm (20in) and equally wide, producing numerous stems from a branching crown and a thick taproot. The opposite leaves are lance-shaped to ovate or elliptic and up to 3.5cm (1.5in) long with entire margins. The flowers bloom in dense heads to 4cm (1.5in) wide, each head subtended by veiny, purplish bracts to 1.5cm (.5in) long and ciliate (with stiff hairs) along the margins. The tubular flowers have five slender lobes and grow to 1.5cm (.5in) long. They are pinkish purple or sometimes whitish, blooming from late spring to late summer. Each flower produces up to four small nutlets.

Cultivation. Full sun or light shade, and well-drained, moist to rather dry soil. More cooperative in the drier climates of Oregon and eastern Washington, but can be grown in wetter places if given excellent drainage and protection from excess sogginess. This is a long-blooming, sweet-smelling plant for rock gardens or troughs. It makes a fine addition to rocky places near paths or benches in the butterfly garden or wildflower meadow.

Propagation. Grow from seed collected in the late summer or fall. Sow the nutlets directly into the garden or into flats of potting soil and leave them outside to cold stratify over winter, or sow them in the spring. It may be possible to propagate this mint from basal cuttings of the stems made in the spring.

Native Habitat and Range. In open, moist to dry, often rocky places at low to fairly high elevations, mainly east of the Cascades in southeastern British Columbia, eastern Washington, and on both sides of the Cascades in Oregon, south through much of California and east to Idaho and Nevada.

Notes. A fragrant tea can be made from this plant, all three subspecies of which occur in our area. *Monardella* includes around 30 species of aromatic herbs native to western North America, primarily California. Siskiyou or serpentine monardella (*M. purpurea*) and robust coyote mint (*M. villosa*) have pink or purplish flowers and range north to southwestern Oregon.

| *Montia parvifolia* | Zones 5a to 9b | Portulacaceae |

streambank spring beauty, small-leaved montia or miner's lettuce

Both flowering stems and stolons grow from the rhizomes of this succulent, delicate perennial, arching or trailing to 30cm (1ft), with small, alternate leaves, and often with small, bulb-like plantlets in the leaf axils. The basal leaves are up to 3cm (1.5in) long and vary from narrow to broadly rounded. The flowers are up to 1.5cm (.5in) long with five petals that vary in color from pale pink with darker veins to deep pink; they bloom from late spring to late summer. A couple of shiny, black seeds ripen in each small capsule.

Cultivation. Full to part shade or dappled light, and moist soil. This little plant can be aggressive, spreading by rhizomes and stolons to form patches, but it is charming among the rocks near the stream or pond. Site it near the woodland garden path or in the moist, shady parts of a rock garden or stone wall.

Propagation. Grow from seed, or from plantlets or bits of stolons, all planted soon after collection, in the summer or fall. Plants in favorable conditions will reproduce vigorously without any assistance.

Native Habitat and Range. In moist, often rocky places near streams, beaches, and in woods at low to mid elevations from Alaska south along the coast to California, east through the mountains to Idaho and Montana.

Notes. The narrow-leaved, pale-flowered *M. p.* ssp. *parvifolia* occurs throughout the range. The lowermost leaf blades of *M. p.* ssp. *flagellaris* are rounded and broad, and the flowers tend to

Montia parvifolia

Narthecium californicum

Nothochelone nemorosa

the darker pink (rose anemone) is found on at the coast from Alaska to southern Oregon. White-flowered *M. chamissoi* (Chamisso's montia, water miner's lettuce) is a similar, stolon-bearing plant of boggy places on both sides of the Cascades, east to the Rocky Mountains and beyond. *Montia* encompasses some eight species in North America, all native to the Pacific Northwest; the stem leaves of *Montia* are alternate in arrangement, or in multiple opposite pairs. More information can be found under *Claytonia* in the section on annuals.

Narthecium californicum	Zones 7b to 9b	Liliaceae

California bog asphodel

This rhizomatous perennial develops narrowly linear basal leaves up to 30cm (1ft) long. The flowering stems grow to 50cm (20in) and have smaller, bract-like leaves. Bright, greenish yellow flowers are about 1cm (.5in) and have six tepals (the sepals and petals are similar), they bloom in narrow racemes to 15cm (6in) long from mid to late summer. The fruits are small capsules.

Cultivation. Full sun to part shade or dappled light, and wet soil. An unusual, showy plant for the pond or bog garden.

Propagation. Collect seeds from dry capsules and plant them into containers or directly into the garden soon after harvest in the fall. Keep the planting medium wet, and allow the seeds to spend the winter outside for germination the following spring. Divisions of the rhizomes can also be made in early spring, but this should be done only with cultivated plants grown from seed.

Native Habitat and Range. In bogs, wet hillsides, and meadows, often among conifers, at mid elevations from southwestern Oregon to central California.

Notes. *Narthecium* is a genus of about six species native to temperate regions of North America, Europe, and Asia.

Nothochelone nemorosa	Zones 5a to 9b	Scrophulariaceae

woodland beardtongue, turtlehead

This perennial produces several stems to 80cm (2.5ft) tall from a branched crown. The leaves are restricted to the stems and are opposite, with short petioles and ovate or lanceolate blades up to 10cm (4in) long with sharply serrated margins. Flowers bloom at the stem tips in an open, glandular-hairy, panicle-like inflorescence. The five-lobed calyx is about 1cm (.5in) long, and the anthers are covered with woolly hairs. The tubular, bilabiate (two-lipped) corolla is pinkish purple and about 2.5cm (1in) long, with the two-lobed upper lip shorter than the three-lobed lower lip. Flowers bloom from mid summer to early fall, and the fruits are rounded capsules to 1.5cm (.5in) long containing many flattened seeds with winged margins.

Cultivation. Full sun to part shade or dappled light, and moist, well-drained soil. This is a lovely perennial for a rocky, wooded slope or large rock garden. Plant it among stones in the hummingbird garden or wildflower meadow, or in openings in the woodland garden.

Propagation. Grow from seed collected in the fall and planted at harvest or in winter. Sow seeds directly into the garden or into flats of potting soil, and leave them outside. Alternatively, stem cuttings can be taken during the summer; treat with hormones, set to root in moist pumice or some other medium, and keep humid until roots form.

Native Habitat and Range. In woods and on moist, rocky slopes at low to fairly high elevations from southwestern British Columbia south to northwestern California, mainly through the Cascades and west through the mountains to the coast, but occasionally in the mountains of eastern Washington and Oregon.

Notes. Sometimes classified as *Penstemon nemorosus*. This plant, the only species of *Nothochelone* in North America, is related to *Penstemon* and also to turtleheads, *Chelone* (*Nothochelone* means "false *Chelone*").

Nuphar lutea ssp. *polysepala*

| **Nuphar lutea ssp. polysepala** | Zones 4a to 9b | Nymphaeaceae |

yellow pond or cow lily, spatterdock

This aquatic perennial produces massive rhizomes that can reach 15cm (6in) across and more than 3m (10ft) long. The heart-shaped leaves usually float on the surface of the water. The leaf blades can grow to 40cm (16in) long on petioles to 2m (6ft). The cup-shaped, fragrant flowers, up to 10cm (4in) across, bloom singly from late spring to late summer. They usually have nine sepals, the outer ones greenish and the inner ones showy and bright yellow, sometimes with a reddish tinge. Ten to 20 smaller, lance-shaped petals, greenish yellow to purplish, surround the many reddish purple stamens and the rayed, disk-shaped stigma. The fruit is a ribbed, flask-shaped capsule to 9cm (3.5in) long containing many seeds.

Cultivation. Full sun to part shade, in water 30cm (1ft) to 1m (3ft) deep with a sandy bed. This impressive plant needs a fairly large pond. It can be planted into containers and then submerged into the water to help keep it from spreading too aggressively.

Propagation. Collect seeds in late summer or fall, plant into containers that are submerged in shallow water, and leave outside for the winter. Can also be propagated from cuttings of the large rhizomes made in the spring.

Native Habitat and Range. In ponds, sandy lake shores, and slow-moving streams at low to mid elevations from Alaska south to California and east to Alberta, south to New Mexico.

Notes. Sometimes classified as *N. polysepala*. This plant was used medicinally by various groups of indigenous people, and the seeds were also eaten. There are probably fewer than 20 species of *Nuphar*, widely distributed in the wet places of the Northern Hemisphere. Among the related water lilies of the genus *Nymphaea*, only one is native to the Pacific Northwest: white-flowered *N. tetragona* (pygmy water-lily) is noted as rare and possibly extirpated from northern Washington but is more common in southern Alaska and western British Columbia. *Brasenia schreberi* (watershield), a similar aquatic plant, lives in sluggish streams and ponds through much of North America; it has floating peltate leaves, purplish flowers, and except for the upper leaf surfaces, the plant is encased in a gelatinous sheath.

Oenothera   Onagraceae

evening-primrose

Around 60 species of *Oenothera* are native to North America; about six occur in the Pacific Northwest. Along with some of the other genera in the evening primrose family, this genus has been the subject of extensive taxonomic revision, but *Oenothera* still includes some of our most beautiful natives. They generally have white or yellow flowers, often fading to shades of red. The flowers have four sepals, four petals, and eight stamens. They are often fragrant and tend to open in the evening. The bases of the sepals, petals, and stamen filaments are fused into the floral tube, or hypanthium, a structure that develops from the top of the inferior ovary, surrounds the style, and differentiates into sepals, petals, and stamens at its tip. The long style ends in a four-lobed stigma, and the fruits are four-parted capsules containing many seeds.

Propagation. Grow from seed collected in the late summer or fall. Plant seeds into containers of potting soil or sow directly into the garden in the autumn, and leave them outside over winter for germination in the spring. Rhizomatous species can also be propagated from divisions of the rhizomes made in the spring.

Oenothera caespitosa   Zones 3b to 9b

desert or tufted evening-primrose

This tufted (cespitose), stemless (acaulescent) perennial grows only to 25cm (10in) tall from a taproot and branching crown. The plants vary from pubescent (hairy) to glabrous (hairless). The leaves are oblanceolate (lance-shaped, widest toward the tip) and tapered to long petioles. They grow to 25cm (10in) long and have entire to coarsely toothed margins. The flowers arise at ground level, sometimes on short peduncles. The somewhat swollen ovary is at the base of the flower, topped by a hypanthium up to 12cm (5in) long. The sepals are up to 3.5cm (1.5in) long, and the petals are white, becoming pinkish with age. The petals are often a bit longer than the sepals and obcordate (heart-shaped, widest toward the tip). The fragrant flowers open in the evening and close during the morning, from late spring to mid summer. The woody capsules are up to 4cm (1.5in) long.

Cultivation. Full sun or light shade, and well-drained, rather dry, rocky soil. A wonderful, drought-tolerant native for gardens east of the Cascades. Plant it near the path in the butterfly garden to attract nocturnal moths, in the rock garden, or among stones near the deck or patio, where its fragrance can be enjoyed in the early summer.

Native Habitat and Range. On dry, stony hills, road cuts, and talus slopes in shrub steppe and ponderosa pine habitats at low to fairly high elevations east of the Cascades from south central Washington south through eastern Oregon to southern California, east through the Rocky Mountains to the Great Plains.

Notes. Both the wide-ranging *O. c.* ssp. *caespitosa* and *O. c.* ssp. *marginata* occur in our area. Birdcage evening-primrose (*O. deltoides*) is a tufted biennial or annual with white flowers aging to pink and pinnately lobed leaves; it lives in dry, sandy soils, ranging as far north as eastern Oregon.

Oenothera caespitosa (photo by Sally A. Simmons)

Oenothera pallida (photo by Sally A. Simmons)

Oxalis oregana

Oenothera pallida   Zones 4a to 9b

pale evening primrose

This rhizomatous perennial produces stems with whitish, exfoliating bark up to 60cm (2ft) tall. The leafy stems are hairy or hairless, simple or branched, and the leaves are linear or narrowly lanceolate, up to 6cm (2.5in) long and less than 1cm (.5in) wide, narrowing to short petioles. The leaf margins vary from entire to toothed or somewhat lobed at the base. The flowers bloom in leafy spikes at the stem tips. The ovary at the base of the flower is topped with a pink or purplish hypanthium to 3.5cm (1.5in) long. The sepals are about 1.5cm (.5in) long, often fused to each other and turned to one side. The petals are about 2.5cm (1in) long with rounded tips, opening white and turning pink with age. The fragrant flowers bloom from late spring to mid summer, opening in the evening and closing in the morning. The capsules are narrow, widest at the base.

Cultivation. Full sun to light shade, and very well-drained, sandy or gravelly soil. This drought-tolerant perennial is a fine addition to the wildlife garden or dry wildflower meadow east of the Cascades (and possibly in southwestern Oregon). Plant it where the fragrant flowers will be enjoyed in the evening or as a nectar plant to attract nocturnal moths in the butterfly garden.

Native Habitat and Range. In sandy or gravelly soil, often on dunes in dry habitats, usually at low elevations from southern British Columbia, mainly east of the Cascades, south through eastern Washington and Oregon, east to Idaho, Wyoming, New Mexico, and Texas.

Notes. The widespread *O. p.* ssp. *pallida* is the only one of the four subspecies that reaches our area. Some of our other native species are even taller, to 1m (3ft), and have yellow or orange flowers, among them *O. villosa* ssp. *strigosa* (*O. strigosa*; hairy evening-primrose), which is found along roadsides and dry hillsides on both sides of the Cascades, and *O. elata* ssp. *hirsutissima* (*O. hookeri*; Hooker's evening-primrose), which is scattered in various habitats throughout the west. Common evening-primrose (*O. biennis*) has leafy stems and a dense spike of showy, yellow flowers; it is generally considered to be of hybrid origin or native to other parts of North America.

Oxalis oregana   Zones 7a to 9b   Oxalidaceae

Oregon oxalis, redwood sorrel

This perennial produces basal leaves and leafless flowering stems from scaly rhizomes. The leaves are ternate or trifoliate, each with three notched, heart-shaped leaflets up to 4cm (1.5in) across on petioles up to 20cm (8in) long. The leaflets tend to fold in bright sunlight and at night. The flowering scapes can grow to 15cm (6in) tall, and each bears a single white to pinkish or pink-veined flower with five petals to 1.5cm (.5in) long. The flowers bloom from mid spring to late summer, and the fruits are five-parted capsules.

Cultivation. Full shade to part sun or dappled light, and moist soil. This charming, low-growing plant competes well with weeds but is very aggressive in moist, shady places. Use it to carpet the ground in the woodland or shade garden, or under ferns and other, taller plants.

Propagation. Most commonly grown from divisions of the rhizomes made in the early spring or fall. Seeds can be collected in the summer and planted in flats of potting soil or directly into the garden in the fall or spring.

Native Habitat and Range. In moist forests at low to mid elevations west of the Cascades from southwestern British Columbia, south to west central California.

Notes. *Oxalis* includes more than 300 species widely distributed in the temperate and subtropical regions of the world; around 20 are native to North America, only a few to our area. *Oxalis suksdorfii* (Suksdorf's wood sorrel, western yellow oxalis) is a rhizomatous but well-behaved perennial with attractive, yellow flowers, blooming from mid spring to late summer; it lives in moist woods and open hillsides from southwestern Washington, south to northwestern California and from the coast to the west slope of the Cascades. *Oxalis trilliifolia* (trillium-leaved wood sorrel) produces a small cluster of white or pinkish flowers from late spring to late summer; it lives in moist woods from the coast, east to mid elevations on the west slope of the Cascades, and from northwestern Washington, south to California, scattered east to Idaho.

Pedicularis   Scrophulariaceae

lousewort

Pedicularis encompasses more than 300 species of mostly perennial herbs. Almost all are native to the temperate, often mountainous regions of the Northern Hemisphere, with a few in South America; around 30 species are native to North America, with about 20 in the Pacific Northwest, especially Alaska. Louseworts are partially parasitic on the roots of other plants; they don't seem to be too host-specific but are often found growing near grasses, sedges, and sunflower relatives. Leaves are alternate and pinnately divided (sometimes merely toothed). The flowers have fused petals and are distinctly two-lipped, often twisted or elongated into odd shapes. The fruits are flattened capsules. The unfortunate common name originates from the belief that livestock could become infested with lice by eating these plants. Their hemi-parasitic nature makes them difficult to cultivate, but many louseworts are beautiful, and determined, expert gardeners will probably have success.

Propagation. Collect seeds in fall when capsules have ripened. Plant them soon after harvest, directly into the garden or into flats of moist or wet potting soil, depending on the species. Seeds should be planted next to other plants of wet places or meadows (grasses, sedges, sunflower relatives) to provide host roots for these partial parasites. Leave planted seeds outside to cold stratify over winter for germination in the spring.

Pedicularis attollens   Zones 5a to 9b

little elephant's head

This fibrous-rooted perennial produces a cluster of unbranched stems to about 60cm (2ft). The plants, especially the inflorescences, are covered with long, woolly hair. The basal leaves are the longest, up to 20cm (8in), and pinnately compound with narrow, sharply toothed leaflets. Flowers bloom in crowded racemes from mid to late summer and are purplish pink or whitish with purple spots, growing to 1cm (.5in) long. The upper lip of the corolla is tipped with a slender, upturned beak that looks like an elephant's trunk, and the lateral lobes of the lower lip resemble the elephant's ears (hence the common name). The flattened capsules are curved.

Cultivation. Full sun to part shade, and wet soil. This is an unusual and wonderful plant for the sunny bog garden, wet meadow, or pond margin. Make sure it has access to neighboring plants to act as hosts for its parasitic roots.

Native Habitat and Range. In wet meadows and seeps at mid to high elevations in the mountains, from northern Oregon, south to California and western Nevada.

Notes. Both *P. a.* ssp. *attollens* and *P. a.* ssp. *protogyna* range into Oregon. *Pedicularis groenlandica* (elephant's head) is similar but is generally hairless (glabrous), and its bigger flowers have a longer, more conspicuous beak (the "elephant trunk"); it inhabits wet meadows and small streams at mid to high elevations from Alaska, British Columbia and Alberta south through the mountains of California and New Mexico, and east across central Canada to Labrador.

Pedicularis attollens

Pedicularis contorta

Pedicularis contorta   Zones 3b to 9a

coiled lousewort

The odd flowers of this species are hard to resist. Plants produce a cluster of stems up to 60cm (2ft) tall from a stout crown. The leaves are pinnately divided into narrow leaflets with serrate margins. The basal leaves are largest, up to 18cm (7in) long. The inflorescence is an open raceme, and the flowers vary from white or yellowish with purple markings to pink or purple. The upper lip of the corolla forms a long beak, curved downward into the lower lip. Flowers reach about 1cm (.5in) in length and bloom from early to late summer, depending on elevation. Seeds ripen in capsules.

Cultivation. Full sun to part shade, and moist to fairly dry soil. An uncommon perennial for the forest opening, woodland margin, or sunny meadow. Be sure to site it near grasses or other plants to provide host roots.

Native Habitat and Range. In fairly dry meadows and open or wooded slopes at mid to high elevations in the mountains, from British Columbia south to northern California and east to Alberta, Montana, Wyoming, and Utah.

Notes. The type, *P. c.* var. *contorta*, has a more western distribution and is found through much of the range; its whitish flowers are usually marked with purple. *Pedicularis c.* var. *rubicunda*, with pink or purple flowers, occurs in western Idaho.

Pedicularis racemosa   Zones 3b to 8b

sickletop lousewort

This lousewort develops a cluster of leafy shoots up to 50cm (20in) from a woody crown. The alternate leaves are lance-shaped to linear and up to 10cm (4in) long with finely serrate margins. The flowers are pink or purplish to white, up to 1.5cm (.5in) long, blooming in leafy racemes from early summer to early fall. The upper lip of the corolla forms a narrow beak that curves downward to touch the three-lobed lower lip. Seeds ripen in capsules.

Cultivation. Full sun to part shade, and moist to fairly dry soil. This is an interesting perennial for the sunny meadow or forest clearing. Be sure to site it near grasses or other plants to provide host roots.

Native Habitat and Range. Among conifers in the mountains, sometimes on open slopes or in fairly dry meadows, at mid to high elevations from British Columbia and Alberta, south to central California and east to Montana, Colorado, and New Mexico.

Notes. *Pedicularis r.* ssp. *racemosa*, with pink or purplish flowers, mainly occurs west of the Cascade crest; white- or yellow-flowered *P. r.* ssp. *alba* grows from the east slope of the Cascades to the Rocky Mountains. Other showy species include red-flowered *P. densiflora* (Indian warrior), native to southwestern Oregon and California, and *P. ornithorhyncha* (bird's beak or duck's bill lousewort), which has interesting pink or purple flowers and ranges from the Washington Cascades, north to Alaska.

Penstemon   Scrophulariaceae

beardtongue

Almost all the more than 200 species in *Penstemon*, some more shrubby than herbaceous, are native to western North America, and the roughly 50 species that occur in our area are among our most beautiful native flowering plants. Penstemons are best known for their brilliantly colored, tubular flowers, attractive to humans and hummingbirds alike. They have opposite leaves, a calyx of five partly fused sepals, and two-lipped (bilabiate) flowers. The four fertile stamens are arranged in pairs; the fifth stamen is a sterile staminode. The fruits are rounded capsules. Penstemons are generally not long-lived, lasting only a few years, but they make up for this with beauty and ease of propagation. They are quite promiscuous, and there is a good chance that fertile hybrid seedlings will appear in your garden if you grow multiple species.

Propagation. Grow from seed collected in the late summer and planted outside in the fall, or stored under cool, dry conditions before planting outside in the early spring. Many species, especially the shrubbier ones, can be grown from semi-hard cuttings taken in mid to late summer, treated with rooting hormones, and set to form roots under humid conditions in pumice or some other rooting medium. Cuttings should be taken only from plants originally grown from seed, never from wild plants. The shrub-like or mat-forming species can be propagated in the garden by layering; nick the underside of a branch and push it slightly into the soil, holding it in place (if necessary) and keeping it moist until roots form.

Penstemon barrettiae   Zones 6a to 9b

Barrett's penstemon

This branched, generally evergreen, shrubby penstemon grows to 40cm (16in) tall. The plants are mostly hairless (glabrous) and glaucous, with a bluish, waxy surface. The opposite leaves are elliptical; the largest ones, near the stem bases, grow to 8cm (3in) long, are tapered to the base,

Pedicularis racemosa

Penstemon barrettiae

and sometimes have a few teeth along the margins. Flowers bloom in racemes at the stem tips from mid to late spring. The corollas vary from rose-purple to lilac and grow to 4cm (1.5in) in length. Angled seeds are produced in the capsules.

Cultivation. Full sun to light shade, and well-drained, rocky or sandy soil. The glaucous foliage makes this an attractive plant even when it's not in flower. Beautiful for the rock garden or trough and an excellent addition to the hot, sunny part of the hummingbird garden.

Native Habitat and Range. In dry, rocky cliffs and talus, sometimes with sagebrush, at low elevations in the Columbia River Gorge of south central Washington and north central Oregon.

Notes. Although it is often cultivated, this species has a very small native range. It is listed as rare in Washington and should never be molested in the wild.

Penstemon cardwellii   Zones 5b to 9b

Cardwell's penstemon

This shrubby evergreen penstemon grows to a height of about 30cm (1ft) and often spreads to form mats. The opposite leaves are elliptic, to 3cm (1.5in) long and (at least the lower, larger leaves) usually toothed along the margins. The flowers bloom in few-flowered racemes at the stem tips. The corollas are lavender or bluish purple and up to 4cm (1.5in) long, blooming from late spring to mid summer, and sometimes again in the fall. The capsules are tough.

Cultivation. Full sun to light shade, and well-drained, dry to rather moist soil. This compact species is often seen growing in volcanic pumice in the wild, but this is not a requirement. Beautiful for the rock garden or sandy area and a fine addition to the low growing plants in a sunny part of the hummingbird garden. Good looking even when it is not blooming.

Penstemon cardwellii

Penstemon davidsonii

Penstemon newberryi ssp. *berryi*

in moist thickets and forests, on rocky slopes, open woods, and forest edges at mid elevations in the Cascades of central Washington, south to southern Oregon and west to the Coast Ranges of Oregon and southern Washington.

Notes. Very similar, with similar cultural requirements, is *P. fruticosus* (shrubby penstemon), a well-branched, evergreen shrublet growing to 40cm (16in). Its racemes are few-flowered, but the light purple to blue-lavender corollas are even longer, to 5cm (2in), and longer blooming too, from late spring to late summer; it lives in open woods and rocky sites at mid to fairly high elevations, mainly east of the Cascades, from southern British Columbia, south to central Oregon and east to Montana and Wyoming. Both it and its widely available selection 'Purple Haze' are excellent plants for the rock garden, dry bank, or hummingbird garden.

Penstemon davidsonii	Zones 5b to 9b

Davidson's penstemon

This mat-forming, slightly shrubby, evergreen penstemon grows only to 10cm (4in) in height and spreads from creeping, woody stems. The small, glossy leaves are tough, rounded, up to 1.5cm (.5in) long, and often shallowly toothed. The flowers are violet-purple to blue-lavender, up to 3.5cm (1.5in) long, and bloom from early to late summer, depending on elevation. Angled seeds ripen in the capsules.

Cultivation. Full sun to part shade, and well-drained soil. This is a beautiful perennial for the rock garden or cement trough on either side of the Cascades, good-looking throughout the year. Plant it in the cracks of a stone fence, especially one bordering the hummingbird garden.

Native Habitat and Range. On rock outcrops, ledges, and talus slopes at mid to high elevations from southern British Columbia, south through the Olympics, Cascades, and Sierra Nevada, east to Nevada.

Notes. *Penstemon d.* var. *davidsonii* occurs throughout the range; the small plants of *P. d.* var. *menziesii* inhabit the northwestern part of the range; and *P. d.* var. *praeteritus* occurs in Oregon and adjacent Nevada.

Penstemon newberryi ssp. berryi	Zones 6b to 9b

Berry's penstemon

This slightly shrubby, mainly evergreen penstemon tends to creep along the ground, producing shoots up to 30cm (1ft) in height. The opposite leaves are elliptical to rounded, up to 3cm (1.5in) long, and usually shallowly toothed along the margins. They are sometimes glaucous, with a bluish, waxy surface. The rose-purple corollas, up to 3cm (1.5in) long, bloom from late spring to late summer, depending on elevation.

Cultivation. Full sun to part shade, and well-drained or rocky soil. Needs excellent drainage west of the Cascades and may need winter protection in the coldest areas on the east side. Excellent for the rock garden, dry bank, or trough or other container, and a great addition to the low-growing edgers at the sunniest border of the hummingbird garden.

Native Habitat and Range. In open, rocky or gravelly places at mid to high elevations in the mountains from southwestern Oregon, south to northwestern California.

Notes. This is the only subspecies of *P. newberryi* that occurs in our area.

Penstemon ovatus   Zones 6b to 9b

broad-leaved penstemon

This penstemon produces deciduous shoots up to 1m (3ft) tall from a somewhat woody base. The plants are hairy, and the opposite leaves have toothed margins. The larger, lower leaves are ovate to deltoid (triangular) in shape, with blades up to 10cm (4in) long. Large, open inflorescences produce many blue-violet flowers to 2cm (1in) long, blooming from late spring to mid summer. The capsules are small and tough.

Cultivation. Full sun or part shade, and moist to rather dry soil. This is a beautiful perennial for the sunny wildflower meadow, dry slope, or woodland margin. The brilliant flowers make it a fine, tall species for the hummingbird garden or perennial border.

Native Habitat and Range. In open woods and rock outcrops west of the Cascades at low to mid elevations, from southwestern British Columbia, south to northwestern Oregon.

Notes. Glaucous penstemon (*P. euglaucus*) and royal or showy penstemon (*P. speciosus*) are similarly lovely herbaceous species native to the Pacific Northwest. Small-flowered penstemon (*P. procerus*) is a fine species for the rock garden or dry wildflower meadow on either side of the Cascades; it produces tufts of slender stems to 40cm (16in) from a woody base, and its deep blue-violet (sometimes whitish) flowers, up to 1cm (.5in) long, bloom in one or more dense whorls around the stems and at their tips from early to late summer, depending on elevation. It lives on open to wooded slopes, dry meadows and rocky or gravelly sites at mid to high elevations in the mountains from Alaska, south to California and east to Saskatchewan, Wyoming, and Colorado.

Penstemon rupicola   Zones 5b to 9b

rock or cliff penstemon

This evergreen penstemon forms dense mats on rocky surfaces and produces flowering shoots up to 8cm (3in) high. The small, tough leaves are rounded, up to 1.5cm (.5in) long, shallowly toothed, and covered with a waxy, whitish coating that gives them a bluish cast. The magenta to rose-purple flowers, up to 3.5cm (1.5in) long, bloom from late spring to late summer, depending on elevation.

Cultivation. Full sun to light shade, and well-drained, rocky or sandy soil. Can be grown on either side of the Cascades but needs especially good drainage in wet climates. This glaucous, blue-leaved mat-former is good-looking even when not in brilliant bloom. Plant it in the cracks of a retaining wall or stone fence, especially one near the hummingbird garden. One of the most beautiful penstemons for the rock garden or cement trough.

Native Habitat and Range. On rocky slopes, cliffs, and outcrops from low (in the Columbia River Gorge) to fairly high elevations from the Cascades of central Washington, south to northern California and west, almost to the coast, in southwestern Oregon.

Notes. The white-flowered selection 'Albus' is sometimes grown in partly shaded areas of the rock garden. Gairdner's penstemon (*P. gairdneri*) grows in very rocky, thin soils in arid regions east of the Cascades in Washington, Oregon, and Idaho. It tends to form tall, open mats from a woody crown and produces flowering stems to 40cm (16in) tall; its flowers, which vary from bluish purple to lavender to pinkish purple, bloom from late spring to early summer.

Penstemon serrulatus   Zones 6a to 9b

Cascade or coast penstemon

This herbaceous penstemon produces yearly shoots up to 60cm (2ft) from a woody base. The opposite leaves are lance-shaped to oblong, sharply toothed and up to 8cm (3in) long, mainly

Penstemon ovatus

Penstemon serrulatus

Penstemon rupicola

growing on the stems instead of at the base of the plant. Flowers bloom in whorls along the stems, or in single clusters at the shoot tips. The corollas grow to 2.5cm (1in) and are lavender-blue to bright purple, blooming from early to late summer. The fruits are tough capsules with many seeds.

Cultivation. Full sun to part shade, and moist or wet soil—one of the few penstemons that will tolerate such soil. Plant near the sunny margin of the pond, bog, or stream. This is a beautiful species for the moist parts of the hummingbird garden or woodland edge, but see cautionary note below.

Native Habitat and Range. Near streams, seeps, and moist, rocky sites at low to fairly high elevations, from southern Alaska, south through the Cascades to central Oregon and west to the coast.

Notes. The white-flowered selection 'Albus' is sometimes encountered. Unfortunately, under warm, humid conditions, the foliage of this species—along with the lovely, pink-flowered cliff dweller, *P. richardsonii* (cut-leaf or Richardson's penstemon), among others—emits an odor so unpleasant that gardeners may be checking the soles of their shoes to see if they stepped in something nasty. Hummingbirds are not discouraged by the smell, but gardeners will want to enjoy these lovely penstemons from a distance and not plant them too close to the deck, patio, or bench.

Penstemon subserratus   Zones 6a to 9a

small-toothed penstemon

This penstemon produces a few shoots up to 80cm (2.5ft) from a woody crown. The basal leaves are the largest, about 10cm (4in) long, elliptic in shape and tapered to the petiole. The stem leaves are sessile (lacking a petiole) and lance-shaped to triangular, usually with some scattered, small teeth. The flowers bloom from late spring to mid summer in few-flowered clusters from the axils of the upper stem leaves; the corollas are about 1.5cm (.5in) long, usually with a violet tube and blue lobes. The fruits are small capsules.

Cultivation. Full sun to part shade or dappled light, and well-drained, rather dry soil. This is a beautiful herbaceous species for the woodland margin, wildflower meadow, rocky hillside, or butterfly garden.

Native Habitat and Range. In open woods and rocky clearings at low to mid elevations, mainly east of the Cascades from south central Washington, south to north central Oregon.

Notes. Other herbaceous species that would suit the rock garden or dry meadow are *P. attenuatus* (narrow-leaved penstemon), with blue or purple (sometimes yellow or white) flowers, and *P. deustus* (hot rock penstemon), whose whitish or yellowish flowers have purplish penciling within the corolla. The former lives in dry meadows or open woods, the latter in dry, rocky places through much of the west.

Petasites frigidus   Zones 3b to 9b   Asteraceae

western or alpine sweet coltsfoot

This bold perennial grows from creeping rhizomes, usually producing flowering stems to 50cm (20in) tall before the leaves. Plants are mostly dioecious, with male and female flowers on separate plants. Flowering shoots have several alternate, leafy bracts to 6cm (2.5in) long. Flowering heads bloom in flat-topped clusters from early spring to mid summer, depending on elevation; each head is about 1cm (.5in) tall, the florets are whitish to purplish, and the rays (on female plants) are small. The large basal leaves expand later in the spring and are rounded to triangular in outline;

Penstemon subserratus

Petasites frigidus var. *palmatus*, flowers

Petasites frigidus var. *palmatus*

leaf blades grow to 40cm (16in) across and vary from deeply palmate to merely shallowly lobed or toothed. The foliage remains beautiful throughout the growing season.

Cultivation. Sun or shade, and wet to very moist soil. Excellent for bog gardens, pond margins, and wet meadows, or in the wet area of the shade or woodland garden.

Propagation. Divide rhizomes in the spring, or at other times of the year. Seeds (available only from female plants) can be planted into wet soil soon after harvest in the summer, or the following spring; cold stratification is not required to break dormancy.

Native Habitat and Range. Near streams, moist meadows, boggy places, and seeps at low to high elevations, circumboreal, ranging south, mostly in and west of the Cascades, through coastal California, east and south to Idaho, Colorado, the Great Lakes, and east coast.

Notes. *Petasites* includes about a dozen species, all native to the chillier parts of the Northern Hemisphere. *Petasites f.* var. *palmatus*, the largest variety in the Pacific Northwest, has large, palmate leaves with deeply cut lobes and toothed margins; it is common west of the Cascades, ranging into California. *Cacaliopsis nardosmia* (*Luina nardosmia*; yellow-pine coltsfoot), also with large, palmate leaves, has yellow flowers with no ray florets; it is found occasionally in open woods and meadows in southern British Columbia, central Washington, and southwestern Oregon to California. *Petasites f.* var. *frigidus* (*P. f.* var. *nivalis*) has coarsely toothed or lobed leaves; both the type and *P. f.* var. *vitifolius* (*P. nivalis*) also occur in our area. *Petasites f.* var. *sagittatus* (*P. sagittatus*; arrowleaf coltsfoot) has arrow-shaped leaves to 30cm (1ft) long with shallow teeth along the margins; it ranges south to Washington and the Rocky Mountains.

Phacelia   Hydrophyllaceae

scorpionweed

Phacelia includes more than 150 species of annual, biennial, and perennial herbs, most native to western North America, with a few occurring in the eastern part of the continent and in South America. Around 30 species are native to the Pacific Northwest. Phacelias produce flowers in helicoid cymes, inflorescences coiled like the tail of a scorpion (hence, the common name). The flowers usually have five petals fused at the base; some butterflies find them very attractive. The alternate leaves vary from entire (smooth-margined) to pinnately compound and are covered with silvery hairs in many species. The fruits are capsules.

Propagation. Collect seeds in late summer or fall and plant soon after harvest. Sow directly into the garden or into flats of potting soil, and leave them outside to stratify under the cool, moist winter conditions for spring germination.

Phacelia argentea   Zones 8b to 9b

silvery or sand dune phacelia

This phacelia produces a cluster of thick, creeping stems up to 40cm (16in) long. Most of the leaves are crowded near the base of the plant. They are usually entire, sometimes with a pair of small leaflets at the base of the main blade; they are elliptical in shape, up to 4cm (1.5in) long, and have distinctive, grooved veins and stiff, silvery hairs. Inflorescences are dense, and the small flowers are usually whitish, blooming from early to late summer.

Cultivation. Full sun, and sandy or gravelly soil. An excellent native for the sandy or pebbly coastal garden, and an interesting subject to try in sandy gardens further inland.

Native Habitat and Range. On beaches and dunes from southwest Oregon to northern California.

Notes. This species has a very tiny range and is listed as threatened in Oregon, so wild plants should never be disturbed. Seed may be available from conservation groups.

Phacelia argentea

Phacelia bolanderi   Zones 7a to 9b

Bolander's phacelia

This phacelia produces upright or sprawling stems to 60cm (2ft) long from a branching taproot. The stems and leaves are hairy and glandular. The leaves are ovate to elliptic, up to 10cm (4in) long and coarsely toothed, often with a pair of small, separate leaflets at the base of the main blade. The bell-shaped flowers are bluish to purplish and about 1.5cm (.5in) wide, blooming from early to mid summer. The capsules are small.

　　Cultivation. Full sun to part shade, and moist to somewhat dry soil. This is a good plant to grow against the rocks at the back of the rock garden. Plant it along dry banks or in the sunny wildflower meadow. It is also a good choice for the butterfly garden or open woodland.

　　Native Habitat and Range. In open woods, banks, and slopes near the coast, at low to mid elevations, from the central California coast, north to southwestern Oregon and disjunct in southwestern Washington.

　　Notes. One of the prettiest of the many perennial phacelias that would be of special interest to rock gardeners is *P. sericea* (silky phacelia), a plant with pinnately compound leaves and purple or blue flowers; it inhabits dry, rocky places in the mountains through much of the west.

Phacelia hastata   Zones 3b to 9b

silverleaf phacelia

This silvery-haired phacelia grows from a taproot and usually produces a branched crown. The stems grow to 50cm (20in) or more and are prostrate to upright in habit. The leaves are broadly

Phacelia bolanderi

Phacelia hastata (photo by Sally A. Simmons)

to narrowly elliptic, and the largest are basal, up to 12cm (5in) long on well-developed petioles. The leaves are mostly entire, but blades sometimes have a pair of lobes at the base. The corollas vary from whitish to lavender, and the stamens extend beyond the petal lobes. Flowers bloom from late spring to late summer, and the capsules are few-seeded.

Cultivation. Full sun to part shade, and well-drained, moist to rather dry soil. Sometimes considered coarse, this plant is nonetheless an interesting addition to the dry bank or sandy wildflower meadow and a good perennial for the butterfly garden.

Native Habitat and Range. In dry, open, often sandy places at low to high elevations from southern British Columbia, south on both sides of the Cascades through California, east to the Great Plains and Colorado.

Notes. Attractive to insects. *Phacelia h.* var. *hastata*, *P. h.* var. *compacta* (compact phacelia), and *P. h.* var. *dasyphylla* (spearleaf phacelia) all occur in the Pacific Northwest. *Phacelia heterophylla* (varileaf phacelia) is a short-lived perennial growing to 1m (3ft) tall, with leaves varying from entire to lobed, and flowers whitish to purplish; it too has a wide range throughout the west. *Phacelia nemoralis* (shade phacelia) can grow to 2m (6ft) tall and has pinnately divided leaves; it has greenish white flowers and grows in open woods and meadows at low elevations west of the Cascades of Washington, south to California.

Phlox   Polemoniaceae

Phlox is a familiar genus of around 60 annual and perennial herbs, mostly native to North America; close to 20 species, some mat-formers and some taller species, are native to the Pacific Northwest. Most of our natives are relatively difficult to cultivate, at least in the wetter parts of our area, but their beauty makes them hard to resist. Leaves are mostly opposite, simple, entire,

Phlox adsurgens

and sometimes needle-like. The flowers are white, pink, or purple and have five petals that are fused into a tube at the base of the corolla, opening into free lobes at the tip. A few seeds are produced in small, three-chambered capsules.

Propagation. Grows well from seed, but seeds are sparse: each capsule usually produces only a single seed in each of the three chambers. Seeds can be collected in late summer or fall and either planted in the fall (and left outside over winter) or stored under cool, dry conditions for spring planting. Plant seeds into flats of potting soil or directly into the garden in fall or spring. Be sure the planting medium is well drained to help protect the seedlings from damping-off. Alternatively, take semi-mature cuttings during the summer, treat with hormones, and set into pumice or some other medium; keep the cuttings in moist, humid conditions until roots form.

Phlox adsurgens	Zones 6b to 9b

woodland phlox

This phlox tends to form a taproot. The stems grow to 30cm (1ft) and are somewhat erect, often leaning on shrubs and other plants. The opposite leaves have smooth margins and are ovate to lance-shaped, up to 3cm (1.5in) long. Flowers up to 2.5cm (1in) across bloom from late spring to mid summer in open clusters at the stem tips; the corolla lobes are rounded and pink, often with a white eye.

Cultivation. Part shade or dappled light, and well-drained, fairly dry soil. This charming little plant is a good phlox for gardens west of the Cascades. Try it in the open woodland or shady edge of the rock garden, positioned next to shrubs, stumps, or boulders that will support its weak stems.

Native Habitat and Range. On rather dry slopes in open woodlands at mid elevations west of the Cascade crest from northern Oregon, south to northern California.

Notes. Better adapted to wetter climates than species of more arid climates.

Phlox diffusa	Zones 3b to 9b

spreading phlox

This taprooted, shrubby phlox forms mats up to 10cm (4in) tall. The leaves are needle-like in shape (but not sharp), more or less evergreen, and about 1.5cm (.5in) long. The showy flowers bloom singly at the tips of the stems from late spring to late summer, depending on elevation; they are about 1.5cm (.5in) wide and pink, lavender, or whitish in color.

Cultivation. Full sun or light shade, and extremely well-drained, gravelly or rocky soil. Though it can be fussy, this is a choice species for the sunny spot in the rock garden. It can also be planted in troughs or other containers.

Native Habitat and Range. On rocky slopes, talus, outcrops, and open forest at low to high elevations in the mountains, from southern British Columbia, south through the Olympics, parts of the Coast Ranges, Cascades, and Sierra Nevada to southern California, east to Montana and Nevada.

Notes. Fairly common west of the Cascades and thus more likely than most mat-forming species to tolerate wet weather. All four subspecies occur in some part of our area.

Phlox hoodii	Zones 3b to 8b

Hood's, spiny, or cushion phlox

This taprooted phlox forms small mats up to 20cm (8in) across and 5cm (2in) tall. The linear leaves are about 1cm (.5in) long and sharply pointed. Single, sessile (lacking a peduncle) flowers bloom from the stem tips. The five-lobed corollas are about 1.5cm (.5in) long, tubular at the base, and white to pink or purplish; flowers bloom from mid spring to early summer.

Cultivation. Full sun or light shade, and rocky, well-drained, rather dry soil. This is an excellent plant for the rock garden or stony, dry slope among sagebrush east of the Cascades. It might survive west-side weather if given shelter from the rain or grown in a deep trough that can be moved to cover.

Native Habitat and Range. In dry, rocky places, often with sagebrush at low to high elevations, east of the Cascades in Washington and Oregon, south through eastern California, east to the Great Plains, Colorado, and New Mexico.

Notes. Five subspecies of this highly variable species reach parts of the Pacific Northwest. *Phlox hendersonii* (Henderson's phlox) is a similar cushion-forming species with needle-like leaves and white to pinkish flowers; native to dry, rocky habitats, it is another choice plant for rock gardeners on either side of the Cascades.

Phlox longifolia	Zones 3b to 8b

longleaf phlox

This phlox forms a taproot and woody-based stems that spread below the ground surface. The shoots usually grow to 40cm (16in) long. The opposite, linear leaves grow to 8cm (3in) long and are well spaced along the stems. The tips are pointed, but not sharp. Five-lobed, tubular flowers bloom in leafy clusters at the stem tips from mid spring to mid summer; they are fragrant, pink to white, and up to 2cm (1in) across.

Phlox diffusa

Phlox hoodii (photo by Sally A. Simmons)

Phlox longifolia (photo by Sally A. Simmons)

Cultivation. Full sun to light shade, and well-drained, rather dry soil. A beautiful, drought-tolerant phlox for wildlife gardens east of the Cascades. In nature, it often grows through the stiffer branches of sagebrush and other shrubs, an effect that can be recreated in the garden.

Native Habitat and Range. On rocky slopes and dry flats, often with sagebrush, at low to fairly high elevations east of the Cascades from southern British Columbia, south to California and east to Montana, Colorado, and New Mexico.

Notes. *Phlox l.* ssp. *longifolia* has a wide range throughout the west.

Phlox speciosa	Zones 3b to 9b

showy phlox

This phlox develops shoots up to 40cm (16in) long from a somewhat shrubby base. The opposite leaves are lance-shaped to linear and up to 7cm (3in) long. The inflorescence is open and leafy. The corollas are about 2.5cm (1in) across, with notched petals varying from pink to white; flowers bloom from mid spring to early summer.

Cultivation. Full sun to part shade, and well-drained or rocky soil. An excellent plant for the rock garden, sagebrush grove, or open pine woodland. Site next to larger shrubs that will act as trellises, or near boulders or logs that will support the weak stems. It will be easier to grow in gardens east of the Cascades, but it does occur in southwestern Oregon and, if given very sharp drainage, can be grown west of the mountains.

Native Habitat and Range. In rocky, dry areas with sagebrush or in open ponderosa pine woods at low to mid elevations, mainly east of the Cascades from southern British Columbia, south to central California (but west of the Cascades in southwestern Oregon) and distributed irregularly east to Idaho, Montana, Nevada, and New Mexico.

Notes. A variable species. Five of the six subspecies occur in our area.

Phoenicaulis cheiranthoides	Zones 4a to 9b	Brassicaceae

dagger pod

This tufted perennial produces a branched crown from a thick taproot. The leaves are mostly basal, clustered into dense rosettes, and gray with their covering of branched hairs. The leaves grow to 15cm (6in) long and are oblanceolate (lance-shaped, but widest toward the tip), tapered to the petiole, and with entire margins. The flowering stems grow to 20cm (8in) and are often prostrate instead of erect. The flowering stems have a few small, clasping leaves, and the inflorescence is a raceme. The many flowers are set on pedicels to 3.5cm (1.5in) long. The four sepals are often pink or purplish, and the petals, growing to 1.5cm (.5in) long, vary from pink to lavender or reddish purple. Flowers bloom from mid spring to early summer. The fruits are narrowly lance-shaped siliques (a slender, dry fruit that splits lengthwise into two halves at maturity, typical of the mustard family) up to 8cm (3in) long, containing several seeds.

Cultivation. Full sun to light shade, and very well-drained, rocky or gravelly soil. Needs especially good drainage in the wettest climates. This is a rock garden beauty with grayish foliage, showy flowers, and interesting fruits. Plant it in the crevices of a rocky outcrop or wall on either side of the Cascades.

Propagation. Collect seeds in summer, before the dried inflorescences break off and blow away, and plant them in the fall, sowing them into containers or directly into the garden. Keep them moist, and leave them outside over winter for germination in the spring.

Native Habitat and Range. On dry, rocky slopes and outcrops near sagebrush or ponderosa pine at fairly low to high elevations east of the Cascades from central Washington, south to the

Phlox speciosa

Phoenicaulis cheiranthoides (photo by Sally A. Simmons)

east slope of the Sierra Nevada in California, west through the Siskiyou Mountains in southwestern Oregon, east through much of Idaho and Nevada.

Notes. This is the only species in the genus. *Draba*, a mustard relative, includes more than 200 species, mostly native to temperate or cold parts of the Northern Hemisphere; more than 40 of the nearly 100 that occur in North America are native to the Pacific Northwest, especially Alaska. Many are small, perennial rock-dwellers and are sometimes grown as rock garden plants. Mount Lassen draba (*D. aureola*), denseleaf draba (*D. densifolia*), fewseed draba (*D. oligosperma*), and Payson's draba (*D. paysonii*) are a few of the yellow-flowered species native to the mountains of our area; lancepod draba (*D. lonchocarpa*) has white flowers, and the yellow flowers of Yellowstone draba (*D. incerta*) turn white with age.

Poa secunda	Zones 3b to 9b	Poaceae

Sandberg's bluegrass

This small, perennial grass produces tufts of short basal leaves and flowering shoots to 30cm (1ft) or a bit taller. The plants are often somewhat purplish, and the leaves tend to curl. The inflorescence is a delicate, open or compressed panicle up to 10cm (4in) long. The tiny flowers (florets) are grouped into spikelets, the typical units of the grass inflorescence, and these are set on the slender, usually upright panicle branches. Two small bracts, the glumes, subtend each spikelet. Each spikelet has up to five florets. Each floret is further enclosed in its own pair of bracts, the lemma and the palea. These bracts lack awns, but are basally hairy. The flowers bloom from mid spring to late summer, depending on elevation, and the fruit is a tiny grain, or caryopsis.

Poa secunda (photo by Sally A. Simmons)

Cultivation. Full sun to part shade, and well-drained, rocky or rather dry soil. This small grass is charming in the rock garden or dry wildflower meadow or bank and is short enough to be planted near a path or trail. It is excellent for drought-tolerant gardens east of the Cascades and for dry, rocky places in west-side gardens.

Propagation. Collect seeds in the late summer or early fall, just as they ripen, and sow in the fall, either directly into the garden or into flats of potting soil. Leave them outside over winter for germination in the spring.

Native Habitat and Range. On rocky, dry ridges, flats, and slopes in the mountains and arid shrub-steppe at low to fairly high elevations from British Columbia to California, throughout the mountains and east to the northern Great Plains.

Notes. A variable species, now including *P. sandbergii* and *P. scabrella*, among others. *Poa* includes more than 100 species, widely distributed in the chillier parts of the world; around 60 are native to North America, more than half to the Pacific Northwest. Other native bluegrasses of arid, rocky sites and mountain meadows are arctic bluegrass (*P. arctica*), alpine bluegrass (*P. alpina*), and Cusick's bluegrass (*P. cusickii*). Marsh bluegrass (*P. leptocoma*) is a tufted grass of wet places at fairly high elevations. Tufted hairgrass (*Deschampsia caespitosa*), another fine bunch-grass with an attractive, open panicle of spikelets, lives in a variety of habitats, from coastal marshes to moist meadows and rocky ridges at high elevation; it is taller, to 1m (3ft). The bent-grasses of *Agrostis* often have a delicate inflorescence, similar to the panicles of bluegrass, but each bentgrass spikelet has only one floret; our native species include *A. exarata* (spike bent-grass), a species of marshes and wet meadows with a narrow inflorescence, and *A. scabra* (rough or hair bentgrass), which occurs in wet to dry habitats, including disturbed areas. *Glyceria* species have graceful inflorescences with several-flowered spikelets; some are widespread plants of very wet habitats, including fowl mannagrass (*G. striata*) and American mannagrass (*G. grandis*), both good additions to the margin of the wetland, pond, or stream.

Polemonium carneum

Polemonium   Polemoniaceae

Jacob's-ladder

The approximately 20 species of *Polemonium* are native to the cooler parts of North and South America and Eurasia, with species diversity centered in western North America; around eight are native to the Pacific Northwest. These herbaceous perennials and annuals have attractive, pinnately compound leaves (hence, Jacob's-ladder) and showy flowers that are typically blue or white. The corollas consist of five petals, fused into a tube at the base and expanding to five petal lobes. The fruits are three-chambered capsules, with few to several seeds in each. The plants are often glandular, and in some species the foliage gives off a strong fragrance of skunk.

Propagation. Easy from seed collected in late summer or fall and planted soon after harvest. Sow seeds into flats of potting soil or directly into the garden, and allow them to stratify outside during the cool, moist winter months for germination the following spring. Garden plants tend to self-sow, and seedlings can be transplanted easily.

Polemonium carneum   Zones 7a to 9b

great or royal Jacob's-ladder

This Jacob's-ladder produces a few stems up to 1m (3ft) tall from a woody base. The alternate leaves are pinnately compound with around 15 lance-shaped leaflets, the longest leaflets up to 4cm (1.5in) long. Flowers bloom from late spring to mid summer in leafy inflorescences at the stem tips; the corollas are about 2.5cm (1in) long and highly variable in color, ranging from salmon or yellowish to lavender or purple, and occasionally blue or white. The capsules are small.

Cultivation. Part shade or dappled light, and moist soil. This is a graceful, easy addition to the taller plants of the perennial bed, the woodland or shade garden, or the edge of a stream or meadow.

Native Habitat and Range. In moist woods, thickets, streambanks, and forest openings at low to mid elevations in the Cascades of Washington and Oregon, west to the Olympic Mountains and south through western Oregon to west central California.

Notes. This species is listed as threatened in Washington and should never be poached from the wild. Western Jacob's-ladder (*P. occidentale*) is likewise tall and blue-flowered; it lives in wet places through much of the west.

Polemonium pulcherrimum var. *calycinum*	Zones 3b to 9b

showy Jacob's-ladder

This herbaceous perennial produces stems up to 35cm (14in) tall. The pinnately compound leaves tend to be clustered at the bases of the stems, and each leaf has up to 25 oval leaflets. The bell-shaped flowers reach a maximum of about 1.5cm (.5in) in length and width; the corollas are usually blue with a yellow eye, but occasionally white. The flowers smell like grape soda and bloom over a long period, from late spring to late summer. Seeds ripen in small capsules.

Cultivation. Full sun, part shade, or dappled light, and moist soil. Although this plant tolerates full sun in moist soil, it is more commonly grown in the partial shade of the woodland garden. Excellent for planting along a path, near the shady bench, or next to the patio, where the ferny foliage, long bloom period, and fragrant flowers can be enjoyed.

Native Habitat and Range. In various habitats, from moist woods and streambanks to rocky, open, fairly dry sites, at low (in the northern parts of the range) to high elevations, from Alaska south to central California, and east in the mountains to Montana, Colorado, and New Mexico.

Notes. Sometimes granted specific status as *P. californicum*. Both *P. p.* ssp. *lindleyi* and the wide-ranging *P. p.* ssp. *pulcherrimum* occur in the Pacific Northwest. Also blue-flowered are some of the dwarf alpine species, or sky pilots; *P. elegans* (elegant polemonium) and *P. viscosum* (sticky or skunk polemonium) are two species that live among the rocks at high elevations. They both have finely divided, skunky-smelling foliage and are charming rock garden plants.

Polygonum	Polygonaceae

knotweed, smartweed

Around 150 species of knotweeds are widely distributed in the temperate parts of the world; most are annual or perennial herbs with distinctive, sometimes papery, stipules at the base of each petiole. The flowers are small and have a single whorl of petal-like appendages or perianth segments, usually with five lobes. The fruits are small, single-seeded achenes. Several of the 20 some species native to the Pacific Northwest have extensive ranges throughout much of North America.

Propagation. Grow from seed collected in the fall and planted outside in fall or winter. Sow seeds into containers of potting soil or directly into the garden for germination in the spring. Well-developed rhizomes can be divided in the spring or fall, but this should be done only with plants originally grown from seed.

Polemonium pulcherrimum var. calycinum

Polygonum bistortoides

Polygonum bistortoides	Zones 3b to 8b

American or western bistort

This knotweed produces one or more unbranched stems to about 60cm (2ft) tall from a short, thick rhizome. Most of the leaves are basal, with oblong blades about 15cm (6in) long and well-developed petioles with brownish stipules sheathing the base of the stem. The stem leaves are much smaller. Flowers bloom from late spring to late summer in dense, spike-like racemes about 4cm (1.5in) long at the shoot tips. Each tiny flower has a white or pinkish petal-like perianth with five lobes. Eight stamens protrude from each blossom. The fruits are three-sided, shiny, yellowish brown achenes.

Cultivation. Full sun to light shade, and moist to wet soil. This is a fine perennial for creating the effect of a mountain meadow, and a good addition to the butterfly garden, where the foliage will provide food for the larvae of some species and the clusters of tiny flowers will attract adults. Plant it in sunny, wet places near a stream or pond.

Native Habitat and Range. Near streams and in moist to wet meadows at mid to high elevations, from southern British Columbia, south through the mountains to California and east to Alberta, Montana, Colorado, and New Mexico.

Notes. The more northern *P. bistorta* (alpine or meadow bistort) barely enters our region, in British Columbia and Alaska. Several other species live in wet soils or standing water, including the perennial *P. hydropiperoides* (swamp smartweed).

Polygonum paronychia — Zones 7b to 9b

beach or black knotweed

This somewhat shrubby knotweed is perhaps more interesting than beautiful, but it has a long bloom period, from mid spring to early fall. Plants produce freely branching, spreading stems to 1m (3ft) long that develop roots where they touch the ground. The leaves, typically clustered at the branch tips, are about 2cm (1in) long, narrowly oblong and with the margins curled under (revolute). The stipules at the bases of the petioles are thin and papery with shredded tips. Small white or pink flowers with five petal-like perianth lobes bloom in small clusters in the axils of the upper leaves from late spring to early fall. The fruits are shiny, black achenes with three sides.

Cultivation. Full sun or light shade, and well-drained, sandy soil. This is an excellent native for very sandy sites, especially the dunes and beaches of coastal gardens and disturbed beach habitats.

Native Habitat and Range. On sandy beaches and dunes along the coast from southern British Columbia, south through much of California.

Notes. Shasta knotweed (*P. shastense*), a very similar species with pink flowers, is native to rocky or gravelly slopes at high elevations in the mountains of southwestern Oregon. Douglas' knotweed (*P. douglasii*) and its several subspecies are small annual natives that often grow in disturbed or dry soils.

Potentilla — Rosaceae

cinquefoil

Potentilla has undergone regular taxonomic revision, but there are probably still upward of 200 species native to the Northern Hemisphere in temperate to arctic climates; almost 30 are native to the Pacific Northwest. Cinquefoils are herbaceous plants with alternate, pinnately or palmately compound leaves. The petals and sepals are in fives, and the petals are usually yellow. The stamens vary in number from several to many, and the fruits consist of one-seeded achenes with small, distinctive styles.

Propagation. Grow from seed collected in the late summer and planted in the fall. Sow seeds into flats of potting soil and leave them outside to spend the winter under cool, moist conditions for germination when the weather warms up in the spring. Well-developed clumps can be propagated from divisions of the rhizomes made in the spring.

Potentilla glandulosa — Zones 3b to 9b

sticky cinquefoil

This perennial cinquefoil can grow to 70cm (28in) from short rhizomes. The foliage has sticky, glandular hairs, and the plant is often reddish. The leaves are up to 30cm (1ft) long and pinnately compound. The leaflets are rounded and have serrate margins. The pale yellow blossoms are about 2cm (1in) across. Flowers bloom in a branched inflorescence from late spring to mid summer. The fruits are small achenes.

Cultivation. Full sun or part shade, and moist to rather dry soil. This is a lovely species for the wildflower meadow, dry bank, or the openings in the woodland or wildlife garden, throughout the Pacific Northwest.

Native Habitat and Range. In moist to rather dry meadows and open woods at low to mid elevations on both sides of the Cascades from southwestern British Columbia, south to northern Mexico and east to Alberta, Montana, and Arizona.

Polygonum paronychia

Potentilla glandulosa

Notes. A highly variable species: seven of its 11 subspecies occur in our area, distinguished by flower size, branching pattern, glands and other types of hairs, and geographic range, among other characters. Other natives include tall cinquefoil (*P. arguta*), mountain meadow or varileaf cinquefoil (*P. diversifolia*), and Newberry's cinquefoil (*P. newberryi*).

Potentilla gracilis	Zones 3b to 9b

graceful or slender cinquefoil

This perennial herb develops stems up to 80cm (2.5ft) from a branched crown. The pubescence varies from short and woolly to long and spreading. The long petioles of the basal leaves can reach 30cm (1ft), and the leaf blades are palmately compound with several leaflets growing to 8cm (3in) in length. Margins of the leaflets vary from toothed to deeply lobed. Bright yellow flowers bloom in branched, flat-topped clusters (cymes) from early to late summer. The fruits are small achenes.

Cultivation. Full sun or light shade, and moist to rather dry soil. A beautiful plant for the perennial border, the wildflower meadow, or the opening in the woodland or wildlife garden.

Native Habitat and Range. In meadows, open forest, and moist places in arid shrub-steppe regions, at low to mid elevations, from Alaska south near the coast to northern Mexico, east to the Great Lakes and south to the Dakotas, Arizona, and New Mexico.

Notes. Four varieties of this highly variable species occur in the Pacific Northwest; distinguishing features include the margins of the leaflets (from serrate or few-toothed to deeply dissected with linear lobes) and the amount and texture of pubescence. Beautiful cinquefoil (*P. pulcherrima*), a similar species, ranges through the western mountains. Drummond's cinquefoil

(*P. drummondii*), high mountain cinquefoil (*P. flabellifolia*), and villous cinquefoil (*P. villosa*) are other attractive natives with showy, yellow flowers.

Prosartes	Liliaceae

fairy bells

Prosartes, a genus of charming, woodland lily relatives, contains about 15 species, most of them Asian; five are native to North America. These branching perennials have numerous, rounded leaves and delicate bell-shaped or tubular flowers with six tepals or perianth segments (the petals and sepals are similar). Flowers bloom at the branch tips, and the fruits are showy, few-seeded, reddish berries.

Propagation. Easy from seed. Collect berries in late summer or fall, remove the seeds from the pulp, and sow them into containers of potting soil or directly into the garden. Leave the planted seeds outside over winter for germination the following spring. Plants should reach blooming size in a couple of years. Larger plants can also be propagated from divisions of the rhizomes made in early spring. Often self-sows.

Prosartes hookeri	Zones 3b to 9b

Hooker's fairy bells

This rhizomatous perennial produces stems to 1m (3ft) tall with a few branches. The oval leaves have prominent veins, pointed tips, and heart-shaped, asymmetrical bases that clasp the stem. Stems, leaves, and leaf margins are finely hairy. The bell-shaped flowers are about 2cm (1in) long and usually bloom in pairs at the branch tips from mid spring to mid summer. The tepals are white, narrow, and flared open to reveal the stamens, style, and developing ovary. The fruit is a few-seeded berry, bright red-orange when ripe.

Cultivation. Full shade to part sun or dappled light, and moist soil with good organic content. A tall, graceful native for the woodland or shade garden or perennial border on either side of the Cascades.

Native Habitat and Range. Moist, wooded areas in light or deep shade at low to mid elevations, from British Columbia south, on both sides of the Cascades to California, east to Alberta, Idaho, and Montana.

Notes. Sometimes classified as *Disporum hookeri*. *Prosartes h.* var. *hookeri*, *P. h.* var. *parvifolia*, and *P. h.* var. *trachyandra* occur in Oregon and California; *P. h.* var. *oregana* ranges from Oregon to the north and east.

Prosartes smithii	Zones 6b to 9b

Smith's fairy lantern

This deciduous perennial develops branched stems close to 1m (3ft) tall from underground rhizomes. The leaves are oval with pointed tips, prominent veins, and rounded bases that clasp the stem. Stems, leaves, and leaf margins have little or no hair. The creamy white flowers are cylindric in shape, about 2.5cm (1in) long, usually blooming in pairs at the stem tips from mid spring to early summer. The overlapping tepals flare only at the tips and conceal the stamens, style, and ovary. The few-seeded berries are yellow or orange when ripe.

Cultivation. Part sun to full shade or dappled light, and moist soil with good organic content. It is a fairly tall plant, but delicate, combining well with ferns and other shade-loving species in the woodland garden or shady perennial bed west of the Cascades.

Potentilla gracilis

Prosartes hookeri

Prosartes smithii

Prosartes smithii, fruits

Native Habitat and Range. Moist places in open woods or deeper forests at low elevations, from southern British Columbia south into California, and from the coast to the west slope of the Cascades.

Notes. Sometimes classified as *Disporum smithii*. Rough-fruited fairy bells (*P. trachycarpa*) inhabits aspen groves and other wooded areas near streams east of the Cascades; it ranges from central British Columbia and Alberta, south to north central and eastern Washington, into the Blue Mountains of northeastern Oregon, and east through the Rocky Mountains.

Prunella vulgaris	Zones 3b to 9b	Lamiaceae

common self-heal or heal-all

This herbaceous perennial is considered weedy by many gardeners, but the flowers are beautiful, and the plants bloom generously over a long period. Plants produce upright or spreading stems from short rhizomes. The opposite leaves are lance-shaped to oval and up to 9cm (3.5in) long. They have well-developed petioles, and the margins are entire or with a few shallow teeth. The tubular, two-lipped (bilabiate) corollas are about 1.5cm (.5in) long, blue-violet (occasionally white or pink) and are surrounded by a spiny-lobed calyx. Flowers bloom in short, dense spikes to 5cm (2in) long at the stem tips, from late spring to early fall. Each flower produces four small nutlets.

Cultivation. Sun to shade, and moist to fairly dry soil. Can be used as a lawn substitute and will flower even when mowed. Plant it in a neglected spot or parking area, or along the edge of the wildflower meadow or butterfly garden.

Propagation. Grow from seed collected in the fall, planted outside into flats of potting soil or directly into the garden, and left to cold stratify over winter for germination the following spring. Alternatively, divide rhizomes in spring.

Native Habitat and Range. In moist fields, lawns, roadsides, disturbed areas, and forest edges at low to mid elevations through much of the Northern Hemisphere.

Notes. This species was used medicinally by many groups of people. *Prunella v.* ssp. *lanceolata*, widely distributed in North America, has narrower leaves and is more common than the type. *Prunella* is a genus of about six species; others are native to Europe, northern Africa, and Asia.

Pseudoroegneria spicata	Zones 3b to 9a	Poaceae

bluebunch wheatgrass

This bunchgrass forms clumps up to 1.5m (5ft) across and flowering stems to 1m (3ft) tall. The leaves are sometimes hairy and generally flat or somewhat inrolled (involute). The inflorescence is an open spike up to 15cm (6in) long. The tiny flowers (florets) are grouped into spikelets, the typical units of the grass inflorescence, and there is usually a single spikelet at each node of the flowering stem. Two narrow bracts, the glumes, subtend each spikelet, and these sometimes have short awns. Each spikelet has up to eight florets. Each floret is further enclosed in its own pair of bracts, the lemma and the palea. The lemma sometimes has a long awn, up to 2cm (1in) long. The flowers bloom from early to late summer, and the fruit is a small grain, or caryopsis.

Cultivation. Full sun or light shade, and rather dry soil. An important rangelands species and an excellent bunchgrass for a dry bank or wildflower meadow, especially east of the Cascades. Plant it with sagebrush and other drought-tolerant species in the wildlife garden; it provides food and cover for many native wildlife species in addition to livestock.

Prunella vulgaris

Pseudoroegneria spicata (photo by Sally A. Simmons)

Propagation. Grow from seed collected in the fall. The seeds can be sown into flats of potting soil or directly into the garden in the fall and left outside over winter; they can also be sown in early spring.

Native Habitat and Range. In dry hills and plains, often with sagebrush, at low to mid elevations from Alaska, south to northeastern California, mainly east of the Cascades, but further west in southern Oregon, east to Alberta, the Dakotas, New Mexico, and Texas.

Notes. Often classified as *Agropyron spicatum*. This is the only species of *Pseudoroegneria* in North America. Other native species of wheatgrass have been moved from *Agropyron* into other genera, especially *Elymus*, these include *E. lanceolatus* (*A. dasystachyum*; thickspike wheatgrass) and *E. scribneri* (*A. scribneri*; spreading wheatgrass).

Ranunculus   Ranunculaceae

buttercup

Most of the more than 200 species of *Ranunculus* occur in the temperate or arctic parts of the Northern Hemisphere; around 70 are native to North America, more than 40 to the Pacific

Northwest. Buttercups are familiar annual or perennial herbs with simple to compound leaves. The flowers have five sepals and yellow (occasionally white), often showy petals, each with a small gland at the base. The stamens vary in number and are often numerous. Each flower has few to many pistils (ovaries, styles, and stigmas), and these develop into rounded or elongated clusters of fruits, the dry, one-seeded achenes. The style at the tip of each achene develops into a straight or curved beak. Buttercups contain compounds that may irritate the skin of some people.

Propagation. Grow from seed collected in late summer and planted in the fall. Sow seeds into flats of moist or wet soil or directly into the garden, and leave them outside over winter for germination when the weather warms in the spring. Rhizomatous species can be divided in the fall or early spring.

Ranunculus alismifolius   Zones 4a to 9b

water-plantain buttercup

This perennial produces stems up to 60cm (2ft) tall from fibrous roots. The leaves are lance-shaped or ovate, with blades up to 15cm (6in) long and entire to finely serrate margins. The basal leaves are tapered to petioles as long or longer than the blade, and the stem leaves have short petioles (or lack them altogether). Flowers develop on long pedicels, up to 15cm (6in) long at the stem tips. Each flower has numerous stamens, five sepals, and five (sometimes more) yellow petals up to 1cm (.5in) long. Flowers bloom from late spring to mid summer, and the fruits are smooth achenes with a straight, short stylar beak.

Cultivation. Full sun or part shade, and very wet soil. A charming buttercup for the margin of the pond or bog, streambank, or wet ditch. Plant it in a wet place in the wildflower meadow on either side of the Cascades. May self-sow once established.

Native Habitat and Range. In wet meadows, swales, streambanks, and pond margins at low to high elevations, from southern Vancouver Island, south on both sides of the Cascades to northern California, east to Montana, Wyoming, and Colorado.

Notes. Four varieties of *R. alismifolius* occur in parts of the Pacific Northwest. Other wide-spread native buttercups of wet or aquatic habitats include *R. aquatilis* (white water buttercup or crowfoot), a plant with white flowers and leaves that are either palmate or very finely dissected, depending on whether or not they are submerged, and *R. cymbalaria* (alkali buttercup), a species of marshes and muddy places that spreads from slender stolons. Yellow water buttercup (*R. flabellaris*) and Macoun's buttercup (*R. macounii*) live in wet places across much of North America. At the opposite end of the habitat spectrum, sagebrush buttercup (*R. glaberrimus*) and Anderson's buttercup (*R. andersonii*) are charming perennials of arid regions dominated by ponderosa pine and sagebrush.

Ranunculus orthorhynchus   Zones 4a to 9b

straight-beaked buttercup

This generally hairy buttercup produces branched shoots to about 60cm (2ft) tall from thick roots. The leaves are two or three times pinnately compound with lobed leaflets. Most of the leaves are basal, with petioles up to 25cm (10in) long and blades to 8cm (3in). Flowers bloom from mid spring to mid summer on pedicels up to 15cm (6in) long. They have five sepals and (usually) five yellow or sometimes purplish petals about 1.5cm (.5in) long. The achenes ripen in a rounded cluster; they are strongly compressed and tipped with a straight stylar beak.

Cultivation. Full sun or part shade, and moist soil. Plant this buttercup on either side of the Cascades, in the moist wildflower meadow, perennial bed, streambank, or slope.

Ranunculus alismifolius

Ranunculus orthorhynchus

Native Habitat and Range. In moist meadows, mountain slopes, and streambanks at low to mid elevations from southern Alaska south to central California and from the coast, east to Montana, Wyoming, and Utah.

Notes. *Ranunculus o.* var. *orthorhynchus* occurs throughout the range; *R. o.* var. *bloomeri* (Bloomer's buttercup) is restricted to Oregon and California. Other buttercups occurring in meadow habitats include western buttercup (*R. occidentalis*) and graceful buttercup (*R. inamoenus*). California buttercup (*R. californicus*) often has more than ten petals and grows on grassy coastal bluffs in our area, most commonly from northwestern Oregon to California. A few buttercups, such as Eschscholtz's buttercup (*R. eschscholtzii*), live in high mountain meadows and talus slopes and are of interest to rock gardeners.

Rudbeckia   Asteraceae

coneflower

All the approximately 20 species of *Rudbeckia* are native to North America, with about three native to our area. Coneflowers are perennial sunflowers with an elongated, conical receptacle holding many small disk florets. Some species also have well-developed ray florets with yellow corollas; others lack rays. *Ratibida* is another small, North American genus commonly called coneflower; these plants have flowering heads with yellow (or yellow and mahogany) ray corollas and with elongated receptacles. Most are native east and south of our area, with upright prairie coneflower (*Ratibida columnifera*) ranging as far west as western Idaho.

Propagation. Easiest from seed collected in the late summer or fall and planted soon after harvest. Sow seeds into containers of potting soil or directly into the garden, and leave them outside to stratify in the cool, moist winter weather for germination the following spring.

Rudbeckia glaucescens   Zones 6b to 9b

waxy or California coneflower

This coneflower produces unbranched stems to 1.5m (5ft) or a bit taller. The plants are glabrous (hairless) and glaucous, whitish with a waxy coating. The basal leaves have slender petioles, and the blades are elliptic to lanceolate, up to 25cm (10in) long, sometimes with a few teeth along the margins. The stem leaves are smaller and sessile (lacking petioles). Single flowering heads bloom on long peduncles. They have brownish disk corollas and up to 20 yellow rays. Flowers bloom from mid summer to early fall, and the fruits are flat achenes with a cup-like, toothed pappus (modified calyx).

Cultivation. Full sun or part shade, and wet soil. This is an unusual perennial for the pond margin, bog garden, or the wet area of the butterfly garden, where the late-blooming flowers will attract insects.

Native Habitat and Range. Near streams, in bogs and wetlands, sometimes on serpentine outcrops and with *Darlingtonia*, at fairly low to mid elevations from southwestern Oregon to northwestern California.

Notes. Sometimes classified as *R. californica* var. *glauca*.

Rudbeckia occidentalis   Zones 3b to 9b

western coneflower

This bold perennial produces simple, sometimes branched, stems up to 2m (6ft) tall from a narrow crown. The basal leaves are largest, usually broadly ovate and up to 25cm (10in) long by 15cm (6in) wide. They are toothed, sometimes lobed, usually with short petioles. The flowering heads grow on long peduncles and lack ray florets. The receptacle, covered with small, dark brownish purple disk florets, is long and conical, up to 6cm (2.5in) long in fruit, with leafy green bracts at the base. The flowers are more interesting than showy, blooming from early to late summer. The fruits are small, four-sided achenes with a pappus (modified calyx) of small teeth.

Cultivation. Full sun to part shade, and soil that is moist or wet, at least early in the season. This large, distinctive coneflower is an attractive plant for the moister places in the wildflower meadow, or butterfly or wildlife garden; insects will be attracted to its nectar, and birds will visit for the small "sunflower" seeds. Plant it on either side of the Cascades near a pond, stream, or seep, as a background for other, more delicate plants.

Native Habitat and Range. Along streams and in moist woods and meadows at mid elevations, from central and eastern Washington, east to Montana and Wyoming, south through the mountains of Oregon to California and Utah.

Notes. *Rudbeckia alpicola*, a smaller plant with lobed leaves, is sometimes included as a variety of *R. occidentalis*; it is endemic to central Washington.

Rumex venosus   Zones 3b to 9b   Polygonaceae

sand or veiny dock

This hairless (glabrous) perennial produces leafy, branching, upright stems to 50cm (20in) tall from woody rhizomes. The leaves are leathery, with the largest toward the top of the stem. The blades are oblong or elliptic and up to 15cm (6in) long. The stipules at the bases of the short petioles are white and up to 3cm (1.5in) long. Tiny flowers bloom in small panicles that develop from the axils of the upper leaves. Flowers lack petals and are not showy, but some of the sepals, or perianth segments, expand greatly as the fruits, small, single-seeded achenes, ripen within them. The enlarged perianth segments are heart-shaped, about 2.5cm (1in) long, reddish, and

Rudbeckia glaucescens

Rudbeckia occidentalis

Rumex venosus (photo by Sally A. Simmons)

Sagittaria latifolia

veiny. Flowers bloom from mid spring until early summer, but the plants are most attractive later in the summer, as the fruits ripen.

Cultivation. Full sun or light shade, and sandy or gravelly, dry to somewhat moist soil. This is an attractive plant for dunes or the sandy places in gardens, especially east of the Cascades. Plant it near sagebrush in the drought-tolerant wildlife garden or bunchgrass meadow.

Propagation. Grow from seed collected in the late summer and planted in the fall. Sow seeds directly into the garden or into containers of potting soil, and leave them outside over winter for germination in the spring. Plants can also be grown from divisions of the woody rhizomes made in the spring, but the rhizomes tend to grow deeply in the soil and may be difficult to work with.

Native Habitat and Range. On sand dunes, gravelly soils, and sandy riverbanks, often near sagebrush, at low to mid elevations east of the Cascades from northern Washington, south to California and east to Saskatchewan, the Dakotas, and Texas.

Notes. *Rumex* (dock, sorrel) is a genus of 100 or more species, native to the temperate parts of the world. Some species, such as golden dock (*R. maritimus*) and willow dock (*R. salicifolius*), are natives with large ranges that include the Pacific Northwest. The closely related *Oxyria digyna* (mountain sorrel) is a charming perennial and a good species for the rock garden, with heart-shaped basal leaves, small reddish or greenish flowers, and a height of 60cm (2ft); it is circumboreal, inhabiting moist, rocky places at mid to high elevations in the mountains of the west, south to California, Arizona, and New Mexico.

Sagittaria latifolia	Zones 3b to 9b	Alismataceae

wapato, broad-leaf arrowhead

This emergent (roots in the water, shoots in the air) perennial produces extensive rhizomes and tubers. The leaves are basal and have arrow-shaped (sagittate) blades up to 25cm (10in) in length, set on long, partly submerged petioles. The leafless flowering stems (scapes) grow to 50cm (20in). The inflorescence is a raceme with several whorls of showy flowers. The flowers have three green sepals and three white petals about 2cm (1in) long. Plants are sometimes dioecious (all the flowers on a plant are one sex only), or with the male flowers developing at the top of the raceme. Flowers usually bloom from mid summer to early fall. The fruits produced by the female flowers are single-seeded, beaked achenes.

Cultivation. Full sun or light shade, in shallow water up to 30cm (1ft) deep. Submerge the roots and tubers of this wonderful pond plant in the mud of a pond, lake margin, or ditch, where the tubers and seeds will provide food for a wide assortment of wildlife species.

Propagation. Easy from divisions of the rhizomes or by transplanting the tubers in the fall or spring. Can also be propagated from seed collected in the fall, planted into mud, either into containers or directly into the pond margin, and left outside over winter for spring germination.

Native Habitat and Range. Usually in shallow water along ponds, lakes, and wet ditches at low elevations from southern British Columbia, south to California and from the Pacific coast, east across much of North America to the Atlantic.

Notes. The tubers of wapato were harvested, baked, and eaten by many indigenous tribes. The widespread *S. cuneata* (arum-leaf arrowhead) is very similar; it lives in wet habitats from Alaska to California, east across much of North America. *Sagittaria* encompasses more than 20 species, mostly native to temperate and tropical parts of the Americas; only a handful are native to our area, and some of these may have been introduced. The closely related species of *Alisma* (water-plantain) live in similar aquatic habitats; narrow-leaf water-plantain (*A. gramineum*) and northern water-plantain (*A. triviale*; often listed as *A. plantago-aquatica*, European water-plantain) are both widespread in North America. *Damasonium californicum* (*Machaerocarpus californicus*; fringed water plantain), another emergent perennial in the water-plantain family, has white flowers with fringed petals that bloom in showy whorls on the racemes from mid spring to

Sanicula arctopoides

late summer; it grows in ditches and sloughs from central California, north to the Columbia River Gorge (it is listed as sensitive in Washington) and east to Idaho and western Nevada.

Sanicula arctopoides	Zones 7b to 9b	Apiaceae

footsteps of spring, beach snakeroot, bear's-foot sanicle

This taprooted perennial produces branching, prostrate or partially upright stems to 30cm (1ft) long. The leaves are yellowish and succulent. Basal leaves have long petioles and form rosettes. The blades are up to 6cm (2.5in) long and 9cm (3.5in) wide, deeply divided into three main segments, the segments lobed and toothed with sharply pointed, but soft, teeth. The leaves of the flowering stems are smaller and oppositely arranged below the branch points. Small umbels, about 1cm (.5in) across, flower at the branch tips. Each umbel is surrounded by a whorl of bracts and consists of up to 25 tiny, yellow flowers that bloom from early to late spring. The fruits are small, dry schizocarps, which split into single-seeded halves at maturity; they are rounded, and the upper half is covered with sturdy prickles, hooked at their tips.

Cultivation. Full sun or light shade, and sandy, well-drained, somewhat dry soil. This attractive plant has not been much cultivated, but it would make a wonderful, early-blooming addition to dunes or sandy bluffs near the beach, or to sandy meadows further inland.

Propagation. Collect the dry fruits in the summer and plant them outside in the fall, directly into the garden or into deep containers that will allow the taproot to develop until seedlings are transplanted. Leave the planted seeds outside to cold stratify over winter for germination the following spring.

Native Habitat and Range. On beaches, open hillsides, and sandy flats at low elevations near the coast from southern Vancouver Island, south to southern California.

Satureja douglasii

Notes. This is an uncommon species, listed as sensitive in Washington State. *Sanicula* includes around 40 species, widely distributed in the world's temperate regions or at high elevations in tropical areas. Eight species occur in the Pacific Northwest, including purple sanicle (*S. bipinnatifida*), Pacific sanicle or black snakeroot (*S. crassicaulis*), northern or Sierra sanicle (*S. graveolens*), coastal black snakeroot (*S. laciniata*), and turkey pea (*S. tuberosa*). Various species were used medicinally by different groups of people, mainly Europeans, but they do contain toxins and may be poisonous.

Satureja douglasii	Zones 5b to 9b	Lamiaceae

yerba buena

This perennial grows from a woody rhizome, and its trailing, prostrate stems grow as stolons, to 1m (3ft) long. The opposite, oval leaves average 2.5cm (1in), are aromatic when crushed, and will generally remain evergreen in mild winters or in a sheltered location. Tiny white or purplish flowers bloom singly in the leaf axils from early to mid summer. The fruits are little nutlets, up to four per flower.

Cultivation. Part shade or dappled light, and well-drained, moist to rather dry soil. A fine groundcover for the woodland garden, especially near paths where it will be stepped on occasionally, releasing its fragrance.

Propagation. Easy from cuttings taken from early summer through early fall. The creeping stems root easily at the nodes where they touch the ground, and these rooted pieces can be detached and transplanted. The tiny nutlets can be collected in late summer and planted into flats of potting soil in the fall or spring.

Native Habitat and Range. On well-drained soil in open coniferous forests and oak woodlands at low to mid elevations from southwest British Columbia south to southern California, mainly west of the Cascade crest, but also east to northern Idaho.

Notes. Sometimes classified as *Clinopodium douglasii*. This "good herb" was used medicinally and also made into a refreshing tea by both indigenous and nonnative people. It is our only native representative of the genus.

Saxifraga   Saxifragaceae

saxifrage

The approximately 300 species of *Saxifraga* are widely distributed, mostly in the arctic and temperate areas of the Northern Hemisphere; around 50 species are native to the Pacific Northwest, some of them restricted to the northernmost parts of our region. The boundaries of the genus have been a source of disagreement among botanists, and some species, especially those with large geographic ranges, have been moved in and out of *Saxifraga*. Many saxifrages are native to rocky, moist habitats, and some form mats. Almost all our native saxifrages are perennial herbs with various leaf shapes; many are notoriously difficult to cultivate. Flowers generally have five white petals and ten stamens; the fruits are capsules with a pair of "beaks" at the top, formed from the two styles.

Propagation. Grow from seed. Collect seeds in the late summer or fall, plant them into the garden or in containers of potting soil soon after harvest, and leave them outside for the winter to cold stratify. Stem cuttings from plants already in cultivation can be taken in spring; treat cuttings with rooting hormones and set them into pumice or some other medium, keeping them moist and humid until roots form. Some species form tiny plantlets, often in place of some of the flowers; these can be collected from the flowering stems during the growing season and planted immediately. Whatever the method, the new plants of many species will take a few years to reach blooming size.

Saxifraga bronchialis   Zones 3b to 8b

spotted saxifrage

This mat-forming saxifrage produces crowded clusters of evergreen leaves, the remains of which persist on the short stems for many years. The small, linear to lance-shaped leaves grow to 1.5cm (.5in) and give the plants a mossy appearance; the flowering stems grow to 15cm (6in) tall and have alternately arranged, spine-like leaves. Each inflorescence produces up to ten flowers about 1.5cm (.5in) across. The five petals are white with purplish or yellow spots and are slightly narrowed at the base. Flowers bloom from early to late summer. The two-beaked capsules are often purplish and contain many brown seeds.

Cultivation. Full sun to light shade, and rocky or gravelly, moist but well-drained soil. This charming cushion plant is relatively cooperative in cultivation and can be grown in a rock garden, stone wall, or similar place in the garden. A mulch of pumice and peat moss may encourage establishment of plants.

Native Habitat and Range. In rock crevices, talus, and open slopes or gravelly flats at low to high elevations, from Alaska south through the Olympic and Cascade Mountains to central Oregon, and east to the Rocky Mountains, south to Utah, Colorado, and New Mexico.

Notes. Of the five subspecies, only *S. b.* ssp. *austromontana* and *S. b.* ssp. *vespertina* range into the Pacific Northwest as far south as Oregon.

Saxifraga bronchialis

Saxifraga caespitosa

Saxifraga caespitosa	Zones 3b to 9a

tufted saxifrage

This saxifrage produces dense or open mats with the old leaf bases remaining on the short branches. The living leaves are wedge-shaped, up to 2cm (1in) long, with three lobes at the tip. Flowering stems have a few, lobed leaves and grow to 15cm (6in) tall. Flowers bloom from mid spring to early fall, depending on latitude and elevation, in loose clusters of one to several per stem and are up to 2cm (1in) across. The sepals are often purplish, and the petals are white. Many dark brown seeds ripen in beaked capsules.

   Cultivation. Full sun to light shade, and moist, well-drained, rocky or gravelly soil. This variable species is small and compact at high elevations, but at low elevations the branches are longer and looser. Grow it in the rock garden, outcrop, or stone wall. A mulch of pumice and peat moss may encourage establishment of plants.

   Native Habitat and Range. On rocky or gravelly slopes, cliffs, and outcrops at low to high elevations, circumboreal, and from Alaska south through Washington and Oregon, from near the coast, east through the mountains to Montana, Wyoming, and New Mexico.

   Notes. *Saxifraga c.* ssp. *caespitosa* and *S. c.* ssp. *subgemmifera* range into Washington and Oregon; *S. c.* ssp. *monticola* occurs from Alaska, south to Idaho and through the Rocky Mountains.

Saxifraga ferruginea	Zones 3b to 9b

rusty or Alaska saxifrage

This saxifrage produces a rosette of leaves from an erect root crown. The wedge-shaped basal leaves grow to 10cm (4in) long and 1.5cm (.5in) wide, with coarse teeth along the margins. The

Saxifraga ferruginea

Saxifraga mertensiana

branched flowering stems grow to 30cm (1ft). The sepals are reflexed and usually reddish. The five petals are white or purplish and narrowed (clawed) at the base, blooming from early to late summer. Three of the petals tend to be larger than the others, and each of these petals has a pair of yellow spots. The flowers are about 1.5cm (.5in) across. Brown seeds, elliptic in shape, ripen in capsules. The flowers are often replaced by small, leafy plantlets that fall before the seeds ripen.

Cultivation. Full sun to part shade, and well-drained but moist soil. This little saxifrage is charming in the mossy, moist places of the streambank, water feature (such as the spray zone near a waterfall), rock garden, or retaining wall.

Native Habitat and Range. Among moist rocks, near streams and other mossy, stony places, at low to high elevations from Alaska south to northwestern California, east from the Coast and Cascade Ranges to Idaho and western Montana.

Notes. A variable species, with *S. f.* var. *ferruginea* and *S. f.* var. *vreelandii* ranging further south than *S. f.* var. *newcombei*. Marshall's saxifrage (*S. marshallii*) is similar and native to Oregon and California. Red-stemmed or Lyall's saxifrage (*S. lyallii*) has fan-shaped leaves with large teeth; it lives in wet places and ranges as far south as northern Washington.

Saxifraga mertensiana	Zones 4a to 9b

wood or Mertens' saxifrage

This perennial produces short rhizomes and sometimes forms large clumps. One to three leaves grow at the base of each flowering shoot. The leaves have long petioles, and the blades are rounded, up to 10cm (4in) across and about equally broad, heart-shaped (cordate) at the base. The leaves are succulent; their margins have coarse lobes, and the lobes are further toothed. Flowering stems grow to 40cm (16in), developing into an open panicle with many flowers. The white flowers are about 1cm (.5in) across. The filaments of the stamens are also white, club-shaped (clavate) and petal-like, with pink anthers. Some of the flowers are replaced by pinkish bulblets, and little plantlets also form in the axils of the basal leaves. Flowering occurs from mid spring to mid summer, and light brown seeds are produced in beaked capsules.

Cultivation. Full sun to part shade, and well-drained, rocky, moist soil. This delicate saxifrage is charming among the mossy, moist rocks along a streambank, pond, rock garden, or retaining wall.

Native Habitat and Range. In the wet rocks or gravel along streams and waterfalls, at low to high elevations, from southern Alaska, south near the coast to northern California, and east to the Cascades, also east in southern British Columbia and the mountains of eastern Washington, Oregon, Idaho, and Montana.

Notes. *Saxifraga odontoloma* (*S. arguta*; brook, stream, or mountain meadow saxifrage), with rounded leaves, is similar.

Saxifraga rufidula	Zones 5a to 9a

rusty-haired saxifrage

This saxifrage often forms clumps from short rhizomes. The leathery leaves grow in a basal rosette and are generally ovate or elliptical, up to 6cm (2.5in) long. The leaf margins have distinctive, even teeth and reddish hairs on their undersides. Flowering stems grow to 20cm (8in) tall, and the inflorescence is flat-topped. The petals are usually white, but the sepals, ovaries, and stems are often reddish and hairy. Flowers are about 1cm (.5in) across and bloom from mid spring to late summer, depending on elevation. The capsules are often reddish and contain thin, brown seeds.

Cultivation. Full to part shade or dappled light, and well-drained, rocky, moist soil. This is a pretty and interesting plant for the shady parts of the rock garden or in a stone wall. Tuck it in the rocks near the pond or stream or in a mossy outcrop in the shade garden.

Native Habitat and Range. In shady places among moist rocks at low to high elevations, mainly west of the Cascade crest to the coast from southern British Columbia, south to northern California, east in the Columbia River Gorge and northeastern Oregon.

Notes. Sometimes classified as *S. occidentalis* var. *rufidula*. Western saxifrage (*S. occidentalis*) is a closely related species with a basal rosette of spoon-shaped, toothed leaves and white or pinkish flowers on stems to 25cm (10in) tall; it occurs in moist to rather dry meadows and rocky clearings at low to high elevations in the mountains and near the coast from southern British Columbia to central Oregon, east to Montana. Grassland saxifrage (*S. integrifolia*) often has a compact inflorescence and leaves with wavy margins or small teeth; it grows in meadows that are moist early in the year. Oregon saxifrage (*S. oregana*) sometimes has entire leaves and prefers boggy meadows. Both grow at low to high elevations.

Saxifraga tolmiei	Zones 4a to 8b

Tolmie's saxifrage

This low-growing, matted saxifrage produces many short shoots covered with the persistent remains of old leaves. The living leaves are small, succulent, and spoon-shaped (spatulate), with slightly inrolled margins; they grow to 1cm (.5in) long and sometimes have stiff hairs at the base. The flowering stems grow to 8cm (3in) tall and have, at most, a few small leaves. Each loose inflorescence produces three or four flowers about 1.5cm (.5in) across. The five petals are white, and the filaments of the stamens are also petal-like, white, and club-shaped (clavate). Flowers bloom from mid to late summer. The capsules are often mottled with purple and contain many light brown seeds.

Saxifraga rufidula

Saxifraga tolmiei

Cultivation. Full sun or light shade, and rocky or gravelly, well-drained but moist soil. This charming mat-former has interesting flowers, foliage, and fruits but is not always cooperative in cultivation; a mulching of pumice and peat moss may help. Grow it in the sunny, moist part of the rock garden, or in a stone wall or similar environment.

Native Habitat and Range. In meadows near streams, in moist rock crevices and talus at high elevations from Alaska south on Vancouver Island and the Olympics and south through the Cascades to the Sierra Nevada of central California, and east in the mountains to Idaho, Montana, and Nevada.

Notes. Purple mountain saxifrage (*S. oppositifolia*) is another cushion-forming perennial with showy, purplish flowers. This circumboreal species occurs on cold alpine cliffs and tundra. Although it is a desirable rock garden plant, the populations native to the Pacific Northwest are difficult to grow, and most cultivated plants are of European origin.

| ***Schoenoplectus acutus*** | Zones 3b to 9b | Cyperaceae |

hardstem bulrush

This large perennial produces stems up to 3m (10ft) tall and forms large colonies from thick rhizomes. The stems (culms) are somewhat angular, pith-filled, and 1cm (.5in) or more in thickness. The few leaves are basal, consisting of well-developed sheathing bases and poorly developed blades. The tiny florets are crowded into spikelets up to 1.5cm (.5in) long and arranged into an open or condensed, branched, umbel-like inflorescence. Each tiny floret is tucked into the axil of a small, gray bract with reddish markings. A pointed involucral bract, to 10cm (4in) long, subtends the inflorescence, appearing to be a continuation of the stem. The flowers bloom from early to late summer, and the fruit is a rounded achene with a pointed tip.

Schoenoplectus acutus var. *occidentalis*

Cultivation. Full sun, and a permanently or seasonally flooded site. Tolerates alkaline conditions. If space is limited, this large emergent plant can be kept in containers sunken into the mud beneath the surface of the water. Excellent for the margin of a lake, large pond, or ditch, providing cover, food, and nesting sites for many wildlife species. It is effective in controlling erosion along shorelines and acts as a filter, improving water quality.

Propagation. Divide rhizomes in early spring or fall. Can also be grown from seed collected in the fall and planted soon after harvest. Sow seeds into very wet soil, either in containers or directly into the muddy margin of the wetland, and leave them outside to cold stratify over winter for germination in the spring.

Native Habitat and Range. In marshes and muddy shores of streams and lakeshores, in water up to 1m (3ft) deep at low elevations throughout much of North America.

Notes. Sometimes classified as *Scirpus acutus*. *Schoenoplectus a.* var. *occidentalis* (tule) is more common from the Pacific Northwest south to California and Arizona, and east to the Rocky Mountains; *S. a.* var. *acutus* (hardstem bulrush), though it also occurs in our area, has a more northern and eastern distribution. *Schoenoplectus* encompasses about 20 species in North America, with about half of these occurring in the Pacific Northwest; all, including American bulrush (*S. americanus*), river bulrush (*S. fluviatilis*), and seashore or cosmopolitan bulrush (*S. maritimus*), will be found under *Scirpus* in many references. Other species, such as hardstem or softstem bulrush (*Scirpus validus* and *S. lacustris*, respectively), have been combined into a single species of *Schoenoplectus*, *S. tabernaemontani*. All these wetlands plants have large ranges in North America. Indigenous people used bulrushes as a lightweight building material with excellent insulating properties. The stems were also used to produce mats, baskets, and other items.

Schoenoplectus acutus var. occidentalis

Scirpus cyperinus

Scirpus   Cyperaceae

bulrush

As was hinted in the previous entry, the genus *Scirpus* used to be larger; many species have been moved to different genera, including *Schoenoplectus*. Approximately 20 of the remaining *Scirpus* species occur in North America, with about half a dozen in our area. These perennial plants of wet places have leafy stems and inflorescences composed of tiny florets grouped into small spikelets. The perianth parts (petals and sepals) are reduced to a few bristles in each floret, and the spikelets of florets are arranged into an umbel-like inflorescence subtended by leafy bracts. The fruits are small, one-seeded achenes.

Propagation. Grow from seed collected in the fall and planted soon after harvest. Sow seeds into wet soil, either in containers or directly into the garden, and leave them outside to cold stratify over winter for germination in the spring. Both rhizomatous and clump-forming species can be divided in the spring.

Scirpus cyperinus   Zones 3b to 9b

wool grass

This clumping perennial produces tufts of stems (culms) to 1.5m (5ft) tall. The stems are angular and leafy, the leaves flat and grass-like with sheathing bases. The numerous spikelets are small, just under 1cm (.5in) and arranged in an open, branched inflorescence at the tip of the stem. Several leaf-like bracts about 10cm (4in) long, with blackish bases, subtend the inflorescence.

Many tiny florets are produced in each spikelet, blooming from the axil of a small, dark scale. The perianth of each floret is composed of six long, wavy, tawny bristles, giving the spikelets a woolly appearance. Flowers bloom from mid to late summer, and the fruits are pale, three-sided achenes.

Cultivation. Full sun or part shade, and wet soil. This is a tall, graceful wetlands species for the margin of the pond or bog, or the low, wet place in the wildflower meadow. The softly woolly flowering spikelets are attractive from summer well into the fall.

Native Habitat and Range. In wet meadows, near lakes and ponds at low elevations, more common in eastern North America, but extending west to Washington and Oregon, where it is scattered on both sides of the Cascades.

Notes. Sometimes confused with *S. atrocinctus* (black-girdle bulrush), a species primarily of eastern North America. Pale bulrush (*S. pallidus*) has spikelets crowded into rounded clusters, the clusters arranged into a larger, umbel-like inflorescence. Nevada bulrush (*S. nevadensis*) has a few, large spikelets, developing without peduncles at the top of the stem. These leafy, rhizomatous perennials are found in wet places, mainly east of the Cascades.

Scirpus microcarpus	Zones 3b to 9b

small-fruited bulrush

This bulrush produces leafy shoots to 1.5m (5ft) from well-developed rhizomes. The stems are somewhat three-angled, and the leaves are flat and grass-like, around 1.5cm (.5in) wide and 20cm (8in) or more in length. The sheaths at the leaf bases are reddish purple where they clasp the stem. Tiny florets bloom in many small spikelets, the spikelets grouped into small clusters and the clusters arranged into a branched, umbel-like inflorescence at the tip of the stem. Leaf-like bracts subtend the inflorescence. Each tiny floret is set behind a blackish or greenish black scale. The perianth consists of a few slender bristles. Flowers bloom from early to late summer, and the fruits are pale, lenticular (lentil-shaped) achenes.

Cultivation. Full sun or part shade, and wet soil. This wetland plant develops extensive rhizomes, making it a good species for controlling erosion on ditch banks and steep pond margins; it also benefits wildlife, providing cover and seed for ducks and other birds. Site it in the bog, or the low, wet place in the wildflower meadow.

Native Habitat and Range. In wet ditches, sloughs, streambanks, and wetlands at low to mid elevations throughout the west, on both sides of the Cascades from Alaska south to California and Arizona, east through the Rocky Mountains, across Canada and the northern United States to the Atlantic.

Notes. *Scirpus congdonii* (Congdon's bulrush) grows to about 60cm (2ft) and looks very much like a dwarf form of *S. microcarpus*; it lives in wet meadows, lake margins, and streambanks at mid elevations in the mountains, from northern Oregon, south into California and Nevada.

Scoliopus hallii	Zones 7b to 9b	Liliaceae

fetid adder's tongue, slink lily or pod

The stems of this perennial lily are subterranean, buried down to 6cm (2.5in), with roots and short rhizomes below this. Stems usually produce two purple-mottled leaves to 20cm (8in) long and broadly oblong. Two to four flowers are produced on pedicels up to 8cm (3in) long and upright at flowering, but elongating and curving downward as the brownish capsules ripen. The flowers, about 2cm (1in) across, are foul-smelling to humans but attractive to pollinating flies. The three sepals are grayish yellow with purple veins, curving back from the flower. The narrow

Scirpus microcarpus

Scoliopus hallii

Scrophularia oregana

petals arch inward over the purple anthers and other flower parts. Fetid adder's tongue blooms from early to mid spring, and the fruits are capsules.

Cultivation. Shade, part sun, or dappled light, and moist, organic soil. An interesting native for the lover of odd plants. Plant it in the woodland garden, bog, or stream.

Propagation. Collect seeds after the capsules have ripened in the summer and sow them soon after harvest, either directly into the garden or into deep containers with enough moist soil to accommodate the underground stems and roots. Leave the planted seeds outside to stratify over winter for spring germination. Plants will take a few years to reach flowering size.

Native Habitat and Range. Near streams and in moist woods, from northwestern Oregon to southwestern Oregon, in the Coast Ranges and the west slope of the Cascades.

Notes. This endemic species, one of only two in the genus, should never be disturbed in nature.

Scrophularia oregana	Zones 7b to 9b	Scrophulariaceae

Oregon figwort

This interesting perennial produces clusters of stems to 1.5m (5ft) tall from thick roots. Basal leaves are lacking, and the stem leaves are opposite with well-developed petioles to 5cm (2in) long. The leaf blades are triangular to broadly lance-shaped, up to 15cm (6in) long by 7cm (3in) wide with sharply serrated margins. Small flowers bloom at the stem tips in branched, leafless inflorescences to 50cm (20in) long. The calyx has five rounded lobes, and the two-lipped (bilabiate) corolla is about 1.5cm (.5in) long and dark maroon. The upper lip of the corolla has two lobes and tends to point forward; the lower lip has three smaller lobes. Each flower has four fertile stamens and a purple or brown staminode (sterile stamen). Flowers bloom from early to late summer, and the fruits are small, rounded capsules with many seeds.

Cultivation. Full sun to part shade, and wet or moist soil. Plant it with other tall perennials in the wet parts of the hummingbird and butterfly garden. A good addition to the pond margin, streambank, or wet place in the wildflower meadow.

Propagation. Grow from seed collected in the late summer or fall, stored under cool, dry conditions, and planted in the early spring.

Native Habitat and Range. Along streams and in moist clearings and thickets at low elevations west of the Cascades in Washington, through southern Oregon.

Notes. Sometimes classified as *S. californica* var. *oregana*. Lanceleaf figwort (*S. lanceolata*), the only other species that occurs in our area, is similar, but its flowers are yellowish green, washed with maroon, and the staminode is yellowish and broad in shape; it lives in moist habitats at low to mid elevations on both sides of the Cascades, from southern British Columbia, south to California and east across much of North America to the Atlantic. Around 100 species of figworts are native to the Northern Hemisphere, but only about a dozen occur in North America.

Scutellaria lateriflora	Zones 3b to 9b	Lamiaceae

blue or mad-dog skullcap, madweed

This deciduous, rhizomatous perennial produces leafy stems to 80cm (2.5ft). The opposite, ovate leaves grow to 8cm (3in) long by 5cm (2in) wide and have toothed margins. Flowering racemes up to 12cm (5in) long develop from the leaf axils and produce many small, blue flowers, up to 1cm (.5in) long, from mid summer to early fall. The fruits, four tiny nutlets, are found inside the calyx after the corollas have dropped off.

Scutellaria lateriflora

Cultivation. Full sun or light shade, and wet soil. This is a good, easily grown species for the margin of a pond, wetland, or ditch. Plant it in the sunny bog or wet place in the wildflower meadow.

Propagation. Divide rhizomes in early to mid spring. Collect seeds in the fall, and sow them into flats of wet potting soil or directly into the garden in autumn or winter for spring germination.

Native Habitat and Range. In ditches, lakeshores, and wet meadows through much of North America from southern British Columbia, east to Newfoundland and south to California and Georgia.

Notes. The calyx is shaped like a helmet (hence, skullcap). The other terms applied to this species are more obscure, since the plants don't seem to have any poisonous properties. *Scutellaria* is a large, cosmopolitan genus of more than 100 species. Five others are native in the Pacific Northwest: those of drier habitats are Danny's skullcap (*S. tuberosa*), narrow-leaved skullcap (*S. angustifolia*), snapdragon skullcap (*S. antirrhinoides*), and dwarf skullcap (*S. nana*); marsh skullcap (*S. galericulata*) occurs in wet places throughout much of the Northern Hemisphere and has larger, blue or purple flowers in pairs at each node.

Sedum   Crassulaceae

stonecrop

Sedum contains around 400 species of mostly low-growing, evergreen, succulent perennials, chiefly native to the temperate regions of the Northern Hemisphere; about 14 are native to the Pacific Northwest. The flowers usually have five sepals and petals, and the fruits are small follicles.

Sedum divergens

Sedum laxum

Stonecrops are generally easy to grow, popular in rock gardens, and attractive to butterflies (some caterpillars eat the foliage). Different species bloom at different times, adding to their appeal.

Propagation. Pieces of stems pushed slightly into the surface of potting soil or pumice will form roots most readily during late spring and early summer. Rooted clumps can be divided in late spring or late summer. Stonecrops can also be grown from seeds collected in the late summer or fall, stored under cool, dry conditions, and planted into flats of potting soil or directly into the garden in early to mid spring. Some species produce tiny plantlets in the leaf axils; these can be detached and planted.

Sedum divergens   Zones 5b to 9b

Cascade or spreading stonecrop

This succulent perennial forms small evergreen mats, rooting freely where stems touch the ground. The fleshy leaves are oval, up to 1cm (.5in) long, and opposite in arrangement. Younger leaves are green; older ones are often bright red. Flowering stems can reach 15cm (6in) and are topped by a cluster of five to 15 blooms. The yellow flowers have five petals and bloom from mid summer to early fall. Each produces five follicles, fused at their bases, with pointed styles.

Cultivation. Full sun to part shade, and moist to rather dry soil that drains quickly. This is an easy little plant—small but brightly colored—for the rock garden or stone wall, or to fill in between paving stones.

Native Habitat and Range. On cliffs, talus, and other rocky places, at mid to high elevations from British Columbia south in the Olympic and Cascade Mountains to northern California.

Notes. A good plant for introducing kids to gardening. Stems look like strings of red and green jellybeans topped with yellow, star-like flowers.

Sedum oreganum

Sedum laxum   Zones 8a to 9b

lax or roseflower stonecrop

This succulent, evergreen perennial grows from branching rhizomes and produces upright stems to 40cm (16in) tall. The leaves are spoon-shaped (spatulate) and relatively large, to 3cm (1.5in) long or more. The large, open inflorescence can grow to 10cm (4in) across. The flowers are pink to violet or whitish, up to 1cm (.5in) long, and bloom from early to mid summer. The follicles are upright and fused at their bases.

   Cultivation. Full sun to part shade, and moist to rather dry soil with good drainage. Another fine, relatively easy stonecrop for the rock garden.

   Native Habitat and Range. On rocky, dry slopes at fairly low to mid elevations from south-western Oregon to northern California.

   Notes. *Sedum l.* ssp. *laxum* includes taller plants with longer, sometimes narrower leaves, often with yellowish flowers; *S. l.* ssp. *heckneri* (Heckner's stonecrop) consists of shorter plants with smaller leaves. Both occur in Oregon.

Sedum oreganum   Zones 5a to 9b

Oregon stonecrop

This succulent, evergreen plant grows from spreading rhizomes, producing flowering stems to 15cm (6in) and shorter sterile shoots. The leaves are spoon-shaped (spatulate), broadest toward the tip and flattened, but fleshy, alternately arranged on the stems. They are green or reddish and somewhat glaucous with a waxy, whitish coating, growing to 2cm (1in) long. Flowering stems are topped with clusters of small flowers, about 1cm (.5in) long, from early to late summer; the petals are yellow, often turning pinkish as they age. The follicles are upright.

Cultivation. Full sun to part shade, and well-drained, moist to rather dry soil. This is a bright, easy little groundcover for the butterfly or rock garden. It can also be used between paving stones or tucked into the crevices of a stone wall.

Native Habitat and Range. In cliffs, gravel, and other rocky places at low to fairly high elevations, from southwestern Alaska and northwestern British Columbia south to northern California, and from near the coast east into the Cascades, occasionally east of the Cascade crest.

Notes. *Sedum o.* ssp. *oreganum* ranges from Alaska to California; *S. o.* ssp. *tenue* is restricted to Washington. 'Glaucum' has foliage with a bluish white, waxy coating.

Sedum oregonense	Zones 5b to 9b

creamy stonecrop

This evergreen, usually wax-coated (glaucous) perennial grows from thick rhizomes. The sterile shoots form rosettes of spoon-shaped (spatulate) leaves up to 3cm (1.5in) long by about 1cm (.5in) wide. The upright flowering shoots grow to 15cm (6in) tall and have much smaller leaves. The inflorescence is elongated and crowded with many pale yellow to creamy flowers that bloom from early to mid summer and turn pinkish as they dry. The follicles are upright, fused only at their bases.

Cultivation. Full sun to light shade, and well-drained, rocky, rather dry soil. A fine plant for the rock garden or border of the butterfly garden.

Native Habitat and Range. On dry, rocky slopes and lava beds at mid to fairly high elevations, from Mt. Hood, south in the Oregon Cascades to southwestern Oregon and northwestern California.

Notes. The flowers are lighter in color than most other species. Sierra stonecrop (*S. obtusatum*) and Applegate or oblong-leaf stonecrop (*S. oblanceolatum*) are similar, with broad leaves and cream-colored or pale yellow flowers; they occur in southwestern Oregon.

Sedum spathulifolium	Zones 5b to 9b

broad-leaved stonecrop

This succulent, evergreen perennial grows from thick rhizomes. Vegetative shoots form compact rosettes of flat, but very fleshy, spoon-shaped (spatulate) leaves to 2cm (1in) long. Older stems and leaves are red; younger foliage is distinctly glaucous, covered with a waxy, bluish white coating. Flowering stems bear alternate leaves and grow to 20cm (8in) tall, topped with clusters of bright yellow flowers. Blossoms are up to 1cm (.5in) long and open from late spring to late summer. The fruits form a ring of slightly spreading follicles, fused at their bases.

Cultivation. Full sun to part shade, and moist to rather dry soil that drains quickly. This lovely little succulent creates a splash of silvery blue-green and red with clusters of bright yellow flowers. A great, easy-to-grow plant for the rock garden, as a groundcover between paving stones, or as edging for the butterfly garden. Tuck rooted pieces into the cracks of a wall or other stone structure for a charming effect.

Native Habitat and Range. In gravelly soils and cliff crevices at low to mid elevations from southwestern British Columbia through California and from the coast, east through the Coast Ranges to the west slope of the Cascades, and in the Columbia River Gorge.

Notes. *Sedum s.* ssp. *spathulifolium* occurs throughout the range; *S. s.* ssp. *purdyi* (Purdy's stonecrop) grows in Oregon and California. This species is the best known and most widely grown of our native sedums; its several selections include 'Cape Blanco' and purple-leaved 'Pur-
pureum'.

Sedum oregonense

Sedum stenopetalum

Sedum spathulifolium

Sedum stenopetalum	Zones 4a to 9b	

wormleaf or narrow-petaled stonecrop

This evergreen, rhizomatous perennial produces linear, succulent leaves to 2cm (1in) long, green with tints of red. The flowering stems grow to 20cm (8in) and are topped with compact clusters of yellow flowers, blooming from late spring to mid summer. The flowering shoots often lose their lower leaves by blooming time, while small plantlets form in the axils of the upper leaves, just below the inflorescence. The follicles spread widely, almost horizontally.

Cultivation. Full sun to part shade, and well-drained, rather dry soil. This species is especially hardy in gardens east of the Cascades, but it's also happy west of the mountains. Great for the rock garden or planted into the cracks of a stone wall, or as a groundcover between paving stones.

Native Habitat and Range. In cliff crevices and dry gravel, low to mid elevations, mainly east of the Cascade crest from British Columbia to California, east to western Montana and Wyoming; occasional in the Willamette Valley and Olympic Mountains.

Notes. *Sedum s.* ssp. *monanthum* has a more western range; *S. s.* ssp. *stenopetalum* has a wider range east of the Cascades. *Sedum lanceolatum* (lance-leaved or spearleaf stonecrop), with narrow leaves and yellow flowers, occurs on both sides of the Cascades and through much of western North America.

Senecio triangularis	Zones 3b to 9b	Asteraceae

arrowleaf groundsel, butterweed, or ragwort

This highly variable perennial produces several leafy stems up to 1.5m (5ft) from rhizomes or fibrous roots. The leaves are generally triangular, the lower ones with well-developed petioles. The largest leaves grow to 20cm (8in) long by 10cm (4in) wide with sharply toothed margins. Several flowering heads bloom in flat-topped inflorescences at the stem tips. The row of involucral bracts surrounding each head grows to 1cm (.5in), and the ray and disk florets are both present. Each head has around eight ray florets with yellow corollas about 1cm (.5in) long. Flowers bloom from early summer to early fall. The fruits are small achenes with a pappus (modified calyx) of long, white bristles.

Cultivation. Full sun to part shade, and moist to rather wet soil. Include this lush, yellow-flowered species with taller perennials near a pond, stream, or bog margin. It's an excellent summer-blooming plant for the wet spots in the wildflower meadow or butterfly garden on either side of the Cascades.

Propagation. Grow from seed collected in the fall and planted outside soon after harvest, either into containers or directly into the garden, and left to stratify over winter for germination in the spring. Plants can also be propagated by dividing clumps in the spring or by taking stem cuttings during the summer.

Native Habitat and Range. Along streams, in wet or moist meadows, open forests, thickets and seeps, usually at mid to high elevations from Alaska, south through the mountains to southern California, east to Saskatchewan, Montana, Colorado, and New Mexico.

Notes. Around 50 species of *Senecio* are native to North America; close to 20 occur in the Pacific Northwest, some of them narrow endemics, others widespread.

Senecio triangularis (photo by Sally A. Simmons)

Sidalcea campestris

Sidalcea   Malvaceae

checkermallow

Sidalcea encompasses a couple dozen species of annual and perennial herbs, all native to western North America, especially California; ten of these occur in our area, and some are listed as rare. Several of our prettiest native wildflowers are checkermallows, which resemble small, delicate hollyhocks. The well-developed basal leaves are palmate or compound, and the alternate stem leaves are smaller, often with narrower lobes. The flowers have five sepals, fused at the base, and five showy petals. The filaments of the numerous stamens are fused into a tube around the style branches. In *Sidalcea*, some of the individual flowers are perfect (the male and female structures are both functional), and these are larger. Other, smaller flowers are functionally pistillate (female), and the anthers are sterile, rudimentary, or missing from the tips of the filaments. The fruit is a schizocarp, consisting of a ring of five to ten carpels (the units of the ovary, like the sections of an orange), each containing a single seed. The individual carpels, or mericarps, eventually dry and break apart at maturity to release the seed. Some caterpillars eat the foliage of checkermallows, making these good plants for the butterfly garden.

Propagation. Grow from seed collected in the late summer or early fall. Sow the seeds into flats or directly into the garden in the fall or winter, and leave them outside to chill for at least a few weeks; they will germinate when the weather warms in the spring. The rhizomes of older plants can be divided in spring, but this should be done only with plants originally grown from seed.

Sidalcea campestris   Zones 5b to 9b

field or meadow checkermallow

This checkermallow produces stems up to 2m (6ft) tall from a taproot and short, thick rhizomes. The plants are usually roughly hairy, and the lower leaves are the largest, with blades up to 15cm (6in) across and set on long petioles. The leaf blades are deeply palmate, with up to nine primary lobes that are secondarily lobed and toothed at their tips. The stem leaves are smaller, palmately compound with narrow leaflets. Loosely flowered racemes develop from the axils of the upper leaves. The cup-like calyx has five lobes. The five petals are up to 2.5cm (1in) long in the larger, bisexual flowers and vary in color from almost white to shell-pink to pale lavender. The flowers bloom in tall, open wands from late spring to mid summer, and the small, dry mericarps are reticulate (net-patterned) on the sides.

Cultivation. Full sun to light shade, and moist to rather dry, well-drained soil. May need some extra moisture in hotter, drier climates. Although uncommon in nature, this lovely perennial is easy to cultivate and grows happily in gardens west and east of the Cascades. Plant it with other tall species in the wildflower meadow, perennial bed, or dry slope.

Native Habitat and Range. In rather dry, grassy fields, slopes, and roadsides, mainly in the Willamette Valley, south to southern Oregon and apparently disjunct in the Puget Sound area.

Notes. Sharing this species' bloom season is *S. nelsoniana* (Nelson's checkermallow), which has a small native range in the gravelly, moist meadows and thickets of the Willamette Valley, rarely to southwestern Washington; it grows only half as tall, to 1m (3ft) tall, and its flowers are pinkish lavender.

Sidalcea hendersonii   Zones 5b to 9b

Henderson's checkermallow

This checkermallow produces flowering stems up to 1.5m (5ft) from a taproot and short, thick rhizomes. The plants are generally purple-tinted and hairless (glabrous). The lowermost leaves have long petioles and rounded blades up to around 10cm (4in) across. The blades are palmate with shallow lobes, and the margins of the lobes are crenate (with rounded teeth). The inflorescences are compound racemes, narrow and spike-like, crowded with flowers. The calyx has five lobes, and the petals are deep pink, sometimes an unusual shade of peachy pink, and up to 2.5cm (1in) long. The flowers bloom from early to late summer, and the dry mericarps are usually smooth.

Cultivation. Full sun to light shade, and moist or wet soil. Needs a bit of shade and extra moisture in hot, dry areas. Although this is a rare plant of coastal habitats, it grows in gardens on both sides of the Cascades and makes an excellent perennial for the moist wildflower meadow or perennial border.

Native Habitat and Range. In tidal marshes and wet meadows near the coast at low elevations from southwestern British Columbia, scattered south to southwestern Oregon.

Notes. Cusick's checkermallow (*S. cusickii*) is restricted to the fields and roadsides of western Oregon, sometimes in heavy soils; its deep rose-pink flowers, carried on stems over 1m (3ft) tall, bloom from late spring to early summer. Sharing this height and bloom season is dwarf checkermallow (*S. malviflora*), a complex species with 13 subspecies, six of which occur in moist meadows and roadsides in western Oregon, rarely Washington; it has pale to deep rose flowers.

Sidalcea hendersonii

Sidalcea hirtipes

Sidalcea hirtipes   Zones 5b to 9b

bristly-stemmed checkermallow

This checkermallow often forms extensive, spreading clumps from short, thick rhizomes. The flowering stems grow to 1m (3ft) tall, and the plants are covered with long, stiff hairs. The basal and lower stem leaves are the largest, palmate, with toothed blades to 6cm (2.5in) across, often on very long petioles. The upper stem leaves are palmate, divided into narrow lobes. The inflorescences are crowded, spike-like, often compound racemes with flowers on small pedicels. The hairy calyx has five lobes, and the five pink to rose-purple petals are about 1.5cm (.5in) long. Flowers bloom from early to mid summer. The small mericarps have a rough surface.

Cultivation. Full sun to part shade, and moist soil. Site this species in the perennial bed or moist place in the wildflower meadow or hillside.

Native Habitat and Range. In moist, open meadows and coastal bluffs at low to mid elevations in the Coast Ranges, endemic from southwestern Washington to the coast of northwestern Oregon.

Notes. Better for east-side gardens is *S. neomexicana* (prairie checkermallow), a subspecies of which occurs in alkaline seeps east of the Cascades in northeastern Oregon and ranges east and south through the Rocky Mountains. Another is *S. oregana* (Oregon checkermallow), which grows in moist meadows and also with sagebrush and ponderosa pine, at low to high elevations, mainly east of the Cascades in southern British Columbia and Washington, but on both sides in Oregon, and south to California, east to the Rocky Mountains. This checkermallow grows from a taproot to 1.5m (5ft) tall, with a branched crown; its light to deep pink flowers bloom from late spring to mid summer.

| **Silene hookeri** | Zones 6a to 9b | Caryophyllaceae |

Hooker's Indian pink or catchfly

This perennial produces prostrate, somewhat rhizomatous stems from a thick taproot and a branched crown. The stems tips are upright to 15cm (6in) tall, and the plants are grayish with pale hairs. The simple, opposite leaves are oblanceolate (lance-shaped, but broadest toward the tip) and tapered to the petiole. The largest leaves develop on the upper parts of the stems and are about 7cm (3in) long. Flowers bloom in small, leafy clusters at the stem tips. The hairy calyx is tubular and about 2cm (1in) long with five teeth at the tip. Each of the five petals has a narrow base (the claw) and a broader, fan-shaped blade to 2cm (1in) long. The petal blades are four-lobed, and the two lateral lobes are usually smaller than the two middle lobes. There are two small, linear appendages on each petal where the blade meets the claw. The flowers, which vary from almost white to bright pink, salmon, or purplish, bloom from mid spring to early summer. The fruits are dry, rounded capsules that open through teeth at the tip and contain numerous blackish seeds.

Cultivation. Full sun or part shade, and well-drained, rocky soil. Allow plants to dry and become dormant in late summer, and protect them from excess moisture in the wetter parts of the Pacific Northwest. Lovely for the rock garden, stone retaining wall, or open woods; on a dry, stony bank; or among the rocks in the sunny part of the wildflower meadow.

Propagation. Grow from seed collected during the summer and planted soon after harvest. Sow seeds into deep containers of light, well-drained potting soil or directly into the garden. Leave the planted seeds outside over fall and winter for germination the following spring. Seedlings spend most of their energy developing a taproot, so plants will not flower for the first year or two. Transplant containerized seedlings early in their second spring, being careful to minimize root disturbance.

Native Habitat and Range. On open, rocky slopes, dry fields, and wooded hillsides at fairly low to mid elevations, west of the Cascades and in the Coast Ranges of northwestern Oregon, south through northern California.

Notes. A variable species. *Silene h.* ssp. *bolanderi* has larger, paler flowers. California Indian pink (*S. californica*) is similar, but the flowers are bright crimson; it grows in open woods at low to mid elevations through California, north to southwestern Oregon and requires dryish garden conditions. *Silene* includes over 200 species, widespread in the temperate or colder parts of the Northern Hemisphere; more than 50 are native to North America, about half of these to the Pacific Northwest, including *S. acaulis* (moss campion, cushion pink), one of our best-known native rock garden species. This tufted perennial forms dense, rounded cushions to 50cm (20in) across, tending to hug the rocky substrate and only growing to about 6cm (2.5in) tall. The pink to lavender (occasionally white) flowers bloom from early to late summer. This plant grows in moist, well-drained, rocky places and is circumpolar, extending to Eurasia and south through the mountains of western North America. *Silene campanulata* (slender campion, bell catchfly) and *S. lemmonii* (Lemmon's catchfly) are taller, with lacy, finely lobed, greenish flower petals; these perennnials live in dry, open woods in southwestern Oregon and California. Other perennial natives include Douglas' or seabluff catchfly (*S. douglasii*), Oregon campion or catchfly (*S. oregana*), Parry's catchfly (*S. parryi*), and Menzies' catchfly or campion (*S. menziesii*); all are widespread in our area, have whitish flowers, and make good additions to the wildflower meadow or perennial bed.

| **Sisyrinchium** | Iridaceae |

blue-eyed grass

These charming little perennials have a fluid taxonomic history. Leaves are linear, folded and flattened (equitant), similar to those of their cousins, but unlike the differentiated petals and

Silene hookeri

Sisyrinchium bellum

sepals of irises, the flowers of *Sisyrinchium* have petals and sepals that are all similar and petaloid. The six "petals" are often referred to as tepals or perianth segments. Seeds ripen in small, rounded capsules with three chambers. In typical *Sisyrinchium* flowers, the filaments of the stamens are fused almost to their tips; in *Olsynium* (grasswidow), a related genus with similar leaves, the filaments are only partially fused and the base of the stamen tube is sometimes inflated. Otherwise, the species of both genera are quite similar. Around 60 species of grasswidows and blue-eyed grasses are native to North America, South America, and the West Indies. About ten of these occur in the Pacific Northwest.

Propagation. Grow from seed. Collect seeds from the small capsules and plant in late summer or fall, soon after they are harvested, or store in cool, dry conditions for early spring planting. If planting in the fall, sow seeds into flats or directly into the garden and leave them outside over winter for germination the following spring. Larger plants sometimes form small clumps, and these can be divided in the early spring or late summer.

Sisyrinchium bellum	Zones 6a to 9b

western blue-eyed grass

This deciduous perennial forms branched flowering stems up to 40cm (16in) tall. The narrow, iris-like basal leaves grow to 20cm (8in) long. In addition to the leaf-like bracts that subtend the flower clusters, there is at least one leaf that develops from a lower node on the stem. Few-flowered, umbel-like inflorescences produce flowers to 2cm (1in) across. The tepals are blue to purplish on the upper surface and pale below, each with a narrow point at the tip, and usually with a yellow eye. Blooming takes place from mid spring to mid summer. The capsules contain several blackish seeds.

Cultivation. Full sun or part shade, and soil that is moist to wet, at least in the spring. This graceful species pairs well with other natives in a border or perennial bed and is a good addition to the seasonally wet vernal pool in the wildflower meadow, pond margin, or other moist, sunny place in the garden. Often self-sows.

Native Habitat and Range. In meadows, seeps, marshes, and ditches that are moist to wet, at least in spring, at low to mid elevations west of the Cascades through Oregon and California.

Notes. This species is sometimes included with Idaho blue-eyed grass (*S. idahoense*) or confused with *S. angustifolium* (narrowleaf blue-eyed grass), which is restricted to eastern North America.

Sisyrinchium californicum	Zones 7a to 9b

golden blue-eyed grass

This small, deciduous perennial forms clumps of basal leaves up to 25cm (10in) tall and less than 1cm (.5in) wide. Two to seven bright yellow flowers bloom at the tips of stems up to 40cm (16in) tall. Flowers are up to 2cm (1in) across and are produced from early to mid summer. The capsules contain black seeds.

Cultivation. Full sun or part shade, and moist to wet soil. This cheerful cousin of iris does well in any wet, sunny spot in the garden. Plant it near a pond or bog, or at the edge of a moist meadow or perennial bed. Self-sows, sometimes aggressively, given sufficient moisture.

Native Habitat and Range. On the margins of lakes, bogs, and other wet places at low elevations west of the Cascades from southern Vancouver Island south to central California.

Notes. Plants from the southern end of the range are generally taller than northern populations. The northern plants have sometimes been considered a separate species, but the differences are not distinctive.

Sisyrinchium douglasii	Zones 5a to 9b

grasswidow, purple-eyed grass, satin flower

This deciduous perennial tends to form clumps up to 30cm (1ft) tall. The lowermost basal leaves are relatively small, to 2cm (1in) long. The leaves on the lower parts of the flowering stems are longer, narrow and grass-like, up to 10cm (4in). The longer of the two bracts at the top of the flowering stem can sometimes grow to 12cm (5in). Flowers are usually produced in pairs and are often turned at right angles from the stem. They are bright reddish purple (sometimes white) and relatively large, up to 4cm (1.5in) across, blooming from early spring to early summer. The capsules contain brown seeds.

Cultivation. Full sun to light shade, and soil that is moist or wet in the early spring, but rather dry by summer. This little plant will do well in the rock garden or in the perennial border on either side of the Cascades. It's beautiful under a grove of oaks or other deciduous trees, or in the seasonally moist parts of the wildflower meadow.

Native Habitat and Range. Open woodlands, rocky slopes, and other places that are moist in early spring, at low to mid elevations west of the Cascades from Vancouver Island south to northern California, east through the Columbia River Gorge and the east base of the Cascades, in central and eastern Washington and Oregon, east to Idaho, Utah, and Nevada.

Notes. Sometimes classified as *Olsynium douglasii*. *Sisyrinchium d.* var. *douglasii* occurs in the western parts of the range; *S. d.* var. *inflatum* is more eastern, growing in sagebrush and ponderosa pine habitats east of the Cascades. In this east-side variety, flower color varies from light lavender to dark purple, and white-flowered plants are common.

Sisyrinchium idahoense

Sisyrinchium californicum

Sisyrinchium douglasii

Sisyrinchium idahoense   Zones 4a to 9b

Idaho blue-eyed grass

This deciduous perennial forms tufts of narrow, grass-like basal leaves to 20cm (8in) long. Unbranched flowering stems can grow to 40cm (16in) and have few leaves except for the bracts that subtend each cluster of one to five flowers. Each blossom is up to 2cm (1in) across, blue to purplish and usually with a yellow eye at the center. Each tepal generally has a narrow point at the tip, and flowers bloom from mid spring to mid summer.

Cultivation. Full sun or part shade, and moist to wet soil. This delicate species is a good addition to the pond margin, bog, or other moist to wet, sunny place in the garden. Site it at the edge of a moist wildflower meadow or with the smaller plants in the perennial bed. Sometimes self-sows.

Native Habitat and Range. In seeps, ditches, meadows, and other places that are moist, at least in the spring, at low to mid elevations from southern British Columbia south to California and east to Montana, Colorado, and New Mexico.

Notes. Sometimes confused with *S. angustifolium* (narrowleaf blue-eyed grass). *Sisyrinchium i.* var. *idahoense*, *S. i.* var. *macounii*, *S. i.* var. *segetum*, and *S. i.* var. *occidentale* occur in the Pacific Northwest. Other native blue-flowered species in our area are Hitchcock's blue-eyed grass (*S. hitchcockii*), Alaska blue-eyed grass (*S. littorale*), Nevada blue-eyed grass (*S. halophilum*), and mountain blue-eyed grass (*S. sarmentosum*).

Solidago   Asteraceae

goldenrod

Solidago is a genus of around 100 species, most of them native to North America. The genera *Euthamia* (which includes about five North American species) and *Oligoneuron* are combined with *Solidago* in many older references; but even considering *Solidago* in the narrow sense (excluding *Euthamia* and *Oligoneuron*), there remain around 70 species in North America, with most of the diversity in the eastern part of the continent. The goldenrods are perennial herbs with fibrous roots and alternate leaves. They generally have small flowering heads clustered into large inflorescences. Both disk and ray florets are usually present, and the fruits, small achenes, have a pappus (modified calyx) of fine bristles. Goldenrods have sometimes been used medicinally, and they have an undeserved reputation for causing hay fever.

Propagation. Easy from divisions of the rhizomes made in mid spring or late summer, or from cuttings of young basal shoots made in the spring. Can also be grown from seed collected in the fall and either planted outside soon after harvest or sown in the spring.

Solidago canadensis   Zones 3b to 9b

Canada goldenrod

This goldenrod produces leafy shoots to 1m (3ft) or even 2m (6ft) from creeping rhizomes. Basal leaves are absent. The largest leaves, to 15cm (6in) long and about 2cm (1in) wide, are in the middle of the stem; they have toothed to entire margins and three distinct veins, and are lance-shaped and tapered to the base, lacking petioles. Flowers bloom at the stem tips, usually in a plume-shaped, panicle-like inflorescence. The tiny heads have yellow ray and disk corollas, and bloom from mid summer to mid fall.

Cultivation. Full sun to part shade, and fairly moist soil. This is a lovely, late-blooming plant for the edge of the woodland garden, wildflower meadow, or pond, and an excellent addition to

Solidago canadensis

Solidago occidentalis

the butterfly garden. Makes a fine cut flower. Under ideal conditions, plants may spread aggressively, but keeping them on the dry side will help to control them.

Native Habitat and Range. In moist meadows, open woods, thickets, and roadsides at low to mid elevations, throughout most of southern Canada and the United States.

Notes. *Solidago c.* var. *salebrosa*, our most common variety, occurs throughout the Pacific Northwest; it has a more elongated inflorescence and is less hairy than *S. c.* var. *gilvocanescens*, a plant of the Great Plains that ranges as far west as eastern Washington. Other species native to our area include giant goldenrod (*S. gigantea*) and Missouri goldenrod (*S. missouriensis*). *Solidago multiradiata* (northern goldenrod) and *S. simplex* (*S. spathulata*; dune or spikelike goldenrod) are more compact plants, suitable for smaller garden spaces. *Solidago simplex* includes two subspecies, but only *S. s.* ssp. *simplex* occurs in the west; dwarf goldenrod (*S. s.* ssp. *s.* var. *nana*), the widespread *S. s.* ssp. *s.* var. *simplex*, and the aromatic, coastal *S. s.* ssp. *s.* var. *spathulata* all occur in our area.

Solidago occidentalis	Zones 3b to 9b

western goldenrod or goldentop

This big goldenrod produces hairless, leafy stems to 2m (6ft) from creeping rhizomes. The many small leaves are narrowly lance-shaped or linear, largest in the middle of the stem, and up to 10cm (4in) long by 1cm (.5in) wide. Flowering heads bloom in small clusters and are organized into larger, flat-topped inflorescences. Each small head is composed of tiny disk and ray florets with golden yellow corollas, blooming from mid summer to mid fall.

Cultivation. Full sun to part shade, and moist soil. Keep plants on the dry side to prevent them from becoming too aggressive. This is a beautiful, late-blooming species, but it gets big and should be planted with other large perennials near the back fence. Excellent for the butterfly garden, or for the edge of the woodland garden, wildflower meadow, or pond.

Native Habitat and Range. Near streams, in meadows, and other open, moist places at low to mid elevations from southern British Columbia and Alberta, south on both sides of the Cascades to southern California, Arizona and, New Mexico.

Notes. Sometimes classified as *Euthamia occidentalis*. Similar in our area is *S. graminifolia* var. *graminifolia* (*E. graminifolia* var. *graminifolia*; bushy or fragrant goldenrod, flat-topped golden-top), which extends from southern British Columbia east across North America.

Sphaeralcea munroana	Zones 5a to 7b	Malvaceae

Munro's globemallow

This thick-rooted perennial produces multiple, leafy stems, and grows to 1m (3ft) tall and 60cm (2ft) wide. Plants are silvery with whitish, star-shaped (stellate) hairs. The leaves are ovate-deltoid (triangular) to reniform (kidney-shaped) and up to 6cm (2.5in) long. The leaf margins are usually pinnately lobed and toothed, and the lower leaves have well-developed petioles. Flowers bloom on short pedicels in simple or compound racemes. Each flower usually has three small, linear bracts (bracteoles) beneath the cup-like, five-lobed calyx. The five showy petals are up to 2cm (1in) long and salmon-pink to bright orange. The filaments of the numerous stamens are fused into a tube around the styles and capitate (head-like) stigmas. The flowers bloom from late spring to late summer. The fruit is a schizocarp, a ring of carpels (the units of the ovary, like the sections of an orange), each containing a single seed, drying and splitting open at maturity.

Cultivation. Full sun or light shade, and well-drained, rather dry soil. This silvery, orange-flowered beauty makes a wonderful addition to gardens east of the Cascades. Plant it among sagebrush in the drought-tolerant wildlife garden, in the wildflower meadow, or with other sun-loving perennials. It is a good plant for the butterfly garden, where the foliage may be eaten by the larvae of some butterflies. It will probably tolerate some gardens west of the Cascades (at least in southwestern Oregon) if protected from excess wetness.

Propagation. Grow from seed collected in the fall and planted soon after harvest. Sow seeds into flats of well-drained potting soil or directly into the garden, and leave them outside over winter for germination in the spring. Another possible method is to take softwood cuttings from young stems in spring; treat them with hormones, set into pumice, and keep humid until roots form.

Native Habitat and Range. In dry, sandy soils and rocky slopes, often with sagebrush, at low to mid elevations east of the Cascades from south central British Columbia, south through eastern Washington and Oregon to northern California, east to Wyoming and Utah.

Notes. *Sphaeralcea* includes around 50 species, most of them native to the warm or arid regions of North and South America. Half of these occur in North America, mainly in the Southwest. Another species that ranges into our area is *S. grossulariifolia* (gooseberry-leaf globemallow); it grows to about 60cm (2ft) and has grayish foliage, reddish orange flowers, and deeply divided, lobed leaves. It blooms in the summer and occurs in the dry plains and foothills of south central Washington and eastern Oregon, to Idaho, Utah, and Nevada. Scarlet globemallow (*S. coccinea*) is similar and ranges as far west as eastern Oregon.

Sphaeralcea munroana (photo by Sally A. Simmons)

Spiranthes romanzoffiana

Spiranthes romanzoffiana   Zones 3b to 9b   Orchidaceae

hooded lady's tresses

This orchid produces flowering shoots up to 60cm (2ft) tall from fleshy, tuber-like roots. The stems bear several narrowly oblong or linear leaves up to 20cm (8in) long, with the largest ones near the base of the stem and the upper leaves reduced to bracts. The inflorescence is a spike of flowers spirally arranged in one to four vertical rows. The small flowers are about 1cm (.5in) long, white to greenish white or creamy. The upper sepal and two lateral petals are fused to form a curved hood. Flowers bloom from mid to late summer. The inferior ovary develops into a small, many seeded capsule.

Cultivation. Full sun to part shade or dappled light, and moist to wet soil high in organic matter. This is an unusual and lovely perennial for the margin of the bog, pond, seep, or streambank. Plants are not especially showy, but the spiraling inflorescence is graceful and fascinating. Do not use fungicides or synthetic fertilizers around orchids (actually, there's no good reason to use any of these chemicals, ever).

Propagation. Possible but difficult from seed. Collect some capsules as soon as they are ripe, along with a bit of soil from around the parent plant. Mix the tiny seeds with the native soil and some mycorrhizal fungal spores, and plant them in the fall, into flats of fine, moist potting soil. Leave the flats outside and keep them protected and moist. With luck, seedlings will germinate and grow, and can be transplanted in a year or so. Orchids should never be dug from the wild.

Native Habitat and Range. In wet meadows, bogs, and streambanks, also in moist to rather dry woods at low to mid elevations, from Alaska south to California, east through the Rocky Mountains to Colorado and New Mexico, and east through much of Canada, the northern Great Plains, and the Great Lakes region to the Atlantic coast.

Notes. Listed as rare in many states, especially in the eastern parts of its range. *Spiranthes* includes somewhere between 100 and 200 species living in temperate areas throughout the world; a couple dozen species of lady's tresses are native to North America. Among these, only *S. porrifolia* (creamy lady's tresses) and the rare *S. diluvialis* (Ute lady's tresses) reach our area (and both are sometimes classified as varieties of *S. romanzoffiana*).

Stachys	Lamiaceae

hedge-nettle

Stachys includes upward of 100 species of herbs and shrubs, widespread in the temperate parts of the Northern Hemisphere and in some subtropical areas to the south. About 25 species are native to North America, with five of these occurring in the Pacific Northwest. Hedge-nettles have simple, opposite leaves and square stems, but lack a minty fragrance. They have a five-lobed calyx and tubular, two-lipped (bilabiate) corolla formed from five fused petals. The flowers have four stamens, and the fruits consist of four nutlets.

Propagation. Divide rhizomes in spring or late summer. Plants can also be grown from seed collected in the fall and stored under cool, dry conditions. Seeds germinate under warm conditions and can be sown into flats of potting soil or directly into the garden from early to mid spring.

Stachys chamissonis var. *cooleyae*	Zones 5a to 9b

Cooley's hedge-nettle

This rhizomatous perennial produces hairy, aromatic (but not minty) shoots to 1.5m (5ft) tall. The stem leaves have ovate blades up to 15cm (6in) long with crenate (round-toothed) margins and well-developed petioles to 4cm (1.5in) long. Flowers bloom in verticils (whorls) near the stem tips. The lobes of the calyx are spine-tipped. The corollas have a three-lobed lower lip and a rounded upper lip. They are deep pink or red-purple and up to 4cm (1.5in) long. Flowers bloom from early to late summer. The four nutlets ripen in the persistent calyx.

Cultivation. Full sun to part shade or dappled light, and moist to wet soil. This is a pretty, pink-flowered perennial for the pond margin, streambank, or wet ditch. Plant it in the wet places in the wildflower meadow or hummingbird garden.

Native Habitat and Range. In wetlands, near streams, and in moist thickets, open woods, and roadsides at low elevations from southern British Columbia, south to central California and from the coast, east to the eastern base of the Cascades.

Notes. Sometimes classified as *S. cooleyae*. *Stachys rigida* (rigid or rough hedge-nettle) has smaller flowers, and its leaves have short petioles, or lack them entirely; it lives in moist habitats on both sides of the Cascades from Washington, south to California and Nevada.

Stachys mexicana	Zones 5b to 9b

Mexican hedge-nettle

This deciduous, rhizomatous perennial develops branched, leafy stems up to 1m (3ft). The foliage is aromatic, some would say unpleasantly so. The leaves are hairy, lanceolate to oblong in shape, and grow to 12cm (5in) long; they have petioles, and the blades have teeth along the margins. The light pink or purplish flowers bloom in whorls (verticils) at the stem tips and leaf axils from early to late summer. The corollas are about 1.5cm (.5in) in length.

Stachys chamissonis var. cooleyae

Stachys mexicana

Cultivation. Full sun to part shade or dappled light, and moist or wet soil. This plant will add diversity to the margin of a large pond, wetland, or other moist to boggy area. Plant it in the wet place in the hummingbird garden or roadside ditch.

Native Habitat and Range. Near streams, wetlands, ditches, and other moist or wet sites at low elevations, generally near the coast, from southern British Columbia, south to California.

Notes. Sometimes classified as *S. ciliata* or *S. emersonii*. *Stachys pilosa* var. *pilosa* (*S. palustris* var. *pilosa*; hairy hedge-nettle) is a widespread taxon found in low, moist places throughout much of North America. The plants grow to about 60cm (2ft), and the flowers are purplish and white. True nettles (*Urtica* spp.), which are often found in the same habitats as hedge-nettle, have drooping clusters of very tiny, greenish flowers and stinging hairs; they are good food plants for butterfly larvae.

Stenanthium occidentale	Zones 4a to 9b	Liliaceae

mountainbells, western featherbells

This deciduous, bulb-forming perennial develops two or three basal leaves to 30cm (1ft) long and 2.5cm (1in) wide. Flowering stems grow to 40cm (16in) and vary from a few-flowered raceme to a branched panicle with up to 25 flowers. The bell-shaped flowers are fragrant, greenish yellow to maroon and up to 1.5cm (.5in) long, blooming from early to late summer. The fruits are capsules to 2cm (1in) long.

Cultivation. Sun or part shade, and moist or wet soil. This plant has a subtle beauty and makes a delicate addition to the woodland glade or moist parts of the rock garden. Add it to the plantings around a bog or pond, where its fragrance can be enjoyed.

Stenanthium occidentale

Streptopus amplexifolius

Propagation. Collect seeds after the capsules have ripened in the fall, and plant them soon after harvest. Sow seeds into containers of potting soil or directly into the garden, and leave them outside to stratify over winter for germination in the spring. Plants will probably take three years to reach flowering size.

Native Habitat and Range. In wet meadows, cliffs, and moist thickets, at low to high elevations from British Columbia south to northern California, and from near the coast, east to Alberta, Idaho, and Montana.

Notes. This species is not often seen in gardens but is worthy of wider cultivation. *Stenanthium* is a genus of four or five species native to North America and eastern Asia.

Streptopus amplexifolius	Zones 3b to 9b	Liliaceae

clasping twisted-stalk

This deciduous, rhizomatous perennial produces branched, leafy stems to 1m (3ft) or more. The leaves are ovate, up to 12cm (5in) long and around 6cm (2.5in) wide. Flowers bloom on bent stalks that develop in the axils of the upper leaves. They are white with yellow-green tints and to 1.5cm (.5in) long, with the tepals strongly reflexed, blooming late spring to mid summer. Fruits are yellow, red, or sometimes purple berries with many seeds.

Cultivation. Shade to part sun or dappled light, and moist soil rich in organic matter. This tall, lush perennial is a good addition to the taller plants of the shade or woodland garden or a planting near a pond or stream.

Propagation. Collect seeds after the berries have ripened, and plant them into containers of potting soil or directly into the garden soon after harvest. Leave planted seeds outside to stratify over winter for spring germination. Plants will probably take a few years to reach flowering size. Another method is to divide rhizomes in mid spring or late summer, but this should be done only with plants already in cultivation and grown from seed.

Native Habitat and Range. Along streambanks and in moist thickets from lowlands to mid elevations, Alaska to California and east through much of Canada and the United States.

Notes. *Streptopus a.* var. *chalazatus* generally occurs east of the Cascades to Idaho and south to Colorado; these plants are glabrous (hairless). The hairier *S. a.* var. *amplexifolius* is found from the west slope of the Cascades to the coast and east through Canada, the Great Lakes, and the eastern United States. The seven species in the genus *Streptopus* are native to the temperate parts of North America, Europe, and Asia. *Streptopus lanceolatus* (rosy twisted-stalk) is another garden-worthy species; our native variety, *S. l.* var. *curvipes*, grows near streams at mid elevations in the mountains from Alaska through western Oregon. The stems of these plants are usually unbranched and shorter, to 30cm (1ft); the flowers are usually pink at the base and white at the tips, but sometimes yellowish with purple streaks. Another species native to the Pacific Northwest is *S. streptopoides* (small twisted-stalk); its stems reach about 20cm (8in) and are usually simple. The flowers are greenish with purple tints, and plants inhabit deep woods at mid elevations in the mountains from Alaska to northern Oregon, east to northern Idaho.

Synthyris	Scrophulariaceae

kittentails

All the approximately nine species of *Synthyris* are native to the mountains of western North America; a handful occur in the Pacific Northwest. Kittentails are small perennials, usually with blue flowers. The petals are fused at the base, and the corolla has four lobes, with one of the lobes larger than the others. The calyx is also four-lobed, and the small capsules are heart-shaped or rounded and flattened, with two chambers. The style and stigma extend from the notch between the lobes. The leaves of most species are rounded with toothed margins. *Besseya* is another small, North American genus of perennials related to *Synthyris*; the two are known to hybridize. *Besseya rubra* (red besseya) has a native range east of the Cascades and can be grown from seed. *Veronica* (speedwell, brooklime) has blue flowers similar to *Synthyris*; *V. americana* (American brooklime) occurs in wet or disturbed habitats in our area and elsewhere.

Propagation. Grow from seed collected from the capsules in summer or fall. Plant seeds soon after harvest, either in containers of potting soil or directly into the garden, and leave them outside over winter for germination in the spring. Plants may take a year or two to reach flowering size. Established garden plants may produce seedlings that can be transplanted. Kittentails should never be poached from the wild.

Synthyris missurica	Zones 4a to 9a

western mountain kittentails

This deciduous perennial produces a cluster of basal leaves and flowering stems from short rhizomes. The leaves have long petioles, and the blades are rounded to reniform (kidney-shaped) or cordate (heart-shaped), up to 8cm (3in) wide and about as long, with shallowly lobed or sharply toothed margins. The flowers bloom in a raceme up to 60cm (2ft) tall from mid spring to mid summer. The corollas are blue or purplish and not quite 1cm (.5in) long. Flattened seeds are produced in a rounded capsule with a shallow notch.

Cultivation. Full sun to part shade or dappled light, and rocky, well-drained, moist to rather dry soil. A charming species for the rock garden, stone wall, or rocky clearing in the woodland garden.

Native Habitat and Range. In moist, open or shaded, rocky slopes at low to mid elevations in the Columbia River Gorge, east to the mountains of southeastern Washington, northeastern Oregon and Idaho, south to central Oregon and northern California.

Notes. *Synthyris m.* ssp. *stellata* is endemic to the Columbia River Gorge; plants are relatively short with more sharply toothed leaves and larger bracts below the inflorescence. *Synthyris m.* ssp. *missurica* has leaves with rounded teeth and the largest range through the Pacific Northwest; *S. m.* ssp. *hirsuta* is restricted to Oregon.

Synthyris reniformis	Zones 6b to 9b

snow queen, spring queen

This species produces a rosette of basal leaves and flowering stems from short rhizomes. The leaves have long petioles, and the blades are up to 8cm (3in) in length and width. The blades are reniform (kidney-shaped) or cordate (heart-shaped), with palmately patterned veins and lobed, toothed margins. The flowers bloom in short racemes at the ends of leafless peduncles up to 15cm (6in) tall. The bell-shaped corollas are blue or purplish and not quite 1cm (.5in) long, blooming from early to late spring. A couple of seeds are produced in each half of the hairy capsules.

Cultivation. Part shade or dappled light, and well-drained, moist to rather dry soil with good organic content, especially in the form of conifer needles. This is a charming little perennial to plant near the path through the woodland or shade garden. It is one of the earliest to bloom, sometimes flowering when snow is still on the ground.

Synthyris missurica ssp. *stellata*

Synthyris reniformis

Native Habitat and Range. In fairly moist, open coniferous woods, glades, and forest edges at low elevations west of the Cascades from western Washington, south to central California, east through the Columbia River Gorge.

Notes. *Synthyris r.* var. *reniformis* inhabits the northern parts of the range; *S. r.* var. *cordata* occurs to the south. Fringepetal kittentails (*S. schizantha*) is another native, restricted to western Washington and northwestern Oregon; its petal lobes are distinctly laciniate (torn or fringed) at the tips. Cut-leaf synthyris (*S. pinnatifida*) includes three varieties of plants with pinnately compound, sometimes hairy leaves; they are native to open, rocky slopes at high altitudes in the Olympic Mountains and east in Idaho, Montana, Wyoming, and Utah. Northern kittentails (*S. borealis*) and Idaho kittentails (*S. platycarpa*) also occur in the west.

Tanacetum camphoratum	Zones 7b to 9b	Asteraceae

dune tansy

This aromatic perennial produces stout, leafy stems to 60cm (2ft) from creeping rhizomes. The leaves are two or three times pinnately divided into fine segments, giving them a ferny look. The largest leaves, up to 20cm (8in) long, are basal or on the lower part of the stem. Flowering stems produce flat-topped clusters of small heads to 1.5cm (.5in) across. The tiny ray and disk florets are both yellow, and the ray corollas are short but visible. The button-like flowering heads bloom from early summer to early fall. The fruits, small achenes, have a pappus (modified calyx) of tiny teeth.

Cultivation. Full sun or light shade, and well-drained, sandy, moist to rather dry soil. This is a lovely, fragrant plant for dunes and sandy soils near the coast, where it often grows with other perennial dune species. It would make an interesting addition to the butterfly garden or wildflower meadow in sandy or gravelly soils away from the immediate coast.

Propagation. Grow from seed collected in the fall and planted in the fall or spring. Plants can also be propagated by dividing the rhizomatous clumps in early to mid spring, or from stem cuttings made during the summer.

Native Habitat and Range. In sand dunes along the coast from southern British Columbia, south to the central coast of California.

Notes. Sometimes classified as *T. douglasii* (*T. camphoratum* is then considered endemic to the San Francisco Bay region, while *T. douglasii* occurs from the coast of extreme northern California, to the north) or *T. bipinnatum* ssp. *huronense* (but Lake Huron tansy is considered to be a more northern and eastern taxon, from Alaska and south to the Great Lakes). *Tanacetum* includes around 50 species of the Northern Hemisphere.

Tellima grandiflora	Zones 5b to 9b	Saxifragaceae

fringecup

This perennial herb grows from short rhizomes. The numerous basal leaves are heart-shaped (cordate) or kidney-shaped (reniform), with toothed margins and a covering of rough hairs. The leaf blades grow to 8cm (3in) in length and width with long petioles. Flowering stems bear smaller leaves and grow to 80cm (2.5ft) tall. Ten to 35 fragrant flowers bloom on each raceme. The flowers have a cup-like calyx. The five, reflexed petals have fringed margins. Flowers open white and become deep pink with age, blooming from mid spring to mid summer. Fruits are small capsules containing many tiny, brown seeds. The basal clumps of leaves remain evergreen during mild winters, often turning reddish in the cold.

Cultivation. Full shade to part sun, and moist soil. Tolerates the dry summer shade under big conifers. This is one of the easiest plants to include among shrubs and other perennials in the shade or woodland garden, or near the edge of the wildflower meadow. Some gardeners west of the Cascades consider it a

Tanacetum camphoratum

Tellima grandiflora

little too easy—once you have it, you will probably have more of it because it spreads enthusiastically from seed. In some ways this is advantageous because fringecup can compete with weeds. If you notice plants suddenly wilting, root weevil damage is a possible cause. Cleaning the curled larvae from the remaining roots and replanting the rosette will often save the plant. Parasitic nematodes are sometimes added to the soil to help control root weevil larvae.

Propagation. Easy from seed collected in late summer and planted at any time. Existing plants will produce seedlings, which can be transplanted. Larger clumps can be divided in early spring.

Native Habitat and Range. In woods, along streams and other moist places, at low to mid elevations from southern Alaska, south near the coast to central California and east to the west slope of the Cascades, the Columbia River Gorge, southeastern British Columbia, northeastern Washington, and northern Idaho.

Notes. This is the only species in the genus *Tellima*, although at various times it has been grouped with other genera of the Saxifragaceae (or other saxifrages have been included with fringecup).

| *Thalictrum occidentale* | Zones 4a to 9b | Ranunculaceae |

western meadowrue

This rhizomatous perennial produces leafy stems up to 1m (3ft) tall. The finely divided leaves are three to four times ternate (divided into threes). The ultimate leaflets are up to 2.5cm (1in) long, varying from lobed and rounded to wedge-shaped (cuneate). The plants are dioecious, either male or female. The flowers have purplish sepals but lack petals and bloom on slender pedicels in open panicles. The male flowers consist of hanging clusters of long, purplish stamens that look like tiny wind chimes. The female flowers are clusters of pinkish ovaries with purplish stigmas, developing into a spreading group of veined, beaked, one-seeded achenes. Flowers bloom from late spring to mid summer.

Cultivation. Full to part shade or dappled light, and moist soil high in organic matter. This is a lovely perennial for the woodland or shade garden on either side of the Cascades. Plant it near the pond or stream, or with taller perennials in the wildflower meadow. Although not especially showy, western meadowrue has wonderful little flowers and airy, fern-like foliage; where both male and female plants are present, it often produces seedlings without assistance.

Propagation. Easy from seed collected in the late summer and planted in the fall. Sow seeds directly into the garden or into flats of potting soil. Leave them outside to stratify over winter for germination in the spring. Plants can also be propagated from divisions of the rhizomes made in the late summer or early spring.

Native Habitat and Range. In moist meadows, thickets near streams, and open woods at low to fairly high elevations from southern Alaska, south on both sides of the Cascades to northern California and east to Alberta, Montana, Wyoming, and Nevada.

Notes. The approximately 100 species of *Thalictrum* are distributed through the temperate mountains and forests of the Northern Hemisphere; around 20 species are native to North America, about six to the Pacific Northwest. Few-flowered meadowrue (*T. sparsiflorum*), Fendler's meadowrue (*T. fendleri*), and purple meadowrue (*T. dasycarpum*) are all tall plants, growing to 1m (3ft). All live in meadows and moist woods through much of North America. Veiny meadowrue (*T. venulosum*) grows to about 60cm (2ft) and ranges through eastern British Columbia and south along the east slope of the Cascades, to the east. Alpine meadowrue (*T. alpinum*) is a small plant to 15cm (6in) tall; it has a wide distribution in the north and is scattered south to northeastern Oregon and through the high mountains of the west.

Thalictrum occidentale, male flowers

Thalictrum occidentale, fruits

Thermopsis montana

| *Thermopsis montana* | Zones 3b to 9a | Fabaceae |

false lupine, mountain golden-pea or goldenbanner

This upright perennial produces leafy shoots to 1m (3ft). Each leaf is compound and trifoliate. The three leaflets are broadly elliptic and can grow to 10cm (4in) long. Each petiole has a pair of large, leafy stipules at its base. Up to 60 bright yellow pea flowers, each about 2.5cm (1in) long, bloom from late spring to late summer in racemes to 30cm (1ft) long. The fruits, slender legumes to 8cm (3in) long, contain up to about five seeds.

Cultivation. Full sun to part shade, and moist or rather wet, well-drained or sandy soil. This is an excellent, long-blooming pea for the perennial bed, wildflower meadow, pond margin, or wildlife garden. Plant it at the woodland edge or on the rocky slope or ditch bank. It is reputedly unattractive to deer and other browsing animals.

Propagation. Usually grown from seed harvested in late summer and planted in the fall. Sow the seeds into containers or directly into the garden, and leave them outside over winter for germination when the weather warms the following spring.

Native Habitat and Range. In moist meadows, roadside ditches, and well-drained sandy or rocky soil at low to fairly high elevations, from southern British Columbia, south to eastern Oregon, mainly east of the Cascades, but also in the Olympic Mountains and parts of southwestern Washington, east to Montana, Colorado, and New Mexico.

Notes. *Thermopsis m.* var. *montana* occurs throughout the range; *T. m.* var. *hitchcockii* is endemic to the Olympic Mountains. *Thermopsis* includes around 20 species, ten of them in North America, the others in northeastern Asia; *T. gracilis* (slender goldenbanner) is the only other in our area.

| *Tiarella trifoliata var. trifoliata* | Zones 5a to 9b | Saxifragaceae |

trefoil foamflower, three-leaflet coolwort

This perennial grows to 60cm (2ft) from short, slender rhizomes. The largest leaves are basal, 4cm (1.5in) long by 6cm (2.5in) wide on 8cm (3in) petioles. Each leaf is somewhat hairy and divided into three leaflets with toothed margins. The leaves are smaller in size on the flowering stems. Tiny, delicate white flowers bloom in panicles up to 35cm (14in) tall from late spring through most of summer and often into autumn. Each small capsule produces a few seeds.

Cultivation. Full to part shade, and moist soil with good organic content. This is a lovely little species for the woodland garden, with a longer bloom period than most native perennials. Plant it near the path in the shade garden, near a pond, or in a perennial bed. Plants are susceptible to attacks from the larvae of root weevils.

Propagation. Grow from seed collected from ripe capsules in summer or fall. Plant seeds outside into flats of potting soil or directly into the garden during the fall or early the following spring. Divisions of the rhizomes can be made in spring or fall.

Native Habitat and Range. Along streambanks, in shady coniferous woods and other moist places, from Alaska to northern Oregon, and from the coast up to mid elevations on the west slope of the Cascades, east in British Columbia to the Rocky Mountains and south to western Idaho.

Notes. *Tiarella t.* var. *unifoliata* (coolwort foamflower, sugar scoop) has leaves that are palmate, not divided; it occurs at mid to higher elevations, from Alaska to California, in the Olympics and Cascades, and east through British Columbia to southwest Alberta, Montana, and northeastern Oregon. *Tiarella t.* var. *laciniata* (cutleaf foamflower) has three leaflets that are divided again into narrow segments; it has a smaller range, from Vancouver Island and the southern mainland of

Tiarella trifoliata var. trifoliata

British Columbia, south through the Gulf and San Juan Islands through the Puget Sound region of Washington and in west central Oregon. All three varieties are sometimes granted specific status. *Tiarella* includes only one other species in eastern North America and another native to Asia. Other small, delicate natives related to *Tiarella* belong to *Suksdorfia* (*S. violacea* and *S. ranunculifolia* are the only species) and *Sullivantia. Sullivantia oregana* (Oregon coolwort) is listed as rare. These plants live in moist, partly shaded sites and can be grown from seed planted outside in fall.

Tolmiea menziesii	Zones 5b to 9b	Saxifragaceae

piggy-back plant, youth-on-age

This perennial spreads to about 80cm (2.5ft) from creeping rhizomes. The basal leaves are hairy, and the lobed, toothed, heart-shaped blades grow to 10cm (4in) wide and almost as long. The flowering stems grow to 30cm (1ft) and bear smaller leaves. The inflorescence is a several-flowered raceme. The small, purplish or maroon flowers bloom from late spring to late summer; they are interesting but not showy and are followed by small capsules.

Cultivation. Full shade to part sun, in moist soil with good organic content. Often remains green where winters are not too fierce. This species is usually grown as a lush groundcover. Plant it around the taller shade-loving perennials and shrubs in the woodland garden, near a pond or bog, or along a path. It can also be grown in a hanging basket or other container on the patio or in the house; when grown as a houseplant, it can be attacked by mealybugs or spider mites.

Propagation. One of the easiest of all our natives. Watch for the appearance of small plantlets at the bases of older leaf blades. Detach the old leaf with young plant and push it into the

Tolmiea menziesii

Townsendia florifer (photo by Sally A. Simmons)

soil surface in the garden or container so that the underside of the "mother" leaf touches the planting medium. This can be done from early summer to early fall, and new plants will quickly form roots in potting soil or in a shady garden bed. It can also be grown from seed collected and planted outside in the fall.

Native Habitat and Range. Near streams and other moist, shady places, along the coast from southern Alaska south to central California, east at low to mid elevations to the west slope of the Cascades.

Notes. This is the only species in the genus. Forms with yellowish leaf mottling are sometimes available.

Townsendia florifer	Zones 4a to 9b	Asteraceae

showy Townsend daisy

This is a small perennial (sometimes biennial or annual), with branched stems only to 15cm (6in) tall. Plants are usually strigose (having long hairs). The basal leaves are the largest, up to 6cm (2.5in) long, spatulate (spoon-shaped) and with entire margins. The flowering heads are relatively large, with a receptacle or disk (holding the disk florets) up to 2cm (1in) across. The ray florets have pale pink corollas, each about 1cm (.5in) long. Flowers bloom from late spring to mid summer. The fruits are hairy achenes, and the pappus (modified calyx) consists of bristles or scales.

Cultivation. Full sun to light shade, and well-drained, rather dry soil. A charming, low-growing daisy for rock or trough gardens on either side of the Cascades. East of the mountains, plant it in front of sagebrush or with other drought-tolerant species in the wildlife or butterfly garden. Although short-lived, plants often self-sow.

Triantha glutinosa

Triantha glutinosa, fruits

Propagation. Collect seeds in the late summer or fall and sow outside in the fall, either directly into the garden or into deep containers, such as tubes. Allow the seeds to cold stratify outside over winter for germination the following spring.

Native Habitat and Range. In open, dry places, often with sagebrush, at low to mid elevations east of the Cascades from central Washington south through eastern Oregon to Nevada and east to Wyoming and Utah.

Notes. *Townsendia* includes around two dozen species, all native to western North America. Wyoming Townsend daisy (*T. alpigena*) and Parry's Townsend daisy (*T. parryi*), both low-growing plants with bluish rays, live in open or rocky places as far west as northeastern Oregon. Hooker's Townsend daisy (*T. hookeri*) ranges to southeastern British Columbia, and tufted Townsend daisy (*T. scapigera*) occurs in southeastern Oregon.

Triantha glutinosa	Zones 3b to 9b	Liliaceae

sticky false asphodel, sticky tofieldia

This deciduous perennial develops stems to 50cm (20in) from upright rhizomes. The linear leaves are mostly basal and up to 30cm (1ft) long. The small, greenish white flowers have six tepals (the petals and sepals are similar) and bloom in compact racemes at the tops of the stems, which are densely covered with glandular hairs. Flowers bloom from early to late summer and are followed by attractive red capsules.

Cultivation. Full sun to part shade, and wet to moist soil. An interesting plant for the edge of an open wetland, bog, pond, or stream.

Propagation. Collect seeds after the capsules have ripened, and plant them soon after harvest into containers of potting soil or directly into the garden. Leave planted seeds outside to stratify under cold, moist winter conditions for spring germination. Plants may take a few years to reach flowering size. Another method is to divide the rhizomes in early spring or late summer, but this should be attempted only with plants originally grown from seed.

Native Habitat and Range. In bogs, streambanks, and wet meadows at low to high elevations, from Alaska south through British Columbia, also in southwestern Oregon and scattered east across the continent.

Notes. Sometimes classified as *Tofieldia glutinosa*. The four species of *Triantha* are native to North America and Japan; another that occurs in our area is *T. occidentalis* (western false asphodel). *Triantha o.* ssp. *brevistyla* is found in the mountains from southern Alaska through Washington and Oregon, east to southeastern British Columbia and Idaho; *T. o.* ssp. *occidentalis* occurs from southwestern Oregon to northern California.

Trientalis   Primulaceae

starflower

All the handful of *Trientalis* species are native to the Northern Hemisphere, with two species in North America and one in northern Eurasia. These delicate plants produce a flowering stem with a whorl of simple leaves from a small, perennial tuber.

Propagation. Grow from seed. Collect seeds in late summer or fall, and plant them shortly after harvest into containers of potting soil or directly into the garden. Allow planted seeds to spend the winter outside for germination in the spring. Transplanting individual stems with their tubers or thickened rhizomes attached is another way to propagate plants, but this should be done only with plants salvaged from destroyed habitat or from cultivated populations.

Trientalis borealis ssp. latifolia   Zones 3b to 9b

Pacific, western, or broad-leaved starflower

This charming little perennial grows from small, upright tubers, about 1.5cm (.5in) long, and also spreads by slender rhizomes. Each plant produces a single stem up to 25cm (10in) tall with a whorl of four to eight leaves at the tip. The leaves are broadly elliptic and up to 10cm (4in) long. The flowers appear singly from the axils of the terminal whorl of leaves. They usually have six or seven petals and are about 1cm (.5in) wide, varying from pale to deeper pink. Flowers bloom from mid spring to mid summer, and each produces a rounded, many-seeded capsule.

Cultivation. Part shade or dappled light, and moist to rather dry soil. Tolerates the dry, shady conditions under large conifers, often carpeting the forest floor. Plant it along paths or among larger species in the woodland or shade garden. Tends to self-sow and form drifts under favorable conditions, but it's really too delicate to be considered weedy.

Native Habitat and Range. In open woods, thickets, and prairies at low to mid elevations from southern British Columbia, east to Alberta and northern Idaho, and south, mainly along the coast and the west slope of the Cascades, to central California.

Notes. Sometimes classified as *T. latifolia* or *T. europaea* ssp. *latifolia*.

Trientalis europaea ssp. arctica   Zones 3b to 9b

arctic starflower

This starflower produces leafy stems up to 20cm (8in) tall from slightly thickened rhizomes. The largest leaves are elliptic, rounded at the tip, and up to 7cm (3in) long. These develop at the tips of the stems, but smaller leaves are also present lower on the stem. Single flowers with up to seven

Trientalis borealis ssp. *latifolia*

Trientalis borealis ssp. *latifolia*

Trientalis europaea ssp. *arctica*

petals are set on slender peduncles at the top of the stem. The flowers are usually white, about 1.5cm (.5in) across, and bloom from late spring to late summer. The fruits are small capsules containing many seeds.

Cultivation. Part shade or dappled light, and moist to wet soil. This delicate long-blooming little perennial is an excellent addition to the bog, shady pond margin, or wet place in the woodland or shade garden.

Native Habitat and Range. In bogs, seeps, and wet meadows and thickets at low to fairly high elevations from Alaska south through the Cascades and along the coast through Oregon to the northwestern tip of California, east across British Columbia to Alberta and Idaho.

Notes. Sometimes granted specific status, as *T. arctica*.

Trifolium   Fabaceae

clover

Clovers are familiar plants, known for their palmately compound leaves, usually with three leaflets (trifoliate or ternate) and tiny pea flowers crowded into heads. The fruits are very small pea pods or legumes that do not split open at maturity and sometimes contain only a single seed. Clovers, like other legumes, are able to fix atmospheric nitrogen with the help of bacteria living in nodules formed on the roots. Most of the approximately 300 species of *Trifolium* are native to the temperate parts of the Northern Hemisphere; more than 30 are native to the Pacific Northwest.

Propagation. Grow from seed collected in late summer or fall and planted soon after harvest. The seeds can be left inside the indehiscent pods or legumes and sown directly into the garden or into containers of potting soil. Leave planted seeds outside to cold stratify over winter for germination the following spring. Clovers can also be propagated from divisions of the rhizomes made in the spring, but this should be done only with cultivated plants originally grown from seed.

Trifolium macrocephalum   Zones 5a to 7b

big-head clover

This perennial clover develops rhizomes from thick roots. The stems are upright and up to 30cm (1ft) tall, sparsely to densely hairy (pubescent). The palmately compound leaves have up to nine leathery leaflets up to 2.5cm (1in) long. Each leaf has a pair of leaf-like stipules with shredded margins at the base of the petiole. The flowering heads lack a subtending bract, or involucre, and can grow to 5cm (2in) or more with up to 100 small pea flowers. Each flower has a rosy pink or pink and white corolla, about 2.5cm (1in) long, and a calyx with long teeth. Flowers bloom from mid spring to early summer, and each small legume usually contains only a single seed.

Cultivation. Full sun or light shade, and well-drained, rocky, rather dry soil. This is one of our most beautiful native clovers and should do well in the dry wildflower meadow, sagebrush garden, or stand of ponderosa pine east of the Cascades. It may be possible to grow it in the well-drained rock garden or trough west of the Cascades.

Native Habitat and Range. In rocky, dry soils, often with sagebrush or in ponderosa pine woods at mid to fairly high elevations east of the Cascades, from central Washington, south through eastern Oregon to northeastern California, east to Idaho and Nevada.

Notes. The rare, magenta-flowered *T. thompsonii* (Thompson's clover) is the only other native clover that typically has more than three leaflets per leaf; it is limited to a few populations growing on rather dry hillsides in north central Washington.

Trifolium macrocephalum

Trifolium wormskioldii

Trifolium wormskioldii	Zones 4a to 9b

springbank or cow clover

This hairless (glabrous), often rhizomatous, taprooted perennial develops somewhat reclining (decumbent) stems to 60cm (2ft) or more. The leaves are trifoliate, each with three elliptic leaflets about 2.5cm (1in) long, and with a pair of leafy stipules up to 4cm (1.5in) long at the base of each petiole. The flowering heads are about 2.5cm (1in) across, and each is subtended by an involucre of sharply toothed bracts. Each head holds up to 60 small flowers, each about 1.5cm (.5in) long, red to purple in color, often with white tips. Flowers bloom from late spring to early fall, and the small legumes often contain more than one seed.

Cultivation. Full sun to part shade, and moist to wet soil. This lovely long-flowering clover makes a fine addition to the edge of the pond or stream. Plant it in the moist or wet places in the wildflower meadow or with other low-growing perennials.

Native Habitat and Range. Near streams, in meadows and coastal dunes at low to mid elevations from Alaska and western British Columbia, south to California and Mexico, and from the coast, east to Wyoming, Colorado, and Texas.

Notes. The fleshy rhizomes were harvested, cooked, and eaten by several coastal tribes. Other attractive, pink-flowered native clovers worthy of a moist place in the wild garden are the widespread *T. variegatum* (whitetip clover) and *T. willdenowii* (tomcat clover), a species most common west of the Cascades.

Trillium	Liliaceae

wakerobin

There are close to 60 species of *Trillium*, the majority of them native to the eastern United States; six species occur in eastern Asia and another half dozen in the Pacific Northwest. Trilliums are distinctive deciduous perennials that grow annual shoots from a short, thick rhizome. Each shoot is topped with a whorl of three leaves and a single flower. In some species, the flower is set flush into the union of the leaves (the sessile trilliums), while in others, the flower is above the leaves, blooming from a peduncle (the pedicellate trilliums). Each flower has three petals and three greenish sepals. Six stamens surround the ovary, style, and three-lobed stigma. The fruit is an angled or rounded, fleshy capsule or berry-like fruit that may split open or simply begin to disintegrate at maturity. The seeds have an eliasome, an oil-rich appendage that attracts ants; the ants eat the eliasome and disperse the seeds. Trilliums should never be picked for cut flowers because this removes the only three leaves—there are no others to conduct photosynthesis for the rest of the growing season. The plants may not die but will likely fail to flower the following year, so enjoy them in the garden or forest.

Propagation. Collect seeds when the ripe fruits begin to open or fall apart in the summer, and plant them into deep containers of potting soil soon after harvest. Leave planted seeds outside in moist soil through the fall and winter for germination the following spring. Seedlings produce a single leaf their first year or so, then three small leaves, and finally three leaves with a lovely flower in the center. They may need protection from slugs. Plants can be salvaged from construction sites during the growing season without harm, but must be dug deeply, to .5m (1.5ft) or so, to capture the rhizomes, roots, and underground stems without breaking them. Some trillium enthusiasts suggest methods for dividing the rhizomes, but this should be tried only with plants grown in cultivation from seed.

Trillium albidum	Zones 5b to 9b

giant white trillium

This lovely perennial produces one to several stems, up to almost 60cm (2ft) tall, from the tip of a short, thick rhizome. The broadly oval leaves grow to 20cm (8in) long and 15cm (6in) across. The leaves are usually mottled with darker green spots, but these may fade as the leaves age. The fragrant, sessile flowers bloom from early to mid spring. The green, lance-shaped sepals can grow to about 6cm (2.5in) long. The petals in large plants are obovate (oval, but widest toward the tip) or sometimes lanceolate, up to 7cm (3in) long and 3cm (1.5in) across; they are usually erect and white or creamy, sometimes pinkish near the petal bases. The fleshy, berry-like fruits are rounded and green or purplish green.

Cultivation. Part shade or dappled light, and moist soil high in organic matter. Though native to warmer climates west of the Cascades, this species can tolerate both cold winters and summer drought. Lovely among other shade-loving plants, in small openings, or near a shady pond or stream. Under favorable conditions, individual plants will become large and often multi-stemmed. Seeds from existing plants may germinate and grow on their own, eventually forming a population. Beware of slugs.

Native Habitat and Range. On moist, forested slopes, streambanks, and thickets in rich, deep soil, at low to mid elevations west of the Cascades from west central Oregon, south through northwestern California.

Notes. In northern Oregon, this species appears to grade into the smaller *T. parviflorum*, and at the southern end of its range, it overlaps with *T. chloropetalum*, an exclusively Californian taxon. In some cases, overlapping species appear to hybridize, adding to the confusion. Case and Case (1997) consider *T. albidum* a well-defined species, at least in the central part of its range.

Trillium albidum

Trillium kurabayashii	Zones 6a to 9b

giant purple trillium or wakerobin

This trillium produces one or two shoots up to 50cm (20in) from a short, thick rhizome. The ovate leaves can grow to 20cm (8in) long by about 15cm (6in) across. They are usually mottled with darker and lighter patches of green. Each stem bears a single, sessile flower. The lanceolate sepals are up to 7cm (3in) long, green, but streaked with purple, especially at the base. The deep, reddish purple petals are usually oblanceolate (lance-shaped, widest at the upper end), up to 10cm (4in) long and 3cm (1.5in) wide. The stamens have purple filaments. Flowers bloom from early to late spring, and the berry like fruit is oval and dark purple.

Cultivation. Part shade or dappled light, and moist soil rich in compost. Tolerates summer drought and, though native to a fairly warm corner of the Pacific coast, this dramatic, purple-flowered species can also tolerate colder winters, though it may be damaged by late frosts. A wonderful specimen for the woodland or shade garden. Plant it near openings in the forest canopy, or near a shady pond or stream. Seeds from existing plants may germinate on their own and eventually form a population. Guard plants from slugs.

Native Habitat and Range. In moist, deep soils near streams and in forests at low elevations near the coast from the tip of southwestern Oregon to the northwestern corner of California.

Notes. Sometimes classified as *T. sessile* var. *californicum*. English and Scottish gardeners have long cultivated this stunning species. *Trillium k*. f. *luteum* has pale, yellow-green flowers. *Trillium petiolatum* (round-leaved trillium) is another sessile species; the three green leaves have long petioles, and the maroon (sometimes green or yellowish) flower, nestled among the petiole bases, barely emerges above the surface of the ground. *Trillium petiolatum* inhabits streambanks and moist woods at fairly low to mid elevations east of the Cascades from central Washington, east to Idaho, and south to the Blue Mountains of Washington and Oregon and north central Oregon.

Trillium kurabayashii

Trillium ovatum

Trillium ovatum   Zones 4a to 9b

Pacific or western trillium or wakerobin

This pedicellate trillium produces shoots to 60cm (2ft) or a bit more from a short, thick rhizome. Older plants or certain individuals can produce multiple shoots. Each stem typically has large, broadly ovate leaves up to 15cm (6in) long and almost as wide. They are usually medium green, rarely mottled. A single flower blooms from early to late spring on a peduncle to 6cm (2.5in) long. The green sepals are lanceolate and up to 5cm (2in) long. The lance-shaped to obovate (oval, but widest toward the tip) petals grow to 6cm (2.5in) long and 4cm (1.5in) wide. They are usually white when they open and fade to deep pink or burgundy as they age. The fruit is a fleshy, angular, yellowish capsule, often splitting when ripe to release the seeds.

Cultivation. Part sun to full shade or dappled light, and moist soil with plenty of organic matter. This is one of our most familiar and best-loved spring wildflowers, a wonderful plant for the woodland or shade garden or near a shady pond or stream. It will tolerate the dry summers of the Pacific Northwest, often by becoming dormant as soon as the surroundings dry out. Often self-sows under favorable conditions, eventually forming gorgeous drifts. Protect plants, especially young ones, from slugs.

Native Habitat and Range. Near streams, in thickets and forests, often where fairly wet in early spring, at low to mid elevations in the mountains, from southern British Columbia south to central California, and from near the coast, east to southwestern Alberta, Idaho, western Montana, Wyoming, and Colorado.

Notes. *Trillium ovatum* f. *hibbersonii* is a dwarf form with pale pink flowers from Vancouver Island; it is sometimes granted specific status, as *T. hibbersonii*.

Trillium parviflorum

Trillium parviflorum	Zones 7b to 9b

small-flowered trillium

This trillium produces shoots to 30cm (1ft) tall from a short, thick rhizome. Some older plants can produce multiple shoots. Each stem generally has large, broadly ovate leaves to 15cm (6 in) long and 8cm (3in) across, mottled with darker blotches. The fragrant sessile flower blooms from early to late spring. The green sepals are narrow and about 2.5cm (1in) long. The narrow petals are up to 5cm (2in) long, creamy white and occasionally purplish at the base. The fleshy, berry-like fruit is rounded and maroon on maturity.

Cultivation. Full shade to part sun or dappled light, and moist soil with plenty of organic matter. Tolerates dry, open sites, but does best in the shade of the woodland garden or near a pond or stream. This isn't the showiest wakerobin, but it is a lovely, relatively unusual plant. If conditions are right, seeds from existing plants may germinate and grow on their own. Beware of slugs.

Native Habitat and Range. In moist woods and thickets, usually at low elevations west of the Cascades, from the south Puget Sound area of western Washington, south to adjacent northwestern Oregon, where it intergrades with *T. albidum*.

Notes. Sometimes confused with *T. chloropetalum* (a taxon native to California), or included with the similar (but more southern) *T. albidum*; it has also been classified as *T. sessile* var. *californicum* or *T. s.* var. *chloropetalum* (but *T. sessile* is an eastern North America native). *Trillium parviflorum* is an endemic species with a very restricted range; it is listed as sensitive in Washington and should never be disturbed in the wild.

Trillium rivale

Trillium rivale	Zones 6b to 9b

brook trillium

This charming pedicellate trillium produces flowering shoots to 15cm (6in) tall from a short, thick rhizome. The ovate leaves grow to about 7cm (3in) long by 6cm (2.5in) wide on distinct petioles to 3cm (1.5in) long. The bluish green leaves are thick and often have silvery patterning along the veins. The flowers bloom on peduncles up to 11cm (4.5in) long. The oblong sepals are green and about 2cm (1in) long. The white petals are usually spotted with purple, ovate in shape, narrowed at the base and tapered at the tip; they grow to 3cm (1.5in) long and almost as wide. Flowers bloom from early to late spring, depending on elevation. The greenish white, berry-like fruit is three-angled, falling from the plant at maturity.

Cultivation. Dappled light or part sun to full shade, and well-drained, moist or rather dry soil, perhaps with some additional conifer needles or bark. This is a delicate plant for the margin of the woodland garden, shadier parts of the rock garden, or stony banks of a stream or pond. Under natural conditions of seasonal drought, the plants wither and become dormant by mid summer.

Native Habitat and Range. In a variety of habitats including rocky hillsides, forest margins, road cuts, shrubby thickets, seep margins, and streambanks at low to mid elevations from southwestern Oregon to northwestern California.

Notes. This narrowly endemic species is available from seed-grown plants. It should be protected throughout its small native range and never disturbed in the wild.

Triteleia	Liliaceae

Triteleia includes about 15 species, all native to western North America, especially California; seven species range into the Pacific Northwest. Each flower has six functional stamens and six tepals or perianth segments (petals and sepals similar to each other and usually petaloid) that are fused together at the base. Plants are occasionally placed in *Brodiaea*; both are genera of graceful, corm-bearing perennials with grass-like leaves and umbels of tubular or trumpet-shaped flowers, but the details of flowers and fruits differ between the two.

Propagation. Collect seeds in the summer or fall, after the papery capsules ripen, and plant them in early fall, sowing them into flats or deeper containers of potting soil, or directly into the garden. Leave the planted seeds outside over winter for germination the following spring, and protect seedlings from slugs. Two or three years of patience will be needed before the corms become big enough to produce flowers. Mature corms can be transplanted to a depth of 7 to 10cm (3 to 4in) in autumn. Small corms sometimes form around the bases of older corms, and these can be detached and transplanted. These small corms should be taken only from cultivated plants originally grown from seed; they will still take a couple of years to reach flowering size.

Triteleia bridgesii	Zones 6b to 9b

Bridges' triteleia or brodiaea

This corm-bearing perennial produces a few linear leaves, to 50cm (20in) long, which are usually still green at flowering time. The leafless flowering stem (scape) grows to 60cm (2ft) tall, producing an umbel of up to 15 flowers. The pedicels of the umbel are up to 6cm (2.5in) long, and the flowers are up to 4cm (1.5in) long, purplish blue to pale lilac, with blue anthers. The tepals are free at their tips and fused at their bases to form a narrow funnel. Flowers bloom from mid spring to early summer, and the fruits are capsules set on top of a small stalk (stipe).

Cultivation. Full sun or light shade, and well-drained, rather dry soil. This is a good bulb for the rock garden or dry parts of the wildflower meadow. Plant it among open shrub borders or along a bank or dry parking area.

Native Habitat and Range. In thickets, forest edges, dry bluffs, and river banks at low to mid elevations from southwestern Oregon, south to central California.

Notes. *Triteleia laxa* (*Brodiaea laxa*; Ithuriel's spear, grass nut) is similar, with funnel-shaped, usually blue purple flowers; it grows in meadows, often in clay soils, at low to mid elevations from the southwestern corner of Oregon, south to southern California.

Triteleia grandiflora	Zones 5b to 9b

large-flowered triteleia

This delicate lily produces one or two basal leaves, still green at flowering time and up to 50cm (20in) long, from the perennial corms. The flowering stems can reach 60cm (2ft), producing a relatively compact umbel with pedicels and flowers both about 2cm (1in) long. The flowers vary in color from deep blue to almost white with a darker vein running along the middle of each tepal. The tepals are free at the tips and fused into a somewhat inflated tube at the base. Flowers bloom from mid spring through early summer; the fruit is a three-sided capsule.

Cultivation. Full sun or light shade, and well-drained, moist to rather dry soil. This is a good species for gardens on either side of the Cascades, but try to find plants propagated from a local seed source. A lovely addition to the woodland margin or oak grove; among the sagebrush in the wildlife garden; in the rock garden on a slope; or in a dry meadow or perennial bed.

Triteleia bridgesii

Triteleia grandiflora

Triteleia hendersonii

Triteleia hyacinthina

Native Habitat and Range. From coastal prairies and meadows to woodlands and arid sagebrush habitats, on both sides of the Cascades from southern British Columbia to Oregon and northern California, east to Idaho, Montana, Wyoming, and Utah.

Notes. *Triteleia g.* var. *grandiflora* (*Brodiaea douglasii*) ranges from eastern British Columbia, Washington, and Oregon, east to the Rocky Mountains; *T. g.* var. *howellii* (*B. howellii, B. d.* var. *howellii*; Howell's triteleia) usually has larger, paler, flowers and a more western distribution from British Columbia through Oregon to California.

Triteleia hendersonii	Zones 5a to 9b

Henderson's triteleia

This corm-forming perennial produces linear leaves up to 40cm (16in) long that are usually still green at flowering time. The leafless flowering stems (scapes) are almost as long as the leaves. Each umbel has four to 15 flowers on slender pedicels about 2.5cm (1in) long. The anthers are blue, and the tepals are fused at their bases to form a funnel-shaped tube. The flowers are about 2cm (1in) long and pale yellow with a purple stripe running down the middle of each tepal. They bloom from late spring to mid summer and then begin to go dormant. The capsules are set on small stalks (stipes).

Cultivation. Full sun or light shade, and well-drained soil. With its unusual flowers, this species makes a lovely addition to the rock garden, sunny slope, or perennial bed. Site in the well-drained part of the wildflower meadow, oak grove, or other semi-dry site. Self-sows under favorable conditions.

Native Habitat and Range. On prairies, dry hills, thickets, and oak or pine woodlands at low to mid elevations from west central Oregon, south to the northern tip of California.

Notes. *Triteleia h.* var. *hendersonii* (*Brodiaea hendersonii*) occurs throughout the range. *Triteleia h.* var. *leachiae* (*Brodiaea leachiae*; Leach's triteleia), which occurs only in the southwestern corner of Oregon, includes smaller plants with white flowers, sometimes tinted blue, and with a purplish blue median stripe running down each tepal.

Triteleia hyacinthina	Zones 5a to 9b

hyacinth triteleia or brodiaea, fool's onion

This corm-bearing perennial produces one or two leaves, up to 40cm (16in) long, which are usually still green when the flowers bloom. The leafless flowering stems (scapes) grow to 60cm (2ft) long, producing an umbel with up to 50 flowers. The tepals are white or pale blue, each with a bluish green midvein and fused into a short tube at the base. The flowers are bell-shaped and up to 1.5cm (.5in) long, blooming from late spring to late summer, depending on elevation. Seeds ripen in small, stalked capsules.

Cultivation. Full sun, and soil that is moist in spring but dry later in the season. This is a beautiful plant to add to the rock garden, stony bank, or wildflower meadow, along with other bulbs and perennials, on either side of the Cascades. It often propagates itself in the garden from seed.

Native Habitat and Range. In open, moist meadows with clay soil and open, rocky flats, sometimes near sagebrush, at low to mid elevations from southwestern British Columbia, south on both sides of the Cascades, through much of California and east to western Nevada and Idaho.

Notes. Sometimes classified as *Brodiaea hyacinthina*. Other *Triteleia* taxa are represented in the Pacific Northwest, ranging north from California into southwestern Oregon. *Triteleia ixioides* (*B. lutea, B. scabra*; pretty face), in its sspp. *scabra* and *anilina*, offers pale to darker yellow tepals and darker midveins, the stamen filaments are forked with two lobes. *Triteleia crocea* var. *crocea* (*B. crocea*; yellow triteleia) has bright yellow flowers, and the stamen filaments are not forked.

| *Typha latifolia* | Zones 3b to 9b | Typhaceae |

cattail, reedmace

This big, aggressive perennial produces annual flowering stems up to 3m (10ft) tall from thick rhizomes. The long, narrow leaves are up to 2cm (1in) wide, their bases sheathing the stems. The tall flowering stem produces a densely flowered spike of tiny flowers. The upper flowers are male (staminate), and the lower flowers are female (pistillate). No gap separates the cylinders of male and female flowers, which bloom from early to mid summer. The male flowers fall away after blooming, leaving the dark brown spike of female flowers, to 20cm (8in) long, to ripen into tiny nutlets. Each nutlet has a tuft of long hairs at its base which helps to disperse it by wind or water.

Cultivation. Full sun or part shade, and very wet mud or shallow water up to 60cm (2ft) deep. This is an emergent (roots in the water, shoots in the air) wetlands plant, excellent for wildlife habitat, erosion control, and improved water quality. Plant it along the margin of a large pond, wetland, or ditch. It does need room, however, and may overwhelm other natives in a small pond; control by planting it in a restricting container.

Propagation. Grow from seed collected and planted in the fall. Plant seeds directly into muddy soil, or into containers filled with potting soil and submerged in water. Leave seeds outside to cold stratify over the winter for germination in the spring. Alternatively, divide the stout rhizomes in spring.

Native Habitat and Range. In shallow, slow-moving or standing water along lakes, ponds, and ditches, at low to mid elevations throughout much of North America; Eurasia and northern Africa.

Notes. The rhizomes are eaten by various wildlife species and sometimes by humans. *Typha ×glauca* encompasses the hybrids between this species and the smaller, nonnative *T. angustifolia* (narrowleaf cattail). *Typha* includes around a dozen species, widely distributed in the temperate and tropical parts of the world. *Acorus americanus* (sweet flag) is an emergent plant that somewhat resembles cattail: the long, narrow leaves can grow to almost 1m (3ft), and tiny, perfect (both male and female) flowers bloom in dense spikes at the base of a leaf-like bract. Sweet flag occurs through southern British Columbia, northern Idaho, and a bit of eastern Washington; disjunct populations suggest it may have been cultivated by indigenous people.

| *Utricularia macrorhiza* | Zones 3b to 9b | Lentibulariaceae |

common bladderwort

This aquatic perennial produces leafy, floating stems to 1m (3ft) long, without apparent roots. The leaves are alternate, up to 5cm (2in) long, and very finely divided into thread-like (filiform) segments interspersed with small valve-lidded bladders that serve to trap tiny, aquatic animals. Up to 20 flowers are produced above the surface of the water, on racemes to 20cm (8in) tall. Each flower has a yellow, bilabiate (two-lipped) corolla that looks much like a snapdragon and has a forward-curving spur at the base. The flowers are up to 2cm (1in) long and bloom from early to late summer. The pedicels curve downward as the flowers fade and the fruits, small, many-seeded capsules, ripen.

Cultivation. Sun or part shade. Common bladderwort is an interesting, carnivorous plant for the pond or lake. It tends to form mats in the water, providing excellent habitat for fish and other aquatic organisms.

Propagation. Grow from broken pieces of stem. It may grow from seed collected in the fall and pressed onto the surface of submerged, mucky soil soon after harvest.

Typha latifolia

Utricularia macrorhiza

Native Habitat and Range. In ponds, lakes, or slow-moving streams at low to mid elevations, circumboreal and extending south in North America to California, Texas, and the Southeast.

Notes. Sometimes classified as *U. vulgaris*. *Utricularia* includes a few hundred species, widely distributed but most diverse in tropical regions; close to 20 occur in North America, around six in our area. Lesser bladderwort (*U. minor*) and flatleaf bladderwort (*U. intermedia*), with the bladders set on specialized stalks separated from the finely divided leaves, are smaller plants and occur in shallow water throughout our area.

| *Valeriana sitchensis* | Zones 3b to 9b | Valerianaceae |

Sitka valerian, mountain heliotrope

This fibrous-rooted perennial produces leafy shoots to 1m (3ft) or more from a thick, branched rhizome or crown. The stems have up to five pairs of opposite leaves up to 25cm (10in) long, with the largest ones near the middle of the stem. The petioles are well developed, and the leaf blades are pinnately divided into several coarsely toothed leaflets, with the terminal leaflet the largest. Small flowers bloom in short, dense clusters at the stem tips. The white to pale pink flowers are less than 1cm (.5in) long, with an inflated, tubular base and five petal lobes. The three stamens and style protrude from the corolla, and the ovary is inferior. The foliage has a sour smell, but the flowers are fragrant and bloom from early to late summer. The fruit is a ribbed, one-seeded achene topped with up to 20 plumose (feathery) calyx branches that help disperse seeds on the wind.

Cultivation. Full sun to part shade, and moist soil. This is a lovely species for the edge of the woodland garden, wildflower meadow, or perennial bed.

Propagation. Grow from seed collected in the late summer or fall and planted soon after harvest. Sow seeds into containers of potting soil or directly into the garden and leave them outside to stratify over winter for germination in the spring. Plants can also be propagated from divisions of rhizomatous clumps made in early spring or summer.

Native Habitat and Range. In moist meadows, woods, streambanks, and thickets at mid to high elevations from southern Alaska, south through the mountains to northern California and east to Idaho and Montana.

Notes. The nearly 200 species of *Valeriana* are widespread throughout the planet; about half of the 15 species native to North America occur in our area. Scouler's valerian (*V. scouleri*) and sharpleaf valerian (*V. acutiloba*) are smaller, less leafy plants; western valerian (*V. occidentalis*) and marsh valerian (*V. dioica*) are small-flowered plants. Tobacco root (*V. edulis* var. *edulis*) and other native valerians have been used medicinally by various groups of people.

| *Vancouveria hexandra* | Zones 7a to 9b | Berberidaceae |

inside-out flower, duck's foot

This deciduous perennial spreads by slender rhizomes. The airy, compound leaves are basal and grow 10 to 40cm (4 to 16in). Each leaflet has three lobes, giving them the shape of a duck's foot (hence one of its common names). Each slender, leafless flowering stem bears ten to 30 nodding, dainty white flowers with the petals flared back, reminiscent of shooting stars. The flowers are about 1cm (.5in) long and bloom from late spring to early summer. The fruits are follicles containing black seeds.

Cultivation. Part shade or dappled light, and moist to rather dry soil high in organic matter. This plant makes an excellent groundcover in any woodland or shade garden west of the Cascades but is especially useful in the dry shade under big conifers or other large trees.

Propagation. Easiest from divisions of the long, slender rhizomes made in late winter or early spring. Plants can also be grown from seed collected in the summer and planted into flats of potting soil soon after harvest; the seeds require warm, rather dry conditions followed by a period of cold, damp stratification over winter for germination the following spring.

Native Habitat and Range. In shady, somewhat moist forests at low to mid elevations, west of the Cascades from the southern part of the Puget Trough, south to northwestern California.

Notes. *Vancouveria*, the namesake of explorer George Vancouver, strongly resembles its close relative, *Epimedium*. There are only two other species in the genus, both of them evergreen and native to western North America. The yellow-flowered *V. chrysantha* (golden inside-out flower) is restricted to southwestern Oregon and northwestern California. *Vancouveria planipetala* (small or redwood inside-out flower) is a smaller version of *V. hexandra*; it occurs in dry woods from southwestern Oregon to the coastal mountains of central California. Both are excellent garden plants but are slower and somewhat harder to grow.

Valeriana sitchensis

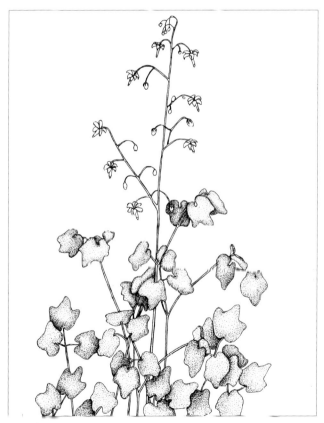

Vancouveria hexandra

Veratrum   Liliaceae

corn lily, false hellebore

There are at least 20 species of *Veratrum* in the Northern Hemisphere, including Europe, and Asia; around ten species occur in North America, with four of them native to our area. Corn lilies produce tall, leafy stems from thick rhizomes. The leaves are broad and deeply veined, and the flowers have six tepals or perianth parts (similar petals and sepals). The flowers are white to yellowish or green and have six stamens; they bloom in large panicles at the shoot tips. The fruits are papery, three-lobed capsules containing numerous seeds. The plants are beautiful but highly poisonous to humans and livestock; they were used medicinally, but with great caution, by many indigenous tribes. Some *Veratrum* species were used as insecticides.

Propagation. Collect seeds when the capsules ripen in the late summer or early fall, and plant them into very moist soil, into containers or directly into the garden, soon after harvest. Leave the planted seeds outside to cold stratify over winter for germination in the spring. It will take several years for seedlings to reach flowering size. Alternatively, divide the thick rhizomes in mid to late spring.

Veratrum californicum   Zones 3b to 9b

California corn lily or false hellebore

This deciduous perennial is attractive even when it doesn't flower. Its stout, unbranched stems, to 2m (6ft) tall, carry strongly veined, broadly ovate leaves; the largest can reach 30cm (1ft) in length and more than 15cm (6in) in width. The numerous flowers are greenish white and about 1.5cm (.5in) long, blooming from early to late summer in upright or spreading panicles.

Cultivation. Full sun to part shade, and moist to wet soil. A good plant for a sunny, boggy spot in the wildflower meadow or as a backdrop for the alpine garden on either side of the Cascades. This is a bold and beautiful species, evocative of damp mountain meadows, but it is highly poisonous and should never be planted where livestock or small children might have access.

Native Habitat and Range. In swamps, wet meadows, and moist woods, at low to high elevations, from western Washington south to southern California and Mexico, east to Idaho, Colorado, and New Mexico.

Notes. The common variety east of the Cascades, *V. c.* var. *californicum*, bears compound panicles almost to the top of the inflorescence; west of the Cascade crest is *V. c.* var. *caudatum*, with an inflorescence whose upper part is unbranched. The species most tolerant of dry conditions is the uncommon *V. insolitum* (Siskiyou corn lily), which lives in thickets, prairies, and dry, rocky woods at low to mid elevations from the Columbia River Gorge, south in western Oregon to northwestern California. It is somewhat shorter, growing only to 1.5m (5ft); its upright panicle is well branched, about 30cm (1ft) tall, and grayish with woolly hair. The yellowish white flowers, about 1.5cm (.5in) long, bloom from mid summer to early fall. This species is listed as sensitive in Washington.

Veratrum viride   Zones 3b to 9b

green corn lily or false hellebore

The unbranched stems of this deciduous perennial grow to 2m (6ft) and carry strongly veined, broadly ovate leaves, the largest of which can reach 35cm (14in) in length and up to 15cm (6in) in width. Many yellowish green or dark green flowers, about 1.5cm (.5in) long, bloom from mid summer to early fall in panicles with drooping branches.

Veratrum californicum

Veratrum viride

Cultivation. Full sun or part shade, and wet soil. A good plant for a sunny, boggy spot in the wildflower meadow or as a taller plant for the alpine garden throughout our area. Plants that are too small to flower have bold, attractive foliage. This big, graceful plant is extremely poisonous; it should never be planted where livestock or small children can get to it.

Native Habitat and Range. In swamps, wet thickets, and meadows, at low to high elevations, from Alaska, south through the Olympics and Cascades to northern California, east to the Rocky Mountains from British Columbia and Alberta to Idaho and Montana, disjunct in eastern North America.

Notes. Populations in the Pacific Northwest have sometimes been considered a separate variety, *V. v.* var. *eschscholzianum*. Many groups of indigenous people carefully used the roots of this highly poisonous plant for a variety of medicinal purposes.

Viola	Violaceae

violet

The more than 300 species of *Viola* are distributed throughout the temperate parts of the world; around 70 occur in North America, and about 30 species are native to the Pacific Northwest. Violets are some of our best-known garden perennials. Our native violets occur in a variety of habitats, from dry shrub-steppe communities east of the Cascades to shady bogs west of the mountains; all are perennial herbs with simple or compound leaves. The flowers have five sepals and five petals. The lowermost petal is the largest and has a spur at the base. All gardeners are familiar with the showy violet flowers that bloom in the spring, but later in the season many violets produce another kind of flower, hidden under the leaves or even beneath the surface of the ground; these cleistogamous flowers, being self-pollinating, never fully open or develop the bright colors and darker penciling attractive to insect pollinators. Violet fruits are three-parted capsules that open explosively to release seed. The seeds are relatively large, and some have an eliasome, an oily appendage, which attracts ants that carry the seeds away, dispersing them.

Propagation. Grow from seed collected in the summer. Sow seeds into flats of potting soil or directly into the garden in autumn or winter, and leave them outside for germination in the spring. Most violets can also be propagated from basal cuttings or divisions of the rhizomes or stolons made during the summer, but this should be done only with plants originally grown from seed.

Viola adunca	Zones 3b to 9b

early blue or hooked-spur violet

This violet produces (usually) leafy stems to 10cm (4in) from slender rhizomes. The leaf blades are usually oval and cordate (heart-shaped) at the base and about 2.5cm (1in) long. The leaf margins are finely crenate (with rounded teeth), and the petioles are well developed, each with a pair of slender stipules at the base. The flowers are about 1.5cm (.5in) long and vary from blue to dark violet with a long, slender, usually hooked, spur. The three lowermost petals are often white at the base and penciled with purple lines; of these petals, the two lateral ones have patches of white hairs at their bases. Flowers bloom from mid spring to early or even late summer. The small capsules contain dark brown seeds.

Cultivation. Sun, part shade, or dappled light, and moist soil. This lovely violet can be grown in gardens on either side of the Cascades; it tolerates a wide range of conditions and may spread under ideal conditions. Plant it along a trail, in the low perennial border, or in sunnier places in the woodland garden. Makes a charming addition to the moist places in the wildflower meadow.

Native Habitat and Range. In open woods, dry to moist meadows, and disturbed places at low to high elevations from southern Alaska, south through California, and from the coast, east through much of northern North America to Quebec and New York.

Notes. The wide-ranging *V. a.* var. *adunca* occurs throughout our area. The similar blue-flowered *V. howellii* (Howell's violet) lives in moist meadows and open woods at low elevations, mainly west of the Cascades from southern British Columbia, south to northern California, but extending east to Klamath Lake in southern Oregon; it blooms from mid spring through early summer, and the spur on the lowest petal is broad and pouched instead of slender and curved. Marsh violet (*V. palustris*) has white, pale blue, or lavender flowers with purple penciling on the lower petals; the leaves and leafless flowering peduncles arise directly from the rhizomes. This species grows near streams and in bogs, seeps, and moist meadows at low to fairly high elevations on both sides of the Cascades from British Columbia to California, east to the Rocky Mountains and across much of Canada. Alaska violet (*V. langsdorfii*) is another rhizomatous perennial with cordate (heart-shaped) leaves and violet flowers on (usually) leafless peduncles; it grows in bogs and moist, rocky places at low to high elevations west of the Cascades, from Alaska, scattered south through Oregon. Olympic violet (*V. flettii*) has lavender or purple flowers and fleshy, purplish, reniform (kidney-shaped) leaves; this endemic, alpine species, native to talus and rock outcrops in the northern Olympic Mountains, is a choice, but difficult, rock garden plant.

Viola adunca

Viola cuneata

Viola cuneata	Zones 6b to 9b

wedge-leaved violet

This hairless (glabrous) perennial produces slender stems up to 20cm (8in) tall from scaly rhizomes. The leaf blades are ovate to deltoid (triangular), cuneate (wedge-shaped) to truncate at the base, and to 2.5cm (1in) long. The purplish petioles are up to 7cm (3in) long with small, greenish stipules at the base. Flowers, about 2cm (1in) across, bloom from early spring to early summer from peduncles in the axils of the stem leaves. The two upper petals are white, sometimes purplish at the base. The two lateral petals each have a purple spot and a tuft of hairs at the base. The lower petal has a yellow base with purple veins and a yellowish, sac-like spur. All the petals are red-violet on the back. The rounded, purplish capsules contain dark brownish purple seeds.

Cultivation. Part shade or dappled light, and moist to somewhat dry, well-drained soil. This attractive little violet makes a lovely addition to the shady parts of the rock garden or low perennial border. Plant it in the open areas of the shade or woodland garden, or along a path.

Native Habitat and Range. In moist to rather dry, open woods, sometimes in rocky, serpentine soils at mid elevations in the mountains from west central Oregon, south to northern California.

Notes. Two-eyed violet (*V. ocellata*) produces triangular leaves with serrate margins and leafy flowering stems up to 30cm (1ft) tall from thick rhizomes. The flowers are white, and the lower three petals have yellow bases with purple penciling. The two lateral petals each have a purple spot at the base, and the upper pair of petals are purplish violet on the back. *Viola ocellata* lives on rocky (often serpentine) banks and woods at low to mid elevations from southwestern Oregon to west central California.

Viola douglasii   Zones 6b to 9b

golden or Douglas' violet

This violet grows from a deep, short rhizome and produces stems to 10cm (4in) long that remain partly underground. The plants are usually pubescent, and the leaf blades are up to 5cm (2in) long, bipinnately compound into linear lobes. The petioles are at least as long as the blades and have small, linear stipules at their bases. The flowers bloom from early to late spring on peduncles that are usually longer than the leaves, up to 12cm (5in). The flowers are about 2.5cm (1in) across and golden yellow, with dark, purplish brown veins at the bases of the lower three petals. The lowermost petal has a short, sac-like spur, and the two lateral petals have yellow hairs at their bases. The two upper petals are dark purplish on the back. The oblong, greenish capsules contain light beige seeds.

Cultivation. Full sun or light shade, and well-drained soil that is moist during the early spring growing season. This is a charming violet with finely divided leaves, an unusual species for the rock garden or deep trough. Plant it in the rocky, vernally moist place in the wildflower meadow or hillside.

Native Habitat and Range. On grassy slopes, meadows, and rocky flats that are wet in the early spring, at low to mid elevations, from north central Oregon, scattered south through California.

Notes. Hall's violet (*V. hallii*) also has deep rhizomes and partially underground stems. Its leaf blades are divided into linear segments; the two upper petals are purple on both surfaces, and the lower three are creamy, with purple penciling. This species lives in open woods and gravelly slopes from southern Oregon to northern California. *Viola praemorsa* (upland yellow violet) and *V. purpurea* (purple-backed or goosefoot violet) are both widespread species, often living in rather dry habitats. Their leaves are entire or toothed, but not compound. They have yellow flowers with purple or brown penciling, and the upper petals are usually maroon on the back.

Viola glabella   Zones 3b to 9b

stream, pioneer, or yellow wood violet

This violet grows from spreading, fleshy rhizomes and produces stems to 30cm (1ft) tall with leaves and flowers developing at the shoot tips. Basal leaves with cordate (heart-shaped) blades also grow directly from the rhizomes. The blades have toothed margins and are set on petioles up to 20cm (8in) long. The petals are bright yellow on both sides; the three lower petals have dark purplish penciling on their bases, and the two lateral petals are bearded at the base. Flowers bloom from early spring to mid summer. The capsules contain brown seeds.

Cultivation. Full or part shade or dappled light, and moist to wet soil. Plant this violet along the streambank, pond, or bog margin. It is also charming in the moist parts of the woodland garden. Once established, it may spread to form a lush carpet in the spring and is a good choice for planting with other moisture- and shade-loving perennials on both sides of the Cascades.

Native Habitat and Range. Along streams and in moist woods and clearings at low to high elevations from Alaska south through northern California, and from the coast, east through the Cascades to Idaho and Montana.

Notes. Canada violet (*V. canadensis*) is similar in form, with flowers and stem leaves clustered at the shoot tips and basal leaves arising singly from rhizomes; it has white flowers with purple penciling and produces stolons in addition to rhizomes. This species has a wide range through much of North America, but only *V. c.* var. *rugulosa* occurs in our area.

Viola douylasii

Viola glabella

Viola sempervirens   Zones 5b to 9b

evergreen, trailing yellow, or redwood violet

This perennial, evergreen violet reaches only about 8cm (3in) in height and spreads mainly by aboveground stolons. The leaves have petioles up to 10cm (4in) long and leathery blades, up to 3cm (1.5in) wide, varying in shape from cordate (heart-shaped) to reniform (kidney shaped). The leaf margins are crenate (with rounded teeth) and often have purple markings underneath. The flowers, which bloom from early spring to early summer, are pale yellow and about 1.5cm (.5in) across. The spur is short and sac-like. The lower three petals have purple penciling, the two lateral petals have yellow hairs at their bases. The purple-spotted capsules contain brown seeds.

Cultivation. Full to part shade or dappled light, and moist soil. This small violet tends to be mat-forming and makes a charming carpet beneath taller plants in the woodland or shade garden. It can also be planted in a rock garden, on a log or stump, or between paving stones along a trail.

Native Habitat and Range. In moist woods at low to mid elevations west of the Cascades, from British Columbia south to west central California and scattered east to northeastern Oregon and northern Idaho.

Notes. *Viola orbiculata* (round-leaved or dark woods violet) is similar, but it lacks stolons, and its sometimes evergreen leaves are thinner in texture and without purple spots; this species lives in meadows and woods at mid to high elevations in the mountains from British Columbia to Oregon, and east to Montana and Wyoming.

Viola trinervata	Zones 5a to 8b

sagebrush violet

This violet produces shoots up to 15cm (6in) tall (the lower parts usually buried) from deep rhizomes. Plants are glabrous (hairless) and generally glaucous, bluish with a waxy coating. The basal leaves are largest, with blades up to 4cm (1.5in) long, palmately divided and with the primary divisions sometimes secondarily divided into narrowly elliptic segments. The leaves have a leathery texture and prominent veins on the lower surface. The flowering stems are leafy, and the flowers, which bloom from early spring to early summer, are about 1.5cm (.5in) long. They are bicolored, with the upper pair of leaves reddish purple and the lower three lilac; the lower petals are yellowish at the base, penciled and blotched with purple.

Cultivation. Full sun to part shade, and well-drained soil that is moist early in the spring. This species becomes dormant when the weather heats up in the summer, but it is unusual and lovely in the spring. This may well be our most beautiful native violet, and gardeners east of the Cascades should consider growing it in the rock garden or dry, rocky meadow, or among the sagebrush in the wildlife garden.

Native Habitat and Range. On rocky hillsides, often under sagebrush, where the soil is moist early in the spring, at low to mid elevations east of the Cascades from north central Washington, south to the Columbia River Gorge, north central, and southeastern Oregon.

Notes. Great Basin or Beckwith's violet (*V. beckwithii*) is a similar species of rocky or dry, clay soils in sagebrush or ponderosa pine habitats, growing at mid elevations, mainly east of the Cascades, from northeastern Oregon, south to northeastern California and east to Idaho and Utah. It has glaucous foliage and leaf blades divided into narrow segments. Flowers bloom from early to late spring; the two upper petals are maroon, and the three lower petals are pale pink or mauve, with yellow bases and purple penciling. Cut-leaf or Shelton's violet (*V. sheltonii*) has glaucous leaves, often purplish underneath, which are rounded in outline and divided into deeply lobed leaflets. The flowers are yellow; the two upper petals are brownish on the back, and the lower three have purple penciling. This species lives in gravelly or loamy soils, often under ponderosa pine or shrubs, from central Washington, south through southwestern Oregon to southern California, east to Idaho and in Colorado.

Wyethia amplexicaulis	Zones 3b to 8b	Asteraceae

northern or smooth mule's ears

This stout, taprooted perennial is completely hairless (glabrous), and the surface of the stems and leaves has a varnished-resinous texture. The stems tend to lean and are up to 80cm (2.5ft) long. The basal leaves are largest, up to 60cm (2ft) long, elliptic in shape, with entire or finely toothed margins and tapered to the petiole. The stem leaves are smaller, alternately arranged and are sessile (lacking petioles), with the base of the blade clasping the stem. Each flowering shoot usually bears several heads with the terminal head the largest and smaller heads growing from the leaf axils. The ray and disk florets are both yellow, and the ray corollas on the larger central heads are up to 4cm (1.5in) long. Flowers bloom from late spring to mid summer. The fruits are achenes with a pappus (modified calyx) of small teeth.

Cultivation. Full sun to light shade, and well-drained, moist to rather dry soil. This is a beautiful, bold yellow daisy for early summer bloom in the wildflower meadow or woodland margin. Plant it near oaks or aspens for a lovely effect.

Propagation. Grow from seed collected in summer and planted in the fall. Seeds can be sown into deep containers, such as tubes (to accommodate the developing taproots) or directly into the garden. Leave planted seeds outside all winter to stratify under cold, moist conditions for

Viola sempervirens

Viola trinervata (photo by Sally A. Simmons)

Wyethia amplexicaulis

Xerophyllum tenax

germination the following spring. Plants will take a few years to reach blooming size, but once established they are long-lived.

Native Habitat and Range. In open woods and vernally moist meadows and hillsides at mid to fairly high elevations from central Washington through eastern Oregon, east to Montana and Colorado.

Notes. *Wyethia* is a genus of perennial plants with sunflower-like heads, all native to western North America; considered in the narrow sense, it includes ten species, half of them native to the Pacific Northwest. *Wyethia helianthoides* (white-rayed mule's ears) occurs in moist to wet meadows at mid elevations in the mountains of eastern Oregon, east to Montana and Wyoming; where it encounters *W. amplexicaulis*, they hybridize to form *W. ×cusickii*, with creamy flowers and other intermediate characters. *Wyethia mollis* (woolly mule's ears) ranges through dry, often wooded areas in the mountains of central California, north into southern Oregon and adjacent Nevada; it has yellow flowers, and the plants are usually white with soft hairs. Narrow-leaved mule's ears (*W. angustifolia*) is a taprooted perennial with stout stems to about 80cm (2.5ft). The leaves are lanceolate and have entire or finely toothed margins. The basal leaves are largest, up to 40cm (16in) long and 10cm (4in) wide, tapered at both ends. Flowering stems usually produce a single yellow sunflower head with ray corollas up to 3.5cm (1.5in), blooming from mid spring to early summer. This species lives in meadows, moist hillsides and rather dry, open ground at low to mid elevations from southern Washington and the Columbia River Gorge, south through northeastern Oregon and the Willamette Valley to central California.

Xerophyllum tenax	Zones 3b to 9a	Liliaceae

beargrass, Indian basket grass

This beautiful member of the lily family is an evergreen perennial that can reach 1.5m (5ft) in height. The narrow, silvery leaves are tough and wiry, forming graceful, arching fountains of foliage. Each flowering stalk bears numerous small, fragrant flowers up to 1cm (.5in) on long pedicels. The flowers have six white tepals or perianth parts (sepals and petals are similar) and six long stamens. The inflorescence is a magnificent, conical raceme. The flowers bloom from late spring to late summer, depending on elevation. The fruit is a few-seeded, three-lobed capsule. Flowering shoots and associated leaves die back after the capsules ripen.

Cultivation. Full sun to part shade or dappled light, and moist, well-drained soil. This clump-forming species is not difficult to grow but is often unwilling to flower: flower initiation probably involves some combination of environmental factors from the previous year. Makes a lovely addition to the alpine or rock garden, the woodland edge, or rocky margin of the wildflower meadow.

Propagation. Grow from seed collected and sown after capsules ripen in late summer or fall. Plant seeds into containers of potting soil or directly into the garden, and leave them outside to cold stratify over winter for germination the following spring.

Native Habitat and Range. In meadows, clearings, and open woods at low to high elevations from southern British Columbia south to northern California, and from the coast, east through the Cascades to Idaho and Wyoming.

Notes. Indigenous people wove beargrass leaves into baskets and other items. Tufts of long-lasting beargrass leaves are often used by florists, but harvesting wild populations may eventually cause their decline.

Zigadenus   Liliaceae

death camas

The fewer than 20 species of *Zigadenus*—attractive but extremely poisonous bulb-bearing perennials all—are native mainly to North America, and also Asia; around five species are native in the Pacific Northwest. The linear leaves are mostly basal, and the flowers consist of six white or yellow-green tepals or perianth parts (petals and sepals are similar) arranged into panicles or racemes. The flowers have six stamens, and the fruits are dry, three-lobed capsules. Although *Zigadenus* was sometimes used, with great caution, as a medicine by indigenous people, the tribal root diggers were careful to avoid it when harvesting camas bulbs.

Propagation. Grow from seed harvested and planted after capsules ripen in late summer. Sow seeds into containers or directly into the garden, and leave them outside to cold stratify over the winter for germination the following spring. It will take a few years for plants to reach flowering size.

Zigadenus paniculatus   Zones 3b to 9b

panicled death camas

This species produces shoots up to 50cm (20in) tall from a perennial bulb. The linear leaves are mostly basal and up to 30cm (1ft) long; there are a few, smaller leaves on the stems. The inflorescence is a branched panicle bearing many small flowers on upright pedicels from early spring to early summer; those on the lower panicle branches are usually male (staminate) and do not produce fruits. The tepals are white or cream, unequal in length, each with a yellowish green gland at the base. The capsules, about 1.5cm (.5in) long, contain light brown seeds.

Cultivation. Full sun to part shade, and well-drained soil that is somewhat moist in early spring. Tolerates dry conditions, which makes it a good choice for gardens east of the Cascades. Attractive in the wildflower meadow or open woods, or planted with sagebrush in the wildlife garden. It can be grown with other bulbs or in the perennial border, but should not be planted where there are small children or livestock nearby.

Native Habitat and Range. In sagebrush habitats and rather dry pine woods at mid elevations east of the Cascades from north central Washington south to the Sierra Nevada of California, east through southern Idaho to Montana, Wyoming, Colorado, and New Mexico.

Notes. Small-flower death camas (*Z. micranthus*) and Fremont's death camas (*Z. fremontii*) occur from southwestern Oregon to California.

Zigadenus venenosus   Zones 3b to 9b

meadow death camas

This bulbous perennial develops shoots up to 50cm (20in) tall. The leaves are linear and mostly basal, reaching 30cm (1ft). The small, creamy flowers are arranged in crowded, often short racemes, sometimes with a few branches, and each tepal has a yellowish green, oval gland at its base. All the flowers are perfect (male and female structures both present and functional) and bloom from mid spring to mid summer. The small, dry capsules contain light brown seeds.

Cultivation. Full sun to part shade, and well-drained soil that is moist in the early spring. An interesting bulb for the wildflower meadow or perennial border, but do not plant it where small children or livestock are present. This species often grows and blooms with true camas (*Camassia* spp.) in nature, making an attractive spring display on either side of the Cascades.

Zigadenus fremontii

Zigadenus venenosus

Native Habitat and Range. In rocky meadows, grassy slopes, sagebrush, and open mountain forests at low to mid elevations from southern British Columbia south to Baja California and from the coast, east to Alberta, southwestern Saskatchewan, the Dakotas, Nebraska, Colorado, and New Mexico.

Notes. *Zigadenus v.* var. *venenosus* is found west of the Cascades, ranging south through Oregon to California and Nevada, and east to southern Idaho, Nevada, and Utah; *Z. v.* var. *gramineus* occurs from the east slope of the Cascades eastward to the Rocky Mountains and the Great Plains. *Zigadenus elegans* (glaucous or mountain death camas) has a large range; our native subspecies, *Z. e.* ssp. *elegans*, is found in grasslands and rocky slopes at mid to high elevations from Alaska and British Columbia to the Olympics and Cascades of Washington, east in the mountains to eastern Oregon, Montana, Alberta, and the Great Lakes, south to Texas and northern Mexico. Stems can grow to 1m (3ft) and produce a raceme with few to several flowers; the flowers are greenish white and each tepal has a heart-shaped gland at the base.

SHRUBS AND TREES

Acer	Aceraceae

maple

Most of the approximately 200 species of maples are deciduous and vary in size from large shrubs to huge trees. Maples are native to northern, temperate areas of the world; around a dozen species are native to North America, but only a few are westerners. Most species have palmate, opposite leaves and small but often attractive flowers. Their characteristic fruit is a double samara, two dry, single-seeded halves, each with a long, papery wing. Maples are used extensively in landscapes, especially as shade trees and for their glowing fall colors. With the exception of clones of a specific plant, individual trees will vary; it is best to select a maple for your garden in the fall if you want particular shades, and remember, when siting, that maples in full sun tend to develop more intense shades of red. A great many cultivars have been developed and selected for their uniform fall color, variegation, and columnar form, among other attributes. Large maples may collect lush growths of mosses, lichens, and licorice ferns (*Polypodium glycyrrhiza*) on their boughs, making a lovely display on gray winter days.

Propagation. Collect seeds just before they ripen in the late summer (at least in the case of *A. circinatum*—*A. macrophyllum* isn't as fussy) or fall and plant them immediately in moist potting soil; leave planted seeds outside to cold stratify over winter for spring germination. Layering too is often successful; nick and bury lower branches that touch the ground. Seedlings and even large plants can be transplanted in winter.

Acer circinatum	Zones 5b to 9b

vine maple

This species is well known for the deep reds, oranges, and yellows of its fall foliage. Vine maples are large shrubs to small trees, often multi-stemmed and reaching 2 to 10m (6 to 30ft). They develop a leggy, vine-like habit in the deep forest and a more compact shape in sun. Branches are slender, and leaves are rounded, about 10cm (4in) wide, with five to 11 lobes. The flowers are attractive with red sepals and white petals, blooming in small clusters from early spring to early summer. The wings of the samaras are widely spread, and the fruits turn red as they ripen.

Cultivation. Full sun to dappled light or part shade (required in the hot summer climates east of the Cascades), and well-drained, fairly moist soil. A fine little tree for the small yard, woodland margin, wildlife garden, or large hedgerow, especially lovely when sited near large boulders or in front of conifers.

377

Acer circinatum

Acer circinatum in fall

Native Habitat and Range. In moist places, often under larger trees, along streambanks and in clearings, at low to mid elevations from southern British Columbia, south to northern California, and from the coast to the east slope of the Cascades.

Notes. 'Monroe' has deeply lobed leaves. The species was used in making a variety of tools; its wood is flexible when fresh and very tough when dry.

Acer glabrum var. *douglasii*	Zones 5a to 9b

Douglas maple

Douglas maple is a shrub or small tree reaching 1 to 10m (3 to 30ft). The twigs are deep red, and the older bark is gray. The leaves are three- to five-lobed, up to 8cm (3in) across, and turn yellow or orange in fall. The flowers may be of one or both sexes. They are greenish yellow and bloom in rounded clusters from mid spring to early summer. Reddish samaras with the wings forming a V-shape follow the flowers.

Cultivation. Full sun to part shade, and moist but well-drained soil. Better adapted to drier, more open sites than *A. circinatum*; use Douglas maple in place of (or with) vine maple, at the edge of a meadow or as part of a large hedgerow. An excellent tree for a small yard, large rock garden, or woodland glade, and a good plant for the winter garden, with its colorful twigs.

Native Habitat and Range. In moist to dry, well-drained, often rocky areas along shores and forest edges at low to mid elevations from southern Alaska, south to California, and from the Pacific coast, east through Idaho and Nevada.

Notes. *Acer g.* var. *torreyi* (Torrey maple) ranges north to Oregon, from California and Nevada; *A. g.* var. *glabrum* (Rocky Mountain maple) ranges east, from western Idaho.

Acer glabrum var. *douglasii*

Acer macrophyllum

Acer macrophyllum   Zones 6a to 9b

bigleaf maple

This big, single or multi-trunked tree grows to 30m (100ft) tall and up to 15m (45ft) across. The bark of older trees is grayish and furrowed; boughs are often covered with mosses and other epiphytes. The large, opposite leaves are deeply three- to five-lobed, up to 30cm (1ft) wide, and usually turn yellow in fall. The greenish yellow flowers bloom in hanging, cylindrical clusters from early spring to early summer and are followed by brown, bristly, winged samaras in late summer and fall.

Cultivation. Full sun to part shade, and well-drained, fairly moist soil. A magnificent tree for shade and wildlife habitat, but this maple requires a lot of space and is not a good choice for the small garden. Don't plant it too close to houses or other buildings, as large branches are brittle and may break during storms. Heavily pruned or logged trees produce large numbers of fast-growing suckers.

Native Habitat and Range. In moist to dry soils with Douglas fir, or in open areas at low to mid elevations, from the coast to the west (and sometimes east) slope of the Cascades and Sierra Nevada, and from southern British Columbia, south to southern California.

Notes. Indigenous people had a variety of uses for this tree. Bigleaf maple is listed as one of the many host plants of *Phytophthora ramorum*, the serious pathogen behind sudden oak death.

Alnus   Betulaceae

alder

Alnus includes around 30 species of deciduous trees and shrubs, mostly native to the Northern Hemisphere; six of these occur in North America, four in the Pacific Northwest. The roots of alders host nitrogen-fixing microorganisms that allow the trees to inhabit poor soils. Alders are often found near water and will tolerate periodic flooding. They are monoecious, with tiny male and female flowers clustered in separate inflorescences on the same plant. Male (staminate) flowers consist of drooping catkins that release pollen in spring before or during the emergence of the leaves. Female (pistillate) catkins are cone-like and woody, producing small nutlets that are winged in some species. After the tiny fruits are released, the "cones" remain on the tree and are attractive through the winter, as are the developing male catkins. Alders are sometimes eaten by tent caterpillars or attacked by borers, but the larvae of more desirable butterflies also eat their foliage: serious butterfly gardeners will want to plant alders.

Propagation. Grow from seed collected in the summer or fall after the "cones" ripen. Plant the tiny nutlets outside in the fall, either into flats of potting soil or directly into the garden, and leave them to stratify in the cold, moist winter weather for germination the following spring.

Alnus rhombifolia   Zones 5a to 9b

white alder

This small, fast-growing tree reaches 25m (75ft) tall and around 10m (30ft) wide. The older bark is light colored, and the young twigs are often finely hairy. The leaf blades are elliptic to oblong, up to 8cm (3in) long, and have serrated margins; they are dark green above, pale and hairy beneath. The male catkins are up to 8cm (3in) long, blooming before the leaves emerge, from mid winter to mid spring. The cone-like female catkins are about 1.5cm (.5in) long, and the tiny nutlets have thin margins but lack papery wings.

Cultivation. Full sun to part shade, and rather wet to even dry soil. This is an attractive small tree for streambanks and pond margins, especially where soils are poor, and a good tree for the boundary of the butterfly garden.

Native Habitat and Range. Along the banks of streams and rivers at low to mid elevations, mainly east of the Cascades in southern Washington and on both sides of the Cascades in Oregon, south through California and east to western Idaho.

Notes. *Alnus incana* ssp. *tenuifolia* (*A. tenuifolia, A. incana* var. *occidentalis*; mountain or thin-leaf alder), another large shrub or small tree that blooms early in the season, occurs from Alaska south, mainly on the east slope of the Cascades in British Columbia, Washington, and Oregon through the Sierra Nevada of California, east to the Rocky Mountains. The pistillate (female) catkins are mounted on short, thick peduncles, and the tiny nutlets are not winged. This species is able to tolerate extremely cold winters and is a good shrub for the streambank or pond margin in mountainous areas.

Alnus rubra   Zones 6a to 9b

red alder

Red alder is a deciduous tree that is fast-growing, to 25m (75ft), but short-lived—old at 50 years. The bark of older trees is smooth and pale gray. The leaves are elliptic to ovate and up to 15cm (6in) long. The leaf margins are toothed and revolute (rolled under). The male flowers are crowded into drooping catkins up to 12cm (5in) long. The female catkins are small, brown, and cone-like when ripe, up to 2cm (1in) long. Flowers bloom from early to mid spring.

Alnus rhombifolia

Alnus rubra

Alnus rubra

Cultivation. Full sun to part shade, and rather dry to moist or seasonally flooded soil. This species can form dense stands on disturbed ground and is therefore considered weedy by some, but it's a great tree for poor soils, streambanks, and areas prone to flooding, and for reclaiming disturbed areas, especially west of the Cascades. Tent caterpillars occasionally disfigure it, but they cause no serious harm. Dead and dying red alders have more wildlife value than young, vigorous trees, especially for cavity-nesting birds. Old snags and stumps are often beautiful and make a garden focal point to plant on and around. An excellent choice for the wildlife garden or tall parts of a hedgerow.

Native Habitat and Range. In moist woods, streams, wetlands, and disturbed areas at low elevations from southern Alaska, south, mainly west of the Cascades through Washington and Oregon, to central California, east in northern Idaho.

Notes. Native people used this species as a medicine and as a source of dye. It remains a valuable source of veneer and other finished wood products, and is often used as firewood or for smoking meat.

Alnus viridis ssp. *sinuata*	Zones 4a to 9b

Sitka alder

This shrubby alder reaches 2 to 5m (6 to 15ft). Young bark is reddish, becoming dark gray with age. The leaves are ovate, up to 10cm (4in) long, with once or twice serrate margins, not much paler underneath than above. The drooping male catkins grow to 10cm (4in) long. The cone-like female catkins grow on slender peduncles at least 2cm (1in) long and bloom from late spring to mid summer. The nutlets have papery wings.

Cultivation. Full sun to part shade, and moist to rather wet soil. This is an excellent shrub for the wildlife or butterfly garden or included in a hedgerow composed of larger plants, and a good plant for the streambank, pond margin, or wetland shore.

Native Habitat and Range. Along streams, in damp woods, and on moist mountain slopes at low to high elevations from Alaska south through the Olympic Mountains and the Cascades of Washington and Oregon to northern California, east through British Columbia, Washington, and northeastern Oregon, to Idaho, Montana, and Wyoming.

Notes. *Alnus v.* ssp. *sinuata* (*A. crispa* ssp. *sinuata*, *A. sinuata*) is the most widespread taxon; the more northern *A. v.* ssp. *fruticosa* (Siberian alder) also occurs in our area.

Amelanchier alnifolia	Zones 3b to 9b	Rosaceae

Saskatoon serviceberry, shadbush, sarviceberry, juneberry

Serviceberry is a small to large shrub, usually 1 to 5m (3 to 15ft) tall and half as wide, that blooms from mid spring to early summer; white flowers, about 2.5cm (1in) wide with five narrow petals, are followed by sweet, deep purple berry-like fruits. The leaves are oval or oblong, up to 4cm (1.5in), and the upper half of the blade is usually serrate. New foliage is reddish, becoming dark blue-green during summer and turning brilliant shades of red and gold in fall.

Cultivation. Full sun to part shade, and moist to rather dry soil. Fall color will be more intense in sunnier sites. This lovely shrub has a place in any Northwest garden and should be planted by all gardeners wishing to attract birds. Excellent for the wildlife garden or hedgerow.

Propagation. Usually grown from cleaned seed planted in fall and cold stratified outside over winter for germination the following spring. Alternatively, semi-hardwood cuttings can be taken in early summer and treated with hormones.

Native Habitat and Range. On hillsides and open woods, at low to high elevations from southern Alaska, south to California and east to the Great Plains, Minnesota, and Colorado.

Alnus viridis ssp. *sinuata*

Amelanchier alnifolia

Notes. A highly variable species. *Amelanchier a.* var. *alnifolia* and *A. a.* var. *cusickii* have the widest ranges east of the Cascades; *A. a.* var. *humptulipensis* and *A. a.* var. *semiintegrifolia* grow on the west side. Several cultivars have been developed for showy flowers; 'Smoky' and 'Northline' both produce larger, sweeter fruits. The approximately 20 species of *Amelanchier* are native to temperate parts of North America and Eurasia. Utah serviceberry (*A. utahensis*) grows in rocky areas and hillsides in eastern Washington, Oregon, and Idaho, ranging south through Texas and east through the Rocky Mountains. Pale serviceberry (*A. pallida*) and dwarf serviceberry (*A. pumila*) also occur in the Pacific Northwest.

Andromeda polifolia	Zones 3b to 9b	Ericaceae

bog rosemary

This low-growing, evergreen shrub reaches 10 to 80cm (4 to 30in) in height and .5 to 1m (1.5 to 3ft) in width. The leaves are narrowly elliptic to linear with entire, revolute (rolled under) margins, dark green above and whitish beneath, vaguely reminiscent of rosemary leaves. Clusters of pink, urn-shaped flowers, about 1cm (.5in) long, bloom from the branch tips from mid spring to early summer. The fruits are small capsules.

Cultivation. Full sun to part shade, and acidic soil with plenty of moisture. Marshy conditions are not otherwise required. This charming little shrub is suited to the sunny bog, pond margin, or rock garden and is also an excellent container plant.

Propagation. Collect seeds after the capsules ripen and plant them outside in the fall, into flats of moist, acidic potting soil; the cold, moist winter conditions will help break dormancy for germination the following spring. It can also be layered. Nick stems and bend them so that the nick is beneath the soil surface; hold the stem in place until roots form. Alternatively, cuttings may be taken during the growing season, treated with hormones, set into pumice or some other medium, and kept in humid conditions until rooted.

Native Habitat and Range. In bogs and swamps at low to high elevations, circumpolar in North America, from Alaska to Labrador and south through British Columbia to northern Idaho, Minnesota, Illinois, and the east coast; northern Europe and Asia.

Notes. At most, *Andromeda* includes only a couple of species, native to the Northern Hemisphere; only *A. p.* var. *polifolia* occurs in the Pacific Northwest. Bog rosemary is lovely in the garden, but it is also poisonous. Cultivars include 'Grandiflora', 'Nana', and 'Blue Ice', a form with bluish foliage.

Arbutus menziesii	Zones 7b to 9b	Ericaceae

Pacific madrone

Whether single or multi-trunked, this evergreen species is one of our best known and most beautiful native trees. It can reach 30m (100ft) but is usually much shorter. The smooth red bark is the best-known feature of madrone, where the older, reddish brown fragments peel away to reveal the younger, greenish to deep red bark beneath. The shiny green leaves are oblong to elliptic and up to 15cm (6in) long on short petioles. The small, fragrant, white flowers are urn-shaped, less than 1cm (.5in) long, and arranged in densely flowered, compound racemes at the branch tips. They bloom from mid to late spring. The fruits are round, bright orange or red berries with a bumpy surface, about 1cm (.5in) wide.

Cultivation. Full sun or light shade, relatively acidic soil, and fast drainage. Difficult to establish. It's not easy to find large madrones for sale, but that's just as well because small plants are

Andromeda polifolia

Arbutus menziesii

more likely to survive. Young trees will need occasional summer water, but after the first year or so they will be able to maintain themselves and begin to grow quickly. Older trees are tolerant of drought and salt spray. Madrone is a beautiful specimen tree and wonderful for the wildlife garden: it provides nectar for butterflies, foliage for butterfly larvae, and evergreen cover for birds, and the berries are eaten by many species. Plant it where the bark and leaf debris it sheds won't be an annoyance.

Propagation. Fairly easy from seed. Collect whatever ripe berries you can in the fall, before the birds eat them, and remove the several seeds from the pulp. Plant them outside, and leave them to cold stratify under cold, moist conditions for germination the following spring. Planting seeds in small, individual containers or tubes, a few seeds to each container, will make seedlings easier to transplant as they grow and will minimize root disturbance. Seedlings are almost impossible to salvage, but container-grown plants are cooperative.

Native Habitat and Range. Open woods, rocky slopes, and relatively dry sites, at low to mid elevations west of the Cascade crest, from southern British Columbia south to southern California.

Notes. *Arbutus* includes a dozen or more species in North America and Eurasia.

Arctostaphylos   Ericaceae

manzanita, bearberry

Arctostaphylos is a well-known genus of around 80 species of evergreen shrubs and groundcovers, most of them native to western North America; approximately ten taxa occur in the Pacific Northwest. Plants have smooth, red bark and alternately arranged, leathery leaves with smooth (entire) margins. The small pink or white flowers have five fused petals and are urn shaped. The anthers release pollen through pores at their tips, and there is a horn-like appendage near each pore. The small fruits are reddish to brownish, somewhat fleshy, and berry-like.

Propagation. Notoriously difficult from seed. Collect ripe fruits and remove seed from the pulp soon after harvest. Put seeds in a dish and pour boiling water over them (some growers use sulfuric acid). Plant the seeds outside into flats or tubes of well-drained potting soil in the fall, and allow them to stratify under cold, moist conditions for sporadic germination the following year. Kinnikinnick (*A. uva-ursi*) and other low-growing species are easier to propagate from cuttings than many of the shrubby species native to our area. Make cuttings about 10cm (4in) long from fall to late winter or spring to early summer. Strip off the lower leaves, treat cut ends with rooting hormones, and set stems into pumice or some other rooting medium. Keep the cuttings under high humidity and out of direct sun until roots form.

Arctostaphylos canescens   Zones 7a to 9b

hoary manzanita

This evergreen shrub can grow to 2m (6ft) tall. The bark is smooth and dark red-brown, and the leaves are pale and often gray with fine hairs. The leaves are ovate to elliptic and up to 4cm (1.5in) long with short petioles. Nodding, white or pink flowers bloom in many small clusters from simple or branched peduncles from late winter to late spring. The reddish fruits are usually hairy.

Cultivation. Full sun or light shade, and well-drained, rather dry, rocky soil. A beautiful plant for the sunny, dry forest margin, large rock garden, or stony bank.

Native Habitat and Range. On dry, rocky slopes and open woods at low to mid elevations from southwestern Oregon, south to northern California.

Notes. This and the other tall, shrubby *Arctostaphylos* species are fine additions to the garden but are difficult to find in nurseries. Many are more tolerant of drought than cold and will probably do best in dry places west of the Cascades; Gasquet or Howell's manzanita (*A. hispidula*), Eastwood's manzanita (*A. glandulosa*), and sticky whiteleaf manzanita (*A. viscida*) range to the north as far as southwestern Oregon. Green manzanita (*A. patula*) should be more tolerant of cold winters; it lives at low to high elevations, ranging north in open conifer forests through Oregon to south central Washington. It is as tall as *A. canescens*, with pink flowers from late spring to early summer and brownish fruits.

Arctostaphylos uva-ursi   Zones 3b to 9b

kinnikinnick

This prostrate, evergreen shrub sends out trailing stems that root where they touch the ground, eventually forming mats to 5m (15ft) across. The branch tips are often upright to 15cm (6in). The bark is smooth and reddish, and the leaves are oblong, leathery, and up to 3cm (1.5in) long on short petioles. The pink flowers, about 1cm (.5in) long, bloom in short racemes of up to eight flowers from mid spring to early summer. The bright red fruits are up to 1cm (.5in) across.

Arctostaphylos canescens

Arctostaphylos uva-ursi

Cultivation. Full sun to light shade, and well-drained, moist to rather dry soil. This is one of our most beautiful and best-known groundcovers, though it may be slow to establish. It is good-looking throughout the year, but tough and drought-tolerant enough for parking lots. It is often planted to help control erosion on dry slopes. In the wildlife garden, kinnikinnick provides foliage for some butterfly larvae; the red fruits often remain on the plants, offering food for birds well into the winter. A handsome addition to the rock garden or stone retaining wall, or as a groundcover in openings among conifers.

Native Habitat and Range. On rocky or sandy slopes and dry, open forest at low to high elevations, from Alaska, south near the coast to central California, east through the Rocky Mountains and across the northern states to Labrador and the Atlantic coast; circumpolar to Eurasia.

Notes. The several cultivars of *A. uva-ursi*, grown from cuttings to maintain uniformity, include 'Alaska' and 'Massachusetts', flat-growing forms with small leaves. 'Vancouver Jade' is also flat-growing but doesn't spread as extensively; its foliage turns bronzy in winter. 'Point Reyes' is more tolerant of heat and drought. Media manzanita (*A.* ×*media*) is a natural hybrid between *A. uva-ursi* and *A. columbiana* (hairy manzanita), a taller plant, to 3m (10ft), which grows along the coast in open, rocky places from northern California to British Columbia. Media manzanita is a spreading shrub, growing to about 60cm (2ft) tall. Pinemat manzanita (*A. nevadensis*) is a prostrate species, very similar to *A. uva-ursi*, but the branches are somewhat stiffer, and the leaves usually have a sharp little point at the tip; it is widespread in the Cascades, blooms from early to mid summer, and produces brownish red fruits.

| *Artemisia tridentata* | Zones 3b to 9b | Asteraceae |

big sagebrush

This evergreen, erect to spreading shrub can grow to more than 2m (6ft) tall, but is often shorter, with a short trunk or branched base. The aromatic, alternate leaves are densely covered with fine, white hairs, giving the foliage a silvery appearance, made more attractive against the dark twigs and shredding bark. The leaves are narrowly wedge-shaped (cuneate), up to 4cm (1.5in) long, with three rounded teeth at the tip. The tiny flowers bloom in small heads arranged in panicles to 20cm (8in) from late summer to mid fall. The fruits are tiny, single-seeded achenes.

Cultivation. Full sun, and well-drained, nonalkaline soil. This truly beautiful, gracefully gnarled, fragrant shrub should be planted more often in gardens east of the Cascades, especially in wildlife gardens. Many animal species depend on sagebrush for food, shelter, and nesting sites, but it has been completely removed from large tracts of land where it once dominated. It is difficult to cultivate west of the Cascades but will survive in the hottest part of the garden, in very fast-draining, sandy or gravelly soil, especially when given some shelter from the abundant rains. This shrub is flammable and should not be planted too close to dwellings; it is killed by fire and does not resprout.

Propagation. Easy from seed. Collect inflorescences when the achenes are ripe, around early December, and store them in paper bags to keep them dry. Plant seeds in spring (or other times of the year) and keep them moist until they germinate within a few weeks. Seedlings grow quickly with a little moisture.

Native Habitat and Range. On dry plains and hills where soils are not alkaline, at low to high elevations, from British Columbia south along the east slope of the Cascades to Mexico, east to the Dakotas, Nebraska, and New Mexico.

Notes. Four subspecies have large ranges that include the Pacific Northwest: *A. t.* ssp. *spiciformis* (big sagebrush), *A. t.* ssp. *tridentata* (basin big sagebrush), *A. t.* ssp. *vaseyana* (mountain big sagebrush), and *A. t.* ssp. *wyomingensis* (Wyoming big sagebrush). Other shrubby sagebrushes native to the mountains or arid regions of the Pacific Northwest include little or low sagebrush

Artemisia tridentata (photo by Sally A. Simmons)

Baccharis pilularis

(*A. arbuscula*), silver sagebrush (*A. cana*), black sagebrush (*A. nova*), Owyhee sage (*A. papposa*), stiff sagebrush (*A. rigida*), and threetip sagebrush (*A. tripartita*). All can be grown from seed. Herbaceous species of *Artemisia* are discussed in the perennials section.

| *Baccharis pilularis* | Zones 8a to 9b | Asteraceae |

coyote brush

This spreading, evergreen shrub grows to a height of about 1m (3ft), sometimes taller, and spreads to 2m (6ft) or more. The small, alternate leaves are wedge shaped (cuneate) at the base, and usually about 1.5cm (.5in) long, with several coarse teeth along the margins. They are bright green and resinous. Plants are dioecious, either male or female. The flower heads produce small, inconspicuous white flowers, blooming from late summer to early winter. Female plants produce tiny achenes with a tuft of hair at one end (the pappus, a modified calyx) that aids in dispersal by wind.

Cultivation. Full sun or light shade, and any kind of well-drained to heavy, moist or rather dry soil. Extremely tolerant of heat and drought but may be damaged by cold. This is an excellent groundcover for a dry, sunny slope or parking area. Plant it at the edge of the large rock garden and prune it to enhance its graceful shape. Deer reputedly avoid this tough species.

Propagation. Grow from seed harvested from female plants in the fall or winter. Seeds germinate without treatment and can be planted in spring for germination within a few weeks. Alternatively, take cuttings from young stem tips in spring or early summer; treat them with hormones and set them into pumice or some other medium, keeping them moist and humid until roots form.

Native Habitat and Range. On dunes and bluffs along the coast at low elevations from northwestern Oregon, south through California.

Notes. *Baccharis p.* ssp. (or var.) *consanguinea* is occasionally applied to taller forms of this species. Cultivars include 'Twin Peaks' (with small, dark green leaves) and the fast-growing 'Pigeon Point' (larger, lighter green leaves). *Baccharis* includes around 300 species, most native to South America. Saltmarsh baccharis (*B. douglasii*) is the only other North American species that ranges as far north as the southwestern corner of Oregon.

Betula papyrifera	Zones 3b to 9a	Betulaceae

paper, white, or canoe birch

This small to medium-sized tree can grow to 30m (100ft) tall and half as wide but is often smaller. The bark, especially in older trees is white, peeling in papery strips, but sometimes the bark is dark reddish or coppery, reminiscent of cherry bark. The alternate leaves are rounded to oval with pointed tips and doubly toothed margins. Leaves grow to 10cm (4in) on short petioles, turning yellow in autumn. The male and female catkins grow to 4cm (1.5in) long, blooming before or with the expansion of the leaves, from early to late spring. Female catkins shatter as the fruits, nutlets or samaras with wings wider than the body of the tiny fruit, ripen and float away on the wind.

Cultivation. Full sun to part shade, and moist soil. Birches are beautiful against green conifers and are a good choice for the edge of the woodland garden or in a tall hedgerow. Honeydew-dripping aphids visit all species of birch, so this is not a good tree for the patio or parking area, but it is a fine tree for the wildlife garden, providing food for some butterfly larvae, and it is more resistant to borers and leaf miners than more commonly planted nonnative species. Many insects are attracted by birch, and they in turn will attract more birds.

Propagation. Easiest from seed. Collect the little fruits in the summer or fall when they are ripe, but before they fall from the catkins. Plant them outside in autumn and leave them to stratify in the cool, moist winter weather for germination the following spring.

Native Habitat and Range. In moist, open to dense forest, and well-drained soils to boggy sites, at low to mid elevations from Alaska south to Washington and northeastern Oregon, east to the Atlantic coast.

Notes. The native variety in the Pacific Northwest, *B. p.* var. *papyrifera*, spans North America. Indigenous people used this species to make canoes and baskets; birch resin was useful as an adhesive, as a medicine, and as chewing gum. *Betula* is a well-known genus of more than 40 species of deciduous shrubs and trees native to the temperate and cooler parts of the Northern Hemisphere; around a dozens species are native to North America. Water birch (*B. occidentalis*), resin birch (*B. glandulosa*), dwarf birch (*B. nana*), and bog birch (*B. pumila*) are also native to the Pacific Northwest.

Cassiope mertensiana	Zones 3b to 9a	Ericaceae

western or white moss heather

This evergreen, mat-forming shrub grows to 30cm (1ft) tall and eventually much wider. The tiny, scale-like leaves are densely arranged in four rows along the slender stems, looking much like a moss. The flowers are small white bells with five fused petals and five reddish sepals, blooming near the branch tips; they are a bit less than 1cm (.5in) long, nodding from pedicels up to 3cm (1.5in) long, and bloom from mid to late summer, earlier at lower elevations. The fruits are rounded capsules with five chambers and many seeds.

Betula papyrifera

Cassiope mertensiana

Cultivation. Sun or part shade, and moist, peaty soil with lots of pumice or other gritty material. May be fussy at low elevations. Tuck this charming heather relative near boulders in the rock garden.

Propagation. Grow from seed collected in summer or fall. Plant seeds into flats or containers in gritty soil, and leave them outside in the cool, moist winter weather for germination in spring or later. Plants can also be propagated by layering, pushing stems under the soil surface and holding them in place until roots form. Another method is to take cuttings of mature twigs in late summer, treat them with hormones, and place them in pumice or some other medium, keeping them humid until they root. These last two methods should be done only with plants that have been grown in cultivation

Native Habitat and Range. In alpine heath and rocky ledges at high elevations, from Alaska, south through the mountains to central California, east to Idaho, Montana, and the Canadian Rockies.

Notes. Of the two varieties, *C. m.* var. *mertensiana* has the more western range, from Alaska, south in the high mountains, to California; *C. m.* var. *gracilis* ranges east to Montana from our area. White arctic or four-angled mountain heather (*C. tetragona*) and club-moss mountain heather (*C. lycopodioides*) also occur in the Pacific Northwest. *Cassiope* is a genus of less than a dozen species native to the chillier, boreal parts of the Northern Hemisphere. The similar *Harrimanella stelleriana* (*C. stelleriana*; Alaskan mountain or moss heather) is another alpine species that ranges as far south as Washington.

Ceanothus	Rhamnaceae

California lilac

Ceanothus includes about 50 species of shrubs and small trees, some deciduous, others evergreen. They are native to North America, mostly to the west, with the majority of species diversity centered in California; fewer than ten occur in the Pacific Northwest. The flowers are tiny, with parts in fives; they bloom in showy, many-flowered panicles or umbels. The fruits are tough capsules composed of three carpels (sections) with a single seed in each carpel. Many of the California species, though beautiful, are not tolerant of the Pacific Northwest climate; thankfully, some of our natives are excellent garden subjects. Most species are nitrogen-fixers and are able to tolerate poor soils; all hybridize readily, and there are many named cultivars. The biggest drawback to these plants may be that the shrubs tend to be short-lived, often dying before their first decade.

Propagation. Grow from seed, but the seeds of many species require pretreatment. Collect seeds from the ripe capsules in late summer or fall, put them into a dish, pour boiling water over them, and leave them to cool overnight. Plant the seeds outside into flats of potting soil, and leave them to stratify in the cold, moist winter conditions for germination the following spring. Many species can be grown from hardwood cuttings taken in late winter or in the fall, treated with rooting hormones, and set to root in pumice or some other medium. Semi-hardwood cuttings can also be taken from early to late summer, treated with hormones, and kept in humid conditions (such as under plastic) until roots form. Ground layering the branches of existing plants is another method that can be used with mat-forming or taller species, but this should be done only with plants grown from seed in cultivation.

Ceanothus integerrimus	Zones 5a to 9b

deer brush

This erect or spreading shrub grows to 4m (12ft) tall and has deciduous, alternate leaves with well-developed petioles. The leaf blades are thin, up to 6cm (2.5in) long, and have entire margins and three main veins spreading from the base. Many tiny white or blue flowers bloom in panicles at the branch tips from late spring to mid summer, and often again in the early fall. The three-lobed capsules have low crests.

Cultivation. Full sun to part shade or dappled light, and well-drained, moist to rather dry soil. This is a fine shrub for the dry parts of the butterfly or woodland garden on either side of the Cascades. Plant it at the back of the rock garden, on a dry bank, or in a parking area or hedgerow.

Native Habitat and Range. In open woods and slopes at low to mid elevations, in southern Washington and northern Oregon, near the Columbia River Gorge, south through western Oregon and California and east to Arizona and New Mexico.

Notes. Redstem ceanothus or Oregon tea tree (*C. sanguineus*), another deciduous shrub but shorter, to 3m (10ft) tall, lives on dry slopes and forest edges at low to mid elevations from southern British Columbia, south on both sides of the Cascades to California and east to Idaho and Montana; it has purplish stems and fragrant white flowers, which bloom in panicles from late spring to mid summer.

Ceanothus prostratus	Zones 4b to 9b

Mahala mat, prostrate ceanothus

This prostrate, evergreen shrub grows to 5cm (2in) in height and forms mats to 2m (6ft) across, the branches sometimes rooting where they touch the ground. The small, opposite leaves are thick and firm, ovate and up to 2.5cm (1in) long, with spiny teeth along the margins. Tiny light

Ceanothus integerrimus

Ceanothus pumilus

Ceanothus prostratus

to dark blue flowers bloom in flat-topped clusters about 2.5cm (1in) across from late spring to mid summer. The small capsules have three short horns at the top.

Cultivation. Full sun or light shade, and fast-draining, sandy or rocky, rather dry soil. It's a beautiful groundcover for the rock garden, stony bank, or clearing among pine trees.

Native Habitat and Range. Openings in dry, coniferous forests at mid elevations along the east slope of the Cascades from central Washington, south through western Oregon to northern California, east to Nevada and Idaho.

Notes. This lovely, trailing shrub is difficult to grow, especially west of the Cascades, but some determined gardeners have success.

Ceanothus pumilus	Zones 6b to 9b

Siskiyou mat, dwarf ceanothus

This prostrate mat-former spreads to 2m (6ft). The opposite, evergreen leaves are small and tough with short petioles. They are cuneate (wedge-shaped, narrowed to the base), whitish underneath, sometimes with a few blunt teeth at the tip and about 1cm (.5in) long. Blue, lavender, or white flowers bloom in small, umbel-like clusters from late spring to early summer, and the capsules are small.

Cultivation. Full sun or very light shade, and fast-draining, sandy or rocky, dry soil. Challenging, especially in extremely wet or cold areas. This charming, evergreen mat-former makes a lovely, small groundcover for the rock garden, stony bank, or slope. Grow from seed.

Native Habitat and Range. On dry, rocky slopes, often in serpentine, at mid to fairly low elevations from southwestern Oregon to northwestern California.

Notes. *Ceanothus cuneatus* (buckbrush), a spiny, branching shrub to 2m (6ft) tall, lives in similar habitats and elevations, on dry, gravelly flats and rocky slopes from western Oregon south through California; its evergreen leaves are thick and gray-green, and its white or pale blue flowers bloom in umbel-like inflorescences on the lateral branches from mid spring to early summer.

Ceanothus thyrsiflorus	Zones 6b to 9b

blueblossom

This evergreen shrub or small tree grows to 6m (18ft). The twigs are angled and green. The alternate leaves are ovate to elliptic, up to 5cm (2in) long, with three prominent veins. They are dark green on the upper surface, paler beneath, with short petioles. Tiny light to dark blue flowers bloom in dense panicles up to 15cm (6in) long from mid spring to early summer, and usually again in the fall. The small capsules turn black when ripe.

Cultivation. Full sun or light shade, and well-drained, rather dry soil. Once established, this plant is drought-tolerant and needs no summer water. Though it is more accepting of summer watering than other species, don't plant it near parts of the garden that are regularly irrigated. This is a beautiful plant for the hedgerow or shrub bed, and an excellent choice for a dry bank or parking strip. It provides evergreen cover, seeds, and insects for birds.

Native Habitat and Range. In dry, wooded canyons and slopes at low elevations from west central Oregon, south near the coast to southern California.

Notes. As one of our best-known native species of *Ceanothus*, this plant and its cultivars are often available in nurseries. 'Skylark' is a shrub to 2m (6ft) tall and almost as wide with deep blue flowers that bloom in spring and again, though less profusely, in fall; 'Snow Flurry' is a taller, wider selection with white flowers. *Ceanothus velutinus* (snowbrush, mountain balm), another spreading, evergreen native, can grow to 3m (10ft) tall and 2m (6ft) or more in width; its addi-

Ceanothus thyrsiflorus

Celtis laevigata var. *reticulata*

tional common names (sticky laurel, tobacco brush, cinnamon bush) are inspired by the resinous fragrance of its foliage. This is a good plant to use as a screen for the deck or patio, where the aromatic foliage can be enjoyed in the summer warmth; its tiny, fragrant, white flowers bloom in dense panicles up to 6cm (2.5in) long from early to late summer.

Celtis laevigata var. *reticulata*	Zones 4b to 9b	Ulmaceae

western or netleaf hackberry

This large shrub or small tree grows to 10m (30ft) tall and just as wide. The older bark is reddish gray, and the new growth is hairy. The deciduous leaves are alternate, and the blades are ovate but oblique (asymmetric) at the base; they grow to 10cm (4in) long and have short petioles and toothed margins. The leaf blades, paler and distinctly veiny beneath, have a rough (scabrous) surface; they turn yellow in the fall. Small clusters of tiny flowers bloom from the leaf axils from mid to late spring. The fruits are small reddish or purplish drupes less than 1cm (.5in) long. The seed is contained in a hard pit surrounded by sweet pulp and a thin outer skin, like a very small cherry.

Cultivation. Full sun or part shade, and soil with some moisture. Tolerates heat, wind, and rocky, poor soil. This is an excellent deciduous tree for streambanks and dry washes east of the Cascades. The berries will attract birds, and people can eat them too, though they're small. It is susceptible to leaf gall, a cosmetic concern that causes no harm to the plant. Include in the wild-life garden or use it as a component of a large hedgerow.

Propagation. Grow from seed collected in the late summer and planted in the fall. Clean some of the pulp from the small drupes, plant the seeds into containers, and leave them outside over winter for spring germination. Plants can also be propagated from hardwood cuttings made in the fall, treated with hormones, and set to root in moist pumice or some other medium.

Native Habitat and Range. On rocky slopes and bluffs, usually near streams and other moist places in dry habitats at low to mid elevations from eastern Washington and Oregon, south to California, New Mexico, and Texas, east to Idaho and Colorado.

Notes. Sometimes classified as *C. reticulata* or *C. douglasii*. There are upward of 50 species of *Celtis* in the temperate regions of the Northern Hemisphere and elsewhere in the tropical parts of the world; around six species are native to North America, but only *C. laevigata*, in its var. *reticulata*, occurs in our area.

| *Cercis orbiculata* | Zones 5a to 9b | Fabaceae |

California or western redbud

This large shrub or small tree is often multi-stemmed and grows to 5m (15ft) in height and width. The deciduous, rounded leaves are alternate, have a heart-shaped (cordate) base, and grow to 9cm (3.5in) across on petioles to 3cm (1.5in). The leaves are blue-green during the growing season and turn yellow or red in the fall. The small, more or less pea-shaped flowers grow to 1cm (.5in) long; they are purplish pink, occasionally white, blooming from early to mid spring. The fruits, reddish pea pods, grow to 9cm (3.5in) long and contain rounded seeds.

Cultivation. Full sun to light shade, and well-drained, rather dry soil. This is a very drought-tolerant species, excellent for a dry bank or parking area. Plant it in the dry parts of the rock garden or hedgerow, or as a small specimen tree near a deck or patio. Flowers best where winters are chilly.

Propagation. Grow from seed harvested in fall or winter and planted outside in late winter or spring. It can also be grown from softwood cuttings taken in the spring, treated with hormones, and set to root in pumice or some other medium. Keep the cuttings humid until roots form.

Native Habitat and Range. On dry slopes and canyons at low to mid elevations in the mountain foothills from northern to southern California, and east to Utah and Arizona.

Notes. Sometimes classified as *C. occidentalis*. We are cheating a bit with this species, as its range doesn't extend further north than northern California, but it is too choice to omit. Its white-flowered selection 'Alba' is a smaller shrub, reaching about 2m (6ft). *Cercis* is a genus of about six species native to North America and Eurasia.

| *Cercocarpus ledifolius* | Zones 3b to 9b | Rosaceae |

curl-leaf mountain mahogany

This gracefully branching, evergreen shrub or small tree grows to 6m (18ft). The small leaves are narrow or elliptic, up to 3cm (1.5in) long, with revolute (inrolled) margins. They are somewhat resinous, dark green above and paler beneath. The small flowers lack petals and bloom singly or in small clusters in the leaf axils from mid spring to early summer. The fruits are more interesting, a small achene with a long, plumed "tail" to 8cm (3in) that develops from the elongated style.

Cultivation. Full sun to very light shade, and well-drained, rocky, rather dry soil. This is a fine species for the dry parts of the garden on either side of the Cascades. Plant it in the background of the rock garden, on a dry bank, or in a parking area or hedgerow.

Propagation. Collect seeds in late summer or early fall, remove the long styles, soak them in water for an hour, and plant them outside into containers of potting soil. Leave them in the cool, moist winter weather for germination the following spring. Plants can also be grown from cuttings taken in the summer, treated with hormones, and kept in pumice or some other medium under humid conditions until roots form.

Cercis orbiculata

Cercocarpus ledifollus

Native Habitat and Range. On rocky mountain slopes and dry foothills at mid elevations, from southeastern Washington, south and west to southwestern Oregon and through California, east to Montana, Colorado, and Arizona.

Notes. *Cercocarpus l.* var. *ledifolius*, which occurs in northeastern Oregon, has elliptic leaves with slightly revolute margins; *C. l.* var. *intercedens* has narrower, strongly inrolled leaves and is more common in our areas. There are only a handful of *Cercocarpus* species, all native to western North America. *Cercocarpus montanus* (*C. betuloides*; alderleaf mountain mahogany) occurs in dry habitats throughout a large area of the western United States, including southwestern Oregon; its leaves are rounded with toothed margins. *Chamaebatiaria millefolium* (desert sweet, fern bush) is another drylands shrub in the rose family, ranging into south central Oregon; it reaches 2m (6ft) and has white flowers from early to late summer. It can be grown in sunny, well-drained parts of the garden on either side of the Cascades, and its finely divided, aromatic foliage will remain evergreen in mild winters.

Clematis ligusticifolia	Zones 4a to 9b	Ranunculaceae

western white clematis

This deciduous vine can produce woody stems to 20m (60ft) long. The leaves are pinnately compound into five to seven leaflets up to 6cm (2.5in) long, with lobed and usually coarsely toothed margins. The plants are dioecious, with male and female flowers on separate plants; the flowers lack petals, but have four small, creamy sepals to 1.5cm (.5in) long. The male (staminate) flowers consist only of stamens; the female (pistillate) flowers usually have sterile stamens surrounding the cluster of pistils. These mature into one-seeded achenes with long, plumose (feather-like) styles up to 5cm (2in) long. Flowers bloom in leafy panicles from early to late summer, but the showy clusters of achenes last into the fall and are at least as attractive.

Cultivation. Full sun or part shade, and well-drained, fairly moist soil. This is one of our few native vines, a good plant to grow on fences, stumps, or larger shrubs and trees on either side of the Cascades. Excellent for a trellis, or allow it to scramble into the hedgerow.

Propagation. Grow from seed collected as soon as it is ripe in late summer or early fall and planted soon after harvest. Sow seeds into containers or directly into the garden, and leave them outside over winter for germination in the spring. Alternatively, take semi-hardwood cuttings in the summer, or tip cuttings in spring. Stems can be layered during the spring.

Native Habitat and Range. Near streams and moist places near sagebrush and ponderosa pine woods at low to mid elevations from British Columbia, east of the Cascades, south to the Columbia River Gorge and on both sides of the Cascades in Oregon, south through California and east to the Dakotas and New Mexico.

Notes. The widespread *C. l.* var. *ligusticifolia* and the more western *C. l.* var. *brevifolia* both occur in our area. *Clematis* includes around 200 species, most of which occur throughout the temperate parts of the Northern Hemisphere; nearly 30 species are native to North America, three others to our area. Rock clematis (*C. columbiana*), another scrambling, vine-like plant, has leaves divided into three leaflets (ternate), nodding blue to purplish flowers, and achenes with long, plumose styles; it grows in dry to moist woods and in talus on the east slope of the Cascades and east through the Rocky Mountains, and is more cooperative in east-side gardens. *Clematis hirsutissima* (hairy clematis, sugar bowls, vase flower) is another species of dry grasslands, sagebrush plains, and ponderosa pine woods east of the Cascades and east through the Rocky Mountains. This upright perennial has single, nodding purplish flowers and grows from a woody crown; plants are generally woolly, the leaves are finely divided into narrow segments, and the hairy achenes have long, plumose styles. Western blue clematis (*C. occidentalis*), with trailing stems to about 2m (6ft), ranges through eastern British Columbia, Washington, and northeastern Oregon.

Clematis ligusticifolia

Cornus   Cornaceae

dogwood

Cornus includes around 30 species, most of them shrubs or small trees. They are primarily native to the temperate parts of North America (the majority in the east), Asia, and Europe, with a few in South America and Africa. The flowers are small, and their parts are in fours, usually arranged in heads or flat-topped clusters. Many species have large, showy, petaloid bracts subtending the inflorescence. Dogwood flowers have inferior ovaries, and the fruit is a berry-like drupe containing a pit (the hardened, innermost wall of the ovary) with two seeds inside. The attractive fruits are red or white.

Propagation. Collect ripe fruits in the fall, and plant them outside into flats of potting soil to stratify in the cold, moist winter weather; unless fruits are being stored, it's not necessary to remove the fleshy part before planting. Even bunchberry (*C. unalaschkensis*), although it is a rhizomatous plant, is most easily propagated from seed, and red-twig dogwood (*C. sericea*) is as easy to grow as willows from hardwood cuttings taken from late fall to late winter. These can be treated with hormones, but they will form roots in a bucket of moist soil without hormones. Cuttings can also be taken during the growing season but must be kept humid until roots form.

Cornus nuttallii   Zones 5b to 9b

Pacific dogwood

This deciduous tree can reach 20m (60ft) but is often shorter, with an angular branching pattern. The leaves are opposite and elliptic to ovate with pointed tips. They have short petioles and are up to 10cm (4in) long, turning red, pink, and yellow in the fall. The small flowers bloom in densely crowded heads and are subtended by four to seven white or pinkish bracts up to 7cm (3in) long. Flowers bloom from mid spring to early summer, and often again in the fall. The fruits are bright red drupes to 1cm (.5in) long, ripening in rounded clusters.

Cultivation. Part shade or dappled light, and moist, well-drained soil. Find an open spot, for good air circulation, but with some shade; this species tends to sunburn. This is one of the best known and most beautiful trees in the Pacific Northwest but also one of the most difficult to grow. It is more susceptible to anthracnose fungus than other dogwoods, a pathogen that is especially damaging in moister climates. Once established, it prefers little or no summer water, so plant it out of the reach of irrigation (it often does well in shady parking strips with conifers). For many gardeners, the spectacular flowers and autumn colors are worth the trouble. Pacific dogwood is also a fine tree for wildlife. The fruits are a favorite of many birds, and caterpillar larvae eat the foliage.

Native Habitat and Range. In moist, well-drained, open to dense forests and near streams at low to mid elevations from southwestern British Columbia, south to southern California, and from the coast through the coastal mountains and east to the west slope of the Cascades and Sierra Nevada; northern Idaho.

Notes. 'Eddie's White Wonder' is a hybrid, the result of a cross between this species and *C. florida*, the best known of the eastern species. Other cultivars include 'Colrigo Giant' and the variegated 'Goldspot', which is propagated from grafts. Indigenous people used the bark of this tree as a medicine and the wood for making various tools. Pacific dogwood is the provincial flower of British Columbia.

Cornus sericea	Zones 3b to 9b

red-twig or red-osier dogwood

This deciduous shrub produces many stems up to 6m (18ft), spreading to form thickets when lower branches grow horizontally and take root where they touch the ground. The older branches have gray-green bark. The bark of the younger stems is smooth and bright red or purplish. The opposite leaves have pointed tips and evenly spaced lateral veins that converge along the leaf margin; they are ovate or elliptic in shape, up to 10cm (4in) long, turning shades of red in autumn. The small, white flowers have four petals and are clustered into flat-topped inflorescences to 6cm (2.5in) across, blooming from late spring to mid summer. The small, berry-like drupes are white or pale bluish.

Cultivation. Full sun to full shade, and moist to wet soil. The bark and fall foliage will be showier when plants have some sun. This versatile shrub is attractive through all seasons and has been in cultivation for many years. Plant it in the hedgerow, shrub border, or wildlife garden: this species provides cover and food for birds, and butterfly larvae eat the foliage. It also does a good job of controlling erosion and tolerates winter flooding, making it an excellent choice for a bog, wetland margin, stream, or ditch bank.

Native Habitat and Range. Along streams, wetlands, and in moist to wet woods at low to mid elevations, throughout much of North America, from Alaska south to California and New Mexico, east through the northern plains to the Atlantic.

Notes. Often classified as *C. stolonifera*. The several cultivars include 'Flaviramea' (the well-known yellow-twig dogwood), 'Insanti' (compact), 'Kelseyi' (dwarf), and the variegated 'Silver and Gold', with yellow branches and green leaves edged with cream. *Cornus s.* ssp. *occidentalis* (western dogwood) is found primarily from the coast to the west slope of the Cascades, ranging east to Idaho and western Montana; *C. s.* ssp. *sericea* occurs throughout the Pacific Northwest and has a wider distribution across the continent. The subspecies vary in characters of the flowers, fruit, and pubescence.

Cornus nuttallii

Cornus sericea in fall

Cornus sericea

Cornus unalaschkensis	Zones 3b to 9b

bunchberry

This trailing, rhizomatous groundcover is woody at the base, but the stems are mainly herbaceous, growing to 20cm (8in) tall. The leaves are green on the upper surface and pale beneath, often evergreen, and growing in whorls of four to seven near the stem tips. They are ovate to elliptic, up to 8cm (3in) long, with parallel veins, and mounted on very short petioles. The lower part of the stem usually has a pair of opposite leaves. The true flowers are tiny, greenish white to purplish and crowded into an umbel-like cluster. The inflorescence is subtended by four white, pinkish or purple-tinged, petaloid bracts up to 2.5cm (1in) long. Flowering takes place from early to late summer. The fruits are shiny red drupes, a bit less than 1cm (.5in) long.

Cultivation. Shade, part sun, or dappled light, and moist, acidic soil with lots of organic matter. Often slow to establish and may benefit by adding some chunks of rotting wood to the planting hole to act as underground "nurse logs." This beautiful little groundcover is lovely among ferns and shrubs in the shade garden. Plant it along paths, in logs or stumps, or near a water feature in the wildlife garden, where birds can enjoy the fruits.

Native Habitat and Range. In moist forests, meadows, and bogs, often growing on logs or stumps at low to fairly high elevations, from Alaska and British Columbia, south to Washington, Oregon, northern Idaho, and northwestern California,

Notes. *Cornus suecica* (Lapland or Swedish cornel) is similar; it has a whorl of leaves at the stem tip, but it also has a couple of pairs of well-developed, opposite leaves on the lower part of the stems. The tiny flowers are purplish. This is a species of arctic distribution, ranging into parts of Alaska and British Columbia. Another bunchberry, *C. canadensis*, occurs in eastern Asia and North America, from Alaska south to northern Washington and Idaho, through the mountains to New Mexico, and east to Greenland; it has a whorl of leaves at the stem tip with a pair of small, opposite bracts on the lower part of the stem. Some consider *C. unalaschkensis* and *C. canadensis* synonymous; others speculate that *C. unalaschkensis* is a natural hybrid between *C. canadensis* and *C. suecica*. Many bunchberries offered in nurseries are *C. canadensis*.

Corylus cornuta	Zones 3b to 9b	Betulaceae

beaked or California hazelnut or filbert

This multi-stemmed, deciduous shrub can grow to 5m (15ft) tall and almost as wide. The alternate leaves are oval, up to 10cm (4in) long, with heart-shaped bases and pointed tips. The leaves have short petioles, are hairy on both surfaces and have doubly serrated margins. They turn yellow in the fall. The plants are monoecious, with male and female flowers in separate structures on the same shrub. Tiny male flowers are crowded into drooping catkins up to 7cm (3in) long. A few female flowers bloom in a small cluster surrounded by bud-like bracts; tiny but colorful, the elongated styles and stigmas of the pistillate flowers look like small, ruby-red spiders. Hazelnuts are some of the earliest plants to bloom, flowering from mid winter to early spring, well before the leaves expand. The fruits are hard-shelled, rounded nuts about 1.5cm (.5in) long and enclosed in a roughly hairy bract, elongated beyond the nut to form a "beak."

Cultivation. Full sun to full shade, and moist to rather dry, well-drained soil. An excellent wildlife plant, providing cover and food, and a good choice for the hedgerow. Site in the sunny or shady, moist or fairly dry parts of the wildlife or woodland garden. Although not aggressive, plants develop suckers and eventually form thickets of arching branches.

Propagation. Easiest from seed. Collect nuts in late summer or early fall, just before they ripen (and the squirrels get them all), while the husks are still a bit green. Plant the nuts, with or without husks, outside soon after harvest in the fall so that they will stratify under cool, moist winter conditions and germinate the following spring. Another method is to remove suckers

Cornus unalaschkensis

Cornus unalaschkensis, fruits

Corylus cornuta var. *californica*

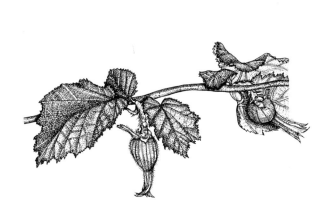

Corylus cornuta var. californica

Crataegus douglasii

from existing plants in late winter or early spring. Hazelnuts can also be layered by nicking a branch, bending it so that the nicked area can be buried, and then holding the branch in place until roots form; this is best done in the fall. They can also be grown from semi-hardwood cuttings taken in late summer or fall.

Native Habitat and Range. In open forests, thickets, clearings, and streambanks, in moist but well-drained soil, at low to mid elevations from British Columbia south to central California, and east to Newfoundland.

Notes. *Corylus c.* var. *californica* has a limited distribution west of the Cascades; it has hairier twigs and the "beak" of the husk is short. *Corylus c.* var. *cornuta* has a much larger range, from northeastern Washington and eastern British Columbia, east to the Atlantic and southeastern states; these plants are less hairy, and the "beak" of the husk is at least twice as long as the nut. *Corylus* includes about a dozen species of deciduous shrubs and trees native to the temperate parts of the Northern Hemisphere, mostly to Asia. Filberts are a major agricultural crop in the Pacific Northwest; most of our orchards are planted with cultivars of the European species *C. avellana* (common filbert) and *C. maxima* (giant filbert). Our native hazelnuts are resistant to eastern filbert blight, but their sale is restricted in Oregon as a precaution to control the disease.

| ***Crataegus douglasii*** | Zones 3b to 9b | Rosaceae |

black hawthorn

This small, deciduous tree or large shrub grows 3 to 10m (9 to 30ft) tall and tends to spread underground, sprouting suckers and forming thickets. The branches have sharp thorns about 2cm (1in) long. The alternate leaves grow to 6cm (2.5in) long and are often doubly serrate as well as shallowly lobed along the upper margins; they are oblong (widest in the middle) to obovate (widest toward the tip) in shape, and turn from green to pretty shades of red in the fall. The flowers bloom in small clusters from late spring to early summer; they are about 1cm (.5in) across and have five white petals. The edible fruits are pomes (like little apples), blackish purple and about 1cm (.5in) long.

Cultivation. Full sun or part shade, and well-drained, moist soil. This is an excellent small tree for the wildlife garden or large hedgerow, providing food, nesting sites, and thorny cover for birds; plants will eventually form thickets if not controlled, however, which may please birds but not all gardeners. Butterflies and hummingbirds also find hawthorns attractive, and deer usually ignore them.

Propagation. Grow from seed collected as soon as pomes ripen in summer, before the birds get them all. Clean the pulp from the seeds, and plant them in containers outside soon after harvest, leaving them to stratify in the cool, moist winter weather. Some seeds will germinate the following spring; others may take longer to break dormancy.

Native Habitat and Range. Along streams and roads, in meadows, thickets, and forest margins at low to mid elevations, from southern Alaska south on both sides of the Cascades to California, and east to the Great Lakes, south to Wyoming and Nevada.

Notes. This species now includes *C. columbiana* (Columbia hawthorn), plants with long thorns and deep reddish fruits. *Crataegus suksdorfii* (*C. d.* var. *suksdorfii*; Suksdorf's hawthorn) has more numerous stamens, a hairless ovary, and leaves that are more oblong in shape; it is scattered from southern Alaska, south through Oregon and east to northern Idaho. *Crataegus* is a genus of a few hundred species, mostly native to the temperate parts of the Northern Hemisphere; only a handful of species are native to the Pacific Northwest. Hawthorn wood is very tough and was used for various tools by many groups of people. The thorns too had many uses, and the bark has been used medicinally. The fruits are edible but dry; they are sometimes made into jelly.

Dasiphora fruticosa ssp. floribunda	Zones 3b to 9b	Rosaceae

shrubby cinquefoil

This deciduous shrub varies from spreading to erect and grows to an average height of 1m (3ft). The bark is reddish brown and shredding. The small leaves are pinnately compound, usually with five leaflets; they grow to 2.5cm (1in), including the petiole, and are generally pubescent with silky hairs. Bright yellow, five-petaled flowers, about 2.5cm (1in) across, bloom in small clusters among the leaves from early to late summer. The fruits are small achenes.

Cultivation. Full sun to part shade, and moist to rather dry soil. This is a good, drought-tolerant shrub to establish along the driveway or in other places where minimum maintenance is desired. Plant it in the low shrub bed, rock garden, or in the hedgerow.

Propagation. Grow from seed collected in the late summer and planted outside into flats of potting soil to spend the winter under cool, moist conditions. Seeds will germinate when the weather warms up in the spring.

Native Habitat and Range. In moist meadows and rocky slopes, from the foothills to high elevations, Alaska, south through the Olympic and Cascade Mountains to the Sierra Nevada of California, Colorado, and New Mexico, east to the Great Lakes and the Atlantic; Eurasia.

Notes. For some time this was the lone woody species in *Potentilla*, as *P. fruticosa*, but it is now back in *Dasiphora*. The many available cultivars of this plant include 'Goldfinger' and 'Jackman's Variety' (bright yellow flowers); 'Gold Star' and 'Klondike' (yellow flowers but low-growing); 'Abbotswood' and 'Mount Everest' (white-flowered); 'Red Ace', 'Sunset', and 'Tangerine' (orange or red flowers, low-growing), and 'Floppy Disc', a low-growing, spreading double pink. Cultivars with deeper-colored flowers will fade in blazing summer sun and may look better in part shade,

Dasiphora fruticosa ssp. *floribunda*

Dryas drummondii

Dryas octopetala

Dryas
Rosaceae

mountain-avens

Dryas is a genus of prostrate, generally evergreen shrubs often grown in rock gardens; perhaps six species are native to arctic or high alpine habitats of the Northern Hemisphere. The woody branches of these mat-forming plants develop roots where they touch the ground. The delicate flowers are followed by equally attractive fruits, achenes with long, plumose styles.

Propagation. Divide rooted clumps or branches in the spring; or make semi-hardwood cuttings from the trailing stems during the summer, treat with hormones, and set to root under humid conditions. Plants can also be grown from seed collected after ripening and planted outside in the fall to spend the winter stratifying under cold, moist conditions. This cold treatment is required to break dormancy, but germination percentage is still likely to be low.

Dryas drummondii   Zones 3b to 8b

yellow mountain-avens

The leaves of this evergreen, mat-forming shrub are ovate to oblong, dark green above and white with woolly hairs beneath; they grow to 3cm (1.5in) long and have small, rounded teeth along the margins. The leafless flowering stems grow to 20cm (8in) tall. Each bears a single, nodding flower, about 2.5cm (1in) across, with eight to ten pale to deep yellow petals. Flowering occurs from late spring to mid summer. The many separate achenes with long, feathery styles are as showy as the flowers.

Cultivation. Full sun to light shade, and well-drained, moist to rather dry soil. This popular rock garden plant will grow in the lowlands as well as at high elevations. Makes a nice groundcover among the rocks and paving stones along a sunny garden path, patio, or driveway.

Native Habitat and Range. On ridges and talus slopes and along streams, from foothills (in the northern part of the range) to high alpine areas, from Alaska through British Columbia, south in the northern Washington Cascades to northeastern Washington, the Wallowa Mountains of northeastern Oregon, and Montana.

Notes. *Dryas d.* var. *drummondii* ranges south into the high mountains of our area.

Dryas octopetala   Zones 3b to 8b

white or eight-petal mountain-avens

The leaves of this usually evergreen, mat-forming shrub are oblong to lanceolate with scalloped margins, dark green above and glandular or white with woolly hairs beneath. They grow to 3cm (1.5in) long and have a crinkly (rugose) surface. The leafless flowering stems grow to 15cm (6in) tall. Each stem bears a single white to creamy flower, about 2.5cm (1in) across, with eight to ten petals. Flowers are produced from early to late summer. The clusters of achenes with long, feathery styles are as attractive as the flowers.

Cultivation. Full sun or light shade, and well-drained, moist to rather dry or rocky soil. This alpine species nevertheless grows well in the lowlands and can tolerate reflected summer heat from pavement. A favorite plant for the rock garden or stone wall, it also makes a nice groundcover among the rocks and paving stones near a sunny garden path or driveway.

Native Habitat and Range. In gravel bars, rocky meadows, and talus slopes, at mid to high elevations, from Alaska, south to the Cascades of Washington, the mountains of northeastern Oregon, Idaho, and the Rocky Mountains to Utah and Colorado, east to Labrador; Europe and Asia.

Notes. North American populations of this species are difficult to propagate, even from cuttings. *Dryas ×suendermannii*, a hybrid between it and *D. drummondii*, has nodding flowers that are yellow in bud, becoming white as they open.

Elaeagnus commutata	Zones 3b to 8b	Elaeagnaceae

silverberry, wolf-willow

This deciduous shrub has an erect or spreading habit, growing 1 to 4m (3 to 12ft) and producing suckers from woody rhizomes. The bark is dark reddish with silvery scales. The leaves are also silvery, sometimes with brownish dots on the undersides; they are alternate, with short petioles and lance-shaped blades to 7cm (3in) long with entire margins. One to three small flowers about 1cm (.5in) long bloom in the leaf axils from late spring to mid summer; they lack petals, consisting only of a tubular hypanthium topped by a four-lobed calyx and four stamens. They are silver on the outside and yellow within, not showy, but sweetly fragrant. The silvery fruits, actually one-seeded achenes surrounded by the dry hypanthium, look like berries or drupes.

Cultivation. Full sun to light shade, and well-drained, moist to rather dry soil. This fast-growing, drought-tolerant shrub is a good choice for a dry bank, parking area, or hedgerow, and an excellent choice for the wildlife garden: although humans will find the fruits dry and mealy, birds think they're delicious. Plant it near a deck or patio, where the fragrance of the tiny flowers can be enjoyed. Tends to sucker and form thickets, adding to habitat value.

Propagation. Easy by removing suckers in late winter or early spring, by layering branches in the fall, from semi-hardwood cuttings made in summer, or from hardwood cuttings made in fall or winter. Plants can also be grown from seed harvested in the fall, planted outside, and left to cold stratify over winter; some seeds will germinate the following spring, but many may take longer.

Native Habitat and Range. In rocky areas, gravelly ledges and along streams from Alaska and British Columbia, mainly east of the Cascades, south to eastern Washington, Idaho, and through the Rocky Mountains to Utah and Colorado, east to Minnesota and Quebec.

Notes. *Elaeagnus* includes around 30 species of shrubs and small trees, almost all native to southern Europe and Asia. This is the only species native to North America.

Elliottia pyroliflorus	Zones 6a to 9b	Ericaceae

copperbush

This deciduous shrub grows to 2m (6ft) or more. The leaves, to 5cm (2in) in length, are light green, alternately arranged, elliptic, and waxy (glaucous) with smooth (entire) margins. The interesting flowers are a light coppery or salmon color. They have five spreading petals, are about 3cm (1.5in) across, and bloom singly from early to mid summer. The fruits are rounded capsules.

Cultivation. Shade or part sun, and moist, acidic soil. With its pale orange flowers, this is an interesting shrub for the edge of the shady bog or pond, or the wet spot in the woodland garden.

Propagation. Collect the capsules just as they are ripening in the fall, allow them to dry, and remove the small seeds. Plant the seeds in late winter in a moist acidic, peaty medium, keeping them out of direct light. It will take a few years for plants to reach blooming size.

Native Habitat and Range. Streambanks, moist forests, and bog margins from foothills to high elevations, from Alaska south through British Columbia, west of the Cascade crest to the Washington Olympics and Saddle Mountain in northwestern Oregon.

Notes. Sometimes classified as *Cladothamnus pyroliflorus*. The only other species in the genus is the rare *E. racemosa*, found in Georgia.

Elaeagnus commutata

Elliottia pyroliflorus

Empetrum nigrum

| *Empetrum nigrum* | Zones 3b to 9b | Empetraceae |

black crowberry

This small, heather-like shrub grows to 15cm (6in) tall, forming mats with its trailing stems to 30cm (1ft) long. The evergreen leaves are linear and less than 1cm (.5in) long, arranged alternately or in whorls of four on the stems. The tiny flowers are purplish but inconspicuous, blooming in the leaf axils from late spring to mid summer. Male and female flowers are on the same plant (monoecious). The attractive fruits are round, black or purplish, berry-like drupes, each containing several one-seeded pits.

Cultivation. Full sun to part shade, and wet to fairly dry soil. This is a charming little shrub for the alpine rock garden, pond, or bog margin. Plant it between the stones of a retaining wall and allow it to cascade gracefully. Most people don't find the fruits very palatable, but they are juicy and used for jam by some, and birds will eat them.

Propagation. Usually from cuttings taken during the growing season. Treat cuttings with hormones and set to root in pumice or some other medium, keeping the cuttings humid until roots form. Plants can be grown from seeds planted in the fall and left outside for spring germination. Layering the branches can also be tried.

Native Habitat and Range. In dry or wet sites, including bogs, rocky coastal bluffs, and alpine tundra, at low to high elevations, generally circumpolar, widespread in British Columbia, south through the mountains of western Washington and near the coast in Oregon to northwestern California east to New York; Eurasia.

Notes. Both *E. n.* ssp. *hermaphroditum* and *E. n.* ssp. *nigrum* occur in our area. There are only a couple of other species in *Empetrum*, native to northeastern North America and South America.

| *Ericameria* | | Asteraceae |

rabbitbrush

Approximately 30 species of *Ericameria* occur in western North America, including *E. bloomeri* (*Haplopappus bloomeri*; rabbitbrush goldenweed), *E. nana* (*H. nanus*; dwarf goldenweed), *E. greenei* (*H. greenei*; Greene's goldenweed), *E. arborescens* (goldenfleece), and *E. discoidea* (whitestem goldenbush), among others. As the synonyms tell you, many (but not all) species of another yellow-flowered group of composites, the goldenweeds (*Haplopappus* spp.) have been moved into *Ericameria*, as have some species that were long placed in *Chrysothamnus*.

Propagation. Grow from seed collected in late fall and planted soon after harvest or stored under cool, dry conditions and sown in the spring. Seeds can be planted directly into the garden or into containers of well-drained potting soil for later transplanting; they need no special pretreatments, but their viability, and so percent germination, is often low. Plants can also be grown from hardwood cuttings made in early spring, before new growth begins, treated with hormones, and set into pumice or some other well-drained medium until roots form.

| *Ericameria nauseosa* | Zones 3b to 9b | |

gray or rubber rabbitbrush

This deciduous shrub can grow to 2m (6ft) but is often much shorter. The twigs and leaves are covered with fine, feltlike white hairs, giving the plants a soft, silvery appearance. The leaves are alternately arranged, linear, and up to 7cm (3in) long. The small flowering heads are arranged into flat-topped clusters at the stem tips. The heads consist only of disk florets with showy,

Ericameria nauseosa (photo by Sally A. Simmons)   Ericameria viscidiflora

golden yellow corollas to 1cm (.5in) long. The flowers bloom from late summer to mid fall, and the fruits, small achenes, are topped with a pappus (modified calyx) of slender bristles.

Cultivation. Full sun or light shade, and well-drained, rather dry soil. This is a lovely, fall-blooming shrub for gardens in dry climates and requires no care once established. Plant it with other drought-tolerant plants in a hedgerow or parking area, or along a road. A good addition to butterfly or wildlife gardens east of the Cascades and in southwestern Oregon.

Native Habitat and Range. In dry, open places, often in alkaline soils, at low to mid elevations from southern British Columbia east to Saskatchewan and south, mainly east of the Cascades (but further west in southern Oregon), through California, Arizona, and Texas, east through the Great Plains.

Notes. Sometimes classified as *Chrysothamnus nauseosus*. This species often grows with *Artemisia tridentata*; but, unlike big sagebrush, it is able to resprout after a fire, so it often forms extensive stands. Both subspecies of this highly variable species occur in our area. *Ericameria n.* ssp. *consimilis* includes eight varieties, most of them native to the Southwest; only *E. n.* ssp. *c.* var. *oreophila* ranges into Oregon and Idaho. *Ericameria n.* ssp. *nauseosa* includes 14 varieties; three range into our area.

Ericameria viscidiflora   Zones 4a to 9b

green rabbitbrush

This small, deciduous shrub grows to 1m (3ft) and about as wide. The brittle stems are glabrous (hairless) or sometimes finely hairy. The linear leaves are alternately arranged, up to 6cm (2.5in) long by 1cm (.5in) wide, and often twisted. Small, sticky flowering heads bloom in flat-topped clusters at the branch tips from mid summer to early fall; the disk florets have bright yellow corollas. The fruits are small achenes with a pappus (modified calyx) of slender bristles.

Cultivation. Full sun or light shade, and well-drained, rather dry soil. An excellent fall-blooming shrub for drought-tolerant gardens east of the Cascades. Plant it with sagebrush and other shrubs in the wildlife garden, hedgerow, parking area, or roadside. It's also a good addition to the butterfly garden.

Native Habitat and Range. In dry, open plains and slopes, often with sagebrush, at low to mid elevations from southern British Columbia, east of the Cascades, south through California and east to Montana, Nebraska, Colorado, and New Mexico.

Notes. Often classified as *Chrysothamnus viscidiflorus*, with three subspecies occurring in our area: ssp. *lanceolatus*, ssp. *puberulus*, and ssp. *viscidiflorus*.

Eriogonum	Polygonaceae

buckwheat

Eriogonum includes more than 200 species of annuals, perennials, and small shrubs, all native to North America, especially the arid regions of the west; about a quarter of these occur in the Pacific Northwest, mostly east of the Cascades, with a few in the rocky places of the high mountains. The small, shrubby species make fine rock garden plants, but they dislike wet climates and are generally easier to grow east of the Cascades. The leaves aren't really evergreen, but after they wither, the old leaves and dried petioles tend to remain on the branches. The three petals and three sepals of the flowers are usually white, yellow, or pinkish, and so similar that they are collectively referred to simply as the perianth. The small flowers are usually clustered into heads or simple to compound umbels. Each small cluster of flowers is subtended by a cup-like involucre (a bract located beneath a group of flowers), and whorls of leaf-like bracts are often present at the branching points or circling the peduncle of the larger inflorescence. Each flower produces a small fruit, a single-seeded, usually three-angled achene. Buckwheat flowers are a good source of nectar for insects, including butterflies and honeybees, and seed-eating birds enjoy the achenes.

Propagation. Grow from seed collected in the summer and planted in the fall. Sow seeds into containers of coarse, well-drained potting soil or directly into the garden, and leave them outside to stratify over winter. Seeds will germinate the following spring and should be kept on the dry side to protect them from damping-off fungus. Established plants may provide seedlings, and these can be transplanted while they are small.

Eriogonum compositum	Zones 5a to 8a

northern or arrowleaf buckwheat

This shrubby perennial develops a branching crown from a woody taproot and tends to form a mat to 30cm (1ft) across. The leaves are basal, about 15cm (6in) long, including the slender petioles. The blades are up to 5cm (2in) wide and triangular to heart-shaped, thinly hairy, and mainly green on the upper surface, and white with dense hairs beneath. Tiny flowers bloom from late spring to mid summer in an inflorescence of compound umbels to up 20cm (8in) across, subtended by linear bracts; flowers vary in color from cream to lemon-yellow. The fruits, small achenes, are somewhat hairy.

Cultivation. Full sun or light shade, and well-drained, rocky or gravelly soil. This is a choice, mat-forming shrublet for the rock garden with distinctive, two-toned leaves and showy flowers. It is also a good plant for the dry parts of the butterfly garden.

Native Habitat and Range. On rocky slopes and talus at low to fairly high elevations, east of the Cascades from central Washington, south to northern California and east to Idaho.

Eriogonum compositum (photo by Sally A. Simmons)

Eriogonum douglasii

Notes. Barestem buckwheat (*E. nudum*), a white, yellowish or pink-flowered subshrub that blooms from early to late summer, is native to sandy or gravelly soils and roadsides on both sides of the Cascades, at low to fairly high elevations; it is common west of the mountains in Oregon and to the south, making it a good choice for rock or butterfly gardens and dry meadows in wetter climates.

Eriogonum douglasii	Zones 5a to 9a

Douglas' buckwheat

This low-growing shrublet forms leafy mats to 10cm (4in) tall. The leaves are linear or spoon-shaped (spatulate), up to 2cm (1in) long, and silvery with white hairs, often on both surfaces. Flowering peduncles grow to 10cm (4in), each with a whorl of leaf-like bracts in the middle. The single, head-like cluster of tiny flowers blooms from a single, cup-like involucre at the tip of the stem. The petal-like perianth segments are usually hairy and vary from cream to pinkish or lemon. The flowers bloom from late spring to mid summer, and the small achenes have hairy tips.

Cultivation. Full sun to light shade, and well-drained, fairly dry soil. This is a small, attractive mat-forming shrublet for the rock garden or crevices in a stone wall. It can also be planted near a trail at the dry edge of the drought-tolerant wildlife or butterfly garden.

Native Habitat and Range. On dry hillsides near sagebrush or ponderosa pine, at fairly low to high elevations east of the Cascades from central Washington, south through the Sierra Nevada of California and east to Nevada.

Notes. *Eriogonum d.* var. *douglasii* occurs throughout the range; *E. d.* var. *sublineare* is restricted to south-central Washington and north-central Oregon.

Eriogonum heracleoides (photo by Sally A. Simmons)

Eriogonum niveum

Eriogonum heracleoides	Zones 3b to 8a

parsnip-flowered buckwheat

This shrubby-based buckwheat forms mats to 60cm (2ft) across and about 30cm (1ft) tall. The leaves are linear to lance- or narrowly spoon-shaped and about 5cm (2in) long. They are covered with gray hair, but sometimes greenish on the upper surface. Flowering peduncles grow to 30cm (1ft) tall and usually have a whorl of leaf-like bracts in the middle. The inflorescence is branched to form a compound umbel with small, leafy bracts developing at the branch points. Small flowers, varying from white to cream or slightly pinkish, bloom from hairy, cup-like involucres. Flowering occurs from late spring to mid summer, and the fruits, small achenes, are hairy on the upper half.

Cultivation. Full sun to light shade, and well-drained, fairly dry soil. This is a small, attractive mat-forming shrublet for the rock garden or crevices in a stone wall. It can also be planted on a dry slope or near a trail at the edge of the drought-tolerant wildlife or butterfly garden.

Native Habitat and Range. In well-drained or gravelly soil in arid shrub-steppe or ponderosa pine habitats at low to fairly high elevations east of the Cascade crest from southern British Columbia, south to northeastern California and east to Montana, Wyoming and Colorado.

Notes. In addition to the widespread *E. h.* var. *heracleoides*, *E. h.* var. *angustifolium* and *E. h.* var. *leucophaeum* also occur in the Pacific Northwest; the three are separated by characteristics of the leaves and the presence of leafy bracts on the flowering stems.

Erlogonum nlveurn   Zones 5a to 8a

snow buckwheat

This plant grows from a branched crown and woody taproot, forming low-growing mats or upright stems to 60cm (2ft). The leaves tend to grow in basal tufts and are about 6cm (2.5in) long, with ovate or elliptic leaf blades and slender petioles. They are silvery with white hairs on both sides. The inflorescence is freely branching and leafy-bracted, with small clusters of flowers blooming at the tips and branching points. The small flowers are white or cream to pinkish, often becoming pink as they age. They bloom late in the season, from mid summer to early fall or a bit later. The small achenes are hairless (glabrous).

Cultivation. Full sun to light shade, and rocky, well-drained soil. An excellent, fall-blooming shrublet for the rock garden or the dry parts of the wildlife or butterfly garden, where the late-season nectar and seeds will be enjoyed by butterflies and birds. Try it spilling over a stone retaining wall.

Native Habitat and Range. On sandy to poorly drained soils and rocky places in arid shrub-steppe to open ponderosa pine woods, at low to mid elevations on the east slope of the Cascades from southern British Columbia, south to central Oregon and east to Idaho.

Notes. The variable *E. strictum* (Blue Mountain or strict buckwheat) is a similar but earlier-blooming species with a branching inflorescence and cream, pink, or yellow flowers; it lives in similar sagebrush habitats from north central Washington, south to California and Nevada and east to Montana.

Eriogonum pyrolifolium   Zones 4a to 8a

alpine or Shasta buckwheat

This buckwheat forms low tufts from a woody taproot and branched crown. The leaves are all basal, with oval to elliptic blades about 5cm (2in) long, including the petiole; they are usually hairy underneath and greenish on the upper surface. The flowering peduncles grow to 15cm (6in) tall and are leafless except for a pair of bracts just beneath the single umbel of flowers. The small flowers vary from white or greenish to reddish and are usually pubescent with reddish hairs; they bloom from mid to late summer and have an unpleasant smell. The anthers are purplish. The achenes are hairy on the upper half.

Cultivation. Full sun, and very well-drained soil high in pumice or gravel. This is an unusual plant for rock, trough, or wildlife gardens in dry climates or at high elevations. The flowers attract butterflies and birds enjoy the seeds.

Native Habitat and Range. In talus, pumice, and rocky ridges at mid to high elevations through the Cascades from south central British Columbia, south to northern California and east to Montana.

Notes. Both *E. p.* var. *pyrolifolium* and *E. p.* var. *coryphaeum* occur in our area; they are separated by degree of pubescence. *Eriogonum ovalifolium* (oval-leaved or cushion buckwheat) is another species native to rocky, alpine ridges as well as ponderosa pine woods and shrub-steppe habitats; the flowers are cream to yellow or purplish and bloom in simple, head-like umbels from late spring to late summer, depending on elevation. This mound-forming plant occurs throughout the west, four of its ten varieties in the Pacific Northwest.

Eriogonum sphaerocephalum   Zones 4b to 8a

rock buckwheat

This branching shrublet grows to 40cm (16in) tall. The numerous leaves are linear to narrowly spoon-shaped, growing in whorls at the branch tips. They are about 2.5cm (1in) long and usually white with woolly hairs beneath, but sometimes greenish on the upper surface. The flowering stems grow to 10cm (4in) and are sometimes branched, with two or more umbels, and leafy-bracted at the branch points. The tiny flowers are usually yellow or white, sometimes creamy or pinkish, blooming from late spring to mid summer. The small achenes have hairy tips.

Cultivation. Full sun or light shade, and well-drained, rather dry soil high in pumice or gravel. This is a lovely mound-forming shrub for the rock garden or other dry, rocky site. Plant it with sagebrush and other drought-tolerant plants in the butterfly or wildlife garden.

Native Habitat and Range. On dry, rocky sites, often near sagebrush or ponderosa pine, at low to fairly high elevations east of the Cascade crest from central Washington south to north-eastern California and east to Idaho and Nevada.

Notes. Both *E. s.* var. *sphaerocephalum* and *E. s.* var. *halimioides*, mainly differentiated by flower color and leaf characters, occur throughout the range.

Eriogonum thymoides   Zones 5a to 8a

thyme-leaf buckwheat

This finely branching, miniature shrub forms a cushion to 15cm (6in) tall. The many small leaves are linear or narrowly spoon-shaped, about 1cm (.5in) long, woolly and curled under along the margins (revolute). The flowering stems grow to 8cm (3in) tall, with a whorl of leaf-like bracts at the middle of the stem. Tiny flowers bloom in compact, simple umbels, from involucres with short, upright lobes. The petal-like perianths are often densely hairy on the outside and vary in color from yellow or creamy to deep rosy pink. Flowers bloom from mid spring to early summer. Thyme-leaf buckwheat plants are dioecious, either male or female. The small, hair-topped achenes will be found only on female plants.

Cultivation. Full sun, and well-drained, stony or gravelly soil. One of the most charming, mat-forming shrublets for the rock or trough garden. It can be planted into the cracks and crevices of a wall or some other stone feature where there is room for the roots to grow.

Native Habitat and Range. On open, rocky ridges and stony ground, often near sagebrush, at fairly low to mid elevations east of the Cascades from north central Washington, south through eastern Oregon to southwestern Idaho.

Notes. These tiny shrubs were once harvested and sold in large numbers, often shipped to Hawaii. They are too slow-growing and uncommon to be dug from the wild and should be grown only from seed.

Eriogonum umbellatum   Zones 4a to 9b

sulfur-flowered buckwheat

This taprooted shrub produces prostrate branches from a woody crown, forming mats to 60cm (2ft) across and up to 30cm (1ft) tall. The leaves are basal and variable, with oval to oblong blades to 3cm (1.5in) long on slender petioles. They are usually gray with woolly hairs underneath and mostly greenish on the upper surface. The flowering stems produce simple or compound umbels, with leafy bracts developing at the branching points of the inflorescence. The tiny flowers are usually light to deep yellow, sometimes creamy or pink-tinted, blooming from early to late summer. The small achenes are hairy at the tips.

Eriogonum pyrolifolium

Eriogonum sphaerocephalum (photo by Sally A. Simmons)

Eriogonum thymoides (photo by Sally A. Simmons)

Eriogonum umbellatum

Cultivation. Full sun or light shade, and dry, stony, well-drained soil. This is an excellent plant for the larger rock garden or dry slope. Thanks to its high variability, it is more cooperative west of the Cascades than most buckwheat species. Makes a fine addition to the dry parts of the butterfly or wildlife garden, where it will provide nectar and seed.

Native Habitat and Range. On gravelly slopes, talus, alpine ridges, and shrub-steppe habitats at mid to high elevations, mainly east of the Cascades in British Columbia, south and west through the mountains of Oregon and California, east to Montana, Colorado, and Arizona.

Notes. An extremely variable species. Nearly half of the 30 varieties occur in the Pacific Northwest; they are separated on the basis of habit, flower color, and pubescence, among other characters. Cultivars include 'Shasta Sulfur' and 'Sierra', both mound-forming plants with yellow flowers.

| *Euonymus occidentale* | Zones 7a to 9b | Celastraceae |

western wahoo, western burning bush

This deciduous shrub can grow to 5m (15ft) tall. The opposite leaves have short petioles, are ovate or oblong, and have pointed tips; they grow to 9cm (3.5in) long and have a thin texture and finely serrate margins. The small, maroon flowers have five petals and usually bloom in clusters of three, from late spring to early summer. The attractive fruits are pinkish capsules, opening to expose the seeds, which have a bright orange covering (aril).

Cultivation. Full to part shade, and moist to wet soil. A little bit of sun will brighten the reds and yellows of the fall foliage. This unusual plant will add diversity to the shady streambank, bog, or pond margin.

Propagation. Easy from semi-hardwood cuttings made during the summer or hardwood cuttings taken from mid to late fall. Treat cuttings with rooting hormones and place them into pumice or some other rooting medium. If cuttings are made during the growing season, keep them under humid, shady conditions until roots form. Plants can also be grown by layering and from seed planted in the fall and left to stratify under cold, moist winter conditions for germination after the weather warms in spring.

Native Habitat and Range. In moist to wet, shady woods and streambanks at low to mid elevations, west of the Cascades and Sierra Nevada from Vancouver Island and south Puget Sound, south through California.

Notes. Sometimes classified as *E. occidentalis*. There are well over 100 species in *Euonymus*, most native to the Northern Hemisphere; this is the only species native to the Pacific Northwest, and only *E. o.* var. *occidentale* occurs in our area, from the northern end of the range to central California.

| *Fraxinus latifolia* | Zones 6a to 9b | Oleaceae |

Oregon ash

These deciduous trees are either male or female (dioecious) and grow to 20m (60ft) with furrowed, gray bark. The opposite leaves are pinnately compound with five to seven leaflets up to 15cm (6in) long; they tend to emerge late in the spring and turn bright yellow early in fall. The tiny flowers are yellowish or greenish and crowded into dense panicles. They bloom from early to late spring, before or with the emergence of the leaves. The pistillate flowers on the female trees develop into clusters of narrow, single-seeded, winged samaras up to 5cm (2in) long.

Cultivation. Full sun to part shade, and moist to wet soil. This tree will tolerate seasonal flooding, making it an excellent choice for wetlands and streambanks west of the Cascades. Oregon

Euonymus occidentale

Fraxinus latifolia

Fraxinus latifolia in fall

ash provides good food, cover, and nesting sites for birds. Leaves are often attacked by a fungal blight late in the growing season, deforming them but not hurting the tree.

Propagation. Easiest from seed. Collect the winged fruits when they ripen in the fall and plant them outside, in containers or in the ground. Leave them to stratify in the cold, moist winter weather for germination the following spring.

Native Habitat and Range. In moist to wet soils of wetlands, streambanks, and floodplains at low elevations from southwestern British Columbia, south to southern California, and from the coast, east to the western foothills of the Cascades.

Notes. Sometimes classified as *F. pennsylvanica* ssp. *oregana* or *F. oregona*. The tough wood of this and other *Fraxinus* species is used in making tool handles and furniture. There are around 50 species of ash, mostly native to the temperate parts of North America (the majority of these in the east) and Eurasia.

Garrya	Garryaceae

silk tassel

Garrya is a genus of about a dozen evergreen shrubs; most species are native to the southwestern United States and Mexico. Plants are dioecious, either male or female. The flowers are tiny and arranged in long, drooping catkins that begin to bloom in winter. The bracts that surround each group of tiny flowers in the catkin have silky hairs, the source of the common name. The male catkins are longer than those of the female plants, but the females produce strings of purple berry-like fruits after flowering, and these remain on the plants all summer or until they are eaten by birds. Both sexes must be present for female plants to set fruit.

Propagation. Fairly easy from seed. Collect ripe fruits, remove some of the pulp or dry fruit wall, and plant the seeds outside in the fall. Allow them to spend three months in cold, moist winter conditions for germination the following spring. The seedlings grow quickly and will be large enough to transplant in a few weeks. Alternatively, hardwood cuttings can be made in late winter or fall, treated with hormones, placed in pumice or some other rooting medium, and kept humid until roots form.

Garrya elliptica	Zones 7b to 9b

wavy-leaved silk tassel

This large shrub can grow to 7m (20ft) tall and almost as wide. The leaves are opposite, and the short petioles are about 1cm (.5in). The leaf blades are leathery and dark green with distinctly undulate (wavy) margins; they are oblong in shape and grow to 8cm (3in). The staminate (male) catkins can reach 15cm (6in). The pistillate (female) catkins are thicker, up to 10cm (4in) long, blooming from mid winter to mid spring; they are followed by dark purple fruits, produced in dense clusters, which are fleshy at first, becoming dry with age.

Cultivation. Full sun or part shade, and moist soil. The beautiful foliage alone makes this shrub a great choice for the hedgerow, for screening, or as a specimen plant, and it will provide food and evergreen cover in the wildlife garden west of the Cascades.

Native Habitat and Range. On hills and bluffs near the coast at low elevations from west central Oregon, south along the coast to southern California.

Notes. Selections from male plants with especially long catkins include 'Evie', with inflorescences to 25cm (10in) long, and 'James Roof', with even longer catkins to 30cm (1ft).

Garrya elliptica

Garrya fremontii

Garrya fremontii   Zones 6a to 9b

Fremont's silk tassel, bear brush

This handsome shrub grows to 3m (10ft) tall and about as wide. The leaves are opposite, yellow-green, ovate to elliptic, up to 8cm (3in) long, and set on petioles up to 1.5cm (.5in). The leaves are shiny, and the margins are smooth. The male and female catkins both grow to about 9cm (3.5in) in length. Silky-haired bracts surround the clusters of tiny flowers that bloom from mid winter to mid spring. The round, berry-like fruits are purple.

Cultivation. Full sun or part shade, and well-drained, moist to rather dry soil. This species survives the heat and cold east of the Cascades better than *G. elliptica* and is quite drought-tolerant. A fine choice for the drier parts of the hedgerow and a good screen, specimen plant, or addition to the wildlife garden, where it will provide food and cover for birds.

Native Habitat and Range. In thickets and open woods, at low to mid elevations, in the Cascades of south central Washington, near the Columbia River Gorge, and south through southwestern Oregon to southern California.

Notes. *Garrya buxifolia* (dwarf or box-leaved silk tassel) is a smaller shrub, growing only to 1.5m (5ft), with a limited distribution from southwestern Oregon to northwestern California.

| *Gaultheria shallon* | Zones 6b to 9b | Ericaceae |

salal

This shrub is variable in height, depending on habitat, ranging from only 50cm (20in) to 3m (10ft) or more. The leathery, evergreen leaves are elliptic, up to 10cm (4in) long and alternately arranged on short petioles. Five to 15 urn-shaped flowers bloom from late spring to mid summer in racemes produced in the upper leaf axils. The nodding flowers are white or pinkish and about 1cm (.5in) long. What appear to be dark purplish berry-like fruits are actually fleshy sepals surrounding a small capsule with many seeds.

Cultivation. Part shade, and moist (not wet) to rather dry soil. Tolerates full sun (where plants will be shorter) to full shade, and poor soil. This is one of the best-known evergreen shrubs west of the Cascades, and one of the few that will tolerate the dry shade under big conifers. Although slow to establish, it is useful for controlling erosion and is an excellent addition to a hedgerow, woodland, or wildlife garden. Butterflies visit the flowers for nectar, and their larvae eat the foliage; all sorts of creatures, including past and present humans, eat the berries.

Propagation. Grow from seed, although this does take some patience. Collect fruits in the fall and remove the tiny seeds from some of the pulp. Mix the seeds and remaining pulp with a bit of ground peat, for easier handling, and sprinkle them on the surface of potting soil in flats or other containers. Leave seeds outside to stratify under cold, moist conditions for spring germination. Protect the tiny seedlings from direct sun while they are small. Another method is to take semi-hardwood cuttings during the summer; treat the cuttings with hormones, set into pumice or some other medium, and keep in humid conditions until roots form. Salal can also be propagated by layering stems in the spring, but established plants do not like to be transplanted and will recover slowly, if at all.

Native Habitat and Range. In dry coniferous forests and rocky sites at low to mid elevations, from British Columbia, south near the coast to southern California, east to the west slope of the Cascades.

Notes. Salal leaves are commonly used in flower arrangements; florists call them "lemon leaves" for their superficial resemblance to the same. *Gaultheria* encompasses approximately 100 species of evergreen shrubs and small trees, most of them native to the Andes of South America but also occurring in North America, Asia, and Australia. Three other species are native to the Pacific Northwest. *Gaultheria hispidula* (creeping snowberry, moxie plum, maidenhair berry) grows in deep coniferous forest or sphagnum bogs from British Columbia to Labrador, dipping south into northeastern Washington and adjacent Idaho, and the Great Lakes states; this delicate little groundcover has white, aromatic fruits. *Gaultheria humifusa* (alpine wintergreen) grows in wet places in the high mountains from British Columbia south through the Olympics and Cascades to northern California, east to the Rocky Mountains; it grows only to 3cm (1.5in) tall with stems 10cm (4in) long. The fruits are red and edible. *Gaultheria ovatifolia* (Oregon wintergreen, western tea-berry) occurs in forests and bogs at mid to fairly high elevations from western British Columbia south to northern California and east to Idaho; the branches trail to 20cm (8in), and the berry-like fruits are bright red. These three species make beautiful small groundcovers, but they are all difficult to propagate and establish in the garden.

| *Grayia spinosa* | Zones 4a to 9b | Chenopodiaceae |

spiny hopsage

This branching, rounded shrub grows to 1.5m (5ft) tall. The tips of the twigs are usually spiny, and the plants have a mealy surface of small, star-like (stellate) hairs. The deciduous leaves are alternately arranged, entire, and fleshy. They are oblanceolate (lance-shaped, but widest

Gaultheria shallon

Grayia spinosa (photo by Sally A. Simmons)

toward the tip), about 2.5cm (1in) long, and tapered to the short petiole. The shrubs are usually dioecious, with male and female flowers on separate plants. The tiny flowers bloom in small clusters, subtended by little bracts, from mid spring to early summer. The flowers are not showy, but the female plants produce utricles (dry, one-seeded fruits) surrounded by two bracts that expand as the seed matures to form a flat, round wing, about 1cm (.5in) across. The fruits are attractive, varying in color from red to whitish.

Cultivation. Full sun or light shade, and dry soil. This is attractive shrub for dry wildlife gardens and drought-tolerant hedgerows east of the Cascades, providing food, cover, and nesting sites for wildlife. Plant it along a dry bank or around a parking area.

Propagation. Grow from seed harvested in the fall and planted soon after collecting. Sow seeds directly into the garden or into containers, and leave them outside to cold stratify over winter for germination in the spring. Though it is more difficult, plants can usually be propagated from hardwood cuttings made in late winter or early spring and treated with rooting hormones.

Native Habitat and Range. On arid slopes and dry valleys, often in alkaline soils, at low to fairly high elevations east of the Cascades from eastern Washington, south to southeastern California and east to Montana, Wyoming, Colorado, and New Mexico.

Notes. Sometimes classified as *Atriplex spinosa*. This species, the only one in *Grayia*, is occasionally planted as browse for livestock.

Holodiscus discolor	Zones 4b to 9b	Rosaceae

oceanspray, creambush

This generally erect shrub grows to 3m (10ft) or taller. The branches are slender, often arching, and the wood is very tough. The leaves are pubescent and alternately arranged on short petioles. The blades are ovate in outline, with shallow lobes and teeth along the margins, reaching about 7cm (3in) in length. Many tiny, five-petaled, creamy flowers bloom in dense, drooping panicles to 20cm (8in) long at the branch tips. The fruits, small, hairy achenes, follow flowering, which takes place from early to late summer. The old panicles turn brown and often hang on the shrubs through the winter.

Cultivation. Full sun to part shade, and moist to dry soil. This drought-tolerant species will help hold the soil on dry slopes, but it is also a beautiful shrub, worthy of a place in the garden or as part of a hedgerow: it is a good nectar plant for the butterfly garden, and birds enjoy the seeds.

Propagation. Fairly easy to grow from hardwood cuttings taken in late fall or winter, treated with rooting hormones, and set to root in pumice or some other medium. Another method is to make semi-hardwood cuttings from mid summer to early fall, but the cuttings must be kept humid while forming roots. Alternatively, grow from seed planted in fall and left outside in cold, moist conditions to germinate the following spring; seeds have a low germination rate, so should be planted thickly.

Native Habitat and Range. Moist to dry, open woods and rocky sites at low to mid elevations, from British Columbia, south near the coast to southern California and east to western Montana and Utah.

Notes. Native tribes had many uses for the hard, strong wood of this species (hence the common names ironwood and Indian arrow wood). *Holodiscus dumosus* (dwarf or gland oceanspray, rock spirea), which grows to 1.5m (5ft), is a species of rocky, dry habitats from north central Oregon, east and south to Idaho, Colorado, and Texas. *Holodiscus* has only a few species, mainly native to western North America.

Holodiscus discolor

Kalmia microphylla

Kalmia microphylla	Zones 3b to 9b	Ericaceae

western bog or alpine laurel

This is a charming plant, but it is poisonous. The slender branches grow to 50cm (20in), sometimes forming roots where they touch the ground. The evergreen leaves are opposite, dark green above and grayish underneath, up to 4cm (1.5in) long; they are elliptic to linear, and the margins are rolled under (revolute). The flowers are pale to deep pink and about 2cm (1in) across with five fused petals, blooming on slender pedicels; the corollas have ten pouches running lengthwise with the anthers tucked into them. Clusters of three to ten flowers develop at the branch tips from early to late summer. The fruits are rounded capsules.

Cultivation. Sun or part shade, and acidic, moist to wet soil. This is a beautiful little shrub for the bog, pond margin, or wet place in the wildflower meadow. Plant it near larger boulders in the rock garden to keep the roots moist.

Propagation. Grow from seed collected from ripe capsules and planted outside in early to mid spring. It can also be layered in late summer or early fall by nicking a branch and bending it so that the nick is under the ground surface. Another method is to make cuttings from semi-ripe wood, treat them with hormones, and insert them into pumice or some other medium in the late summer or early fall.

Native Habitat and Range. Bogs and wet meadows at low to high elevations from Alaska, south through the Olympics and Cascades into the mountains of California, and east to the Rocky Mountains.

Notes. Sometimes classified as *K. microphylla* ssp. (or var.) *occidentalis*, *K. polifolia* ssp. (or var.) *microphylla*. *Kalmia polifolia* (*K. polifolia* var. *polifolia*; bog laurel) occurs across much of Canada, dipping south to Montana, the Great Lakes states, and the northeastern United States. There are only moderation species of *Kalmia*, all native to eastern North America.

Kalmiopsis leachiana

Krascheninnikovia lanata (photo by Sally A. Simmons)

Kalmiopsis leachiana　　　　　　Zones 7a to 9b　　　　　　Ericaceae

This small, evergreen shrub grows slowly to 30cm (1ft) in height and twice as broad. The slender branches bear many alternate, elliptical, dark green leaves, about 1cm (.5in) long, with glandular dots on the undersides. Numerous flowers are arranged in flat-topped clusters of five to eight blooms, each set on a thin pedicel to 2cm (1in) long. The calyx is red, and the deep pink corolla consists of five petals, fused at the base, up to 1.5cm (.5in) across. The shrubs flower from early to mid spring, and sometimes again later in the season. The fruits are flattened capsules.

Cultivation. Part shade or dappled light, and somewhat acidic soil, on the dry side of moist, with excellent drainage and good organic content. This is a beloved and beautiful rock garden plant. It is fussy but not impossible.

Propagation. Grow from seed, collected in the summer or fall, stored under dry, cool conditions, and planted into flats or other containers in late winter or early spring. New plants can be grown from cuttings taken during summer or fall, treated with hormones, and set to root in pumice. Keep the cuttings humid until roots form. Cuttings should be taken only from plants grown in cultivation from seed.

Native Habitat and Range. Narrowly endemic to dry, rocky slopes at mid elevations in the Siskiyou Mountains and vicinity of the North Umpqua River in southwestern Oregon.

Notes. This is, so far, the only species in the genus: populations in the North Umpqua River watershed have several differences (including fragrant flowers) and may merit recognition as a separate taxon. *Kalmiopsis* ("looks like *Kalmia*") is similar to *Kalmia*, but the leaves are different, and the corolla of *Kalmiopsis* lacks longitudinal pouches.

Krascheninnikovia lanata   Zones 3b to 9b   Chenopodiaceae

winterfat

This small, erect or spreading shrub grows to a maximum height of about 60cm (2ft), producing annual shoots from a woody base. The entire plant is densely hairy with white or reddish hairs. The numerous lance-shaped or linear leaves are alternately arranged and grow to 4cm (1.5in) long; their entire margins are often rolled under (revolute). The plants are monoecious, producing small male and female flowers on the same plant. The male (staminate) flowers fall after releasing pollen; the tiny female (pistillate) flowers are surrounded by two small, densely hairy bracts that completely enclose the single-seeded fruit (utricle). The flowers bloom from late spring to mid summer, but the woolly fruits are the most attractive feature.

Cultivation. Full sun or light shade, and rather dry or rocky soil. An excellent plant for alkaline or salty soils east of the Cascades, and with good drainage, it may survive the wetter climates west of the mountains. Include this very attractive, silvery shrub with sagebrush and other drought-tolerant species in the arid wildlife garden.

Propagation. Grow from seed collected when they are ripe in mid fall. The seeds lose viability when stored at room temperature, so should be planted soon after harvest. Plant them into containers or directly into the garden, and leave them outside over winter for germination the following spring.

Native Habitat and Range. In rocky foothills and dry plains, often in alkaline or saline soils, at low to mid elevations east of the Cascades, from eastern Washington, south to southern California, east to Saskatchewan, the Dakotas, and Texas.

Notes. Sometimes classified as *Eurotia lanata* or *Ceratoides lanata*. As the common name suggests, winterfat is highly regarded as a browse plant, especially for livestock but also for deer, and has long been used in range restoration; it is also known as winter or white sage but is related neither to sagebrush (*Artemisia* spp.) nor to true sage (*Salvia* spp.). It is the only species in the genus, at least in North America.

Ledum   Ericaceae

Labrador tea

The approximately four species of *Ledum*, all aromatic shrubs with evergreen leaves related to *Rhododendron*, are native to cold, acidic bogs in North America and Eurasia. Although tea is sometimes made from *L. groenlandicum*, all species are poisonous to livestock, and we humans should approach them with caution.

Propagation. Grow from seed collected from ripe capsules in fall, stored in cool, dry conditions, and planted outside in early to mid spring. Plants can also be grown from semi-hardwood cuttings made during the late summer or early fall, treated with hormones, and set into pumice or another medium; keep the cuttings humid. Another method to try is layering in late summer or early fall. Nick a branch and bend it, so that the nick is beneath the ground surface; keep the stem in place until roots form.

Ledum glandulosum   Zones 3b to 9b

Pacific or trapper's tea

This small, evergreen shrub grows to about 1m (3ft). The young stems are hairy, and the aromatic, alternate leaves are elliptic, growing to 5cm (2in) in length. The leaves are entire, not strongly inrolled (revolute), and the undersides have whitish hairs and resinous dots. Clusters of 15 to 30

Ledum glandulosum

Ledum groenlandicum

Leucothoe davisiae

white flowers, about 2cm (1in) across, with five petals bloom on slender pedicels from early to late summer. The fruits are rounded capsules.

Cultivation. Full sun to part shade, and acidic, wet to moist soil. This species makes a fine addition to the margin of the pond, bog, or the wet spot in the meadow. Plant it near a trail or bench, where its aroma can be enjoyed.

Native Habitat and Range. In boggy places at low to high elevations, from British Columbia, south to California, mostly in and east of the Cascades, in the Blue Mountains and west coast of Oregon, and east to the Rocky Mountains

Notes. Despite its common names, this species is considered toxic; it can be most easily differentiated from *L. groenlandicum* by the white, not rusty, hairs on its lower leaf surfaces. Another native to our area is *L. palustre* (northern or marsh Labrador tea), which occurs in southwestern Alaska and northern British Columbia, as well as in northern Europe and Asia.

Ledum groenlandicum	Zones 3b to 9b	

Labrador tea

This aromatic, evergreen shrub grows to 1.5m (5ft). The leathery leaves are linear to elliptic, alternately arranged, and to 6cm (2.5in). The leaf margins are rolled under (revolute), and the undersides are covered with rusty, woolly hairs. The white flowers are about 1cm (.5in) across, blooming in clusters of 15 or more at the branch tips, from late spring to mid summer. The fruits are small capsules.

Cultivation. Full sun to part shade, and acidic, wet to moist soil. This medium-sized shrub is attractive in flower and can be used as an evergreen background for smaller bog-loving species. Plant it near the bench by the pond, where its resinous fragrance can be enjoyed.

Native Habitat and Range. Acidic bogs and wet forests at low to mid elevations across North America, from Greenland to Alaska, south through British Columbia to the Olympic Peninsula of Washington.

Notes. Some people make tea from the leaves of this species, and indigenous people used it for medicinal purposes, but it should not be confused with other species of *Ledum* or related ericads, several of which are toxic. The rusty hairs on the undersides of its leaves are a good identifying feature. It should be consumed only in small quantities. *Ledum* ×*columbianum*, a naturally occurring hybrid between this species and *L. glandulosum*, ranges from western Washington south to California.

Leucothoe davisiae	Zones 6b to 9b	Ericaceae

western leucothoe, Sierra laurel

This small, evergreen shrub grows to 1.5m (5ft) and at least as wide. The glossy, alternate leaves are oblong, up to 6cm (2.5in) long, with entire or finely toothed margins. Nodding flowers bloom in racemes to 15cm (6in) long on the branch tips. The white, urn-shaped flowers consist of five fused petals and are about 1cm (.5in) long, blooming from late spring to early summer and sometimes later. The fruits are small, round capsules.

Cultivation. Part shade or dappled light, and wet to moist soil. This good-looking shrub is an excellent addition to the shade or woodland garden. It makes a handsome evergreen background for smaller herbs.

Propagation. Grow from seed. Collect seeds from ripe capsules and plant them outside in early to mid spring; keep seedlings moist and protect them from direct sun. Can also be grown from cuttings made from semi-ripe wood in the late summer or early fall, treated with hormones, and inserted into pumice or some other medium; keep cuttings moist and humid until roots form.

Native Habitat and Range. In bogs and other wet places from foothills to high elevations, southwestern Oregon to central California.

Notes. The genus encompasses around 30 species, native to North and South America and eastern Asia; this is the only species in the Pacific Northwest.

Linnaea borealis	Zones 3b to 9b	Caprifoliaceae

twinflower

This charming evergreen subshrub has slender, trailing, woody stems to 1m (3ft) long that root where they touch the ground, often forming mats. The small, glossy, opposite leaves are elliptic to rounded in shape and often have a few shallow teeth; they have short petioles and are up to 2.5cm (1in) long. Upright flowering stems grow to 10cm (4in) and flower at the tips. The fragrant, pink flowers are funnel-shaped and grow to 1.5cm (.5in). They are produced in pairs from a slender, forked peduncle, blooming from early summer to early fall. The small, nut-like fruits contain a single seed.

Cultivation. Full shade, part shade, or dappled light, and moist soil. Tolerates the dry shade under conifers, but prefers some moisture, especially in drier climates. Use as a groundcover under taller plants or along the path in the woodland or shade garden. Once established, it will spread, but it is not aggressive.

Propagation. Usually increased by dividing the rooted sections of stems, or by taking hardwood cuttings and rooting them during the growing season. It can also be grown from seeds, harvested and planted in the fall into flats of potting soil and left outside for the winter.

Native Habitat and Range. In shady or open woods and moist to rather dry soil, at low to fairly high elevations, circumpolar, extending south through much of the Pacific Northwest to California, the Rocky Mountains, the Great Lakes, and the northeastern United States.

Notes. Both subspecies, *L. b.* ssp. *longiflora*, with longer flowers and more variable leaves, and *L. b.* ssp. *americana*, occur in our area. The former is more common here, ranging as far south as Oregon and east to Idaho; the latter is widespread in North America. This is the only species in the genus; plants are not happy living in small containers for any length of time, so they are difficult to find at nurseries.

Lithocarpus densiflorus	Zones 6b to 9b	Fagaceae

tan or tanbark oak

This evergreen tree can grow up to around 30m (100ft) in height and 10m (30ft) in width, but is often shorter and broader in cultivation. The bark is thick and fissured. The gray-green leaves are alternately arranged, up to 12cm (5in) long with toothed margins and prominent lateral veins. Twigs and leaves are woolly when young. The trees are monoecious, with male and female flowers in different structures, but on the same plant. The tiny male (staminate) flowers bloom in upright, branching catkins (some people dislike their smell), and the little female (pistillate) flowers bloom at the bases of the male catkins. Flowers bloom from early to late summer. The fruits, acorns, require two years to reach maturity. They are up to 3.5cm (1.5in) long, set into a shallow cup to 2.5cm (1in) across with narrow, spreading scales.

Cultivation. Full sun or part shade, and moist to rather dry soil. This is a beautiful specimen tree or addition to the woodland garden, where it will tolerate the shade of other trees but not extreme cold. The foliage adds a different shade to the backyard forest, and the trees provide food, cover, and nesting sites for wildlife. The shrubby *L. d.* var. *echinoides* is a good choice for the hedgerow.

Linnaea borealis

Lithocarpus densiflorus

Propagation. Collect ripe, two-year-old acorns (some will probably contain insect larvae) in the fall and plant them shortly after harvest. They can be planted directly into the garden or into deep containers, in moist, well-drained soil, and left outside for the winter.

Native Habitat and Range. On wooded, sometimes dry slopes at low to fairly high elevations from southwestern Oregon, south to southern California, mainly in the Coast Ranges and the west slope of the Sierra Nevada.

Notes. Susceptible to sudden oak death (*Phytophthora ramorum*), as are many other species, related and unrelated. *Lithocarpus d.* var. *densiflorus* is the taller variety; *L. d.* var. *echinoides* (dwarf tanbark) is a shrub to 3m (10ft) tall, often found at higher elevations in the mountains. The genus includes upward of 100 species; all except *L. densiflorus* are native to Asia. The fruits of this species were eaten by indigenous tribes, and the bark was used in tanning leather. A related genus, *Chrysolepis* (*Castanopsis*; chinquapin), is mostly Asian, but two handsome, evergreen species are native to the Pacific Northwest. *Chrysolepis chrysophylla* (giant chinquapin) can become a tree to 30m (100ft) tall; it is found in dry woods and open areas at low to mid elevations west of the Cascades. It is infrequent in western Washington, becoming more common in western Oregon, ranging south to west central California. *Chrysolepis sempervirens* (bush chinquapin) is a spreading shrub up to 2m (6ft) tall; it lives in woods from southwestern Oregon, south through much of California. Both chinquapins are lovely, but difficult to propagate or cultivate.

Lonicera   Caprifoliaceae

honeysuckle, twinberry

Lonicera is a well-known genus of around 150 species of woody vines and shrubs, most of them native to temperate and subtropical regions of the Northern Hemisphere. Fewer than 20 are native to North America; seven occur in our area. The tubular flowers, formed from five fused petals, are sometimes showy and fragrant and typically attractive to hummingbirds. The ovaries are inferior, and the fruits are berries (the floral tube or hypanthium contributes to the fruit). The berries are often showy and are very attractive to birds; those of at least some honeysuckles are reputed to be poisonous to humans. Although the best-known honeysuckles are vines, most of our native species are upright shrubs.

Propagation. *Lonicera ciliosa* and other vine-like species can be grown from hardwood cuttings taken in the late fall or from young stems cut during the summer and kept under humid conditions until roots form. *Lonicera involucrata* is easy to propagate from cuttings taken at any time of year, but hardwood cuttings made in late fall or winter are easier to work with because they don't require humid conditions. Plants can also be grown from seed. Collect berries in late summer, before the birds get them all, and plant them, pulp and all (unless they are to be stored), into flats of potting soil. Leave the planted seeds outside to stratify under cold, moist conditions for germination the following spring.

Lonicera ciliosa   Zones 4a to 9b

orange honeysuckle

This slender, woody, twining vine can grow to a height of 6m (18ft). The deciduous leaves are opposite, broadly elliptic, and up to 10cm (4in) long, with hair-like cilia along the margins. The uppermost pairs of leaves are completely fused around the stems and inflorescences. The orange-yellow to red-orange flowers bloom in clusters at the branch tips from late spring to mid summer; they are tubular and up to 4cm (1.5in) in length. The fruits are translucent red-orange berries, up to 1cm (.5in) wide, ripening in clusters.

Cultivation. Part sun or dappled light, and moist to rather dry soil. This honeysuckle is happiest growing up the trees and shrubs in the partial shade at the edge of the woodland or hedgerow; it also does well on a trellis or growing on a fence, and is perfect for the hummingbird or wildlife garden, with its tubular orange flowers and red berries. The foliage is susceptible to mildew in the late summer, which is often more of a problem for plants grown in full sun.

Native Habitat and Range. In open woods, thickets, and forest margins at low to mid elevations from southern British Columbia south to northern California, more common west of the Cascades, but ranging east to western Montana and Utah.

Notes. Birds love the red berries, which are reputedly poisonous to humans. *Lonicera interrupta* (chaparral honeysuckle), another vining species with tubular, cream-colored flowers and red berries, ranges from southwestern Oregon south to California and Arizona. *Lonicera hispidula* (hairy or pink honeysuckle) is a woody vine or trailing shrub that can grow to 3m (10ft) or more. The flowers are tubular, pink or pinkish yellow, and up to 2cm (1in) long, blooming in clusters from early to late summer, followed by red berries; it lives in open woods, thickets, streambanks, and rocky places at low elevations, from southwestern British Columbia, west of the Cascades, south through California.

Lonicera ciliosa

Lonicera ciliosa, fruits

Lonicera involucrata, fruits

Lonicera involucrata   Zones 3b to 9b

black twinberry

This upright, deciduous shrub is fast-growing, to 3m (10ft) or more. The young branches have four angles in cross-section. The leaves are opposite, elliptic in shape, and up to 15cm (6in) long, on short petioles. Peduncles about 2.5cm (1in) long develop from the leaf axils, each bearing a pair of tubular, yellow flowers, 2cm (1in) in length. Flowers bloom from mid spring to late summer. Each pair of flowers is subtended by two pairs of showy bracts that turn reddish purple as the flowers fade and the fruits ripen. The bracts form a shallow cup around the pair of shiny, black berries.

Cultivation. Full sun to full shade, and moist to wet soil. Site in the moister soils of a hedgerow or near the margin of a stream, pond, or bog. This handsome shrub is also an excellent plant for the hummingbird or wildlife garden on either side of the Cascades; although the flowers are small, hummingbirds visit them, and the berries, inedible to humans, are enjoyed by fruit-eating birds.

Native Habitat and Range. Moist forests and thickets, streambanks, and swampy sites at low to fairly high elevations, from Alaska south through California to Mexico, and east to the Rocky Mountains, occasionally to the Great Lakes.

Notes. *Lonicera i.* var. *involucrata* is the wide-ranging variety; *L. i.* var. *ledebourii* is taller, has reddish flowers, and occurs along the coasts of Oregon and California. Other shrubby species include *L. caerulea* (bluefly honeysuckle),with yellow flowers and blue berries; its var. *cauriana* is native to moist places at mid elevations from south central Washington, south through Oregon to California, east to Montana and Wyoming. Another is *L. conjugialis* (purpleflower or wedded honeysuckle), with reddish purple flowers, ranging from south central Washington, south through the mountains of Oregon to central California. *Lonicera utahensis* (Utah honeysuckle) is an upright shrub to 2m (6ft), with whitish or yellowish flowers and red berries; it occurs in moist areas at mid to high elevations in the mountains from southern British Columbia through Oregon to California, east to Alberta and Montana, and south to New Mexico.

Luetkea pectinata   Zones 3b to 9b   Rosaceae

partridgefoot

This lovely, evergreen semi-shrub spreads by underground rhizomes and also by stolons that creep along the ground surface to form mats. The leaves grow mostly in basal tufts and are about 2cm (1in) long, including the petiole. They are wedge-shaped and pectinate, divided into linear segments like the teeth of a comb. The upright flowering stems grow to 15cm (6in) and are topped by compact racemes, each with eight to 20 small flowers with five, creamy white petals. Flowers bloom from early to late summer and are followed by little follicles.

Cultivation. Full sun or part shade, and well-drained, moist soil. Beautiful as a groundcover under taller shrubs or along the path in the woodland garden. It is also a fine plant for the moist or shadier parts of the rock garden, keeping its good looks through the winter.

Propagation. Divide rhizomes, with leaves and roots attached, during the growing season. Can also be grown from seed, collected and planted in autumn, then left outside to stratify under cold, moist conditions for spring germination.

Native Habitat and Range. Moist meadows, rocky or shady sites at mid to high elevations in the mountains of western North America, from Alaska south in the Olympics and Cascades to northern California, in eastern British Columbia and southwestern Alberta, south to Idaho and Montana.

Notes. Often called mountain or creeping spirea for its similarity to that rosaceous genus; it also resembles, at least superficially, many saxifrages, and was at one time classified as *Saxifraga*

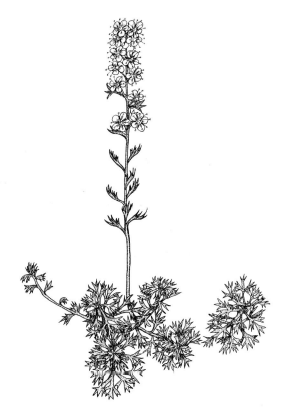

Luetkea pectinata

pectinata. Although it is most common at high elevations, partridgefoot is quite happy in the lowlands and is one of the most cooperative alpine species. It is the only species in the monotypic *Luetkea*.

Mahonia	Berberidaceae

Oregon grape, holly grape

The approximately 100 species of *Mahonia* are native to Asia and North and Central America; of the ten that occur in western North America, four are native in our area. *Mahonia* is sometimes included in *Berberis*; the two genera are similar and known to hybridize. Holly grapes are evergreen shrubs with pinnately compound leaves and usually prickly leaflets; the leaflets often resemble the leaves of holly (*Ilex* spp.). The yellow flowers bloom in short racemes. The perianth parts (petals and sepals) are unusual in that they are arranged in whorls of three, all colored and petaloid; the two upper whorls are often considered to be the six petals, the next two whorls as six sepals, and the lowermost whorl as three bracts that subtend the other parts. The fruits, dark blue berries, are glaucous, covered with a waxy, whitish bloom. The berries are sour but edible and reputedly make a fine jelly. The plants are sometimes used medicinally, and a yellow dye can be made from the inner bark of the stems and roots.

Propagation. Easiest from seed. Collect ripe berries in the summer, remove some of the pulp, and plant the seeds into flats of potting soil soon after harvest. Leave them outside during the fall and winter to stratify in the cold, moist weather for germination in the spring. Oregon grape is difficult to propagate vegetatively but can sometimes be grown from bud or hardwood cuttings made in early spring. Established plants do not like their long roots disturbed and may die or take years to recover when transplanted.

Mahonia aquifolium, fruits

Mahonia aquifolium	Zones 5a to 9b

tall Oregon grape

This handsome, evergreen shrub grows erect, branched stems up to 3m (10ft) and spreads by tough rhizomes. The alternate leaves are pinnately compound, each with up to seven leaflets with spiny margins. The glossy leaflets are ovate and up to 8cm (3in) long. Small, yellow flowers bloom from early to late spring in racemes up to 8cm (3in) long, clustered at the branch tips. They are fragrant and are followed by the berries, which are about 1cm (.5in) long. Cold, sun, and age cause the leaflets to turn attractive shades of burgundy and red.

Cultivation. Full shade to full sun (some shade where summers are hot), and moist to rather dry soil. Tolerates the dry shade under big trees. An excellent screen, barrier, or component of a hedgerow, and a fine plant for the wildlife garden, providing cover and food for birds. Although it can be pruned back, it tends to spread, and the foliage is fiercely prickly, so it's best not to plant it too close to a path.

Native Habitat and Range. Moist to rather dry or rocky wooded slopes and thickets at low to mid elevations, from southern British Columbia south to California, and from the coast east through the Columbia River Gorge to eastern Washington, northeastern Oregon, northern Idaho, and Montana.

Notes. The state flower of Oregon. Its popular selection 'Compacta' grows only to 1m (3ft) tall but can spread to 2m (6ft); 'Orange Flame' grows to a similar size, turns burgundy in the winter cold, and has bronzy new growth.

Mahonia aquifolium

Mahonia nervosa

Mahonia nervosa   Zones 5a to 9b

Cascade, long-leaved, or dull Oregon grape

This low-growing, evergreen shrub spreads by rhizomes and produces erect stems to about 60cm (2ft) or a bit more. The pinnately compound leaves tend to grow in tufts at the branch tips. Each leaf has up to 15 ovate, leathery leaflets to about 6cm (2.5in) long. The leaflets have asymmetric bases, spiny margins, and three or more distinct veins radiating from the point of attachment. The fragrant, pale yellow flowers bloom in racemes up to 20cm (8in) long from early spring to early summer; the berries are about 1cm (.5in) long. The foliage turns a wine color in cold or sun, and older leaflets turn bright red before they fall.

Cultivation. Full shade to part sun, and moist to rather dry soil. This is an especially good shrub for dry shade under big trees. Plant it in the well-drained dry spots of the shade or woodland garden, or at the base of the hedgerow, where its year-around beauty can be enjoyed. Excellent for the wildlife garden, providing cover and food for birds.

Native Habitat and Range. Moist to dry forested areas at low to mid elevations from southern British Columbia south to central California, mainly from the coast to the west slope of the Cascades, occasionally east to Idaho.

Notes. *Mahonia pinnata* (wavyleaf or California barberry) occurs near the coast from southwestern Oregon to southern California; it too is on the low-growing side, with stems to 1m (3ft) tall, but its leaves are more similar to those of *M. aquifolium*.

Mahonia repens   Zones 3b to 9b

low Oregon grape

This evergreen groundcover grows erect stems up to 30cm (1ft) or somewhat taller, and spreads to 1m (3ft) by rhizomes. The alternate leaves are similar to *M. aquifolium*, pinnately compound, each with five to seven leaflets. The leaflets are ovate and up to 8cm (3in) long, and the spines along the margins are often weak. The upper surfaces of the leaflets are usually dull, and the lower surface is waxy. Fragrant, small yellow flowers bloom from mid spring to early summer in racemes up to 8cm (3in) long, crowded at the branch tips. Clusters of berries, about 1cm (.5in) long, follow the flowers. The foliage becomes bronzy in full sun or winter cold.

Cultivation. Full sun to full shade, and well-drained, moist to dry soil. Although slow-growing at first, this is one of the best groundcovers for dry shade and is quite drought-tolerant once established, even in full sun. Plant it along banks, in parking areas or at the base of the taller shrubs in a hedgerow on either side of the Cascades. This is a good evergreen for the dry parts of the wildlife garden, where it will provide cover and food for ground-feeding birds.

Native Habitat and Range. Canyons and dry, forested slopes at low to mid elevations, from southern British Columbia and eastern Washington, east to Montana and the Dakotas, south through Oregon to northern California, and east to Colorado and New Mexico.

Notes. Considered a noxious weed in some parts of the eastern United States. An even lower form with especially stiff, waxy-coated leaflets (sometimes granted specific status as *M. pumila*, dwarf western Oregon grape) occurs in southwestern Oregon and northern California.

Malus fusca   Zones 6a to 9b   Rosaceae

Pacific or western crabapple

This small, deciduous tree grows to a maximum height of about 12m (35ft). Small shoots are often sharp and thorn-like. The leaves are alternately arranged on the stems and the blades can grow to 10cm (4in) long; they have small teeth along the margins and usually one or two larger lobes. Leaves turn shades of red and orange in the fall. The flowers, up to 2.5cm (1in) across, have five white or pinkish petals; they are arranged in clusters of five to 12 and bloom from mid spring to early summer. The fruits are small, fleshy pomes about 1.5cm (.5in) long, turning yellow or reddish when ripe.

Cultivation. Full sun to part shade, and moist to wet soil. Survives near salt water and will tolerate flooding. An excellent plant for streams, ponds, and boggy sites, or the wet places in the wildlife garden. Birds and other animals enjoy crabapples, and these pretty little trees provide good nesting and cover, making them excellent additions to a hedgerow or thicket.

Propagation. Grow from seed separated from the fruit pulp and planted outside in fall to stratify under cold, moist conditions for germination the following spring. Seedlings will probably grow slowly their first few years. Existing plants can be layered by cutting a nick in a branch, bending it to the ground, burying the nicked area in soil, and staking the branch in place until roots form. This method is slow; it may take a couple of years for roots to form.

Native Habitat and Range. Wetlands, bogs, streambanks, and moist woods, at low to mid elevations from southern Alaska, south to northern California, and from the coast east to the west slope of the Cascades.

Notes. Sometimes classified as *Pyrus fusca*. *Malus* is a genus of about 25 species of small trees native to the temperate regions of the Northern Hemisphere; only a few species are native to North America. Western crabapples are small but edible, and were eaten, fresh or preserved, by coastal tribes.

Mahonia repens

Menziesia ferruginea

Malus fusca

| *Menziesia ferruginea* | Zones 4a to 9b | Ericaceae |

rusty menziesia, false azalea, fool's huckleberry

This deciduous shrub has slender branches and can grow to 2m (6ft) or more. The leaves are alternate and light green, often covered with fine brownish hairs and glands. The ovate to elliptic leaves tend to grow in clusters at the branch tips and are up to 6cm (2.5in) long with finely serrated margins; they turn to brilliant oranges and crimsons in the fall. The interesting flowers are urn-shaped, formed from four fused petals and vary in color from pinkish to yellow or orange; they are about 1cm (.5in) long and bloom in small clusters from late spring to late summer. The fruits are dry capsules containing many seeds.

Cultivation. Full sun or part shade, and moist, acidic soil rich in organic matter. The fall foliage display will be more intense where plants get some sun. A good plant for the shrub border or as part of the hedgerow. Site it at the woodland edge or as a background shrub in the large rock garden.

Propagation. Collect ripe capsules in the fall, mix the tiny seeds with some ground peat for easier handling, and sprinkle them on potting soil in flats. Leave the flats outside in cool, moist winter conditions for spring germination. Can also be grown from cuttings made from semi-hardwood during the summer, treated with rooting hormones, and set to root under humid conditions in pumice or some other medium.

Native Habitat and Range. Near streams and in moist woods at low to fairly high elevations, from Alaska south along the coast to northern California, east across southern British Columbia and northern Washington to Alberta, Montana, and Wyoming.

Notes. The approximately six species in this genus are native to North America and Japan.

| *Morella californica* | Zones 7b to 9b | Myricaceae |

Pacific or California wax myrtle

This fragrant evergreen shrub can grow to 6m (18ft) or taller, usually from multiple trunks. The alternate leaves are narrowly elliptic and about 8cm (3in) long, with small black dots (wax glands); they are dark green and glossy above, paler beneath, and with at least a few teeth along the margins. The tiny flowers are of separate sexes, produced in male or female spikes up to 2cm (1in) long, growing in the leaf axils of the same plant (monoecious). Male (staminate) spikes generally develop in the axils of the lower leaves; female (pistillate) spikes, often with some male flowers mixed in, are higher on the branches, blooming from mid to late spring. The fruits are small, a bit less than 1cm (.5in) in width; they are purplish and drupe-like, with a waxy, warty surface surrounding the seed.

Cultivation. Full sun to part shade, and moist to rather dry soil. Moderately drought-tolerant, once established. This is a tough and beautiful evergreen shrub for a screen or as part of a large hedgerow. Plant it in the wildlife garden, where the birds can enjoy the fruits and humans can enjoy the aromatic (but not overpowering) foliage.

Propagation. Usually grown from seed. Collect fruits in the fall, remove some of the outer wax, and plant the pits outside, allowing the seeds to stratify in the cold, moist winter weather for germination the following spring and summer. Wax myrtle can also be grown by layering. Nick a branch, and bury the nicked section underground until roots form in a month or two; once rooted, the branch can be removed from the parent plant. Another method is to take semi-hardwood cuttings during the summer or hardwood in winter; treat with hormones, set into pumice or some other medium, and keep humid under plastic or glass.

Native Habitat and Range. Canyons, thickets, and moist slopes at low elevations near the central Washington coast, south to southern California; apparently disjunct on the west coast of Vancouver Island.

Morella californica

Myrica gale

Oemleria cerasiformis

Notes. Sometimes classified as *Myrica californica* (many wax myrtles and bayberries are classified as either *Morella* or *Myrica*). *Morella* includes perhaps 25 species, native to temperate and tropical parts of the world; the approximately six North American species are mainly distributed in the southeastern United States.

| *Myrica gale* | Zones 3b to 9a | Myricaceae |

sweet gale

This aromatic, deciduous shrub usually grows to 1.5m (5ft). Plants are either male or female (dioecious), and the flowers appear before the leaves. The male (staminate) catkins are about 2cm (1in) long, and the female spikes grow to 1cm (.5in), blooming from mid spring to early summer. The alternate leaves are usually oblanceolate (lance-shaped, but broadest toward the tip) and up to 6cm (2.5in) long. The leaves have entire margins or with a few coarse teeth along the upper halves; they are finely hairy, at least on the lower surface, and dotted with yellow wax glands. The tiny fruits are nutlets, covered with a yellowish wax and crowded into brown spikes.

Cultivation. Full sun to part shade, and wet to very moist soil. This nitrogen-fixing species is a good choice for wetland restorations or sites with poor soils. Plant it at the edge of the pond or bog, or along the shore of a larger wetland to improve diversity and habitat value.

Propagation. Tends to spread by suckers, which can be separated in late winter or early spring to produce new plants. To layer plants, nick a branch and bury the nicked section underground until roots form in a month or two, then remove the rooted branch from the parent plant. Sweet gale can also be grown from seed. Collect fruits in the fall, remove some of the outer wax and plant the fruits outside into flats of potting soil, allowing the seeds to stratify in the cold, moist winter weather for germination the following spring.

Native Habitat and Range. In the wet soils near bogs, lakes, and coastal swamps at low to mid elevations, from Alaska south, west of the Cascades, scattered to southwestern Oregon and east to Newfoundland, the Great Lakes region, and the Atlantic coast; Eurasia.

Notes. The only other species of *Myrica* is native to California.

| *Oemleria cerasiformis* | Zones 7a to 9b | Rosaceae |

Indian plum, osoberry

This deciduous shrub or small tree can grow to 5m (15ft). The alternate leaves have short petioles, are elliptic or lanceolate, and grow to 10cm (4in). The leaf margins are entire (smooth) and crushed leaves smell like cucumbers. The greenish white flowers bloom in drooping racemes as the leaves are expanding. The blossoms are bell-shaped and about 1cm (.5in) across, blooming from late winter to mid spring. Unlike the majority of rose relatives, Indian plums are either male or female (dioecious), and only female plants produce the small plums (drupes). These are about 1cm (.5in) long, orange or red when young, ripening to blue-black.

Cultivation. Part shade or dappled light, and moist to rather dry soil. Usually tolerates full sun. This little tree is common in the forest understory and is a good plant for the dry shade under big conifers in the woodland garden. It is among the very earliest to bloom, usually in March or even February. Hungry hummingbirds returning from winter migration are attracted to them. The little plums produced by female plants ripen early in summer and are much loved by fruit-eating birds, so this is certainly a species worth adding to the wildlife garden or hedgerow.

Propagation. Easy from seed, but you will have to race the birds to harvest them in early summer as they ripen. It is not necessary to remove the seed from the fleshy outer layers, or stony inner fruit walls unless the seeds are being stored for a long period of time. Dry the fruits, and plant them outside in the fall. Stratification under cold, moist winter conditions will break dormancy, and seeds will begin to germinate by spring, or sometimes sooner. Plants are also easy to grow from hardwood cuttings made in late winter and treated with rooting hormones. Root cuttings and layering are other possibilities.

Native Habitat and Range. In fairly dry to moist woods, along roads and streams, mainly at low elevations from southwestern British Columbia, south near the coast to southern California, east to the west slope of the Cascades and Sierra Nevada.

Notes. Sometimes classified as *Osmaronia cerasiformis*. It is the only species in the genus. As one common name suggests, indigenous people ate the fruits, in spite of the large pits. This plant is such an early bloomer, it is tempting to bring some branches inside as cut flowers, if you do this, make sure there is good ventilation, as the flowers emit an odor reminiscent of cat spray.

| *Oplopanax horridus* | Zones 3b to 9b | Araliaceae |

devil's club

This deciduous shrub grows thick, often unbranched stems to 3m (10ft) tall. The large maple-like leaves are alternate and palmate, up to 30cm (1ft) across with equally long petioles. The stems, petioles, and undersides of the leaves bristle with yellowish spines to 1cm (.5in) long. The small, greenish white flowers are arranged in compact umbels, and these are secondarily arranged into conical racemes or panicles, up to 25cm (10in) long, blooming at the stem tips from late spring to mid summer. The fruits are bright red, flattened few-seeded berries.

Cultivation. Part to full shade, and soil that is wet to very moist, but with some drainage. Site near a stream, seep, or pond. This is a bold, dramatic, almost tropical-looking plant, especially when the red berries ripen. It is best enjoyed from a distance and shouldn't be planted near paths or other places where humans might encounter the vicious spines. On the other hand, it makes a most effective barrier.

Propagation. Fairly easy from hardwood cuttings taken in late winter, treated with hormones, and set to root in pumice or some other medium. It can also be grown from seed collected in the fall and planted outside in flats of moist potting soil to stratify in the cool, wet winter weather. Germination may be slow and sporadic.

Native Habitat and Range. In moist to wet woods, seeps, and streambanks at low to mid elevations (higher elevations in the south) from Alaska, south through western Oregon, east throughout British Columbia and in northern Washington to northern Idaho and Montana, also in Ontario and Michigan.

Notes. Related to ginseng (*Panax* spp.). Indigenous tribes used devil's club to treat everything from dandruff to diabetes.

| *Opuntia polyacantha* | Zones 3b to 9b | Cactaceae |

Plains prickly-pear cactus

This mat-forming cactus grows only to 30cm (1ft) tall but often forms extensive clumps. The jointed stems, or pads, are rounded in outline and strongly flattened, growing to 15cm (6in) long; they have small bristles in addition to straight spines up to 5cm (2in) long. The flowers have greenish sepals and numerous yellow or reddish petals up to 7cm (3in) long; they have many stamens and a lobed stigma, and bloom from late spring to early summer. The inferior ovary develops into a rather dry, berry like fruit, the "prickly pear."

Cultivation. Full sun or light shade, and sandy, well-drained soil. This is an excellent plant for the drought-tolerant wildlife or large rock garden east of the Cascades. It also makes a fine, low-

Oplopanax horridus

Opuntia polyacantha var. *polyacantha* (photo by Sally A. Simmons)

Paxistima myrsinites

growing barrier once the plants expand. It can be grown in containers in wetter climates west of the Cascades.

Propagation. Easy by rooting the pads, which break loose whenever the plants are disturbed. Collect some pads during the spring or early summer, and allow them to dry for a few days. Plant them into sand or pumice, pushing the base of the pad a little way into the growing medium. Keep them moist until roots form.

Native Habitat and Range. In dry, sandy soils, often with sagebrush, at low to mid elevations east of the Cascades from southern British Columbia, south to central and eastern Washington, northeastern Oregon, and southeastern California, east through the Rocky Mountains to the Great Plains.

Notes. Only the widespread *O. p.* var. *polyacantha* occurs in our area. *Opuntia* is a large, taxonomically fluid genus of North and South America. Around 40 species are recognized in North America, but most occur south of us; only a couple other species occur in the Pacific Northwest. *Opuntia fragilis* (brittle prickly-pear) forms low, spiny mats to 15cm (6in) tall, and the joints of the stems tend to be more rounded than flattened. The yellow flowers are about 5cm (2in) across, blooming from late spring to early summer. This plant has a wide range across much of western North America, from southern British Columbia to California at low to mid elevations; in our area, it lives on dry, sandy soils, mainly east of the Cascades, but also in dry places around Vancouver Island, Puget Sound, and southwestern Oregon. Many of the prickly-pear populations in our area are thought to be *O. ×columbiana* (grizzly bear prickly-pear), a natural hybrid between *O. polyacantha* and *O. fragilis*. *Pediocactus simpsonii* (Simpson's hedgehog cactus) is our only other native cactus. This small, barrel-shaped plant produces stems singly or in clusters to 20cm (8in) tall and to 12cm (5in) thick. The flowers are yellowish green to purple, and the rounded fruits contain black seeds. It lives in arid valleys and dry hillsides east of the Cascades, from central Washington and eastern Oregon, east through the Rocky Mountains. Both *P. s.* var. *robustior* and *P. s.* var. *simpsonii* occur in our area. This is a tempting cactus for rock gardeners, but the plants are slow-growing and should be propagated from seed only, never dug from their wild homes unless they are to be destroyed.

| *Paxistima myrsinites* | Zones 3b to 9b | Celastraceae |

Oregon boxwood, mountain-lover

This handsome, evergreen shrub is mostly grown for its glossy foliage. Plants grow to 1m (3ft) tall and just as wide. The small, leathery leaves are opposite and mounted on very short petioles; they are generally oblong in shape and about 2.5cm (1in) long, with serrate margins. The tiny flowers have four maroon petals and bloom from mid spring to mid summer. The fruits are small, few-seeded capsules.

Cultivation. Part shade or dappled light, and moist to fairly dry, well-drained soil. Tolerates the dry shade under big trees on either side of the Cascades. Plant it at the edge of the shade garden or near a woodland clearing, or add it to the background plantings in the rock garden. Looks good near logs or stumps. It makes a fine, evergreen addition to a low-growing hedgerow, but deer may eat it during the winter.

Propagation. Fairly easy from semi-hardwood cuttings made during the summer, treated with hormones, set into pumice or some other medium, and kept humid under plastic or glass until roots form. It can probably be grown from seeds planted outside in the fall.

Native Habitat and Range. In moist to fairly dry coniferous forests and rocky clearings at low to mid elevations from British Columbia south to central California, and from the coast, east across southern British Columbia, northern Washington, and northern Oregon to Alberta and Montana, south through the Rocky Mountains to New Mexico.

Notes. The only other species in the genus, *P. canbyi*, occurs in the mountains of the eastern United States.

Paxistima myrsinites

| *Philadelphus lewisii* | Zones 4a to 9b | Hydrangeaceae |

Lewis' mock orange, syringa

This deciduous shrub has long been cultivated for its beautiful, fragrant flowers. Plants can grow to 3m (10ft) tall. The opposite leaves are ovate to elliptic and up to 7cm (3in) long on short petioles. The leaves have three veins running from the base, and the margins are smooth, ciliate, or sometimes with a few teeth. The white flowers are up to 4cm (1.5in) across, blooming in racemes at the tips of lateral branches from late spring to mid summer. The petals (typically four), anthers, and ovary are usually somewhat hairy (pubescent). The fruits, capsules to 1cm (.5in) long, are filled with many small seeds.

Cultivation. Full sun to part shade, and well-drained, moist to rather dry soil. Quite drought-tolerant once established, and therefore a good choice for the dry bank, driveway, or parking area. Plant this native on either side of the Cascades in the hedgerow or butterfly garden, or near a deck or patio, where the scent of its flowers can easily be enjoyed.

Propagation. Easy from hardwood cuttings taken in autumn, or from semi-hardwood cuttings taken in summer. Treat cuttings with rooting hormones and set them to root in pumice or some other medium. If working with leafy, semi-mature wood, be sure to keep cuttings humid until roots form. Can also be grown from seed. Shake the tiny seeds from the capsules onto the surface of soil-filled flats in the fall. Leave them outside to stratify in the cold, moist winter weather for germination the following spring.

Native Habitat and Range. In various habitats, from dry, rocky areas near sagebrush to streambanks and moist forest openings near the coast, at low to mid elevations, from British Columbia south to northern California, east through southern British Columbia, Washington, and most of Oregon to Idaho.

Notes. Sometimes classified as *P. gordonianus*, or *P. lewisii* ssp. (or var.) *gordonianus*. This species is the state flower of Idaho; its cultivar 'Goose Creek' has double flowers. *Philadelphus* includes approximately 50 species, mostly native to temperate and subtropical areas of North America, Europe, and Asia; around 20 species occur in North America, five others, all highly variable, in our area. Family relation *Whipplea modesta* (whipplevine, yerba de selva) makes a nice trailing groundcover for dry, sunny or shady woodland trails and rock gardens west of the Cascades, producing upright flowering shoots bearing clusters of small, white flowers from mid spring to mid summer; it occurs in open forests, dry, rocky sites, and roadsides at low to mid elevations from northwestern Washington, south through western Oregon (where it is more common) to central California.

| *Phyllodoce empetriformis* | Zones 3b to 8b | Ericaceae |

pink mountain-heather

This small, evergreen shrub grows to 40cm (16in) and tends to form mats. The needle-like leaves grow to 1.5cm (.5in) long and are grooved along the lower surface. The bell-shaped flowers are formed from five fused, rose-pink petals. They are small, less than 1cm (.5in) long, and bloom from early to late summer, earlier at lower elevations. The fruits are tiny, rounded capsules.

Cultivation. Full sun or part shade, and moist, well-drained, fairly acidic soil. A charming plant for the rock garden or stone retaining wall, but somewhat fussy at low elevations. Adding peat and pumice or gritty sand to the soil may help keep this little shrub happy. Locating plants near large boulders will help keep the roots cool.

Propagation. Grow from semi-hardwood cuttings made during the summer, treated with hormones, set into pumice or some other medium, and kept humid until roots form. Can also be increased by layering; push the small branches of shrubs growing in cultivation under the ground surface during the early spring and detach the pieces after roots form. Plants can be grown from

Philadelphus lewisii

Phyllodoce empetriformis

the tiny seed, collected and planted in the fall, and left outside to cold stratify over winter for spring germination.

Native Habitat and Range. On open, rocky sites and seeps at high elevations from Alaska, south through the mountains to northern California, east across British Columbia to Idaho, Montana, and Wyoming.

Notes. A genus of fewer than ten species, native to the chilly, northern parts of North America and Eurasia. *Phyllodoce glanduliflora* (yellow mountain-heather) has yellowish or greenish white, urn-shaped flowers; it grows at mid to high elevations from Alaska, south through the mountains of Oregon, and east to Montana and Wyoming. *Phyllodoce ×intermedia*, with light pink flowers, is the naturally occuring hybrid between *P. empetriformis* and *P. glanduliflora*.

Physocarpus capitatus   Zones 6a to 9b   Rosaceae

Pacific ninebark

This erect or spreading, deciduous shrub grows to 4m (12ft). The attractive bark is shredded, peeling away in thin strips to reveal layers underneath. The leaves are alternately arranged and broadly ovate in outline, with three to five large, palmate lobes with serrated margins; the blades grow to 8cm (3in) on petioles to 3cm (1.5in) long. Each inflorescence produces 20 to 40 small, white flowers in a rounded cluster, each blossom about 1cm (.5in) across. Flowers bloom from late spring to early summer and are followed by attractive, pinkish brown clusters of follicles that tend to remain on the plants.

Cultivation. Full sun to part shade, and moist to fairly wet soil. An excellent plant for a stream-bank, pond, or ditch margin. Site it in the moist parts of the hedgerow or edge of the woodland garden, where it can be enjoyed throughout the year. Ninebark has a naturally graceful shape, which can be enhanced with pruning.

Propagation. Very easy from hardwood cuttings taken in fall or winter, treated with hormones, and stuck into moist pumice or some other medium to form roots. Can also be grown from seed collected when the follicles are ripe and planted outside in the fall to stratify under cold, moist conditions. Some seeds will germinate the following spring, but the percentage will probably be low.

Native Habitat and Range. Near lakes, streams, wetlands, and in moist woods at low to mid elevations from southwestern Alaska, south near the coast to southern California, east to the west slope of the Cascades, and occasionally east to northern Idaho.

Notes. Mallow ninebark (*P. malvaceus*) is similar but smaller, has fewer flowers, and lives in drier, colder habitats; it occurs in canyons and coniferous forests east of the Cascades from south central British Columbia, south through eastern Washington and Oregon, and east to southwest Alberta, Montana, Wyoming, and Utah. Four of the approximately ten species of *Physocarpus* are of western North American origin; the rest are from eastern North America and Asia.

Populus   Salicaceae

cottonwood

Populus is a genus of familiar deciduous trees, many with attractive, pale bark and golden fall foliage. Cottonwoods have tiny, wind-pollinated flowers in long, drooping catkins. The trees are either male or female (dioecious), and only the females produce capsules that contain the wind-dispersed, white-haired seed. The approximately 40 species of the genus are widely distributed in the Northern Hemisphere; about six are native to North America. No *Populus* species should ever be planted near septic systems or drain fields: the roots will seek out the lines (especially perforated pipe) and clog them, with unpleasant results.

Physocarpus capitatus

Populus balsamifera ssp. trichocarpa

Propagation. Grow from hardwood cuttings taken any time during the winter; these often form roots even without the application of hormones. Trees can also be grown as live stakes, by pushing dormant branches directly into the ground where they will form roots under moist conditions. This method is inexpensive, but the mortality of live stakes is high if the soil dries out too quickly. Aspens and other cottonwoods can be grown by removing and transplanting suckers during late winter or early spring. Plants can also be grown from the tiny, hairy seed. Collect seeds in late spring or early summer, and plant immediately by sprinkling them onto the surface of potting soil. Keep soil wet until the seeds germinate within a few weeks.

Populus balsamifera ssp. *trichocarpa*	Zones 3b to 9b

black cottonwood

This rough-barked, deciduous tree can grow to 50m (150ft) tall and 10m (30ft) wide, though it is usually smaller. The dormant buds are large, pointed, and shiny with a sticky resin that is deliciously fragrant in the early spring. The alternate leaves vary in shape, with a cordate (heart-shaped) to rounded base, and a pointed tip; they are broadest below the middle, up to 15cm (6in) long and have small, rounded teeth along the margins. The leaves turn golden in the fall. The petioles are about 7cm (3in) long and rounded in cross-section, often with a pair of glands where the petiole meets the leaf blade. The undersides of the leaves are pale or rusty with brown resin. Flowers bloom in catkins from late winter to mid spring, before the leaves fully expand. The male (staminate) catkins are about 3cm (1.5in) long; the female (pistillate) catkins, when mature, are up to 20cm (8in). Each female flower has three large stigmas and produces a capsule filled with cotton-tufted seed that is dispersed by the wind, sometimes in large quantities.

Cultivation. Full sun, and moist to wet soil. Tolerates winter flooding. This fast-growing tree is an excellent choice to begin habitat restoration on a large site. Cottonwoods are relatively short-lived, but old or standing dead trees make some of the best habitat (as long as they're not too close to your house) for wood ducks, woodpeckers, and other cavity-nesting creatures. Don't plant where the dropping leaves, flowers, and twigs will be a problem. The wood is brittle, and the surface roots can heave pavement, making this a tree to be enjoyed at a bit of a distance. Trunk borers sometimes attack young trees.

Native Habitat and Range. Along streams, lakeshores, floodplains, and other wet or moist places at low to mid elevations, from Alaska south through southern California, and from the coast east to southwestern Alberta, Montana, North Dakota, Wyoming, and Utah.

Notes. This subspecies, among the most common trees along rivers and streams in our area, is sometimes given specific status, as *P. trichocarpa*. Indigenous tribes had many uses for its resin-coated buds and other parts. Narrow-leaved cottonwood (*P. angustifolia*) is a smaller, more slender tree to 20m (60ft) with narrow, lanceolate leaves; it grows near streams in dry mountains and high plains from eastern Oregon and central Idaho, south through eastern California to Texas and Mexico, east to the Great Plains.

Populus tremuloides	Zones 3b to 9a

quaking aspen

This graceful, deciduous tree grows to 20m (60ft) but is often shorter. Aspens readily reproduce from suckers, forming extensive colonies where all the trees are of a single sex, since the trees are either male or female (dioecious). The bark is smooth and greenish white, becoming dark and rough on old trees. The leaves vary from rounded-ovate to heart-shaped (cordate), with pointed tips. The leaves are paler on the undersides, have finely toothed or wavy margins, and can grow

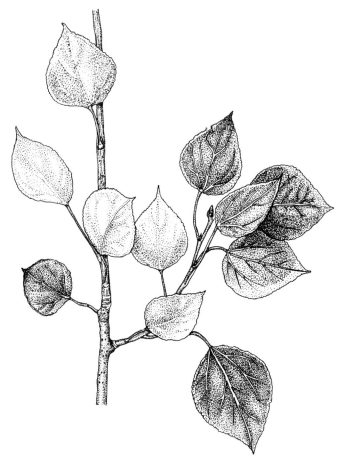

Populus tremuloides

to 9cm (3.5in) long by 8cm (3in) wide; they turn yellow and gold in autumn. The slender petioles are at least half as long as the leaves and strongly flattened at right angles to the blades, causing them to flutter in the slightest breeze. The male (staminate) catkins grow to 3cm (1.5in) before releasing their pollen and falling from the tree. Female (pistillate) catkins can grow to 10cm (4in) and bloom from mid spring to early summer. The capsules are ovate with two lobed stigmas at the tip.

Cultivation. Full sun, and moist soil. Tolerates a little shade. May do poorly in lowland areas where climates are mild—this species prefers a winter chill. May suffer from the sudden blackening of foliage and dieback of branches, but some individuals are more resistant than others. Trees are sometimes attacked by borers. Despite these liabilities, a small grove of quaking aspens is a beautiful focal point for the wildflower meadow, pond margin, or streambank. They are especially lovely against a background of conifers and are often planted near windows, decks, and patios, so that their fluttering leaves, pale bark, and golden fall colors can be enjoyed.

Native Habitat and Range. Near streams and on moist to dry slopes at high to (less often) low elevations from Alaska south to California and northern Mexico, and from near the coast (less commonly), east through the Rocky Mountains and much of North America to Labrador and the Atlantic coast.

Notes. Although this tree is most closely associated with the Rocky Mountains, it is fairly common in the Pacific Northwest, especially in the mountains and east of the Cascades. Its selection 'Pendula' has drooping branches.

Prunus   Rosaceae

cherry, plum

The economically important genus *Prunus* includes upward of 200 species, most native to the temperate regions of the Northern Hemisphere; about 30 species are native to North America but only a few occur in our area. Plums, cherries, apricots, peaches, and almonds—the "stone fruits"—are all members of *Prunus* (in the broad sense). Flowers are typically rosaceous, with five petals and many stamens. The fruits are drupes, a fleshy fruit with an ovary wall (pericarp) consisting of a thin outer skin (exocarp), a fleshy middle layer (mesocarp), and a stony inner layer (endocarp). A single seed, surrounded by a seed coat, develops inside the stony endocarp. Hundreds of cultivars have been developed, some for their fruit, others for their ornamental flowers.

Propagation. Easiest from seed. Collect ripe fruits and remove the fleshy part of the drupe. Plant the pits outside in the fall, and allow them to stratify under cold, moist conditions for spring germination. Can also be grown from cuttings of young, growing shoot tips made in mid to late spring, from semi-hardwood cuttings in mid to late summer, or from hardwood cuttings in late winter or fall, but these are more difficult methods.

Prunus emarginata   Zones 4a to 9b

bitter cherry

These deciduous shrubs or small trees are often multi-trunked and can vary in height from 2 to 15m (6 to 45ft). The bark is shiny and reddish or gray. The leaves are alternate, and the petioles are about 1cm (.5in). The blades are ovate to oblong and up to 8cm (3in) long. The leaves are usually rounded at the tips and have finely toothed margins; they turn yellow in autumn. The white to pinkish flowers bloom from mid spring to early summer in flat-topped clusters of up to ten; they are around 1.5cm (.5in) across. The small drupes are red to almost black when ripe and about 1cm (.5in) long.

Cultivation. Full sun or part shade, and moist to rather dry soil. As far as humans are concerned, this tree lives up to its common name, but birds relish the cherries, making this an excellent tree for the wildlife garden or hedgerow on either side of the Cascades. It is also a pretty tree for open places in the woodland garden.

Native Habitat and Range. In moist, open woods or near streams in drier habitats at low to mid elevations from British Columbia south to southern California, and from the coast east to Montana, Utah, and Arizona.

Notes. *Prunus e.* var. *emarginata* generally occurs east of the Cascades; it is often shrubbier, and the leaves tend to be only sparsely hairy or glabrous. *Prunus e.* var. *mollis* is more common west of the Cascades; it is usually more of a tree than a shrub and tends to be hairier, especially on the undersides of the leaves.

Prunus virginiana   Zones 3b to 9b

chokecherry

This attractive, deciduous shrub grows to about 4m (12ft) tall. The bark is shiny and purplish. The leaves, up to 10cm (4in) long, are oblong to elliptic with finely serrated margins. There are one or two glands where the blade meets the petiole, and leaves turn red or yellow in the fall. Numerous white flowers about 1cm (.5in) across bloom in long racemes, to 15cm (6in), at the branch tips from late spring to mid summer. Small red or purple drupes about 1cm (.5in) long follow the flowers.

Prunus emarginata

Prunus virginiana (photo by Sally A. Simmons)

Cultivation. Full sun, and moist to rather dry soil. Tolerates some shade. Birds are very fond of chokecherries, making this an excellent large shrub for any wildlife garden. Plant it in a hedgerow, near the back fence, or in a sunny spot in the woodland garden.

Native Habitat and Range. In various habitats, from coastal bluffs, to streambanks in the arid shrub-steppe, to open woods at low to mid elevations from British Columbia east to Newfoundland and south through our area to southern California.

Notes. *Prunus v.* var. *melanocarpa* is a larger shrub with dark red or purple fruits; it ranges from British Columbia south along the east slope of the Cascades, then west to the coast in southern Oregon and California, east to the Great Plains and New Mexico. *Prunus v.* var. *demissa* is a smaller shrub with dark purple drupes. In this variety, the undersides of the leaves are hairy; it occurs on both sides of the Cascades from British Columbia through California, scattered south and east to Texas. Western or Klamath plum (*P. subcordata*) is native in much of California, with a range extending north as far as southern Oregon.

Purshia tridentata	Zones 3b to 9b	Rosaceae

antelope bitterbrush

This is a lovely deciduous shrub with an open, angular branching pattern, growing to 2m (6ft) tall and almost as wide. The small leaves are wedge-shaped (cuneate), up to 2cm (1in) long with three narrow lobes or teeth at the tip; they are green on the upper surface and densely gray-haired underneath. The beautiful, fragrant flowers bloom singly on short twigs from mid spring to early summer. The pale yellow blossoms have five petals and are about 1.5cm (.5in) across. Each flower produces one single-seeded achene about 1.5cm (.5in) long.

Cultivation. Full sun or very light shade, and well-drained, moist to dry soil. An excellent plant for the wildlife garden and an especially good choice for large rock gardens, hedgerows, and shrub borders east of the Cascades. It is possible to grow this species west of the Cascades in full sun with sandy or rocky soil.

Propagation. Best from seed collected in summer and planted outside in fall to stratify under cold, moist conditions for germination the following spring. Existing plants can be layered by cutting a nick in a branch, bending it to the ground, burying the nicked area in soil, and staking the branch in place. This is a slow method; it may take some months for roots to form.

Native Habitat and Range. From grasslands and sagebrush plains to juniper or ponderosa pine forest, at low to mid elevations, from southern British Columbia south along the east slope of the Cascades in Washington, ranging further west in southern Oregon, south through California, east to western Montana, Wyoming, Colorado, and New Mexico.

Notes. This species is one of the most important browse plants for large herbivores, both wild and domestic, in the dry regions of the west. There are about six other species of *Purshia*, mostly native to southwestern North America, with Stansbury's cliffrose (*P. stansburiana*) reaching western Idaho.

Quercus		Fagaceae

oak

Quercus is a familiar genus of approximately 300 species of deciduous or evergreen trees and shrubs, most of them native to the temperate parts of the Northern Hemisphere, with a few occurring in the mountains of tropical regions to the south. Close to 100 species are native to North America; quite a few oaks are native to California, but only five range north into Oregon. Oaks are extraordinarily promiscuous (many hybrid populations occur in nature) and monoecious,

Purshia tridentata (photo by Sally A. Simmons)

with male and female flowers blooming in separate structures, but on the same plant. The male (staminate) flowers are slender, drooping catkins, and the female (pistillate) flowers bloom in small clusters, eventually developing into an acorn, a one-seeded nut surrounded by a series of bracts that form a cup-like involucre. Several bird species eat acorns, and the western gray squirrel, whose populations are declining, depends on oaks for survival. Oaks are an excellent choice for creating habitat in large expanses of lawn or pasture. Plant oaks in groves and, once they have grown a bit, begin adding understory species to recreate an oak woodland. *Phytophthora ramorum*, which causes sudden oak death, was first noticed when such large stands of oaks began to die in California; it has since been discovered to be pathogenic to many other, unrelated plant species, and efforts are being made to control it.

Propagation. Grow from seed, but acorns are sometimes difficult to find: trees may not pro duce crops every year, and in years when acorns are plentiful, they are quickly consumed by wildlife. Collect acorns as soon as they are ripe. If the seeds have been attacked by weevils (leaving a small hole in the acorn wall), try soaking them in hot water at 49C (120F) for half an hour before planting. The acorns of some oaks germinate in the fall, extending a long taproot into the soil soon after they drop from the tree, so they should be planted soon after harvest, either into deep containers or directly into the garden. Shoots will appear when the weather warms in the spring. If trees are to be held in containers, lateral roots can be encouraged by pruning or allowing the taproot to be "air pruned" when it tries to grow out of the container and into the ground. Another suggestion for encouraging lateral root development is to plant the acorns in a box with copper mesh at the bottom, about 15cm (6in) below the seeds; the taproot will stop when it touches the copper mesh and lateral roots will begin to form. This will give young oaks a better chance of survival when transplanted.

Quercus chrysolepis   Zones 6b to 9b

canyon live oak

This evergreen tree has a rounded shape and grows to 20m (60ft) in height and width, sometimes larger, but sometimes small and shrubby. The bark of young trees is smooth and pale, becoming darker gray and scaly or checked with age. The alternate leaves are leathery, mostly oblong and up to 6cm (2.5in) long. The margins vary from entire to spiny-toothed, and the petioles are short. Tiny flowers bloom from mid to late spring. The acorns are oblong and about 2.5cm (1in) long or longer and almost as wide. The involucral cup is well developed, and the scales are covered with dense, felt-like hairs.

Cultivation. Full sun or light shade, and well-drained, moist to rather dry soil. Tolerates drought once established. This is an adaptable oak for many gardens west of the Cascades, but it needs full sun and good drainage in the wettest climates. It should do well in many dry gardens east of the Cascades, but may not be tolerant of extreme cold. An excellent specimen tree for the wildlife garden or oak grove and a fine addition to the large hedgerow, where it will provide evergreen cover, nesting sites, and food for birds and other wildlife. Prune it or plant it in dry soil to keep it small.

Native Habitat and Range. In canyons, on moist slopes, and in open woods at low to mid elevations, from southwestern Oregon, south through California and Arizona.

Notes. *Quercus c.* var. *chrysolepis*, which occurs throughout the range, is extremely variable in size and other characteristics.

Quercus garryana   Zones 5b to 9b

Oregon white oak, Garry oak

This deciduous tree can grow to a massive size, reaching 25m (75ft) or more in height and up to 20m (60ft) in width, but is often small and shrubby. The bark is furrowed and scaly, and the trunk can grow to 1m (3ft) in diameter. The alternate leaves have petioles to 2.5cm (1in) long. The leaf blades are oblong in outline, to 12cm (5in) long and deeply lobed with three to seven rounded lobes on each side. Their upper surface is shiny and dark green; the lower surface is paler and hairy. The leaves turn yellow-brown in the fall. The tiny male (staminate) flowers bloom in drooping catkins; the female (pistillate) flowers bloom singly or in few-flowered clusters. Flowers bloom as the leaves appear, from mid spring to early summer. The acorns are up to 3cm (1.5in) long, surrounded by a shallow, scaly cup and maturing in one year. They are edible, but crops are not produced every year.

Cultivation. Full sun or light shade, and moist to fairly dry, well-drained soil. Although the species' habitat includes forested wetlands and floodplains, planting trees in saturated soils may be risky. Rather slow-growing, a full-sized Oregon white oak is nevertheless a magnificent tree, if you have the time and the room, and it can be kept small if planted in rocky, dry soil.

Native Habitat and Range. In rocky bluffs and dry slopes to (usually) well-drained, deep soils of floodplains and river banks, at fairly low elevations from southwestern British Columbia, south to southern California, mostly west of the Cascades, but also east through the Columbia River Gorge and north along the east slope of the Cascades to central Washington.

Notes. *Quercus g.* var. *garryana* has the widest range and is the common variety throughout the Northwest; plants are often shrub-like in dry, rocky habitats. *Quercus g.* var. *fruticosa* is a spreading shrub to 3m (10ft) with smooth, gray bark and hairy leaves to 5cm (2in); it occurs from west central Oregon south to northern California. *Quercus g.* var. *semota*, a somewhat larger, multi-stemmed shrub to 5m (15ft), occurs in dry woods in southern Oregon.

Quercus chrysolepis

Quercus kelloggii

Quercus garryana

Quercus kelloggii   Zones 6b to 9b

California black oak

This deciduous tree grows to 25m (75ft) or more in height and about as wide. The trunk can grow to be 1m (3ft) across, and the dark bark is smooth in young trees, becoming fissured in age. The leaves are alternate and have petioles to 4cm (1.5in) long and oblong blades to 15cm (6in) or more. The blades are bright green above and paler underneath. The leaf margins are deeply pinnately lobed, and the lobes have coarse teeth with long bristles at the tips. The new spring growth is pinkish, and the leaves turn yellow-orange or yellow in the fall. The tiny flowers bloom from mid spring to early summer, and the acorns require two years to mature. The oblong acorns are about 2.5cm (1in) long, enclosed about halfway in a cup with thin scales.

Cultivation. Full sun or part shade, and moist to rather dry soil. This is a lovely, drought-tolerant oak for drier gardens west of the Cascades; it may not survive the colder places east of the Cascades. Plant it as a specimen tree in a lawn or field, or as part of the woodland garden or oak grove. It provides food, cover, and nesting sites for wildlife, and seasonal beauty for gardeners.

Native Habitat and Range. On forested, rather dry hills at low to fairly high elevations from west central Oregon, south through the mountains to southern California.

Notes. *Quercus* ×*moreha* (oracle oak) is a hybrid between this species and *Q. wislizeni* (interior live oak), a native of California

Quercus sadleriana   Zones 6a to 9b

deer oak

This spreading evergreen shrub has smooth, gray bark and grows to 2m (6ft) tall. The alternate leaves are usually oblong in shape, and the pinnate veins are prominent. The leaves grow to 12cm (5in) long, and the margins are sharply serrate. The small flowers bloom in the leaf axils from mid spring to early summer and produce one to several acorns, to 2cm (1in) long, in a thin-scaled cup.

Cultivation. Full sun or part shade, and well-drained, fairly dry soil. This is a beautiful and uncommon evergreen shrub for the wildlife garden or hedgerow. Plant it in a rocky glade or at the edge of the wooded wildlife garden.

Native Habitat and Range. On open slopes and dry forested ridges at mid to fairly high elevations from southwestern Oregon to northwestern California.

Notes. Huckleberry oak (*Q. vacciniifolia*) is also evergreen, about 1.5m (5ft) in height and 3m (10ft) in width. Its ovate, gray-green leaves have smooth margins, growing to 3cm (1.5in) long; the acorns are small and rounded. This oak, native to dry, stony slopes and thickets at mid elevations from southwestern Oregon south through the mountains of California, makes a good rock garden shrub and may be more tolerant of cold than some other native shrubs.

Rhamnus purshiana   Zones 4a to 9b   Rhamnaceae

cascara

This small, deciduous tree has smooth, gray bark and grows to 10m (30ft). The alternate leaves are oblong, with blades up to 13cm (5in) on stout petioles. The glossy, dark green leaves have margins with very fine teeth and prominent lateral veins running parallel from the midvein. The flowers are tiny and greenish, blooming in umbels of up to 25 from mid spring to early summer. The berry-like fruits are purplish black and about 1cm (.5in) long.

Cultivation. Full sun to full shade, and moist soil. The peachy-yellow fall foliage will be brighter if plants have some sun. This is one of the best berry-producing trees for birds and a good choice

Quercus sadleriana

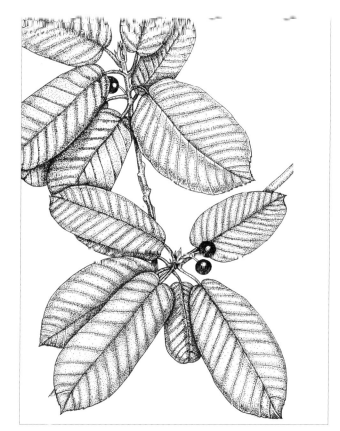

Rhamnus purshiana

Rhamnus purshiana

for the sunny or shady wildlife garden, or taller sections of a hedgerow. The berries can also be eaten by humans but are not very flavorful.

Propagation. Easiest from seed. Collect ripe fruits in the fall (you will have to race the birds), clean some of the pulp from the seeds (actually small pits, each with a few seeds inside), and plant them in the fall. Leave planted seeds outside to stratify in cold, moist winter conditions for germination the following spring.

Native Habitat and Range. In wet to fairly dry woods, forest edges, and marshy clearings at low to mid elevations from southern British Columbia south to central California, mainly west of the Cascades, but also east to northeastern Oregon, through Idaho to western Montana.

Notes. Often classified as *Frangula purshiana*. The bark of this tree is still used as a laxative. *Rhamnus californica* (*F. californica*; California coffeeberry) is an evergreen shrub of the Southwest that ranges as far north as southwestern Oregon. The 100 or more species of *Rhamnus* and *Frangula* (in which genus cascara and other species are sometimes placed) occur throughout the world in temperate and subtropical areas.

Rhododendron   Ericaceae

Rhododendron includes more than 700 species, the vast majority of which are native to southeastern Asia; 20 or more species are native to the eastern and southeastern United States, and only a handful evolved in our region—though rhododendrons generally grow so happily here that they are taken for natives by many. Included in the genus are the big, evergreen rhodies with leathery leaves and also all the azaleas. Some of these shrubs are deciduous or small in size, but all have typical flowers of five petals fused at their bases, anthers that release pollen through pores at their tips, and five-celled capsules.

Propagation. Both *R. albiflorum* and *R. macrophyllum* are fairly easy to grow from cuttings taken from semi-ripe wood in summer or fall, treated with rooting hormone, and set into pumice or some other medium until roots form. *Rhododendron occidentale* is more easily grown from seed. Collect the seeds as the capsules dry and plant them outside into flats of potting soil in late winter or early spring, keeping the planting medium, seeds, and seedlings warm, moist, and shaded.

Rhododendron albiflorum   Zones 3b to 8a

white-flowered or Cascade rhododendron

This deciduous slender-branched rhododendron grows to 2m (6ft). The leaves are alternate and tend to grow in clusters; they are elliptic in shape, growing to 9cm (3.5in) in length, with smooth (entire) margins, and turn orange and crimson in fall. The bell-shaped flowers, about 2cm (1in) long, are white or creamy and grow in small clusters along the stems; they bloom from early to late summer and are followed by capsules.

Cultivation. Part shade or dappled light, and well-drained but moist or wet soil with good organic content. This species is notoriously difficult to grow, but some gardeners have had success. When it cooperates, it is a lovely shrub for the shady woodland garden or pond margin.

Native Habitat and Range. Usually in wet places along streams and in moist forests, but sometimes on well-drained sites at mid to fairly high elevations in the mountains from British Columbia south through the mountains to central Oregon and east to western Montana.

Notes. *Rhododendron a.* var. *albiflorum* has a large range through the Pacific Northwest but is an unusually difficult garden subject, perhaps lacking particular mycorrhizae or other soil symbionts.

Rhododendron albiflorum

Rhododendron occidentale

Rhododendron macrophyllum

Rhododendron macrophyllum   Zones 7a to 9b

Pacific or western rhododendron, California rose-bay

This large, evergreen rhododendron can reach 8m (26ft) in height but is usually shorter. It typically has an open (some would say leggy) habit and can form thickets. The leaves are oblong and leathery, 8 to 20cm (3 to 8in) in length. Flowers vary from light pink to rose-purple and are up to 4cm (1.5in) long. They bloom in clusters at the branch tips from late spring to mid summer. Capsules follow the flowers.

Cultivation. Part shade or dappled light, and moist to somewhat dry soil with high organic content. Tolerates deep shade but will produce more flowers when planted at the edge of the forest or in part sun. Excellent under the big trees in the woodland garden or as part of a hedgerow. With luck, deer will leave this shrub alone, but it may be toxic to humans.

Native Habitat and Range. In moist to rather dry forests at low to mid elevations from southwestern British Columbia south to northern California, and from the west slope of the Cascades to the coast.

Notes. This species is the state flower of Washington.

Rhododendron occidentale   Zones 6b to 9b

western azalea

This deciduous shrub grows 1 to 3m (3 to 10ft) or taller and has oblong, thin-textured leaves to 8cm (3in) long on short petioles. In fall, the foliage turns bright shades of orange and red. The wonderfully fragrant flowers vary in color from white to pink with yellow or rose blotches; they bloom in clusters from late spring to mid summer, after the shrubs have developed leaves. The oblong capsules are about 2cm (1in) long.

Cultivation. Part shade or dappled light (under taller trees or near a building), and moist soil. Plant this lovely native in the hedgerow or opening in the woodland garden, where it can be seen throughout the year.

Native Habitat and Range. Moist woods and streambanks at low to mid elevations from the coast of southwestern Oregon, east to the west slope of the Cascades and south to southern California.

Notes. *Rhododendron o.* var. *occidentale* occurs in Oregon and California; it generally has white flowers with yellow streaking, pink-tinged at the base. 'Leonard Frisbie' is a noteworthy selection, and the species is also a parent to many hybrids. The related *Loiseleuria procumbens* (alpine azalea) is a little mat-forming shrub that grows only to 10cm (4in) tall, with stems spreading to 30cm (1ft); its opposite, oblong leaves are leathery and evergreen, less than 1cm (.5in) long, and its tiny flowers, bell-shaped and pink, with five petal lobes, grow in clusters at the stem tips. This species lives in lowland bogs and alpine heath. It has a circumpolar range, dipping as far south in the Pacific Northwest as northern Washington; it is often cultivated among the cool, moist boulders of the rock garden and can be propagated from cuttings, by layering, and probably from seed.

Rhus   Anacardiaceae

sumac

Rhus includes around 100 species, distributed throughout the temperate and subtropical parts of the world; fewer than 20 are North American natives, and only two of these occur in our area. The fruits are used to make tea. Also native to the Pacific Northwest—and carefully avoided—

Rhus glabra

are related plants that cause contact dermatitis, lately classified in *Toxicodendron* ("poison tree"): *T. diversilobum* (*R. diversiloba*; Pacific poison oak) and *T. rydbergii* (*R. radicans*, *R. radicans* var. *rydbergii*; western poison ivy).

Propagation. In late winter, separate and transplant some of the many rooted suckers that are produced from the woody rhizomes. Sumacs can also be grown from cuttings made during the late summer from semi-hardwood stems treated with hormones, stuck into pumice or some other medium, and kept under humid conditions until roots form. Another method is to make root cuttings during the winter. Alternatively, collect and sow seeds in fall, place them in a dish, pour boiling water over them, and sow outside, after cooling, leaving them to stratify under cold, moist winter conditions; expect sporadic germination the following spring.

Rhus glabra	Zones 3b to 9b

smooth sumac

These fast-growing, deciduous shrubs spread by woody rhizomes and produce glabrous (hairless) stems to 3m (10ft). The pinnately compound, alternate leaves are up to 40cm (16in) long with up to 25 leaflets. The leaflets are lanceolate to elliptic, up to 12cm (5in) long with serrate margins. They are dark green above and pale below during the growing season, turning brilliant shades of red and orange in the fall. Tiny greenish yellow flowers (some functionally male, others female) bloom in dense panicles from mid spring to mid summer. The fruits are dry, flattened, berry-like drupes that turn scarlet in fall and remain in conical clusters on the branch tips into the winter.

Cultivation. Full sun, and moist (not wet) to dry, well-drained soil. This species has a bonsai look in the winter, a tropical look in the summer, and the spectacular fall foliage is unsurpassed.

The more a gardener disturbs the soil at the shrub's base, the more it will spread, but this feature makes it a good plant for erosion control on dry banks. Unwanted suckers can be cut back, transplanted, or mowed. A beautiful addition to the hedgerow, dry parking strip, or along the sunny border of the wildlife garden on either side of the Cascades.

Native Habitat and Range. In fairly arid, rocky canyons and washes at low to mid elevations from southern British Columbia, south, mainly on the east side of the Cascades (but also on the west side) through Oregon and Nevada to Mexico, east through the United States.

Notes. In the selection 'Laciniata', the leaflets are deeply lobed, giving the foliage a ferny effect.

Rhus trilobata	Zones 3b to 9b

lemonade or skunkbush sumac

This deciduous shrub grows to 2m (6ft) in height or less, with at least the same spread. Each alternate leaf grows to about 7cm (3in) long and has three leaflets with lobed margins. The middle leaflet is largest and fan-shaped, and the leaves turn red in the fall. Tiny, greenish yellow flowers bloom in small clusters near the branch tips from late spring to mid summer. The fruits are red-orange drupes, not quite 1cm (.5in) long.

Cultivation. Full sun, and dry to somewhat moist soil. Some gardeners find the smell of the foliage unpleasant, but this plant tends to form clumps instead of suckering, making it a fine choice for the medium-sized hedgerow. Plant it in the wildlife garden, along a dry bank, or near a parking area, where its bright fall colors and attractive fruits can be enjoyed.

Native Habitat and Range. Along streams, hillsides, and canyons at low to mid elevations, mainly east of the Cascades from Alberta, south in southeastern Washington and near the Snake River in eastern Oregon, in southwestern Oregon, and south through California to Mexico, east through the Rocky Mountains to the Great Plains.

Notes. *Rhus t.* var. *anisophylla*, *R. t.* var. *quinata*, and *R. t.* var. *simplicifolia*, mainly native to the Southwest, just enter our area in southern Oregon; *R. t.* var. *trilobata* has a wider range through the west, including the eastern edge of the Pacific Northwest.

Ribes	Grossulariaceae

currant, gooseberry

Ribes includes about 150 species of shrubs, mostly native to temperate regions of the Northern Hemisphere, and also extending south into the Andes; about 50 are native to North America, half to the Pacific Northwest. Gooseberries are thorny, with long spines at the nodes and sometimes bristly internodes; currants usually lack thorns and are different in other ways, leading some to split gooseberries and currants into two separate genera (*Grossularia* and *Ribes*, respectively). Both currants and gooseberries are shrubs with palmate leaves and five-part flowers. The bases of the sepals, petals, and stamens are fused to form a floral tube, or hypanthium, above the inferior ovary; the hypanthium and the free tips of the petals and sepals are usually colored, and some species produce showy flowers. Several cultivars, often of European or Asian origin, have been developed for their fruits, which are enjoyed by birds and sometimes used in pies and jams. Some *Ribes* species are alternate hosts for white pine blister rust and may be banned in certain areas.

Propagation. Remove seeds from the berries and plant them into flats of potting soil in the fall. Leave them outside where the winter weather will chill the seeds and help to break dormancy for spring germination. Plants can also be propagated from semi-hard or hardwood cuttings taken in late summer or fall, treated with rooting hormones, and set into pumice or some other medium until roots form.

Rhus trilobata

Ribes aureum var. *aureum*

Ribes aureum var. aureum   Zones 3b to 9b

golden currant

This thornless, deciduous shrub grows to a height of 1 to 2m (3 to 6ft). The light green leaves are smooth and three-lobed, reaching about 5cm (2in) in length. Each raceme bears up to 15 tubular, golden yellow, sometimes fragrant flowers that turn orange as they age. Flowers usually bloom from mid to late spring. Red or purplish berries follow the flowers.

Cultivation. Sun or light shade, and moist to fairly dry soil, with occasional water in hot climates. This species is often found east of the Cascades and is tolerant of heat and cold, but will also do well on the wetter west side. A fine plant for the hedgerow or wildlife garden; hummingbirds will visit the flowers, and fruit-eating birds will enjoy the berries.

Native Habitat and Range. Near streams and in floodplains in ponderosa pine and sagebrush country at low to fairly high elevations on the east slope of the Cascades, from north central Washington to California, east to the east side of the Rocky Mountains from Saskatchewan and South Dakota to New Mexico.

Notes. *Ribes a.* var. *aureum* is the only variety encountered in our area.

Ribes bracteosum   Zones 6a to 9b

stink currant

This open, thornless shrub is deciduous and can grow to 3m (10ft) tall. The alternate leaves are maple like, up to 20cm (8in) across, and have an odor that some people find unpleasant. White to greenish flowers bloom from late spring to early summer in upright racemes to 30cm (1ft)

Ribes bracteosum

Ribes cereum (photo by Sally A. Simmons)

long, often with small leaves at the base. The flowers are saucer-shaped, and there are 20 to 40 in each inflorescence. The berries are rounded, about 1cm (.5in) long, black and glaucous, covered with a waxy, white coating.

Cultivation. Shade, part sun, or dappled light, and wet to very moist soil. This is an excellent, lush shrub for the streambank, pond margin, or bog. Plant it in the wet, shady spot in the wildlife garden, where birds will have access to the berries.

Native Habitat and Range. In moist to wet woods, thickets, and along streams, at low to fairly high elevations, from Alaska, south to northern California, mainly from the coast to the west slope of the Cascades.

Notes. The berries are variable in flavor; some people like them, and many of the coastal tribes consumed them in large numbers. Maple-leaf currant (*R. acerifolium*) and red swamp currant (*R. triste*) have smaller but similar maple-like leaves with large, pointed lobes; in these species, the saucer-shaped flowers are reddish and arranged in relatively short racemes.

Ribes cereum	Zones 3b to 9b

wax currant

This thornless, deciduous shrub is usually rounded in shape and grows to 1.5m (5ft). The small leaves are shallowly lobed and fan-shaped, about 2.5cm (1in) in length and width, and are sometimes hairy (pubescent) as well as glandular. The tubular flowers are white or pinkish and about 1cm (.5in) long. They bloom in small clusters at the branch tips from mid spring to early summer. The red berries are attractive, but most humans consider them inedible; they are better left for the birds.

Ribes cruentum

Cultivation. Full sun to part shade or dappled light, and dry to moist, well-drained soil. This is an excellent small shrub for gardens east of the Cascades or in southwestern Oregon; it is less cooperative in wetter climates unless the soil is very well drained. Plant this pretty shrub in the sunny hedgerow, wildlife garden, or large rock garden.

Native Habitat and Range. In arid sagebrush habitats and rocky ridges, at fairly low to high elevations, mainly east of the Cascade crest (further west in southern Oregon) from southern British Columbia, south to California and Arizona, east to the Dakotas, Colorado, and New Mexico.

Notes. *Ribes c.* var. *cereum* has deeply lobed, fan-shaped bracts beneath each small inflorescence and occurs throughout most of the western part of the range. *Ribes c.* var. *pedicellare* (*R. c.* var. *inebrians*) has very small, ovate bracts and ranges from western Idaho to the east and south. *Ribes c.* var. *colubrinum* has ovate bracts and is relatively hairless (glabrous); it is restricted to the Snake River Canyon and its tributaries in southeastern Washington, northeastern Oregon, and western Idaho.

Ribes cruentum	Zones 6b to 9b

shiny-leaf currant

This deciduous shrub produces multiple stems to 1.5m (5ft) tall. Each node has three slightly curved spines to 1cm (.5in) long. The glabrous (hairless) leaves are rounded and about 2cm (1in) across. The blades usually have three shallow lobes with finely toothed margins. Flowers bloom singly or in pairs from short, drooping peduncles. The cylindric hypanthium is red, and the narrow calyx lobes are flared back. The petals are pinkish or white and have fringed (erose) margins. The flowers are about 1.5cm (.5in) long and bloom from early to late spring. The round berries are about 1cm (.5in) long, red or purple, and quite spiny—best left for the birds.

Cultivation. Full sun to part shade or dappled light, and moist, well-drained soil. A good thorny shrub for the wildlife and hummingbird garden or hedgerow, providing food, nesting sites, and cover for birds.

Native Habitat and Range. Near rivers, in stream gravel, canyons, and ridges at low to fairly high elevations west of the Cascades from west central Oregon, south to northern California.

Notes. *Ribes c.* var. *cruentum* and *R. c.* var. *oregonense* both occur in Oregon.

Ribes divaricatum	Zones 6a to 9b

spreading or wild gooseberry

This thorny, deciduous, arching shrub can grow to 2m (6ft) tall. A few brown spines, up to 2cm (1in) long, occur at the stem nodes (where leaves are attached), but the internodes are smooth or merely bristly. The leaves are broadly oval in outline, usually with three main lobes; the lobes have toothed margins, and the blades grow to 6cm (2.5in) in length and width, on petioles as long as the leaves. The flowers are about 1cm (.5in) long with a narrowly bell-shaped, reddish floral tube and reflexed calyx lobes. The tiny petals are white or reddish, and flowers bloom in small racemes from mid to late spring. The edible berries are rounded and smooth, purple-black, and about 1cm (.5in) long.

Cultivation. Full sun to part shade or dappled light, and moist soil. A good barrier and an excellent shrub for the damp places in the wildlife garden or hedgerow, providing food, nesting sites, and thorny cover for birds.

Native Habitat and Range. In moist, open woods, canyons, hillsides, and clearings at low elevations from southwestern British Columbia, south to southern California, mainly west of the Cascades but east in the Columbia River Gorge.

Notes. *Ribes d.* var. *divaricatum* occurs from British Columbia, south to Oregon; *R. d.* var. *pubiflorum* has a range near the coast from southwestern Oregon to California. Another deciduous, thorny shrub, *R. lacustre* (prickly or black swamp gooseberry), grows as tall, and it too makes an excellent barrier plant; though its nodal spines are smaller, the stems are covered with slender prickles. Its flowers, broadly saucer-shaped and reddish to maroon, are borne later, from mid spring to mid summer in drooping racemes; the deep purple berries are slightly smaller and bland. It grows in various habitats, from dry, forested slopes and ridges to streambanks and moist woods at mid elevations, on both sides of the Cascades from Alaska south to California, east to the Great Lakes and Atlantic coast. Site it and culture it as you would *R. divaricatum*.

Ribes laxiflorum	Zones 4a to 9b

trailing black currant

This spreading, deciduous shrub usually grows to 1m (3ft) tall but can become vine-like and grow to 5m (15ft) or more in deep woods. The stems are thornless and reddish brown. The leaf blades are maple-like, growing to about 8cm (3in) across. They have well-developed petioles, and the five lobes are triangular and have coarsely serrated margins. Up to 18 flowers bloom in erect racemes that are usually shorter than the leaves. The flowers are saucer-shaped, about 1cm (.5in) across, and bloom from mid spring to mid summer. The floral tube and calyx lobes vary from greenish white to reddish purple, and the small, crescent-shaped petals are red. The blackish purple fruits are glaucous, with a waxy, whitish coating, and have some glandular hairs.

Cultivation. Shade, sun, or dappled light, and rather wet to moist soil. This is a pretty, trailing shrub for the pond margin, woodland garden, moist slope, or damp spot in the wildlife garden or hedgerow, where birds will enjoy the berries.

Ribes divaricatum

Ribes laxiflorum

Native Habitat and Range. In wet coastal forests, roadsides, and mountain slopes at low to mid elevations from Alaska south along the coast to northern California, mainly west of the Cascades, but east across British Columbia to Idaho, south to Colorado and New Mexico.

Notes. The berries were eaten by some of the northwestern tribes, but most people do not consider them very palatable.

Ribes menziesii	Zones 8a to 9b

canyon gooseberry

This upright, deciduous shrub grows to 2m (6ft) tall. The branches are gray, bristly, and glandular with three spreading spines to 1.5cm (.5in) long at each node. The petiolate leaf blades are up to 4cm (1.5in) wide; the three main lobes have toothed margins. One or two flowers bloom from the short racemes that develop from the nodes. The narrowly bell-shaped floral tube and reflexed calyx lobes are red, and the small fan-shaped petals vary from white to pinkish or yellow and tend to have inrolled margins. The flowers are about 1cm (.5in) long and bloom from early to late spring. The round, reddish purple berries are about 1cm (.5in) long and glandular-hairy.

Cultivation. Full sun or part shade, and moist, well-drained soil. Not especially tolerant of cold but fairly drought-tolerant. A good shrub for the hummingbird or wildlife garden or hedgerow west of the Cascades. It can be used as a thorny barrier and makes good nesting habitat, but only birds will find the berries palatable.

Native Habitat and Range. In canyons, woods, and flats, generally at low elevations in the Coast Ranges of central Oregon, south through much of western California.

Notes. Only one variety, *R. m.* var. *menziesii*, occurs in our area.

Ribes sanguineum	Zones 5b to 9b

red-flowering or blood currant

This lovely thornless, deciduous shrub grows from 1 to 3m (3 to 10ft). The rounded leaves are 3 to 7cm (1.5 to 3in) wide, pubescent and sometimes glandular, with three to five toothed lobes. Drooping racemes each bear ten to 20 tubular flowers with a pale pink to deep red floral tube and calyx, and pink to whitish petals. Flowers are occasionally white and bloom from early spring to early summer. The black berries are glaucous, waxy and whitish; they are edible but not very good—best left for the birds.

Cultivation. Sun to part shade, and moist to fairly dry, well-drained soil. This is a wonderful plant in the hummingbird or wildlife garden, or as part of a hedgerow, blooming just about the time when hummingbirds are migrating to their summer breeding grounds.

Native Habitat and Range. On rocky slopes and moist to rather dry woods and valleys at low to mid elevations from southwestern British Columbia south to west central California, and from near the coast to the west slope of the Cascades, occasionally east of the Cascades in British Columbia and northern Washington, Idaho, and the Columbia River Gorge.

Notes. *Ribes s.* var. *glutinosum* grows along the coast from Oregon to California; *R. s.* var. *sanguineum* occurs throughout the range. One of our best-loved native shrubs, this species has been cultivated for years. Selections include 'Album', 'White Icicle', and 'Inverness White' (white flowers); 'Claremont' and 'Spring Showers' (pink); and 'Elk River Red' and 'King Edward VII' (deeper red). *Ribes lobbii* (gummy gooseberry), with showy red and white flowers, is a spiny, spreading shrub to 1m (3ft) and a desirable garden plant; it lives near streams and in forests and rock outcrops at low to mid elevations, from southwestern British Columbia, south to northwestern California, and from the coast to the west slope of the Cascades, east of the Cascades in Washington and in the Columbia River Gorge.

Ribes menziesii

Ribes sanguineum

Rosa	Rosaceae

rose

Rosa encompasses more than 100 species, mostly native to temperate parts of the Northern Hemisphere; fewer than ten of the 20 species native to North America occur in our area. Humans have been tending, selecting, and crossing roses for millennia, resulting in something like 20,000 cultivated varieties. Roses are also grown for fragrant oil and for their hips, which are a good source of vitamin C. The hip is the fleshy, red hypanthium, or floral tube, the fused bases of the sepals, petals, and stamen filaments that surround the single-seeded achenes, which are the true fruits.

Propagation. Collect hips just as they ripen, remove the achenes, and plant them into flats of potting soil in the fall. Leave them outside and allow them to cold stratify over winter for germination the following spring. Woody rose rhizomes can often be cut apart in early spring, and root cuttings can be made in winter. Roses are sometimes grown from semi-hardwood cuttings taken in the summer and from hardwood cuttings made in mid to late fall, treated with hormones, and set to root in pumice, but this method is more difficult.

Rosa gymnocarpa	Zones 5a to 9b

baldhip or dwarf rose

The slender stems of this rhizomatous shrub usually grow no taller than about 1.5m (5ft). Branches vary from being quite bristly to having only a few thin thorns. The leaves are sparsely glandular and pinnately compound, composed of five to nine leaflets, the largest up to 4cm

Rosa gymnocarpa

Rosa nutkana

Rosa gymnocarpa, hips

(1.5in) long. The small, fragrant flowers bloom at the branch tips, singly or in few-flowered clusters, from late spring to late summer. The little roses are about 2.5cm (1in) across, with five, light to dark pink petals. As the fruits mature, the hips turn scarlet, and the five sepals fall from the top of the hip, leaving it "bald."

Cultivation. Full sun to part shade, and moist (but not wet) to rather dry soil. This drought-tolerant rose will survive in the dry shade under big conifers. Good for the edge of the shade garden or woodland, in the wildlife garden, or as a low-growing component of the hedgerow.

Native Habitat and Range. In dry to moist woods or forest openings at low to mid elevations, from southern British Columbia, south on both sides of the Cascades, to southern California, east to Montana and Idaho.

Notes. *Rosa spithamea* (ground rose) grows to a maximum of 30cm (1ft) and is native to dry woods in southwestern Oregon and California.

Rosa nutkana	Zones 4a to 9b

Nootka rose

The stems of this rhizomatous shrub can grow to 2m (6ft) or more. Branches vary from being quite prickly to almost thornless, except for the slender spines at the nodes. The pinnately compound leaves have five to seven leaflets with serrate margins, up to 7cm (3in) long. The fragrant flowers usually bloom singly at the tips of new branches, from late spring to mid summer; they can reach 8cm (3in) across, with five petals varying from light to dark pink. The hips are rounded, turning dark red or purplish and often hanging on the shrub through much of the winter.

Cultivation. Full sun to part shade, and fairly dry to wet soil. Tolerates sites prone to occasional flooding or affected by salt water. This is a beautiful native shrub throughout the year: the pink flowers are deliciously rose-scented, attracting butterflies as well as humans, and the red hips are a beautiful sight in winter and an important food source for birds. Will spread by rhizomes, suckering and forming thickets that provide habitat and help control erosion on moist banks.

Native Habitat and Range. In woods and meadows, along roadsides and near streams at low to mid elevations, from Alaska and British Columbia, south to northern California, and from the coast to the Cascades and east to eastern Washington, Oregon, and in the Rocky Mountains to Colorado, Utah, and New Mexico.

Notes. *Rosa n.* var. *nutkana* usually occurs west of the Cascades; *R. n.* var. *hispida* is more common east of the crest. *Rosa woodsii* (Woods' rose), a similar species, usually occurs east of the Cascades, often at lower elevations than *R. nutkana*, but the two hybridize when the opportunity presents itself. It too is a deciduous shrub, growing from 1 to 2m (3 to 6ft) tall and varies from prickly to almost thornless. Its sweetly scented, light to deep pink flowers are smaller, to 5cm (2in) across; they bloom in clusters of up to several flowers, from late spring to mid summer, and are followed by red hips. *Rosa w.* var. *ultramontana*, the common variety in our area, grows near streams, in open woods and rocky slopes at low to mid elevations, east of the Cascades from British Columbia, south to California and east to the Great Plains; although it prefers full sun to part shade and moist soil, it's the best native rose for gardens east of the Cascades, able to tolerate hot, dry summers and cold winters.

Rosa pisocarpa	Zones 7b to 9b

peafruit, swamp, or clustered wild rose

This rhizomatous shrub grows to 2m (6ft). Branches may be prickly or almost thornless. The leaves are pinnately compound, composed of five to nine leaflets, each one up to 4cm (1.5in) long. The small, fragrant flowers bloom in clusters of three or more at the tips of young stems, from late spring to mid summer. The roses are small, up to 4cm (1.5in) across, with five pink petals. As the fruits mature, the clusters of small hips turn dark red or purplish, tending to remain on the plants into the winter.

Cultivation. Full sun to part shade, and fairly dry to very wet or swampy soil, including sites prone to flooding. Site it along a streambank or wetland margin, or in the soggy spot of the hedgerow. This is also a good nectar plant for the butterfly garden, and the attractive hips provide winter food for birds.

Native Habitat and Range. Along streams and wetland thickets at low to mid elevations west of the Cascade crest, from British Columbia south to northern California, east through the Columbia River Gorge and northern Oregon to Idaho.

Notes. Similar is *R. californica* (California rose), a variable species primarily native to California, but ranging as far north as western Oregon. *Rosa acicularis* (prickly rose), a species of the far north, extends south from Alaska, throughout British Columbia, to the Rocky Mountains, Great Lakes, and Atlantic coast.

Rubus   Rosaceae

blackberry, raspberry, bramble

Rubus is a complex, cosmopolitan genus of a few hundred species, the highest concentration of which occur in the temperate parts of the Northern Hemisphere. Most of the nearly 200 species native to North America are in the northeast, many of them endemics; only 15 or so species are Northwest natives. Many cultivars of *Rubus*, including raspberries, boysenberries, and blackberries, are grown commercially for their fruit. The flowers of *Rubus* have five sepals, five petals, and many stamens. The fruits consist of tiny, individual drupelets, each with a style and stigma and a fleshy outer ovary containing a single seed. A cluster of these drupelets forms an aggregate fruit. In blackberries, the drupelets are fused to the receptacle and the two structures break off as a single unit; in raspberries, the drupelets are fused to each other but only weakly attached to the receptacle, falling away from it like a little cap. Some of our best-known native shrubs and groundcovers are species of *Rubus*, as are some of our most notorious weeds.

Propagation. Upright, shrubby species can be grown from hardwood cuttings taken in winter or semi-hardwood in summer, treated with rooting hormones, and set in pumice, potting soil, or another medium. Plants can also be propagated from divisions of the rhizomes made from late fall to early spring. Stolon-forming species can be propagated from rooted sections of the prostrate stems divided from late winter to spring. *Rubus* can also be grown from seed collected from the small fruits, cleaned of pulp, planted outside into flats of potting soil in fall, and left to stratify in the cold, moist winter weather for germination the following spring.

Rubus lasiococcus   Zones 5b to 9b

dwarf bramble, creeping raspberry

This thornless, trailing groundcover is only about 10cm (4in) tall, but each stem (stolon) can spread to 2m (6ft), rooting at the nodes. The leaves grow in clusters of up to three, are heart-shaped (cordate) in outline, and are palmately three-lobed. They are up to 6cm (2.5in) across and usually deciduous, but sometimes remain evergreen. One or two small, white flowers to 1.5cm (.5in) across bloom on pedicels to 5cm (2in) from early to late summer. The tiny, raspberry-like fruits, less than 1cm (.5in) across, are red and covered with gray hairs.

Cultivation. Full sun to full shade, and moist to rather dry soil. This is a charming groundcover for the woodland or shade garden. Plant it near a path or around taller shrubs and perennials.

Rosa pisocarpa

Rubus lasiococcus

Native Habitat and Range. In thickets, woods, and clearings at mid to fairly high elevations, from southwestern British Columbia, south in the Olympic and Cascade Mountains to northern California.

Notes. *Rubus arcticus* (arctic or dwarf blackberry, nagoonberry) is another thornless, trailing species with pink flowers and red fruits. Two of its subspecies, *R. a.* ssp. *arcticus* and *R. a.* ssp. *stellatus*, occur in northern bogs and meadows in southwestern Alaska and British Columbia; *R. a.* ssp. *acaulis* crosses North America, dipping south through British Columbia to the Cascades of northern Washington, the Rocky Mountains, the Great Lakes, and east.

Rubus parviflorus	Zones 4a to 9b

thimbleberry

This deciduous, thornless shrub spreads from woody rhizomes. The upright stems grow to 2m (6ft). The leaves are palmate and alternately arranged on the stems, growing 15cm (6in) long and at least as wide. The showy flowers are about 4cm (1.5in) across and have five white petals. They bloom in clusters of three to seven at the branch tips from late spring to mid summer. The drupelets are red when ripe, detaching from the receptacle like a shallow thimble (or raspberry).

Cultivation. Full sun to part shade, and moist to fairly dry soil. This plant will form suckers, making it a good species for erosion control on hillsides. Some gardeners find it too aggressive, but it is a fine plant for the hedgerow or wildlife garden on either side of the Cascades, providing cover and fruit for birds and nectar for butterflies. Many people enjoy the fruits.

Native Habitat and Range. Clearings and open woods in moist to rather dry soil, at low to fairly high elevations from Alaska south to southern California, and from the coast east to the Great Lakes, Wyoming, Colorado, and New Mexico.

Notes. A wide-ranging, variable species; the more common northern populations we see are *R. p.* var. *parviflorus*. Barton's raspberry (*R. bartonianus*) is similar, an upright shrub with no thorns and palmate leaves; it is endemic to the Snake River Canyon in northeastern Oregon and adjacent Idaho.

Rubus pedatus	Zones 4a to 9b

five-leaved or strawberry bramble

This thornless, mat-forming plant produces prostrate runners (stolons) to 1m (3ft) that form roots where the nodes touch the ground. Short stems to 2cm (1in) tall are produced at the nodes, each with around three leaves and a single flower on a slender peduncle to 6cm (2.5in) long. The sometimes evergreen leaves have well-developed petioles and are palmately compound into three leaflets, with the lateral leaflets again divided almost to the base. The leaflets are up to 3cm (1.5in) long and strongly toothed. The single white flowers bloom from late spring to mid summer. The fruits are small clusters of up to six (sometimes only one) bright red drupelets; they are tiny but tasty.

Cultivation. Part to full shade or dappled light, and moist to rather wet soil. This is a charming groundcover for the woodland or shade garden. Plant it near the bog, mossy streambank, or path.

Native Habitat and Range. Along streams and in boggy or mossy forests at low to fairly high elevations from Alaska, south to west central Oregon and from the coast east through southern British Columbia and western Washington to western Alberta, northern Idaho, and western Montana.

Rubus parviflorus

Rubus pedatus

Notes. *Rubus chamaemorus* (cloudberry), another thornless, low-growing, boreal species, has white flowers and yellowish berries; it inhabits northern bogs at low elevations, ranging as far south as southwestern British Columbia, Minnesota, and New York.

Rubus spectabilis   Zones 6a to 9b

salmonberry

This rhizomatous shrub can form thickets to 3m (10ft) or more in height. The stems are upright or arching and vary from quite thorny to almost thornless. The leaves consist of three leaflets with toothed margins, the longest leaflet growing to 9cm (3.5in) long. One or two flowers bloom on short branches from early spring to early summer. The flowers are about 3cm (1.5in) across, and the petals are dark pink to magenta. The fruits are small orange to reddish drupelets, separating from the elongated receptacle like a raspberry.

Cultivation. Full sun to full shade, and moist to rather wet soil. If given perfect conditions, this species will spread aggressively; one good way to control it is to plant it where the soil is a bit on the dry side. An excellent plant for the hummingbird and butterfly garden, despite its aggressive tendencies; its flowers open just as the hummingbirds are returning to their summer breeding grounds. Some people love salmonberries, others don't, and the flavor of the fruits can vary among plants. But if people don't eat them, the birds surely will, making this a fine shrub for the wildlife garden or hedgerow.

Native Habitat and Range. Along streams, wetlands, ditches, and in moist woods at low to mid elevations, from Alaska south to northwestern California, and from the coast, east to the west slope of the Cascades, occasionally east of the crest to northern Idaho.

Notes. *Rubus s.* var. *spectabilis*, the common form in our area, is one of the earliest fruits to ripen, adding to its wildlife value. Every indigenous tribe that lived within the range of salmonberry ate the shoots and fruits. Another upright species, *R. leucodermis* (blackcap, black raspberry), grows to 2m (6ft). The arching stems are prickly and strongly glaucous, waxy white; the flowers are white, and the purple or black drupelets form a tasty raspberry. Blackcaps grow in open forests, thickets, and disturbed sites from southern British Columbia south through California and from the coast, east to Montana and Arizona. Red raspberry (*R. idaeus*) is similarly sized, with somewhat prickly, brown-barked stems; its leaves also have three (to five) leaflets, but its white flowers eventually give way to red fruits. This plant grows along streams, in woods and talus, more commonly east of the Cascades, from Alaska south through California and east across much of North America and Eurasia; *R. i.* ssp. *idaeus* and *R. i.* ssp. *strigosus* occur in the Pacific Northwest.

Rubus ursinus   Zones 5b to 9b

trailing blackberry, dewberry

This is the trailing vine that catches unwary hikers by the ankles; it produces prickly, prostrate, glaucous (covered with a waxy, white bloom) stems to 5m (15ft) or more. The alternate leaves have three leaflets with toothed to lobed margins, the largest leaflets to 7cm (3in) long; they turn red in the fall. The plants are dioecious, producing either male or female flowers in flat-topped clusters. The flowers are white or pinkish and up to 4cm (1.5in) across, blooming from mid spring to mid summer. The fruits are black, up to 2.5cm (1in) long, and the drupelets are fused to the receptacle so that they break off as a unit, as in a typical blackberry.

Cultivation. Full sun or part shade, and moist to rather dry soil. Often behaves as a colonizing species on newly disturbed sites and can be ferociously aggressive in the garden. On the other

Rubus spectabilis

Rubus ursinus

hand, it produces what some consider the most delicious of all blackberries when female plants are present. Plant on a disturbed slope or in the far corner of the wildlife or woodland garden; drape the stems over a low fence or trellis to make the berries easier to harvest.

Native Habitat and Range. In woods, on prairies and disturbed sites, such as logged or burned areas, at low to mid elevations from southwestern British Columbia, south through California and from the coast, through the Cascades, occasionally east to northeastern Oregon, southeastern Washington, and central Idaho.

Notes. *Rubus u.* ssp. *macropetalus* occurs throughout the range; *R. u.* ssp. *ursinus* is more southern, native to California and southwestern Oregon. Because of its excellent flavor, this native blackberry has been used in developing several cultivated varieties such as boysenberries and loganberries. *Rubus nivalis* (snow bramble, raspberry, or dewberry) is another trailing plant with prickly stems to 2m (6ft) long. The evergreen leaves are broadly oval, sometimes three-lobed and usually simple, but sometimes divided into three leaflets. The flowers are pink, and the fruits are red and blackberry-like. This plant makes a charming groundcover and lives in moist woods at mid elevations in the mountains from southern British Columbia, west of the Cascades and south to northwestern California, sometimes east to Idaho.

Salix   Salicaceae

willow

Salix is a familiar genus of shrubs and trees, encompassing some 300 species. Most are native to the temperate and colder parts of the Northern Hemisphere, close to a hundred are native to North America, about half to the Pacific Northwest. Some species are large enough to be considered trees, but most willows are shrubs, and several are low and mat-forming. Willows are deciduous and have simple, alternate leaves. A single scale that lacks any sort of resinous surface covers each winter bud. The plants are dioecious, either male or female. The catkins (aments) are spike-like, small stems crowded with tiny flowers that lack petals or sepals. Each flower has a scale (a small bract) beneath it, and the catkins are upright or spreading, not usually drooping. The flowers may bloom before the leaves appear, or during, or after they expand, depending on the species. The fruits are tiny capsules, and the seeds have tufts of hair. Willows can be difficult to identify for a number of reasons. The sexes are separate, and the flowers of male plants fall soon after blooming; the leaves and stipules can be much larger in vigorous plants than in plants under stress; and other vegetative characters are also highly variable. The tendency of willows to hybridize only adds to the confusion. Willows are common along streams and other wet places. All improve wildlife habitat by providing excellent cover, nesting sites, and food for birds, butterfly larvae, and other insects. They should never be planted near drain fields or perforated pipe; be careful to site them away from septic systems, and all water and sewer lines.

Propagation. Easy from hardwood cuttings taken from late fall to late winter and set to root in pumice or moist potting soil until roots form; hormones can be used on the cut stems but are not necessary. Rooted suckers can be transplanted, and branches can be used as live stakes in moist to wet soils. Species from high elevations are sometimes grown from stem tip cuttings made just as the shoots are leafing out, treated with hormones, and rooted under humid conditions. Willows can also be grown from the tiny seed, collected as soon as it is ripe in summer or early fall and planted soon after harvest. Sow seeds onto the surface of flats of potting soil, and water them in without covering them. They will germinate in the fall or the following spring. Keep seedlings moist until they are large enough to transplant. Some species will self-sow.

Salix exigua	Zones 3b to 9b

narrowleaf or coyote willow

This deciduous shrub spreads by woody rhizomes to form thickets of reddish stems up to 3m (10ft) tall, but sometimes the plant forms a slender, taller tree up to 8m (26ft). The alternate leaves are narrowly lance-shaped or linear, up to 15cm (6in) long and 1.5cm (.5in) wide. The petioles are very short, and the tiny stipules quickly fall from them. The leaves have entire margins or small teeth; the new growth is softly hairy, but often hairless when older, turning yellow in the fall. The catkins are short and dense, up to 5cm (2in) long, with yellow scales. Male flowers have two stamens; female flowers have short stigma lobes. The flowers bloom during and after the expansion of the leaves, from early to late spring.

Cultivation. Full sun to part shade, and wet to moist soil. Tolerates long periods of flooding. An attractive, thicket-forming shrub for an open, wet site. Its rhizomatous habit makes it useful along ditch banks and wetland margins, especially where erosion control is needed.

Native Habitat and Range. Along the banks of streams and other wet places, often in dry climates at low to mid elevations, east of the Cascades in British Columbia and northern Washington and on both sides of the Cascades in Oregon, south through California, and east to Montana, Colorado, New Mexico, and Texas.

Notes. Sometimes classified as *S. hindsiana* (or various subgroups of this species), *S. nevadensis*, and varieties of *S. sessilifolia*, among other names. Willow taxonomy can be an ugly thing, and *S. exigua* has a long list of older synonyms.

Salix exigua (photo by Sally A. Simmons)

Salix hookeriana

Salix hookeriana   Zones 6a to 9b

Hooker's or dune willow

This large, branching shrub or small tree grows to 6m (18ft) tall. The alternate leaves are broadly elliptic to obovate (oval, but widest toward the tip), up to 12cm (5in) long and usually woolly beneath. The petioles are up to 2cm (1in) long, and the stipules may be small and deciduous or better developed. The leaf margins vary from entire to somewhat serrated, and the flowers generally appear before the leaves. The catkins are woolly, and the scales are dark brown, blooming from early to mid spring. The male catkins are up to 4cm (1.5in) long, and each flower has two stamens. Female catkins are up to 12cm (5in) by the time the small capsules mature.

Cultivation. Full sun to part shade, and wet to moist soil. This is an excellent willow for gardens near the coast, where it often lives in moist places among sand dunes. It will tolerate flooding, making it useful along ditches and wetland margins, especially where erosion control is needed. An excellent shrub for the wet place in a large hedgerow or as a shrub in the wildlife garden.

Native Habitat and Range. In streams, ditches, and near coastal dunes at low to mid elevations, from southern Alaska, south along the coast to northern California and east to the west slope of the Cascades and the Columbia River Gorge.

Notes. Includes *S. piperi* (Piper's willow). "Splitters" consider *S. hookeriana* a coastal species, similar to and hybridizing with *S. piperi*, which has a more interior range up the west slope of the Cascades.

Salix lucida

Salix lucida   Zones 3b to 9b

shining willow

This deciduous shrub or small tree can grow to 15m (45ft), with one or more main trunks. The bark of older trunks is fissured; younger branches are smooth and brown or grayish, and the twigs are glossy. The alternate leaves are lance-shaped, up to 15cm (6in) long, and tapered to a long, pointed tip. There are glands at the base of the leaf blade and on the stipules, when present. Young leaves are hairy, but older leaves may have little hair. The undersides of the leaves are sometimes glaucous, with a waxy, whitish surface. The dormant buds tend to be flattened, looking something like a duck's bill. Flowers bloom in catkins at the same time as the leaves emerge, from early to late spring. Male catkins grow to 7cm (3in), and each flower typically has five stamens. Female catkins can grow to 12cm (5in) when the capsules are mature, and tiny flowers of both sexes each have a yellowish bract at the base. Fall foliage is yellow.

Cultivation. Full sun to part shade, and wet to moist soil. Tolerates long periods of flooding, making this willow useful along ditches and wetland margins, especially where erosion control is needed. An attractive tree for an open, wet site.

Native Habitat and Range. Along streams and wetlands, often in standing water, at low to mid elevations, Alaska and Yukon, south to southern California, east to Saskatchewan, South Dakota, and New Mexico.

Notes. Sometimes classified as *S. lasiandra*. *Salix l.* ssp. *lasiandra* (Pacific willow) is most common west of the Cascades, but also occurs to the east in British Columbia, Idaho, Montana, and Oregon, to Arizona and New Mexico; the undersides of the leaves are glaucous. *Salix l.* ssp. *caudata* (greenleaf willow), by contrast, has leaves that are green on both surfaces; it lives east of the Cascades, from British Columbia south to California and east to South Dakota and Colorado. Peachleaf willow (*S. amygdaloides*) is similar to *S. lucida*; it occurs in wet places in generally arid

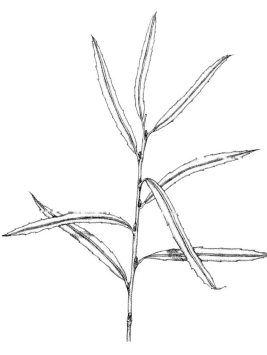

Salix melanopsis

regions east of the Cascades, east to the Atlantic, and like all willows is an excellent tree for the wildlife garden.

Salix melanopsis	Zones 4a to 9b

dusky or Columbia River willow

This shrub or small tree grows to 6m (18ft) tall. The leaves are finely hairy when young, but generally hairless (glabrous) with age. The undersides of the leaves and also the twigs tend to be glaucous, whitish with a waxy coating. The leaves have very short petioles and small, deciduous stipules. The narrow leaf blades are lance-shaped to linear, up to 15cm (6in) long and 1.5cm (.5in) wide. The leaf margins are entire or have a few teeth. The catkins bloom after the leaves appear, from early to mid summer, and a yellow scale subtends each tiny flower. The catkins have some woolly hairs, and male flowers have two stamens. The female catkins can grow to 10cm (4in) long as the small capsules mature.

Cultivation. Full sun to part shade, and wet to moist soil. This slender, graceful willow will tolerate long periods of flooding and produce suckers, making it useful along ditches and wetland margins, especially where erosion control is needed. It is an attractive tree for an open, wet site or for the moist place in the hedgerow or wildlife garden.

Native Habitat and Range. In moist or wet soils along the banks of streams at low to mid elevations from southern British Columbia, mainly east of the Cascades in Washington, south through Oregon on both sides of the Cascades and through California, east to Idaho, Wyoming Utah, and Colorado.

Notes. Sometimes classified as *S. fluviatilis* or *S. exigua* ssp. *melanopsis*. *Salix melanopsis* has a larger range than *S. fluviatilis*, a plant described in older references as being restricted to parts of the Columbia River and some of its major tributaries, including the Willamette.

Salix scouleriana   Zones 3b to 9b

Scouler's willow

This deciduous shrub or small tree can grow to 12m (35ft) and is often multi-stemmed with brown or yellowish branches. The alternate leaves are variable, up to 8cm (3in) long and obovate (oval, but widest toward the tip). The leaf tips are rounded or pointed, and the stipules at the base of the petiole are variable, when they persist. Young leaves are hairy, but older leaves may have little hair. They are dark green above and whitish with a waxy surface (glaucous) beneath. The leaves commonly have some felt-textured, usually rust-colored hairs on the underside. The dormant buds tend to be rounded and smooth, pressed close to the stem. Flowers bloom in catkins, usually before the leaves emerge, from early to late spring. Male catkins grow to 4cm (1.5in), and each flower has two stamens. Female catkins can grow to 6cm (2.5in), and tiny flowers of both sexes each have a black or brown bract at the base. The small capsules have dense, short hairs and are narrowed to the stigmas at the tip.

Cultivation. Full sun to part shade, and wet to rather dry soil. This relatively drought-tolerant willow makes an attractive addition to the hedgerow. Excellent for either upland or wet areas, especially where erosion control is needed, and a good tree for the wildlife garden.

Native Habitat and Range. Streambanks and wetland edges to upland woods and thickets, at low to mid elevations, Alaska south to southern California, east to Manitoba, South Dakota, and New Mexico.

Notes. This is one of the most common willows, especially in upland areas west of the Cascades. Alaska or felt-leaved willow (*S. alaxensis*) is another tall species, to around 8m (26ft), with similar leaves that are woolly underneath; this is a northern species, living at low to high elevations but only ranging as far south as southern British Columbia.

Salix sessilifolia   Zones 5b to 9b

soft-leaved or northwest sandbar willow

This upright, deciduous shrub or small tree grows to 8m (26ft) with gray bark and velvety twigs. The alternate leaves grow to 10cm (4in) long and 3cm (1.5in) or less in width. They are lance-shaped or elliptic, and the leaf margins sometimes have a few scattered teeth. The petioles are very short, and the small stipules are deciduous. Young leaves have dense, soft, white hairs on both surfaces, but older leaves may have thinner hair. Flowers bloom in catkins after the leaves have expanded, from late spring to mid summer. Male and female catkins grow to about 6cm (2.5in) long. Each male flower has two stamens, and the tiny flowers of both sexes each have a yellow bract at the base. The small capsules ripen in the late summer.

Cultivation. Full sun to part shade, and moist to wet soil. Though it can produce suckers aggressively, this graceful species is one of the most attractive willows and brings a soft, silvery touch to the moist or wet parts of the hedgerow. Site it in wet or seasonally flooded areas and use it for erosion control along ditches and banks.

Native Habitat and Range. Along lakes and streams, in wet clearings at low to mid elevations, from southern British Columbia, mainly west of the Cascades, south to northwestern California, east up the Columbia River Gorge and into northeastern Oregon.

Notes. This species is considered threatened in Washington. *Salix fluviatilis* (river willow) is now partially included with *S. sessilifolia*; other varieties of *S. fluviatilis* have been placed with *S. melanopsis*, *S. exigua*, and other similarly narrow-leaved willow species.

Salix scouleriana

Salix sessilifolia

Salix sessilifolia

Salix sitchensis   Zones 4b to 9b

Sitka willow

This deciduous shrub or small tree can grow to 8m (26ft) and has smooth, gray bark and finely hairy twigs. The alternate leaves vary in size, growing to 9cm (3.5in) long, and are elliptic or obovate (oval, but widest toward the tip). The stipules at the base of the petiole are variable and may be large on fast-growing branches. The leaves are bright green with a few hairs on the upper surface and densely hairy below, but not pale or waxy (glaucous). The hairs beneath the leaves are gray to white and flattened, giving them a satiny texture. The dormant buds tend to be oblong and grooved, angling away from the stem. Flowers bloom in catkins before the leaves, or with them, as they emerge, from early to mid spring. Male catkins grow to 5cm (2in), and each flower has a single stamen. Female catkins are 8cm (3in) at maturity, when the small capsules ripen. The tiny flowers of both sexes each have a brown to blackish bract at the base.

Cultivation. Full sun to part shade, and wet to moist soil. This is an excellent willow for wet or seasonally flooded areas, especially along ditches and banks where erosion control is needed. Makes an attractive addition to the moist or wet parts of the hedgerow.

Native Habitat and Range. Thickets near streams, lakes, and wetlands, wet clearings, and forest margins at low to mid elevations from southern Alaska to central California, mainly west of the Cascades, but ranging into eastern Washington, Oregon, and British Columbia, to northern Idaho and western Montana.

Notes. In addition to the taller, easily cultivated willows of relatively low elevations, there are also some charming, low-growing mountain species. Arctic willow (*S. arctica*) is a mat-forming shrub that spreads along the ground by rhizomes and grows to 10cm (4in), sometimes taller; its leaves are around 5cm (2in) long and the flowers appear with them. This plant grows on alpine ridges and mountain meadows in Alaska and in the northern parts of North America, occurring south as far as southern British Columbia, northern Washington, and Montana. Snow willow (*S. nivalis*) is another low-growing species of talus slopes and high mountain ridges; it has a more southern distribution, from southern British Columbia and Alberta, south through the mountains to California, Nevada, Colorado, and New Mexico. Cascade willow (*S. cascadensis*) is another low-growing willow, living in talus and high mountain meadows in southern British Columbia and northern Washington, south to Wyoming and Utah. These willows are sometimes difficult to grow at low elevations but are lovely plants for rock and trough gardens, requiring moist, gritty soil.

Salvia dorrii   Zones 4b to 9b   Lamiaceae

grayball or purple sage

This small, aromatic, evergreen shrub grows to 50cm (20in) in height and at least as wide, with spiny branches. The opposite leaves are elliptic to spoon-shaped (spatulate), up to 3cm (1.5in) long, tapered to the petiole. They generally have a silvery, mealy surface. The blue-violet (rarely white) tubular flowers are two-lipped (bilabiate) and have five petal lobes. They bloom in whorls (verticils) at the stem tips and are subtended by rounded, reddish bracts. The corollas are about 1cm (.5in) long, with the two stamens and style extending far beyond the petal lobes. Flowers bloom from late spring to early summer, and the fruits consist of four small nutlets.

Cultivation. Full sun or light shade, and well-drained, rocky or sandy, dry soil. This pretty little shrub does well in the dry climate east of the Cascades (and probably in southwestern Oregon) and is a good plant for the rock garden or xeric shrub bed. Won't be happy in the wet regions.

Propagation. Collect seeds in late summer or fall and plant them outside soon after harvest to spend the winter in cold, moist conditions for germination the following spring. Plants can also

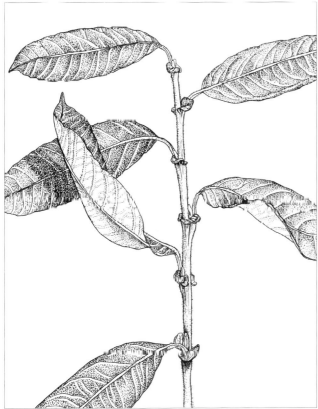

Salix sitchensis

Salvia dorrii (photo by Sally A. Simmons)

be propagated from softwood cuttings of young shoots. Treat cuttings with hormones and set them in pumice or some other medium under humid conditions until roots form.

Native Habitat and Range. Dry slopes, flats, and rocky places, often with sagebrush, at low to fairly high elevations, east of the Cascades in Washington and Oregon, south through California and east to Idaho, Utah, and Arizona.

Notes. *Salvia d.* ssp. *dorrii* (*S. carnosa*), in its varieties *dorrii* and *incana*, occurs in in the arid parts of the Pacific Northwest. *Salvia* is a genus of at least 500 species, widely distributed in the warm or temperate parts of the world, especially the dry, subtropical, or tropical parts of the Americas. Approximately 50 species are native to North America; this is the only one that occurs in our area.

Sambucus   Caprifoliaceae

elderberry

Sambucus is a genus of around 20 species of large shrubs or small trees occurring in temperate regions or at high elevations in tropical areas of the world; only a couple of species are native to North America and the Pacific Northwest. Elderberries are characterized by their pinnately compound, opposite leaves and woody stems filled with spongy pith. The tiny flowers have five petals and inferior ovaries; they bloom in dense many-flowered inflorescences. The fruits are berries. Elderberries are excellent wildlife shrubs, providing nectar for butterflies and colorful berries that are enjoyed by many species of birds. A couple of them long, fleshy roots that do not fare poorly in containers.

Propagation. Easy from hardwood cuttings taken from mid fall to early winter, treated with hormones, and set to root in pumice or another medium. Plants can also be grown from cuttings taken during the growing season, but these must be kept humid until roots form. Alternatively, grow from seed collected in late summer or fall; remove some of the pulp from the seeds, and plant them outside into flats of potting soil, leaving them to cold stratify over winter for germination the following spring.

Sambucus nigra ssp. *caerulea*	Zones 4a to 9b

blue elderberry

This deciduous shrub or small tree is usually multi-stemmed, growing 3 to 10m (10 to 30ft) tall and to 6m (18ft) across. The leaves are opposite and pinnately compound, with five to nine leaflets, the leaflets reaching up to 15cm (6in) in length. The leaflets are commonly lance-shaped and have serrated margins. The tiny, creamy flowers are arranged in large, flat-topped clusters that can reach 15cm (6in) or more in width, blooming from late spring to mid summer. They are followed by dark blue berries with a white, waxy coating.

Cultivation. Full sun, and moist to rather dry soil. Tolerates part shade and is fairly drought-tolerant, especially west of the Cascades. This is a wonderful small tree for the wildlife or butterfly garden, hedgerow, or open field on either side of the Cascades.

Native Habitat and Range. In moist to rather dry, open woods and valleys at low to mid elevations from southern British Columbia south to California, and from near the coast, east to Montana, Colorado, New Mexico, and Texas.

Notes. Sometimes classified as *S. mexicana* or *S. cerulea*. The fruits can be used in jams, pies, and wine, and some people like to cook with the flowers.

Sambucus racemosa var. *racemosa*	Zones 3b to 9b

red elderberry

Red elderberry is a large deciduous shrub that grows to about 3m (10ft) tall and just as wide. The pinnately compound leaves are oppositely arranged and usually have five to seven leaflets. The leaflets are lance-shaped, have serrate margins, and can reach 15cm (6in) in length. Conical clusters of tiny, white flowers bloom from early spring to mid summer and are followed by berries that are bright red (sometimes yellow or white). The raw fruits are inedible and reputedly mildly toxic to humans; cooked fruits were used by indigenous poeple. The other parts of the plant are poisonous.

Cultivation. Full sun to fairly deep shade, and moist to rather wet soil. Tolerates the dry shade under conifers. An excellent shrub for the wildlife or butterfly garden, hedgerow, or pond margin on either side of the Cascades.

Native Habitat and Range. In moist, open forests, streambanks, clearings, and swampy sites, at low to mid elevations, circumboreal and throughout much of North America.

Notes. *Sambucus r.* var. *racemosa* (*S. racemosa* ssp. *pubens* var. *arborescens*), our typical red elderberry, ranges through much of the continent; *S. r.* var. *melanocarpa* (black elderberry) has purplish black fruits and occurs in the Rocky Mountains, extending west to eastern Washington, Oregon, and northern California.

Sambucus nigra ssp. *caerulea*

Sambucus nigra ssp. *caerulea*, fruits

Sambucus racemosa var. *racemosa*

| *Shepherdia canadensis* | Zones 3b to 8b | Elaeagnaceae |

Canadian buffaloberry, soopolallie, soapberry

This deciduous, spreading shrub usually grows to 2.5m (8ft) in height and width. The opposite leaves are oval, up to 6cm (2.5in) long, green on the upper surface, silvery and dotted with rusty scales underneath. Plants are dioecious, with male and female flowers on separate plants. The tiny, brownish flowers bloom in few-flowered clusters in the spring, and fruits ripen in mid summer. Female plants bear bright red or yellowish, berry-like fruits, bitter to the taste and soapy to the touch.

Cultivation. Full sun to part shade, and dry to moist, well-drained or rocky soil. More tolerant of the drought, heat, and cold east of the Cascades, but it will be happy if given sun and good drainage even on the soggy west side. An attractive shrub for the hedgerow or wildlife garden. Birds enjoy the fruits, and they can also be used to make a tart jam.

Propagation. Grow from seed collected in the summer, cleaned from the pulp, covered with hot water, allowed to cool, and planted outside in the fall into flats of potting soil. Leave seeds to stratify in the cold, moist winter weather for germination the following spring. Can also be grown from softwood cuttings taken in spring, treated with hormones, set into pumice, and kept humid.

Native Habitat and Range. In dry, open woods and rocky sites to moist thickets, at low to mid elevations, from Alaska through much of British Columbia, south through eastern Oregon, east and south through the Rocky Mountains to Arizona, east to the Great Lakes and Atlantic coast; also present west of the Cascades, as on southern Vancouver Island and along Puget Sound, but more common east of the mountains.

Notes. Buffaloberries were used by various groups of indigenous people to make "Indian ice cream." The fleshy fruits were added to water, whipped until they became frothy, and sweetened with other plants. *Shepherdia* is a genus of three species, all native to North America. Another desirable garden plant, silver buffaloberry (*S. argentea*), occurs in eastern British Columbia, eastern Idaho, and southeastern Oregon, becoming more widespread in the Rocky Mountains and Great Plains; this tough, spiny shrub grows to 4m (12ft). The leaves are silvery on both surfaces, and the berries are edible.

| *Sorbus sitchensis* | Zones 3b to 8b | Rosaceae |

Sitka mountain ash

This upright, multi-trunked shrub, to 4m (12ft) and with reddish bark, offers beauty throughout the seasons. The alternate leaves are pinnately compound into seven to 11 leaflets. The leaflets are oblong, have blunt tips, and turn yellow and red in the fall; they grow to 5cm (2in) long, and the margins are toothed above the middle. The tiny, white flowers have five petals and bloom in branched, flat-topped clusters to 8cm (3in) across, from early to mid summer. The fruits are small, berry-like pomes (like tiny apples), red or orange, with a waxy, bluish (glaucous) surface.

Cultivation. Full sun to part shade, and moist, well-drained soil. Prefers cold winter climates and generally dislikes life in a container. This is an excellent shrub for the wildlife garden, hedgerow, or woodland edge. The fruits are edible and are sometimes made into a tart jelly to accompany meat, but only birds find them palatable in their fresh state.

Propagation. Grow from seed cleaned from the fruits and planted into flats of potting soil in the fall. Leave them outside to stratify in the cold, moist winter weather for germination in the spring. Can also be propagated from semi-hardwood cuttings made in summer, but may be slow to form roots.

Shepherdia canadensis

Sorbus sitchensis

Native Habitat and Range. Along streams, in open woods, rocky slopes, and meadow margins, usually at mid to high elevations, from Alaska, south through the Olympic and Cascade Mountains to northern California, east to eastern British Columbia, northern Idaho, and northwestern Montana.

Notes. *Sorbus s.* var. *grayi* occupies the southern and western parts of the range, from British Columbia to northern California; in this variety, the leaflets are toothed only at the tips. *Sorbus s.* var. *sitchensis* has leaflets with teeth on at least the upper half and is scattered from Alaska to Washington, east to Alberta and Montana. Western mountain ash (*S. scopulina*), another native shrub of mid to high elevations, differs in its pointed leaflet tips and shiny fruits, among other features. *Sorbus scopulina* var. *cascadensis* grows mostly on the west slope of the Olympics and Cascades, from British Columbia, south to the mountains of northern California. *Sorbus s.* var. *scopulina* has a larger range, from Alaska south, mainly east of the Cascade crest, to California and Arizona, east to the Rocky Mountains. California mountain ash (*S. californica*) lives in the mountains of California and Nevada, ranging as far north as southern Oregon. There are around 50 species of *Sorbus*, native to temperate or subarctic parts of the north, with about six species native to North America; these hybridize with each other and with other rosaceous genera.

Spiraea   Rosaceae

spirea

Spiraea, a genus of pink- or white-flowering shrubs, many of them well known ornamentals, contains some 70 species, most native to the temperate parts of the Northern Hemisphere; fewer than ten species are native to North America, a handful to the Pacific Northwest. The five-petaled flowers are tiny, but numerous, blooming in dense panicles or flat-topped clusters that butterflies find attractive. The fruits are small follicles, and the simple leaves are alternately arranged.

Propagation. Grow from seed collected in late summer or fall after the small follicles have started to open. Sow seeds into flats of potting soil in the fall, and leave them outside to cold stratify during winter for spring germination. Plants should reach blooming size in a couple of years. Spireas can also be grown from hardwood cuttings made during late fall, treated with hormones, and set to root in pumice or some other medium. Divide plants with woody rhizomes or make root cuttings in early spring or late fall. Cuttings can also be taken from semi-mature wood during the summer, treated with hormones, and kept humid under mist or plastic until roots form.

Spiraea betulifolia var. *lucida*   Zones 3b to 9a

shiny-leaved spirea

This rhizomatous, deciduous shrub usually grows to 60cm (2ft). The leaves are oblong and grow to about 6cm (2.5in) long with coarsely toothed margins, dark green above and pale beneath. Tiny white or pinkish flowers bloom in flat-topped clusters up to 8cm (3in) across from early to mid summer.

Cultivation. Full sun to part shade or dappled light, and moist to rather dry soil. This is a pretty little plant for a low-growing hedgerow, butterfly garden, shrub border, or pond margin. It is able to tolerate the dry shade near big trees, making it a good choice for the woodland or shade garden.

Native Habitat and Range. Along streams and lakes, in woods and rocky hillsides, at low to high (in the eastern part of the range) elevations, from British Columbia south through the Cascades to southern Oregon and east to Saskatchewan, Wyoming, and South Dakota.

Notes. The type is native to Japan and northeastern Asia; this is the only variety that occurs in our area.

Spiraea douglasii   Zones 4a to 9b

Douglas' or western spirea, hardhack, steeplebush

This spirea, an erect shrub that can reach 2m (6ft), is able to spread by rhizomes, forming thickets. The leaves are oblong, usually toothed on the upper half, and grow to 10cm (4in) long. Many small flowers bloom in dense, spire-like panicles to 20cm (8in) long. The flowers are light to dark pink, blooming from early to late summer. The small follicles are shiny.

Cultivation. Full sun or part shade, and wet to moist soil. This is an excellent plant for restoring wetlands and controlling erosion on ditch banks or other wet areas, though it may become too aggressive in some situations. It won't grow in deep water or dry sites, so its tendency to spread can be minimized by planting it close to these ecological barriers. Can be grown in shrub beds or as part of a hedgerow. The many, tiny flowers make it a good nectar plant for the butterfly garden.

Native Habitat and Range. Along streams, bogs, and wet meadows, at low to mid elevations from southern Alaska, south to northern California, mainly from the coast to the west slope of the Cascades, also east to eastern British Columbia, Idaho, western Montana, and northeastern Oregon.

Notes. Sometimes classified as *S. menziesii*. *Spiraea d.* var. *douglasii* is finely pubescent with grayish hairs, especially on the undersides of the leaves; it is the common variety near the coast and west slope of the Cascades, from British Columbia to California. *Spiraea d.* var. *menziesii* has finely hairy leaves, but they are not grayish beneath; it occurs from Alaska through the Cascades to northern Oregon and east to northeastern Oregon, northern Idaho, and western Montana. This species hybridizes with *S. betulifolia* var. *lucida* to form *S.* ×*pyramidata* (pyramidal spirea),

Spiraea betulifolia var. lucida

Spiraea douglasii

which is similar to *S. douglasii* but with broader panicles of pink-tinted, white flowers; it is native near water or among rocks from southern British Columbia, south along the east slope of the Cascades to northern Oregon and east to central Idaho.

Spiraea splendens* var. *splendens	Zones 3b to 9b

subalpine or mountain spirea

This erect or spreading shrub grows to 70cm (28in). The leaves are oval, finely toothed (at least on the upper half), and up to 4cm (1.5in) long; they turn to lovely shades of red and orange in the fall. The small, deep pink flowers bloom in dense, flat-topped clusters to 4cm (1.5in) across, from early to late summer. The small follicles split open along one suture when ripe to release the small seeds.

Cultivation. Full sun or part shade, and moist soil. The fall foliage will be more brightly colored in a sunnier location. Although this species is native to mountain habitats, it seems quite happy at low elevations. An excellent plant for the rock garden, hedgerow, shrub border, or along a sunny garden path, and a good source of nectar for the butterfly garden.

Native Habitat and Range. Near lakes and streams, woods, and open, rocky slopes at mid to high elevations, British Columbia south through the Olympic and Cascade Mountains and Sierra Nevada of California, east to southeastern British Columbia, Montana, Idaho, and northeastern Oregon.

Notes. Sometimes classified as *S. densiflora* or *S. densiflora* ssp. (or var.) *splendens*. Its cultivar 'Summer Song' has bronzy foliage in the spring and fall. *Spiraea stevenii* (*S. beauverdiana*; Steven's spirea) has white flowers and grows in similar habitats at low to alpine elevations in Alaska and British Columbia.

Spiraea splendens var. *splendens*

Symphoricarpos albus

Symphoricarpos albus   Zones 3b to 9b   Caprifoliaceae

common snowberry, waxberry

This branching shrub reaches a maximum height of about 2m (6ft) and spreads by woody rhizomes. The leaves are opposite and generally rounded but often lobed on young shoots; they grow to 5cm (2in) long. The flowers are small, less than 1cm (.5in) long, pink and tubular; they bloom in short, few-flowered clusters from late spring to late summer. The round, white berries, about 1cm (.5in) wide, tend to hang on the plants through much of the winter.

Cultivation. Full sun or part shade, and moist to rather dry, even poor soil. Fairly drought-tolerant once established. Plants do a good job of controlling erosion on banks and are a worthy addition to any wildlife garden or hedgerow, providing fruit for birds in winter, even if they're not a favorite. The distinctive berries are eye-catching in the winter and look especially lovely with rose hips.

Propagation. Best from hardwood cuttings made in late fall or winter, or semi-hardwood cuttings in late spring. The clumps of woody rhizomes can also be divided when plants are dormant. Can be grown from seed, but after cleaning the seeds from the pulp, they generally require months of warm, and then cold stratification before they will germinate. Sow them into flats of potting soil in the fall, and expect germination the second spring.

Native Habitat and Range. Widespread in moist to dry thickets, rocky slopes and open woods at low to mid elevations from Alaska to Quebec and south to California, Colorado, and many of the eastern states.

Notes. The common variety here, *S. a.* var. *laevigatus*, also occurs east of the Great Plains; *S. a.* var. *albus* is more widespread east of the Continental Divide. Another Pacific Northwest

Umbellularia californica

Umbellularia californica, flowers

species is trailing snowberry (*S. hesperius*), which ranges from southwestern British Columbia to California, mainly west of the Cascades but also east to northern Idaho and southeastern Washington. Western snowberry or wolfberry (*S. occidentalis*) and mountain snowberry (*S. oreophilus*) are more common east of the Cascades and in the Rocky Mountains. Desert snowberry (*S. longiflorus*) occurs in dry areas of southeastern Oregon, California, and Nevada, south and east to Texas. The toxicity of snowberries is minor; a few tribes used them in small amounts. There are fewer than 20 species of *Symphoricarpos*, most of them native to North America.

Umbellularia californica	Zones 7b to 9b	Lauraceae

Oregon myrtlewood, California bay or laurel

In the forest, this evergreen tree can reach 25m (75ft) in height and 30m (100ft) in width with greenish to reddish brown bark. In harsher environments and in the garden it is usually much smaller, up to 10m (30ft) in height and width. The powerfully aromatic, leathery leaves are oblong to lance-shaped, about 8cm (3in) long, deep yellow-green, and alternately arranged; older leaves turn yellowish and drop in autumn. The small, yellowish flowers bloom in umbels in the leaf axils from mid winter to late spring. The ripe fruit is a rounded, inedible, purplish drupe to 2.5cm (1in) long.

Cultivation. Full sun to full shade, and moist to dry soil. Grows slowly, but will be a bit quicker in moist, deep soil. This is a good species for the tall hedgerow or as a screen or background plant west of the Cascades. Plants provide dense, evergreen cover for birds and can be thinned if they cast too much shade; they are sometimes attacked by aphids or scale insects and are susceptible to sudden oak death, a disease caused by the fungus-like pathogen *Phytophthora ramorum*.

Propagation. Grow from seed collected from the purple drupes in the fall and planted outside to spend the winter under cool, moist conditions for germination in the spring. Mature plants often produce seedlings without assistance.

Native Habitat and Range. In canyons, woods, and thickets, at low to mid elevations, from west central Oregon, south on the west side of the Cascades through California.

Notes. The wood of Oregon myrtlewood is hard and strong, often used in woodworking to make beautiful furniture and fine bowls, and although they are more strongly flavored, its leaves can be used as a substitute for the related sweet bay (*Laurus nobilis*). This is the only species in the monotypic *Umbellularia*, and *U. c.* var. *californica* occurs throughout the range.

Vaccinium   Ericaceae

huckleberry, blueberry, bilberry, cranberry

Vaccinium includes around 150 species of deciduous or evergreen shrubs, mostly native to the colder, mountainous areas of the Northern Hemisphere, especially North America and eastern Asia; more than 30 species are native to North America, and about half of these occur in the Pacific Northwest. Flowers are small and urn-shaped, composed of five fused petals. The anthers release pollen through a pair of tubes at their tips; in some species the anthers have horn-like projections (awns). The ovaries are inferior, and the hypanthium, or floral tube (fused bases of sepals, petals, and stamens), contributes to the fruit, a fleshy, edible berry.

Propagation. Collect berries in the summer, and remove the tiny seeds from some of the pulp. Mix the seeds and remaining pulp with a bit of ground peat, for easier handling, and then sprinkle the mixture on the surface of potting soil in flats or other containers. Leave seed flats outside after planting to stratify under cold, moist winter conditions for spring (sometimes fall) germination. Seedlings are tiny and must be protected while young. Plants can also be propagated from tip cuttings taken in the spring or from semi-hardwood cuttings taken in summer or fall; treat cuttings with hormones, set into pumice or some other medium, and keep them under humid conditions until roots form. Another method is to layer stems in the spring; nick a stem, bend it, and bury the nicked section in ground, anchoring it in place until roots form. *Vaccinium ovatum* and other species may seed themselves when growing in a suitable location in the garden. Small seedlings can be transplanted, but larger, established plants do not like to be relocated.

Vaccinium membranaceum   Zones 3b to 9b

black, mountain, or thinleaf huckleberry

This deciduous shrub reaches a maximum height of 2m (6ft). The older branches have shredding bark; the younger twigs are angled. The alternate leaves are elliptic, up to 5cm (2in) long, have pointed tips and finely toothed margins. They turn beautiful shades of magenta and red in the fall. The flowers are yellowish pink and less than 1cm (.5in) wide, blooming from mid spring to early summer. The berries are purplish or reddish black and shiny.

Cultivation. Full sun to full shade, and moist to fairly dry, acidic soil. Plants will produce more fruit if they get some sun, and the display of autumn foliage will be more intense. The fruits have excellent flavor and are very attractive to birds as well as humans. Site at the edge of the woodland garden, under big conifers, or in the hedgerow on either side of the Cascades.

Native Habitat and Range. In moist to rather dry woods and open mountain slopes at mid to high elevations from British Columbia to northern California, in the Olympics and both sides of the Cascades, east to Montana and the Great Lakes, south to Utah and Arizona.

Vaccinium membranaceum

Notes. The fruits of this species, one of the tastiest of our native huckleberries, were highly valued by indigenous people. Dwarf bilberry or blueberry (*V. caespitosum*) is a smaller plant that produces sweet, edible fruits; it grows to 30cm (1ft) tall in bogs, forests, and wet meadows at low to high elevations throughout the west and east to the northern Atlantic coast. A species of similar size, *V. deliciosum* (Cascade or blue-leaved huckleberry), grows in the mid to high mountains of the Pacific Northwest, and huckleberry pickers often visit the populations for their excellent berries; unfortunately, these plants do not do well in low-elevation gardens.

Vaccinium ovalifolium   Zones 3b to 9a

oval-leaved huckleberry

This spreading, deciduous shrub can grow to 2m (6ft) tall. The older stems are grayish, and the young twigs are hairless (glabrous), reddish or yellowish green, and strongly angled. The alternate leaves are ovate to elliptic and up to 4cm (1.5in) long, green above and glaucous, waxy and whitish below. The leaf margins are entire or finely toothed. The flowers are broadly urn-shaped, less than 1cm (.5in) long, and pinkish, blooming singly from the leaf axils from late spring to mid summer, as the leaves are expanding. The edible blue-black fruits are glaucous, with a whitish bloom, and about 1cm (.5in) long.

Cultivation. Full to part shade or dappled light, and moist to rather wet soil high in organic matter. The fruits of this species generally ripen earlier than other huckleberries. Plant it next to the bog or shady pond on either side of the Cascades, or in moist parts of the woodland or shade garden, under big conifers.

Vaccinium ovalifolium

Native Habitat and Range. In bogs, moist forests, and clearings at low (in the north) to mid or fairly high elevations from Alaska south through northern Oregon and from near the coast, east to Montana, the Great Lakes, and across Canada.

Notes. Often seen with this species in the forest understory is *V. alaskaense* (Alaska blueberry), another spreading or upright shrub to 2m (6ft) tall. The flowers are pinkish or bronzy, and the berries are purplish black and shiny, often not glaucous; this species grows in moist forests and clearings at low to fairly high elevations from Alaska to northern Oregon and from the coast to the Cascades.

Vaccinium ovatum   Zones 7a to 9b

evergreen huckleberry

This good-looking evergreen shrub has been used as an ornamental for many years. It has a spreading or upright habit and can grow to 4m (12ft). The small, alternate leaves are ovate and up to 5cm (2in) long with finely toothed margins. The new growth is bronzy, and older leaves are leathery, glossy, and dark green. The pink flowers, almost 1cm (.5in) long, bloom in small clusters in the leaf axils from mid spring to late summer. The berries are small but numerous, edible, and purplish black.

Cultivation. Full sun to part shade, and moist, well-drained soil. Will be shorter in full sun and may become leggy in deep shade. This is a handsome addition to the more open areas of the woodland garden, hedgerow, or shrub border; it provides excellent cover and food for birds, and butterflies visit the flowers. Can also be grown in containers.

Native Habitat and Range. In coniferous forests, clearings, and near beaches, at low elevations, from British Columbia, south along the coast to southern California, east to the west slope

Vaccinium ovatum

Vaccinium ovatum, fruits

of the Cascades.

Notes. This species was collected by all indigenous tribes within its range. Even small plants will produce many berries, and some believe evergreen huckleberries are sweeter if harvested after the first frost. The "leatherleaf" branches are often used in floral arrangements.

Vaccinium parvifolium	Zones 4a to 9b

red huckleberry

This lacy, deciduous shrub has an upright habit and can grow to 4m (12ft) tall, though it's typically shorter. The young twigs are green and distinctly angled. The leaves are alternate, oval, and up to 2.5cm (1in) long. The greenish or pinkish flowers are less than 1cm (.5in) wide, blooming singly in the leaf axils from mid spring to early summer. The berries are bright red, sour but tasty, and about 1cm (.5in) wide.

Cultivation. Shade to part sun or dappled light, and moist, acidic soil with lots of decaying organic matter. This is a graceful, airy shrub for the woodland or wildlife garden, where birds and people can both enjoy the berries. Plant it near a water feature or into old stumps.

Native Habitat and Range. In moist, coniferous forests, often on logs or stumps, at low to mid elevations from southeastern Alaska south to central California, and from the coast to the west slope of the Cascades, occasional east of the crest.

Notes. Dwarf bilberry (*V. myrtillus*) and grouseberry (*V. scoparium*) are other species with reddish berries; both are smaller shrubs with a wide range through the west. Bog cranberry (*V. oxycoccos*) is a creeping evergreen shrub with slender, vine-like stems; it produces pink or red berries and grows in acidic bogs and wet meadows at low to mid elevations in our area, and

Vaccinium parvifolium

Vaccinium uliginosum

east through Canada and the northern United States. Lingonberry or mountain cranberry (*V. vitis-idaea*) is a low-growing, evergreen species native to the far north, extending south to coastal Alaska and scattered through British Columbia, as well as the Great Lakes and Atlantic coast; it is cultivated for its red berries and ornamental qualities.

Vaccinium uliginosum	Zones 3b to 9b

bog blueberry

This spreading, deciduous shrub grows to 30cm (1ft) tall. The twigs are yellow-green and finely hairy, but more rounded than angled. The leaves are obovate (oval, but widest toward the tip), up to 3cm (1.5in) long, and have entire margins. They are distinctly veiny underneath and turn burgundy in the fall. Up to four pink flowers bloom from each leaf axil from late spring to mid summer. The tasty berries are about 1cm (.5in) wide, dark blue and glaucous, covered with a whitish, powdery bloom.

Cultivation. Full sun or part shade, and wet to moist or rather dry, well-drained soil, on the acidic side, high in organic matter. The fall foliage display is most intense in sunny sites. This is a fine shrub for the sunny bog, pond margin, or rock garden. Birds and humans will both enjoy the berries.

Native Habitat and Range. In bogs near the coast and in rocky, alpine heath, at low to high elevations, circumboreal, from Alaska south to California near the coast and east to Montana, Wyoming, and Utah, east to the Great Lakes and Atlantic coast; Eurasia

Notes. This species is listed as rare in some of the eastern parts of its range. Its fruits remain an important food to some indigenous tribes.

Viburnum	Caprifoliaceae

highbush cranberry, cranberrybush

The famously ornamental genus *Viburnum* includes more than 100 species of shrubs or small trees, mostly native to mountains or temperate parts of North America, Europe, and Asia; around 15 species are native to North America, but only three occur in our area. The leaves are usually opposite and simple, often with lobed or toothed margins. The flowers are arranged in umbels or panicles. They have five petals and inferior ovaries. The fruits are small drupes, like a plum, with a stony inner fruit wall enclosing the seed. Viburnums are appreciated throughout the year for their showy flowers, bright fall foliage, and attractive fruits, which are enjoyed by birds and sometimes by humans.

Propagation. Grow from seed collected and cleaned from the pulp in the fall and planted soon after harvest. Sow seeds into flats of potting soil and leave them outside to cold stratify over winter for germination in the spring. Plants can be propagated from hardwood cuttings or divisions of rhizomes taken in late winter or mid fall, treated with rooting hormones, and set into pumice or some other medium until roots form. They can also be increased from tip cuttings made during the spring, or from cuttings of semi-ripe wood taken during the summer; keep cuttings under humid conditions until roots form. Layering branches by nicking and burying part of the stem in autumn will also produce plants.

Viburnum edule   Zones 3b to 9a

highbush cranberry, squashberry, mooseberry

This rhizomatous, deciduous shrub produces erect to lax stems up to 3m (10ft) or a bit taller. The opposite leaves have three-lobed (sometimes without lobes), rounded blades to 10cm (4in) in length and width. The leaf margins are sharply toothed, and the blades are hairy underneath. The leaves turn brilliant shades of red in the fall. Small, flat-topped inflorescences to 2.5cm (1in) wide bloom from axillary shoots, each shoot with a single pair of leaves. The small, white flowers are all similar, with five-lobed corollas less than 1cm (.5in) across; they bloom from late spring to mid summer. The red to orange drupes are up to 1.5cm (.5in) long and ripen in small clusters. They are tart and edible.

Cultivation. Full sun to part shade or dappled light, and moist to rather wet soil. This is a beautiful shrub for the hedgerow, pond margin, or wildlife garden on either side of the Cascades. The drupes make a good "cranberry" sauce, if the birds don't eat them first.

Native Habitat and Range. In moist woods, wetland margins, and thickets at low to mid elevations from Alaska east to Newfoundland, south near the coast and in the mountains to northwestern Oregon, the Rocky Mountains, the Great Lakes, and northeastern United States.

Notes. Listed as rare in several states near the Great Lakes and Atlantic coast. Indigenous tribes considered the drupes an excellent food.

Viburnum ellipticum   Zones 5b to 9b

oval-leaved viburnum

This deciduous shrub grows to 3m (10ft) tall. The opposite leaves have hairy petioles to 2cm (1in) long. The blades are rounded to broadly elliptic, up to 8cm (3in) long, and turn red in the fall. The leaf margins have coarse teeth; they are sometimes palmately veined but lack lobes. Flat-topped inflorescences to 5cm (2in) across flower at the tips of leafy stems. The flowers are all similar, with five petal lobes and a whitish corolla about 1cm (.5in) wide. Flowers bloom from late spring to early summer. The red fruits are elliptical in shape and about 1.5cm (.5in) long with a flattened pit.

Cultivation. Full sun to part shade or dappled light, and moist soil. This excellent shrub brings three-season interest to the woodland margin, hedgerow, or wildlife garden.

Native Habitat and Range. In thickets and open woods at low to mid elevations from southwestern Washington, south through northern California, mainly west of the Cascade crest, but further east in southern Oregon.

Notes. This species tolerates drier conditions than *V. edule*, but it may not be as cold hardy.

Viburnum opulus var. americanum   Zones 3b to 8b

American cranberrybush

This deciduous shrub or small tree can grow to 4m (12ft) tall. The opposite leaves have petioles to 3cm (1.5in) long and are hairless (glabrous) except for a few glands; they turn yellow to red-purple in fall. The leaf blades are palmately veined and lobed, up to 12cm (5in) long and almost as wide; they usually have three relatively long, pointed lobes, and the margins are entire or sometimes with a few teeth. Flat-topped inflorescences up to 15cm (6in) across develop at the stem tips. The flowers around the margin of the flower cluster are large and showy, to 2.5cm (1in) across, white, and sterile; the fertile flowers are much smaller and bloom from late spring to mid summer. The translucent, red drupes are tart and up to 1.5cm (.5in) long.

Viburnum edule

Viburnum ellipticum

Viburnum opulus var. americanum

Vitis californica

Cultivation. Full sun to part shade, and moist soil. This is a lovely big shrub for the hedgerow or wildlife garden, often planted primarily for its fall foliage display. The fruits make good sauce, if the birds don't get them first. Plants are sometimes attacked by aphids.

Native Habitat and Range. In moist woods and lake shores at low to mid elevations from central British Columbia, south, scattered on both sides of the Cascades in Washington, east across much of North America, where it is more common.

Notes. Sometimes classified as *V. opulus* ssp. *trilobum* or *V. trilobum*.

Vitis californica	Zones 6b to 9b	Vitaceae

California wild grape

This deciduous vine, often grown for its fall color, produces stems to 10m (30ft) or more with shredding bark. The leaves are generally pubescent, and the blades are about 12cm (5in) across; they are usually cordate (heart-shaped) at the base, and the blades have three, sometimes shallow lobes. The margins usually have blunt teeth, and the leaves turn brilliant shades of red in the fall. Small, fragrant, greenish yellow flowers bloom in panicles up to 15cm (6in) long from late spring to early summer. The round berries are about 1cm (.5in) wide, purplish and glaucous, with a whitish bloom.

Cultivation. Full sun or light shade, and well-drained, moist to rather dry soil. This is a fine vine for a trellis or fence at the edge of the wildlife garden on either side of the Cascades, though plants may be sensitive in the colder parts of our area. The berries are edible but perhaps more interesting to birds than to people.

Propagation. Grow from seed collected in the fall, cleaned from the pulp, and planted into containers of potting soil in the late fall or early winter. Leave the planted seeds outside to cold stratify for germination when the weather warms in the spring. Can also be grown from hardwood cuttings taken in fall or winter, or from semi-hardwood cuttings taken in summer, treated with rooting hormones, stuck into pumice, and kept humid until roots form. Layering the flexible branches by nicking a stem and burying the nicked section in the ground during the spring is another method.

Native Habitat and Range. Near streams and in canyons at low to mid elevations from southwestern Oregon, south to southern California.

Notes. Cultivars include 'Roger's Red' and the smaller 'Walker Ridge'. There are upward of 50 species of *Vitis*, mostly native to the temperate parts of the Northern Hemisphere; about 15 are native to North America. The other grapes seen here are probably escapes from cultivation.

PLANTS FOR SPECIAL SITUATIONS AND PURPOSES

The following are suggested species for particular garden situations. See the entry for each genus or species listed below for a discussion of additional possibilities.

Drought-tolerant plants

Unless they live by the water, many plants in the Pacific Northwest must endure some seasonal drought. This list includes plants that are especially drought-tolerant, but excludes species that require wet soil early in the spring. Most will also tolerate cold, but some may not survive the soggy winters in the northwestern parts of our area. Species listed here typically live in sunny, arid conditions (see "Plants for Shade" for ones that will tolerate the dry shade under big trees); some, especially the ferns, live among rocks where moisture is actually available for much of the year. Drought-tolerant annuals generally set seed and die when their surroundings dry out too much, producing a new generation the following year.

FERNS

Cheilanthes gracillima
Cryptogramma acrostichoides
Cystopteris fragilis
Pentagramma triangularis

CONIFERS

Calocedrus decurrens
Cupressus bakeri
Juniperus spp.
Pinus attenuata
Pinus contorta var. *latifolia*
Pinus jeffreyi
Pinus lambertiana
Pinus ponderosa

ANNUALS

Amsinckia menziesii
Clarkia spp.
Claytonia exigua
Collomia grandiflora
Crocidium multicaule
Gilia capitata
Helianthus annuus
Lupinus bicolor
Madia elegans
Phacelia linearis
Platystemon californicus
Triphysaria eriantha

PERENNIALS

Achillea millefolium

Achnatherum hymenoides
Agastache occidentalis
Allium acuminatum
Allium falcifolium
Antennaria rosea
Arabis aculeolata
Artemisia dracunculus
Asclepias spp.
Astragalus spp.
Balsamorhiza spp.
Brodiaea spp.
Calochortus spp.
Cerastium arvense
Cistanthe umbellata
Danthonia californica
Dichelostemma capitatum
Elymus elymoides

Epilobium canum ssp. *latifolium*
Erigeron filifolius
Erigeron linearis
Erigeron poliospermus
Eriophyllum lanatum
Erysimum capitatum
Eschscholzia californica
Festuca idahoensis
Fritillaria pudica
Fritillaria recurva
Helianthus cusickii
Hesperostipa comata
Heterotheca villosa
Ipomopsis aggregata
Leptosiphon nuttallii
Lewisia spp

Leymus cinereus
Lilium bolanderi
Lilium washingtonianum
Linum lewisii
Lithospermum ruderale
Lomatium columbianum
Lomatium dissectum
Lomatium grayi
Lupinus lepidus
Lupinus leucophyllus
Lupinus sulphureus
Machaeranthera canescens
Mentzelia laevicaulis
Mimulus aurantiacus
Monardella odoratissima
Oenothera spp.

Penstemon spp. (most)
Phacelia hastata
Phlox spp.
Phoenicaulis cheiranthoides
Poa secunda
Pseudoroegneria spicata
Rumex venosus
Sedum spp.
Sphaeralcea munroana
Townsendia florifer
Trifolium macrocephalum
Triteleia spp.
Viola trinervata
Zigadenus paniculatus

SHRUBS AND TREES

Arctostaphylos spp.
Artemisia tridentata
Baccharis pilularis
Ceanothus spp.
Cercis orbiculata
Cercocarpus ledifolius
Dasiphora fruticosa ssp.
    floribunda
Elaeagnus commutata
Ericameria spp.
Eriogonum spp.
Garrya fremontii
Grayia spinosa
Holodiscus discolor

Krascheninnikovia lanata
Opuntia polyacantha var.
    polyacantha
Philadelphus lewisii
Purshia tridentata
Rhus spp.
Ribes cereum
Salvia dorrii
Sambucus nigra ssp.
    caerulea
Shepherdia canadensis
Symphoricarpos albus
Umbellularia californica

Plants for bogs, wetlands, streams, and ponds

Plants are respiring organisms and require molecular oxygen just as we animals do; although they produce more oxygen than they use and conduct gas exchange through tiny pores (stomata) in their leaves, most terrestrial plants take up atmospheric oxygen through their roots and will drown and die from lack of oxygen if flooded for any length of time. All the plants listed here will tolerate but may not require wet soils; species that live in wet soils are tolerant of low oxygen levels in the muddy soil or have other features, such as stems filled with spongy tissue, to assist with gas exchange. Here too, besides plants that will tolerate seasonal flooding, are three plants that are normally emergent (E), with their roots under water and their shoots in the air, and three plants that are fully aquatic (A), floating in the water or on the surface with their roots, usually, in the mud below.

FERNS

Adiantum aleuticum
Athyrium filix-femina
Blechnum spicant
Equisetum spp.
Woodwardia fimbriata

CONIFERS

Chamaecyparis nootkatensis
Larix occidentalis
Picea sitchensis
Pinus contorta var. contorta
Pinus contorta var. latifolia
Thuja plicata
Tsuga spp.

ANNUALS

Coreopsis tinctoria var.
    atkinsoniana
Impatiens capensis
Lasthenia californica
Limnanthes douglasii
Mimulus alsinoides

PERENNIALS

Aconitum columbianum
Argentina egedii
Arnica amplexicaulis
Artemisia lindleyana
Aster subspicatus
Caltha leptosepala
Cardamine occidentalis
Carex spp.
Coptis laciniata

Corydalis scouleri
Cyperus strigosus
Darlingtonia californica
Darmera peltata
Dodecatheon jeffreyi
Dodecatheon pulchellum
Drosera rotundifolia
Dulichium arundinaceum
Epilobium luteum
Epipactis gigantea
Erigeron peregrinus
Eriophorum spp.
Erythronium revolutum
Eupatoriadelphus maculatus
Gentiana spp.
Grindelia stricta
Helenium bolanderi
Heracleum maximum
Hypericum anagalloides
Iris missouriensis

Juncus spp.
Lilium occidentale
Lilium pardalinum ssp.
    vollmeri
Lotus formosissimus
Lupinus polyphyllus
Lysichiton americanus
Mentha arvensis
Menyanthes trifoliata (A)
Mertensia paniculata
Mimulus guttatus
Mimulus lewisii
Mitella ovalis
Narthecium californicum
Nuphar lutea ssp. polysepala
    (A)
Pedicularis attollens
Penstemon serrulatus
Petasites frigidus
Polygonum bistortoides

Ranunculus alismifolius
Rudbeckia spp.
Sagittaria latifolia (E)
Schoenoplectus acutus (E)
Scirpus spp.
Scrophularia oregana
Scutellaria lateriflora
Senecio triangularis
Sidalcea hendersonii
Sisyrinchium spp.
Spiranthes romanzoffiana
Stachys spp.
Stenanthium occidentale
Triantha glutinosa

Trientalis europaea ssp.
   arctica
Trifolium wormskioldii
Typha latifolia (E)
Utricularia macrorhiza (A)
Veratrum spp.
Viola glabella

SHRUBS AND TREES

Alnus spp.
Andromeda polifolia
Betula papyrifera
Cornus sericea
Empetrum nigrum

Euonymus occidentalis
Fraxinus latifolia
Kalmia microphylla
Ledum spp.
Leucothoe davisiae
Lonicera involucrata
Malus fusca
Myrica gale
Oplopanax horridus
Physocarpus capitatus
Populus balsamifera ssp.
   trichocarpa
Rhamnus purshiana
Ribes bracteosum
Ribes laxiflorum

Rosa nutkana
Rosa pisocarpa
Rubus pedatus
Rubus spectabilis
Salix spp.
Sambucus racemosa var.
   racemosa
Spiraea douglasii
Vaccinium ovalifolium
Vaccinium uliginosum
Viburnum edule

Plants for hedgerows

The difference between a hedgerow and a mere hedge is that hedgerows are composed of a variety of plants instead of a single species pruned into some unnatural shape. As the British discovered long ago, hedgerows not only serve as fences, they also make excellent wildlife habitat because of their diversity. This diversity will please the gardener almost as much as the birds because, rather than being a uniform green rectangle, a hedgerow is an ever-changing part of the garden. Different species will bloom and set fruit at different times of the year. Some plants will turn bright colors and then lose their leaves in the fall; others will be evergreen. Birds, squirrels, reptiles, amphibians, butterflies (and their caterpillars), and many other insects will make the hedgerow a happy home. In addition, a hedgerow may sometimes serve as a corridor that connects one piece of habitat to another, countering some of the fragmentation that we disruptive human inhabitants have caused. This list includes only shrubs and relatively small trees, beginning with conifers. Of course, vines and many herbaceous plants can be added at the base of the hedgerow.

CONIFERS

Pinus contorta var. *contorta*
Pinus monticola
Taxus brevifolia

SHRUBS AND TREES

Acer circinatum
Acer glabrum var. *douglasii*
Amelanchier alnifolia
Arbutus menziesii
Arctostaphylos spp.
Artemisia tridentata
Baccharis pilularis
Betula glandulosa
Betula occidentalis
Ceanothus spp.
Cercis orbiculata
Cercocarpus ledifolius

Chrysothamnus spp.
Clematis ligusticifolia (vine)
Cornus nuttallii
Cornus sericea
Corylus cornuta var.
   californica
Crataegus douglasii
Dasiphora fruticosa ssp.
   floribunda
Elaeagnus commutata
Elliottia pyroliflorus
Euonymus occidentale
Fraxinus latifolia
Garrya spp.
Gaultheria shallon
Grayia spinosa
Holodiscus discolor
Ledum spp.
Leucothoe davisiae

Lonicera ciliosa (vine)
Lonicera involucrata
Mahonia spp.
Malus fusca
Menziesia ferruginea
Morella californica
Myrica gale
Oemleria cerasiformis
Oplopanax horridus
Opuntia polyacantha
Paxistima myrsinites
Philadelphus lewisii
Physocarpus capitatus
Populus tremuloides
Prunus spp.
Purshia tridentata
Quercus sadleriana
Rhamnus purshiana
Rhododendron spp.

Rhus spp.
Ribes spp.
Rosa spp.
Rubus spp. (shrubby forms)
Salix spp.
Salvia dorrii
Sambucus spp.
Shepherdia canadensis
Sorbus sitchensis
Spiraea spp.
Symphoricarpos albus
Umbellularia californica
Vaccinium spp.
Viburnum spp.

Plants for shade

The plants listed here prefer to be in shade for half the day or more, or will do reasonably well under such conditions. Dry shade under big conifers and other trees is often a difficult garden situation. Some species are fairly tolerant of dry shade; others, especially species living under deciduous trees such as oaks, flower early in the year and become dormant as the trees leaf out and the soil dries up. Plants that take dry shade (DS) are noted. Note that almost all our native ferns live in shady places; ferns for dry, rocky sites and ferns for wet places appear in other lists. *Polystichum munitum* is one of the best ferns for shady, dry conditions, especially west of the Cascades.

CONIFERS

Abies spp.
Chamaecyparis spp.
Larix occidentalis
Picea spp.
Sequoia sempervirens
Taxus brevifolia
Thuja plicata
Tsuga spp.

ANNUALS

Claytonia perfoliata
Claytonia sibirica
Collinsia grandiflora
Collomia grandiflora
Gilia capitata
Impatiens capensis
Mimulus alsinoides
Nemophila menziesii
Platystemon californicus

PERENNIALS

Achillea millefolium
Achlys triphylla
Aconitum columbianum
Actaea rubra
Agastache urticifolia
Allium cernuum
Anemone deltoidea
Anemone multifida
Anemone oregana
Antennaria rosea
Apocynum cannabinum
Aquilegia spp.
Aralia californica

Argentina egedii
Arnica spp.
Aruncus dioicus
Asarum caudatum
Aster spp.
Bensoniella oregana
Bolandra oregana
Boykinia major
Calochortus subalpinus
Calochortus tolmiei
Caltha leptosepala
Campanula rotundifolia
Cardamine spp.
Carex spp.
Castilleja spp.
Chamerion angustifolium
Clintonia uniflora
Coptis laciniata
Corydalis scouleri
Cynoglossum grande (DS)
Danthonia californica (DS)
Darlingtonia californica
Darmera peltata
Delphinium nudicaule
Delphinium trolliifolium
Dicentra spp.
Dodecatheon spp.
Douglasia laevigata
Drosera rotundifolia
Epilobium luteum
Epipactis gigantea
Erigeron peregrinus
Erigeron speciosus
Erythronium spp.
Fragaria vesca
Fragaria virginiana
Fritillaria affinis
Fritillaria recurva

Galium oreganum
Gentiana spp.
Geranium viscosissimum
Geum macrophyllum (DS)
Goodyera oblongifolia (DS)
Heracleum maximum
Heuchera spp.
Horkelia fusca
Hydrophyllum spp.
Hypericum anagalloides
Iris chrysophylla (DS)
Iris innominata (DS)
Iris tenax (DS)
Juncus effusus
Juncus ensifolius
Lathyrus vestitus ssp.
    bolanderi
Lewisia tweedyi (DS)
Lilium spp.
Lithophragma spp.
Lotus formosissimus
Lupinus latifolius (DS)
Lupinus polyphyllus
Lysichiton americanus
Maianthemum spp.
Mentha arvensis
Menyanthes trifoliata
Mertensia paniculata
Mimulus aurantiacus (DS)
Mimulus dentatus
Mitella ovalis
Montia parvifolia
Narthecium californicum
Nothochelone nemorosa
Nuphar lutea ssp. *polysepala*
Oxalis oregana
Pedicularis spp.
Penstemon ovatus (DS)

Penstemon serrulatus
Penstemon subserratus (DS)
Petasites frigidus
Phacelia bolanderi (DS)
Phlox adsurgens (DS)
Phlox speciosa (DS)
Polemonium spp.
Potentilla spp.
Prosartes spp.
Prunella vulgaris (DS)
Ranunculus spp.
Rudbeckia spp.
Satureja douglasii (DS)
Saxifraga ferruginea
Saxifraga mertensiana
Saxifraga rufidula
Scirpus spp.
Scoliopus hallii
Scrophularia oregana
Senecio triangularis
Silene hookeri (DS)
Sisyrinchium spp.
Solidago canadensis
Spiranthes romanzoffiana
Stachys spp.
Stenanthium occidentale
Streptopus amplexifolius
Synthyris spp.
Tellima grandiflora (DS)
Thalictrum occidentale
Tiarella trifoliata var.
    trifoliata
Tolmiea menziesii
Triantha glutinosa
Trientalis borealis ssp.
    latifolia (DS)
Trientalis europaea ssp.
    arctica

Trifolium wormskioldii
Trillium spp.
Triteleia hendersonii (DS)
Utricularia macrorhiza
Valeriana sitchensis
Vancouveria hexandra (DS)
Veratrum spp.
Viola adunca
Viola cuneata (DS)
Viola glabella
Viola sempervirens
Wyethia amplexicaulis (DS)
Xerophyllum tenax
Zigadenus paniculatus (DS)
Zigadenus venenosus

SHRUBS AND TREES

Acer spp.
Alnus spp.
Alnus rubra (DS)
Amelanchier alnifolia (DS)

Andromeda polifolia
Betula papyrifera
Cassiope mertensiana
Ceanothus integerrimus (DS)
Celtis laevigata var.
    reticulata
Clematis ligusticifolia
Cornus spp.
Corylus cornuta (DS)
Crataegus douglasii
Elliottia pyroliflorus
Empetrum nigrum (DS)
Euonymus occidentale
Fraxinus latifolia
Garrya elliptica
Garrya fremontii (DS)
Gaultheria shallon (DS)
Holodiscus discolor (DS)
Kalmia microphylla
Kalmiopsis leachiana (DS)
Ledum spp.
Leucothoe davisiae

Linnaea borealis (DS)
Lithocarpus densiflorus (DS)
Lonicera ciliosa (DS)
Lonicera involucrata
Luetkea pectinata
Mahonia spp. (DS)
Malus fusca
Menziesia ferruginea
Morella californica (DS)
Myrica gale
Oemleria cerasiformis (DS)
Oplopanax horridus
Paxistima myrsinites (DS)
Philadelphus lewisii (DS)
Phyllodoce empetriformis
Physocarpus capitatus
Prunus emarginata (DS)
Quercus kelloggii (DS)
Quercus sadleriana (DS)
Rhamnus purshiana
Rhododendron spp.

Ribes spp.
Rosa spp.
Rosa gymnocarpa (DS)
Rubus spp.
Rubus lasiococcus (DS)
Rubus parviflorus (DS)
Rubus ursinus (DS)
Salix spp.
Salix scouleriana (DS)
Sambucus racemosa var.
    racemosa
Shepherdia canadensis (DS)
Sorbus sitchensis
Spiraea spp.
Spiraea betulifolia var.
    lucida (DS)
Symphoricarpos albus (DS)
Umbellularia californica
    (DS)
Vaccinium spp.
Viburnum spp.

Plants for wildflower meadows

Just about any herbaceous plant can be included in a wildflower meadow, but here is a selection of starting possibilities, including native grasses. All these plants will tolerate full sun but have varying moisture needs, depending on the species. Some live in dry meadows; others require wetter soils, at least early in the spring. Check the other lists and plant descriptions for additional details. Most annuals are good additions to the wildflower meadow and can be planted from seed; the perennials listed here are best planted out from small containers.

FERNS

Pteridium aquilinum

PERENNIALS

Achillea millefolium
Achnatherum hymenoides
Aconitum columbianum
Agastache spp.
Agoseris aurantiaca
Allium spp.
Anaphalis margaritacea
Anemone multifida
Anemone occidentalis
Angelica lucida

Antennaria rosea
Apocynum cannabinum
Aquilegia spp.
Argentina egedii
Arnica spp.
Artemisia suksdorfii
Asclepias spp.
Aster spp.
Astragalus spp.
Balsamorhiza spp.
Brodiaea spp.
Calochortus spp.
Caltha leptosepala
Camassia spp.
Campanula rotundifolia
Carex spp.

Castilleja spp.
Cerastium arvense
Chamerion angustifolium
Cistanthe umbellata
Cynoglossum grande
Danthonia californica
Darmera peltata
Delphinium menziesii
Dichelostemma spp.
Dodecatheon spp.
Drosera rotundifolia
Elymus elymoides
Epilobium canum ssp.
    latifolium
Erigeron spp.
Eriophyllum lanatum

Erysimum capitatum
Erythronium spp.
Eschscholzia californica
Eupatoriadelphus maculatus
Festuca idahoensis
Fragaria spp.
Fritillaria spp.
Gaillardia aristata
Galium oreganum
Gentiana spp.
Geranium viscosissimum
Geum spp.
Grindelia stricta
Helenium bolanderi
Helianthus cusickii
Heracleum maximum

Hesperochiron pumilus
Hesperostipa comata
Heterotheca villosa
Horkelia fusca
Hypericum anagalloides
Hymenoxys hoopesii
Iliamna rivularis
Ipomopsis aggregata
Iris spp.
Juncus spp.
Lathyrus vestitus ssp.
    bolanderi
Leptosiphon nuttallii
Leymus cinereus
Lilium columbianum
Lilium pardalinum ssp.
    vollmeri
Linum lewisii
Lithophragma spp.
Lithospermum ruderale

Lomatium spp.
Lotus formosissimus
Lupinus spp.
Machaeranthera canescens
Maianthemum racemosum
Maianthemum stellatum
Mentha arvensis
Mentzelia laevicaulis
Mertensia paniculata
Mimulus spp.
Monarda fistulosa
Monardella odoratissima
Narthecium californicum
Nothochelone nemorosa
Oenothera spp.
Pedicularis spp.
Penstemon ovatus
Penstemon serrulatus
Penstemon subserratus
Petasites frigidus

Phacelia bolanderi
Phacelia hastata
Phoenicaulis cheiranthoides
Poa secunda
Polemonium pulcherrimum
Polygonum bistortoides
Potentilla spp.
Prunella vulgaris
Pseudoroegneria spicata
Ranunculus spp.
Rudbeckia spp.
Rumex venosus
Sanicula arctopoides
Saxifraga spp.
Scirpus spp.
Scrophularia oregana
Scutellaria lateriflora
Senecio triangularis
Sidalcea spp.
Silene hookeri

Sisyrinchium spp.
Solidago spp.
Sphaeralcea munroana
Stachys spp.
Stenanthium occidentale
Thalictrum occidentale
Thermopsis montana
Townsendia florifer
Triantha glutinosa
Trifolium spp.
Triteleia spp.
Valeriana sitchensis
Veratrum spp.
Viola adunca
Viola douglasii
Viola trinervata
Wyethia amplexicaulis
Xerophyllum tenax
Zigadenus spp.

Plants for rock gardens

Many plants inhabit rocky places, where they have both excellent drainage and available moisture through much of the growing season. The dwarf cultivars of some native conifers make good additions to the rock garden (the mat-forming *Juniperus communis* makes a good rock garden plant in its natural form), but most of them are larger trees in their wild state and do not make this list. The plants that follow normally live in moist to dry, sunny or shady places among boulders or gravel. Plants of dry climates often cooperate in the wetter parts of the Pacific Northwest when planted in a rocky substrate. Many of these species are also good choices for trough gardens. Additional species are discussed in the plant descriptions, and avid rock gardeners will probably know of others.

FERNS

Asplenium trichomanes
Cheilanthes gracillima
Cryptogramma
    acrostichoides
Cystopteris fragilis
Pentagramma triangularis
Polypodium spp.

ANNUALS

Calandrinia ciliata
Clarkia spp.
Claytonia exigua
Collinsia grandiflora

Crocidium multicaule
Gilia capitata
Lupinus bicolor
Mimulus alsinoides
Plectritis congesta

PERENNIALS

Achillea millefolium
Agastache occidentalis
Allium spp.
Anaphalis margaritacea
Anemone multifida
Anemone occidentalis
Antennaria rosea

Arabis aculeolata
Armeria maritima
Astragalus spp.
Balsamorhiza rosea
Bolandra oregana
Brodiaea spp.
Calochortus spp.
Campanula rotundifolia
Cerastium arvense
Cistanthe umbellata
Danthonia californica
Delphinium glareosum
Delphinium menziesii
Dichelostemma spp.
Dodecatheon spp.

Douglasia laevigata
Elymus elymoides
Epilobium canum ssp.
    latifolium
Eriophyllum lanatum
Erysimum capitatum
Erythronium spp.
Festuca idahoensis
Fragaria chiloensis
Fritillaria pudica
Geum triflorum
Helianthus cusickii
Hesperochiron pumilus
Hesperostipa comata
Heterotheca villosa

Trichium spp.
Hackelia fusca
Ipomopsis aggregata
Iris douglasiana
Iris tenax
Leptosiphon nuttallii
Lewisia spp.
Lilium bolanderi
Linum lewisii
Lithophragma spp
Lithospermum ruderale
Lomatium spp.
Lupinus lepidus
Lupinus leucophyllus
Mentzelia laevicaulis
Mimulus aurantiacus
Monardella odoratissima
Montia parvifolia
Nothochelone nemorosa
Oenothera spp.
Penstemon spp.

Phlox spp.
Phoenicaulis cheiranthoides
Poa secunda
Polemonium pulcherrimum
Saxifraga spp.
Sedum spp.
Silene hookeri
Sisyrinchium douglasii
Sphaeralcea munroana
Stenanthium occidentale
Synthyris missurica
Townsendia florifer
Trifolium macrocephalum
Trillium rivale
Triteleia spp.
Viola cuneata
Viola douglasii
Viola trinervata
Zigadenus venenosus

SHRUBS AND TREES

Acer glabrum var. *douglasii*
Andromeda polifolia
Arbutus menziesii
Arctostaphylos spp.
Artemisia tridentata
Baccharis pilularis
Cassiope mertensiana
Ceanothus prostratus
Ceanothus pumilus
Cercis orbiculata
Cercocarpus ledifolius
Dasiphora fruticosa ssp
   floribunda
Dryas spp.
Elaeagnus commutata
Empetrum nigrum
Eriogonum spp.
Holodiscus discolor
Kalmiopsis leachiana

Kruckebergia lanata
Luetkea pectinata
Opuntia polyacantha
Paxistima myrsinites
Philadelphus lewisii
Phyllodoce empetriformis
Purshia tridentata
Quercus garryana
Quercus sadleriana
Ribes cereum
Ribes cruentum
Ribes sanguineum
Salvia dorrii
Shepherdia canadensis
Sorbus sitchensis
Spiraea betulifolia var
   lucida
Spiraea splendens var.
   splendens
Symphoricarpos albus

Groundcovers

Groundcovers are plants that tend to grow horizontally, often developing lateral stems that grow above (stolons) or below (rhizomes) the surface of the soil, producing new roots and shoots as they go. Some are deciduous; those that are evergreen (E) are so noted. The amount of light and moisture each requires will vary from species to species. Most of the other more compact or cushion-forming plants are in the previous list, "Plants for Rock Gardens."

FERNS

Gymnocarpium dryopteris
Polypodium glycyrrhiza

CONIFERS

Juniperus communis (E)

PERENNIALS

Achlys triphylla
Antennaria rosea
Argentina egedii
Armeria maritima (E)
Arnica spp.
Asarum caudatum (E)
Coptis laciniata

Dicentra formosa
Erigeron glaucus
Fragaria spp.
Galium oreganum
Goodyera oblongifolia (E)
Hydrophyllum tenuipes
Hypericum anagalloides
Lupinus lepidus
Lupinus littoralis
Maianthemum spp.
Mentha arvensis
Montia parvifolia
Oxalis oregana
Penstemon cardwellii (E)
Penstemon davidsonii (E)
Penstemon newberryi ssp.
   berryi (E)
Penstemon rupicola (E)

Petasites frigidus
Phlox spp. (E, sometimes)
Polygonum paronychia
Prunella vulgaris
Rumex venosus
Satureja douglasii
Sedum spp. (E)
Tanacetum camphoratum
Tolmiea menziesii
Trifolium spp.
Vancouveria hexandra
Viola spp.

SHRUBS AND TREES

Andromeda polifolia (E)
Arctostaphylos uva-ursi (E)
Baccharis pilularis (E)

Cassiope mertensiana (E)
Ceanothus prostratus (E)
Ceanothus pumilus (E)
Cornus unalaschkensis (E,
   often)
Dryas spp. (E, often)
Empetrum nigrum (E)
Eriogonum spp.
Gaultheria shallon (E)
Linnaea borealis (E)
Luetkea pectinata (E)
Mahonia nervosa (E)
Mahonia repens (E)
Opuntia polyacantha (E)
Phyllodoce empetriformis (E)
Rubus lasiococcus
Rubus pedatus
Rubus ursinus

Plants for butterflies

Since adult butterflies do well only when their larvae thrive, the serious butterfly gardener will want to provide nectar plants for adults as well as food plants for herbivorous caterpillars. Butterflies may visit a wide variety of flowering plants as they search for nectar, but plants with many tiny flowers that bloom in crowded inflorescences are often favorites. The butterfly can park on a single flower cluster and drink from many small flowers without having to move. Other plants, including trees and grasses, make good forage for the caterpillars. The following is a list of plants likely to attract butterflies as nectar sources as well as good egg-laying sites. Additional species are discussed under the descriptions of these plants.

CONIFERS

Pinus spp.
Pseudotsuga menziesii
Thuja plicata

ANNUALS

Coreopsis tinctoria var. *atkinsoniana*
Crocidium multicaule
Gilia capitata
Helianthus annuus
Lasthenia californica
Lupinus bicolor
Madia elegans
Plectritis congesta

PERENNIALS

Abronia spp.
Achillea millefolium
Achnatherum hymenoides
Agastache spp.
Agoseris aurantiaca
Allium spp.
Anaphalis margaritacea
Angelica lucida
Antennaria rosea
Apocynum cannabinum
Aquilegia spp.
Arabis aculeolata
Armeria maritima
Arnica spp.
Artemisia spp.
Aruncus dioicus
Asclepias spp.

Aster spp.
Astragalus spp.
Balsamorhiza spp.
Cardamine spp.
Carex spp.
Chamerion angustifolium
Cynoglossum grande
Danthonia californica
Delphinium spp.
Dicentra spp.
Elymus elymoides
Erigeron spp.
Eriophyllum lanatum
Erysimum capitatum
Eupatoriadelphus maculatus
Festuca idahoensis
Fragaria spp.
Gaillardia aristata
Glehnia littoralis ssp. *leiocarpa*
Grindelia stricta
Helenium bolanderi
Helianthus cusickii
Heracleum maximum
Hesperostipa comata
Heterotheca villosa
Heuchera spp.
Hymenoxys hoopesii
Lathyrus vestitus ssp. *bolanderi*
Leymus cinereus
Lilium spp.
Lomatium spp.
Lotus formosissimus
Lupinus spp.
Machaeranthera canescens
Mentha arvensis

Monarda fistulosa
Monardella odoratissima
Oenothera spp.
Penstemon spp.
Petasites frigidus
Phacelia spp.
Phlox spp.
Phoenicaulis cheiranthoides
Poa secunda
Polygonum spp.
Prunella vulgaris
Pseudoroegneria spicata
Rudbeckia spp.
Rumex venosus
Sanicula arctopoides
Scutellaria lateriflora
Sedum spp.
Senecio triangularis
Sidalcea spp.
Solidago spp.
Sphaeralcea munroana
Stachys spp.
Tanacetum camphoratum
Thermopsis montana
Townsendia florifer
Trifolium spp.
Valeriana sitchensis
Viola spp.
Wyethia amplexicaulis

SHRUBS AND TREES

Acer spp.
Alnus spp.
Arbutus menziesii
Arctostaphylos spp.
Artemisia tridentata

Baccharis pilularis
Betula papyrifera
Ceanothus spp.
Celtis laevigata var. *reticulata*
Cornus spp.
Crataegus douglasii
Ericameria spp.
Eriogonum spp.
Gaultheria shallon
Holodiscus discolor
Lithocarpus densiflorus
Mahonia spp.
Malus fusca
Philadelphus lewisii
Populus spp.
Prunus spp.
Quercus spp.
Rhamnus purshiana
Rhododendron spp.
Rhus spp.
Ribes spp.
Rosa spp.
Rubus spp.
Salix spp.
Salvia dorrii
Sambucus spp.
Sorbus sitchensis
Spiraea spp.
Symphoricarpos albus
Vaccinium spp.
Viburnum spp.

Plants for hummingbirds

Conifers provide nesting sites and insects for hummingbirds, making them good additions to the hummingbird garden. What's listed here are the expected hummingbird plants those with nectar-filled, tubular red flowers. But hummers visit other plants—sometimes because of their early flowering, sometimes because they attract the tasty insects that are a critical component of a hummingbird's diet. Some of these less "classic" but still hummingbird-attractive plants are included as well.

ANNUALS

Centaurium muehlenbergii
Clarkia spp.
Collomia grandiflora
Impatiens capensis

PERENNIALS

Agastache spp.
Aquilegia spp.
Castilleja spp.

Chamerion angustifolium
Delphinium spp.
Dichelostemma ida-maia
Epilobium canum ssp.
    latifolium
Heuchera spp.
Iliamna rivularis
Ipomopsis aggregata
Lilium spp.
Lupinus spp.
Mimulus spp.

Monarda fistulosa
Nothochelone nemorosa
Penstemon spp.
Scrophularia oregana
Sidalcea spp.
Sphaeralcea munroana
Stachys spp.

SHRUBS AND TREES

Arctostaphylos spp.

Ceanothus spp.
Cercis orbiculata
Lonicera spp.
Oemleria cerasiformis
Ribes spp.
Rubus spectabilis
Salvia dorrii
Sambucus spp.
Vaccinium spp.

Plants for fruit- and seed-eating birds

There is no plant that is not eaten by some creature, but here are some species especially favored by birds that eat fruits and seeds—plants that offer fleshy fruits such as berries, pomes (tiny apples), and drupes (plums and cherries); plants that provide dry fruits, such as the achenes of sunflowers; and other species with tasty seeds. Most conifers, for instance, provide seed (as well as cover and nesting sites) for birds; if space is a concern, try *Pinus contorta* var. *contorta*, one of our smallest native conifers.

ANNUALS

Coreopsis tinctoria var.
    atkinsoniana
Helianthus annuus
Madia elegans

PERENNIALS

Achnatherum hymenoides
Actaea rubra
Aquilegia spp.
Aralia californica

Balsamorhiza spp.
Carex spp.
Clintonia uniflora
Danthonia californica
Elymus elymoides
Eupatoriadelphus maculatus
Festuca idahoensis
Fragaria spp.
Gaillardia aristata
Helenium bolanderi
Helianthus cusickii
Hesperostipa comata
Hymenoxys hoopesii

Leymus cinereus
Lupinus spp.
Maianthemum spp.
Prosartes spp.
Pseudoroegneria spicata
Rudbeckia spp.
Sagittaria latifolia
Schoenoplectus acutus
Scirpus spp.
Senecio triangularis
Streptopus amplexifolius
Thermopsis montana
Typha latifolia

Wyethia amplexicaulis

SHRUBS AND TREES

Acer spp.
Alnus spp.
Amelanchier alnifolia
Arbutus menziesii
Arctostaphylos spp.
Artemisia tridentata
Ceanothus spp.
Celtis laevigata var.
    reticulata

Cornus spp.
Corylus cornuta
Crataegus douglasii
Elaeagnus commutata
Empetrum nigrum
Ericameria spp.
Eriogonum spp.
Fraxinus latifolia
Garrya spp.
Gaultheria shallon

Grayia spinosa
Holodiscus discolor
Krascheninnikovia lanata
Lithocarpus densiflorus
Lonicera spp.
Mahonia spp.
Malus fusca
Morella californica
Myrica gale
Oemleria cerasiformis

Physocarpus capitatus
Prunus spp.
Purshia tridentata
Quercus spp.
Rhamnus purshiana
Rhus spp.
Ribes spp.
Rosa spp.
Rubus spp.

Salix spp.
Sambucus spp.
Shepherdia canadensis
Sorbus sitchensis
Symphoricarpos albus
Umbellularia californica
Vaccinium spp.
Viburnum spp.
Vitis californica

Plants for sandy beaches and dunes

Many plants grow in rocks, near the coast or in the arid shrub-steppe, but this list includes only plants that can live in very sandy soil. Some will do best in sandy gardens and beaches. Others grow in dunes further east, where the summers are often hotter and the winters colder. Still others are widely distributed and will grow in dunes or very sandy soils throughout our area.

FERNS

Pteridium aquilinum

CONIFERS

Pinus contorta var. *contorta*

ANNUALS

Crocidium multicaule
Phacelia linearis

PERENNIALS

Abronia spp.
Achillea millefolium
Achnatherum hymenoides
Allium cernuum
Argentina egedii
Armeria maritima
Artemisia suksdorfii
Asclepias speciosa
Astragalus succumbens
Calystegia soldanella
Camissonia cheiranthifolia
Castilleja affinis ssp.
    litoralis
Cistanthe umbellata

Erigeron filifolius
Erigeron glaucus
Erysimum capitatum
Fragaria chiloensis
Glehnia littoralis ssp.
    leiocarpa
Grindelia stricta
Helianthus cusickii
Heterotheca villosa
Juncus breweri
Leymus spp.
Lupinus littoralis
Oenothera pallida
Phacelia argentea
Phacelia hastata

Polygonum paronychia
Rumex venosus
Sanicula arctopoides
Sphaeralcea munroana
Tanacetum camphoratum

SHRUBS AND TREES

Arctostaphylos uva-ursi
Baccharis pilularis
Eriogonum niveum
Opuntia polyacantha
Salix hookeriana

Plants for erosion control

Many plants are rhizomatous, but the plants in this list are especially likely to spread. Some species may be too aggressive for many garden situations, but their tendency to form rooted mats or colonies of vigorous suckers makes them ideal for stabilizing hills, banks, and shorelines.

CONIFERS

Juniperus communis

PERENNIALS

Carex obnupta
Chamerion angustifolium
Dulichium arundinaceum

Erigeron glaucus
Eriophorum spp.
Iris missouriensis
Juncus spp.
Leymus spp.
Schoenoplectus acutus
Scirpus microcarpus
Solidago spp.
Typha latifolia

SHRUBS AND TREES

Arctostaphylos uva-ursi
Baccharis pilularis
Cornus sericea
Crataegus douglasii
Elaeagnus commutata
Gaultheria shallon
Holodiscus discolor
Mahonia spp.
Myrica gale

Opuntia polyacantha
Populus tremuloides
Rhus glabra
Rosa spp.
Rubus parviflorus
Rubus spectabilis
Rubus ursinus
Salix spp.
Spiraea douglasii
Symphoricarpos albus

REFERENCES

Much of the taxonomy in the older floras has changed, but they are hard to beat for accurate, detailed information on the plants themselves and their habitat. In addition to floras and field guides, here are several good books on gardening and growing plants, native and otherwise. The USDA Plants Database (http://plants.usda.gov/) is an excellent resource for updated taxonomy, general range maps, and links to other reliable sources of information.

Bailey, L. H., and E. Z. Bailey. 1976. *Hortus Third*. New York: Macmillan Publishing.

Brenzel, K. N., ed. 2001. *Sunset Western Garden Book*. Menlo Park, California: Sunset Publishing.

Case, F. R., and R. C. Case. 1997. *Trilliums*. Portland, Oregon: Timber Press.

Hartmann, H. T., and D. E. Kester. 1975. *Plant Propagation*. 3d ed. Englewood Cliffs, New Jersey: Prentice-Hall.

Hitchcock, C. L., and A. Cronquist. 1973. *Flora of the Pacific Northwest*. Seattle: University of Washington Press.

Hitchcock, C. L., A. Cronquist, M. Ownbey, and J. W. Thompson. 1969. *Vascular Plants of the Pacific Northwest*. 5 vols. Seattle: University of Washington Press.

Kozloff, E. N. 2005. *Plants of Western Oregon, Washington, and British Columbia*. Portland, Oregon: Timber Press.

Kruckeberg, A. R. 1982. *Gardening with Native Plants of the Pacific Northwest*. Seattle: University of Washington Press.

Leigh, M. 1997. *Grow Your Own Native Landscape*. Washington State University Cooperative Extension–Thurston County: Native Plant Salvage Project.

Peck, M. E. 1961. *A Manual of the Higher Plants of Oregon*. 2d ed. Portland, Oregon: Binfords and Mort.

Pojar, J., and A. MacKinnon, eds. 1994. *Plants of the Pacific Northwest Coast*. Vancouver, British Columbia: Lone Pine Publishing.

Stokes, D. W., L. Q. Stokes, and E. Williams. 1991. *Stokes Butterfly Book*. Boston: Little, Brown and Company.

Thompson, P. 2005. *Creative Propagation*. 2d ed. Portland, Oregon: Timber Press.

Turner, M., and P. Gustafson. 2006. *Wildflowers of the Pacific Northwest*. Portland, Oregon: Timber Press.

Young, J. A., and C. G. Young. 1986. *Collecting, Processing, and Germinating Seeds of Wildland Plants*. Portland, Oregon: Timber Press.

INDEX